USSR

TURCOMANS

GORGAN

E KAVIR
DESERT)

DASHT-E

Kerm

Bandar 'Abbas

QESHM

Straits of Hormuz

NB

SA

RAB
TES

OMAN

Musandam Peninsula

Gulf of Oman

Chah Bahar

ISTAN

The Pahlavi Crown

IRAN
Under The
PAHLAVIS

IRAN
Under The
PAHLAVIS

GEORGE LENCZOWSKI

Editor

HOOVER INSTITUTION PRESS
·Stanford University • Stanford, California

*The Hoover Institution on War, Revolution and Peace, founded at
Stanford University in 1919 by the late President Herbert Hoover,
is an interdisciplinary research center for advanced study on
domestic and international affairs in the twentieth century. The views
expressed in its publications are entirely those of the authors
and do not necessarily reflect the views of the staff, officers,
or Board of Overseers of the Hoover Institution.*

Hoover Institution Publication 164

© 1978 by the Board of Trustees of the
   Leland Stanford Junior University
All rights reserved
International Standard Book Number: 0-8179-6641-2
Library of Congress Catalog Card Number: 76-26773
Printed in the United States of America

This book is dedicated to
the people of Iran
whose ancient and unique civilization
is experiencing in the mid-twentieth century
a spectacular resurgence and progress
for the benefit of their own
and the world at large.

Contents

Preface

This book was conceived as an attempt to portray and evaluate the changes that have occurred in Iran since the coming to power of the Pahlavi dynasty. During this period Iran emerged from her semimedieval slumber to become one of Asia's principal modernizing states and a leading military power in the Persian Gulf region. Since this progress was achieved under the aegis of the monarchy, an institution with deep roots in Iran's remote past, the volume has a dual focus, on the process of modernization and on the role of the traditional concept of kingship.

The chapters that follow represent the efforts of an international team of scholars whose fields of specialization range over a wide spectrum, from the history of religion to oil economics and contemporary international affairs. Although they are citizens of countries other than Iran, all have been linked to Iran by ties of sustained interest, research, and, in some cases, prolonged residence there.

The editor wishes to express his thanks to the University of California at Berkeley for granting him a sabbatical leave in the course of the academic year 1975-76 to enable him to concentrate on this book.

The contributors to the present volume have benefited from the assistance and courtesies extended to them during their research and journeys to Iran by a number of Iranian public institutions, including Iranian Universities, the Library of the Majles, and various ministries and agencies of the government. Individuals and departments concerned are too many to be enumerated here. The editor would like, however, to mention the Ministry of the Imperial Court and, more specifically, HE Mr. Assadollah Alam, the Minister; Ambassador Amir Khosrow Afshar; and Mr. Homayoun Bahadori, Undersecretary, whose thoughtful help in securing audiences and appointments and guiding the authors through the extensive government apparatus in search of materials has proved of inestimable value. The editor wishes also to thank Dr. Ahmad Ghoreichi, Dean of the Faculty of Law of the National University and chairman of the Executive Committee of the Rastakhiz party, for supplying him with information about the concept and structure of the party; and Dr. Youssef Samadzadeh, Undersecretary in the Ministry of Higher Education, for his assistance in selecting historical photographs from the archives of the Imperial Court and the permission to reproduce them. Thanks are also due to the Iranian Embassy in Washington for providing the pictures of the Royal Family and the permission to reproduce them.

The editor, in his capacity as author of chapter 12, acknowledges with gratitude the permission granted by HIM the Shahanshah Aryamehr to quote from his book *Mission for My Country*.

As is often the case in studies pertaining to the Middle East, selection of an appropriate method of transliterating Persian words and names has posed a problem. In trying to cope with it we have adopted three guidelines: first, to eliminate the long-vowel signs, so as to make the text easier to follow by non-specialized readers; second, to ensure maximum possible consistency in italicized Persian terms; and third, to observe established usage in English for a number of familiar, commonly used words, especially personal and place names.

G.L.

Berkeley, California
April 1977

Notes on Contributors

PETER J. CHELKOWSKI is Professor of Persian and Iranian Studies, Director of the Hagop Kevorkian Center for Near Eastern Studies, and Chairman of the Department of Near Eastern Languages and Literatures at New York University. He holds degrees from the Jagellonian University of Cracow, the University of London, and the University of Tehran (Ph.D., 1967). His publications include *Iran: Continuity and Variety* (1971); *The Scholar and the Saint: Studies in Commemoration of Abu'l-Rayhan al-Biruni and Jalal al-Din al-Rumi,* editor (1974); and *Mirror of the Invisible World: Tales from the Khamseh of Nizami* (1975).

ALVIN J. COTTRELL (Ph.D., University of Pennsylvania) is Director of Research at the Georgetown University Center for Strategic and International Studies. He has taught at the University of Pennsylvania and was Professor of Foreign Affairs at the National War College. Among his recent publications are *The Indian Ocean: Its Political, Economic, and Military Importance,* coeditor (1972); *Iran, Afghanistan and Pakistan: Tensions and Dilemmas* (1974); and *Iran: Diplomacy in a Regional and Global Context* (1975).

DONALD R. DENMAN is Professor and Head of the Department of Land Economy and Fellow of Pembroke College, Cambridge University. Holder of degrees from London University (Ph.D., 1945) and Cambridge (M.A., 1948), he is Vice-President of the Commonwealth Human Ecology Council and has served in a number of advisory posts to foreign governments and international organizations. His publications include *Origins of Ownership: A Brief History of Landownership and Tenure* (1958); *Land Use and the Constitution of Property* (1969); and *The King's Vista: A Land Reform Which Has Changed the Face of Persia* (1973).

WILHELM EILERS is Professor Emeritus at the Julius Maximilian University in Würzburg. Holder of degrees from the universities of Leipzig and Berlin (Dr. Juris), he served as representative of the German Archaeological Institute in Isfahan and was associated with the American Luristan Expedition. He is editor of the Iranian branch of the *Orientalistische Literaturzeitung* (Leipzig) and member of the learned societies focusing on Iran in London, Liège, and New York. His recent publications include *Deutsch-Persisches Wörterbuch* (1967); *Semiramis* (1971); *Westiranische Mundarten aus der Sammlung Wilh. Eilers* (1976); and *Festgabe Deutscher Orientalisten zur 2500 Jahrfeier Irans,* editor (1971).

LAURENCE P. ELWELL-SUTTON is Professor of Persian at the University of Edinburgh. Educated at the School of Oriental Studies, London University (B.A. Hons; Arabic, 1st class), he served in Iran as Press Attaché at the British Embassy in Tehran (1943-47). He was also Chairman of the British Association of Orientalists (1971-72). His major publications are *Modern Iran* (1941); *Guide to Iranian Area Study* (1952); *Persian Oil: A Study in Power Politics* (1955); and *The Persian Metres* (1976).

PIO FILIPPANI-RONCONI is Professor of Religions and Philosophies of India and Professor of Sanskrit at the Oriental Institute, University of Naples. Educated at the University of Rome (Ph.D.), he was awarded a doctorate honoris causa from the Tehran University and admitted to membership in the Royal Academy of Cordoba. His major publications include *Il Roseto (Golestan)* editor and translator (1965); *Religioni dell'India,* 2 vols. (1965); *Upanisad Antiche e Medie* (rev. ed. 1968); and *Ismaeliti ed Assassini* (1973).

WILLIAM E. GRIFFITH is Ford Professor of Political Science at Massachusetts Institute of Technology and Adjunct Professor of Diplomatic History at the Fletcher School of Law and Diplomacy, Tufts University. A holder of degrees from Hamilton College and Harvard University (Ph.D., 1950), he is General Editor of the MIT series *Studies in Communism, Revisionism and Revolution,* of which twenty-one volumes have appeared thus far. His major works are *The Sino-Soviet Rift* (1964); *Sino-Soviet Relations, 1964-1965* (1967); and *The Germanies and East Europe* (in press).

CHARLES P. ISSAWI is Bayard Dodge Professor of Near Eastern Studies at Princeton University. Holder of degrees from Oxford University, he was Professor of Economics and Director of Near and Middle East Institute at Columbia University, and served as consultant to the Food and Agriculture Organization and the United Nations. His publications include *Egypt in Revolution* (1963); *Economics of Middle Eastern Oil* (1962); and *The Economic History of Iran* (1971).

GEORGE LENCZOWSKI is Professor of Political Science, University of California at Berkeley. Educated at the universities of Warsaw, Paris and Lille (J.S.D.), he has served as Director, Middle East Research Project, American Enterprise Institute for Public Policy Research (nine studies published), and member of the Board of Iran Foundation in New York. He is Chairman of the Committee for the Middle East, Hoover Institution, and member of the Board of Governors of the Middle East Institute in Washington. His major works include *Russia and the West in Iran* (1949); *Oil and State in the Middle East* (1960); *The Middle East in World Affairs* (3rd ed., 1962); *Soviet Advances in the Middle East* (1972); and *Political Elites in the Middle East,* editor (1975).

HARALD MEHNER is Managing Director of the Study Center for Tropical and Subtropical Agriculture and Forestry of the University of Göttingen. Educated at the universities of Berlin, Frankfurt, and Giessen (Ph.D., 1950), he served as representative of the German Ministry of Economic Development in Iran in 1967, and is adviser to the German Development Aid Organization. He is the author of *Stand und Formen der Mechanisierung der Landwirtschaft in den Asiatischen Ländern* (1965-68). He also coedited and coauthored (with Ulrich Gehrke) *Iran: Natur, Bevölkerung, Geschichte, Kultur, Staat und Wirtschaft* (1975).

ROGER M. SAVORY is Professor of Islamic Studies, University of Toronto. Educated at Oxford and the University of London (Ph.D., 1958), he served as Chairman of the Department of Islamic Studies at Toronto, 1968-73, and as Vice-President, Middle East Studies Association of North America, 1973. A member of the Editorial Board of the *International Journal of Middle East Studies,* he has contributed numerous articles on Iran to learned journals as well as to the *Encyclopaedia of Islam, Encyclopaedia International,* and the *Cambridge History of Islam.* He has edited *Introduction to Islamic Civilization* (1976), and translated *The History of Shah Abbas the Great* (in press).

ROBERT B. STOBAUGH is Professor of Business Administration and Coordinator, Energy Project, Harvard University Graduate School of Business Administration. Educated in engineering at Louisiana State University and holder of a degree from Harvard (D.B.A., 1968), he has served as a consultant to President Nixon's Cabinet Task Force on Oil Import Control in 1970, and as a member of President Johnson's Advisory Committee on Trade Policy in 1968. His publications include *Petrochemical Manufacturing and Marketing Guide* (2 vols., 1966 and 1968); *Money in the Multinational Enterprise* (with Sidney M. Robbins, 1973); and *Nine Investments Abroad and Their Impact at Home* (1976).

GEORGE LENCZOWSKI

Introduction

From Assertion of Independence to the White Revolution

In 1976 Iran celebrated a major landmark in her modern history, fifty years of growth and development under the aegis of the Pahlavi dynasty. Half a century may not appear a long period if compared with twenty-five hundred years of existence as a political entity and distinct civilization since the ancient Iranian empire was founded by Cyrus the Great. By the standards of modern history, however, which has witnessed unprecedented changes in every sphere of human life throughout the world as a result of advances in science and technology, half a century is a sufficiently long stretch of time for a nation to undergo radical and dramatic changes. Both domestically and externally, such changes have indeed occurred in the life of Iran.

In the sociopolitical sense, the twentieth century will go down in history as an era of revolution and modernization, particularly as regards the areas of the world situated outside western Europe and North America. The continent of Asia has experienced probably more dramatic changes in a short span of time than any other area of the world. In the 1950s and 1960s there was a tendency among social scientists to concentrate on two countries at the extremities of the Asian continent, Japan and Turkey, as subjects of their studies inasmuch as the two represented, each in her own way, a radical process of modernization outside the Communist orbit. Perhaps this selection was justified at the time when it was made. By the 1970s, however, it was certain that Iran should not only be included as a subject of such investigation but that she might even claim primacy. This was so because Iran had experienced a transformation not less profound and, in many respects, more spectacular than the other two countries. This claim to attention could be based on three reasons: Iran's transition from weakness to strength, from backwardness to progress, and from poverty to wealth.

REZA SHAH

The new era in Iran's history opened in the 1920s with the coming to power of Reza Khan, a towering figure whose unique personality and unique career left a deep imprint upon the life of his nation. Reza Khan's rapid ascent from common soldier to King could be compared with the rise of Napoleon in France or Bernadotte in Sweden; however, it was more striking in terms of the social distance covered. Napoleon had the advantage of going to a military academy before embarking on a regular army career. Bernadotte was indeed a soldier who carried "the marshal's baton" in his knapsack and ended as king, but a king in a foreign country, to some extent imposed by external influence. Not so Reza Shah, who grew up in a purely Iranian environment, assumed the imperial rank among his own people, and thus created a real saga of a self-made man against the background of Iran's monarchical tradition.

In his national policies two main features stood out: nationalism and modernization. In this respect he could be compared to Peter the Great, who launched Russia from her medieval slumber upon a path of modernity. Among his contemporaries Reza Shah was frequently compared to his neighbor, Kemal Ataturk, of whose attitudes and reforms he was fully aware. The two leaders had certainly a good deal in common: their burning nationalism, their determination to modernize their countries, and their critical attitude towards the intrusion of religion into the public life of their respective nations. But the two also differed considerably from each other. While Ataturk was willing to burn the bridges with the past, Reza Shah not only maintained the institution of monarchy but also promoted a revived consciousness of ancient Achaemenian glory, particularly through architectural symbolism. In this sense, of course, he was more fortunate because his nation had had a long record of civilized life when the Turks were still leading a nomadic existence in the steppes of central Asia.

In the subsequent chapters a group of specialists will review in greater detail the achievements of both Reza Shah and his son and successor, Mohammad Reza. In these introductory remarks we will limit ourselves to the main points in the work and struggles of these two rulers. Reza Shah's achievements could be summed up under three headings: building up the infrastructure of a modern state, asserting independence from foreign domination, and launching sociocultural reforms. With regard to the first, Reza Shah did indeed lay down the foundations without which a modern state could not function. These included assertion of government authority and national unification in the face of various centrifugal and anarchistic forces; the creation of a reliable army under national command; establishment of a modern fiscal system based on rational organization; and development of the minimum of communications and transportation facilities compatible with the requirements of a modern state.

Assertion of independence from foreign occupation and control was the second major achievement of Reza Shah. At the very outset of his rule he had to face the threat of militant Communism imported into Iran with the advancing Red Army which, despite the repudiation by the Bolsheviks of czarist Russia's imperialistic practices, fell into the old pattern of occupying the northern provinces of Iran and threatening the integrity of the entire state. This struggle for emancipation from foreign control was marked by two crises. The first was the Soviet attempt to set up a separatist Communist government in the province of Gilan. This required both military and diplomatic countermeasures, the outcome being the conclusion of the Soviet-Iranian Treaty of February 1921 and the subsequent withdrawal of Soviet troops from Iranian territory. The treaty, however, was negotiated by Iranian representatives in Moscow while Reza Khan, not yet fully in power, was personally commanding military operations against the northern rebels and their Soviet allies. This perhaps explains why the treaty was burdened with an onerous clause in the form of article 6 authorizing entry of Soviet troops into Iranian territory, should the latter become a base for anti-Soviet aggression. Although the attached memoranda made it clear that the provision in question comprised only the toleration by the Iranian government of the anti-Soviet activities of White Russian elements against the Soviet territory, in subsequent years Moscow tended to give a more comprehensive interpretation to this clause by including in it Iran's formal ties with Western powers during the period following World War II, which clearly was not encompassed by the terms of the original clause. Regardless, however, of the text of the treaty in question, Reza Shah succeeded in removing the Soviet presence in Iran and in effectively curbing the activities of Soviet agents and their Communist allies inside the country.

The second crisis that the Shah faced was the one with Great Britain. It revolved around oil, the concession for which was held by the Anglo-Iranian Oil Company, the latter in turn controlled by the British Admiralty. Relations between Great Britain and Iran profoundly differed from those between Iran and Russia. While Britain exercised imperial control in India, the Persian Gulf, and the Middle East, she was essentially a status quo power not bent on territorial aggrandizement and not guided by a militant or aggressive ideology. Her interest in Iran focused largely on the preservation of such economic advantages as she or her citizens had achieved in that country. Therefore, from the point of view of Iran's independence, Britain was not only a country in a different category from the Soviet Union, but even could be counted upon as providing a counterbalance to the Soviets' actual or potential aggressive designs. This, however, did not diminish Britain's economic self-interest, which was based on somewhat outmoded notions regarding the relationship between the metropolis and the colonies or semicolonies. Although the showdown between Reza Shah and the British over oil in the early 1930s abounded in moments of tension and recrimination, it ended by a compromise in which rationality and restraint were displayed by both parties.

In his pursuit of policies aiming at the safeguarding of national independence and security, Reza Shah was ready to cooperate with the neighboring states which, like Iran, were anxious to safeguard their integrity against possible Soviet expansion and subversion. To this end he entered, in 1937, into a regional alliance known as the Saadabad Pact, the other signatories being Turkey, Iraq, and Afghanistan. Furthermore, not unlike his Constitutionalist predecessors of the period preceding World War I, Reza Shah was inclined to look for a friendly third force that would help Iran free herself from Soviet menace and British influence. Thus he repeated the experiment of 1911 when an American expert, Morgan Shuster, had been brought to Iran to reorganize Persian finances, by inviting in the early 1920s another American, Dr. Arthur Chester Millspaugh, to assist in the reorganization of the Iranian treasury. After some years a German, Dr. Kurt Lindenblatt, was appointed governor of the national bank, while numerous German technicians were invited to advise Iran in developing her industry and communications. Although these contacts with the United States and Germany respectively did not represent a movement toward political or military alliance, nevertheless they were conceived by the Shah and his ministers as a material factor in reducing Iran's dependence upon her two powerful imperial neighbors.

The task of rebuilding, unifying, and strengthening the state consumed so much time and energy that to an outside observer it is little short of amazing that Reza Shah found enough strength to enact a number of social and cultural reforms, some of which had to be imposed against fierce opposition from various entrenched interests. The main thrust of these reforms was to transform the hitherto lethargic masses into a new and enlightened citizenry that would actively participate in the development of the country. Reza Shah was thus a pioneer in introducing what we may call a meritocracy in Iran's national life. Under his reign it was not inherited wealth or connections that counted but actual competence and performance. He was impatient with slothful and lazy officials and prone to dismiss or punish those who failed in their tasks or betrayed his trust. Having a dim view of the role played in the society by reactionary and often semiliterate *mollas,* he took away from the religious establishment its judicial and educational responsibilities while developing under the state auspices a modern school system with the University of Tehran, opened in the 1930s, at its apex.* He was also the first ruler in Iran to call for the emancipation and education of women. Aware of the shortage of the skilled manpower in his country, Reza Shah was willing to

---

*Persian words that appear frequently in this book are defined in the Selected Glossary of Persian Terms, printed with the appendix.

employ foreign experts. However, to avoid encouraging the foreign political influence that such experts might represent, he made it a point to hire them on an individual basis and to place them under Iranian control. Such experts, for instance, were employed in constructing the Shah's cherished project, the Trans-Iranian Railway. However, he took care not to rely on technicians of any single nationality and, furthermore, deliberately avoided dependence on foreign governments by providing exclusively Iranian financing of the project. Above all, he instilled in his people a sense of pride and self-reliance.

TRAUMA OF WORLD WAR II

During World War II Iran experienced a double tragedy. She suffered occupation by the Soviet Union and Britain—and she was deprived of the leadership of her great king just at a time when a strong, experienced hand was needed to steer her destinies. Two factors appear to have combined to produce this sad outcome: Iran's strategic position and Reza Shah's authoritarian personality. As for the first, geopolitics had cast Iran into the difficult position of being the only practical route of access for Western military supplies to the hard-pressed Soviet allies. With regard to the second factor, the fear that Reza Shah inspired even in his closest collaborators prevented them from telling him the full truth about what they knew concerning the real intentions and attitudes of both Britain and the Soviet Union. Had the Shah not been deceived by this misleading and incomplete information, perhaps he would have made adjustments in his policy in a way that would have satisfied both London and Moscow and thus obviated the necessity for military occupation of Iran. Forced to abdicate in favor of his son and go into exile, Reza Shah left his native land with the sad awareness that much of his great work was undone and that his beloved country was suffering a general relapse.

Indeed, the war years witnessed a reappearance of many evil features of the past, while the military presence of foreign powers on Iranian soil encouraged attitudes of treachery and an unscrupulous search for personal gain.

To fill the cup of bitterness, moreover, it became clear that Communist Russia had entered Iran not merely for the purpose of assuring the smooth flow of supplies from the West to her own territory. Her designs were definitely more ambitious. They were starkly revealed in the Molotov-Hitler agreement of November 26, 1940, in which the Soviet government demanded and obtained the consent of the Axis powers that "the area south of Batum and Baku in the general direction of the Persian Gulf is recognized as the center of the aspirations of the Soviet Union."* Thus Iran faced not only an

---

*The complete text of the agreement can be found in Raymond J. Sontag and James S. Beddie, eds., *Nazi-Soviet Relations 1939-1941: Documents from the Archives of the German Foreign Office* (Washington, D.C.: U.S. Department of State, 1948), p. 259.

actual foreign occupation but a concrete threat to her very existence as an independent state.

MOHAMMAD REZA SHAH

Mohammad Reza Shah ascended the throne on September 16, 1941, when he was a few weeks short of his twenty-second birthday (October 26). At the time of the golden jubilee of the Pahlavi dynasty he had ruled for thirty-five years, thus more than doubling the period during which his father directed Iran's policies as head of state. Basically, Mohammad Reza Shah's reign displayed the same two trends as were characteristic of his father's period, nationalism and modernization. There were other similarities as well: the new King faced at the beginning foreign occupation and interference, he was challenged by tribal rebellion and unrest, and was beset by an upsurge of provincial separatism and communism. He also had to wage a struggle for economic independence from British dominance of the oil sector. And, like his father, he searched for a friendly third force that would counterbalance both the Soviet and the British influence.

But there were also important differences between the two rulers and the periods during which they reigned. Reza Shah had begun his personal rule from a position of strength. Although his country was in a state of weakness and chaos and foreign troops were present on her soil, Britain was gradually relinquishing her responsibilities in Iran while the Soviet Union, despite a show of aggressive tendencies, was not the colossus she became after World War II, having in the 1920s barely emerged from the struggle for life and death against the counterrevolution of the Whites and foreign intervention. Faced with this situation, Reza Shah commanded the only reliable military force in Iran and the opposition to him, whether in the center or in the tribal areas, could never muster enough strength to overcome his skill, organization, and mobility. By contrast, Mohammad Reza Shah began his reign from a position of weakness dictated by the circumstances. Powerful armies of occupation had just entered his country and intended to stay there at least for the duration of the war. Following the conclusion of World War II, the hasty departure of the British and American troops (the latter were not an occupation force) was a mixed blessing inasmuch as it left Iran exposed to face alone a powerful Soviet military presence.

This leads us to another contrast: in the struggle for independence that both rulers had waged, at the time of Mohammad Reza Shah the stakes were higher and the tension greater because the Soviets were both more aggressive and stronger and also because, with the gradual abandonment by Britain of her imperial position east of Suez, the resulting power vacuum threatened the entire area of the Middle East. Most significant in this respect was Britain's conceding of independence to India in the late 1940s and two decades later her decision to relinquish imperial responsibilities in the Persian Gulf. True enough, the search for a friendly third force this time brought not only positive results but actually secured for Iran an ally in the form of the strongest yet most benevolent power in the world—the United States. But before this alliance was concluded, there was an early tense period during which the availability of this third force was by no means certain. For one thing, the United States was geographically remote; for another, American policy makers needed to be educated in the realities of the power play in the Middle East in general and in Iran in particular. This "educational" process was not an easy matter inasmuch as throughout World War II the United States had conducted a consistent policy of close alliance with the Soviet Union, and the entire American government propaganda apparatus was geared to present the Soviets to the American public as respectable allies, unjustly attacked by the Nazi war monster, peace-loving (hence proper candidates to cosponsor the United Nations), and displaying encouraging democratic tendencies. In this respect, it is worth noting, Soviet intrigue in Azerbaijan coupled with the Soviet bid to extend control over Iran's central government constituted a vital factor in the radical reorientation of American attitudes that eventually found expression in the policy of containment formalized by the Truman Doctrine of 1947. Iran, however, although thus playing a key role in the process of policy change, was a potential victim if the process faltered, and she could have ended in a position similar to that of the Eastern European satellite states. To emerge victorious from these trials required strong nerves, cool courage, and singleness of purpose.

There was still another difference between the father and the son. While Reza Shah had to nurture only one nationalist movement during his reign, namely his own, Mohammad Reza Shah had to deal with competing forces that interpreted nationalist objectives and priorities in a different way from his own. This in particular referred to the definition and designation of friends and enemies of Iran. There were elements during his rule that viewed Western, particularly British, imperialism as the only true danger to Iran. With such an approach, a possibility existed of effecting an alliance between this type of nationalist and the Communists who, by virtue of their ideologies and loyalties, regarded the West as an enemy. This possibility became an actual reality in the early 1950s and the alliance thus formed attempted to overthrow not only the government but the institution of monarchy as well. The Shah's own nationalism, which he described as "positive" in contrast with the negative, anti-Western brand of the competing forces, had as its objective not only a strong and independent Iran but also close links between Iran, the United States, and her Western friends, both of the latter being viewed as allies in the struggle to preserve Iranian independence and integrity.

Moreover, the Shah did not want to limit Iran's role to that of a "junior partner" in a broader alliance to contain Soviet expansionism. He felt that the political situation in the Middle East called for a strong Iran that would play a stabilizing role in the region. For this reason he insisted on and secured the development of a well-equipped and trained military establishment that, under his rule, not only enlarged and modernized its land forces but also branched out into military aviation and the navy. By the mid-1970s Iran could be described as enjoying military hegemony in the Persian Gulf region while protecting the vital sea-lanes through which eighteen million barrels of oil per day were being carried to overseas destinations.

Mohammad Reza Shah's reign differed also from that of his father's in the scope and content of modernization measures. True enough, both kings were reformers, but the reforms carried out during Mohammad Reza's time were more comprehensive and more concerned with social justice and the welfare of the masses. Launched in 1963 and known under the general name of the White Revolution, these reforms contained an original six-point program with land reform as its central objective, later enlarged into seventeen points that embraced a variety of social, economic, and cultural measures. The program represented a broad attack in every conceivable sector against the old ills of the Iranian society. Its many features are reviewed in the chapters that follow. The reforms were accompanied by economic planning and development that in the 1960s and 1970s achieved one of the highest growth rates anywhere in the world. These impressive attainments were further bolstered by the substantial increase in national revenue through a truly revolutionary raising of the prices of exported oil. The latter represented the Shah's own achievement inasmuch as since the middle 1950s he had assumed personal leadership in all matters pertaining to the development of petroleum resources in the country. In this respect, he not only secured Iran's full control over her oil industry but also led the victorious regional campaign of oil-producing states to ensure that their major natural resource would obtain on world markets a price commensurate with the rising prices of manufactured commodities produced in advanced industrialized states.

In spite of the tragic interruption experienced at the time of World War II and its aftermath, the two reigns of the Pahlavi period had this in common that they represented a continuous struggle of strong-willed rulers to elevate their nation from the level of weakness and backwardness to a higher level of strength and modernity. It was indeed a struggle in which many opposing forces both at home and abroad had to be overcome. There were setbacks but there were also spectacular victories. The story of these trials and achievements is told in the chapters that follow.

1

Reza Shah the Great: Founder of the Pahlavi Dynasty

The little British India steamer that sailed from Bandar 'Abbas in the Persian Gulf on September 28, 1941, was carrying a complement of passengers that differed markedly from the usual motley crowd that had covered its decks during its twenty-seven years of sailing up and down the gulf to and from Karachi. On this occasion the S.S. *Bandra* (3,194 tons, registered in Glasgow, where it was built in 1914) had only twenty passengers, of whom nine had comparatively humble status. The remaining eleven consisted of Reza Shah Pahlavi, until twelve days previously ruler of Iran; his fourth wife; eight of his ten children; and his son-in-law, son of his minister of court and husband of his eldest daughter.

On September 16 in Tehran, Reza Shah had addressed a dignified letter to the prime minister, Mohammad 'Ali Forughi:

> As I have during these past years devoted all my powers to the affairs of the country and am exhausted, I feel that the time has come for a younger strength to take charge of the affairs of the country, which require constant attention, and thereby to ensure the well-being and prosperity of the nation. I have therefore handed over the sovereign power to my heir and successor and retired from active life. From today, Shahrivar 25, 1320 [September 16, 1941], let the whole people, military and civil, recognize my legal heir and successor as sovereign, and offer to him in furtherance of the interests of the country what they have offered to me.[1]

The same day the ex-Shah had left for Isfahan, where his family, apart from his eldest son, the new Shah Mohammad Reza, and his second daughter, the young Shah's twin sister Princess Ashraf, were waiting for him. Together they had continued their melancholy progress through Yazd and Kerman to Bandar 'Abbas. It was a far cry from the tours of inspection he had so often carried out in the past. Though he was not a man for empty forms and ceremonials, his arrival in a city had always been the occasion of much hurrying to and fro of officials, of hasty finishing of unfinished jobs, of top hats and morning coats. Now his coming was almost unnoticed; there was no official reception, and accommodation for his party was provided reluctantly.

In Kerman the ex-Shah was unwell, suffering from an ear infection; but the British consul, considering himself once again a power in the land, hurried him on southwards without even time to gather together the bare necessities of travel. When the party arrived in Bandar 'Abbas, the *Bandra* was already lying offshore (there was no harbor), ready to sail in the morning. The Shah sent his family on board, but insisted himself on spending his last night in Iranian territory on land. The next day, as the little ship plowed its way down the Persian Gulf towards India, Reza Shah stood gazing back at the land that he loved, and that he was never to see again.

In Karachi he suffered further indignities. Contrary to his expectations, he was not allowed to land, and after five frustrating days he and his family were transferred to the Henderson liner S.S. *Burma* (7,281 tons)—also by an odd coincidence built on the Clyde in 1914—and conveyed to the little Indian Ocean island of Mauritius. They arrived on October 15, in time for the onset of the hot season in this isolated, humid little patch of ocean-bound land. No doubt British officialdom thought such a climate appropriate for someone from Iran, but the scorching humidity of the Persian Gulf, with which the visitors were most familiar, was far from typical of the whole country; and a man accustomed to the dry, temperate altitude of Tehran, 4,000 feet above sea level, would find it hard to adapt to sea level in the tropics. The ex-monarch's health continued to suffer until, on March 27, 1942, he was permitted to transfer to South Africa and the moderate climate of Johannesburg. There he spent the remaining two years of his life until his death, of sheer weariness of spirit, on July 26, 1944.

His spirits could hardly have been raised by the news filtering through from his own country. Even as he left Tehran, British and Russian troops were closing in on the capital. Although the main bodies were withdrawn a month later, the presence of Allied forces—British, Russian, American, French, Polish, and the rest—continued to be a prominent feature of the city's life for the next four years. His beloved railway was taken over by the military and devoted almost exclusively to the transport of supplies to the Soviet Union. The tiny navy had been wiped out; the 200,000-strong army, virtually his personal creation, had been disbanded even before his abdication, an action that landed the over-hasty war minister temporarily in jail. Before they could be rounded up again, large quantities of small arms and ammunition had found their way into the hands of the tribes, who were once again flexing their muscles as they saw the strong hand of the central government removed. Once again it became unsafe to travel in Iran without an escort. It was several years before the tribes could be reduced to the state of subserviency they had known under Reza Shah, and he himself was never to see this happen. The careful posture of neutrality in the world war was abandoned, and Iran found herself a belligerent when, on September 9, 1943, she declared war on Germany. Not that these gestures towards the Allied cause earned much respect for Iran; it was symbolic that early in 1942 Anthony Eden, the British foreign secretary, announced that the country was in future to be described in the West as "Persia" instead of "Iran,"—and added insult to injury by coupling this announcement with the similar substitution of "Siam" for "Thailand," an Axis sympathizer.

The country seemed to be falling apart. The insatiable demands of the Allied forces and the hoarding of supplies by profiteers were causing not only rampant inflation—a sevenfold increase in the cost of living between the autumn of 1941 and the spring of 1944—but also acute food shortages, amounting in many areas to actual famine. "Famine in Tehran?" exclaimed Reza Shah on hearing this incredible news. "What's the meaning of famine? Have the Iranians got to provide the foreigners with bread as well? They made out that they were going to provide the people of Iran with bread! They were going to make everything fine for them. Fine indeed! But they're trying to blame it all on me."[2] To the casual observer, it looked as though the whole structure laboriously built up over the preceding twenty years was being systematically dismantled by the Allied powers and the new political groupings springing up everywhere—politicians of the old regime, the new men trained by the Pahlavi system, left-wing activists released from the political prisons, right-wing fanatics modeling themselves on the German Nazis, middle-of-the-road democrats, place-seekers—contained no one capable of taking a firm hold of the situation.

It must have seemed like the end of everything to the exiled monarch gazing across the sea towards his beloved country. To most people it must have seemed like the end of an era. But looking back from the vantage point of thirty-five years on, we can see that the disaster was not as great as it seemed then, that the foundations of the new structure were still sound. The crisis marked only the end of a beginning, the beginning of Iran's transformation from a semimedieval kingdom ignored or exploited by international powers to a powerful modern state with a dominant role in world affairs.

Iran had not reached that stage in 1941; the long haul back to independence and self-respect was still ahead. But to understand how that was
possible, we must turn back the pages of history to see how it all started.

WHO WAS REZA KHAN?

The story begins in 1878 in the little village of Elasht, in the district of
Savadkuh, deep in the heart of the Elborz Mountains some 110 kilometers
northeast of Tehran as the crow flies, or 300 by road. Today Elasht is
undergoing changes; selected with other villages throughout the country as
an experimental area, it has seen in recent years the introduction of
electricity and piped water, the building of a primary school, the opening of
shops, the establishment of a health center, library and meeting hall, and
even the institution of a supermarket and a bank (a branch of the Army
Bank, the first bank founded by Reza Shah). Yet it is still more remote from
city life than the actual distance suggests, so remote indeed that most
Tehranis do not know how to pronounce its name. Even now travel to it is
restricted in winter by weather conditions, the rough road leading thither
being frequently blocked by snow. But a hundred years ago there were no
roads at all, and the only means of access were narrow winding tracks over,
through, and around the precipitous mountain gorges, negotiable only on
foot or by mule and horse. Clinging to the slopes of these forbidding valleys
at altitudes ranging up to ten thousand feet are little villages, seldom of more
than a thousand inhabitants, the little stone-and-plaster-built cottages
huddled on top of one another for warmth and security. Their occupants
subsist mainly on the products of their flocks of sheep and goats grazing on
the mountainside above their homes, supplemented by patches of vegetables
and cereals.

The Elborz Mountains have always been the least accessible part of Iran.
When the Arabs poured on to the central plateau in the seventh century A.D.,
this was one part of the country that they were obliged for many years to
bypass. Secure in their remote valleys, the hardy mountain folk long
remained impervious to Arab culture and Islamic religion, and when later
they adopted Islam they gave it fanatical devotion and at the same time
incorporated into it many of the beliefs and practices they had inherited
from their Iranian ancestors. In these mountains Hasan Sabbah, the Isma'ili
leader known to the European world as the Old Man of the Mountain and
Chief of the Assassins, had his impregnable castle of Alamut. The tenth-
century poet Ferdowsi, author of *Shahnameh*—the "Book of Kings" embody-
ing the legendary history of Iran—sets many of his scenes in these valleys,

peopling them with kings and heroes, demons, giants, and dragons.

The people of Mazandaran pride themselves on their pure Iranian ancestry. Hardy, long-lived men and women of striking appearance, they have long provided some of the best fighting men in the Iranian army.

Elasht itself lies at an altitude of 6,000 feet, and has a population of about 2,500, fairly large for a village in this area; although no reliable records exist, it was probably much the same a century ago. In a little house that is still standing to this day, there was born on March 16, 1878, Reza, the youngest son of Abbas 'Ali Khan, familiarly known as Dadash Beg, a major in the Savadkuh Regiment and son of Morad 'Ali Khan Soltan, also an officer of the same regiment, who was killed at the siege of Herat in 1856. A book written in 1893 mentions the latter as the brother of a distinguished theologian who died at the age of 45 in about 1810, so that the family combined in its tradition the two most prominent aspects of Mazandarani society, the military and the religious.[3] To this element in Reza's makeup was added the Caucasian contribution of his mother, Nush-Afarin Khanom, whose family, though of Iranian stock, came originally from Erivan when that city was conquered by the Russians early in the nineteenth century.

Reza's father died some months after his birth, and the following spring his mother decided to return to Tehran, where she had been born and brought up. In later years the tough Cossack general often told the story of how he had almost died in the bitterly cold journey through the mountains. However, the experience does not seem to have harmed him, for he grew up to be a tall, strong young man, who then as all his life towered over his fellows. While still a youngster (the exact age is given differently in various accounts, but he was probably between twelve and fifteen) he joined the Russian-officered Cossack Brigade, in which one of his uncles was an officer, and rose steadily from the ranks to officer level. In his thirties he was in command of a machine gun detachment, an early instance of the fascination that technical and mechanical things held for him all through his life. He took part in a number of military campaigns against unruly tribes in the mountain areas of Mazandaran, Gilan, and Azarbayjan, and by the time he was forty he had achieved the rank of *mir panj,* approximately equivalent to brigadier, and was in command of the Hamadan *otryad* (detachment) of the Cossack Division. So for the first half of his adult life Reza Khan was a soldier pure and simple, following in the steps of his ancestors, and had there not been something exceptional about him, there would have been no reason for him to have become anything more. But it would appear that mentally as well as physically he was in advance of his neighbors. He not only, as we have seen, achieved competence in the technical field of machine gunnery, a qualification that might have been expected of anyone in his position; he also taught himself to read and write, which was a rather less usual accomplishment at that time, when education was considered to be a privilege of the wealthy classes.

But Reza Khan's military career gave him more than literacy and technical know-how. With these came awareness, born of endless and wearisome campaigning against rebellious tribesmen, of the wretched state of his country. Though he had at that time never been abroad—and indeed only twice left Iran before his final departure in 1941—he could hardly have failed to realize that a land in which vast wealth existed side by side with grinding poverty, in which travel was rendered virtually impossible both by lack of roads and by robbery and banditry, in which the great and powerful sought office primarily for their own ends, and in which bribery and corruption were the fuel that drove the government machine, was a land that compared unfavorably even with its immediate neighbors, let alone with the technologically advanced countries of the West, whose products he could see flooding the markets and changing the habits of his countrymen. He quickly developed a soldier's contempt for the bungling and self-seeking politicians of Tehran, whose eloquence and rhetoric served merely to conceal their incompetence and greed. But even more to the point, his service as an ordinary private soldier under the command of Russian officers taught him that no foreigner, however well-intentioned, would ever put the interests of Iran before those of his own country. "After I had chosen the soldier's profession," he wrote, "I became ever more sunk in grief, as I saw the destinies of Iran's forces determined by Russian officers, who intervened directly in all the affairs of the army and compelled the Iranian officers to accept their dictatorial ways. These Russian officers were ostensibly in the service of the Shah, but in reality gave priority to the interests of their own country."[4] This suspicion of foreigners, and particularly of Iran's most powerful neighbors, Russia and Britain, was to stay with him all his life. And it is difficult to blame him, when one looks back at the history of Iran during the past century.

THE STRANGLING OF IRAN

The Cossack Brigade was formed not long after Reza Khan's birth in 1878. In that year Naser ad-Din Shah paid his second visit to Europe, and accepted an offer from the tsar to train an armed force on Russian lines that could serve as a personal bodyguard for the Shah. For about forty years this force, which at times numbered as many as 10,000 cavalry and infantry, was officered entirely by Russians, and even the noncommissioned ranks were rarely filled by Iranians. Given this fact, and given the course of Iranian history during these years, it is scarcely surprising that the Cossack Brigade served far more as an instrument of Russian policy than as a servant of the Shah of Iran. By the end of the nineteenth century the absolute monarchy of the Qajars was drawing to an end, and the stability of the regime was being threatened from two entirely different sources. On the one hand the growing commercial, financial, and political interests of Britain and Russia were compelling them ever more blatantly to influence the Iranian government's policies in directions more profitable to themselves, and by the same token to keep that government as weak as was practicable without total collapse. So long indeed as the interests of the two powers were in conflict, Iranian politicians could indulge in the game of playing one off against the other. But neither Shah nor ministers proved themselves strong or determined enough to strike out on a line of their own; instead, they remained content to react negatively towards each fresh crisis or encroachment on their sovereignty.

But the very circumstances that brought the foreign powers to Iran also brought with them other disturbing factors. The passive acceptance of a divinely appointed absolute ruler began to be undermined by doctrines and teachings that had been familiar in Europe for a century. Democracy, constitution, limited monarchy, nationalism, freedom of speech, and other such unfamiliar concepts, brought not so much by Europeans themselves as by Iranians sent to Europe to learn the techniques necessary for men who were to use and operate the new weapons and machines, became the common coin of political discussion. In spite of every effort by the regime to suppress them, they finally surged up into an outburst of popular feeling that was potent enough to wrest a constitution from an unwilling Shah and even to cast down from his throne his reactionary successor, who had sought to turn back the clock. Yet even these domestic crises were not allowed to pass without the intervention of the two European powers, and while we do not need to go as far as the party-political abuse that charged one or the other side with merely acting on the orders of foreigners, we have yet to recognize that British support of the constitutionalists and Russian support of the royalists was neither ineffectual nor disinterested. The immediate effect of the Constitutional Revolution of 1906, as seen from the practical viewpoint of a patriotic Iranian soldier, was the delivery of the country helpless into the hands of the powers. At the very time that Britain and Russia were taking opposite sides in Iran's domestic affairs, they were calmly and secretly dividing the country between themselves into spheres of influence, Russia in the north, Britain in the south. As if further to seal Iran's doom, the abdication of Mohammad 'Ali Shah and his subsequent unsuccessful attempt to regain his throne was followed with hardly a gap by the outbreak of World War I and the irruption into neutral Iran of Russian,

Turkish, and British forces. For the next four years Iran found herself, if not a battlefield, at least maneuvering ground for the rival armies. In the south German agents stirred up the tribes, and were finally hunted down and suppressed by the British-officered South Persia Rifles. Another British force in the east guarded the approaches to India. The Cossacks continued to take their orders from St. Petersburg until the Russian Revolution of 1917, when—most of their officers being supporters of the old regime—they slipped out of the control of the new Moscow government, without however necessarily aligning themselves with either the Shah or their former allies and rivals, the British.

Reza Khan himself played a small but significant part in these developments. During 1917 the White Russian commander of the Cossack Brigade was replaced by a Kerensky nominee, Colonel Klerzhé, who brought with him as second-in-command a former comrade-in-arms, Colonel Staroselsky. When the Kerensky regime fell and was replaced by the Bolsheviks, the loyalties of these two officers diverged: Klerzhé inclined towards the Bolsheviks, while Staroselsky owed allegiance to the White Russian General Denikin, then campaigning in south Russia. To Reza Khan, already advancing up the officer ladder, both these officers seemed disloyal to Iran; but he was also conscious that the most serious danger to Iran came from the Bolsheviks, who were already seeking to advance the frontiers of their influence in Asia by encouraging dissident movements in northern Iran. He was therefore willing as a first step to support Staroselsky in the forcible removal of Klerzhé, even though this resulted in no more than the transfer of command to another Russian officer.[5] Indeed, the only alternative seriously put forward at the time was the appointment of a prince of the royal house, which in Reza Khan's eyes would hardly have been an improvement. So the position by 1920 was that the Cossack Division (as it now was), the only substantial Iranian armed force, could not be trusted to fight loyally for or against either of the two neighboring powers, or even to support its own nominal masters.

By 1920 the situation in Iran had sunk to its lowest level for over a century. The nationalist-constitutionalist movement that had begun with such high hopes was grinding to a halt amid a welter of argument, recriminations, and party bickering. Cabinet succeeded cabinet with high-sounding aims and corrupt intentions. The ruler himself, catapulted onto the throne as a child by his father's abdication, was still a young, inexperienced, cowardly, and corrupt individual, whose first thought was for his personal well-being, and whose confidence in the future of his country was so diminished that he could think of nothing but ways of escape from his responsibilities. In any case the writ of his government scarcely ran outside Tehran and a few other large towns, and even in those towns the chief

His Imperial Majesty Reza Shah the Great

authority was the provincial governor, whose power derived from his control of a private army, and who owed to the central government only as much allegiance as he thought fit. Travel between cities was impossible without an escort, always assuming the escort could be trusted. The only organized armed forces in the country were under the control of foreigners. Apart from the Russian-officered Cossack Division, numbering some six thousand men, there still remained in the south the British-officered South Persia Rifles, a force of comparable size, and distributed throughout the country the ragged remains of the Swedish-officered gendarmerie, founded in 1911. There was also in Tehran a 600-strong Central Brigade. Torn apart by six years of war and civil disorder, the country seemed indeed to be falling to pieces. In every corner of the land local chiefs and tribal khans were taking the law into their own hands—Turcomans in the northeast, Kurds in the northwest, Bakhtiaris and Qashqa'is in the south, Baluchis in Kerman and Bulchistan, Lurs in the mountain ranges of the west. In Khuzistan, the Arab Shaykh Khaz'al reigned as an independent ruler, confident in the support of his British allies. In Gilan, Mirza Kuchek Khan established an independent, republican regime from his Jangali "forest" headquarters, and collaborated with other rebels and Bolshevik troops along the whole coast of the Caspian Sea.

The Bolshevik Revolution of 1917 brought little relief. The main White Russian resistance was concentrated in the Caucasus across Iran's northwestern border, and although the immediate effect of the revolution was the withdrawal of Russian interest in Iran, Iranian territory served as a route and base for the British force sent under the command of General Dunsterville to conduct a hopeless three-cornered campaign with two colors of Russians, the Turks, and local republican and nationalist movements in the Caucasus. This British force later fell back into Iran to form a weak line of defense along the route from Tehran to Baghdad. Meanwhile the defeat of the White Russian General Denikin had deprived the Cossack Division of its last links abroad, while at the same time ships of the White Russian fleet carrying large number of refugees sought asylum in the harbor of the Iranian port of Enzeli, there to offer a tempting bait to the victorious Red forces, now in full occupation of the Caucasian provinces.

BRITAIN AND THE "PERSIAN QUESTION"

The British situation in Iran was at this time determined by the lines of policy laid down by Lord Curzon, who had been foreign secretary since 1919. Viceroy of India from 1899 to 1905, Lord Curzon had as early as 1889, when he published his book *Russia in Central Asia,* been a firm advocate of a policy in Asia that combined a form of imperialism with the containment of Russia. Seen from this point of view, Iran was a handy buffer state, not necessarily to be absorbed but rather to be maintained as a barrier against possible Russian designs on India, the jewel in Britain's imperial crown. With Germany defeated and Russia in the toils of civil war, the time seemed ripe for Britain, unhampered by other powers, to turn Iran into a docile and well-run protectorate.

The first step towards this was the negotiation of the Anglo-Persian Treaty, signed on August 19, 1919, the general effect of which, though it nominally recognized the independence of Iran, was to place the country under British tutelage, with British advisers at all sensitive points, particularly the military and financial. Although this treaty required ratification by the Majles (the lower house of the Iranian legislature), which had not been reelected since the expiry of its third session in 1916 (and was not to be reconstituted until 1921), it was supposed that this was no more than a formality. To mark British pleasure the young Ahmad Shah was brought to London and feted by the British government, to whom, as Lord Curzon later put it, "he more than once gave expression to the most cordial acceptance of the Agreement."[6] Meanwhile, the provisions of the treaty began to be put into effect immediately. A military mission headed by Brigadier General W.E.R. Dickson, former commander of the East Persia Cordon Field Force, and a financial one led by Sydney Armitage-Smith, duly arrived. Among the problems that confronted the military mission was the future of the various existing forces, the Cossack Division, the South Persia Rifles, and the gendarmerie. It soon became clear that the line that was going to be advocated was the incorporation of all three into a British-officered force, thus at one stroke eliminating the dangers posed by the presence of Russian and Swedish officers, neither of whom could be expected to cooperate happily with Britain.

Before this plan could be brought to fruition, a number of problems emerged. One of these was the discovery that Bolshevik Russia was not, after all, a factor to be ignored, even though the defeat of the Red Army in the West by the Polish Marshal Pilsudski certainly made the threat of Bolshevik adventures less likely. All the same the British government, influenced by Curzon, was extremely reluctant to leave the defense of India's border to a Persian force, however well-trained. On the other hand, the prevailing sentiment in Britain was in favor of disentanglement from complicated adventures in the East. The small British forces in Iran, the South Persia Rifles and the North Persia Force ("Norperforce"), the remnants of Dunsterville's force, were hardly enough to block a determined Bolshevik advance, and there was no point in leaving them there merely "to strew leaves from a Persian rosegarden in front of the advancing Bolsheviks," as one British critic put it.[7] But in the long run, far more important was the almost universal condemnation of the treaty in Iran itself. It was widely supposed that even the ministers who had negotiated and signed it had only done so after considerable financial persuasion; apart from them, members of all political groups were astonishingly unanimous in condemning the whole scheme. Above all, the proposal to replace the Russian Cossack officers with British aroused the greatest indignation of all. Others besides Reza Khan saw that the essential first step was to bring the armed forces of the country under national control, free of all foreign influence; but only Reza Khan had the courage and determination to do it. He was by no means alone in his hatred of foreign interference, born though that was of personal experience. The flames of nationalism may have been damped by the experiences of the past fifteen years, but they had certainly not been quenched. More and more, people were beginning to see that Iran's only hope lay in a genuine revival of nationalist feeling led by personalities whose only interest was in the rebirth and revitalization of their country.

Incredible as it may appear, the British government sought to cash in even on this situation. Lord Curzon's dispatches to Tehran show increasing disillusion with the prospects of the successful ratification of the treaty; he was becoming more inclined to cut loose from Iran. Before the end of 1920 it was clear that the British government had decided to withdraw all its forces—South Persia Rifles, Norperforce, East Persian Cordon Field Force. Nevertheless, instinctive caution suggested the unwisdom of completely leaving Iran to her fate. The problem, as Lord Curzon saw it, was to ensure a stable Iran after a British withdrawal. He hoped to achieve this by himself selecting a suitable prime minister (the candidate was a Qajar prince, Nosrat ad-Dowleh Firuz, present in London to negotiate a government loan).[8] Events however moved too quickly for him, and for once a vacuum in Iran was filled not by a foreign power but by a purely national movement.

Certainly the world atmosphere was favorable to such movements. The end of the war in Europe, the defeat of the German, Austro-Hungarian, Russian and Ottoman empires, and the consequent breakup of those conglomerations had brought independence to more than one hitherto subject people. The peace settlement was being worked out along the lines of self-determination, and by 1920 the map of Europe showed not only new frontiers but also new names—Yugoslavia, Czechoslovakia, Estonia, Lithuania, Latvia. Most of these new or revived states chose the republican form of government, for in the new world atmosphere republicanism seemed to be the natural complement to ethnic nationalism. In Asia the prospect was not quite so attractive; true, there were short-lived independent republics in Armenia, Azarbayjan, and Georgia, but elsewhere the old imperialist game was still being played—though even here it was being given a covering of respectability and even a considerable degree of impermanence by the new mandatory system, supervised by the League of Nations. Territories like Syria, Iraq, and Palestine were nominally independent, and indeed the mandate system was not formally introduced until 1921. Genuine independence was a long time in coming, but nevertheless there would have been little international sympathy for any power seeking openly to extend its territorial empire. Moreover, in a few more years the world was to see more than one nationalist revolutionary movement led by an outstanding personality—Kemal Pasha in Turkey, Mussolini in Italy, Hitler in Germany. The era of the dictators was at hand.

THE WIND OF CHANGE

In Iran the whole situation was to change in the twelve months between the spring of 1920 and the spring of 1921. The sequence of events began with the arrival of a Bolshevik fleet off the Caspian coast of Iran; it demanded the surrender of the White Russian ships interned in the port of Enzeli. The demand was rammed home by the bombardment of Enzeli and Rasht and the landing of Bolshevik troops. These towns were held by part of the former "Dunsterforce" (General Dunsterville's army), now under the command of Brigadier General Champain, who decided that he could not maintain his position. Leaving behind him considerable quantities of ammunition, stores, and petrol, he withdrew rather ignominiously through the newly established Bolshevik lines to take up a more secure position north of Qazvin.[9] Meanwhile the Cossack forces, including the detachment commanded by Reza Khan, moved up into Gilan and Mazandaran and engaged with the Bolshevik forces, which had not linked up with Kuchek Khan and Amir Mo'ayyad (rebel leader operating in Gilan and Mazandaran who cooperated with the Red Army); for a time their efforts were successful, and they even recaptured Rasht. The defeated British commander was meanwhile replaced by Major General Ironside, who reorganized the British defense position at the Manjil Pass, only shortly before the collapse and retreat of the Cossacks. As they filtered back through the British lines to regroup at the Agha Baba camp west of Qazvin, Iranian anger at what they described as the treachery of their Russian officers came to a head, and when the demoralized division was instructed by Staroselsky to follow him to Tehran, it refused to do so; instead the Russian commander found on his arrival at the capital that the reluctant Shah had been compelled to dismiss him and his Russian colleagues and to appoint an Iranian commander in his place. The latter turned out to be, not a soldier, but a member of the Iranian imperial family whose primary function appeared to be to ensure the loyalty of the division to the

Shah. A competent commander was still needed, but the circumstances were such that the appointment of a British officer would not have been acceptable either in Iran or in London. It was at this point that General Ironside and Colonel Smythe, the British military adviser with special responsibility for the Cossacks, began to notice the work of the Hamadan *otryad*.[10] They were the only detachment that seemed to be taking a genuine interest in their training, and this enthusiasm was clearly due to their commanding officer, a tall, vigorous, and distinguished looking man by the name of Reza Khan. To Ironside and Smythe it was obvious that he was the only man capable of taking command of the Cossack Division, and in due course the Shah's nominee faded from the picture and Reza Khan became the de facto commander.

Reza Khan had no hesitation in blaming the treachery and incompetence of the Russian officers for the disasters in Gilan and Mazandaran, a view fully confirmed by what was discovered of their corruption and peculation. At the same time the fiasco of the British retreat from Rasht (which finally decided the British cabinet, against the urging of Lord Curzon, on total withdrawal from Iran) can hardly have predisposed him in favor of a British-officered force. Instead he was reinforced in his long-held belief that the only salvation for Iran lay in the creation of a wholly Iranian force, armed and trained to the highest degree possible, and as we have seen he was determined that the troops under his command should show what was possible given single-minded direction and freedom from foreign or political control.

We are now on the eve of the event that, with hindsight, can be seen as the turning point in Iran's history, the moment when the country ceased to drift into chaos, and began to follow a straight and positive course towards independence and self-sufficiency. Strangely, for an event of such climacteric importance, the full facts are still obscure, and perhaps never will be known. Instead we are obliged to try to come at the truth on the basis of what we know of the political and military forces involved, the personalities concerned, and the results that finally emerged. This is indeed an indication of the nature of the problem. Most of the individuals concerned have given their own account of what happened, often with a view to enhancing the importance of their own role. Contemporary observers have told us what they saw, but not what was hidden from them. Later writers, working from documents and memoirs, have sought primarily to justify a particular political line, this was especially true of the polemical works that appeared after 1941, when the fashion was to attack the recently fallen monarch with any weapon that lay to hand, without too strict a regard for the truth. What is quite certain is that Iran at the beginning of 1921 was ripe for some kind of upheaval. Reformist and revolutionary currents were in the air, and it may have been no more than a matter of time and chance which took precedence.

Already in Gilan there was the semi-Communist regime of Kuchek Khan, not perhaps firmly enough based and certainly too torn by ideological differences to provide a starting point for a national revolution; but there had been some attempts at agrarian reforms and other measures designed to combat some of the worst social abuses in Iran. In Tehran more than one liberal and democratic political grouping was talking in terms of some drastic action, though few were doing more than talk. Of these the group led by Seyyed Ziya ad-Din Tabataba'i, a young, idealistic journalist from a religious background, was coming to the fore. Finally, Reza Khan's ambitions were by no means limited to the creation of a modern army; how far he saw himself at this stage as the leader of an Iranian renaissance we cannot tell, but that he was convinced of the need for such a renaissance there can be no doubt, and it was also clear that, as the commander of the only efficient armed force in the country, he alone had the means to bring it about.

Though Reza Khan was first and foremost a simple soldier, he had a full share of the Iranian capacity for political intrigue and manipulation. The way in which he succeeded in weaving together and converting to his own use the various conflicting interests, without their even being aware of it, marks him out as a man destined to rule. Two main strands were present: the nationalist reformist groupings, led by Seyyed Ziya; and the British, still in effective control of most of the country but anxious to be rid of their responsibilities. As for the others, the Shah was almost negligible; frightened for his very life, he seems to have been thinking of nothing but how he would most conveniently leave the country. The older politicians were largely discredited as a result of the confusion of the past decade. The Bolshevik Russians were beginning to realize that they had overreached themselves, and were talking of withdrawal; and without their support Kuchek Khan would not last very long.

It was popular at one time in Iranian political circles to attribute the coup d'état of 1921, together with Reza Khan's consequent rise to supreme power, to a deep-laid British plot to establish in Iran a regime that could be counted on to serve British interests. If such a plot ever existed, it was a highly unsuccessful one, for the period from 1921 to 1941 marked the rapid decline and almost complete elimination of British influence from Iran (with the possible exception of the oil area in the southwest), an influence that was to return briefly in 1941 until it was finally expunged after the events of 1951-53. But the belief in the all-pervading power of the British Intelligence Service, given the substantial backing of fact that it undoubtedly once had, dies hard in Iran, and the British are still blamed in jest for the shortcomings of the weather or the taste of the tea.

Certainly there was a full measure of British intrigue at the time we are discussing. It could hardly have been otherwise, given the dominating position that Britain still held as a result of the partial implementation of the unratified Anglo-Persian Treaty. But official British policy was by now a negative one: how to withdraw gracefully from Iran without leaving behind a situation of chaos that could be exploited by Russia, in the British book (and not without reason) still the main rival despite the change of regime. That this was the British government's purpose seemed to be generally understood by British officials; there was less unanimity on how it could be achieved. Indeed, we are faced with the curious spectacle of rival diplomats and soldiers trying to play a Machiavellian role by encouraging one group or another, not realizing that they were themselves being used by a far more skilled operator. In London, as we have seen, the official candidate was Nosrat ad-Dowleh Firuz, who had been dispatched posthaste to Iran but arrived too late to stop the course of events. He was arrested by Seyyed Ziya, and is credited with having after his release started the story about the coup d'état being a British plot. British diplomatic officials on the spot seem rather to have favored the seyyed; certainly some of them, though possibly not the British minister Norman himself, had been in frequent touch with him. In an interview with Norman on February 25, 1921, shortly after he had been appointed prime minister, Seyyed Ziya warned the British envoy not to press too hard for the appointment to the army of British officers (a proposal that the seyyed himself had made as far back as the summer of 1920). Significantly, he continued that "if Great Britain wished to secure her position here she must sacrifice shadow for substance, remain in the background and help Persia effectively but unostentatiously. He [Seyyed Ziya] was sure that this policy would in the end gain for Britain most of the advantages she had expected to obtain from an impracticable agreement."[11] On March 3 he gave Norman a further assurance that he was determined to employ British officers for the armed forces.[12]

We should not, perhaps, read too much into all this. Norman may have felt that he was influencing events, and certainly in his cables to Lord Curzon in London he was vigorous in urging Seyyed Ziya's claims to support from Britain—urgings that fell on deaf ears, for Curzon was now fully committed to withdrawal. But Seyyed Ziya was also playing a subtle game. He needed support, and he did not care particularly where it came from. At the same time he was a visionary rather than a man of action; his political failure in 1921, as again after 1943, was largely because of his inability to combine his idealism with the practical business of government and politics. When he did embark on political intrigue, he became as often as not the victim rather than the victor. This certainly seems to have been the case when he sought to remedy the most obvious weakness in his position by calling on the Cossack Division for aid.

This was probably the first contact between Seyyed Ziya and Reza Khan, and it offered the latter the chance for which he had been waiting. One can imagine that Reza Khan quickly saw through Seyyed Ziya's weaknesses, while accepting him as a useful political ally, someone who could help him to achieve the first of his ambitions, the creation of a strong unified army. It is significant that, although by all accounts Reza Khan was one of the leading personalities in the coup d'état, he did not take a ministerial post but contented himself with the post of commander in chief of the armed forces. Given his personality, outlook and subsequent record, the suggestion that he also came to power by virtue of British support strikes one as even less likely than the same charge made against Seyyed Ziya. It does not seem as though Reza Khan had had any contact with British Legation officials, indeed, even after February 21. Norman described him as "an honest and capable officer without political ambitions."[13] Nevertheless it is the case that both Ironside and Smythe later claimed some responsibility for the coup d'état, though perhaps again it was a case of the tail wagging the dog.[14] Early in 1921 Smythe had been in contact with Seyyed Ziya and a group of officers (not of the Cossack Brigade) who supported him, including Major Mas'ud Khan and Captain Qasem Khan, whose names will be heard again. The most positive role was played by Ironside, who according to his own account had discussed with Reza Khan the possibility of a coup d'état and on February 12 indicated that, if Reza Khan embarked on one, Norperforce would not hinder him, provided that he did not propose to overthrow the Shah. Ironside even claims that at his audience with Ahmad Shah on February 15 he tried unsuccessfully to persuade the Shah to appoint Reza Khan to a position of power.[15]

It is clear from Ironside's comments that he shared Reza Khan's disillusion with Ahmad Shah and the Tehran politicians. But the basic aims of the two men were entirely different. Reza Khan was looking forward to a fundamental revolution in the affairs of Iran, a revolution that would bring about profound social changes in the country, changes such as those he did in fact achieve during his years of power. Ironside, on the other hand, was concerned merely to establish Iran as a buffer against the further advance of Communism; he was not concerned with social revolution, and indeed his insistence that there should be no threat to the position of the Shah shows that his outlook was essentially a conservative one. Reza Khan too at this stage may not have been thinking of anything as disturbing as the downfall of the Qajar house; but even if he could see that such would be the inevitable outcome of the line he was pursuing, it was evidently not a matter of high priority with him, as is shown by the readiness with which he gave the undertaking for which Ironside asked and the punctiliousness with which he later sought to be released from it.

However, the significant point is that on February 14 Ironside had received unexpected orders to hand over the command of Norperforce to Major General Sir George Cory, and to proceed to Baghdad and Cairo to take part in a conference headed by Churchill, secretary of state for the colonies, on the future of the mandated territory of Iraq.[16] He left Qazvin by air at dawn on February 18. As his replacement did not arrive until some days later, neither of them was present when Reza Khan, on the evening of February 18, ordered the Cossack troops to begin their march in the direction of Tehran.

THE COUP D'ÉTAT

The story of the coup d'état of February 1921 has often been told. The Cossack Division, rested and reequipped after their traumatic experiences in Gilan, marched briskly from Qazvin to Karaj, about thirty miles west of Tehran, ignoring instructions from the government and from their nominal commander, Sardar Homayun, to return to their headquarters. They were now joined by Seyyed Ziya and a group of officers from Tehran, and at a meeting with Reza Khan they finalized their plans for the occupation of Tehran. They then moved on to Mehrabad (the present site of Tehran Airport, but in those days some miles outside the city walls), and here were met by a delegation consisting of a representative each of the Shah and the cabinet, and two members of the British legation staff. Their mission was to try to dissuade the Cossacks from entering the town, but in this they were unsuccessful. The most authentic account of this meeting comes in the report that Norman subsequently sent to Lord Curzon:

> Reza Khan said that Cossacks who had had experience of Bolsheviks and knew what they were, were tired of seeing one inefficient Government succeed another at Tehran where apparently nobody was making any preparations to oppose Bolshevik advance which would follow withdrawal of British troops. They were therefore coming to Tehran to establish strong Government, which would see to this matter. They professed loyalty and devotion to the Shah, but were determined to set aside the evil counsellors by whom he had been surrounded.[17]

Meanwhile Sardar Homayun had been received in audience by Ahmad Shah, who relieved him of his command and appointed Reza Khan in his place. On February 20 Reza Khan issued his first order of the day: "I have been appointed by His Majesty to the command of His Majesty's Cossack Division. I hereby present myself to all the units, officers, and men of the division, and inform them that as from the second of Hut [February 20] they are to regard my orders as mandatory and to carry them out accordingly." Later the same day he made a short, emotional speech to the troops:

Fellow-soldiers! You have offered every possible sacrifice in the defense of the land of your fathers. All of us have, in the forests and marshes of Gilan, with empty stomachs and ragged uniforms in the pelting rain, together exposed our breasts to the bullets of the Bolsheviks and the rebels. But we have to confess that all our loyalty has served merely to preserve the interests of a handful of traitors in the capital. In spite of all our sacrifices, the unfeeling politicians of the capital, seeing us in the grip of the crimes of our Russian officers, have made no attempt to collaborate with us. They have no welcome for those who risk their lives for their country. These insignificant men are the same treacherous elements who have sucked the last drop of the nation's blood, and have betrayed their fatherland and their patriotic soldiers. Now we are on our way to recover our rights and to revenge ourselves on these corrupt and worthless elements. In order that you may not enter the city empty-handed and so be ashamed before your children, I have ordered that thirty tomans shall be paid to each officer and twenty tomans to each Cossack.[18]

Half an hour after midnight the Cossack troops, numbering about three thousand, entered Tehran and began to occupy key points. They encountered virtually no resistance, whether out of general sympathy with their purposes or because orders to that effect had already been issued from the highest quarters. At all events the Central Brigade troops stationed in Tehran either joined the Cossacks or remained in their barracks. There was brief resistance at the gendarmerie headquarters, where the Swedish General Westdahl was in command; but after the brief exchange of shots and the loss of one man the gendarmerie withdrew, and the Cossacks occupied this and other gendarmerie and police posts throughout the city. By the time the citizens of Tehran awoke on the morning of February 21, the occupation of the city was complete.

A proclamation signed by Reza Khan, posted throughout Tehran, told them the facts—the establishment of martial law and a curfew, the suspension of the press, the banning of meetings, the shutdown of places of entertainment, and the closing of government departments including post and telegraph offices. Captain Qasem Khan, one of the coup d'état leaders, was named as town commandant. Meanwhile Seyyed Ziya was being received by the Shah, who appointed him prime minister, and was busy forming his cabinet, which included Major Mas'ud Khan as minister of war, but otherwise consisted of men already comparatively well-known in public life. Reza Khan was commander in chief of the armed forces, and regularly attended cabinet meetings, even though he was not officially a member. He also received the rank and title of *sardar-e sepah* (marshal of the army).

The brief three-months' premiership of Seyyed Ziya turned out much as might have been expected. The idealist, faced with the practical problems of government, found himself out of his depth. Within a week of his appointment he produced a grandiose program calling for the reorganization of finance and justice; abolition of the capitulatory system; division of state lands among the peasants and improvement of relations between landlords and peasants; encouragement of trade and industry and opening up of communications, roads, etc.; and the establishment of schools.[19] All these indeed were projects that eventually were carried out—but not by Seyyed Ziya. One positive achievement, though it was merely a matter of putting the final touches to what had already been negotiated in Moscow, was the establishment of friendly relations with Soviet Russia by the signing of the treaty already under negotiation in Moscow, by which Russia recognized the independence of Iran and surrendered most of the concessions granted to Tsarist Russia. At the same time the Anglo-Persian Treaty of 1919 was finally abandoned, and the suggestion was made (though not carried out) that certain other foreign concessions ought to be reconsidered. But for the most part the achievements of Seyyed Ziya's government were negative and even disruptive in character. He seems to have tried to cover up his inadequacies by arresting not only his open opponents, like Nosrat ad-Dowleh Firuz, but anyone else who might conceivably cause trouble. The tensions within his cabinet were there from the start. Mas'ud Khan tried to resign in March, and did so definitively in April, whereupon his place was taken by Reza Khan, who indeed even before he entered the cabinet was already largely directing its discussions. Indeed this resignation was only one sign that there could not be more than one master, though Reza Khan, immersed in his own problems, was not yet ready to take over full control. But his disillusionment with Seyyed Ziya was obvious. Whether the break came over the prime minister's indiscriminate policy of arrests, or his rather too obvious pro-British leanings, or his reliance on the support of conservative politicians opposed to radical change, or even his attempts to fulfill his promises to the British minister, we cannot know, nor is it a matter of great significance. He had lost the confidence of Reza Khan, and he had to go.

Reza Khan was the one significant personality there, and when on the first anniversary of the coup d'état he issued a proclamation declaring that he was its real author, and pouring contempt and even threats on those newspaper editors who dared to suggest anything to the contrary, he was merely stating the obvious.[20] If the coup d'état was to be regarded not simply as an isolated historical event but as the beginning of a revolution in Iranian affairs, then Reza Khan was clearly the only man with any claim to be the author of that revolution, for it was only in the sphere of government under his control, the military, that significant progress was made either during the term of office of Seyyed Ziya or during the two years following.

Reza Khan was not too worried about the slow progress towards social, economic, educational, and judicial reforms. These were desperately needed.

But before anything else could be done, the country had to be reunited, rebels and dissidents suppressed, and security and government authority established throughout the land. And this meant the building of a unified and efficient national army. Reza Khan's natural inclination as a soldier coincided with what he saw to be the prior necessity for Iran. So the first months and years of his control of the Ministry of War (itself a creation of the new regime) were devoted almost exclusively to this task. The various armed units in the capital and the north of the country—the Cossack Division, the Central Brigade in Tehran—were concentrated in a new base. Next, the Swedish commander and officers of the gendarmerie were dismissed and replaced by Iranians, and the whole force transferred from the Ministry of the Interior to the Ministry of War and incorporated into a single centralized body with a common uniform. On November 25, 1921, Reza Khan summoned the gendarmerie officers and addressed them: "Gentlemen! Iran, your dear fatherland and mine, has more than ever need of its brave sons. You must exert every effort like men in the service of your country and the pursuit of its independence. You may be confident that the principles of concentration and unity of speech will send the best possible fruits of greatness to welcome you. Be alert! The dust of Ardashir is watching you. Be prepared!"[21] At the same time the terms "Cossack" and "gendarme" were abolished and replaced by the single term *qoshun* (army), a word that was itself later supplanted by *artesh* as part of the general Iranianization of military terminology. A systematic hierarchy of ranks was introduced. As the size of the force under arms grew, there developed a systematic organization into divisions and brigades, while the gendarmerie under the title of *amniye* (security forces), was once again separated, though still under the Ministry of War.

Reza Khan succeeded in incorporating the remnants of the British-officered South Persia Rifles, though in this task he had no cooperation from the British authorities; Curzon, angry at the failure of his policy as represented by the Anglo-Persian Treaty, was not in a mood to be helpful, and all negotiations for the retention of the force under arms, but with Iranian instead of British officers, were firmly rejected. On September 13, 1921, the British minister informed the Iranian government that the disbandment of the force would continue, and added that none of its arms and equipment would be disposed of in Iran. In spite of this, it was some time before the British government could be induced to drop its claims to compensation from the Iranian government for the "services" of the South Persia Rifles, nor was it until March 1926 that the last small detachments of British Indian troops were finally withdrawn from the British Residency and Consulate General at Bushire and the British Consulate at Bandar 'Abbas.[22]

Reza Khan was also well aware of the necessity for a sound financial backing for his military reforms. A successful army had to be well-equipped, properly fed and clothed, and promptly paid, all novelties where the soldiers of Iran were concerned. So long as the provision of finance was dependent on the decidedly haphazard tax-collecting methods of the Ministry of Finance, this could not be ensured. He therefore insisted on the transfer to his ministry of a number of revenue-providing departments, in particular the Administration of Public Domains and of Indirect Taxation, from which sources he could ensure the funds he needed. This remained the position until the arrival of the American financial adviser, A.C. Millspaugh, in November 1922, when Reza Khan, recognizing the importance of a centralized, efficiently run financial administration, agreed to the reincorporation of these offices into the Ministry of Finance, in exchange for a guarantee of regular revenue for the army.[23] He further played his part by using the government's newly found military strength as a backing for Millspaugh's unpopular but badly needed tax-collection measures.

STRENGTH IN UNITY

Reza Khan's wise policy paid off over the next two years, grueling years of military campaigning in the course of which rebellious movements throughout the country were systematically suppressed and the authority of the central government reestablished. Some of these rebellions were political in inspiration: the rising in Tabriz of the gendarmerie officer Abol-Qasem Lahuti, who eventually fled across the Russian border and died there many years later after establishing a reputation as a propagandist poet; or that of Mohammad Taqi Khan Pesyan, another gendarmerie officer, who headed a mutiny in Mashhad and was defeated and killed. Kuchek Khan and his ally Amir Mo'ayyad were still active in Gilan and Mazandaran, supported by small detachments of Russian troops in spite of the provisions of the treaty of February 1921; Kuchek Khan himself, after a split with his Communist allies, died of exposure in a remote part of the Elborz Mountains on November 25, 1921, and by the following summer the remaining dissident elements had been rounded up or driven across the border, and the two provinces were once more peaceful. Elsewhere the trouble was caused mainly by the tribes exercising their immemorial claim to autonomy. The most serious threat came from the Kurds of the northwest, led by Isma'il Aqa Simitqu; by the autumn of 1922 the area was largely pacified, though Isma'il Aqa himself was not finally eliminated until 1926, when he rashly crossed back into Iran from Turkey, where he had taken refuge, and was captured and killed.

The other main problem area was the south, where the great tribal conglomerates of the Qashqa'i and Bakhtiari, not content with leading their independent nomadic existence, enhanced their living standards by banditry and robbery, and posed a constant threat to orderly travel about the country. A series of successful campaigns in Fars, Baluchistan, and Khuzistan was in due course followed by their disarmament and the establishment of a network of military posts throughout the area. Though pacification never became total, and cases of minor banditry occurred in the more remote parts from time to time, these tribes did not until after 1941 pose a threat to central authority. By the middle of 1923 there remained only one part of the country not fully subject to the rule of Tehran, the semiautonomous shaykhdom of Shaykh Khaz'al Sardar-e Aqdas; but before this problem could be dealt with, important political changes were taking place in the capital.

With the fall of Seyyed Ziya the political system in Iran seemed to slip back into its old routine. Between June 1921 and October 1923 there were five different cabinets headed by three different prime ministers, holding office for anything between three and eight months. Most of the members of these cabinets were professional politicians, and it might almost have seemed as though nothing had changed at all. The one thing however that distinguished these cabinets from all others past and future was the unshakability of the minister of war. One could scarcely ask for any better confirmation of the claims made by Reza Khan to authorship of the revolution. If, for the time being, he was allowing the old political maneuverings to take their course, it was only because he was more urgently occupied with his campaigns to settle and pacify the country. All the time his own stature was growing, and he was steadily being recognized on all sides as the most powerful and significant figure in the country. That this was the case was clear not only from the honors showered on him by the Majles, the growing imbalance between his position and that of the unhappy Ahmad Shah, who complained bitterly but unavailingly of the contempt with which his minister of war treated him, and the panic that ensued when he threatened to resign if he did not receive better cooperation from the politicians, but also the ever more desperate efforts of his enemies by propaganda, rumor, and plot to get rid of him. With the completion of the first stages of his plan to reunite the country, it seemed to Reza Khan that the time had come for him to intervene more effectively in the affairs of the country.

On October 28, 1923, Reza Khan, while retaining the post of minister of war, became prime minister. It was no more than the logical next step in the course upon which he had embarked two and a half years earlier. Whatever the politicians may have thought about him, his standing in the country was unquestioned. To the "man in the street," the peasant in his village, and above all the soldier in his barracks, he was the embodiment of nationalism, of patriotic pride and national resurgence. He was the only man who looked in the least capable of leading the country towards the future, the only man who possessed the necessary qualities of leadership and enjoyed the confidence of most parties and groupings in the country. If this confidence was based less on past achievement than on future promise, it has to be admitted that this promise was amply fulfilled during both his premiership and after he became Shah, though not necessarily in the way that many of his supporters may have expected.

How far Reza Khan saw at this stage into the future that lay before him it is impossible to say. The immediate reaction of Ahmad Shah, after signing the rescript appointing Reza Khan prime minister, was to announce his intention of traveling once again to Europe (he had been there in 1919 and 1921, and had evidently found it to his taste) for medical treatment. He actually left Tehran on November 3, and was accompanied as far as the frontier by his new prime minister (he had left his younger brother, Mohammad Hosayn Mirza, as regent in his place). There could hardly have been a sharper indication of the relative status of the two men; but there was even greater historical irony in the fact that the young Shah's departure by way of Baghdad and Beirut coincided with the abdication of the Ottoman Sultan Mohammad VI and the declaration of a republic in Turkey. Neither Ahmad Shah nor Reza Khan can have been unaware of the symbolism; and it can hardly have been mere coincidence that a few months later, in March 1924, the Iranian press began to be full of articles advocating the creation of a republic in Iran. Telegrams from the provinces, poems, and cartoons were published attacking Ahmad Shah and the whole Qajar dynasty. Less often mentioned by name, but clearly dominating the whole scene, was the figure of Reza Khan, the only possible candidate for the office of president. It is not altogether clear how far he himself was involved in this agitation. He certainly had little use for the weakling Shah, as his conduct towards him had shown. The record of the Qajar monarchy as a whole was unimpressive. If it was clearly shown to be the will of the country, he was not averse to stepping into the vacant seat. But the sudden campaign, by whomever launched, had merely taken the opposition by surprise, and as March wore on they began to rally their forces. It was not merely the monarchists and conservatives who opposed the republican idea. The religious hierarchy, so often in the history of Iran on the side of revolution, had become alarmed at republican Turkey's abolition on March 3 of the caliphate, long if somewhat dubiously held by the Ottoman sultans. Republicanism suddenly became offensive to Islam, the tide began to swing the other way, and Reza Khan, never fully committed to the movement, broke free from those who were trying to push him in that direction, and in a statement issued on April 1 called on his countrymen to refrain in the future from all republican talk.

Fellow countrymen! Experience has shown that governments should never oppose popular opinion, a policy that has been followed by the present government, which has never sought to restrain public feeling, no matter from what quarter it comes. At the same time my own policy from the very first has always been confined to the preservation of the majesty of Islam and the independence of Iran, and the furthering of the interests of the nation and the people. I regard any opponent of this policy as an enemy of the people and will fight relentlessly against him; I am determined to pursue the same policy in the future. In recent days popular feeling has been confused, and this confusion may lead to results contrary to those I have in mind for the maintenance of security and order and sound government. From the first day, I and every man in the armed forces has held before him the high ideal of the preservation of the splendor of Islam. We have always striven to ensure that Islam thrives and spreads, and that the status of our religious leaders is respected and honored. Recently I visited Qom and spoke with the divines of that holy city. We discussed the present situation, and in consequence we came to the decision to recommend to our fellow countrymen that they should cease all talk of a republic and instead devote all their energies to removing the obstacles to reform, and cooperate with me in strengthening the foundations of our faith, the independence of the country, and the national government. I therefore urge all patriots to desist from demanding a republic, and to work together with me for the achievement of our common goal.[24]

A few days later he withdrew to the little mountain village of Rudehen, some thirty miles east of Tehran, whence he addressed telegrams to the Majles and the army announcing his resignation. As no doubt he had calculated, the result was panic; his position in the country was now such that few could imagine governing without his guiding hand, or face the prospect of a relapse into the chaos of earlier years. Telegrams, petitions and delegations poured into Rudehen, and in due course, after an overwhelming vote in the Majles in his favor, he agreed to return, his position immeasurably strengthened. It was another striking example of the understanding and mastery that this simple soldier had acquired of the arts of political maneuver and stratagem, especially as practiced in Iran. By now, too, the way ahead must have been becoming clear to him. But first of all he had one unfinished task to complete.

THE SHAYKH OF MOHAMMARA

The southwestern corner of Iran, part of the province of Khuzistan, had more than one reason for regarding itself as an autonomous region not subject to the orders of Tehran. The population was largely Arabic-speaking, having more in common culturally as well as linguistically with the inhabitants of Iraq just across the border. It included within its bounds the vast untapped reserves of oil that the Anglo-Persian Oil Company had begun to exploit in 1908, and which were only now revealing their full potential; this was a prize that the wily British were not likely to release into the hands of a central government that would be far less easy to control than the local shaykh. And finally this shaykh, Shaykh Khaz'al Sardar-e Aqdas of Mohammara, had not only enjoyed virtual independence for many years, but also had good reason to think that he would be protected by the British government against any attempt to interfere with that independence. None of these claims to the right of self-rule made much impression on the strong-minded prime minister; the shaykh was an Iranian subject, and like every other Iranian subject he had to accept the decrees of the government. Above all, he had to pay his taxes. Already in 1923 Reza Khan had authorized the American financial advisers to put pressure on Shaykh Khaz'al to meet the tax payments due from him; this had resulted in a small token payment, but during the following year there were signs that the shaykh was intriguing to bring about the downfall of the central government and the recognition of his independent status. He formed the Sa'adat (Prosperity) Party, or Committee, into which he attracted a number of Bakhtiari and Luri chieftains; its main purpose was to oppose the movement of central government troops into Khuzistan. Supporters were found in the Majles, and an envoy was sent during the summer to Europe, where he gained the support of the Shah in Paris and also interviewed British government and oil company officials in London.[25] Meanwhile a long telegram from Khaz'al reached the president of the Majles attacking Reza Khan as an enemy of the Shah and Islam, and the British minister called on the premier to remind him of Britain's interests in the area, the possible dangers of any military operations to the oil installations, and the strength of Shaykh Khaz'al's support in the country. When these moves appeared to have no effect, telegrams were sent to the Shah in Paris begging him to return, while at the same time, with fine inconsistency, the shaykh began to intrigue with the Iraqi government with a view to securing the annexation of Khuzistan to its Arab neighbor. Further warnings from the British government were accompanied by the appearance of British warships in the Persian Gulf.

A lesser man might have been intimidated by all this; but the shaykh and his supporters had sadly miscalculated the psychology of the *sardar-e sepah*. The more the threats and intrigues from at home and abroad multiplied, the more determined he became to settle the matter once and for all. Indeed, his own instinctive understanding of the situation seems to have been far superior to that of his opponents. At the beginning of November he announced to the Majles his intention of taking personal command of the campaign in the southwest, the first time an Iranian prime minister had ever taken part in fighting. As the telegrams and protests of the shaykh became ever more frantic, Iranian forces moved towards his capital in a relentless threefold pincer movement. Bakhtiari and Luri resistance melted away, the hoped-for intervention from Britain failed to materialize, and on November 15, on his arrival in Shiraz en route for the south, Reza Khan received a groveling telegram of surrender from the shaykh of Mohammara. He sent a curt reply, demanding unconditional surrender, and continued his advance, arriving at Mohammara by gunboat on November 28. By the middle of December the whole affair was concluded, an Iranian governor-general appointed, and military, administrative, and financial machinery initiated. Reza Khan himself crossed into Iraq (the first time he had ever left Iranian territory) in order to make the pilgrimage to the holy cities of Najaf and Kerbela, and returned to Tehran on January 1, 1925.

The ecstatic and triumphal reception that greeted him there served only to confirm what he now knew: that the resolute pursuit of a single-minded course of action would overcome all obstacles and turn opposition into support. By his successful action against the shaykh of Mohammara he had won over to his side almost all the opposition groups; he had deflated the last murmurings of opposition among the unruly tribes of the south; and—perhaps most significant of all—he had successfully defied the expressed wishes of Iran's most powerful neighbor. The British diplomatic defeat was so complete that when a few months later (it was now April) the shaykh was rash enough to seek an interview in Basra with the British colonial secretary, L.S. Amery, the only result was his arrest—in the middle of a party on board his yacht off Mohammara—and removal to Tehran, followed by confiscation of all his property.[26] A plaintive protest in the British House of Commons by Anthony Eden received an evasive answer from the foreign secretary, Sir Austen Chamberlain, and the now friendless shaykh, courteously received by Reza Khan, entered upon the life of an honored exile in the capital, where he remained until his death some years later.

By now it was becoming clear that no one, not even Reza Khan himself, could stop his headlong career towards supreme power. In the earlier stages he may have envisaged Ahmad Shah as a constitutional monarch, reigning but not ruling; though he was well aware of the Shah's lack of interest in the affairs of his country, he may even have regarded this as a recommendation. But Ahmad Shah's encouragement of the seditious activities of the shaykh of Mohammara must have convinced Reza Khan that the monarch could not be trusted even with the role of a figurehead, and by the time of his return to Tehran he had made up his mind that the revolutionary program he was planning for the country could only be carried out if he himself were the one unquestioned supreme authority. Nor was there any need for violent or unconstitutional measures; the force of public opinion behind him, the confidence reposed in him by the vast majority of the political leaders and Majles deputies, would be quite adequate to carry through the necessary processes of law.

On February 14, 1925, the Majles voted by a large majority to entrust to Reza Khan supreme command of all the defensive and security forces in the country. A few weeks later a special committee of the Majles was formed to collaborate with the prime minister in the drafting of a program of reform. Gradually, as the year wore on, there developed in the press a vigorous campaign against Ahmad Shah and the Qajar dynasty in general. So far the name of Reza Khan was not mentioned as a substitute, but the significance of the pointed contrast between a century of stagnation under the Qajars and four years of progress under Reza Khan was not lost on the supporters of both sides. By a strange irony Ahmad Shah's father, the reactionary Mohammad 'Ali, died in exile in February. The monarchist party, headed by the Crown Prince and Regent, Mohammad Hosayn Mirza, began to panic; telegrams were sent to Ahmad Shah in Paris urging him to return, while his envoy in London tried vainly to win the support of the British government. But the weight was all on the other side of the scales; even Ahmad Shah, urged by some of his supporters to plot the assassination of his prime minister, refused to do so on the grounds that Reza Khan was the only man capable of leading the country.[27] Although in the middle of September he announced his intention of returning to Iran, it seems that this was only a trial balloon flown to test the atmosphere there. Whether or not he meant it seriously, the reaction must have been enough to frighten him off; meetings and demonstrations were held throughout the country, telegrams poured into the capital, and in a climax to the campaign, the Majles on October 31 passed a bill deposing the Qajar dynasty, setting up a Constituent Assembly, and appointing Reza Khan temporary head of state pending the assembly's decision.

A Dynasty is Founded

On December 12, 1925, the Constituent Assembly after a week of debate voted by 257 affirmative votes to 3 abstentions to amend articles 36, 37, and 38 of the Supplementary Fundamental Law of October 7, 1907, so as to vest the monarchy in the person of Reza Shah Pahlavi and his successors in the male line, and specifically to exclude any member of the Qajar house from the succession or the regency.[28] Three days later Reza Shah took the following solemn oath before the deputies of the Majles:

As God is my witness, I swear on the Word of God and on all that is revered in the eyes of God that I will devote all my efforts to the preservation of the independence of Iran, and will preserve and defend the territorial integrity of the kingdom and the rights of the nation. I will guard the Fundamental Laws of the Constitution of Iran and reign in accordance with those laws. I shall strive for the propagation of the Ja'fari Ithna'ashari Faith, and recognizing that God Almighty is watching over all my actions, I shall hold no purpose but the welfare and greatness of the state and nation of Iran. I pray to God Most High for success in the service of the advancement of Iran, and I seek the aid of the righteous spirits of the saints of Islam.[29]

Four months later, on April 25, 1926, a dramatic and colorful ceremony took place at the Golestan Palace in Tehran: Reza Shah Pahlavi placed the new Pahlavi crown on his head, at the same time confirming his six-year-old son (the present Shah) as Crown Prince, and so formally inaugurating the new Pahlavi dynasty of Iran. The speech he made is worth quoting in full, for it enshrines in miniature the principles by which he was to rule the country for the next fifteen years:

On this occasion, as I perform the ceremonies of my coronation, I wish to bring to the attention of the whole people my views regarding the carrying out of fundamental reforms in our country. The expression of these views may serve both as a comprehensive instruction to my governments and a guide to the people. Firstly, my particular attention has been and always will be directed to the preservation of the principles and foundations of religion, for in my opinion one of the most effective means of ensuring national unity and strengthening the spirit of community of the Iranians is the fortifying of the bases of religious faith.

Secondly, I have under God Most High and with the support of the Immaculate Emams always preferred action to speech, and any position that I may have achieved in the task of reforming our country has only been the result of work and effort. I desire therefore that every employee of the state and every individual in the realm shall understand this general truth and shall set this fundamental principle before him as the watchword of his life of duty. All must know that the advancement of any project, the fulfilment of any plan, can only be achieved under the stimulus of serious purpose and as a result of work and effort. My imperial governments must therefore remember without fail that the duty of carrying out the fundamental reform of the country—the establishment of security, the spread of education, proper attention to public health, the improvement of the economic situation, the increase of national wealth, the completion of communications, the welfare of agriculture and commerce, and urgent reform of the judicial system—leave no time for contemplation and laxity. They must bring the utmost sense of urgency to the execution of these reforms, all of which are of the highest degree of importance, so that my views may be implemented as I expect. I am especially determined that, in anticipation of the opening of the Sixth National Consultative Assembly [the Majles], the necessary plans and preliminaries to these reforms shall be prepared by the government. Government officials must provide an example of industry, high morality, and firmness of purpose, and strive for the health, strength, education and wealth of the people, so that well-being and prosperity may be available to all in accordance with my expectations.[30]

THE PATH OF REFORM

The extent to which Reza Shah achieved the ambitions set forth in his inaugural speech may best be judged from a thematic examination of the policies that he adopted through the sixteen years of his reign, of the motives and attitudes that inspired his actions, and of the methods that he employed. Perhaps they can all be summed up in one sentence: he wanted to see Iran independent, self-reliant, and respected in the community of nations, an Iran capable of running her own affairs without direction or protection from any other quarter, an Iran great not by virtue of empire but through wealth in natural and human resources and in morale. This was his interpretation of nationalism—a revolutionary one in the sense that, when he began to take power in 1921, not one of these objectives was within sight of achievement. However, Reza Khan was also that rare combination, an idealist who was at the same time a practical man of action, and so he was not content with a distant prospect or with hopeful theorizing. Indeed, he never elaborated his ideas in the way that Kemal Ataturk did; but from his actions it is clear that he saw the stages ahead under three heads. First, it was necessary to establish efficient machinery of government. We have already seen the initial steps he took towards the creation of a unified army. Later, conscription was introduced, a small navy and air force set up, and trainees sent regularly to France. At home military academies were established, as well as a medical corps, hospitals, military police, and similar ancillary services to an efficient army. As major rebellions declined (there was trouble in Kurdistan in 1926, and in Baluchistan in 1928) the *amniye* road guards organization was developed under the aegis of the army, while in the cities the police force was reformed and strengthened. By the thirties it was possible to travel safely in most parts of the country, and one of the major tasks entrusted to the army was the disarming and settlement of the nomadic tribes, a task carried out with a considerable degree of ruthlessness and harshness. To the progressive-minded monarch it was inconceivable that the outdated way of life of the nomad could continue to be a part of the modern society for which he was striving. Of course there were also sound military and administrative reasons for discouraging a system that did not lend itself to bureaucratic control. It was for this kind of purpose that the small 40,000-strong standing army was formed; it was never intended to be confronted with the unimaginable fact of invasion from outside.

Next to the security forces in importance was the formation of an orderly bureaucratic structure. Under this head was included everything from the systematic grading and classification of civil servants, the distribution of responsibilities between ministries, departments, and offices, and the elimination of bribery and corruption, to the registration of births, deaths and marriages and the issue of identity cards. Given the lack of experience in these fields, it was inevitable that there would be abuses. Officialdom often got out of hand, resulting in local tyranny, and at the same time the measures taken to counteract this led to overcentralization in Tehran and lack of local initiative. These are characteristic faults of bureaucracy, and Iran at that time was no exception. Yet even this excessive rigidity was preferable to the total absence of order and method that had prevailed earlier, and it could be justified as a necessary intermediate stage.

Centralization of government machinery would only work if communications were adequate, and there was undertaken an ambitious program of road building, which resulted by 1940 in the completion of over 15,000 miles of motorable roads, many of them through precipitous mountain areas. Few of these were asphalted, and by European standards they were still very primitive. But to a country that had hardly known rapid means of transit since the courier services of Darius the Great, they were a great advance. The transport of passengers, goods, and mails from one part of the country to another now became a matter of days rather than months. But the greatest achievement in this area was the completion of the Trans-Iranian Railway. Even at the opening of the first trunk road, the Tehran-Ahwaz highway, on October 24, 1928, the Shah could not refrain from expressing the hope that it would soon be paralleled by a railway. On October 15 of the previous year, when he cut the first sod at the site of the Tehran station, he referred to the railway as one of his oldest dreams, "one of the most powerful factors in the progress and prosperity of the country." On August 26, 1938, as he tightened the last golden bolt at the mountain station of Safid Chashmeh, forty-two miles south of Arak, he described the occasion as one of the proudest days in the history of Iran, and praised the people of Iran for the tenacity, self-sacrifice, and strength of purpose they had displayed in bringing the task to a successful completion.[31] To Reza Shah the building of the railway was not merely an economic or even a military asset; it was a symbol of the new Iran, capable of carrying through successfully the most daunting tasks, and at this level it was beyond criticism.

It is not necessary in this brief survey to dwell on the other administrative reforms that owed their inception to Reza Shah—the reform of the financial structure, the systematization of taxation and government budgeting, the establishment of banks and insurance companies, and the issue of bank notes; nor on the reform of the judicial system and the drawing up of civil and criminal codes of law, measures that made possible the abolition of the hated capitulations, which gave to aliens the privilege of being tried in their own consular courts. In the international sphere, too, Iran played a role aimed at the maintenance of her own territorial integrity and security by means of international agreement and the establishment of world peace. She was an early member of the League of Nations, signed the Kellogg Pact, and generally encouraged the peaceful settlement of disputes. Reza Shah saw early the importance of establishing good relations with his immediate neighbors, and this policy, which led to a series of agreements over disputed frontiers, was crowned with the signing of the Sa'dabad Pact in 1937 between Iran, Turkey, Iraq, and Afghanistan. His attitude towards European countries was a little more guarded; he was well aware of Iran's need for the expertise of western technology, but he did his best to limit Iranian dependence on foreign experts to the smaller countries who could not be suspected of imperialist designs. The major powers he kept at a friendly arm's length, allowing them only a minimal share in Iranian projects, for example the railway, and above all avoiding foreign indebtedness. The one serious clash came in 1932 with the cancellation of the Anglo-Persian Oil Company's concession. Although the final outcome of this dispute was not as favorable to Iran as at first sight seemed to be the case (considerable advantages were secured, but the company's quid pro quo, the thirty-two year extension of the concession, was worth a great deal more than Reza Shah realized at the time), the compromise was the result of balancing national self-esteem against the necessity of keeping Iran's biggest natural asset in full-time operation. It was to be another forty years before Iran fully achieved Reza Shah's ambition to control the country's major natural resource.

NATURAL AND HUMAN RESOURCES

The second of Reza Shah's basic principles was to ensure the fullest possible use of Iran's natural resources for the benefit of her people. The Shah's constant journeying round the country, on a scale seldom practiced by any earlier ruler, made him aware of the vast unexploited wealth that existed in it, and he was determined that this should be used both to enrich Iranian life and society and to reduce dependence on foreign products, even if the native article was not always as good. This was one reason why the emphasis tended to be on industrialization to the relative neglect of the more traditional aspects of the economy, such as agriculture. It is not entirely true to say that the land was neglected by Reza Shah; on his own estates in Mazandaran there was a good deal of experimentation in new methods, and one justification for the acquisition of such estates was that there was more chance of their being properly used than if they were left in the hands of absentee landlords. In more than one place, model villages and farms, agricultural and veterinary institutes, were established under government auspices; under private enterprise they would certainly never have been completed. Elsewhere the mining of coal, iron, and copper was developed. Above all the importance of irrigation was stressed, and the construction of dams begun in order to provide water for agricultural purposes as well as to meet city needs. Perhaps an even more effective step was the construction by the state of factories making use of native agricultural products—sugar beet, silk, cotton, tobacco, fruit, and fish, to mention a few.

This was a good example of the combining of natural resources with the other aspect of economic development that undoubtedly appealed far more to Reza Shah—industrialization, modernization, the learning and use of western technology. While he did not despise the traditional crafts, and indeed introduced measures to improve them, for instance the banning of chemical dyes in the manufacture of carpets, his own taste was for the mechanical and technical. The full weight of government support was placed behind the opening of new factories, not only in the fields mentioned above, but also in light and heavy industries like textiles, glass, paper, chemicals, soap and fats, building materials, iron foundries, small arms, aircraft assembly, and even shipbuilding. In all these activities the stress was on state enterprise; though Reza Shah was no dogmatist and never evolved theories comparable to the *étatisme* of his neighbor Kemal Ataturk, from a purely pragmatic point of view it seemed wise to keep the initiative in the hands of the state until private enterprise in Iran had developed a more progressive outlook. By the end of the reign some 150 state factories had been established, while a number of products—sugar, tea, tobacco, for example—were controlled by government monopolies. At the same time, in spite of his phobia about foreign loans, Reza Shah recognized the need to attract foreign capital for major industrial projects. In his address to the "economic" Eighth Majles on February 3, 1931, he stressed that "to embark on major works and large factories calls for greater attention than can be provided out of current funds, so of course capital must be attracted from abroad, to complement the exploitation of the country's natural resources."[32]

He was indeed by no means isolationist in his economic outlook. He saw the need for foreign trade as a means of diversifying the country's wealth, and the controls established through monopolies, protective tariffs, and currency restrictions were an attempt to strike a balance between Iran's requirements in the way of foreign products and the encouragement of home industries. Oil was still the country's biggest export, but the Shah looked forward to other possibilities. Opening an industrial exhibition in Shiraz in March 1937, he asked for greater attention to be paid to agriculture. "Our raw materials and agricultural products," he said, "are becoming of increasing interest to the world; our export categories do not include any luxury goods, so whatever we produce will find a good market."[33]

But above all Reza Shah was interested in people, and so we come to the third pillar of his reform, the best possible use of Iran's human resources. As in the political and economic fields, so in the social and cultural the Shah wanted Iranians to be self-sufficient and self-confident. Since the peoples of the western world seemed to have achieved many of the things that he desired for his own country, it seemed to him that some aspects of their life must be worth copying, if only for the sake of placing Iran firmly in the mainstream of modern culture. To this end it was necessary to abandon the old ways, where these were no longer adaptable to the requirements of the new age. The whole way of life in town and country needed to change. This was the stimulus behind the rebuilding and replanning of towns and cities, crude though the execution may often have been. The narrow lanes and covered bazaars, negotiable only by donkey or on foot, had to be replaced by broad, well-paved avenues accessible to motor transport. At the time that they were cut through cities like Tehran, Shiraz, Tabriz, with little regard for what stood in their way, they may have seemed like wasteful luxuries; now they are hardly wide enough to cope with the flow of today's vehicles. The new ideas on town planning spread well beyond the big cities, and a standard pattern—a broad avenue with a square at each end acting as the spine of the built-up area—came to be adopted for most small towns, as they expanded rapidly under the pressure of easier communications. Villages that lay along the main routes were similarly affected, but those off the beaten track long remained untouched, and in general the life of the peasant, in spite of sporadic essays in reforming the land tenure system, saw little change. Reza Shah may well have argued that reform of urban life, as the social base for his industrialization program, was of higher priority; but one unfortunate effect, combined with the centralization of government in the capital, was a steady flight from the land into the towns, a trend that had gathered so much momentum in his time that it actually increased in volume during the years following his reign, and has scarcely been reversed even now.

Reza Shah indeed paid more attention to the tribes than to the peasants. In his view the nomadic way of life was a more serious handicap to the modernization of the country, and he would gladly have eliminated it altogether. This was beyond even his autocratic powers, but nevertheless the policy of disarmament was followed as far as possible by attempts to settle the tribesmen on the land, a policy that of course meant a complete undermining of their traditional economic and social structure. It would seem that the Shah's view of the tribal problem was formed mainly by his military experience, and took too little account of the other implications of the enforced adoption of an alien way of life. It was an unavoidable aspect of the general trend of his reform, which was to encourage the growth of facilities and services that were only consistent with a settled urban lifestyle. He was concerned about public health and hygiene, but his answers tended more towards large, well-run hospitals than to small rural clinics. He encouraged physical education and sport, but the sportsgrounds and stadia were situated in the cities. Similarly, in the case of education, great attention was paid to the establishment of a university in Tehran and technical colleges there and in other cities, though on the credit side it must be pointed out that Reza Shah expanded the educational system from a handful of mission and privately owned institutions to a complete school system that provided the possibility of universal education in most towns and even in some of the larger villages. Common sense dictated that this should start where the larger school populations were and gradually grow outwards. Reza Shah's educational system also took the first steps towards the education of adults and the gradual elimination of illiteracy.

But certainly the most spectacular of Reza Shah's humanitarian reforms was the extension of the rights of citizenship and education to the female half of the population. As he himself put it in his speech on January 8, 1936 (the Dey 17, celebrated thereafter as a feminist festival, when the removal of the veil became compulsory): "We must never forget that one-half of the population of our country has not been taken into account, that is to say, one-half of the country's working force has been idle."[34] Once again, the motive uppermost in his mind was the more effective use of Iran's human resources. Nevertheless he also stressed the need for women to have rights equal with men, and to enjoy the same educational and social benefits as they did, for, as he reminded his hearers, "the happiness of the future is in your hands. You are the educators of the coming generation, you have the possibility to become good teachers and to bring up good citizens." In fact, girls had already been attending school on equal terms with boys, and when Tehran University was opened for classes in the following year, the Shah insisted—against the expectation of the university authorities—that women students should be admitted to all classes. Of the twelve who actually took up the offer, almost all subsequently achieved high positions in education, medicine and public affairs.[35]

The fact that by the 1970s two of these women had become senators would certainly have pleased the late Shah, for while he could not have been described as a democrat in the conventional sense of that term, he firmly believed that everyone had a duty to participate in the work of governing and administering the country. Though the forms of constitutional government were retained intact, with elections taking place at the allotted intervals and the Majles meeting regularly to pass legislation, what Reza Shah had in mind was rather the constant contact and exchange of information between electors and elected, so that everyone would understand and fulfil his function in society. In a speech to the Majles deputies on July 1, 1929, he urged them to go out into the country and tell the people what the government and the Majles were doing: "I am personally most anxious that, wherever the deputies come across faults in national and public affairs that are not of a purely private character but are of general concern, they should inform me personally, so that steps may be taken to set matters right."[36]

Above everything else, Reza Shah stressed the necessity of hard work and unflagging activity. It was a constant theme in all his speeches—to the Majles deputies, to the parties of students leaving for Europe, to engineers, teachers, doctors, and government officials. To a certain degree this was no more than a recognition of the obvious facts; but the Shah also knew his countrymen well. He was well aware of their proclivity for talk rather than action, and he was determined to lift them by force out of the lethargy that had submerged Iranian society ever since the Middle Ages. Reza Shah's greatest personal asset was his intimate understanding of his own people, of their strengths and their weaknesses—strengths that can still be used, weaknesses that still have to be combatted. Iranians have many qualities that can be turned into assets under the right leadership. An extreme individualism contrasts with a readiness to accept authority. A tendency to zealotry and fanaticism, especially in religious matters, struggles with negativism and passivity, with acceptance of fate and concealment of one's real feelings. Iranians have an intense interest in the new and exotic, coupled with a marked capacity for learning and absorbing; but they are also sceptics, with a strong sense of humor and a distrust of pretension and pomposity. They are famed for their politeness, hospitality, and *ta'arof* (courtly phrases); they can also be obstinate, sensitive to criticism, and touchy where their dignity is concerned. They can be hard-working and efficient when they choose, and their readiness to delay and procrastinate is proverbial. There is a deep, underlying patriotism coupled with a suspicion of alien influences, but this does not prevent some from succumbing to the blandishments of foreign interests.

IRAN'S SOCIAL REVOLUTION

Reza Shah's genius lay in his ability to cut through the maze of contradictions in the national character, and to bring about in the course of twenty years a revolution in Iranian life and society that would have seemed inconceivable only a year or two earlier. A major factor in his success was his own capacity for hard work. It showed itself in his indefatigable interest in every aspect of the country's affairs, his ceaseless tours of inspection, his remarkable grasp of the details of a problem. In spite of his reputation for bullying and impatience, he was more inclined to favor a gradualist approach; he preferred to see small, well-thought-out steps rather than grandiose schemes that were liable to collapse under their own weight. His biggest undertaking, like the Trans-Iranian Railway, took eleven years to complete. Unlike Kemal in Turkey, who succeeded, or Amanullah in Afghanistan, who failed, he never took any major step without preparing the ground well beforehand. Though he was a soldier by training, he showed himself to be a skillful politician with a gift for manipulating people; he seldom went headlong at an obstacle, preferring to find a way round it. Nevertheless he understood very well when more forceful methods were needed, or more to the point, when they would work; and he made effective use of his carefully built-up reputation for violence of temper and sharpness of retribution, characteristics that he seldom had actually to bring into play. It is true though that he was more apt to chastise than to reward; proper fulfilment of a task was no more than an act of duty, the minimum to be expected of anyone. This tendency doubtless increased during his latter years, when his authority was more firmly established and his patience less.

It can hardly be disputed that he was an authoritarian by instinct. Accustomed to the military chain of command, he saw nothing unreasonable in the concept of a revolution from above; indeed he would probably have argued that a revolution from below could lead only to chaos. The kind of effort that he believed was needed to bring Iran into the modern world could be made only by a united nation; from some such feeling as this sprang, not merely his hatred of communism, but his instinctive distrust of political activity of any kind. The political party system, hardly to be dignified by that term, that had developed in Iran since the 1906 constitution, was not geared to the production of constructive results, and as soon as he was firmly established he did away with it. His reluctance to encourage the 1924 republican movement may have stemmed from similar feelings. If the instinctive Iranian acceptance of authority was to be uppermost, it was more likely to be given readily to a Shah than to a president. This emphasis on unity found expression in various ways; for instance, the abolition of titles in 1935, while it might at first sight have seemed to conflict with the stress on authority, was intended rather to make everyone equal under the sovereign.

In fact Reza Shah had little use for the older generation, whom he regarded as largely responsible for most of Iran's ills. His constant emphasis on the importance of education, his annual addresses to the parties of government students leaving for Europe, his encouragement of youth and scout movements, his fostering of athletics and sport, all show clearly that he saw the future of the country in the hands of young people who were not limited and blinkered by the habits and beliefs of their elders. But at the same time he wanted to ensure that the young men and women acquired the right moral attitudes and habits of thought. "Man is not naturally immoral, when he is born man is good; it is bad companions and associates that corrupt him. So avoid association with bad characters, because the full advantage of your education will depend on your moral upbringing. If your moral upbringing is not good, your efforts will never have any result."[37]

In these precepts we see a reflection of Reza Shah's own way of life. The qualities that appealed to him most were sound morals, simplicity of life, austerity, discipline, self-reliance—qualities that he felt had been lacking in Iran in recent years. Neglect of them lay at the root of the ignorance, superstition, and fanaticism that handicapped his people, and so these were the qualities that were preached incessantly in the press, from the radio, and through official and semiofficial propaganda organizations and publications. The same high moral tone pervaded everything; frivolity, triviality, sensationalism, and crime were banned from the newspapers, from the cinema, broadcasts, and even novels and short stories, for all these were either government-controlled or subject to official censorship. In all this propaganda an equation was made between reform, both social and moral, and patriotism—patriotism not in the romantic, flag-wagging sense prevalent in Europe, the negative attitude of "My country right or wrong," but the forward-looking aim of making Iran as good as any other country and better than most. But Reza Shah also saw that successfully to instil this outlook it was necessary to build up a sense of pride in one's country. Since present-day Iran was still relatively near the bottom of the ladder of progress, he urged his countrymen to look back to the great days of Iranian history, to the age of the Achaemenid kings, Cyrus, Darius and Xerxes; to the Sasanids of the pre-Islamic period, especially Shapur the Great, humbler of the Roman emperors Valerian, and—greatest of all—Anushirvan the Just. It may well be, as has often been related, that Reza Shah's awareness of this great past was stimulated by the work of the American art historian, Arthur Upham Pope.[38] If so, it was certainly increased by his visits to Persepolis, Susa, and other archaeological sites, and the founding of the Archaeological Museum in Tehran and of the National Monuments Society owed much to his interest.

As if to keep a constant reminder before the popular eye, many of the new buildings with which Tehran and other cities were enriched were designed or decorated in the style of these ancient times; the Police Headquarters and the National Bank reflected the architecture of Persepolis, while the Archaeological Museum was modelled on the Sasanid palace at Ctesiphon. The first major international congress to be held in Iran celebrated the millenary in 1934 of the birth of the poet Ferdowsi; it was attended by some forty scholars from sixteen countries other than Iran. The mausoleum opened at Tus on this occasion by the Shah ingeniously combined pre-Islamic and Islamic motifs.

But in general the Islamic era in Iran's history was played down, though an exception was made in respect of Karim Khan Zand, the last noteworthy Iranian ruler before the Qajars (who were not yet ripe for rehabilitation); his bones, which had been buried by the first Qajar ruler where he could walk over them daily, were exhumed and reinterred in the holy shrine at Qom. And although the more primitive and picturesque aspects of Iranian society tended to be kept under wraps, an exception was made in the establishment in 1933 of the Ethnographic Museum, where examples of tribal costumes and traditional arts and crafts were preserved.

Some of the measures seem to have been primarily cosmetic—the adoption of names of Persian origin for the months, for instance, and for a number of cities, which lost their traditional Arabic names; thus Mohammara became Khorramshahr, Soltanabad became Arak, Aliabad Shahi, while even Tehran had its Arabic "t" replaced by a Persian one. This was all part of a wider program of language reform, the purpose of which was to replace European and Arabic words, especially those used for new inventions like aeroplanes, elevators, and torpedoes, and as scientific and medical terms. The search was pursued vigorously by the Farhangestan (Iranian Academy) for about five years, but was virtually dropped after the abdication of Reza Shah, and never achieved anything approaching the wholesale purge carried out in Turkey; indeed, some of its more eccentric inventions were personally vetoed by the Shah. The example of Turkey was not followed in another respect, in that the traditional alphabet and spelling, though of Arabic origin, were retained, and in 1935 it was even decreed that Latin lettering was not to be publicly displayed, for instance, in cinema posters and shop signs. While much of this may seem rather trivial, it was all part of the policy of creating a psychological atmosphere in which Iranian things would be regarded as of at least equal value with foreign.

There were some apparent inconsistencies with this policy of giving an Iranian coloring and veneer to ordinary life, of which the most obvious was the wholesale adoption of European or "international" dress, and the banning of traditional and tribal costume. In this case the motive was modernization: the old dress recalled the old way of life, with its passivity, subservience to alien interests, and sense of inferiority in the modern world—all weaknesses that Reza Shah was trying to eliminate. It was also a unifying factor, something he had learned as a soldier in uniform. Similarly, the European practice of using surnames replaced the old, complicated, and sometimes unintelligible system of patronymics, *laqabs* (nicknames), *konyeh* (surnames), and the rest, because it made possible an orderly system of registration. The line between what should be adopted from the West and what should be rejected was a seemingly arbitrary one; on the one hand technology, dress, law, on the other language, art, history. When the line is looked at in that way, a certain pattern emerges: what was retained was the permanent element in Iranian culture, those aspects that could not be matched by any modern equivalent. Reza Shah had a great love for what he considered to be the progressive features of modern civilization, but he was also very conscious of Iran's capacity for absorbing and converting to her own use, without losing her own identity, the external and alien cultures with which she came into contact. The one thing that has struck all students of Iran's history is the continuity of her culture; poised at the crossroads of civilization as she is, she might have been expected to become a mere amalgam of Middle Eastern, Asian and European elements; but in fact there is a recognizable solid core that has proved indigestible to all outsiders, attitudes and ideas that hardly seem to have changed since the beginnings of Iranian civilization three thousand years ago. Reza Shah may not have thought consciously in these terms, but he had an instinctive awareness of what could be discarded and what had to be preserved.

With certain sections of the Iranian community Reza Shah was never on easy terms. The well-entrenched ecclesiastical hierarchy he viewed both as a possible unifying force and as an obstruction to reform. He was himself a Moslem of average piety; after the settlement of the Shaykh Khaz'al problem he made a pilgrimage of thanksgiving to Najaf and Kerbela, and was presented by the Shi'a divines with a portrait of 'Ali. Speaking to the Majles on March 1, 1937, on the occasion of a religious festival, he warned them not to make the mistake of assuming that

> reform and the acceptance of the civilization of the world today mean the abandonment of the principles of the faith and of the religious law, or that there is any conflict between reform and modernization on the one hand and religion and faith on the other. If the Great Lawgiver of Islam were alive today to see the progress of the world, he would confirm the complete harmony of his true teachings with the basis and institutions of the civilization of today. Unfortunately those noble and lucid ideas have with the passing of time been misused by certain people, and in consequence our country has fallen into decline. For thirteen centuries, in each of which the country ought to have taken a great leap forward, it has remained motionless and backward. We are now faced with the consequences of this neglect, and must make amends for the torpor of the past.[39]

So it was the reactionary and obstructive aspects of Islam in Iran that Reza Shah wished to eliminate. Much of the ignorance and superstition that bedeviled the path of the reformer had its origin in the narrow outlook and limited education of the *mollas* (teachers of Moslem law and doctrine), and it was from them that the chief opposition came to such reforms as the unveiling of women, or such innovations as the dissection of human bodies in the new medical faculty of the university. Reza Shah felt himself strong enough to brush aside this religion-based opposition; the anecdote of his incursion, booted and spurred, into the shrine at Qom to chastise the ecclesiastic who had attacked the Queen for unveiling her face may not be true in detail, but it is certainly ben trovato.[40] He swept away the mourning processions and spectacles performed annually in the month of Moharram, discouraged the activities of dervishes and fortune-tellers, forbade the practice of sacrificing camels and sheep, and even threw open certain mosques to foreign tourists. He abolished the ecclesiastical courts, and replaced the Koranic *maktabs* by modern primary schools. To ensure that the "church" was prepared to cooperate fully with the reform movement, he restricted the right to practice as a teacher of religion to those who had undergone a course of training and passed tests prescribed by the Moslem hierarchy under his direction. There was no room in this scheme either for the incompetent and ignorant or, less happily, the unorthodox, for either could act as a brake on the rapid movement forward. In addition, there was a tendency among the more articulate supporters of the reform movement to blame Islam and the Islamic outlook for the stagnation of Iranian life during the preceding centuries. The lack of an educational system, the seclusion of women, the passive acceptance of fate, were all failings of Iranian society that could be attributed to the baleful influence of Islam. Some extremists even went so far as to advocate a revival of the ancient Mazdaean religion, hitherto the faith of a handful of Zoroastrians in Yazd, Kerman, and one or two other centers; but there is no evidence that Reza Shah himself took any interest in this proposal, in spite of his interest in pre-Islamic Iran.

The other social group that found itself in conflict with the Shah's ideas was to some extent a product of his own reforms. The widening of educational opportunities, the encouragement of higher education, and the regular dispatch of groups of students to Europe and the United States all contributed to the growth of a new intelligentsia, who indeed were not opposed to the modernization program, but at the same time criticized either the slow pace at which it was proceeding or deplored the restrictions on personal freedom that it brought. They welcomed his nationalism, but deplored his undermining of democratic forms. Many of those who returned from the West brought back with them advanced political and social ideas, and while the vast majority were not Communists some undoubtedly were. Reza Shah was strongly suspicious of Marxism, both as a political creed subversive of orderly authoritarian society, but still more as the vanguard of his powerful neighbor to the north, whose politics might have changed in 1917, but whose international policies and plans had not. The outlawing of Communist parties and movements in 1931 and the series of actions against left-wing politicians and "freedom-loving" writers culminated in the mass arrest and trial of "the Fifty-Three" in 1937, some of whom on their release in 1941 formed the nucleus of the left-wing, Russian-oriented Tudeh party. Unfortunately, the Shah's alarm at the activities of these minority groups was extended to embrace intellectuals of all colors, so that the cream of the educated population, who ought to have been in the lead of the new movement, tended to find themselves alienated from it.

THE REAL TRAITORS

However, the worst crime in Reza Shah's eyes was subservience to foreign interests, no matter from what direction they came. In the proclamation he issued on November 12, 1923, shortly after he became prime minister, he gave particularly vigorous expressions to this:

> There are certain people who have abandoned the moral courage of their own nation and have used foreign interests to further their personal plans and designs. This kind of conduct not only degrades the Iranian people, who have always been known for their pride and courage, in the eyes of the world; if it is allowed to continue, it will destroy our true national order and undermine totally the foundations of our society. . . . If in future it is seen that this kind of disgraceful behavior is continuing and that unauthorized individuals are engaged in discussions with external bodies, such people will be regarded as out-and-out traitors. A traitor has no right to live within the community of his country, he will be condemned by state and nation alike, and I shall inflict on him the punishment he so richly deserves.[41]

After his return in January 1925 from the successful Mohammara campaign, he addressed the Majles:

> Before I took office, not only were all questions settled in principle by foreigners, but even the minor details of internal affairs were dealt with by them according to their inclinations. Even minor clerks in ministries and departments could only be employed on their recommendation and intervention. This kind of illegal intervention permeated all official organizations; most of them became accustomed to this meddling, and in consequence the tribes and clans who pinned their last hopes on the destruction of the central authority seized the opportunity to engage in tyranny and oppression, robbery and banditry.[42]

It is against this kind of background that one has to regard the often petty restrictions that were placed on foreigners, especially diplomats, living or traveling in Iran. On one occasion, he responded to a request for special facilities for the travel of foreign diplomats around the country: "Under no circumstances can such a request be entertained. In the first place we would make ourselves look like their servants; in the second place we would imply lack of confidence in the security of the country."[43] Similarly, it was made difficult for foreign governments (in this case the Russians were particularly in mind) to set up reading rooms or publish newspapers. Foreign embassies and legations were required to correspond in Persian, and contact and correspondence with foreign representatives except through the Ministry of Foreign Affairs was forbidden. One minister was dismissed for attending a reception at the French Legation at a time when relations with France were under a cloud.[44]

It was of course understandable that Reza Shah should have been suspicious of the activities of a huge foreign organization like the Anglo-Iranian Oil Company, and that he should have missed no opportunity of indicating his displeasure, particularly since circumstances made it difficult for him to impose any major restrictions. When he toured the south in 1937, he pointedly refrained from visiting any AIOC installations or meeting senior officials, and it is said that, when he sailed back down the Shatt al-Arab in an Iranian warship, he turned his back as the vessel passed the Abadan waterfront. He was even reluctant to attribute honest motives to foreign advisers directly employed by the Iranian government. The Millspaugh financial mission was dismissed in 1927 after 4½ years of efficient service because, as the Shah told the American minister in the course of an audience, Millspaugh had "one serious fault, lack of consideration for the dignity of the government and the state." This one fault, the Shah explained, outweighed all his other good qualities. "The government," he concluded, "would rather put up with difficulties and preserve its independence than have everything running smoothly and enjoy no freedom of action."[45] This policy was followed consistently; foreign advisers were progressively eliminated from government departments, the customs, and—after a scandal involving the two German managers—the National Bank. To the extent that foreign experts were needed, their powers and duties were carefully circumscribed; in the building of the railway, for example, the whole project was divided into small lots and each farmed out to a different company, so that no one group and still more important no one country could achieve a dominating position. Specialists from small countries were favored above nationals of the big powers, and especially of Iran's two traditional enemies, Britain and Russia. Another measure designed to restrict foreign influence was the gradual elimination of foreign schools, or their takeover and incorporation into the state system.

Whereas in Qajar times Iran had survived by pursuing a "policy of balance," of playing off one powerful neighbor against another, Reza Shah's aim was to create an independent role for Iran, free of pressures from either side. In part, this involved building the image of Iran in foreign eyes as a viable, progressive state. He was all too conscious that in the past westerners had looked on his country with a degree of contempt, as a backward, debilitated society without a future. He was himself convinced that this was false; but he also had to prove it false to the outside world. The progress that was being made in Iran had to be forced on the attention of foreign observers and visitors, and often this could best be done through the symbolism of relatively trivial matters. His insistence on the use in diplomatic correspondence of the Persian name of the country, Iran, instead of the European form, Persia, was intended to underline the country's break with the past, to stress that Iran was no longer a mere appendage of Europe. He wanted foreigners to visit Iran, and with the limited resources available tried to encourage tourism; but it had to be ensured that they saw, or at least carried away with them, only those aspects that would do Iran credit. The removal of beggars from the streets was partly humanitarian, but it also had a cosmetic motive, as did such seeming absurdities as the ban on photographing camels.

The reverse of this coin was the heated reaction of the Shah to unfavorable references to himself and to Iran in the foreign press. Indeed, he was less concerned about serious, objective criticism of his policies than he was about frivolous or scurrilous stories whose only purpose seemed to him to be the bringing of his country into contempt. In some cases these were felt to be serious enough to warrant a rupture of diplomatic relations: an article in the *Münchener Illustrierte Presse* in 1931 nearly caused such a breach with Germany; in 1936 relations with the United States were suspended for nearly two years; while a month's break with France followed a facetious caption to a photograph of a cat in the *Petit Parisien* in December 1938.[46] In bringing to an end this last quarrel Reza Shah wrote personally to President Albert Lebrun:

> Our decision was not solely the outcome of certain offensive articles in certain papers. We have had the impression that for a number of years insufficient notice has been taken in France of the changes that have taken place in our country, and that no effort has been made to understand correctly the new Iran. It was these attitudes, echoed in the French press, that impelled us to break off relations between the two countries until such time as France should show willingness to appreciate our country in its true light.[47]

On an earlier occasion retribution had fallen on two of his ministers. The Shah, irritated at French articles on Iran, refused collaboration in a Persian art exhibition in Paris, and so instructed the minister of foreign affairs; but the latter forgot to tell the minister of education, who sent a telegram of greetings at the opening. *L'Intransigeant* headlined its report, "The Shah says yes, but the minister says no." Both ministers were dismissed.[48]

In some respects, evidently, Reza Shah was not well-informed about western attitudes and practices. He never understood the concept of a free press, whose comments were individual and not necessarily inspired by government policy. At the same time his knowledge of world events and trends was remarkable for a man who, until his final exile in 1941, had only twice been outside his own country, and had never traveled as far as Europe. The careers of men like Lenin, Kemal, Mussolini, Gandhi, Hitler, even the failed Amanullah, all had their effect on his thinking. In each of them he saw the rebel against the established world of the great powers and the imperialists. Perhaps he did not always see clearly enough where they were going. Superficially there seemed to be something in common between the outlook of Nazi Germany and his own, as indeed he so informed the retiring German minister in 1935.[49] But in fact Reza Shah's objective of a confident, self-sufficient Iranian nation could hardly have been further from the aggressive, "master-race" outlook of the German dictator. Like many of his compatriots, Reza Shah had a great admiration for France; all the early groups of students were sent there, and to some of them he explained the reasons:

> You are being sent to a land which not only possesses the greatest and best-organized army in the world, but whose actions also provide an example to every other country of national feeling, loyalty, and unwavering patriotism. In the recent world war she sacrificed thousands of victims for the independence and integrity of her territory and proved to the world once again her right to life and existence. . . . You are being sent by a monarchical government to a republican country solely in order that you may take the patriotism of the French as your model, bury it deep in your hearts, and make courage and patriotism the key to your endeavors.[50]

PATRIOTISM AND HARD WORK

Certainly, his personal experiences as a Cossack soldier, as a minister of the crown, and finally as Shah, provided the most formative element in the building of Reza Shah's outlook and character. His was a very practical mind; he saw what was wrong, and set out to put it right. Iran's ills were ignorance and illiteracy, selfishness and treachery, incompetence and lack of confidence, subservience to foreigners. A self-educated man, he had no theories about government, and made no seven-day speeches like Kemal Ataturk's address to the Turkish National Assembly in 1927. Patriotism and hard work were the qualities that he valued, and beyond stressing these he saw no need for talk. He had a great gift for getting the best out of his subordinates, something that would not have been possible if the only inducement at his disposal had been fear of consequences. In fact he managed to gather round him a talented body of ministers and advisers, men like Shaybani and Yazdanpanah in the military sphere, 'Ala and Davar in the political, Hekmat and Sadiq in education. At the same time he never became wholly dependent on them, and he was ruthless in discarding anyone who had served his purpose or had failed. He had his errors of judgment too; it is questionable how far a man like Mokhtari, the notorious chief of police at the end of his reign who was responsible for the evil reputation of the political prisons, was capable of truly interpreting his master's wishes.

Reza Shah was by no means unwilling to listen to advice. There are many anecdotes that serve to illustrate this. At the time of the unveiling a leading Moslem divine drew his attention to the fact that a new café had been opened, where unveiled women were frequently seen, immediately opposite the British Legation at Qolhak; the man of God, doubtless none too happy about the new reform, suggested to the Shah that the juxtaposition of this blatant flaunting of the new freedom with the headquarters of the most corrupting foreign influence in Iran was something to be avoided. The Shah saw the point, and the café was closed. It was unfortunate that his reputation for severity and unapproachability must often have deprived him of valuable information and points of view, for he more than once requested officials and Majles deputies to keep him informed of what was wrong in the country. His weekly meetings with the Majles deputies were maintained throughout the greater part of his reign. Nevertheless he was a firm believer in authoritarian government, without which he believed people would sink into communism and chaos; his paternalistic manner comes over very clearly in his speeches. He was never confident of the ability of the governing elite to carry on without his guidance, and one of his aims was to place the administration of the country on a footing that would enable it to continue uninterrupted after his death. He also knew enough of Iran's history to appreciate the importance of a secure succession, and his nomination of his eldest son as Crown Prince simultaneously with his own accession, as also the stringent and comprehensive education and preparation for his duties that he gave him, did in the result ensure an orderly transfer of power in 1941.

Reza Shah was unusually tall, and all the photographs of him from his days with the Cossacks onwards show him towering over his fellows. This natural advantage was matched with a dignity and even aloofness that sat well on the shoulders of a man who was to occupy the throne of the ancient monarchy of Iran. He did not confide readily in others, made no attempt to court popularity by the exercise of personal charm, and throughout his life remained personally isolated from all but a few members of his family. Even as Shah he felt most at ease in the company of soldiers. During the days following his abdication, the Iranian press was full of stories and anecdotes about the late monarch, many hostile, a few friendly; but friend and foe alike recalled in him the same qualities—his directness of speech, his forthright brusqueness, his formidable temper (which he used not as an uncontrolled outlet but as a conscious weapon), his ruthlessness in enforcing what he believed to be right, even—rather unexpectedly—his boisterous sense of humor. On being shown a specimen of iron ore at an exhibition, he commented, "A people who have such a valuable mineral at their disposal and can't make use of it ought to have their brains knocked out with it."[51] At one time, it was said, there was a rule that, whenever the Shah visited a city, the governor should first come in ordinary dress to welcome him some twenty miles outside it, and then return to greet him in official rig at the governorate. On one occasion the governor of Hamadan, having performed the first part of this duty, leapt into his car to return to the city, but found himself trapped behind the Shah's vehicle. The royal escort observed the intruder and tried to bring him to a halt by sounding their horns, without effect until the Shah himself noticed the commotion, stopped his car and so the whole procession, and dismounted to see what the trouble was. To his astonishment he was greeted by a blushing, tongue-tied governor in his shirt and underwear, caught in the middle of changing into his official costume. The Shah's anger quickly gave way to amusement when the matter was explained, and thereafter the rules were changed.[52]

Visiting an industrial exhibition, the Shah was offered a glass of beer at the brewery stand, which he drank with relish, commenting, "This beer is not bad." The minister of court, an elderly and conscientious teetotaler, hastened to agree with him, whereupon the Shah retorted, "You don't drink. How do you know it's good?" The Minister was nonplussed for a moment only. "Your Majesty," he replied, "I am not the servant of the beer, I am Your Majesty's servant. If you say it is good, then I too say it is good; if you deny it, I too shall deny it." This reply, made in the classic courtly tradition, appealed to the Shah's sense of humor, and he continued the tour in high spirits.[53]

In general, however, Reza Shah had little use for the conventional forms of flattery, just as he disliked pretentiousness and pomposity of any kind, and in his own life eschewed the ceremonial and show that had been regarded in the past as the normal environment of a Shah. He invariably wore military uniform, and usually of a very simple kind; he ate modestly and drank little, and slept on a mattress on the floor in the traditional Iranian manner. In his personal life he adhered to the same high moral standards that he preached for others. Though he was married several times, he took no other interest in women, and it is told of him that once in Turkey, attending an air display by the seashore, he kept his eyes firmly fixed on the aircraft even though there was a party of pretty girls bathing in the sea immediately in front of him. He had a strict soldier's sense of honor, never more vividly illustrated than in his dispatch in 1925 of a special envoy to General Ironside, then commandant of the Staff College at Camberley, to seek release from the undertaking he had given in 1921 not to overthrow Ahmad Shah.[54]

He was indefatigably hard-working, with an insatiable appetite for detail and an extraordinary memory. It was this characteristic that perhaps gave the impression that he was inclined to make snap decisions without sufficient thought; certainly once he had made up his mind to a course of action, he wanted to see it carried out without delay. He was impatient of delay and inefficiency, and intolerant of neglect and waste. He himself lost little time on small talk and the niceties of social intercourse. His daily routine was strictly timetabled, and he was a strenuous advocate of order, neatness, discipline, and punctuality. One of the most widely publicized photographs shows him at the window of a railway carriage smilingly consulting his watch as the train (evidently) draws in on time. Nor was he inclined to leave the enforcement of discipline and cleanliness to others. When honored guests were due to arrive, he personally inspected their quarters. Once, early in his reign, the press reported that he had turned up at the Ministry of Foreign Affairs at the starting time of seven o'clock, only to find that none of the officials had arrived; when at length they did so, he took the opportunity of delivering them a serious lecture on duty and punctuality.[55] He did not like to be put off by trivial difficulties. When it was suggested that his opening of Tehran University might be postponed if it was raining, he retorted that he would be there even if it rained stones.[56]

The period between the two world wars was for Iran the period of Reza Shah. Perhaps no monarch before him had ever left so distinctive an imprint. He found a semimedieval, feudalistic, anachronistic conglomerate of tribes, huge landed estates, and backward peasants, freed it from foreign political and economic domination, and converted it forcibly and irresistibly into the beginnings of a modern state. As he said in one of his last speeches at the twentieth anniversary of the coup d'état on February 20, 1941, "The greatest achievement of the past twenty years of effort, whose true worth will be confirmed by history, is the readiness of the country for further progress."[57] Reza Shah's reforms provided the social, educational, and psychological foundation for a progressive, self-governing society. It is doubtful whether any of the developments in Iran from 1941 to the present day could have taken place if the country had not first passed through the mill of his revolution. The educated middle class, from which today is drawn the personnel of the new political and economic structure of Iran, could not have existed without the educational and cultural background from which they sprang, and which was directly or indirectly the creation of Reza Shah. It is significant that, without indeed any conscious purpose on his part, the political and social advances were parallelled by equally significant developments in literature and the arts. The dramatic break with the classical traditions of the past made by such writers as Sadeq Hedayat and Bozorg Alavi, however reluctant they and their followers may have been to acknowledge it, was a natural product of the new intellectual environment of Reza Shah's regime. The fact that these writers often felt themselves stifled by censorship merely emphasizes the paradox, and there is further irony in the fact that the intellectuals later spearheaded the condemnation of Reza Shah. They, like their opposite numbers in the West, tended to look at the phenomenon of Reza Shah through Marxist eyes, just as their parents had seen him as a product of international political interests. Both were wrong. Reza Shah was the right man thrown up at the right time in a country that needed such a man.

THE FINAL TRAGEDY

The tragedy of Reza Shah's career was that he was never allowed to finish his task. During the earlier years of his reign, and indeed until close to the end, it may have seemed as though international events would pass Iran by, and that she would be left in peace to follow her own inclinations. Happenings in Europe were far away, and to begin with at any rate seemed to be aimed at establishing international peace and security. Imperialism appeared to be on the decline. Even the rise of the dictators, precipitated by the worldwide economic crisis of the early thirties, seemed hardly a matter for concern in Iran. Many of the expressed ideas of Adolf Hitler—moral regeneration, discipline, hard work—were much like those preached by Reza Shah. The Iranians had a better title to the name "Aryan" than the Germans. And the German engineers and experts who came to Iran to assist in the setting up of factories and railways were efficient, cooperative, and apparently nonpolitical. Mussolini's Abyssinian war was a little nearer home, but neither that conflict, nor the absorption by Germany of the Saar, Austria, the Sudetenland, and Czechoslovakia, nor the outbreak of the Spanish civil war made much impact in Iran. Nearer at hand the Arabs of Palestine were rebelling against the British mandate and the Zionist incursion, while in India Gandhi's drive for self-government was gaining in speed and force. With these struggles Iran, as an Asian country, might be expected to feel some sympathy, but in the meantime she was an oasis of comparative peace and orderly progress.

The outbreak of war in 1939 following the signing of the Russo-German nonaggression pact must have caused Reza Shah some anxiety. Germany was known so far only as a friend, but Russia was the traditional enemy, long suspected of territorial ambitions on Iran. Suddenly the German presence in Iran seemed a little more disquieting. He hastened to declare his country's neutrality, and did his best according to his lights to maintain it; he did not consider that he was under any obligation to dismiss the six hundred or so German technicians scattered about the country, for he was confident that his security organizations were well up to the task of keeping track of them. Considerably more alarming were rumors of secret talks between Ribbentrop and Molotov, at which plans were said to have been made for the partition of the Middle East between the two powers, Germany taking the western part including the Iranian oil fields, and Russia occupying the rest of Iran,

Afghanistan, and eventually India. Reza Shah began to concentrate on security, and the pace of reform slowed down. In a speech to Majles deputies and newspaper editors on June 29, 1940, he stressed the dangers of the changing situation, and criticized his ministers and advisers for constantly fobbing him off with "May the blessed mind of His Majesty rest assured!" "Certainly we can count on our disciplined forces and our neutrality, but that is not enough. Every individual in the country must be ready and prepared for difficult times, and this is something that, in spite of all our facilities, has been forgotten."[58] He ordered all the organs of government propaganda, together with the press, to concentrate on the task of informing the people accurately about the world situation.

Disaster struck with the German attack on Russia in June 1941. True, the threat of Russo-German collaboration was gone, but instead there was an alliance between Iran's oldest enemies, the two powers who according to Iran's traditional policies must always be kept apart. Whichever way the course of the war went, Iran was doomed to be the victim. If the Germans succeeded in thrusting through and penetrating into the Caucasus, there would be nothing to stop them moving down into Iran to form the eastern arm of a pincer movement against the British position in the Middle East. This could only be avoided if Britain could bolster Russian resistance, and to do this the inescapable conclusion was that military supplies from the west would have to be routed through Iran. Iran, then, would have to be brought into the war, and since it was unlikely that the strong-minded independent Shah could be persuaded diplomatically to allow his territory to be made available for this purpose, other methods had to be sought. For a few weeks, notes of growing asperity passed between the two Allied powers and the government of Iran; the excuse—a somewhat flimsy one—was the presence of a number of German technicians in the country. Meanwhile plans were being coordinated for a joint military invasion, which duly took place on August 25. The Iranian army, Reza Shah's creation, was adequate for normal duties, but could never have been expected to offer more than token resistance to the two most powerful armies in the world. But even this three-day victory was not enough for the Allies. Their aims included the destruction of the Pahlavi regime, which they sought to achieve by military, diplomatic, and propaganda means; British and Russian forces began to move towards Tehran, the two Allied envoys stepped up their diplomatic pressure, and from London BBC programs personally attacked the Shah in a series of increasingly scurrilous broadcasts. Reza Shah was wise enough to perceive the direction in which events were moving; his personal dignity could not permit of effective collaboration between himself and the violators of Iran's integrity. If anything at all was to be saved from the wreck of what he had created, he would have to withdraw from the scene. In a last patriotic gesture he announced his abdication and called on his people to give their allegiance to his son and heir, the Crown Prince.

His departure from the seat of power was accompanied by a stream of invective from the previously sycophantic press and politicians that must have reminded him of the reaction to his dismissal in 1932 of his minister of court, Taymurtash. On that occasion two newspaper editors who had earlier been lavish in their praises of the minister and were now being equally lavish in their abuse were ordered by the Shah to take brooms and sweep Sepah Square in Tehran as a penalty for their fickleness.[59] No such punishment was meted out to the disloyal editors of 1941, but it was not many years before the mood began to change; even before Reza Shah's death in 1944 there could be heard nostalgic voices in his favor, and the traumatic days of 1946, when it seemed as though the country was on the point of being torn apart, completed the conversion of many. By 1950 public opinion had swung right round. A resolution of the Majles had awarded the late Shah the title of "Great," and in March of that year his body was brought from Cairo, where it had been temporarily housed, and interred with great ceremony in a marble mausoleum in the south of Tehran, whose solid, austere lines mirror well the character of the man who almost single-handed changed the course of his country's history, dragged it from its medieval slough, and hurled it into the twentieth century. Whatever the subsequent achievements of Iran, however great her future, her people can never forget the ruler who by his personality and single-minded determination laid the foundations that made all the rest possible.

2

The Tradition of
Sacred Kingship in Iran

The heritage handed down by Iran to the West and still living in its ideological conceptions and cultural institutions is manifold. If its patterns are sometimes difficult to recognize and trace back to their origin, that is due to the fact that this legacy has been received through intermediate cultures and Westernized models.

THE LEGACY OF IRAN

The leading elements of what we could call the "vertical organization" of the state are part of this age-old heritage. They were handed over to the modern world through the late Roman imperial structure and its medieval renaissance, through the institutions of chivalry and knighthood that, obscurely transmitted to European society in a Celtic-Germanic garb, were later Christianized. The original bearers of this heritage were probably the Alans and other nomadic tribes of Iranic issue, who formed the bulk of the barbarian cavalry in the Roman army, and hence were settled in places ranging from Gaul to Pannonia.

In the religious realm the Western world received from Iran a fair number of conceptions and mystical symbols that in the course of centuries have acquired citizenship in our innermost spiritual life. Among these are the angelic structure of the other world, whose hierarchies are conceived as the cosmic intermediaries between God and man. From the same source comes the "Lord God of the celestial host" *(Dominus Deus Sabaoth)*, continuously engaged in the fight against the Evil One, who figures in the Catholic mass, as well as the figures of some angels, such as Michael and Gabriel, borrowed through late Judaism from the Iranic "Venerable Ones" *(yazata, izad)*

Mithra and Sraosha (etymologically, "Companionship" and "Obeisance"), apart from Seraphiel, a replica of the Iranic Rashnu, the judge of the deceased.

The same eschatological function that is ascribed to Jesus as "Resurrector of the Dead" was prefigured in the apocalyptic books of the Avesta, and in its epitomes and commentaries, such as the *Abyatkar i Zhamaspik*.[1] It continued in the Islamic age through the gnostic theorizing of the Isma'ilis and later through the Sufis; also in this category is the theory of the *rastakhiz,* or (Ancient Persian) *qiyamat-e qiyamat* ("the Resurrection of Resurrections"). This also explains the gifts traditionally offered by the Iranic Magi to the newborn Lord.

If we want to remind ourselves of some current representations of pure Iranic origin that belong even to the popular religious life, they range from the aureola of saints and kings (a derivation from the Avestic *khvarenah,* the mystical halo surrounding the heads of the consecrated sovereigns of ancient Iran) to the very picture of the Holy Grail, already known in Persian traditions as the "cup showing the world" (*jam-e jahan-nomay*), on account of the clairvoyance it bestowed on the primordial King Yima Khshaeta (Jamshid, in Neo-Persian), who subsequently lost it for his unworthiness.[2]

In addition to various elements of material civilization, such as the culture of various fruit and nut trees (peaches, almonds, pomegranates, etc.), of state organization, such as the principal ministries and secretaries, and of visible symbols of rank and dignity (such as the pontifical tiara, a color to show court or military rank, the triple trumpet blast summoning attention in the army), we can point to a number of ideas, representations, philosophical or metaphysical conceptions, and devices of social and political organization that are all of remote Iranic origin, and that have seeped into our daily life over the ages. If we want to recognize a character common to them all, whatever field they may belong to, we must go back to the remote ideologies of Iranic origin to which a broad range of inspired writings bear witness. Among these are the later part of the Avesta, the *Denkart,* and the *Bundaheshn,* sacred books of the Zoroastrians; epic works, such as the Pahlavi edition of the *Khwatay Namak,* which is practically continued and resumed by the famous (Neo-Persian) *Shahnameh,* "The Book of Kings" of Ferdowsi (eleventh century A.D.); a great number of mystical writings of innumerable philosophers, both Zoroastrian and Moslem, who build a golden chain of thinkers from hoary antiquity down to our days.

Quite unlike the Indian civilization, which commonly considers human life on earth, with its hopes and sorrows, to be pure Illusion *(maya),* the Iranian culture, from the prophet Zarathustra (our "Zoroaster," about the tenth century B.C.) has always given a positive value to the human struggle in the world.[3] Man, *following his own free choice,* has come to earth leaving a blessed existence "in Heaven" to stand by the Sire of Light and Truth, Ahura Mazda ("the Thinking Lord") in His millennial fight against Darkness and Falsehood, embodied in Anra Mainyu ("the Evil Spirit").

In this connection it is told that before the existence of time, Ahura Mazda had made His own choice for the Good. He asked the Fravashis (the angelic doubles of men) whether they preferred to remain eternally blest and immortal in the world of archetypes, or if they considered it worthier to come down into the material world to live in physical bodies, limited in space and time, and engage themselves in combat against the principle of Evil. "They decided upon coming down in the material world, so they could become again immortal and perfect at the end of the world's life, for the eternity and sempiternal progress."[4]

The same conception, characterized by strong positivistic "Western" features, is to be found embedded in quite different traditions, like the Islamic one, probably inspired in this case by an Iranian example. The Qor'an emphasizes this meaning dramatically when it says: "God quoth 'Verily did I offer the trust of Our secrets to heavens, to earth, to mountains. They all refused to take it on and shuddered from it: only the MAN backed it, for he is a madman, a fool!'."[5]

In both cases, body and time, the conditions for earthly existence are by no means Illusion, as in Indian pantheism, but the right instruments for the everyday victory over the Spirit of Negation and Falsehood *(druj).* As for time, the scenery of this cosmic fight, it has been meditated upon with keen attention by the Persians since the beginning of their civilization. Time, in effect, is linked to the last destination of man, inasmuch as he will be rewarded or punished according to what action he has performed as long as "he was in time," namely, during his earthly life.[6] Therefore, the very notion of time has been recognized by Persian gnosis as a reality arising from action and will, far beyond the common awareness of man who, being caught in its flow, is unable to grasp its essence.

The reality of time is considered from three aspects. First, it exists as the unmoving point of Eternity that transcends each single moment in the stream of events. This is the field of divine action, and its presence actualizes itself into the same human will emerging to sheer awareness of itself. The Persians symbolized it by the all-devouring lion-man, surrounded by the seven spires of the serpent—the emblem of the *Zrvan Akerena,* the "Infinite Aeon."[7] Second, there is the "duration" or "cycle" *(zamaneh),* which is the experience of time by the Angelical Entities: it brings about the meaning, the significance of a cosmic or historic period taken as a whole. In this connection, the Persians thought that every human occurrence, as a meeting of persons or facts, gave birth to an invisible creature evolving into the future. It was from Persia, then, that the late Greek gnosis received this conception, identifying it with that of the *egregoroön* ("the Wake One"). Third, there is the level from which the common experience of time arises, namely the flow of successive and somehow disconnected moments that proceed from past to future. This last forms the basis for the common perception of matter and its relation to abstract thought.

Persian philosophical meditation, subsequently Zoroastrian and Moslem, conceived this dimension of "material time," in which every man lives within his waking condition, as arising from the same necessity that drives him to recover his former Edenic existence. This gives a reason for man's combat against Evil in a limited way of life bound by time and space. As hinted above, man subscribes to this peculiar experience because he has willed to join the cause of Ahura Mazda, engaging himself in the worldly struggle.

In contrast, some Islamic sects of Iranic issue, such as the Isma'ilis and Eshraqis, believe that man sank into this bewildering condition (as the result of a kind of spiritual dizziness that befell him, when he became suddenly aware of his own original separateness from the Creation). Hence, time was subjectively born as the distance of his actual being from his true essence, the latter to be won back through diurnal fight during the physical life.[8]

However, according to the tenets of Zoroastrianism, and quite differently from other religions (even those of Iranic origin, such as Manichaeism), *matter has a positive value,* inasmuch as the whole of Reality is considered under two heads: the ideal one—*menok,* or "mind-like"—which is spiritual, comprehending all ideas and archetypes, the so-called Lords of Species; and the material—*geti,* or "worldly"—which is physical, because in it these principles become personified as the visible manifoldness of material existence.[9]

Thus the Iranians have given a metaphysical justification since the earliest times for what we deem to be *our* concrete, Western evaluation of life and action, time and matter. We will see that these are the grounds on which the same notions of kingship, state, government, administration, and so on, were founded in Ancient Iran.

As for the meaning of this life, it is worth observing that the concept of angel proceeds from a psychological attitude of the ancient Iranians who, when confronted by an event or a physical occurrence, instead of asking themselves, *What* is that? rather inquired, *Who* is this one? i.e., What does it mean? Whence does it come, and whither is it driving me?—implying a cyclical conception of time as "a lump," not a series of incongruous instants due to melt away from this moment to the next.[10]

The actual realization of such a vision means to be enlightened, to be a "potential king." It is something more than a feeling. It is a vocation that runs through the whole of the religious and philosophical world of Iran. For the ancient Mazdaeans, no gap existed between prayer, worship, and meditation, on the one hand, and, on the other, proper cultivation of the land, raising good cattle, hunting wolves, and repelling marauders *(mairyas)*.[11] Witnessing the presence of man on earth was like a spiritual crescendo in which he displayed his militancy on behalf of the Good Spirit beyond space and time. Conversely, the earth revealed her inner dimension, her own significance: in Pahlavi language *zam* and *zamyad* are two words that both signify "earth," the former as "meaning of the earth," or Earth Goddess, the latter as "material earth." *Zam* was personified by the stately appearance of the female angel, Spenta Armaiti, (Devotion; Well-Connected Thought,) hence the Living Spirit of Earth. What does it mean? It is not, by any means, a fantastic conception merely dreamed up by the mythopoetic imagination of the ancient Persians; rather it is the transposition into mythology of a process of pure spiritual enlightenment. The sense experience regarding the "facts" of external being conveys to man a series of abstract or perceivable data that form the practical field of his relational life. But the fact that the human mind is able to find an objective connection between these data, transforming them into spiritual "acts" of knowledge, is due to the working "inwardness" of such a Spirit, which forms the link between man and his realm, the Earth. As an angelic symbol, the Earth Goddess reflects like a mirror the spiritual identity (Avestic *daena*, Middle Persian *den*, Neo-Persian *din*, this latter also meaning "good Religion") of the righteous man.[12]

Thus for the Old Zoroastrians the significance of work as an activity was that it actualized the meaning of things surrounding a man, by transforming the physical reality into his own spiritual essence.[13] The fulcrum of this grasp of the divine message hidden in the objects and the forms of nature was conceived to be the "intelligent will" (Avestic *khratu*, the same word as the Vedic *kratu*, which means "sacrificial offering," and the Greek *kratos*, which means "strength").[14]

Action in the world and a selfless consecration of its results are the seed for the renewal of the whole Creation, called in Old Persian *frasha-kereti*, the actual realization of the archtype hidden in the physical appearance, a realization that is the aim of the Good Creator's work on earth. Further on we will see how the apotheosis of man—following the ideology of the ancient Iranians, as propounded by the inscriptions of Darius in Persepolis—abides in his power of collaborating during his everyday life with the cosmic designs that lie beyond the veil of Creation. In this view, *man begins to be a king.*

SPIRITUAL FEATURES
OF THE KINGSHIP IN IRAN

The old Iranian traditions knew two ways for the continuation of Ahura Mazda's work on earth and the reintegration of man in His universal designs. The former was the priesthood, the way for the *zaotar* (invoker), or *athravan* (fire-priest), who called on revelation through the sacral office or the ecstasy of the *haoma,* the enrapturing juice. The latter was the way of the warrior *(rathaeshtar)* who in contrast worked on the material, visible stage of the world, arousing himself the cosmic will of Ahura Mazda.[15]

To put it in different terms, we deal with two quite different types, respectively culminating in the figure of the prophet, as Zarathustra was for Ancient Iran (whose spiritual tendency he shaped into a positive religion, Mazdaism), and the character of the king, *khshayathiya,* typified by the primordial kings Haoshyanha and Yima—especially the latter, for his connection with the victorious halo of glory, the *khvarenah.*

Kingship and Priesthood are thus considered to be the two fundamental poles of human society, and this tradition has been firmly maintained throughout the millennial history of Iran, notwithstanding the radical conversion of almost all Iranians from one religion to a quite different one, namely from Mazdaism to Islam. Even now, the Shahanshah on the one hand and the Shi'ite clergy on the other preserve the continuity of this ambivalent national ideology, conserved from the Aryan origins to the present time. Probably even the expectations of today's Iranian Shi'ites for the return of the hidden imam, the Mahdi (the prophet Mohammad's true legatee) continues in the new religion as the old expectation for the *Saoshyant,* the Savior to come in the future, who as believed by the Mazdaeans will bear in one person *(pat evak tan)* the kingly Glory *(khvarrah-e khvatayih)* and the Good Religion *(veh den);* and consequently will destroy the Evil Spirit *(Evak Menok).*

To stress this point there is an important passage in the *Denkart* ("Religion's Acts"):

> The event against which the Evil Spirit is most stubbornly opposed is the conjunction in one single person and with the outmost intensity of the kingly *khvarrah* and the Good Religion: for it is this conjunction that will drive him to destruction. *(2)* Because, should the kingly *khvarrah* in its utmost degree of intensity, as it was in Yam, be joined with that of the Good Religion, or should the *khvarrah* of the Good Religion in its utmost degree of intensity, as it was in Zartusht, be coupled with that of the kingship in its utmost intensity, as it was in Yam, then the Evil Spirit would have perished and the creatures could have been preserved from the assault, and the Renovation of Existence would have taken place. . . . *(3).*[16]

It is worth observing that the ancient Persians did not actually consider the kingship necessarily dependent on a particular religion, even on the Mazdaism that was considered the only valid one. Basically, this was the attitude that allowed the royal ideology to pass almost unscathed from Zoroastrian antiquity to the Islamic Middle Ages, and safely reach modern times.

In any case, sufficient evidence has been found to prove that kingship, though not connected with any religion in particular, gradually evolved into a religious institution. The king's cosmic nature was proclaimed in his honorific titles; he was Lord of the Seven Climes (Middle Persian *haft keshvar khvatay)*, as well as King of the Age *(shah-e zaman)*. The famous Roman historian Ammianus Marcellinus has recorded for posterity the titles assumed by the Persian Emperor Shahpur II in a letter sent to his Roman colleague Constantius ("Chlorus"): "I Shahpur, King of Kings [Shahanshah], partner with the stars, brother of the Sun and the Moon. . . ."[17]

Even in the case of alien kings, there was religious meaning involved in kingship; here the testimony of Pliny the Elder, in his *Natural History,* is very significant.[18] As Nero invested his Armenian vassal Tiridates, himself a magus of Parthian descent, with the royal diadem, the latter wanted in return to initiate his Roman lord to the dignity of kingship as it was traditionally practiced in Iran. But he failed, "for Nero had not the intellect necessary for receiving this art from him."

As for the separation of the concept of kingship from a specific religion, the second chapter of the *Videvdat,* a sacred Zoroastrian book, gives a fair account of Yima Khshaeta's refusal when the same Ahura Mazda proposed to him that he should receive the Good Religion (i.e., Mazdaism) along with the insignia of the sacral kingship. Yima Khshaeta limited himself to accepting the second grant without further involvement; notwithstanding, Ahura Mazda bestowed on him the royal symbols such as the crown, the throne, the golden dagger, and the royal seal (Middle Persian *mohr,* sometimes read as *mehr,* "sun").

Then Yima Khshaeta alighted on earth, among mankind, resplendent and bright like a human sun. People thus beheld an exceptional event: one sun was following his usual course across the sky and another—a human one—was descending upon the earth.[19]

This descent of the kingly principle in solar garb forms one of the pivots on which turns the national tradition of Iranians of all times. We would like to believe that the very title of *Aryamehr* (Old Persian *Arya-mithra,* "Sun [or Friend] of the Aryan community"), assumed by Mohammad Reza Shah to characterize his sovereignty, is a living reminder of this remote and venerable conception, never obliterated in the popular memory of the Iranians.

The legitimate king was supposed to be the embodiment of what we could call the Mithra-principle. As Ahura Mazda was the strict custodian of the essential law of Reality *(arta, asha),* so was Mithra the keeper of power *(khshathra)* among men and creatures of Nature, in which realm he provided for the health of herds and the richness of crops.[20] He was also the loyal friend *(mithram,* in the accusative case, also means "friend," "lover" [Neo-Persian *mehr])* to the warrior and the supporter of the lawful emperor. This aspect, as we shall show later, was especially prominent in the Roman Empire, as the result of a clear Iranian influence on its religious and military ideology.

G. Widengren has observed that Mithra was "the Great King" par excellence, whose human incarnation was eagerly awaited as bringer of salvation to mankind in the centuries preceding and following the Christian era. It is said that when Mithradates Eupator, the King of Pontus who claimed to be a descendant of the Achaemenian royal family, was born, a star was shining with such radiance that all the heavens seemed to be ablaze for seventy days: the same event was repeated when the coronation of this king took place, some twenty years later (112/11 B.C.).[21]

Such celestial signs were supposed to appear on the eve of birth of a King-Savior, like King Hushetar, who would redeem humanity from the grip of the evil principle. The pious magi who came to Bethlehem following the comet behaved according to an Iranic pattern: they knew from a tradition of old that this was a sign for the appearance on earth of a King-Savior.

But it is only in the Mazdaean tradition that we can find the conception of the solar Mithra-element being embodied in the royal person, or of a relationship between heaven and earth, as well as a link between godhead and humanity, that refers to him. This sort of mediation attributed to the ideal sovereign is a persistent feature that characterizes not only the state ideologies but Persian mysticism at all times. We find it in Mithraism, later successfully diffused among the military class of the Roman administration, as well as in Manichaeism and, in more recent times, in different forms of Persian *'erfan* (viz., the spiritual mediation of Islam) referring to 'Ali, the cousin of Mohammad and fourth caliph, or to the Hidden Imam, the true legatee of the Prophet after the Shi'a, who possesses the kingly endowments and mystical prerogatives already held by the Great Kings of Ancient Persia.

Thus the Great King is at the same time conceived as the accomplished, Perfect Man—the *adam-e kamel,* as it presently sounds in Persian.[22] He is also the Column of Light (Arabic *'amud as-subh),* connecting the upper world of ideas and archetypes with the lower world of concrete facts. The renowned Manichaean documents known as *Acta Archelai* (8.7) set forth the conception of "columna gloriae [which corresponds exactly to the Arabic *'amud as-subh*], quod vocatur vir perfectus"—"the Pillar of Glory, that is called 'the Perfect Man'."

Nine centuries later, the so-called illuminati *(Eshraqiyun),* in a fully Islamic age, considered it a fundamental achievement for the mystic to be the personal realization of the aforementioned "pillar of glory" by which the "Holy Spirit" (Arabic *ruh al-gods)* alights upon him.[23] Of course, in a case like this one, the mystic deals with the imaginative interiorization of the "Great World" (Neo-Persian *'alam-e bozorg)* into his human individuality, namely his "Little World" (Neo-Persian *'alam-e kuchek).* The symbol, the "Exemplary World"

(Neo-Persian and Arabic *'alam-e mesal),* is the instrument working out the mediation between the two.

This, besides its mystical assumption by the initiated, is the *arcanum* of the sacral kingship in a nutshell. Therefore, the procedure of interiorization of the symbol, to be realized by the individual, affords a clue to the deep concern with which myths like this one still affect the modern Eastern mind. We read, in the *Denkart* (245.3-246.5), that every man is the synthesis of all elements *(chehr)* and forces *(nerok)* belonging to animate and inanimate creation alike; by analogy, the king is viewed as one who condenses in his actual being and function all the social classes, for he naturally owns the principle and essence of each one.

The *Shahnameh* of Ferdowsi, although composed in the Islamic age by a Moslem, still recalls how the mythical King Jamshid (Yima Khshaeta), after having discovered the metals and established the different skills and crafts, divided the people into four classes (priests, warriors, farmers, and artisans), each appointed for what we call "a fragment of the kingly task." The vertex of such a society, the king, is fitted to his own undertaking *(khweshkarih)* by three qualities, thus illustrated by the *Zatspram,* a late Zoroastrian book: "Relentlessly fighting—night and day—against his own *druj* [namely, the power of Falsehood abiding in himself], as long as his life lasteth: never disowning his Religion: never failing in the fulfillment of his own Duty...."[24]

The people's happiness and good fortune were conceived as totally dependent on the king's behavior and the fulfillment of his task, which—as the *Denkart* witnesses—consists in "releasing people from poverty, anguish, need, illness and disorder.... The worthiest of estimation amongst the Sovereigns is that one who has delivered the people of his country from every sort of need and possible illness, the one under whose rule the poor ignore misery, and there is no malady to which remedy might not be borne...."[25]

For the same reason, cosmic matters such as the due course of seasons, hence the fertility of land and so on, were conceived as a reflection of king's virtues. Even the Persian title for "Great" (Old Persian *vazra-ka,* Neo-Persian *bozorg),* applied to the king (Old Persian Cuneiform *khshayathiya vazraka,* translated into Classical Greek as *megas basileus,* the "Great King") involves an etymological meaning of this kind. Gösta Liebel relates the term *vazraka* to the noun *vazra,* "club," "thunderbolt," viz., the weapon brandished by the God-King Verethraghna, the protector of warriors, in Plutarch's account of the birth of Mithradates. This author explains *vazra-ka* as "club-bearer," hence "bestower of fertility," as was his German counterpart Donar-Thorr, with his magic hammer Mjölnir, killing foes and fiends, and at the same time, consecrating legitimate wedlock.[26]

It is astounding to observe how the memory of this relation between the king and the fertility of the soil has been conserved from hoary antiquity up to the presen: day. To limit ourselves to antiquity, we may quote two Zoroastrian texts, separated by an interval of some fourteen centuries, describing almost in the same words but, obviously, in two different languages the image of the mythical Yima Khshaeta's kingdom: a description, we observe, that has been handed down nearly intact to the present popular tradition. The former is the *Avesta Yasht* 19, portraying the blessed conditions of Yima's realm: "Yima, the good shepherd, became the kingly glory, the *khvarenah,* during all the time he exercised his lordship over the earth of the seven climes [the seven *keshvars* related, as already said, to the lines marking the magical cup owned by the same king], over *daevas* [viz., the goblins] and human beings, over *Yatus* [viz., the fiends] and the *Pairikas* [a kind of witch], over the good people and the tyrants, the blind and the deaf; *(32)* Yima, the one who took from the hands of the *daevas* riches and weal, suet and herds, prosperity and glory, under whose reign the kinds of food were endless under the teeth of the eaters; when herds and mankind were freed from the hindrance of death, when water and plants did not suffer from drouth; *(33)* under whose reign there was neither cold nor heat, neither old age nor envy prompted by the *daevas*. . . ."

Now let us look at chapter 6 of the *Abyatkar i Zhamaspik* ("The Memoirs of Zhamasp"), an apocalyptic text, which runs as follows:

> and Yamshet, the one of the fine cattle, was endowed with majesty, with glorious bravery, with splendid victory; *(14)* and he took the seven climates under his sway, which was exerted on men and on devs during 616 years and 6 months. . . .
> *(15)* During his age, clouds, winds and rain were submitted to his will and he gave the devs and the paris as slaves to men; *(16)* and the devs made ready the food for men, who lived therefore in peace and comfort. *(17)* Under his domination, there existed no frost, no heat, no nuisance of old age, no death, no envy created by the devs. . . ."[27]

Therefore, the essence of the Iranian kingship was not mere enhancement of the human function on earth, but rather supernatural power aiming at *"renewing" the world after a celestial pattern.* We have seen that such a renewal, religiously expressed by the adverb *frasha*—apparently derived from the stem *fra-ank,* "proceeding forward"—"advancing to completion"—is a *re-creation* that, in the case of the king's work, does not abide in the realm of abstractions; rather, it must appear as embedded in a physically *visible* mold.[28] As a matter of fact, if we read the inscriptions of Darius the Great, who reigned between 522 and 485 B.C., we continually stumble upon the expression *frasha tya vainataiy,* viz., "the regeneration *which is seen.*" That means: "What thus far belonged to the mere world of ideas, has now been engraved into the realm of material certitude."

Such a "material certitude" was subjectively considered by the ancient

Persians to belong to what they deemed to be "active goodness" (Old Persian *naiba,* Middle Persian *nevak,* Neo-Persian *niku*), the opposite to *vohu* (Middle Persian *bih,* Neo-Persian *beh*), which was "abstract, religious goodness."[29] The former applied to warriors, farmers, and kings, the latter— naturally—was developed by the priestly people. Both were founded on the Universal Harmony, the Essential Rule, *arta* or *asha* (from the root *ar,* "to move towards," "to adapt to each other").

Thus if material life is fundamentally "good," every form of psychological anguish or physical pain arising in men must be rooted in the violation of such a cosmic rule or harmony, especially when pains are suffered by the community as a result of the king's misuse of his own power, and his failure to fulfill his duties. This is the reason why Iranian rulers willingly stressed the moral value of their lordship, rather than the naked fact of their power, as other Eastern sovereigns did. Darius, stating his accomplishments, gives an account of the ethical virtues that made him worthy of being the legitimate king as opposed to false pretenders (such as the magus *Gaumata*), and deserving "Ahuramazda's" bounty and blessing: *"(4)* when Ahuramazda beheld this country fallen in disarray, He delivered it to me. He made a King of me. I am king by Ahuramazda's will: I have put the earth in order." The reasons follow:

> A great God indeed is Ahuramazda, who created all these fair things *that are to be seen* [translator's emphasis], who created happiness for man, who poured intelligence over King Darius, who made King Darius a king, the only king for the many, the unique leader over the many. King Darius speaketh: "By Ahuramazda's will I am of such nature that I am a friend to the just: I am no friend to the unjust. It is not my wish that either the weak might suffer injustice from the strong one, or the strong one from the deceiver. What is right, that is my desire. I am no friend to the man that followeth Falsehood. I do not easily set myself in anger: what ariseth in me when I might feel anger, that I do strongly restrain by my thought. I do strongly rule my inclinations. . . ."[30]

And now the final prayer of the Great King, engraved on the southern wall of the apadana (great staircase) at Persepolis; it invokes the help of Ahura Mazda for his enterprises as confirmation of the legitimacy of his lordship: "May neither foe, nor dearth, nor any form of Falsehood overcome this country! This do I pray Ahuramazda and all the gods to grant me as a gift. May Ahuramazda, with all the gods, give this to me!"

It is worth observing that the aforesaid calamities of Falsehood *(drauga),* Enmity *(haina),* and Famine *(dushiyara)* exactly correspond, but in reverse, to the functions performed by the first three classes of the Persian people, namely the priests, the warriors, and the producers of material wealth, on whose mutual balance is founded the empire's progress and happiness.

Therefore, the personal realization by the king of these social virtues—the religious awe and righteousness of the priests, the bravery and loyalty of the warriors, the industry of the farmers and tillers—was considered the only token for obtaining the grace of God and everlasting continuity for the kingdom.[31]

Every king was thus expected to renew, in his own age, the image of his primeval predecessor Yima, ruling the entire world, starting from the blessed clime of Khwaniratha where was set the fabulous country of the Aryans, the *Airyana Vaejah,* in which "the whole year lasted but one day and one night"—a symbol for a "polar" condition, psychological rather than geographical.[32] It is worth remembering that even in Islamic times, in Persian Sufism, the "pole" (Arabic *al-qotb*) was meant as an interior quality, the realization of the so-called *mani manī* ("the I of the I-ness").[33] This is the "pillar of light," already mentioned, that connects Heaven and Earth through the Perfect Man personified by the ruling king.

The royal function of renewing the world (already described as *frasho-kereti*) is further related to the possession by the king of the Victorious Light, the aforesaid *khvarenah.* The ancient Persians, however, did not regard this aureola as a mere poetic abstraction; on the contrary, it was a *visible energy*— thus says the third book of the *Denkart*—strictly *bound to the destiny of each man,* inasmuch as it allowed the fulfillment of the duty proper to his social class, the *khweskarih.* As for the king, the actual presence of the *khvarenah* depended on his loyalty to the Essential Rule *(arta, asha),* and was therefore granted in accordance with his personal worth *(arzih).*[34] It was a gift that not only the king, but actually every man received from the Creator: it was said that the same Ohrmazd (Middle Persian for Ahura Mazda) drew the *khvarenahs* from the Endless Light *(anaghr roshnih)* and delivered them to the Holy Geniuses *(yazatas)* who ruled the Fire *(Atar)* and the Waters *(Apo).*

These two species of entities transfer the Victorious Light from the spiritual to the physical world, from the *menok* to the *gete,* this latter ruled by chronological time *(aban,* or *zaman),* assigning individual *khvarenahs* to different kinds of beings, as the principle supporting their terrestrial life.[35] In man this *khvarenah* is susceptible to developing itself (for instance, in the case of the common man who becomes a king), for it is continuously nourished by wisdom, energy and virtues. Its presence within man actually depends on his spiritual awareness, that is, the extent to which he is conscious of his own original I-ness.

As a principle supporting human life, the *khvarenah* forms the paradisiacal particle that works the miracle of generation. Time itself, which, during the earthly life, forms the scenario in which the *khvarenah* brings about the destiny of man, is brought back by the same *khvarenah* to its celestial pattern, to the achronic, all-devouring Infinite Aeon, the *Zrvan Akerena.* Originally, "king" meant a man capable of realizing, in full awareness, his own destiny by developing his inborn *khvarenah.*

Many legends have been told in Iran about such a Victorious Light, sometimes called *a-khvaretem khvarenah,* which, by the amphibology of the verb *khvar/hvar,* meaning both "to devour" and "to shine," might mean "the splendor which is never consumed," hinting at the celestial principle present in every man which remains intact through all his life on earth. In Middle Persian this meaning is conveyed by the translation *agrift khvarrah,* i.e., unseizable *khvarrah,* eventually ascribed by the *Denkart* to the priestly class *(han-i asronan).*[36] Inasmuch as the *Denkart* was edited *after* the Arab invasion and subsequent fall of the Iranian monarchy, the implication was that no king, no matter who, was capable of bearing the holy aureola properly!

It is the *Denkart,* too, that gives an account of the vicissitudes suffered by many princely personages in their struggles to acquire the victorious halo.[37] The *khvarenah* was originally designed by the Good Creator to preserve the earthly, physical creation *(dam-i astvant),* and was for that reason bestowed in its totality on King Yima. Then, after the king's disgrace and fall, the *khvarenah* divided itself into three parts, corresponding to the three social functions: the aforesaid *agrift khvarrah* belong to the priests; the *khvarrah-e Kayan* was shared by the princes and warriors; and the *khvarrah-e Iran* was owned by the body of the Aryan community, the common people.

The nineteenth Yasht of the Avesta reports that, after Yima's disgrace, the threefold *khvarenah* was assumed first by Mithra, the solar spirit par excellence, then by Atar the fire-genius who, in trying to rescue it from the usurper Azhi Dahaka, sank it into the depths of the sacred Vouru Kasha lake.[38] There it remained unscathed under the watch of Apam Napat, "the Born from the Waters," another manifestation of the Original Fire, awaiting the return of the legitimate sovereign of Iran, upon whom it should be bestowed.

On the same grounds, many legends stressed how illegitimacy, or moral evil, made a number of princes unable to get hold of this token of kingship. Such was the Turanian tyrant Franhrasyan (the Afrasyab of the *Shahnameh),* who tried three times to seize it—and three times failed. In the shape of a royal hawk (or a phoenix, Neo-Persian *homa-ye homayun),* the *khvarenah* later appeared in the country of Iran to crown two kingly heroes, first, Thraetaona (the Indian Trita Aptya, Fereydun in Neo-Persian) and after him Kereshaspa (the Indian Krshasya, Garshasp in Neo-Persian), who became Universal King as a reward for having saved the freedom of the Iranian people and of mankind by rescuing them from a number of tyrants and monsters.

It is also said that at the end of time the three parts of the *khvarenah* will be reunited to help the final Savior, Saoshyant, in his task of *relieving all humanity* from evil, distress, malady, and death, forever. Thus the theory of the sacral kingship in ancient Iran appears to convey a meaning far beyond a class ideology; indeed, it points to an eschatological ideal regarding the mystical liberation of humankind as such. The Iranian people, through the tormented vicissitudes of their history, even after major changes of religion, have never lost sight of this ideal, sometimes personified as a worthy monarch or as a righteous dynasty; rather they have always kept the ideal of what was actually meant by the myth of kingship, never discarding the hope that, some day in the future, myth and history would again converge for the happiness of all mankind.

The Iranian Kingship and
Its Influence on the Roman Empire

If we want to look into the causes of the successful diffusion in the Western world of certain institutions connected with kingship, in either the religious or the lay domain, we must go back to the Roman Empire, which was the first Western state to absorb a great deal of such outside influence, especially in its political and administrative institutions regarding the status of the Emperor, his retinue and household. In particular, the legal position of his patrimony and treasure and, above all, his religious and institutional standing, were subject to this influence.

On this basis, in the course of time, many civil and military institutions of our traditional West, such as the prerogatives of the chief of state, or the state ministries and secretaries, were established. In the beginning, nothing was so far from the Roman mentality as to ascribe a transcendent character to the personality of national warlords and statesmen, not even to the most successful among them, like Gnaeus Cornelius Scipio, still less to acknowledge them as having godlike qualities. The early Romans were rather inclined to drag these men before a jury and eventually behead them, if they were faintly suspected of aspiring to kingly dignity. Even the *rex sacrificulus* (king of the sacrifices) was only a shadow of the former kings, a functionary whose activities were limited merely to the performance of religious ceremonies; indeed, he was obliged to leave the city once a year as a reminder of the *regifugium,* the king's flight, or expulsion.

Gaius Iulius Caesar, a dictator who was practically a king, refused to accept the title of king when it was presented to him by the Roman people; nevertheless, he was killed for endangering the republic. For these reasons, when the monarchy was re-established in Rome, it was formed *not* after the old Italian, Etruscan, or Celtic pattern, but, strangely enough, following in broad outlines the Hellenistic-Iranian example.

For all practical purposes, it was during the grueling campaigns in Asia

Minor, against or for the local Hellenistic kings, that the Romans learned something of the Iranian ideology and institutions of the top state hierarchies—Iranian despite their Greek trappings—and came to grips with the religious and mystical elements underlying them.

Lucius Cornelius Sulla (138-68 B.C.), the lonely aristocrat, one of the coolest statesmen and most successful Roman warlords, was soon attracted by Persian-Anatolian mysticism, whose devotee was his stubborn adversary, Mithradates Eupator, king of Pontus. Soon, in 92 B.C., he was recognized by the Persian magus accompanying the satrap Orobazes on his embassy to the Roman army as an embodied godhead—as we are told by the historians Velleius Paterculus and Plutarch.[39]

When he seized total power in Rome, after the crushing defeat of the Italian mutinies (82 B.C.), he also assumed the enigmatic surname of Felix, "the Lucky One." He did so in order to establish his personal connection with the goddess Venus (Aphrodite in Greek), bearer of such a title, into whose mysteries he had been initiated at her temple at Comana. On that occasion, he had adopted the title of Epaphroditos, "attached to Aphrodite." Scandal and fear arose in Rome, for the goddess was not only believed to keep under her sway the realm of love, but—more important to the practical Romans—also that of irresistible victory.[40]

They knew besides that the terrible dictator was imbued with Eastern ideas; and on his entering Rome, where he put to sword almost all his adversaries, he was displaying his kinship not so much with the mild Western Venus, as with her Iranian counterpart Anahita ("the Unscathed"), who personified the terrible aspect of the kingly power, the *khvarenah* itself!

A few years later another Roman, Gaius Iulius Caesar, ascribed to himself descent from the same divine person, through the Albanian kings and their ancestor Aeneas, the Phrygian fugitive from Troy who was Venus's son by Anchises, a mortal. From that time onward, Venus-Victoria became the Patroness and Mother Goddess of all Romans.[41]

The heir and legatee of Caesar, Octavian, having established his absolute power over the Roman world (whose republican frame had already collapsed during the civil wars), founded an empire on a conception that was originally quite foreign to his people. The same title of emperor, "imperator," had been until then granted by the Senate to generals in the field, but only to stress their full power, which was provisional, and could be exercised only when abroad. In contrast, Octavian was recognized as sovereign like a Persian Shahanshah, although he never interfered with the prerogatives of the Senate and other state magistracies, protected as he was by the same Venus-Victoria, who was now his ancestress. His power was symbolized by the eagle—the bird of Jupiter, but also the occidental interpretation of the Iranian *saena-merego* (Neo-Persian *simorgh*), the royal bird of prey personifying the *khvarenah*. In addition, on January 16, 27 B.C. he was given the title and name of Augustus, which is an exact translation and even phonetic transposition of the Avestic adjective *aojishta*, "possessor of the most increasing force," generally attributed to the Fravashis, the angelic doubles of eminent or godlike personalities.[42]

The meaning of *ojas* (the stem of *aoj-ishta*) was "the irresistible life-energy of human seed"; at the same time, it hinted at the dazzling power of the *khvarenah* (as shown by the attributive expression *khvarena-anuhastamo*, "most endowed in *khvarenah*"). Augustus's person was held to be semidivine during his life and completely divinized after his death, when an eagle was loosed upon his blazing pyre.

The very Iranian ideology of kingship in its Hellenistic interpretation had fatally attracted Caesar's and Octavian's antagonists Gnaeus Pompeius and Marcus Antonius, who both failed in their separate dreams of universal empire, though they were better qualified for it than their adversaries, because they came to disown their loyalty to Roman institutions. Their attempts to realize an ideal, the taste of which they had relished when commanding in the Orient, were premature. However, the Roman atmosphere was becoming ripe to receive the more stimulating impulses just mentioned. A mystical sense of expectancy was creeping into the society: at least, the enlightened aristocracy wanted to grasp the meaning of its own mission. The Fourth Eclogue of Vergil beautifully expresses such a climate when it celebrates the birth of the infant who will restore the Golden Age among men—a well-known motif in Persian lore. The Iranian myth of the King-Savior supplied the idea.

Another purely Iranian feature of sacral kingship was related to the cult of Mithra, introduced into the Roman dominions by the Cilician pirates reduced to captivity by Pompeius after a hard and bloody campaign. The cult of the Sun God, whose mysteries were spread by these half-Iranians amidst their former enemies, combined with the growing militarization of the empire, increased the Iranic elements present in the Roman Empire from its very beginning, to the point that the Emperor Aurelian, upon his triumph in 274 A.D., ordered that the Sun God, of whom he was the high priest, was to be worshipped as official protector of the state and the personal patron of the emperor himself.[43] He also established at the inauguration of his temple that the same date—December 25—was to be considered the birthday of the God *(Dies natalis Solis Mithrae)*. This same date was later adopted by Christians for the Savior's Nativity, probably at the suggestion of the same emperor (himself a "heathen"!), who shortly before had personally settled a contest between Christian bishops about the supremacy of the Roman See.

So intimately was the idea of the Savior connected with the image of the Persian god, that we find the date definitely recognized by Pope Liberius a century later, in 354, when the empire was already officially Christianized, in place of the previously celebrated dates of November 20 or January 6. Similarly, the Epiphany, which marks the beginning of the Savior's earthly mission, was closely associated with the homage of the Persian Magi to the newborn King, as we see beautifully represented in the mosaics of St. Apollinaris's cathedral in Ravenna, where the images of the three Magi personify the three human ages.

Thus, from Nero initiated into the mysteries of Mithra, bestowing the *Persian* kingly diadem on Tiridates of Armenia—a Roman vassal, belonging to the Parthian royal family—to Julian the Apostate receiving a Mithraean rank (probably that of "Persian" or "Eagle") the day of his ascent to the throne, in December 361 A.D., the Roman hierarchies were subjected over three centuries to an increasing Iranian influence, especially in the institutional sphere.

In this tale, Diocletian and Constantine represent important landmarks. The former introduced the full Iranian etiquette into the court ritual, including (in 288 A.D.)the Persian "adoration" of the Genius of the Emperor, the so-called *proskynesis*. He established a Privy Council *(consistorium)* like the one in Ctesiphon, and divided the empire into four military headquarters after the Sassanian pattern *(Apakhtar, Khavar,* etc.), each ruled by a quasi-emperor with a range of authority similar to the jurisdiction of the *espahbads* (military governors) of the neighboring Persian Empire.[44]

As for Constantine, until 312 A.D. he was officially considered an earthly Sun. His dynasty claimed descent from Claudius II (reigned 268-70 A.D.), himself believed to be a scion of the same godhead.[45] On his conversion to Christianity Constantine renounced the radiant solar crown, but still retained the Persian diadem, a token of consecration that enhanced his lofty qualifications. Although the Roman title *divus* (divine) was exchanged for the Greek Christian one, *isapostolos* (equal to the Apostles), his position remained identical.

The same institutions (with a stronger Eastern character, however) were preserved by the subsequent Byzantine Empire up to its fall before the Turkish onslaught in 1453, eleven centuries later. The Ottoman Turks, first through the Abbasid Caliphate (already extinguished before the rising of the Ottoman branch from the Seljuk realm) and later through the Seljuks of Asia Minor, had previously adopted a number of originally Persian institutions that affected the political, military, economic, and royal domains.

In this connection, the historian Ibn Bibi, describing the Seljuk ruler's accession to the throne, gives an account of a number of Iranian and even Indo-Iranian traditions followed on that occasion, such as the release of captives.[46] These attest to the overwhelming influence of Persian patterns that preserved the traits of an Indo-European protohistorical tradition.

The Byzantine court and state and later the Papacy, preserved symbols and institutions, received from Iran in different ages, that were then transmitted, for the second time, to all European monarchies. In this case, however, the intermediary was the Holy Roman Empire, restored by Charlemagne on his coronation, in A.D. 800, by Pope Leo III. It would be interesting to dwell upon the Iranic elements on which this ceremony was founded. Einhard, in his *Vita Caroli Magni,* tells us how Pope Leo, upon finishing the mass, approached the kingly throne, kneeled, made obeisance (viz., the Persian *proskynesis*), then got up and placed the imperial crown on Charles's head. At that moment the people present, the priests and the men-of-war, both Roman and Frank, shouted three times: "Life and Victory to the 'August' Charles, crowned by God, great and pacific Emperor!"

"Life" and "victory" are the two opposite poles of the kingly function; the former is proper to priesthood, characterized by the white dress (the dress of the magi) worn under the red garb, which symbolizes the latter pole, that of warriorship. The same Iranian combination of royal and priestly robes was formerly worn by Persian Armenian kings, to stress the double power they held, the power also symbolized by the globe and the scepter or sword. The same parallelism between two functions simultaneously held by the king may be seen in his double title ("Great and Pacific").

The Syriac text *The Cave of Treasures* states explicitly that the so-called heathen kings (of Persia) "were dressed in the clothing of the Magi, whenever they sacrificed or offered gifts to their gods."[48] Six centuries after the fall of the Sassanian Empire under the Islamic onslaught, we still find the Norman kings of Sicily donning white episcopal dress when attending religious assemblies in Palermo, thus to enhance their priestly prerogatives. Even now, during the so-called Vacant See, when a pope is deceased and another one has not yet been elected, the red-and-white striped banner (the imperial canopy) is hoisted on the sacred keys, the state symbol, as a reminder of the emperor's protection of the Holy See during such a period, granted as it was in times of yore. In this way the Iranian symbology of sacral kingship has traveled to the West during the millennia, impregnating with its zest and emotional force the supreme emblems of power in our world.

CONTINUITY OF THE ROYAL TRADITION
AFTER THE INTRODUCTION OF ISLAM

If the sudden conquest of Persian by the ragged host of the bedouin Sa'd ibn Abi Waqqas (636-52) appears little less than a miracle, we feel no small wonder when we consider that, after the establishment of Islam in Iran and the apparently total erasure of the political and religious institutions on which its empire and its social organization were founded, not only did Iran keep its peculiar character, but it was also able to impose its way of life, political organization, and (however partially) its spiritual orientation, in an Islamic form and sometimes in the Arabic language, upon a political and religious empire stretching from Spain to the boundaries of China. Shortly after the Arab invasion, the Persians—already converted to the new creed—began spreading the patterns of their superior civilization to a number of Moslem countries and kingdoms. Such was the caliphate of Baghdad whose capital, which Caliph al-Mansur built in 763 practically under Persian superintendence, not far from the old Sassanian capital of Ctesiphon, retained a Persian name (Bagh-dad, "created by God") and was no longer a real Arab city.

Still more did the Ghaznavid and Seljuk realms, and later the Ottoman Empire (not to mention the Samanid, Buwayhid, and Ziyarite kingdoms, which were pure Iranian, or the Ismailite anticaliphate of Cairo, which was a purely Iranian creation) undergo such a Persian influence. Iran gave numerous great figures to Islam: statesmen, such as Nezam al-Molk, the organizer of the Seljuk sultanate (d. 1092); warriors, such as the renowned Saladin (Salah ad-Din), mirror of chivalry; philosophers, such as Avicenna (Ibn Sina) and al-Ghazali; even refined "Arab" literati such as Hamadhani, grammarians such as Sibawayh, mathematicians such as al-Khwarizmi, historians such as at-Tabari, and encyclopedic geniuses such as al-Biruni.

Most of "Arab" philosophy and some of Islamic theology appears to be of Persian origin. This is a paradox, since being a "Persian" meant for many philosophers the charge of heterodoxy and even of mystical extravagance. The tragic cases of al-Hallaj, Bashshar ibn Burd, and Sohravardi bear witness to the seriousness of this charge: they ended their meditations and raptures on the scaffold.

The resurgence of Iran in the Islamic period was something more than a rebirth: it was a new creation.

When the Persian *espahbad* Rostahm, son of the other generalissimo Farrukh Hormizd, lost his noble life on the third day of the Battle of Qadisiyya (A.D. 636), and the sacred banner of Iran (*derafsh-e Kayani,* made out of the apron of the mythical blacksmith Kaveh, vanquisher of the tyrant Azhi Dahaka) fell into the hands of the Arabs; when the last emperor, Yazdagard III, was compelled to a flight that ended with a wretched death (A.D. 651); when the Sassanian scions Aparvez, in A.D. 674, and his son Narseh, in A.D. 707, took shelter in distant China; then it seemed as if a splendid past were gone forever. Yet a similar invasion by Alexander of Macedon ten centuries before, an invasion that uprooted the Achaemenian dynasty and the secular establishment of the Persian ruling class, had not meant such a calamity, because Alexander did not intend to annihilate the Empire. Rather, he meant to enlarge it and rule over it as the continuator of the former dynasty. Hence he gladly yielded to Iranian usages, rites, creeds, and beliefs, and persuaded his Greek followers to do the same thing. (The Medo-Persian legends, though cursing him, accredited the rumor that he was a spurious scion of the Achaemenids.) After him, the Hellenistic kingdoms were more or less a Greek-Iranian creation. In contrast, the Arab invasion, brought about by the tidal wave of fresh, enthusiastic faith of newborn Islam, swept across the old Persian Empire reaping a rich territorial and human harvest.

The Zarathustrian Church, without the support of the national state and losing its hold on the newly converted masses, although it was tolerated by the conquerors, withered and nearly disappeared. Even the national language was superseded by the new parlance, the Arabic "tongue of God," common idiom for all Moslems. All this signified the near waning away of national identity, a tendency that was strengthened by the immigration and implantation of entire Arab tribes, such as the Banu Qays and other tribes, exiled in the number of fifty thousand to the distant Khorasan in A.D. 668 by the Omayyad Caliph Mu'awiya.

The reaction was not delayed. It began to rise in Khorasan, the eastern border of the Moslem Empire that comprised, in addition to the homonym province of Persia, the present Afghanistan, Tadjikistan, Uzbekistan, and Turkmenistan. This border country was the shelter and sometimes the hideout of all the mutineers and rebels, either Arab or Persian: dissatisfied Arab chieftains, Persian landowners attached to the old traditions, Shi'ites (supporters of 'Ali, the Prophet's cousin and son-in-law who died in 661, for the caliphate), supports of 'Abbas (another of the Prophet's next of kin), Zarathustrians of different trends, beside Mazdakites (followers of the fifth-century Zoroastrian priest Mazdak), and heterodox groups of every kind. They were a colorful, seething mass, ready to surge after any charismatic leader. Such a leader was the Persian, Abu-Moslem, who succeeded in rallying this heterogenous crowd around the Abbasid pretender Abol-'Abbas as-Saffah (A.D. 747).

The accession to the caliphate of the Abbasids, in A.D. 750, meant a radical transformation of the Moslem Empire, which from an Arab commonwealth, governed—as it was under the Omayyads—in a patriarchal way, changed into an autocratic State, politically organized more or less after the Sassanian or Byzantine pattern. Civil administration—tax levies, army structure, court etiquette—assumed an unmistakable Persian appearance. The caliph, brought to the throne by a revolution occurring in a Persian country, prepared and led by a Persian general, became himself the Islamic portrait of a Sassanian ruler, the same who had reigned till a century before in the now smoldering Ctesiphon, a few miles from the newly built Baghdad. Even if the shrewd Abu-Moslem was infamously rewarded by the ungrateful as-Saffah, who soon let him be killed, the weight of the immense empire only devolved onto the shoulders of another Persian, the *vazir* (an Iranian word, meaning "minister"), who during the first half-century of Abbasid rule was always a member of the Barmakids, a family that had formerly been fire-priests in Balkh but were soon converted to Islam.

The minister, following the Sassanian pattern, immediately organized a number of departments *(divan)* in the interest of an efficient state administration. These included the "ministry of treasure" *(al-kharaj)*, the "court of accounts" *(divan al-azemmeh)*, the "ministry of war" *(divan al-jond)*, the "ministry of communications" *(divan al-barid)*, the "ministry of police" *divan ash-shorteh)*, and the privy seal *(divan al-khatam)*.[49] The genius of three Persian converts *(mavali)* had already been evident. For instance, at the time of the Caliph Omar II (717-20), the Iranian Sulayman ibn Abis-Sari organized a mail service connecting Damascus with the distant Khorasan and Transoxiana—an astounding achievement for those days and even later, especially in Europe.

As a symptom of the early Iranization of the Arabs settled east of Iraq, the historian at-Tabari recollects how the Arab governor of Khorasan, Asad ibn Abdallah, celebrated Mihragan, the festival of Mithra, along with the local aristocracy, offering a delicious meal to the local Persian *dehqans* and the Arab generals as well. In return, the *dehqans* offered him the same presents that a few years before they used to give the Sassanian feudal lord, as the king's representative.[50]

Other episodes of this kind bear witness that the Persian people, even as they changed religions, still retained the old usages and customs and stuck to their traditions, many of them dating back to pre-Zoroastrian antiquity (before the eleventh century B.C.). They included traditions related to the cardinal feasts—Nowruz (first day of spring, beginning of the Persian year), Sadeh (the feast of fire, at the Winter solstice), Mihragan (at the autumnal equinox)—and the beliefs regarding elements, especially fire and water, faithfully observed nowadays in Khorasan.[51]

This conservative element, so consonant with the ease the Persians showed in accepting the new religion, explains the instinctive maintenance of many ideologies, especially if they were related to the universal and social order, like those regarding the sacral kingship.

In the old regime the sacral kingship had two sources of support. On the one hand, it was linked to the primeval myths of the Universal King dating back to Indo-European antiquity; on the other, it was supported by the pious legends of Zarathustra, particularly those regarding the Three Saviors of Humankind, i.e., Ushetar, Ushetar Mah, and Soshans, who were to be born, in the last three millennia, from the seed of Zarathustra miraculously preserved in the boreal Lake Vouru-kasha.[52] The popular conscience of Islamic Iranians, though, still retaining in the background the warriorlike myths of Jamshid, Fereidun, Peshotan, Sami Nareman, etc., handed down even by such Moslem authors as Daqiqi and Ferdowsi, relegated Zarathustra to a dim limbo of effaced memories. They replaced his person and those of his future descendants and missionaries with the charismatic ones of the martyrs for the faith: 'Ali and his son al-Husayn (viciously killed at Karbala in A.D. 680 by the Omayyad troops), who were branded by the glowing fire of prophecy—an unequaled token indeed, and one that played the role of the old *khvarenah*.

Besides, these imams ("directors of prayer," later "leaders of the Shi'a," the party of 'Ali), bearing in their veins not only the blood of the prophet Mohammad but, from 'Ali "Zaynul-Abedin," also that of the Sassanian house (Zaynul-Abedin, "the Jewel of the Worshippers," is believed to have married the daughter of the last Sassanid emperor, the Shahbanou or "Imperial Lady"), enjoyed a double legitimacy, both Arab and Iranian. Such a legitimacy, ascribed to the Holy House of the "Fourteen Blessed Ones" (Mohammad, 'Ali, and Fatima, daughter of the Prophet and wife to 'Ali, with their eleven descendants), inevitably led to the resurrection in Islamic garb of the sacral kingship—which, however, followed the old Iranian pattern.

When, in A.D. 873, the twelfth descendant of that line disappeared at the well of Samarra, he became the Hidden Imam, the "Lord of Time" (Sahib az-Zaman), and the expectation of his return reproduced in a non-Islamic mold the earlier expectation of the Savior (Old Persian *Saoshyant*, Middle Persian *Soshans*) who would come at the end of time—a belief that had been fundamental to all Mazdaeans.[53]

The evolution of the Shi'a from a political party, as it was in the beginning, into a gnostic sect (especially its Ismailite branch), with all its overwhelming influence on the formation of the Islamic mystic philosophy, was a determining factor for the conservation and even the enrichment of the conceptions related to the sacral kingship, and so repugnant in principle to the equalitarian outlook set forth by the Arab Islam. We know that the fifth and the sixth imams, Mohammad Baqir and Ja'far as-Sadiq, as witnessed by their contemporaries al-Kulayni and Mohammad ar-Razi (d. 941), actively contributed to the *Ikhwan as-Safa* ("Encyclopedia of the Brethren of Purity"). These fifty-one books constituted the "Summa" of ancient wisdom and science, arranged in an organic frame of thought that responsively reflected a hierarchic vision of reality in its different manifestations.

In this connection, it is worth reminding ourselves that the pivot of imamite ideology was the so-called convocation *(da'vat)* of elects, whose gathering was viewed as reflecting on an earthly plane the archetypal "full number" (Greek *pleroma*, also meaning "perfection") that exists in heaven. Its first emanation was the Primordial Man *(adam-e qadim)*, or Spiritual Man *(adam-e ruhani)*, whose projection in the temporal world is the imam as Universal King. The Imams, from 'Ali downwards, were conceived as the initiators of the cycle of the so-called *valayat* (from the Arabic *vali*, "neighbor," "friend," "confidant"), after the close of that of *nobovvat* (prophecy), sealed up by the last prophet, Mohammad.

The latter handed down the last revelation, the former were the keepers of its secret meaning *(baten)*. The Supreme Proof *(hojjat)*, or evidence supporting the authenticity of an experience, belonged entirely to the chosen group of the *da'vat*. The imam had not only a general theological value, but was conceived as subjectively abiding in the very heart of each supporter of his mission, as his innermost actual being. "The imam's light abiding in the faithful's heart" was "more resplendent than a sun spreading daylight," because "the imam, as the Primordial Being," was "always present within the hearts of all his loyal people." It was also said that "the one who knows himself knows his own imam. The one who dies without having known his own imam passes away without having realized his own innermost self."[54]

In this way the Shi'a, instead of effacing the ideology of the sacral kingship, enhanced it further by propounding its spiritual dimension as an object of personal experience, lying within the power of every mystic devout.

The figure of the Eternal King was further personalized in this heterodox ambience by the famous Haft Bab-e Sayyidna ("The Eight Gates of Our Lord"), Hassan-e Sabbah, the terrible master of the "new" Ismailites (d.1124), identifying him with the same Melki-tzedeq (i.e., Melchizedek), priest-king of Ur, who anointed Abraham, and is also mentioned in the Pauline *Epistle to the Hebrews.* He was to come at the end as the "Resurrector" *(qa'em)*, thus—we add—recovering the function already attributed by the Mazdaeans to the Savior. His ideal adept was homologized to the *Persian* Salman, the freedman and counselor of Mohammad.[55] In this way, as it happened in the ancient mysteries of Mithra, the man who ascended to a stage approaching the royal dignity was considered ipso facto to be "a Persian"! In later Ismailism, the imam was homologized to the rank of the First Intelligence *('aql-e kulli).*

These mystical ideas regarding the kingly function, attributed by the Shi'ites to the successive leaders of the Holy House of the Fourteen Blessed Ones were not, as might be supposed, the abstract concoction of some philosophical elite; rather, they filled a popular need that was particularly felt in the regions already belonging to the Sassanian Empire.

Around 750, coinciding with the Abbasid accession to the caliphate, a number of mutinies and political rebellions with a messianic hue, beginning with the Ravandiyyeh that, paradoxically enough, ascribed the same Godhead to Caliph al-Mansur, burst out in Khorasan and other parts of Iran. They all retained some characteristics in common: "the concentration of divinity" attributed to their leaders (especially if dead!), a divinity to be shared with other partners who were recognized as having the function of "expected king" and deliverer from wrong and misery; their millenarism, or predictions of the end of human time; their mixture of heretical tenets, both Islamic and

Zarathustrian; and the belief that their leaders were possibly the reincarnation of some successful general, such as Abu-Moslem, or some unsuccessful missionary who eventually suffered martyrdom. (As a matter of fact, the deceased personalities did *not*, in any way, share during their life the beliefs of their enthusiastic later supporters: the importance ascribed to them lay uniquely in the "magical halo," or power of suggestion—practically a sort of *khvarenah*—that enveloped them throughout their lifetime.)

Such, for instance, was the mutiny of the magus Bihafrid, or Behzad, who suddenly showed himself, in 750, on the top of an inaccessible dome to the people of Nishapur, proclaiming himself the prophet sent by God to restore the "true" religion of Zoroaster (in effect, a mixture of modified Mazdaism and Islam). He had an enormous number of supporters, about 30,000, but after some time he was put to the sword by Abu-Moslem, who in turn was unaware that, after his own death, he would be "deified" and raised to a mystical kingship by a still greater number of supporters!

First of these was his own lieutenant Sindbad, or Peroz Espahbad ("the Victorious General") who, after the slaughter of his commander, raised a long and terrible revolution in northern Iran, claiming himself to be the prophet (Arabic *rasul*) of the same Abu-Moslem, who obviously had not died but, on the point of death, had escaped the fatal blow by invoking the Supreme Name (Arabic *esm-e a'zam*). Transforming himself into a white dove, he fled to a copper castle in the heavens, where he still lived in the company of the Mahdi (the future Messiah) and Mazdak (the famous Persian heresiarch put to death by King Khosrow in A.D. 529.

In Sindbad's doctrines, besides the old Gnostic-Mazdaean ideas (the Supreme Name, the Three Saviors, the Dove Spirit), there appears for the first time the so-called *récit visionnaire* (visionary tale)—viz., the Castle, etc.—which was to become a commonplace in the mystical literature of Avicenna, Sohravardi and other philosophers, who used it to introduce the adept through ecstasy into an esoteric dimension of Reality.

Next was the mutiny of Ustad Sis (about 767) in Tokharistan (the region of Balkh), who launched the movement of Bihafrid: it ended, shortly after, in the usual way. It was, however, followed by the serious insurrection led by a remarkable personage, a former missionary *(da'i)* of Abu-Moslem in Khorasan, probably named Hashim ibn Hakim but better known by the nickname of al-Muqanna' (Arabic "the Veiled One"), because he usually kept his face hidden by a veil, saying that otherwise its radiance would have burned all who beheld it. As a matter of fact, the "burning radiance" of the King's face is a mythical feature of the sacral kingship. Even in the Qajars' time it was courtly etiquette to shout, when being introduced to the royal presence, *misuzam* ("I burn!"), and cover one's own face with both hands.

Narshakhi, in his *History of Bukhara,* gives a fair account of the adventures of this strange character, who proclaimed himself *tout court*, the embodied God. Already, according to the Veiled One, God had appeared among men under the semblances of Adam, Noah, Abraham, Moses, Mohammad and Abu-Moslem; now he himself was that semblance, a kind of spiritual *(ruhani)* essence, capable of assuming any shape, and even of impregnating the souls of living people. He worked a number of miracles, including the famous "rising of the moon from the well of Nakhshab," and shortly after this miracle a great part of eastern Iran fell under his sway. Caliph al-Mahdi, in A.D. 783, was compelled to send against him a regular army, which besieged his castle on the mountain Sitam, near Kish, for fourteen years. At last, seeing no escape from his awkward situation, al-Muqanna' poisoned his retinue, including one hundred ladies (daughters of local *dehqans* forming his harem) and boldly threw himself into a burning furnace, in order not to leave any trace of himself and to keep the people waiting for his return from the next world. He was unfortunately betrayed by a shrewd girl who did not drink the poison and was therefore able to witness the gruesome end of her master.

Other forms of religious enthusiasm spread in the western regions of Persia, namely, Iraq 'Ajemi and Azarbayjan, under the leadership of the Persian Javidan ibn Sohrak and his disciple 'Abdollah Papak, whose ideology and social customs have been related rather imperfectly by some Moslem historians.[56] Their adherents, called *khorramis* (the "happy ones") were noted for their lenient domestic and social habits, and considered all religions to be fundamentally true. They believed in two principles, Good and Evil; in repeated incarnations on earth (metempsychosis); and in the unity of the Divine Inspiration, which was always present among men and from time to time descended upon the prophets. They also held fast to the old Iranian traditions regarding the sacral kingship, whose emblems and insignia Papak himself ended by wearing.

All this is only to characterize the psychological atmosphere prevailing in the eastern lands of the caliphate during the first two centuries of Islam (Papak died in 838), which was endemically shaken by messianic movements. The ideologies of these movements, even when they represented no more than a revival of Mazdaean beliefs, owed their emergence to the new and energetic faith of Islam, which in some way catalyzed the religious energies slumbering in the common people.

Another remarkable contribution to this flood of devotion was late pagan gnosticism, still practiced in many cities along the old border between Iran and Mesopotamia, especially among the so-called Sabaeans of Harran, whose outer wisdom and science, later reflected in the then emergent Islamic philosophy, probably rested on an inner foundation supplied by some kind of ecstatic experience. Such an atmosphere, in which the mystical trends did not necessarily contradict the acceptance and outward practice of Islam, led on the one hand to the formation of extremist sects under the Shiʻa—for instance, that of al-Khattab, who propounded the divinity of the sixth imam, Jaʻfar as-Sadeq, although the latter disavowed it, or that of the Ismailites—and, on the other, favored the formation of independent Iranian kingdoms of Shiʻite tendency. Among these kingdoms were that of the Samanids in Balkh (ninth to tenth centuries), who were descendants of the royal family of Bahram Chubin (d. 591), and the Ziyarids (928-1077) in Tabaristan, south of the Caspian Sea, made famous by a number of statesmen and writers such as Qabus (976-1012) and, some fifty years later, by his descendant Kay-Kaʻus.

They were followed by another Persian dynasty, that of the Buwayhids, one of whose members, Ahmad, entered Baghdad in 945 and imposed himself, a Shiʻite, on the caliph as lord protector. To the same family belongs ʻAzod ad-Dowleh ("Arm of the State," d. 983), who succeeded in unifying under his scepter the whole of Iraq and Persia.

Thus, under the orthodox caliphate and without disavowing the Moslem faith, Iran gradually rose again to possession of its own national identity and ethnic consciousness. A landmark in this process was the accession to the throne of Mardavej, son of Ziyar, who became independent in 928 and seized the whole region extending from Qazvin to Rayy and Isfahan, then northwards to embrace the whole of Gorgan (ancient Hyrcania) and adjacent countries. Masʻudi tells in his *Golden Prairies* that Mardavej, when he reached the height of his power, wanted to be dressed as a king in every respect after the old Iranian traditions; for the astrologers had said that *he* was to become the Universal King. Then

> he caused a golden throne embedded with precious stones to be built, he clad himself in a *badanah* [sleeveless tunic], and he crowned himself with a golden *taj* [kingly tiara] studded with jewels. He had already noticed the designs of the crowns previously worn by the kings of Persia, and selected for himself that of Khosrow Anoshervan. His secretaries, along with the soothsayers and quacks who gathered around him, revealed to him that the celestial bodies worked by their irradiation a special influence on Isfahan; that a new religion would be revealed in that city, where all the treasures of the earth would be conveyed; that the king who ruled it would bear yellow marks on his feet; that his body would be marked by such and such a sign; that he would reign for so many years. . . . Mardavej eventually agreed that he was the yellow-dyed man due to reign over the whole world.[57]

Apart from the fact that Mardavej was considered to be a kind of adherent to Mazdaism, it is worth observing how the Persian people still remembered the old doctrines of what kingship should be—doctrines that dated back not so much to Zoroastrian antiquity as to common Indo-European lore and even earlier. The signs marking the Universal King's body are a tradition that still lives in India, as is the case for the Buddha, whose kingly signs *(laksanas)* were easily recognized upon his birth. The motif of the "Yellow Emperor" is even more commonly found in a number of traditions, such as in China (Huang Ti), not to mention the current ideas regarding the solar king, Yima (Yama in India), who was also characterized by the yellow hue, etc.

It is interesting to note how many elements of the traditional civilization of Iran, which was already oriented toward monotheism and a strong ethical life by Zarathustrianism, received a further impulse toward gnosticism, with its symbolic view of worldly life and functions, from the stern morality of Islam. Indeed, it was Islam that served as the vehicle for the introduction, if not the return, of Neoplatonism to Iranian civilization.[58]

At the beginning of the eleventh century of the Christian era, the gradual rise of powerful dynasties of Iranian stock and, in general, of the Shi'ite faith and of some Isma'ili tendencies, as exemplified by the Samanids, Buwayhids, and Ziyarites, suffered a quite violent setback, if not a definite collapse, as a result of the growing power of Turkish tribes led by energetic chieftains recently converted to Sunni Islam. Such were the Ghaznavids, descendants of a Turkish slave, Alp Tegin, who first belonged to the Samanid ruler, and later became his governor-general of Khorasan. His descendant Mahmud, the famous raider of India, totally dispossessed his former lords in 999, receiving—as we are told by the Persian historian Gardizi—the insignia of his investiture *('ahd)* from Caliph al-Qadir Bi'llah (d. 1031). The aforesaid writer gives a short account of the ceremony by which Mahmud was given the titles of "Right Arm of the Caliphate" *yamin ad-dawlat)* and "Trustee of the Community" *(amin al-milla),* along with such symbols of his official dignity as the banner *(liwa),* the robe of honor *(khel'at),* and the crown *(taj).* Upon receiving these insignia, he duly sat on the throne like a Persian king of old.

Although racially and culturally foreign to the Iranic civilization, this dynasty, like the Seljuk dynasty that succeeded it (and which, like it, was of pure Turkish stock), gave a tremendous impetus to Persian culture, so that Iran really became the heart of Islam. At the death of Mahmud (1030), his kingdom stretched from Samarqand in Central Asia to Gujerat in India, from Kashmir to Iraq. Although narrow-minded, bigoted, and strictly Sunni, his plans did not include founding any civilizations that were not to be both Iranian and Islamic, and with this aim he enriched his court in Ghazna (the present Afghanistan) with literary men, scientists, and philosophers virtually kidnapped from every corner of his empire. The great philosopher and physician Ibn Sina (Avicenna), the scientist and historian al-Biruni, the philosopher Abu Sahl al-Masihi ("the Christian"), and the so-called Pleiad consisting of such Persian poets as 'Unsuri, Farrukhi, Asadi, and Ferdowsi were sometimes his enforced guests.

Although the Turks (in their psychology) and the orthodox Moslems (from a religious point of view) were spiritual strangers to the intimate soul of Persian civilization, the Ghaznavids and later the Seljuks (from 1047 on), with the fervor of new converts, fostered the Persian civilization within the Islamic frame, spreading its language, forms, and customs to the countries they conquered, as happened in India. Conversely, under these same dynasties, there began the slow but irresistible Turkization of outer Iran— Tokharistan and Ferghana—which has not yet been completely accomplished (Soviet Tadjikistan is still culturally and linguistically an Iranian country).

Such a process was initially brought about by the partly heathen Ilek-khan and Ghuzz clans, later reinforced by the Mongol onslaught of 1217, followed by the settlement of Turkish tribes coming from central Asia. The rulers, however, whether Timurid, Moghul, or Shaybanid, continued to assert their spiritual adherence to Persian civilization, and sometimes found room for brilliant centers of Persian art and literature in their Eastern capitals. But as far as the political side is concerned, no doubt the Seljuk Empire, under the nominal rule of the caliph of Baghdad, represented the peak of Iranian influence on Eastern Islam. It is sufficient to recall two names: Nezam al-Molk, the grand *vazir* of Malek Shah (d. 1092), one of the greatest statesmen of the Moslem countries; and the theologian al-Ghazali (d. 1111), who settled once and for all the reciprocal relations between faith, mysticism, and philosophy in Islam.[59]

Contemporary with the Seljuks; the anticaliphate of Cairo created by the Fatimids represented another creation of the Persian genius, this time in a heterodox pattern: the Isma'ilite one, whose philosophical accomplishments, no less than the political ones, cannot be disregarded due to the mystical, literary, and artistic achievements they led to.

As for the subject of the sacral kingship, the Isma'ili imam, the "anticaliph" of Mahdiyya and later of Cairo, for almost two centuries (909-1171) was considered an almost godlike person, a projection on the earthly plane of the primordial Adam, and even the very Word of God. On a more practical level, the power and prerogatives of the former Persian emperor, even if not directly invoked, were practically enforced, as was the court etiquette, to the point at which many heresiologies clearly stated that the formidable sect of the Isma'ilis and its later offshoot, the "Assassins" of Persia and Syria, represented a sort of historic vengeance of the Iranians on the Arabs for their imposition of orthodox Islam.[60]

The Mongol invasion (1217), with the radical destruction, "including cats and dogs," of a great part of Iran, the ruin of the 'Abbasid caliphate of Baghdad (1258) and the Isma'ili order, with the wholesale massacres that ensued, signified the definite decline of a splendid civilization whose features we have briefly outlined. The rise of Timur-e Lang (Tamerlane, 1381) and his conquest of an empire comparable to that of Genghiz Khan did not improve the situation of Iran and its institutions even though his descendants—Shah

Rokh, Ulugh Beg, Baisonqor, Abu Sai'd (d. 1468)—fostered the Persian civilization, and even though a great-grandson of his, Baber (1483-1530), transplanted this civilization into newly conquered India. For the resurgence of the Iranian state in a national sense, although supported by an army partly of Turkish race (for instance, the seven tribes that formed the *Shah-sevan*—"the Shah's loving people"—were Shamlu, Rumlu, Ustajlu, Tekelu, Afshar, Qajar, and Zulqadar), we must wait until 1501, when the sixteen-year-old lad Isma'il Safavi, descendant of the pious Shayhk Ishaq Safi ad-Din (d. 1334), seized Tabriz, *assuming the title of Shahanshah-e Iran.*

Thus after nine centuries a true Iranian, even if believed to be a seyyed descendant of the seventh imam, Reza, took upon himself the burden of the imperial dignity, *intending to reign over all Iran with a national and religious outlook worthy of his sacred mission.* It is not necessary to speak here of the astounding achievements of this young man, nor of those of his great-grandson Shah 'Abbas the Great, the contemporary of Akbar the Moghol, emperor of India, of Elizabeth I and Philip II, with whom he maintained some relations. Eventually Persia came to be the most splendid realm of the East. Here, we would like to dwell only upon some features of his kingship, considered from a typological point of view.

In this context it is worth considering that Isma'il wanted to be proclaimed Shahanshah when only sixteen years old, the "mystical age" of the Accomplished or Perfect Man (*adame-e qadim,* which corresponds etymologically, even, to the cabalistic *adam qadmon*), as evidenced by a number of Mazdaean and Islamic books (e.g., *Al-Hayy ibn al-Yaqzan,* "The Living, Son of the Wake," of Avicenna, and the *Motarehat* of Sohravardi. He was soon divinized, as was his grandfather, Shaykh Junayd, who ruled the Safavid order from 1447 to 1456. Upon his accession to the throne he completely and sometimes ruthlessly unified his kingdom even on the spiritual level, imposing the Shi'ite rite and thus isolating the Persians from the Ottoman Turks and Central Asian Turkomans, both of whom belonged to the Sunni confession. During a period when religious confession was a primary factor in the national consciousness, the Safavids were to some extent the real builders of modern Iranian unity (we still cannot speak of the Iranian state in the modern sense, since it is a creation of the present Pahlavis).

As for the sacral kingship, Shah Isma'il declared in his *Songbook* that every great personality that in some way manifested the "signs" or tokens of God was in its essence "beyond time and space," its historical character being a mere appearance of this essence:

> Today I came down to earth: I am lord and king! Know as true that I am
> Hadar's son! [Haydar was the name of Isma'il's father, and a
> name of 'Ali.]
> I am Fereydun, I am Khosrow, I am Jamshid and I am Zahhak [his enemy], I

am Rustam son of Zal, I am Alexander!
The mystery of *ana'l-Haqq* ["I am God," the famous cry of al-Hallaj] is
hidden in this heart of mine, for I am the Absolute Reality and
Reality is that which I do utter![61]

In this way, even in exaggerated accents, the sacral meaning of kingship was
enhanced in terms of its independence from any empirical form of religion, as
it had been at the very beginning in ancient Iran, by a man who practically was
the restorer of a religion, or at least its most authoritative proponent. In this
original orientation, which established itself even at an institutional level, Iran
saw an astounding flourishing of mystical experience, philosophy, and
metaphysic wisdom that to some extent went beyond the confessional limit of
Islam and influenced other religions, such as Judaism, Zoroastrianism, and
Hinduism. This was due to a chain of thinkers strongly affected by the
"illuminative" Neoplatonism of Shehab ad-Din Yahya Sohravardi (d. 1191),
who before suffering martyrdom at the hands of the bigoted clergy of Aleppo
had achieved an amazing synthesis between the prophetic philosophy of Islam
and the ancient wisdom of old Mazdaean Persia *(hekmat-e khosrovani)*.[62] His
philosophical example was followed by Sharazuri (d. 1250), who inspired
Qutb ad-Din Shirazi (d. 1311), Ibn Kammuna (d. 1277), Haravi (d. 1300), and
Davvani (d. 1501)—men who brought about the fusion of imami Shi'ism and
Sohravardian Neoplatonism.

The apogee of this school, centered on the relations between being and
existence and on belief in the archetypal stages of the latter, was reached by
Mir Damad (d. 1631) and Molla Sadra of Shiraz, who inspired the philosophical outlook of the Zoroastrian high priest of Shiraz, Azar Kayvan, later
an emigrant to Patna, India, where (one century later) the greatest Persian
poet of India, Mirza Bidel, would be born and nourished by this same school.

It was the same spiritual orientation, we should add, that inspired the
religious reform of Akbar, the Grand Moghol, in its synthesis of Islam,
Zoroastrianism, Hinduism, and Christianity. Very likely, even if the matter
has not yet been investigated, this flow of Iranian gnosticism somehow
nourished the powerful conceptions of the Jewish philosopher of Cairo, Isaac
Luria (d. 1572), as propounded in his *'Esh Hayyim* ("The Tree of Life") and in
the cabalistic works of his followers, such as the *'Emeq ha-Melek* ("The Valley
of the Kings").

THE PAHLAVI REVIVAL
OF THE SACRAL KINGSHIP

The philosophical and mystical renaissance brought about by the above
thinkers, especially Mir Damad and Molla Sadra, formed the spiritual

atmosphere that surrounded the actual rebirth of the sacral kingship—a rebirth that did not result from but rather caused the reuniting and full independence of the Iranian nation.

Neither political and military misfortunes nor the fall of the Safavid dynasty (1722) affected in any way the core notion of the kingship that had been formed in its early years. To such an extent was this true that the following period, with all its ups and downs, such as the Afghan invasion (1722-25), the ascent of Nadar Shah with his conquest of Delhi (1738), the beneficent intermission of the Zands (1758-94) and, finally, the national decline and stagnation during the Qajar dynasty (1795-1925), added nothing to the ideal that had been created under the Safavids. From the fall of this dynasty to the granting of the constitution in 1906, we witness a period of decadence on the one hand and, on the other, incubation of the seed that Shah Isma'il and Shah 'Abbas had sown deeply into the national conscience of Iran.

On the eve of World War I, after a century of decay that included not only the loss of Georgia (1813) and Armenia (1828) but the renunciation of Herat and Afghanistan, not to mention the abandoning of every claim to the old Central Asian provinces, long since occupied by Russia (1874), Iran had practically become a colonized country, politically, economically, and militarily subject to Russia and Britain (1907).

Although this unbearable situation weighed most heavily on the humblest classes in the country, the reaction to it was brought about by a movement led by intellectuals, clergy, and merchants, classes traditionally aware of the country's destiny, who launched the constitutional movement (1906-1909) that came to its revolutionary climax in Tabriz and Tehran (1908-1909). But the actual transformation of the country and its definite emergence in a modern shape was the achievement of an until then unknown soldier, a tough army officer from Mazandaran, Reza Khan, who emerged at the head of his Cossack Brigade in February 1921, overcoming the wave of disorder that was sweeping across the unfortunate and nearly dismembered country.

It is not our task to recapitulate the astounding transformation that Iran underwent in the period between 1921 and 1941, rising from a shabby feudal country into an actively self-modernizing nation. In the words of the poet, "The wrinkled hand of an old man has turned into the smooth palm of a young boy." Rather, we shall emphasize how this transformation perfectly fitted the *renovatio imperii* energetically brought about by the new emperor, this imposing warrior "come out from the mountains," like Ardashir Papakan, founder of the Sassanian dynasty, or Arshak, the first of the Parthians, or— mythically—like the future Savior-Heroes Manushchithra and Keresaspa, presently asleep in the mountains of Tabaristan. It is worth observing how Reza Shah, though anxious and even eager to modernize his country, preferred, when it came to the moment of assuming power, to conform to the traditional pattern of the *Shahanshahi-ye Iran,* viz., the sacral royalty of Iran, thus giving new blood and life to the venerable institution, and shunning the temptation of following the republican example of Kemal Ataturk.[63]

In this connection, the evidence supplied by the Western science of history and comparative religions was welcomed by the Shah, for it gave an outward support, built upon dates and facts, to what already was both his and his people's intuition of the proper meaning and innate working power of the holy kingship embodied in his person. In the days of Reza Shah, what had formerly been intended as *farreh-ye kayan,* the Neo-Persian periphrasis of *khvarenah* shone with the unerring light of sheer facts: the best incarnation of what the Achaemenids meant by *frasha tya vainatay* (the renewal that is visible), or *frasho-kereti* (the renovation), was the immense work performed by the old emperor.

The fact has already been mentioned that, even if the Safavids were to some extent the builders of national Iranian unity in modern times, the modern Iranian state, along with the structures that maintain its functioning, is undoubtedly an achievement of the Pahlavi dynasty. In the short span of twenty years Reza Shah literally sculptured a new nation out of a raw material that nobody even dreamed could have been pure marble, still less tempered steel. He possessed not only the talent of actually seeing what was to be done and the willpower of causing it to be carried out, but still more the persuasive force to awaken a whole people so that they could realize the capabilities, till then ineffective and slumbering, that lay in their innermost soul.

Now as far as we are concerned, one might ask, without falling into unnecessary eulogizing and mythologizing, whether the institutional, political, and economic improvements brought about by Reza Shah may somehow be considered as fitting into the frame of the sacral kingship. In other words, what relation might there be between a thing apparently so mystically abstract as the royal ideology and the concrete facts of putting an entire country under the control of a newly created central administration, of modernizing its institutions, maintaining the integrity of its frontiers, establishing a new code of common law, creating a national bank as a firm basis for the national currency and business, designing a modern pattern for the national education, founding universities and schools of all grades and levels, building a railway that is one of the greatest feats of modern times, erecting factories for the production of common goods, developing modern industries, socially reforming the country from its roots, repressing if not totally obliterating secular abuses and corruption, liberating womenfolk from the veil and making them eligible for every degree of instruction and advancement, and putting an end to the foreign exploitation of the natural richness of Iranian soil?

If we want to find an answer to this complex question, we need only skim through an old volume of scripture, the *Denkart,* book 3, whose chapter 133 carefully enumerates the twenty-one moral qualities and the factual capacity to be possessed by a king striving to be "representative of Ahura Mazda the Radiant and Glorious." The actual personality of Reza Shah is exactly portrayed there, as in the next chapter the deeds of the Good Kingship are further explained.[64]

The old Shah, though feverishly engrossed in his task, could not see what fruit would be borne by the plant he had so carefully set in the ground. He, a man born to war and yet striving for peace and progress, was doomed to die of a broken heart in captivity, while his country was again trodden by foreign armies engaged in a war that was not his own. When his sacrifice was consummated, it seemed as if all the internal and external foes that he had defeated or kept at bay during his life had worked their revenge upon him. They incarnated the eternal ills—hatred, ignorance, falsehood, poverty, spiritual and physical malady—that spread among the people with renewed force.

Last was the attempt to dismember the country, an attempt made when Azarbayjan seceded in 1946. In those dim years, recovery was possible because one institution remained unscathed and preserved, both through the strength of its representative and through the determined will of the people: the monarchy.

The assumption by Mohammad Reza Shah of the title of Aryamehr reaffirmed this revival of the primordial spirit of Iran fostered by a monarchy whose aim was to combine the continuity of the ancient principles with modern transformations.[65] It was in the same vein that the Majles in March 1976 adopted a new calendar that begins with the accession to the throne of Cyrus II ("the Great") 2,535 years earlier. This decision was designed to further strengthen the country's attachment to the national Iranian tradition, which had been inseparably interwoven with the institution of monarchy.

Thus the notion of sacral kingship still appeared to be consciously cultivated in Iran twenty-five centuries after the foundation of the Achaemenian Empire. The guiding idea was not only to preserve the monarchy but, through reforms instituted from above, to equate it with virtue, according to an old prayer in the Avesta: "May good sovereigns have sway, may not wicked sovereigns rule us, thus by the deeds of good wisdom, O Armaiti."[66]

3

Social Development in Iran during the Pahlavi Era

That appears [to thee] in the form of inversion [illusion]
from the top of the pear-tree: come down, O youth!
The pear-tree is the tree of [phenomenal] existence: whilst
thou art there, the new appears old.
Whilst thou art there, thou wilt see [only] a thorn-brake
full of the scorpions of wrath and full of snakes,
When thou comest down, thou wilt behold, free of cost, a
world filled with rose-cheeked [beauties] and [their] nurses.

Jalal ad-Din Rumi*

Iran is a country in which, perhaps more than is the case in most countries, things are not necessarily what they seem to be on the surface. As an outsider, therefore, it is with extreme diffidence that I approach the task of giving an account of social development in Iran during the last fifty years. I derive some comfort from the saying, "The onlooker sees most of the game," and from the fact that for more than thirty of these fifty years I have been an eyewitness of social change in Iran. Nevertheless, the task of describing within such a small compass the immense changes that have taken place during this period is a daunting one, and clearly it will not be possible for me to do more than sketch in the main outlines.

In order to avoid confusion, I will discuss the many aspects of social development under certain principal heads, but none of these sections can be entirely self-contained, and there will inevitably be some degree of overlapping. Nor is it possible to divorce the question of social development from some mention, however brief, of the political and economic environment in which this development takes place, because much social change is initiated

---

* *Masnavi-ye ma'navi,* iv, 3540-43 (Nicholson's translation).

by political action or economic decisions. Finally, I would aver that no discussion of social development in modern Iran can profitably be carried on without some reference to the long Iranian historical and cultural tradition. If one is to make any realistic assessment of social development within a given period, one must have a yardstick against which to measure the amount of change. It would therefore seem logical to begin this chapter with some account of the state of affairs prevailing in Iran during the early part of this century, in the period immediately prior to the coup d'état of 1921 and the establishment of the Pahlavi dynasty.

"ONE OF THE MOST BACKWARD COUNTRIES IN THE WORLD" THE CONDITION OF IRAN IN 1900

In 1900, Iran[1] was

a fairly primitive, almost isolated state, barely distinguishable as an economic entity. About one-fifth of the population of about 10 million lived in small towns; another quarter consisted of nomadic tribes; while the rest eked out an existence in poor villages. Agriculture was the primary occupation, and the almost complete lack of roads, railways or other transport facilities made it essential for each geographic region to be self-sufficient in foodstuffs. Industrial activity was sparse, with no serious attempts having been made to explore or exploit a potentially vast array of natural resources. Oil, the future life-blood of the economy, had still not been discovered in commercial quantities, while the economy had less than ten years' experience of modern banking institutions.[2]

Urban conditions had not advanced since the Middle Ages. The streets of Tehran, "narrow, without sidewalks, covered with several inches of dust in summer and the same amount of mud in winter, were dirty, uneven, winding, and full of holes. At night, darkness reigned."[3] As a result, lawlessness was rife; bands of *lutis* (ruffians) rampaged through the streets at night, and rival gangs did battle with one another even in daylight. The army suffered from lack of training, and was subject to many administrative abuses such as padded rolls, a disproportionately high ratio of officers to other ranks, inadequate pay, and a hereditary system of commissions.[4] The average life expectancy was less than thirty years. "Families were large; women had no rights; men could have as many as four wives; and male children were strongly preferred. In order to keep the peasants ignorant and poor, the landowners opposed the establishment of schools or clinics."[5] The urban picture that emerges is one of the "wealthier people maintaining a reasonably good life behind secure walls while the majority lived in poverty, disease, illiteracy, and slum conditions."[6] Educational instruction consisted of the *maktab,* a single classroom presided over by a *molla,* in which boys from the age of seven upwards followed a strictly traditional curriculum: reading and writing, calligraphy, Arabic grammar, and a lot of rote learning involving the memorization of passages from the Qor'an, verses of poetry, the Shi'i catechism, and so on. Secondary education was carried on mainly through the services of private tutors. The only exceptions to this general picture were the *madrasehs,* which were primarily theological seminaries, the foreign mission schools, and schools run by non-Moslem minority groups such as the Jews and Armenians. The last two categories of schools were the only ones providing education for girls. The *maktabs,* and many of the *madrasehs,* were kept going solely by private donations and *vaqf* funds (i.e., funds from charitable foundations). The only institution of higher learning was the Dar al-Fonun (Polytechnic College), founded in 1851 by Naser ad-Din Shah Qajar for the purpose of training officials and administrators for the bureaucracy. The general practice was for those parents who could afford it to send their sons abroad for their secondary and university education. Over 95 percent of the population was illiterate.[7]

FROM THE CONSTITUTION TO THE
ACCESSION OF REZA SHAH (1906-1925)

The promulgation of the constitutional documents of 1906-1907 in theory converted Iran from a traditional society to a constitutional monarchy, but from the outset the path of constitutional government in Iran was fraught with difficulties. For one thing, many uneducated and illiterate Iranians simply did not understand what was meant by a constitution. "In the mouth of a Lur the word *mashruteh,* constitution, is simply a synonym for 'disorder.' He will say, 'So and so is making constitution,' i.e., he is playing Old Harry somewhere."[8] For another, the political pressure of the Great Powers was unrelenting. In 1907, Britain and Russia divided Iran into "zones of influence." In 1908 an intransigent Mohammad 'Ali Shah introduced martial law and closed the National Consultative Assembly (*Majles-e Showra-ye Melli,* or "Majles"), and in 1911 Russian pressure resulted in its closure for the second time.

By 1911, wrote Sir Arnold Wilson, the country was in a "miserable state," and ready to accept any form of government that would give it security. "The destruction of property is great," he said, "and the misery of the poor pitiful to behold. It will be ten years or more before this country recovers from the anarchy of the last three."[9] The situation deteriorated still further between 1914 and 1918, when British, Russian, and Turkish troops ignored Iran's declaration of neutrality and operated on Iranian soil. At the same time, a strong German diplomatic effort was successful in dividing the cabinet and the Majles and in establishing a rival "government" at Kermanshah. As a result, there was a complete breakdown of the authority of the central government. At the end of World War I, the treasury was empty, famine conditions prevailed, and Iran "seemed weaker than at any time in the 19th century."[10] At least 100,000 people died of starvation in Iran during World War I.[11] Following the famine, typhus and typhoid epidemics are said to have carried off 50,000 people in Tehran out of a total population of 300,000.

The turbulent political events of this period prevented Iran from making any real progress along the path of social and economic reform. A Ministry of Education, Vaqfs and Fine Arts was set up in 1910, and attempts were made at educational reform. A number of elementary and secondary schools were founded on French lines, but a shortage of funds, and the opposition of the *'olama* (men learned in theology), restricted these efforts. The French jurist Adolph Perni completed the draft of a penal code which was submitted to the Majles in 1912; the signatories to this document included three *mojtaheds* (Shi'a theologians)—a significant admission on the part of these high-ranking theologians that the *shari'at* (religious law) was no longer adequate.[12]

.However, serious rifts began to appear in the ranks of the three groups primarily responsible for the establishment of constitutional government: the intellectuals; the religious classes; and the bazaar (merchants, skilled craftsmen, and members of trade guilds). It has often been assumed in the West that the intellectuals were the most important of these groups but, while it is true that they gave impetus to the demand for reform, it is equally true that they alone could never have brought about the granting of the constitution in 1906. For this, they needed the support of the lower-middle-class groups from the bazaar and of the religious classes, who were inspired more by their hatred of social injustice and autocratic oppression, and by their dislike of interference by foreign powers in the internal affairs of Iran, than by any strong desire for constitutional government. When it became clear that the constitution was to be the prelude to modernization, the support of some of the *'olama* changed into active opposition. An analysis of the background of the deputies to the First Majles is revealing. More than 40 percent of the deputies bore a title like *hajj* or *seyyed*, indicative of religious piety and middle-class background. Similarly, the long list of different trades and crafts represented among the deputies testifies to the strength of bazaar support. In other words, the two most important elements in the Iranian constitutional movement were not Western-inspired at all, but traditional Islamic. Even the so-called *farangima'ab*—Iranians who had returned to Iran after the completion of their higher education abroad—remained "overwhelmingly Persian" in their homes, family relations, marriages, and personal habits. In 1920, Iran was still "a totally Oriental nation."[13]

In addition to the dissensions among the various groups that had initially pressed for the granting of a constitution, dissensions which became more acute as time went on, there was a fundamental paradox in the constitutional documents, a paradox that has not been resolved to this day. As Amin Banani has noted, the Constitution of 1906 tried to accept all the tenets of Western liberal democracy, which was of course based on seventeenth- and eighteenth-century concepts of natural law and the rights of man, and at the same time make all legal enactments of parliament subject to strict conformity with the *shari'at* and to the approval of the *'olama*.[14] In other words, it set out to establish a liberal democracy with secular institutions but without the basic prerequisite of such a system—the separation of Church and State.[15] It is this basic contradiction which has marred the relations between the Shah and the *'olama* throughout the Pahlavi period.

By the last months of 1920, Iran

> seemed to be on the verge of collapse, about to disintegrate into a number of separate parts some of which might be absorbed into neighboring states. Hunger, poverty, insecurity, despair and apathy reigned. . . . It seemed as if Iran could survive as a nation and as an entity only if such survival would serve the interests of Great Britain and Soviet Russia. No one could believe that any efforts by the Persians themselves could alter this situation.[16]

Certainly Great Britain did not believe it, and Lord Curzon, the British foreign secretary, saw the reorganization and control of the Persian army by British officers, and the loan of such advisers as might be necessary to control the police and the civil administration, as the only solution to the problem of Iran's chronic weakness. The Soviet Union, which had taken over control of the Jangali nationalist movement in Gilan, had established the Autonomous Soviet Socialist Republic of Gilan on June 4, 1920, and had officially formed the Persian Communist Party, hoped that from this nucleus its influence might spread to other parts of Iran. No less an authority than Comte de Gobineau gave it as his considered opinion that no oriental country was capable of pulling itself up by its own bootstraps without the benefit of a European protectorate or mandate.

It is against this background that the coup d'état of February 1921 must be viewed. If Iran was to continue in being as an independent nation, the paramount need was for a strong hand to restore the authority of the central government in the provinces, and to rid Iran of the economic and political pressure of the Great Powers in order to reestablish Iran's sovereignty. On

December 12, 1925, when the Constituent Assembly, by a majority of 257 to 3, voted to vest the monarchy in Reza Khan, it was clear that the majority of Iranians thought that he alone stood a chance of achieving these goals. In the following sections, Reza Shah's policies will be discussed from the viewpoint of their effect on Iran's social development.

THE FOUNDATIONS ARE LAID: SOCIAL DEVELOPMENT DURING THE REIGN OF REZA SHAH THE GREAT (1925-1941)

Education

The creation of an educated and informed population is probably the most important key to the reform of society. In Iran, in which the mass of the population was illiterate at the time of the establishment of the Pahlavi dynasty, the fight against illiteracy was one of the most extreme urgency. Considering that Reza Shah had had little formal education himself, it is to his credit that he moved with his customary vigor and dispatch to set up a comprehensive system of state education comprising six years of elementary and six years of secondary education based on modern curricula. The modernization of the curriculum alone was a courageous act at a time when the attitude of the 'olama "was such that they would refer to anyone who dared to try to study a European language as an infidel, and that such a person would possibly suffer physical abuse as well for his temerity."[17]

At the time of the accession of Reza Shah in 1925, only some ten thousand boys were enrolled in national (state and private nonreligious) schools.[18] By 1928-29, 138,947 boys and girls were enrolled in 1,038 primary schools, and a further 9,661 in 25 secondary schools.[19] From 1928 onwards, 100 top secondary school students were sent annually to Europe, on bursaries, for a university education in the fields of medicine, dentistry, mining, engineering, and agriculture. Nine-tenths of these students went to France.[20]

Apart from the general impetus toward modernization afforded by Reza Shah's establishment of a state education system, his educational policies had two particularly important effects on society: first, since educational instruction had hitherto been virtually the monopoly of the religious classes, the secularization of education necessarily dealt a severe blow to the power of the 'olama; second, the conceding of the principle that education should not be confined to boys was the first step toward the social emancipation of women.

Initially, there was a shortage of qualified teachers. The creation of teachers' training colleges lagged far behind the construction of schools, and until 1934 the original Teachers' Training College (founded 1918) was the only one of its kind; by 1941, however, there were 36. In 1935, the development of state education was carried to its logical conclusion by the establishment of Iran's first university, the University of Tehran, with five faculties: arts, science, medicine, law, and engineering. Theology, fine arts, and agriculture were added later. For years, however, students and graduates of the University of Tehran suffered from the fact that any degree from a European institution automatically carried greater social prestige and was a more marketable product in economic terms than were degrees from Tehran. The *farangi-ma'ab* continued to be a "social lion."[21] The young man educated in Europe was much sought after on the marriage market; but he also did a great deal towards breaking down the old system of arranged marriages.[22]

Another aspect of education during the reign of Reza Shah that had far-reaching social effects was the adult education program, begun in 1936. Its aims were to combat illiteracy and to give training in the principles of good citizenship. Evening classes were begun at both the elementary and secondary school levels and, in the first year of the program's operation, 9,356 adults received certificates of literacy. By 1940, over 150,000 adults from every walk of life were enrolled in these evening classes, and students of school age were also admitted to them if, for economic reasons, they had to work during the day.[23]

In sum, Reza Shah's educational reforms represented a drastic break with Islamic tradition, and caused a major upheaval in the traditional social order.

Reform of the Legal System

There is no doubt that, of all the classes of Iranian society, the *'olama* bore the brunt of the reforms of Reza Shah. It was inevitable that this should be so, because any move in the direction of westernization and modernization—two of the primary goals of Reza Shah's policies—involved a degree of secularization, a separation of powers between the political institution and the religious institution, and consequently impinged on sectors of social and economic life in which the *'olama* had either a controlling or at least a strong influence.

Having removed the educational system from the control of the *'olama,* Reza Shah turned his attention to the reform of the judiciary. Here, an overriding political consideration prompted the reform. One of the most hated symbols of foreign influence in Iran was the system of "capitulations," that is, extraterritorial privileges granted to foreign nationals resident in Iran. These privileges included the right of foreign nationals to be tried by their own consular courts. The reasons put forward by foreign powers to justify this right included the corruption of the courts, the maladministration of justice, but above all, the conflict of jurisdiction between the religious courts *(mahakem-e shar')* and the state courts, which tried cases on the basis of customary law *('orf)*. The reform of the judiciary was therefore a necessary prerequisite to abolition of the capitulations, which Reza Shah announced on May 1, 1928. Under the energetic direction of a young *farangi-ma'ab* named Davar, who had a law degree from Geneva, a new draft penal code was ready in 1926, and a draft civil code in 1928. In 1927, Davar was appointed head of the newly created Ministry of Justice. The Civil Code was a compromise: the first ten articles were a translation of the French *Code Civil,* but the articles relating to personal status represented "a codification, simplification, and unification of the *shari'at.*"[24] However, this was merely the first step. The process of refining and amending both this and the Penal Code went on almost continuously throughout the reign of Reza Shah. Each successive step meant a further erosion of the power of the *'olama,* and a particularly severe blow was dealt to them in 1932, when a law was enacted that required the registration of documents and property to be handled by secular courts only. The *'olama* had derived a large proportion of their income from the discharge of this business, and many were now forced to "abandon the robe and seek secular employment."[25] In 1936, the secularization of the judiciary was further emphasized by legislation that required judges to hold a degree from the Tehran Faculty of Law or from a foreign university; any judge not holding such a degree was required to pass an examination in order to continue in the employ of the ministry, and many of the *'olama* left the judiciary at this point.

In no area of law did the *shari'at* show greater tenacity than in the area of family law. Although the laws relating to marriage, divorce, and crimes against morality (rape, prostitution, homosexuality, etc.) were modified many times between 1926 and 1940, vestiges of *shari'at* remained. For instance, a man might still legally marry up to four wives, and temporary marriage was still permitted. Not infrequently, the attempt to combine Western concepts with *shari'at* law resulted in inconsistencies and paradoxes. Moreover, some articles of the new legislation remained inoperative because of contrary social pressures; for example, the articles stipulating that the consent of both parties was a necessary condition of marriage were largely ignored except by westernized Iranians, and arranged marriages continued to be the norm.

Public Health Legislation

Prior to the Pahlavi era, public health was nonexistent in Iran. In 1924, there were only 905 physicians in the whole country, and only 253 of these had been trained in accredited schools.[26] Such efforts as had been made in the field of public health prior to the accession of Reza Shah had proved largely abortive, in many cases because of the opposition of the religious classes. The League of Nations *Report on an Investigation into the Sanitary Conditions in*

Persia (1925), quoted by Banani, stated clearly the magnitude of the difficulties confronting any such efforts on the part of the government:

> The beliefs of the people and the teachings of the religious instructors or *mullas,* as they are called, have not only an effect on the character of the people but also prevent the introduction of sanitary and other reforms. The opinions of the leaders of Moslem thought are important factors in all affairs of state. . . .
>
> Many of the customs of the people are interpretations of the Koran. The manner of killing the animals in the slaughterhouses, the washing of the dead, and their burial, are all performed in the manner laid down by the religious laws. The belief that all running water which is open to the air is good and safe for drinking is taught by the religion. Dissection or postmortem examination of bodies is forbidden.[27]

The "most efficient part of the Persian Sanitary Administration," in the opinion of the authors of the League of Nations report, was the Pasteur Institute, founded in 1923.[28] However, because of the total lack of any program of immunization or hygiene, such diseases as malaria, trachoma and dysentery were endemic. Between 1927 and 1930, stringent regulations were enacted regarding the licensing of physicians, and by 1935 the ratio of doctors to population was 1:4,000 compared with 1:11,000 in 1924; unfortunately, however, a high proportion of the doctors continued to be concentrated in Tehran. By 1941, all the recommendations of the 1925 League of Nations report had been implemented with the exception of the provision of a piped water supply for the major cities and of sewage disposal schemes. The scheme to supply Tehran with piped water was ready for implementation in 1941, but the occupation of Iran by Allied troops in that year led to its postponement, and in fact it was fifteen years before it was implemented.

The increased importance attached to public health was reflected in the establishment of the Ministry of Health in 1940, and the Public Health Law of 1941 contained some important provisions: compulsory vaccination against smallpox; compulsory disclosure and treatment of venereal disease; free medication for poor patients; and the certification of brothels. Under Reza Shah, the improvement in public health was slow but steady, but even after 1940 the system continued to rely heavily on *farangi-ma'abs* for qualified doctors. There had already been significant shifts in the attitude of the *'olama* toward medical care; for instance, whereas in 1925 the dissection of corpses as an aid in the teaching of anatomy was not permitted, by 1930 this interdict was no longer enforced. The construction of hospitals was also put in hand. Prior to the accession of Reza Shah, the only good hospitals in Iran were those founded by British and American missionaries, in some cases nearly a hundred years previously. Reza Shah ordered the construction of an up-to-date hospital in Mashhad staffed by German doctors, and of a 1,000-bed hospital attached to the University of Tehran. The Shah was also responsible for the establishment of various charitable organizations such as the Red Lion and Sun Society (the Persian Red Cross), the Organization for the Care of Mothers and Children, and orphanages.[29]

The Rise of the New Professional/Bureaucratic Middle Class

The reforms of Reza Shah in the three areas mentioned above—education, the legal system and public health—accelerated the development of the middle classes, but the new middle class was different in character from the old bourgeoisie, which had consisted of members of the entrepreneurial, business, and merchant classes, together with the old-style clerical staff of the government offices and members of the religious classes. Few, if any, of the old bourgeoisie had had a Western education. The essential qualification for admittance to the new professional/bureaucratic middle class was a Western education or an education on Western lines to the extent that this was now available in Iran. The common denominator among members of the new "professional/bureaucratic intelligentsia" was the expertise (professional, technical, cultural, intellectual, or administrative) acquired through a modern education.[30] The rise of this class was a direct result of Reza Shah's legislation requiring, for example, a law degree for the holding of judicial posts, and setting Western standards for the certification of doctors. Precisely the same effect was achieved by the Civil Service Law of 1922, which laid down entrance requirements, promotion scales, pension provisions, and the like, based on Western models. As Reza Shah's policies of state capitalism and centralized administration developed, civil servants increased not only in prestige but also in numbers. The students sent abroad annually from 1928 onwards for their university education formed, on their return to Iran, the core of the new professional middle class.[31]

The Rise of the Industrial Working Class

James Bill, in his analysis of Iranian politics, has noted the emergence of two new classes of society in Iran since the beginning of the twentieth century: first, the professional/bureaucratic intelligentsia already mentioned; and, second, the industrial working class.[32] Again, the origins of the industrial working class must be sought in the reign of Reza Shah, for it was he who tried to make Iran less dependent on foreign imports by laying the foundations of industrial development. The corporate structure of traditional Islamic society, in which the "social cement" consisted of a wide variety of religio-socio-political organisms at the level of the city ward, the village, the craft guild, the zurkhaneh ("house of strength") and the like, had begun to disintegrate during the Zand-Qajar civil war and had continued to grow weaker during the nineteenth century. In its place, Reza Shah sought to put the cohesive strength of a state with a highly centralized bureaucracy and an economy based largely on state capitalism. State factories were run by the Department of Industry and Mines, a branch of the Ministry of National Economy. At the managerial level, these factories provided jobs for engineers returning from Europe and for graduates of local technical colleges, all of whom, of course, formed part of the new professional bureaucratic middle class.

The Military Sector

A discussion of Reza Shah's reorganization of the army has no place in this chapter, but reference must be made to those military reforms which had social implications. In the first place, hereditary commissions were abolished and, commencing in 1922, a group of officer cadets was sent annually for the next ten years to French military academies. Second, conscription was introduced in 1925 to provide men for the new unified standing army. During their two years on active service, the men were taught to read and write and received instruction in a trade. Since many of them came from rural areas, this instruction had important social effects when they returned to their villages. Conscription thus contributed materially to "the amalgamation of society, the rise of literacy, the urbanization of the young rural and tribal population, and the breakdown of isolation."[33] In 1938, the fact that men possessing a higher standard of education, the products of the system of compulsory education introduced by Reza Shah, were now becoming available for service in the armed forces, was acknowledged by legislation that provided for more rapid promotion for graduates of secondary schools and universities. At the same time the *'olama*, formerly exempt from military service, became liable for the two years of active duty, although they continued to be exempt from service with the reserve.[34]

The Agricultural Sector

One sector of society that Reza Shah signally failed to reform was the agricultural one. In 1900, 90 percent of the labor force were agricultural workers.[35] Despite the fact that oil was discovered in Iran in 1908, in 1946 as much as 75 percent of the work force was still engaged in agriculture.[36] The basic obstacle to agricultural reform was the system of land tenure itself, which had undergone little change since Sasanid times. With the exception of a small number of peasant proprietors or smallholders *(khordehmalek)*, the peasants in general did not own the land they tilled, but were either tenants, paying a fixed sum annually to the landlord, or sharecroppers, the crop being divided between landlord and peasant on the basis of the "five elements" *('avamel-e panjganeh):* land, water, seed, draft animals, and labor. If the peasant contributed nothing but his labor, he might in theory receive only one-fifth of the crop, but in practice he rarely received less than one-quarter. The peasant was frequently subject to corve'es imposed by the landlord, such as the construction of roads, bridges, and mosques, and the digging of ditches and watercourses. The peasant had no security of tenure; after harvest, the landlord could appropriate his plot and turn him out of the village. Although in theory the peasant was free to leave his village and go elsewhere, in practice he was usually in debt to the landlord, and consequently could not do so; further, he probably lived in a house that belonged to the landlord, and would be reluctant to give up what he had and launch out into the unknown. But weighing even more heavily on the peasant than any load of financial debt were the psychological burdens of the sharecropping system and of the fact that he did not own the land. A peasant who had to hand over up to 75 percent of his crop to the landlord had no incentive to improve his land or increase production. Without radical change in the whole peasant-landlord relationship, no real improvement could be effected.

During the first fifteen years after the 1921 coup d'état, no steps were taken to change this relationship. The Civil Code ignored it. Some advances were made during this period: an agricultural college was opened at Karaj (1929); an agricultural bank was established (1930); from 1925 onwards, foreign experts were brought in to conduct experimental programs designed to improve the quality of stock and of seed. In 1932, money was allocated to a forestry conservation program (the first of its kind in Iran), to try and preserve Iran's dwindling woodlands; but the fundamental socioeconomic problem remained untouched. Indeed, there was some evidence that the introduction of farm machinery, without any reform of the system of tenure, merely weighted the scales more heavily against the peasant. For example, combines would deprive the village women ot their traditional right of gleaning, which often produced enough grain to provide a peasant family with bread for six weeks.[37]

In 1937, Reza Shah introduced the Land Development Act, which was designed to encourage the optimum use of land on the part of both landlord and peasant. Unfortunately, the act remained a dead letter, because its implementation was entrusted to the landlords. Those landlords who disliked the act, did nothing; those who attempted improvements met with opposition from the peasants, who saw no point in increasing production until the sharecropping scheme was changed. In 1939, the Majles authorized the Ministry of Justice to examine possibilities of reforming sharecropping agreements, but no action was taken.[38]

From ancient times, an important part of the agricultural scene in Iran has consisted not of settled cultivators, but of transhumant tribes, which travel in the late spring from the lowlands to the high mountain valleys in search of pasture, and return in the fall when the first snows begin to fly. Of these tribes, some, like the Kurds and Lurs, are of Aryan stock; others, like the tribes of Azarbayjan and Khorasan, are of Turkic stock; others again, like the tribes of Fars, are of mixed Turkish and Persian, or Turkish and Arab blood, while many of the tribesmen in Khuzistan are of Arab stock. The large flocks of sheep and goats that are tended by these tribesmen constitute an important source of meat, skins, and milk products, and from the wool the women weave rugs and a wide variety of other articles. These tribes have always been unruly and ready to take up arms against the government of the day. Brigandage has often been a way of life to them. To Reza Shah they represented not only a threat to internal security and a challenge to his policy of centralization, but an administrative problem and an anachronism in the modern society he was endeavoring to build. It was not easy to levy taxes on tribesmen who were on the move for several months of the year; nor could the benefits of state education readily be brought to them. The answer, he thought, lay in the forcible settlement of the tribes. But the army and gendarmerie, who were ordered to carry out this policy, frequently treated the tribesmen harshly and unjustly, and the land set aside for the tribes was often unsuitable for cultivation. Tribal chiefs were taken to Tehran and kept under surveillance as hostages for the good behavior of their tribes. These policies left a legacy of bitterness. Although after 1941 the tribes regained much of their freedom, they never regained their former power.[39]

The Status of Women

By introducing a system of compulsory education for girls as well as boys, Reza Shah had early given notice that the emancipation of women was one of the planks in his program of reform. The principal symbol of the subordinate status of women was the all-enveloping *chador* of funereal black cloth, without which no respectable woman would be seen abroad. At Nowruz (New Year) 1928, the Queen Mother visited the shrine at Qom wearing only a light *chador* instead of the traditional black one; for her temerity, she was chided by one of the *'olama*. When he heard of the incident, an enraged Reza Shah went at top speed to Qom, strode into the shrine without removing his boots, and beat the offender with his riding crop.[40] Later the same year, there were demonstrations at Tabriz against the proposed unveiling of women.[41] But Reza Shah was not to be deflected from his purpose. In 1934, women teachers and students were first allowed, and then ordered, to appear in school without the *chador*. The same year, women were admitted to the School of Medicine and the Law School in Tehran. In Mashhad, as a protest against these measures, a *shaykh* took *bast* (the traditional form of sanctuary).[42] But the sanctuary was violated by the army which quelled the resultant riots. "An innovation occurred in June 1935; the Prime Minister Forughi gave a tea at the Iran Club for cabinet ministers and their under-secretaries and they were instructed to bring their wives along. Other mixed teas soon followed."[43] Early in 1936, the Shah, the Queen Mother and two of the royal princesses attended a ceremony at the Normal School at which the Queen Mother was to distribute the diplomas to women graduates of the Faculty of Medicine and other schools. Neither the Queen Mother nor the princesses wore the *chador*. Reza Shah made a speech on the rights and status of women:

> I am exceedingly pleased to observe that, as a result of knowledge and learning, women have come alive to their condition, rights and privileges. . . . We should not forget that up to this time one-half of the population of the country was not taken into account. No statistics of the female population were taken. . . . I am not trying to point out contrasts between today and the old days but you ladies should consider this as a great day. You should avail yourselves of the opportunities which you now have to improve your country.[44]

Finally, on February 1, 1936, the law designed to bring about the abandonment of the *chador* came into effect. "As of that date any officials of the *Ministry of Finance* whose wives were found to be wearing the *chador* were subject to dismissal. Women wearing the *chador* were not allowed in cinema houses or in public baths, and taxi and bus drivers were liable to fines if they accepted veiled women as passengers."[45] The decisive step on the long road toward the emancipation of women had been taken. There were many setbacks. It is said that some women, particularly of the older generation, stayed indoors until after the abdication of Reza Shah rather than be forced to go outside unveiled; at all events, there was considerable backsliding after 1941, and even in the mid-1970s it was obviously going to be some time before the *chador* was abandoned altogether. Many younger women who normally went about in Western dress were reverting to the wearing of the *chador* in special circumstances, for instance, for saying prayers or in the presence of members of the older generation who they knew disapproved of their not wearing the *chador;* and the wearing of the *chador* remained de rigueur in the holy places of the Shi'is.

Summary

Reza Shah has with justification been called the "father of modern Iran," because his accession marked the end of an epoch. In his determination to modernize Iran, to rid the country of foreign influence and to make it politically and economically independent, he initiated legislation that brought about a major upheaval in the traditional social order and abolished or modified many existing, mainly Islamic, social institutions. There was a marked diminution in the influence of the *'olama,* whose power was attacked at a number of points: education; the administration of justice; *owqaf* (lands held in mortmain); and so on. In general, the *'olama* were opposed to any social change which could be attributed to Western provenance, or considered to be un-Islamic, or both; for example, the unveiling of women, and the dissection of corpses for the purposes of anatomy classes. Reza Shah's educational reforms began to make inroads into the country's massive illiteracy problem, and as more and more people acquired a secondary education inevitably their expectations increased and their attitudes changed. The professional/bureaucratic middle class and the industrial working class came into being and developed steadily to form an increasingly large bourgeoisie. Improved communications, better travel facilities and, above all, the introduction of conscription, began to break down the static and compart-mentalized nature of rural life and to bring people of different social classes into contact with one another. Improved communications also meant that more goods found their way into the hands of more people more cheaply, and this meant that the standard of living began to rise. In 1925, it was still cheaper to supply Tehran with imported Russian oil than it was to truck Iran's home-produced oil from Khuzistan. By 1929, however, the number of vehicles on the roads had jumped from 1,000 to 14,000, and by 1938 travel time by road from Bushire to Tehran had been cut from 30 days to 3.[46] By 1935, all major cities had electricity and this brought radio broadcasting within the reach of a large proportion of the Iranian population. Radio facilitated the process of education and unification, at the same time accelerating the process of social change. The Uniform Dress Law of December 1928, which introduced Iranians to Western dress and the Pahlavi cap, was as drastic a social change in its way as the later ban on the wearing of the *chador.* None of this would have been possible, however, if Reza Shah had not first restored law and order to the country. The lawless conditions and lack of security on the roads that prevailed prior to his accession have already been mentioned; one year after the coup d'état of 1921, however, the Imperial Bank of Persia was able to report that "for the first time in seven years not one of its twenty branches had been closed by disturbances."[47] Only the position of the peasants, who in 1900 constituted 90 percent of the labor force and in 1946 still 75 percent, had changed but little.

SETBACKS AND DISAPPOINTMENTS

On August 25, 1941 British and Russian forces invaded Iran, and two days later, on August 27, Reza Shah ordered all resistance to cease. On September 16, the Shah abdicated in favor of his son, Mohammad Reza, who was then some six weeks short of his twenty-second birthday.

This is not the place to comment on the political background to "the events of Shahrivar," as the Iranians called them, but they had far-reaching social repercussions. The army was demoralized, not so much by the fact of its defeat as by the manner in which it had occurred. The liberalization of the regime not only permitted the reemergence of political forces of a markedly illiberal character, both of the extreme Right and the extreme Left, but enabled various social groups that had suffered a diminution of power and influence under Reza Shah to reassert themselves. Foremost among these groups were the 'olama and the landowning aristocracy. In the Fourteenth Majles, the first Majles to be elected since the Allied occupation, which was convened in 1943, the landlord/tribal *khan* group was stronger than in the Thirteenth Majles.[48] Indeed, it constituted some 70 percent of the deputies.[49] With few exceptions, cabinets represented the landlord/*khan*/'olama majority. This necessarily meant a slowing down of the pace of social development, because the landowning class, with a vested interest in the status quo, opposed any policies that might require more technology, which might lead to the expansion of the trade and money economy, and which might thus increase the size and influence of the middle class. From the ranks of the 'olama, who sought to regain the power and prestige they had lost under Reza Shah, was formed an extreme right-wing religious group named the *feda'iyyan-e eslam*. This group soon demonstrated its willingness to resort to assassination to gain its end. Seyyed Ahmad Kasravi, the noted scholar, had made a violent attack on Shi'ism and on the authoritarianism of the 'olama. It was planned to take legal action against him—action that was welcomed by Kasravi as it afforded him an opportunity to engage in debate with his opponents—but before the trial took place both Kasravi and his secretary were stabbed to death in broad daylight by two members of the *feda'iyyan-e eslam*. The government took no action against the murderers, a fact that in itself indicated the extent to which the 'olama had regained their power. A leading figure of the *feda'iyyan*, Abol-Qasem Kashani, had a long history of militant political activity directed against both the British and Pahlavi dynasty.[50] Paradoxically, the force of the extreme Left, represented by the Tudeh party, the successor to the Persian Communist party banned by Reza Shah in 1931, was able to broaden the social base of its support by recruiting members from the two new social classes brought into being by his reforms: the professional/bureaucratic intelligentsia and the industrial working class. The Tudeh party, at first taking pains to obscure its Soviet connections and claiming to be a "democratic" movement using a "socialist method based on the masses," recruited many of the younger intellectuals who, "often Western-trained and frustrated in their ambitions because of the outmoded social system, constituted a chronically discontented class."[51]

Until the withdrawal of the last foreign troops from Iranian soil in May 1946, Mohammad Reza Shah was not master in his own house. Even then, the social and economic problems that were the legacy of the Allied occupation continued to make the task of government a most difficult one. For example, between 1941 and 1945 the cost-of-living index rose from 154.1 to 1,108.[52] The efficiency of much of the plant in the textile industry installed by Reza Shah declined between 1941 and 1946 because Allied control of transportation prevented adequate replacement of machinery and acquisition of spare parts.[53] At the same time, the Shah was faced by political problems of the first magnitude: in Azarbayjan as in Kurdistan, separatist movements had, with Soviet support, succeeded in wresting the provinces from the control of the Iranian government. In 1946, the Shah took his first positive political stand by refusing to ratify the agreement that had been signed by the prime minister, Qavam as-Saltaneh, and the leader of the Azarbayjan regime, Pishevari, because this agreement represented a recognition of, and capitulation to, the Azarbayjan regime's demands. In 1947, seeking to challenge the monopoly control of the trade unions exercised by the Tudeh party, the government formed a non-Communist labor movement called the Union of Iranian Workers' Syndicates (ESKI). A bitter struggle at once ensued between ESKI and the Tudeh-controlled unions. The Tudeh party, now at the height of its power, decided at its Second Party Congress in 1948 to make a strong bid to win the support of university students both in Iran and abroad. Within a year, the Tudeh party claimed that 50 percent of politically active students had joined its ranks.[54] Thus began the era of student strikes and demonstrations, and the process of alienating from support of the Pahlavi regime a majority of Iranian students receiving their higher education abroad.

The year 1949 was a crucial year in the social development of modern Iran. As always, social, economic, and political factors were inextricably mixed and, as so often, a political event supplied the impetus for social reform. On February 4, 1949, an attempt was made to assassinate the Shah. The would-be assassin apparently had connections with both right-wing religious elements and the Tudeh party.[55] This incident convinced the Shah that the polarization of politics in Iran was now such that he could no longer with safety try to steer a middle course between the Scylla of the *feda'iyyan-e eslam* and the Charybdis of the Tudeh party. This conviction led him to take the decision to play a larger role in government than he had done hitherto, and this decision in turn was directly responsible for setting Iran once more in motion along the path of social development.

On February 15, 1949, the First National Development Plan was legislated, and the Plan Organization was set up to implement it. If there is one feature

that more than another distinguishes the reign of Mohammad Reza Shah from his father's, it is precisely this all-important element of planning, which was conspicuously absent under Reza Shah. The First Plan and its successors have not only led to the economic development of Iran, but have changed the social and cultural life of the country. The First Plan was envisaged primarily as a blueprint for economic development, but gradually, as the social implications of economic planning came to be realized to a greater extent, the plans have been used more and more consciously as instruments for the achievement of social and cultural goals. In particular, the Fourth and Fifth Plans laid stress on measures to deal with the problems that arise during a period of social upheaval.

In February 1950, the Shah established the Imperial Organization of Social Services, and transferred to it, for distribution to the peasants, the royal estates. With strong support from the prime minister, General 'Ali Razmara, the Shah also took strong measures against corruption in the bureaucracy, as a prerequisite of more efficient administration. But, as in 1941, political events once again intervened to place obstacles in the path of social development. On March 7, 1951, General Razmara was assassinated by a member of the *feda'iyyan-e eslam*. In an atmosphere of mounting excitement, the Shah was obliged to accept Dr. Mosaddegh as prime minister on April 29 and to sign his bill for the nationalization of the Anglo-Iranian Oil Company on May 2. Production of oil virtually ceased for three years, and this brought to a sudden stop the First National Development Plan, which was financed mainly from oil revenue.

Dr. Mosaddegh was prime minister from April 1951 until August 1953, and for more than half this period he held dictatorial powers. He possessed the power to effect a social revolution, but seemed devoid of ideas once his goal of the nationalization of oil had been achieved. Far from introducing a program of land reform, he stopped the distribution of crown lands initiated by the Shah in January 1951. In 1952, Dr. Mosaddegh introduced measures ostensibly designed to reduce the landlord's share of the crop and to abolish certain dues and services, but these measures were as ineffectual as Reza Shah's 1937 Land Development Act. In fact, "these decrees seemed designed to prolong the life of the existing land system by minor concessions which at first glance appeared substantial, but which were in fact either negligible or impractical. They did nothing to give the peasant security of tenure, which was fundamental to reform."[56]

As disenchantment with Dr. Mosaddegh increased, both the Communists and the ultra-right religious faction gained recruits from the ranks of disillusioned intellectuals. The *'olama* adopted the slogan, "the pragmatic, materialist West can satisfy your body, but only Islam can satisfy your soul."

The popularity of the works of Kafka and Sartre reflected the cynicism prevalent among intellectuals who believed that only a Communist revolution could accomplish reforms. The Tudeh party, already strong among the industrial working class, intellectuals, and students, further extended its influence by sending agents among the tribes and into the villages to make recruits. In addition, it established a widespread network among army officers.

Dr. Mosaddegh fell from power in August 1953, and oil production was resumed the following year. The political atmosphere continued to be highly charged and dangerous, and until April 1957 martial law was necessary for the maintenance of law and order. An attempt by the *feda'iyyan-e eslam* to assassinate Prime Minister 'Ala in November 1955 was swiftly followed by the execution of his assailant and also of the murderer of the former Prime Minister Razmara; the latter had been released from jail by Dr. Mosaddegh. This straw in the wind was indicative of the Shah's new resolve to rule rather than to reign.

Despite the turbulent political situation, the Shah pressed ahead with social reform. He resumed the sale of crown lands, hoping that the large landowners would follow his example, but the Majles was "still a parliament of the privileged classes, composed of men of means and of education, a formidable combine drawn from the traditional élite of Iran. More than 90 percent were landlords or members of the powerful bureaucratic class."[57] In 1956, the Shah inaugurated the Second National Development Plan. Already social benefits were going hand in hand with economic progress: "the number of schools increased; health conditions improved; malaria was largely eradicated . . . the peasantry became more mobile."[58] But a fundamental change in the system of land tenure—the only change that would liberate the peasants—seemed as far away as ever. Although by 1958 more than half a million acres of crown lands had been distributed to 25,000 peasants, none of the landowners appeared inclined to follow suit. In February 1960 the leading *mojtahed* of the day, Ayatollah Borujerdi, "had issued a statement . . . that any step limiting the size of landed estates would be contrary to Islam."[59] In March "an ill-conceived and badly drafted bill limiting the amount of land that anyone could hold to 400 hectares (988 acres) of irrigated land or 800 hectares (1,976 acres) of unirrigated land" was actually passed by the Majles, but the bill was watered down during passage, and the law "remained a dead letter, reinforcing the belief of the landowning classes . . . that they had little to fear from the talk of land reform. . . . Bills might be drafted, but no one believed that they would ever be implemented."[60] It is interesting to note that *vaqf* lands (i.e., lands held in mortmain) were exempted from the provisions of the 1960 Land Reform Act.

THE WHITE REVOLUTION

Mohammad Reza Shah, frustrated in his hopes of achieving land reform by constitutional means, and surrounded by people who claimed to be advocates of social revolution but in reality were actively opposed to any social and economic reforms that might break down the existing structure of society and so weaken their own position, decided on drastic measures. After appointing on May 6, 1961, 'Ali Amini, Dr. Mosaddegh's minister of national economy, his new prime minister, the Shah proceeded on May 9 to dissolve both the Majles and the Senate "for the protection of the nation's rights and interests and to safeguard the Constitution"; he was desirous that "no obstacles should hinder the strong Government appointed to institute fundamental reforms." The Majles did not sit again until October 1963. During this period of twenty-nine months of rule by decree, the Shah promulgated and began to implement a Six-Point Reform Program that marked the beginning of his White Revolution.

This Six-Point Program was overwhelmingly approved by national referendum on Bahman 6, 1341 (January 26, 1963), a date "which must be considered as the starting point of Iran's modern history."[61] The original six principles were: (1) land reform; (2) nationalization of forests and pastures; (3) sale of state-owned factories to the private sector as security for land reform; (4) a profit-sharing scheme for employees in industry; (5) reform of the electoral laws; (6) creation of the Literacy Corps to combat illiteracy, particularly in rural areas. Six other principles were subsequently added to the revolution's program: (7) creation of the Health Corps (1964); (8) creation of the Reconstruction and Development Corps (1964); (9) establishment of *khanehha-ye ensaf* (Houses of Equity), which were village courts of law (the first House of Equity was established in 1963 but the system was not declared to be the ninth principle of the White Revolution until 1965); (10) nationalization of water resources in order to guarantee adequate supplies for irrigation and industry; (11) urban and rural reconstruction (i.e., elimination of slums, improvement of the environment, and raising of the standard of life); (12) reorganization of all government administrative structures and of the educational system, including the decentralization of the administrative system.

It goes without saying that the implementation of the principles of the White Revolution has had a profound effect on social development in Iran. Indeed, as the Shah said in an address to the nation on January 28, 1963, two days after the revolution's first six principles had been endorsed in a national referendum, perhaps in the whole course of Iranian history the basis of Iranian society had never been so profoundly and fundamentally transformed, to "assume a new form based on social justice."[62] Although the Six-

Point Program had been enunciated by decree, in the absence of Parliament, the legality of the Shah's action was based on article 26 of the Supplementary Fundamental Law of the Constitution, which states that "the powers of the realm are all derived from the people." In other words, the Shah, frustrated in his attempts to reform society through parliamentary channels, had bypassed Parliament and had appealed directly to the people, particularly the peasants, and the five-and-half million people who voted for the Six-Point Reform Program on January 26, 1963, had indicated their strong support for the kind of social revolution that he was proposing. For this reason, the Shah is in the habit of referring to it as the "White Revolution of the Shah and the People" *(enqelab-e safid-e shah o mardom)*. On the second anniversary of the promulgation of the Six-Point Program, January 26, 1965, the Shah was able to declare confidently that the foundations of a new society had been laid.

It is unfortunately not possible within the scope of a single chapter to describe the effects of the White Revolution in detail. Each of the twelve principles could be made the subject of a separate book—indeed, the first principle, land reform, has already been the subject of numerous articles and two books.[63] However, an attempt will be made to give a brief description of those principles which have had the greatest impact on Iranian society.

Land Reform

The pernicious effects of the sharecropping system in force at the time of the promulgation of the Land Reform Law of January 9, 1962, have already been mentioned. "Between the landowner and the peasant there was often an attitude of mutual suspicion. The landowner saw the peasant as a drudge who would cheat him of his profits if not handled with severity. . . . Education, hygiene, and suitable housing were regarded as unimportant, except by a minority of enlightened landowners."[64]

The Land Reform Law of 1962 has been called by an Iranian historian the "greatest single piece of legislation in twenty-five centuries of Persian history."[65] It was supplemented by additional legislation on January 17, 1963, and July 25, 1964. "The law," writes Ann K.S. Lambton, "had the touch of genius. It was admirably simple in conception and, what was extremely important, capable of immediate implementation in spite of the fact that there was no cadastral survey for the whole country, no land survey department, and no body of officials trained in land reform or kindred matters."[66] The Shah, on his own initiative, had decided to take action in order finally to break the power of the landowning class, which of course included members of the religious classes as well as lay persons. The magnitude of the task may be judged from the fact that, prior to the 1962 act, 56 percent of the land was in the hands of 1 percent of the population.[67] Thus, although considerable economic benefits accrued from the implementation of the act, its primary object was not economic benefit but social reform.

The most important provision of "phase one" of land reform was the limitation of landholdings to a maximum of one village (orchards, tea plantations, and woodlands were exempt, as were lands cultivated by hired laborers). All land in excess of one village was to be sold to the government at a valuation based on the taxes paid by the landlord prior to 1962. The compensation to the landlords was to be paid in ten (later increased to fifteen) installments. The land thus acquired by the government was to be sold to the peasants, together with the relevant water rights, and paid for by the peasants in fifteen annual installments; the peasants actually cultivating the land were given the first option to purchase. Membership in a cooperative society was made a condition of sale. This was a necessary measure because the peasants would need help with such things as the marketing of crops (formerly carried out by the landlord) and the purchase of agricultural machinery. The cooperatives were also to provide credit for the purchase of seed and other necessities.

This historic law was first put into operation at Maragheh in Azarbayjan, and thereafter its application was rapidly extended to the whole country. Predictably, there was opposition to its implementation but, astonishingly, little violence and almost no loss of life. The landlords naturally adopted delaying tactics and resorted to evasion. Those who had previously criticized the government for inaction now criticized it for moving too fast. "Haste meant that mistakes would inevitably occur, but delay would have enabled the opposition to muster their forces and block all effective action. The extreme Left was hostile to the reform and probably would have been satisfied with nothing short of collective farms."[68] The intellectuals, on the other hand, "wanted a 'textbook' reform, whereas the reform was essentially pragmatic and devised to suit Persian conditions."[69] Relations between landlord and peasant in the landowners' "chosen" villages remained on a sharecropping basis, but regulations were introduced to effect a drastic improvement in the sharecropping agreement: the landlord was forced to fulfil his obligations in regard to the provision of free schools, bathhouses, and dwellings; sharecroppers were granted security of tenure; there was a flat-rate increase in the peasants' share of the crop of 5 percent on irrigated land and 10 percent on dry-farming operations. Some 8,000 villages, or approximately one-seventh of the total number of villages in Iran, were affected by the phase one legislation of January 1962.

On January 8, 1963, some 4,700 peasants attended a national congress in Tehran. "For the first time in the history of the country, peasants from different parts of the country were brought into contact with each other, and for the first time, they felt a sense of unity and strength. Many of those who took part still remember the congress as a great landmark in the change that has taken place in their conditions."[70] Already, the peasants felt liberated, and there was a striking rise in the morale of peasants living in the villages directly affected by phase one. In the land reform villages, "peasants were eating better food, had better clothes, and more household goods than formerly. In many districts, there was also a marked increase in school attendance."[71] Most important of all, the ingrained submissive attitudes of centuries were beginning to break down. For the first time, the peasant felt that "his voice counted for something and even that he had a responsibility towards the country and the community."[72]

Meanwhile, on January 17, 1963, additional land reform legislation was promulgated. This new legislation, which became known as "phase two," affected landlords who owned one village or less. This time, upwards of 33,000 villages, or about 60 percent of all villages, were affected. Under phase one, the peasants in villages by the legislation of January 9, 1962, received the title deeds to the land; under phase two, the emphasis was on tenancy agreements. Landlords were given three options: *(1)* to lease their land to the actual cultivators, the rent being calculated on the basis of the average annual revenue over the last three years multiplied by the Land Reform Organization's regional coefficient of land values; *(2)* to sell the land to the actual cultivators; *(3)* to divide the land with the peasant in the same proportion as under the existing crop-sharing agreement, the peasant paying two-fifths of the value of the land in equal installments over a period of ten years. Further phase two legislation was promulgated on July 25, 1964, and at that time two more options were added; *(4)* the formation, to cultivate the land, of a joint agricultural unit with a managing committee consisting of a representative of the landlord, a representative of the peasants, and a person chosen by mutual agreement between landlord and peasants; *(5)* the purchase by the landlord of the peasants' rights *(haqq-e risheh)* up to a stated maximum acreage. "The decision to bring charitable *owqaf* [*vaqf*] within the scope of the law aroused the hostility of some sections of the religious classes."[73] Under the phase two legislation, public *vaqf* land was to be leased to the occupying peasants for a period of ninety-nine years.

In the event, the option preferred in a majority of cases was number one; as a result, most of the peasants in villages affected by phase two became tenant farmers. As in the phase one villages, there was improvement in the peasants' standard of living and in the standards of cultivation.[74] The peasants built themselves better houses, because the fear of eviction had gone. Communal effort was also directed toward the provision of schools, public baths, and rural roads. In general, the peasants' level of debt decreased. In this latter regard, as in many other aspects of land reform, the Rural Cooperative Societies played a vital part. The amount of the loan repayment installments made by the peasants was frequently less than they formerly paid to the landlord. Freed from corvées and traditional dues, the peasant worked harder and productivity rose. His social contacts were much broader, and he gradually learned to stand on his own feet in his dealings with government officials—those from the Agricultural Bank, for instance, or the Ministries of Agriculture and Justice.

In 1963, the Central Organization for Rural Cooperation (CORC) was formed and took over the functions of the Land Reform Organization and the Agricultural Bank. Under the direction of CORC, the Rural Cooperative Societies provided the peasants with credit, seed, fertilizers, insecticides, cloth, etc., and purchased some of the crops, including rice, pulses, dates, and citrus fruits. [75] Apart from this, the work of the cooperative societies had enormous social implications, because it gave "the peasants some education in business" and taught them "the connection between better farming, better living and better business."[76] "By the spring of 1968, 8,652 societies with a membership of 1,105,402 persons serving some 20,803 villages had been established."[77] CORC had done a magnificent job in the four years of its existence prior to its incorporation in the new Ministry of Land Reform and Rural Cooperation in 1967. "The officials of CORC are a keen and dedicated body of men," wrote Ann K.S. Lambton in 1969. "They have succeeded in gaining the trust of the peasants in a country in which the gulf between the government and the governed has seldom been bridged. I cannot speak too highly of their work."[78]

The main function of the rural cooperative societies was to provide the peasants with credit, but the federations of societies in a given area had much wider functions than that. They provided their members with consumer goods, such as cloth, soap, rice, pulses, and some household commodities.[79] They also helped them to market their crops; provided them with fertilizers, pesticides and sprayers; encouraged them to use improved strains of seed; acted as agencies for the National Iranian Oil Company (NIOC) and supplied their members, on a regular basis and at a fixed price, with oil products including kerosene; and encouraged handicrafts, such as the weaving of rugs, which brought in additional revenue to the society. "Steadily, relations of trust and confidence are being built up on the basis of the small society, the members of which know each other intimately, and a wider sense of unity is being developed through the federations."[80] In this way, the societies helped to develop to the full the hitherto unsuspected talents of the peasants, and thus to contribute to the social well-being of the nation. Not the least of these unsuspected talents was the ability displayed by peasants in their capacity as managers of rural cooperative societies. If well chosen, the working peasant enjoyed the confidence of his fellows and made the best type of manager because he not only knew the problems best but cared more. CORC ran courses of instruction for managers of rural cooperatives that were highly successful. "Most of the managers who took part were working peasants, many of them middle-aged. It is a tribute to their keenness that they were prepared to give up several weeks of their time at a busy season of the year in order to learn how to run their societies better. Whereas formerly it was the exception rather than the rule for the managers to write up their books, now the majority of them write up most of the books."[81]

The primary object of phase one of land reform had been to destroy the power of the large landowners; that of phase two was to improve the condition of the peasants in the villages not affected by phase one. Phase three of land reform, launched in 1966, tackled the politically and socially delicate question of the consolidation of parcels of land into economic units, consolidation that permitted a greater degree of mechanization and a more efficient exploitation of the land. Prior to land reform, there had been a strip system designed to give each peasant a fair share of the good land and the bad in each village.

The first part of the legislation for phase three was passed by the Majles and the Senate in December 1967 and January 1968, respectively. It provided for the establishment of joint stock agricultural companies, or agricultural corporations, comprising two or more villages. Initially, the government was to control their operation and to inject considerable sums of money into them. Apart from the benefits mentioned above, it was hoped that the creation of these corporations would induce peasants to leave the areas of the poorest land. In areas where the corporations were established, the peasant gave up his land in return for shares in the joint stock company, and was employed by the company as an agricultural laborer (not all the peasants in a given area were hired by the joint stock company).

The second part of the phase three legislation became law in January 1969. It abolished all tenancies except in the case of land constituted as charitable *owqaf*, and required that the land be sold to the occupying peasants. The land was to be divided between landlord and tenant in the same proportion as the crop had been divided under the old crop-sharing agreement. The tenants were to pay a cash sum equal to 10 times 40 percent of the annual rent less 15 percent, or 12 installments totaling 12 times 40 percent of the annual rent less 15 percent, and were required to become members of a rural cooperative society.[82] This legislation had been rendered necessary primarily because under phase two of land reform the preferred option had been number one, namely, the renting of the land to the peasants. As a result, although the "new tenancies had no taint of bondage about them,"[83] nevertheless "the landlord and tenant relationship reminded the villages of the old order."[84] To prevent the process from dragging on indefinitely, a terminus ad quem was imposed by the Shah: September 22, 1971. September 23, 1971, was declared "Farmers' Day," and as of that date any land still in dispute was deemed to have been sold to the tenants. This day, almost ten years after the introduction of the Land Reform Law of 1962, marked the official end of the land reform program. The last gap in the land reform legislation was plugged when the Shah "gave notice of the Government's intention to legislate for the transfer of full ownership of the land to tenants holding long leases in public *vaqf* lands."[85]

Land reform has effected a social revolution in Iran. The large landowners have been removed from the rural scene, but they have not been lost to the economy; they have not been put to death, nor have their lands been confiscated. Their sphere of action has been transferred from agriculture to industry. Their place in rural areas has been taken by city-bred members of the middle classes: surveyors, mechanical and hydraulic engineers, agricultural advisers, veterinarians, officials connected with health and welfare, and above all, members of the various corps established by the White Revolution program. At the same time, the expectations of the emancipated peasants have increased.

> The former peasant no longer sees any reason why his children should remain illiterate. He begins to develop a new attitude toward civic rights and personal property: why shouldn't he have good schools, health clinics, better housing and food, and the other niceties of urban, industrial life? . . . He is more willing to allow his wife to work outside the home. . . . He rears his daughters to go without the veil and may even approve miniskirts as a symbol of the new way of life.[86]

The Three Corps

After land reform itself, the principles of the White Revolution that have effected the greatest changes in Iranian society have been the ones establishing the three corps: the Literacy Corps *(sepah-e danesh)*, founded in 1963, to which women were admitted in 1968; the Health Corps *(sepah-e behdasht)*, founded in 1964; and the Reconstruction and Development Corps *(sepah-e tarvij va abadani)*, also founded in 1964. These three corps together formed the spearhead of the attack on the basic problems existing in rural areas. Foremost among these was illiteracy, which despite the fact that compulsory state education had been on the statute books since the early days of Reza Shah, still ran as high as 80 to 85 percent in some areas because of the lack of facilities, the teachers' reluctance to work in the villages, and resistance on the part of the peasants and tribesmen themselves to the idea of sending their children to school when their labor was needed in the fields or in the minding of flocks.[87] Although some 70 percent of the population was still rural, 75 percent of the teachers were concentrated in the urban areas. Equally formidable were the problems of public health, sanitation, and hygiene. The Health

Corps was designed specifically "to provide medical facilities to the common man in the villages and rural areas." In addition, it concerned itself with such matters as the provision of a pure water supply (which frequently involved the digging of wells, the installation of pumps, etc.); the construction of latrines; and the construction of hygienic public baths. The Reconstruction and Development Corps was designed primarily to supplement the work of the Plan Organization in rural areas. Its members trained the peasants in improved agricultural techniques, and were concerned with such matters as the improvement of the quality of stock; the proper use of fertilizers and pesticides; and the operation of experimental farms and orchards.

Each of the three corps mentioned above was made up largely of high school graduates and university students who had been called up for military service. The conscripts were given basic army training, followed by the appropriate specialized training. Conscripts who had taken courses at university in medicine, veterinary science, or agriculture were naturally given preference for entry into the Health Corps and the Reconstruction and Development Corps. On completion of their four- or six-month training period, the corpsmen were dispatched to the villages, where they served the remainder of the period of their military service. Service in one of the Corps entitled one to take precedence when applying for a job in the Civil Service. University correspondence courses were available to the girls serving with the Reconstruction and Development Corps.

On arrival in a village, the first duty of a literacy corpsman was the formal education of the children of the village. In addition, the corpsman was expected to be able to give help and advice to villagers on a wide range of health, agricultural, and community problems. If no school existed in the village, but the inhabitants expressed the wish to have one, the corpsman made the necessary arrangements with the authorities. The school was built, and the cost of construction borne, by the villagers themselves, with the exception of a maximum grant from the government of $75 for the purchase of essential building materials that the villagers could not supply.[88] In this way, the villagers came to feel pride in their local school.

> Villagers on the whole seem to cooperate willingly with Literacy Corpsmen. They provide all labour for building schools, baths, roads, bridges, mosques, etc. Most of the villages have a community fund to which they all contribute. This fund is cash on hand and permits some otherwise unfinanced projects to be carried out. When records are kept, it is usually the corpsman and the village chief who handle the books.[89]

Many of the literacy corpsmen decided to remain in the villages as civilian teachers after the completion of their period of military service—if only because they were not trained to do any other type of job.[90] Boys and girls studied in mixed classes, usually with a preponderance of boys. Attendance was very good, except in summer, when the need for labor in the fields still caused a sharp decline in enrollment.[91] Parents still tended to burst into the classroom and haul their offspring off to look for a lost cow or deal with some common farming occurrence.[92] Despite the fact that not all corpsmen were dedicated to their task, in general the villagers showed great respect for their teachers, whose presence "in the traditional village, away from their own rather conservative homes," they took as a signal that "a great social transformation" had begun to take place in Iranian society.[93] The Literacy Corps program provided instruction up to grade six. In the mid-1970s, however, the problem of how to provide instruction beyond that grade remained a very real and pressing one.

In 1969, when women were for the first time admitted to the Literacy Corps, it was thought advisable to allocate them to villages near their home. This enabled them to live at home (thereby avoiding possible problems associated with their lodging in the village), and to travel by bus each day to their village. Between April 1963 and September 1969, 52,601 corpsmen were sent to the villages, and, between October 1968 and September 1969, 2,720 corpswomen, all volunteers, were also sent.[94]

As literacy increased, so too did the rate of migration from the land to the cities. Agricultural workers constituted 90 percent of the total labor force in 1900, 75 percent in 1946, 46 percent in 1966.[95] By 1972, they were less than 40 percent.[96] This massive influx of people into the cities caused an acute housing shortage and the appearance in south Tehran of shanty towns that rapidly became slums. The government was not slow to act.

> Large sums were allocated during the Third and Fourth Plans for slum clearance and the construction of low-cost housing. . . . During the Third Plan, low-cost housing projects were implemented by extending loans through the Mortgage Bank. The newly created Ministry of Housing and Development has initiated large-scale programs for slum clearance, particularly in large cities. The Fourth Plan provides for the construction of at least 55,000 housing units per year, either through direct investment by the public sector or by providing loans to the private sector on easy terms.[97]

Government assistance to low-income groups was necessitated by the extremely high cost of accommodation in the private sector. For example, in 1976 a two-bedroom apartment in a good residential district of midtown Tehran rented for $1,000 a month. On the other hand, salaries were also high: during the same period, a junior executive with seven years' experience could make $2,000 a month; a typist with some knowledge of English $500; and an unskilled laborer in the construction industry $7 a day. The minimum wage as of 1975 was $3 a day, but the average monthly income of workers in this category was $164. Workers' cash extras included a share of the profits, overtime, bonuses, family allowances, and a New Year's bonus; their noncash bonuses included free transportation to work, free lunches at work, and other benefits.

Despite the mass migration from the land to the cities, agricultural production rose by 23 percent in the first decade after land reform.[98] Moreover, the peasants who remained on the land were no longer in debt. As soon as the Land Reform Law granted the peasants independence from the landlords, and set up a new framework of rural society that permitted a genuine amelioration of their social condition, they demonstrated a surprising degree of adaptability. There was a striking improvement in their morale because "the peasant for the first time began to feel that his voice counted for something."[99]

The health corpsmen were organized into mobile health teams each consisting of at least the following: a doctor; two assistants with a high school graduating diploma; and a driver. In the larger teams, the physician had three assistants, and a dentist and a psychiatrist were also attached to the team. Each team had a van equipped with pharmaceuticals, instruments, and an examination table. All teams met once a month at the regional center to discuss mutual problems. The assistants were qualified to perform vaccinations and give inoculations, and the Health Corps has achieved some striking results through its program of vaccination against cholera, smallpox, and other diseases. Iran was the first country in the Middle East to implement a program of universal vaccination against measles in rural areas; as a result, the incidence of this disease declined from about 400 per 100,000 per month in 1966 to between 30 and 40 per 100,000 per month in 1970.

To make the most effective use of their resources, the Health Corps teams in most cases were not continually on the move, but established clinics that served a number of villages; if the number of villages in the area warranted it, subclinics were established in the larger ones and were visited by the physician according to a fixed schedule. Prior to 1962, a few clinics existed in rural areas, but they had no water or electricity, and there were no doctors in attendance. About one-third of the corpsmen, and about two-thirds of the corpswomen continued to serve in rural areas after the completion of their period of military service. All the women who served in the various corps were volunteers. Although, by virtue of the saying, "A doctor is more sacred than a husband," male physicians were admitted to peasants' houses and were allowed to examine female patients, nevertheless, women were even more acceptable in the villages. The Health Corps was one of a number of agencies, both government and private, that disseminated family planning information. Before a husband and wife decided to practice birth control, both were interviewed by Health Corps staff. Birth control was represented as a means of raising the standard of living; a slogan frequently used was: *bachcheh-ye kam-tar zendegi-ye behtar* ("Fewer children mean better living").

An acute shortage of doctors was the biggest problem that faced the Health Corps and one that restricted the expansion of medical facilities in general. By 1976, Iran was graduating about seven hundred doctors annually, but this number was completely inadequate to meet the need. In 1974, the doctor-to-population ratio was still only about 1:3,000. By 1976, some 420 recruits were being drafted into the Health Corps every six months, but only a small proportion of these were doctors. Since the number of doctors available to the Health Corps was variable, there might be periods when a Health Corps clinic was left without a physician. To meet this need, Iran imported large numbers of doctors from Pakistan, India, and the Philippines. The Filipino doctors came to Iran under contract to their own government and were required to bank half their salary in the Philippines. The Indian and Pakistani doctors came on a two-year contract, and managed to save a large proportion of the salary of $1,000 a month that they earned in Iran.

In 1976, although the quality of doctors was reasonably good, and that of specialists was high, that of hospital medical services in general, and particularly of nursing, was low. Middle-class patients, especially, complained about the high cost and low quality of medical services, and those who had the time and money still went abroad for medical treatment. There were probably almost as many Iranian doctors practicing abroad as there were in Iran, although 89 percent of doctors and dentists had received their training in Iran. Of the expatriate doctors, 70 percent were in West Germany and the United States. The reasons given by these doctors to justify their remaining abroad included better pay, less bureaucracy, the feeling of being close to the mainstream of professional life, access to research laboratories and medical libraries, and dislike of the two-year period of military service, which, in the opinion of some doctors, retarded their professional development. The government made concessions to the doctors in an effort to check this braindrain. Doctors were allowed to spend their period of military service working in either military or civilian hospitals with regular salary, and were also permitted to carry on private practice in their spare time. In addition, the government promised more money for medical research; in the mid-1970s, Iran was spending less on this than the 1 percent of GNP set by the United Nations as the recommended minimum for research in developing countries.[100] Three-year specialist training courses were made available at Shiraz and Firuzgard as an attractive alternative to spending six or seven years abroad (the first two of which are usually spent acquiring fluency in the appropriate foreign language). Specialist courses, taught by leading professors of the Faculty of Medicine, were available in anesthesiology, pediatrics, and gynecology.[101]

The members of the three corps, by penetrating into many previously ignored and isolated regions, have played a major role in accelerating the pace of social development in Iran. Closely connected with the work of the corps has been that of the Houses of Equity. The establishment of these tribunals began in 1963, and in 1965 was declared to be the ninth principle of the White Revolution; by 1969, 2,000 such tribunals had been set up across the country.[102] The object of these tribunals was to make available to the rural population arbitration in and settlement of minor disputes. It was considered that the most effective arbitrators in this type of dispute would be persons with knowledge of local conditions, and so the magistrates who constituted these tribunals were chosen by and from the local inhabitants. They received no salary, and even illiterates were eligible to serve. Very often, a literacy corpsman was appointed clerk of the court. The tribunals have been remarkably successful. In the past, the peasant, with neither time nor money to have recourse to the provincial courts, would not infrequently resort to violence to resolve his disputes. The work of the Houses of Equity therefore contributed to rural tranquillity; in fact, they proved so successful that the system was extended to urban areas, in order to alleviate the burden on the courts of a large number of minor cases of a marital or domestic nature.

The Changing Status of Women

Reza Shah had started the process of the emancipation of women by decreeing that for the first time girls should receive an education, and by ordering that the *chador* be no longer worn; as already mentioned, the latter order was far from effective. The decisive step, however, which admitted women finally not only to an equal place in society but also opened to them the doors of political power, was Mohammad Reza Shah's decree granting every woman of legal age the right to cast an electoral ballot for, and to be elected to, the Majles and the Senate. The fifth principle of the White Revolution had called for the establishment of universal suffrage but, on January 22, 1963, four days before the date set for the national referendum on this program, the *'olama* organized a violent demonstration aimed at obstructing the referendum "by terrorizing the public, and one of its specific aims was to strike against the growing popular acceptance" of female participation in the referendum.[103] As a result of this opposition by the religious classes, the government approached the question of female suffrage with extreme caution. Only on the morning of the referendum itself, January 26, 1963, did Tehran radio broadcast an announcement that women would be permitted to vote in the referendum. Even then, they were to use separate ballot boxes, and their votes, although counted, would not be included in the grand total.[104] Encouraged by the result of the referendum, the Shah instructed the government to implement the Six-Point Program as the law of the land

and, a few days later, the female suffrage law was enacted. Religious opposition was not at an end, however, and in the riots of June 1963 the Tehran mob "made a particular effort to frighten women and to demonstrate that their new rights exposed them to serious menace."[105] Nevertheless, the die had been cast, and six women were elected to the Twenty-first Majles in September 1963, and two to the Senate.

From 1963 onwards, the status of women in Iranian society rose steadily, and, as more women became literate, there could be no doubt that their participation in the social and political life of the country would become even greater. Although the position of women in the large urban centers had improved between 1910 and 1960, in the provincial towns and rural areas the traditional family structure still prevailed at the time of the White Revolution:

> Marriages were arranged for girls at an early age; sometimes even before they reached puberty. A man could have as many as four wives and might well have another family of which the wife had no knowledge. . . . Governed by strict conventions and traditions, women's lives were hard. A wife was subject to the will of her husband, and beating was the accepted remedy for a disobedient woman. . . . A man could divorce a wife without her permission or even her knowledge. Temporary marriages were allowed. . . . The Persian women lived solely in the home.[106]

In 1956, literacy among rural women was still as low as 1 percent (compared with 20.6 percent among urban females); in 1965 it was 3 percent; by 1971 it had risen to 9 percent. In contrast, literacy among women in urban areas had increased from 20.6 percent in 1956 to 36.3 percent in 1965. The overall literacy rate among women in 1971 was 26.3 percent.[107] In 1972 it was 31 percent, and was expected to rise to 47 percent by 1978.[108] In 1967, legislation was passed to prevent a man from marrying a second wife unless the first wife agreed. From 1968 onward, women were admitted as volunteers to the three corps of the White Revolution. In 1974, the minimum legal age for marriage for girls was raised from sixteen to eighteen. In 1975, Iranian women were accorded signal recognition when Princess Ashraf Pahlavi was unanimously elected to chair the Consultative Committee for the World Wide Conference of International Women's Year, in New York City. In particular, the emancipation of women has meant a great upsurge of concern for social welfare, and both Empress Farah Pahlavi and Princess Ashraf Pahlavi have given a strong lead in directing and encouraging a wide variety of programs aimed at remedying social ills.

Social Welfare

Social welfare in Iran is the concern not only of government ministries and the three corps of the White Revolution, but also of government-sponsored agencies such as the Women's Organization of Iran *(Sazeman-e Zanan-e Iran),* the president of which is HIH Princess Ashraf Pahlavi, and of independent institutions such as the Tehran School of Social Work, the founder and director of which is Miss Sattareh Farmanfarmayan. The School of Social Work offers a four-year B.A. degree and an M.A. program in social work administration, and in 1960 was accepted for membership in the International Association of Schools of Social Work.

The social problems that had to be tackled were both numerous and daunting in their magnitude. The low literacy rate among women, which put them at a disadvantage in regard to playing their proper part in society, was only one obstacle to be overcome. Another urgent need was to liberate women from the burden of excessively large families. Directly after its first field experiences in 1958 the Tehran School of Social Work realized that its work for the welfare of the people could not be successful without the addition of family planning *(tanzim-e khanavadeh)* to the range of services offered. The school therefore cooperated in the establishment of the Family Planning Association of Iran the same year; in 1976, the association had nine clinics in Tehran and nine branches in the provinces. The limitation of families was not only an urgent social need but an economic necessity. As a result of improved health standards, the infant mortality rate has dropped steadily. Twenty-five years ago, a woman who bore eight live children could expect to rear four to adulthood. In 1976, the figure was six or even seven. At the same time, life expectancy rose from 35 years in 1960 to 51.6 years in 1975. The average rate of population increase for the years 1970-73 was 3 percent. When one remembers that more than 50 percent of the country is uncultivable, it is not surprising that Iran is no longer able to grow all the food it needs. Moreover, new sources of drinking water are hard to find and, if the population growth is not checked, the conversion of sea water to fresh water by the expensive desalination process may be the only answer.

The urgent need for effective family planning is indicated by the fact that, if the 1976 estimated growth rate of 3.2 percent is not checked, the population will double in twenty-one years. The rate of population growth is boosted by the tendency of females to marry at a much earlier age than males. In the 15-19 age group in 1966, 6 percent of males but 47 percent of females were married. "Young marriage means a prolonged period of fertility, a greater number of children, and, with the increased chances of survival, an increase in the youthfulness of the population."[109] Despite these facts, social opposition to the concept of limiting family size has been tremendous. The religious classes, which one might have expected to oppose family planning, while not wildly enthusiastic about it, have not actively opposed it. The *'olama* have been much more concerned with the preservation of the family unit against erosion. The opposition has come from the parents themselves. Traditionally, parents had large families to allow for "wastage" from children's diseases and epidemics. In a primarily agricultural society, many hands were needed in the fields, and sons were regarded as insurance against sickness, crop failures and old age.

The family planning program was initially aimed at women aged twenty-six to thirty-five who had already had two or three children. Social workers soon found, however, that only women with five children or more would listen to government propaganda that emphasized the economic problems arising from large families. Import of the pill was legalized in Iran in 1961, and government production began in 1967. Ingenious methods are sometimes used to ensure that women do not forget to take their birth control pills: for instance, they may be instructed to place the pills at the side of their prayer rugs. Sometimes, incentives are used: at one family welfare center, for instance, women who enrolled in the family planning program received free milk for their children, but this was discontinued if the woman became pregnant.[110] Birth control information was widely disseminated at such places as universities, barracks, police stations, and factories. At the same time, improved prenatal care for expectant mothers was provided by Mother and Child Clinics established in most towns with a population of more than 10,000. For the Fifth Development Plan, current in the mid-1970s, the goal was to reduce the estimated growth rate of 3.2 percent per year to 2.4 percent.[111]

The community (or family) welfare centers *(markaz-e refah-e khanavadeh)* continue to represent one of the most important aspects of social work in Iran. These centers developed out of an emergency project, supervised by the staff of the Tehran School of Social Work, to give relief to victims of flooding in the low-income Tehran suburb of Javadiyyeh in 1962. This project revealed the urgent need for social work among the families who had been pouring into the capital from rural areas. In the absence of adequate housing, these families lived in overcrowded, unsanitary quarters. "Most of the women, in addition to being illiterate, lacked any knowledge of sanitation, hygiene or proper diet. Since their husbands, lacking education and skills, were often unable to provide for their families, many women were forced into employment, thus leaving the families further uncared for."[112] With the help of a grant from the Empress, and the donation of a site by the mayor of Tehran, the first community welfare center was opened at Javadieh in 1966; students of the School of Social Work had "contacted construction companies and obtained bricks, tile, cement and other materials. Other students saw merchants and obtained donations of curtains, food, furniture, refrigerators, kitchen equipment and other equipment and supplies."[113]

The services provided by the community welfare centers included day care, family planning instruction, and maternal and child health care. The family planning advice was provided free of charge by doctors and members of the Health Corps, in cooperation with the Ministry of Health. Students from the School of Social Work carried out a program of intensive home visits in the areas around the community welfare centers, in order to acquaint families with the services that they offer. Prigmore reports that after the women began to take advantage of the family planning instruction, follow-up visits were still needed to counter their own and their neighbors' and relatives' anxieties.[114] Vocational training programs helped women to augment the wages of their husbands, who were often unskilled laborers. The men were given help in finding employment, and legal counsel was available to the women regarding their rights in matters affecting marriage, divorce, child custody and working conditions. Social workers and lawyers were available to give assistance to women in court cases.

By 1970, there were some half dozen community welfare centers operating in working-class districts of Tehran, including one in the red light district that catered specifically to the needs of prostitutes. In that year, these and other similar centers established by the Ministry of Labor were brought under the supervision of a new body, the Community Welfare Center of Iran. The success of these centers was such that many more were opened in the provinces, beginning in 1964 with one at Yazd that was designed to help workers in the handloom industry who had been hard hit by industrialization. In 1976, there were over 70 centers operating in the provinces, and the government was committed to increasing the number to 200 by 1978.

The primary purpose of the Women's Organization of Iran is, in the words of its constitution, to "raise the cultural, social and economic knowledge of the women of Iran and to make them aware of their family, social and economic rights, duties and responsibilities."[115] Some of the organization's activities in the field of social welfare overlap with, or are complementary to, the activities of other organizations, both government and independent. In 1969, the Women's Organization established a School of Social Work at Varamin. The 175 students enrolled at this school were to follow a two-year program at the end of which they would receive a diploma equivalent to an Associate of Arts Degree in Social Work. The program was an integrated one of classroom study and weekly field work. Similar schools under construction at Ahwaz and Tabriz were expected to open in 1976-77.

An important project carried out by the Women's Organization of Iran was the Saveh experiment in functional literacy in a rural environment. In 1973, the organization set up a research unit to collect the statistical data and other information needed to build up a detailed descriptive profile of the rural Iranian woman and her environment. Sixty villages were included in the survey and three questionnaires administered: to married women up to forty-five years of age; to unmarried girls aged nine to fourteen; and to unmarried women aged fifteen to twenty-two. The surveys completed, and teaching materials prepared, the first six-month cycle of classes was held between June and December 1974. Educational elements included language, arithmetic, basic science, technical information, civic education, and simple illustrative arts, all carefully planned in relation to each other according to the philosophy of functional literacy. Of the findings and suggestions contained in the report published after the completion of this experimental project, two had highly significant social implications. First, it was discovered that to make rural women literate without at the same time providing similar facilities for illiterate rural men merely set up disruptive social tensions in the village. Second, the report stated that "programs for rural Iranian communities must include religious content and recognize the strong religious sentiments of participants." It was a mistake, the report continued, to concentrate entirely on "the so-called practical aspects of the villagers' daily life."[116] This is a theme to which we shall return in the concluding portion of this chapter.

The social and welfare services administered directly by the government are extensive. Formerly, they were administered by a number of ministries including the Ministry of Health and the Ministry of Labor and Social Affairs. But on April 27, 1974, the Shah created the new Ministry of Social Welfare, which was designed to "coordinate the hitherto dispersed and isolated resources and activities of a large number of existing government institutions and non-government organizations and agencies, and collate their functions in order to avoid duplication, conflicts, complications and consequent wastages of time, effort and money."[117] All social welfare policies and programs of government ministries and departments, with those of nongovernment organizations and agencies, were brought under the supervision of the High Council for Social Affairs, which was presided over by HIM Empress Farah Pahlavi.[118] The lengthy list of these organizations and agencies made the need for coordination obvious and indicated the magnitude of the task. The Ministry of Social Welfare itself was subdivided into four field-service organizations: the Social Security Organization; the Health Insurance and Medical Care Organization; the Rehabilitation Services Organization; and the Social Welfare Services Organization. The first three of these had formerly been attached to other ministries and had been brought under the umbrella of the new ministry in April 1974.[119] All four organizations were directed by a new Ministerial Department of Parliamentary and Administrative Affairs. In addition,

a large number of non-government organizations provide all kinds and types of social welfare services at all levels through the country. Prominent among them are the Farah Pahlavi Charitable Foundation; the Imperial Organization of Social Services; the Pahlavi Foundation (1961); the National Association for the

Protection of Children (1968); the Iranian Women's Organization; Youth Palaces and Homes; the Red Lion and Sun Society (1923); the Association for the Rehabilitation of the Disabled (1968), and the Universal Welfare Legion. . . .[120]

To these must be added the National Organization for Family Welfare; the Boy Scouts and Girl Guides; and the Students' Welfare Organization (1969). Nor is this all. "Quite a few government ministries and departments, autonomous and semi-autonomous organizations of the Government also provide widespread social welfare services to their employees and specific groups of the community, e.g. the Owqaf Organization, Ministry of Cooperatives and Rural Affairs, Ministry of Justice, Ministry of Labour and Social Affairs, Ministry of Education, Ministry of Health, and the National Iranian Oil Company."[121] To help meet the shortage of personnel, special emphasis has been placed on the "intensive training of 'social welfare corpswomen' and their maximum utilization thereafter in the government and non-government agencies. Some 300 Social Welfare Corpswomen are trained every six months and placed in the field service agencies."[122] Every effort was thus being made to deal with the many social problems caused by growing urbanization and a period of rapid social change.

One of the first acts of the Ministerial Department of Parliamentary and Administrative Affairs was to revise the Social Security Law and secure parliamentary approval for this (February 10, 1975). The revised law extended social security coverage to "all categories of government and non-government employees, workers, farmers, civil servants, professionals, and self-employed persons."[123] Social security insurance, among other things, gave the employee protection against disability and accidents; it paid compensatory wages during illness, and an old age pension. With the passage of the 1975 Social Security Law, the government began for the first time to pay a share of the social security contributions. The premium amounted to 30 percent of the employee's wages and was paid in the following proportions: government, 3 percent; employee, 7 percent; employer, 20 percent.

The Industrial Sector

The emergence of a new class of industrial workers during the reign of Reza Shah has already been noted. In addition to the workers in the factories established by Reza Shah, one must not forget the 20,000 workers employed by the Anglo-Persian Oil Company, who enjoyed medical, recreational, and other facilities unmatched in any other part of the industrial sector at that time. Of the manufacturing industries, the textile industry had been from the start Iran's largest in terms both of production value and total labor force, and in 1947 it employed over 60 percent of the workers in this sector.[124] Between 1947 and 1952 there was an industrial recession in Iran, due partly to foreign competition, partly to the diversion of investment funds to the booming construction industry, and partly to mismanagement and other factors.[125] The period 1956-60, however, was one of rapid industrial growth: the number of industrial enterprises increased from 45,000 in 1957 to 70,000 in 1960.[126] The number of workers employed in the manufacturing industries rose from 815,000 in 1956 to 1,402,000 (of whom some 40 percent were women) in 1968, and to 1,890,000 in 1972-1973.[127] Labor was becoming more mobile. For example, many Gilani workers who had worked on the Manjil and Latian dams elected to work also on the Shah 'Abbas Dam near *Isfahan,* despite the separation from their families that this entailed.[128]

With the increase in the size of the labor force, working conditions and the welfare of the workers became matters of urgent concern. Two principles of the White Revolution related to the industrial sector: number three, which called for the sale of state-owned factories to the private sector (the state still owned 98 factories in 1960); and number four, which directed that a profit-sharing scheme for workers in industry be brought into being. The Labor Profit Sharing Law offered workers the incentive of higher wages for increased productivity, and led not only to increased productivity but to improved labor-management relations. Under this law, management must either distribute to the workers 20 percent of net profits, or

> prescribe extra compensations based on production norms, through higher productivity or less waste. In practice, efficient factories (mostly large, modern enterprises) have set both the salary and production norms, and served as a model for collective bargaining agreements in smaller, more traditional work-shops. . . . Contrary to some dire predictions, the implementation of the law did not adversely affect investment in the industrial sector, and owing partly to improved labour relations, such investments have actually increased."[129]

On April 24, 1974 an imperial *farman* (decree) was promulgated that provided for the sale of industrial shares to the workers. The scope of this legislation went far beyond anything envisaged by the governments of most Western capitalist countries and, like other aspects of the White Revolution program, sustained the Shah's claim that this was a revolution of the Shah and the people, directed from above. Ultimately, all firms with a capital stock of more than 100 million rials, with fixed assets of more than 200 million rials, or with an annual sales turnover of more than 250 million rials, were to fall within the scope of the law provided that they had been in production for more than five years. The purchase of industrial shares by the government and their sale to the workers was to proceed gradually. In the first place, 320 companies were affected, and 49 percent of the shares of these companies had to be transferred by Mehr 1357 (September-October 1978). Workers employ-ed by the company in question got first option to purchase these shares; after that, any remaining shares up to the limit of 49 percent were offered to workers in other companies, to cultivators, and to the general public, in that order. To enable the workers to purchase the shares, the government agreed to loan each worker a sum up to 100,000 rials ($1,500), repayable over 10 years at 4 percent interest. Any worker with three years of continuous service with his company was eligible to purchase the shares, and farmers might buy them through their rural cooperative societies. The steel industry and the oil industry were exempt from the provisions of this legislation. Foreign-owned firms were required to conform with its provisions on the same terms as their Iranian counterparts. The government anticipated that 50 percent of the shares would be purchased by workers, 20 percent by cultivators, and 30 percent by the general public, but in 1976 it was not yet possible to say whether this projection was accurate.[130] However, the workers' response to the sale of the shares was tremendous and exceeded all expectations: many of them paid cash. The psychological impact of this legislation, on both factory owners and workers, was of course enormous.

By 1976, working conditions in the factories were on the whole good and, in the larger factories, excellent. At the national automobile company, founded twelve years ago as a product of the White Revolution and employing nearly 8,000 people, a wide variety of social amenities were available, including a mosque, a hospital, and food stores; the sports facilities included football, basketball, and swimming. Two thousand apartments varying in size from one to five bedrooms were let to employees free of charge. Men and women received equal pay for equal work. The factory canteen provided the workers with a subsidized lunch at a cost to the worker of 17 cents (actual cost to the employer, $1.00). At a plant in south Tehran established 11 years ago as a family business, 1,200 workers were provided with free transportation to the factory, free meals while on duty, and free protective boots.

The social revolution in the status of women has been reflected in the great increase in the number of women who are working and also in the greater variety of jobs available to women. In 1976, of some 1,500,000 women in employment, about one-third had jobs in industry. "They work in the textile, electronics and food industries, and in a variety of other industrial units."[132] There has been a significant increase too in the number of women working in the service-based occupations. Not only has "the bulk of the new openings in secretarial and clerical jobs over the past decade . . . been filled by women," but "women have also moved in large numbers into sales," where they staff "shops, department stores, supermarkets and other retail outlets."[133] The third most significant change had been in the number of women employed as teachers. "In 1957 only 12% of students in teacher training schools and colleges were women. Today the figure stands at over 50%." In general, there had been a clear shift away from agriculture to industry and services. In 1976, however, women filled few posts in the higher echelons of the public and private sectors. A start had been made, but the role of women in decision-making was not yet commensurate with their numbers. Traditional attitudes, too, still constituted a formidable barrier to the employment of women. As one manufacturer put it: "You can hardly expect me to send a woman out to try to sell paint to a small shopkeeper with a bazaari mentality."[134]

The New Technocrats

As already noted, the policies of Reza Shah had brought into being a new type of middle class whose principal distinguishing characteristic was the possession of a university education acquired in Europe. The establishment of the Plan Organization in 1949, the nationalization of the oil industry in 1951, and the endorsement of the White Revolution program in 1963, rapidly accelerated the development of this class. Large numbers of technicians, bureaucrats, and professional people were needed at short notice to implement the schemes for economic and industrial development. The Shah himself identified the shortage of skilled manpower as one of the most serious problems that continued to beset Iran in 1975. [135]

Although men and women with the necessary expertise still did not exist in Iran in sufficient numbers, the caliber of many of the younger technocrats, administrators, and managers was impressive. Since 1955, certain *dowrehs* (political and professional coteries) had come into being whose membership was largely middle-class, and many of Iran's present leaders, including the prime minister himself, had made their way to the top by this route.[136] Of the thirty persons identified by James Bill as constituting the Pahlavi political elite, other than the Shah, fifteen were of "upper-class origin" and fifteen of "low-middle and middle-class origin."[137]

The magnitude of the problem may be gauged by the fact that, for instance, "the Ministry of Economy tripled in employment while the Ministries of Education and Agriculture doubled in size" in the seven years between 1956 and 1963. But whereas in 1956 "less than one-twelfth of the bureaucracy had received any kind of higher education . . . in 1963 nearly one-fourth could claim such training." During the same period, "the total number of university graduates employed in all governmental agencies increased from 12,561 to 23,142." "By the mid-1960s, the bourgeois and professional middle classes together accounted for nearly 17% of the employed Iranian population."[138] Between 1965 and 1975, the professional middle class increased in size even more rapidly in response to the accelerating pace of economic development. Between 1900 and 1930, according to Jalal Al-e Ahmad, intellectuals were drawn from the ranks of the nobility, religious classes, landlords, and tribal chiefs. By 1976, the professional middle class included not only the sons but the *daughters* of landlords, military officers, clerics, shopkeepers, bureaucrats, servants and mule drivers.[139] Most of the intelligentsia were not practicing Shi'is.[140] This led to tensions between those who were wedded to Western beliefs in economic progress, and those who were more traditionally minded: I shall return to this problem in my conclusion.

In 1976, the bazaar remained a stronghold of traditional values and viewpoints. Many small businessmen, according to Gustav Thaiss, still refused to allow their children, especially sons, to be educated beyond the sixth class of elementary school, despite government laws to the contrary. The reason usually given was the fear that the children would "lose their religion," and also that they were "needed in the father's business."[141] Nevertheless, as economic and professional opportunities increased in Iran, fewer children followed their father's professions.[142] In the past, too, the bazaar was the place where kinship ties were strongest, and a large proportion of the marriages were contracted between bazaar families. By the mid-1970s, this was no longer the case. Indeed, as the pace of social change accelerated, the family unit, as in the West, was placed under severe and often intolerable strains. The divorce rate increased substantially.[143] As in the West, mass culture had "bred family disorganization and the alienation of the individual from tradition and old value patterns."[144] As in the West, there were complaints that too much violence in films shown on television encouraged violence in society at large. Despite the pace of social change, however, it was still unheard of for a boy or girl under the age of fourteen to be allowed to go out with a member of the opposite sex, and in certain sections of society the ban extended to much later ages. Sexual deprivation was thought by some psychiatrists to be a major cause of neuroses among Iranians.[145] At the same time, films were shown that were much more sexually stimulating than would have been permitted in the past and this, combined with the fact that traditional family and cultural relationships still militated against free heterosexual relationships, was thought to be a contributory factor in the increase of crimes such as rape. The *'olama* were extremely concerned about the increasing emphasis on nudity and sex in films and magazines.

CONCLUSION

During the first fifty years of the Pahlavi era, certain irreversible social trends were initiated. Among these were the movement from the villages to the cities; the breaking of the power of the landlords and the emancipation of the peasants; the reduction in adult illiteracy; the ever wider dissemination of education; the emancipation and enfranchisement of women; social mobility; and the trend toward secularization, which may indeed be irreversible but which has at least been checked to a degree by the recent revival of religion. The combined effect of these and other trends might well have meant that the Iranian monarchy was itself in transition. On the other hand, Mohammad Reza Shah, by cultivating—much to the puzzlement of the representatives of the Western media, liberal intellectuals, etc.—a revolutionary rather than a sacral image had demonstrated a flexibility that seemed likely to enable the institution of the monarchy to pass this crucial test with flying colors.

Since the inauguration of the First National Development Plan in 1949, the emphasis in Iran has been on the economic and technological development needed to build up the industrial infrastructure that will be so vital to Iran in the days ahead when its oil resources are exhausted. Since Iran's oil revenues increased in 1974, the pace of this development has been breakneck. With it, however, have come some problems, familiar to the West, of a social or environmental nature, such as pollution, traffic congestion, housing shortages, and slums. The Fourth Plan (1968-73) took cognizance of these problems by placing its main emphasis on public welfare.[146] Similarly, in the Fifth Plan (1973-78), the first objective was "to raise the quality of life for all social groups." This objective was placed before the maintenance of "rapid, balanced and sustained economic growth." Again, objective (f) was "to preserve, rehabilitate and improve the environment, and raise the quality of life, particularly in larger centres of population," and objective (j) was "to maintain and resuscitate the nation's valuable cultural heritage."[147]

It is clear that this represented a significant shift in thinking on the part of some of those who direct Iran's affairs. In the Iran of 1976, as in the West, there were those who were concerned about traditional values, the environment and the ecology. Of particular importance in this regard were the various "think tanks" (goruh-e motafakkerin) set up by the Shah to ponder the question of Iran's priorities, and the strong lead given by the Empress to those concerned about the preservation of traditional arts and craft. There were a number of straws in the wind: for instance, a revival of interest in Islamic philosophy and religion among university students. There were also signs of a return to traditional themes and models in art, music, and architecture.[148]

Early in this century, the respected Iranian intellectual Taqizadeh declared, "We must Westernize ourselves, body and soul." By 1976, however, many Iranian intellectuals realized that Western technology had not produced human happiness. The psychic disorders prevalent in the West, the direct result of the psyche's being deprived of its basic relationship with the nonrational, or spiritual, had given Iranian thinkers pause. Both Marxists and so-called Massachusetts-trained technocrats were now seen by some as alien to Iranian society. In some quarters, all modernizers (keravati: literally, "those who wear a tie") were hated equally whether they were foreigners or Iranians. This is not to say that there was a call for a return to a stifling traditionalism, but rather the call was for a distinctively Iranian solution to the problems of the human condition. Six hundred years ago, the Iranian poet Hafez asserted that such a solution lay within the grasp of Iranians.[149] In 1976, Prime Minister Hoveyda echoed Hafez when he declared that it "is not by discarding our past that we mean to create our future."[150]

It seems that an appropriate motto for Iranian reformers might therefore be "Hasten slowly." "Introducing change through traditional institutions preserves the continuity in the culture and prevents large-scale social disintegration."[151] However, Iranians were not deterred by the risks involved in social development. As the Shahbanou (Empress) had said: "In Iran, while we are proudly committed to our rich heritage and traditions, we shall not hesitate to create an environment conducive to achieving the human aspects of our aspired goals. This may well entail a new set of values under which a greater balance will be achieved between the material and the spiritual needs of man."[152]

The single most important factor in social development in Iran during the Pahlavi era has been a psychological rather than a material one. The numb apathy of the past has gone. The problems continue to be great, but now there is the will—and, increasingly, the expertise—with which to solve them. "What Iran is seeking to accomplish holds great significance not only for Iran, but . . . for all the countries of the world."[153]

4

The Iranian Economy 1925-1975: Fifty Years of Economic Development

At the beginning of the nineteenth century Iran's economy stood at a level roughly comparable to that of her main neighbors, Turkey, Egypt, and India, but unlike them she did not participate in the general movement of progress that marked that century. For this there were several reasons. First, Iran's unfavorable location, lying off the main sea routes that carried the flow of merchandise, men, and ideas; matters were not greatly improved by the opening of Suez Canal which, while it enabled steamers to sail from Europe to the Persian Gulf, may have further diverted some trade from the land routes to the sea routes. Second, the country's physical structure, with a short and inhospitable coast on the Persian Gulf and huge mountain chains shutting off her fertile and productive areas from the open seas. Third, the weakness of her government, which was unable effectively to control the country and ensure law and order, much less carry out a policy of economic development. And even had it been stronger at home, the government's capacity to act would still have been severely restricted by the external constraints to which it was subjected: the capitulations, the commercial treaties which deprived it of fiscal autonomy, and the concessions it had granted to British, Russian, and other foreign companies. Last, there was the baleful influence of the Anglo-Russian rivalry, with each country strong enough to thwart any constructive schemes proposed by the other and both agreeing only on one point: that a weak and undeveloped Iran would best serve their interests.

As a result, at the outbreak of World War I Iran had practically no railways, only a few hundred kilometers of paved roads, and only one port, Enzeli (Pahlavi), that had undergone any improvement. Her handicrafts had declined, but no factory industry had risen to replace them; of the few plants that had been set up some had failed and the others were struggling hard to meet foreign competition. Her agriculture had remained almost untouched by modern developments. Her cities lacked almost all amenities. Her financial and fiscal institutions were archaic and rudimentary, and incapable of meeting the needs of the economy. And Iran had contracted a large foreign debt for which there was little positive to show.[1]

This feeble structure was further strained by the disruptions and hardships endured by Iran during World War I. The transport system deteriorated, crops failed in many areas, and the ensuing famines and epidemics took tens of thousands of lives. The shortage of goods, and the large expenditures by the Iranian government and the warring armies of Britain, Russia, and Turkey, sent up the price of staple foodstuffs and other commodities five to tenfold. The government had lost control over many parts of the country, its revenues had declined, and its finances were in utter disorder, to the point where it was unable to pay its officials and troops.

The Reign of Reza Shah, 1925-1941

When Reza Shah came to power, the economy of Iran was near collapse: World War I had imposed great strains on a very weak economic structure and brought it to its breaking point.

Table 4.1
IRAN, EGYPT, AND TURKEY, 1925:
SELECTED INDICATORS OF DEVELOPMENT

	IRAN	EGYPT	TURKEY
Population (millions)	(12.5)	14	13.1
Imports (millions of dollars)[a]	88	250	246
Railways (kilometers)	250	4,555	4,700
Automobiles[b]	4,450	17,740	7,500
Cement output (metric tons)	—	90,000[c]	59,000[c]
Refined sugar output (metric tons)	—	109,000[c]	5,000[c]
Students in schools	74,000	635,000	413,000

SOURCES: League of Nations, *International Statistical Yearbook, 1926* and *1927;* United Nations, *The Development of Manufacturing Industry in Egypt, Israel and Turkey; al-ihsa al-Sanawi; Istatistik Yilligi;* Overseas Consultants.

a. Exports are omitted, since both the inclusion and the exclusion of petroleum would be misleading.

b. 1926.

c. 1928.

Iran's lack of development at the beginning of Reza Shah's reign may be judged by comparing her with two other Middle Eastern countries with roughly equal populations and a similar historical and cultural background. Table 4.1 shows how far Iran stood behind Turkey, and still more Egypt.

To get the Iranian economy moving a "big push" was required, and Reza Shah provided this by abolishing the capitulations and commercial treaties, repealing or revising the concessions, and concentrating his efforts on the development of transport and industry, the reform of fiscal and financial institutions, and the control of foreign trade.[2] In this period the petroleum industry played only a marginal role, although both its output and the revenues it paid to the government increased severalfold; as late as 1937/38, oil revenues accounted for only 13 percent of total government receipts and almost all were spent on military equipment.*

In transport, there was much roadbuilding and by 1938 Iran's roads were officially stated to total 24,000 kilometers; of these, only 50 kilometers were asphalted but the total length of gravel roads had risen to 12,000 kilometers, compared to 2,400 at the beginning of the reign.[3] This rough but serviceable network carried a rapidly expanding volume of motor transport: between 1928 and 1937, consumption of motor fuel rose more than sevenfold, the average duration of a journey fell to about one-tenth of the prewar figure, and the cost of transport was cut by some three-quarters. An air service between the main cities was also started, in 1926, and expanded in the 1930s. And by 1935 telephone lines totaling over 10,000 kilometers connected the principal towns.

But the most ambitious transport project was the Trans-Iranian Railway, linking the Caspian port of Bandar Shah with the Persian Gulf port of Bandar Shahpur, a distance of 1,394 kilometers. Begun in 1927 it was opened to traffic in 1938, at a total cost of about $150 million. The extension of the line northward to Tabriz and eastward to Mashhad was interrupted by the invasion of Iran in 1941, after 853 of the 1,553 kilometers of line had been completed.

Private industry was encouraged by exemptions from customs duties and certain other taxes, by rebates and preferences, by credit supplied by the Agricultural and Industrial Bank founded in 1933, and by protective measures including tariffs, quotas, and exchange control. In addition the government set up and ran several plants in textiles, sugar refining, cement, and other industries, and a steel mill and iron foundry were under construction in 1941. By then, the cement, textile, food, drink, and tobacco industries met a large part of domestic consumption.

Agriculture received comparatively little help from the government. The

---

* Dates such as "1937/38" refer to the Iranian solar year, which begins with the spring equinox.

only major irrigation project, in Khuzistan, was rather unsuccessful and no major change was made in land tenure or organization. However, farmers did benefit from price support and credit, some agricultural research and extension was undertaken, and particular emphasis was put on industrial crops such as silk, sugar beets, tobacco, tea, and cotton, for which the necessary processing plants (for ginning, husking, drying, etc.) were built. Output of these crops rose sharply, and—although no reliable figures are available—it would seem that the production of grain kept up with the population growth.

The fiscal system was reorganized and modernized and, for the first time in Iran's history, the government exercised effective control over expenditure. The achievement of tariff autonomy in 1928 made it possible to raise duties for revenue and protection, and a further important source of revenue were the twenty-seven monopolies in tobacco, sugar, tea, and other goods. From 229 million rials in 1922 revenues rose to 400 million in 1931—converting a substantial deficit into a small surplus—and to 1,376 million in 1938 and 3,200 million in 1941. Defense absorbed much of expenditure, but its share fell from over 50 percent in the 1920s to 26 percent in 1939, while that of public works and social services rose steadily to 30 percent.

In the financial field, a law was passed in 1930 changing the basis of the currency from silver to gold, but the world crisis and the fall in the price of silver prevented its implementation. Instead Iran moved to a paper currency, issued by the Bank Melli, which had been founded in 1927 to perform some of the functions of a central bank and to which, in 1931, the note-issuing functions of the British-owned Imperial Bank were transferred. Other specialized banks were established by the government and total deposits in the banking system rose from 560 million rials in 1936 to 1,320 million in 1939 and 2,000 million by the middle of 1941.

A drastic change in the foreign trade system was the introduction of monopoly in 1931 and exchange control in 1936. Both were responses to the world crisis, which drove down the price of Iran's exports of primary products and saddled her with increasing import surpluses. They also served to raise revenue, protect Iranian industries, and strengthen the government's hands in dealing with the state-controlled trade of her two leading partners, the Soviet Union and Germany. But there is some evidence that this bilateral trade with its more powerful partners raised Iran's import prices and worsened her terms of trade.

In summing up the economic results of Reza Shah's reign, one is struck by both the magnitude of the effort and the results achieved. The effort may be judged by the investment of about $260 million in railways and another $260 million in industry—over half the latter coming from the private sector. These figures represent a very high investment ratio for an economy of the size and level of Iran. The results appear in table 4.2, which shows that, although still lagging far behind Egypt and Turkey, Iran had somewhat narrowed the gap.

Table 4.2
IRAN, EGYPT, AND TURKEY, 1938
SELECTED INDICATORS OF DEVELOPMENT

	IRAN	EGYPT	TURKEY
Population (millions)	15	16.4	17.1
Imports (millions of dollars)	55	184	119
Railways (kilometers)	1,700	5,606	7,324
Automobiles	(15,000)	33,700	11,300
Cement output (metric tons)	65,000	375,000	287,000
Refined sugar output (metric tons)	22,000	238,000	247,000
Cereal output (million metric tons)[a]	3.09	3.63	6.46
Cotton output (metric tons)[b]	34,000	400,000	52,000
Energy consumption[c]	1.55	2.05	2.18
Students in schools[d]	234,000	1,309,000	810,000

SOURCES: League of Nations, *International Statistical Yearbook, 1939/40;* United Nations, *Review of Economic Conditions in the Middle East, 1949-50; ibid., 1951-52; al-ihsa al-sanawi; Istatistik Yilligi.*
a. Wheat, barley, maize, rice—annual average, 1934-38.
b. Lint—annual average, 1934-38.
c. Million metric tons of coal equivalent.
d. 1936/37.

One last, important point should be noted: this development was carried out without any foreign financial assistance. Offers of foreign loans were turned down, for fear they might jeopardize the country's independence and, as noted before, oil revenues were allocated to military uses. The cost of the whole development program was met by taxes, mainly on consumption. Needless to say, in this as in all similar strenuous attempts to accelerate development, there was considerable waste and the cost to the consumer and taxpayer was high.

War and Oil Nationalization, 1941-1953

The presence in Iran of British, Soviet, and American troops from 1941 to 1946 had a deeply disruptive effect on her economy. The government lost control over the northern provinces and its revenues fell off sharply, causing large budgetary deficits. Huge amounts of money were spent by the Allied authorities and troops. At the same time, there were crop failures and, owing to the shortage of shipping, the quantum of imports decreased considerably. Prices therefore rose sharply, the cost-of-living index advancing from 100 in 1939 and 152 in 1941 to 756 in 1944—an increase well above that of the other Middle Eastern countries and India. Iran did, however, derive two benefits from the presence of foreign troops: her foreign exchange reserves rose by some $200 million and the carrying capacity of her railways, roads, and ports was greatly expanded, to facilitate the moving of 4 million tons of equipment to the Soviet Union.

In the postwar years, the main preoccupations were political, not economic: first the effort to end the Soviet occupation of the northern provinces, and then the movement that culminated in the nationalization of the petroleum industry in 1951, which in turn led to the virtual cessation of oil production. In 1949 the First National Development Plan, providing for a total expenditure

Table 4.3
IRAN, EGYPT, AND TURKEY, 1950
SELECTED INDICATORS OF DEVELOPMENT

	IRAN	EGYPT	TURKEY
Population (millions)	19.3	20.4	20.9
Imports (millions of dollars)	191	564	286
Railways (kilometers)	3,180	6,092	7,634
Automobiles	38,300	77,900	32,600
Cement output (metric tons)	54,000	1,022,000	396,000
Refined sugar output (metric tons)	69,000	218,000	186,000
Cereals output (million metric tons)[a]	3.09	3.72	6.74
Cotton output (metric tons)[b]	26,000	364,000	99,000
Electricity output (million kwh)[c]	200	642	676
Energy consumption[d]	4.51	4.42	5.40
Students in schools	743,000	1,597,000[e]	1,798,000

SOURCES: United Nations, *Review of Economic Conditions in the Middle East, 1949-50; ibid., 1951-52;* United Nations, *Statistical Yearbook,* 1951.

a.   Wheat, barley, maize, rice—annual average, 1947-51.
b.   Lint—annual average, 1947-51.
c.   1948.
d.   Million metric tons of coal equivalent.
e.   1949.

of 21,000 million rials ($656 million), was approved. This sum was to be covered by the allocation of all petroleum revenues, by hard-currency loans from the International Bank for Reconstruction and Development (IBRD), and by internal loans from Bank Melli. But, because of nationalization, oil revenues disappeared, the IBRD did not make any loans to Iran and, by the end of 1954, only 4,200 million rials had been actually spent on implementation. Private investment, in industry, agriculture, transport, and especially housing, continued but on a small scale.

Hence the amount of economic progress in this period was very limited. Agriculture benefited from some minor irrigation schemes and the introduction of machinery, fertilizers, pesticides, and selected seeds, but its output does not seem to have kept pace with population growth. Industry enjoyed a good deal of protection, partly caused by the foreign exchange shortage, and the capacity of some branches was considerably expanded. So was that of power and transport. But, as table 4.3 shows clearly, the gap between Iran on the one hand and Egypt and Turkey on the other, which had narrowed in the period 1925-38, once more widened.

Recovery and Imbalance, 1954-1962

The rapid rise of oil production and revenues in the period 1954-58 and the substantial aid provided by the United States led to a sharp recovery in Iran's economy. The investment ratio shot up and a high growth rate was achieved. But this advance was accompanied by severe inflationary pressures, which both pushed up the price indices and unbalanced Iran's foreign transactions, leading to a large drop in foreign exchange reserves. In addition, both oil revenues and foreign aid slowed down in 1959 and 1960. Iran was therefore forced to turn to the International Monetary Fund and to carry out a drastic deflationary policy, cutting down public expenditure, restricting credit, and reducing imports. This produced the desired effect: the rise in prices was slowed down and, for over a decade, stood at one of the lowest rates in the world; similarly, the large reduction in imports, together with a renewed increase in oil revenues, enabled Iran to surmount its foreign exchange difficulties. But, of course, the usual price of deflation was paid: according to official figures, GNP rose by only 2.4 percent in 1961/62 and by 2.5 percent in 1962/63; i.e., in both years it failed to keep pace with the population growth.

The White Revolution and the Upsurge, 1962-1971

During the period 1962-71 Iran benefited from a political stability and an interest in economic and social development on the part of the government that had no precedent in her modern history. Three landmarks stand out: the White Revolution of 1962/63; and the Third (1962/63-1967/68) and Fourth

(1968/69-1972/73) National Development Plans. The White Revolution removed or loosened many obstacles impeding Iran's development, by its land reform, social task forces such as the Health Corps, profit-sharing provisions in industry, and the measures taken to increase the participaton of women in the country's political, social, and economic activities. The plans channeled a huge amount of public development funds—204.6 billion rials ($2.73 billion) and 506.8 billion ($6.75 billion) respectively—into the various sectors of the

Table 4.4
IRAN, EGYPT, AND TURKEY, 1972:
SELECTED INDICATORS OF DEVELOPMENT

	IRAN	EGYPT	TURKEY
Population (millions)	31.2	34.8	37.0
Per capita GNP (dollars)	490	240	370
Per capita energy consumption[a]	954	324	564
Per capita steel consumption (kilograms)	59	30	55
Per capita textile consumption (kilograms)[b]	5.1	4.6	6.7
Per capita sugar consumption (kilograms)	28	16	20
Imports (million dollars)	2,410	899	1,508
Railways (kilometers)	4,944	5,500	8,133
Railway freight (million ton-kilometers)	3,693	2,976	6,641
Automobiles (thousands)	481	206	372
Cement output (thousand metric tons)	3,372	3,822	8,424
Refined sugar output (thousand metric tons)	598	550	811
Electricity output (million kwh)	9,100	8,030	11,242
Cereals output (million metric tons)[c]	7.7	6.7	17.1
Cotton output (thousand metric tons)[d]	209	495	536
Students in schools (thousands)[e]	4,820	5,708	6,720

SOURCES: United Nations, *Statistical Yearbook, 1974;* IBRD, *World Atlas, 1974; Statesman's Yearbook, 1974;* Food and Agricultural Organization, *Production Yearbook, 1974.*

a. Coal equivalent, kilograms.

b. 1971-72.

c. Wheat, barley, maize, and rice, annual average 1972-74.

d. Lint, annual average 1972-74.

e. 1971.

economy. In addition private enterprise, actively encouraged by the government, invested some two-thirds to three-quarters as much as the public sector during the two plans. The result was a real rate of growth in the period 1960-72 of over 9 percent per annum, a figure matched by a bare handful of countries. Both investment and growth will be studied in more detail below. At this point, perhaps the best way of showing how far Iran had advanced is once more to compare it with the two other major Middle Eastern countries (table 4.4). It will be seen that, on most counts, Iran stood ahead of both Egypt and Turkey, and in the last three years Iran has surged still more rapidly ahead.[4]

The Multiplication of Oil Revenues
and the Fifth Plan, 1972-1975

The Tripoli-Tehran agreements of 1970 and 1971 resulted in a sharp rise in oil revenues that was greatly accelerated by the quadrupling of oil prices at the end of 1973. Iran's oil revenues shot up from $1.1 billion in 1970 to $2.4 billion in 1972 and $17.4 billion in 1974.[5] They were estimated at $20 billion in 1975. Naturally, this huge influx caused an explosive growth in Iran's economy: in 1972/73 real gross national income grew by 13 percent, in 1973/74 by 34 percent, and in 1974/75 by 42 percent. Equally naturally, such rates of growth produced severe imbalances in the economy, in the shape of physical bottlenecks—manifested perhaps most clearly in the transport system and labor markets—and a sharp rise in prices; thus the cost-of-living index shot up by 11.2 percent in 1973/74, by 15.5 percent in 1974/75, and continued its rapid climb in 1975. Clearly, Iran is faced with an unmatched opportunity which, however, carries with it great difficulties and potential dangers. There is no precedent in the whole world's history for such rapid growth and no way of evaluating the strain it can put on the social fabric of the country experiencing it. The benefits are plain, the pitfalls less obvious but none the less real. Iran's response to this unique challenge will have consequences extending well beyond her borders.

THE TREND OF THE ECONOMY:
EMPLOYMENT AND INCOME

Iran's population has been growing rapidly, from 19.1 million in 1956 to 26.1 million in 1966 and an estimated 34 million in 1975. The rate of natural increase has been steadily rising, from about 2.5 percent per annum in the early 1950s to 3 percent in the late 1970s, when natural increase in rural areas was put at 3.5 percent and in urban at 2.4 percent. However, because of large-scale immigration from the countryside, the population of the towns was actually growing at about 4.4 percent a year, compared to 5.5 percent in the period 1956-66.[6] As a result, the share of the urban population in the total had risen from 31 percent in 1956 to 38 percent in 1966 and about 45 percent in 1975, and was expected to approach 60 percent by the end of the 1980s.

As in other developing countries, Iran's rapid demographic growth is due to a high birth rate accompanied by a sharply declining death rate. The crude

Table 4.5
EMPLOYED POPULATION (000)

	1956	1966	1972
Agriculture	3,326	3,774	3,800
Percent	56%	50%	43%
Industry			
Mining and manufacturing (incl. handicrafts)	816	1,324	1,820
Oil	25	26	40
Construction	336	520	710
Utilities	12	53	60
TOTAL	1,189	1,923	2,630
Percent	20%	25%	30%
Services			
Transport and communications	208	224	255
Commerce	355	513	650
Government	248	474	640
Other services	582	650	900
TOTAL	1,393	1,861	2,445
Percent	24%	25%	27%
Total fully or seasonally employed	5,908	7,558	8,875
Wholly unemployed	158	284	320
Total labor force	6,066	7,842	9,195

SOURCE: ILO, op. cit., p. 31.

death rate fell from 2.22 percent in 1956 to 1.78 in 1966 and an estimated 1.2 in 1975—1.5 in rural areas and 0.8 in urban. The birth rate has declined much less: from 4.85 to 4.65 and an estimated 4.2, the present rural rate being put at about 5.0 and the urban at 3.2. The last figure suggests that, with increasing urbanization, Iran's birth rate may fall; certainly, the government is promoting family planning.[7] However, all projections foresee a continued rapid growth in population, to about 36 million by 1977, 47 to 48 million by 1987, and some 60 million by the end of this century.[8] Even with 60 million inhabitants, Iran would have a lower density of population than most countries.

Labor Force

The combination of high birth rates and relatively low death rates has produced a very youthful population, 46 percent being under 15 years of age, 51 percent between 15 and 64, and only 3 percent 65 or over. The resulting high ratio of dependents to people of working age is a handicap that will be overcome only very gradually, as Iran's population slowly ages. The age structure, and the relatively restricted role of women in economic life, have kept the activity rate (ratio of economically active population aged 12 or over to total population) at the low level of 46 percent—77 percent for males and 14 percent for females; this is not expected to change significantly during the next few years since a rise in the school population and a consequent decline in the male activity rate should offset the anticipated rise in female activity brought about by increased literacy and urbanization, a higher age of marriage, and the general emancipation of women.[9] But although the activity rate is low, the absolute size of the labor force has been increasing fast because of the high population growth. Table 4.5 shows the breakdown of the labor force in the period 1956-72 and brings out the relative decline in agricultural employment and the very rapid growth of the industrial work force.

The table indicates that unemployment stood at the relatively low level of 3 percent (2 percent in rural areas and 6 percent in urban), but this figure is misleading. In Iran, as in other predominantly rural countries, underemployment rather than open unemployment is the main problem and there is no doubt that this has been—and, in spite of the large exodus from the countryside still remains—high in the villages.[10]

In spite of Iran's very rapid economic growth in the 1960s, employment seems, if anything, to have lagged behind the increase in the labor force of some 250,000 a year. There was an acute shortage of skilled workers, whose wages rose sharply, but unskilled labor remained overabundant and its wages low. This situation however changed markedly in the 1970s. By the end of 1972 the unemployment rate was reported as only 1.2 percent and the underemployment rate at 2.2 percent.[11] Perhaps more significant is the behavior of the index of wages of unskilled construction workers (1969/70 = 100), which by 1971/72 had risen to only 106.7 but shot up to 125.2 in 1972/73, 146.1 in 1973/74, and 192.5 in 1974/75.[12]

The Fifth Plan anticipated a serious labor shortage, since the number of new jobs created was put at 2,112,000 and the additional supply of labor at only 1,391,000. This shortage was expected at both the professional level (engineers, demand 36,000, supply 20,000; medical personnel, demand 44,000, supply 21,000; technicians, 117,000 and 75,000, etc.) and among skilled and semi-skilled workers.[13] To fill the gap efforts were being made to increase female employment and to upgrade the labor force through greatly expanded education and vocational training. Tens of thousands of Iranians were also being sent abroad, for advanced education and training, and tens of thousands of foreigners had been hired, from Europe, the United States, and Asia. But it seemed likely that labor markets would remain tight for many years to come.[14]

As regards sectoral distribution, the Fifth Plan foresaw a rise of only 130,000 jobs, or 6 percent of the total, in agriculture. The main increases were in industry and mining, with 846,000 jobs or 40 percent of the total; in construction, with 528,000 or 25 percent; and in services, with 552,000 or 26 percent. This expansion in urban activities, and the larger ones foreseen for the next two decades, were presumably going to be met by the natural increase of the town population and continued migration from the countryside. It need hardly be pointed out that the ensuing expansion of the cities, and particularly of Tehran, were about to pose the severe social problems that had been encountered in other countries.

Gross National Product

Iran's economic development since the early 1960s may be studied in terms of a simple model composed of three sectors: oil; the modern sector, consisting of manufacturing and services; and the traditional sector, agriculture.[15] The oil industry, which to an overwhelming degree produces for export, provides the capital needed for the growth of the other two sectors but—because of its very capital-intensive and advanced technological nature and the underdevelopment of the other sectors—does not receive a substantial flow of resources from them. To an increasing extent, oil has contributed both capital and foreign exchange, thus freeing Iran from the constraints that have impeded the development of so many countries.

The modern sector draws on the oil industry for capital and on the traditional sector for labor and raw materials, and sells much of its output to the traditional sector and an increasing proportion to itself. As it develops, it increasingly generates its own capital and begins to draw from the oil sector growing amounts of raw materials and energy. Eventually, as oil reserves are depleted and output declines, the once dominant oil sector will become integrated in, and subordinate to, the other two sectors, especially manufacturing.

The traditional sector both draws on the products of the other two (fuel, machinery, consumer goods, etc.) and supplies them with food and raw materials. At the same time, through migration to the towns, it supplies the modern sector with labor. Its relative importance is therefore bound to decline, but it is essential that its absolute output continue to grow, as it has a vital part to play in economic development. This can be done by modernizing agriculture and greatly raising the productivity of those farmers who remain on the land.

Before studying the sectoral composition of the gross national product (GNP) it is necessary to survey its overall growth. In current rials, GNP at market prices rose from 284 billion rials ($3.8 billion) in 1959/60 to 798 billion rials ($10.6 billion) in 1970/71, or by 181 percent, i.e. at a compound rate of just under 10 percent.[16] After that, mainly because of the huge increase in oil revenues but also owing to greater industrial and other activity, the rate of growth accelerated. GNP stood at 979 billion rials in 1971/72, 1,183 billion rials in 1972/73, 1,743 billion rials in 1973/74, and 2,975 billion rials ($44.4 billion) in 1974/75. In other words, GNP was multiplied 3.7 times.

Until the end of 1971 prices in Iran rose very little (see below) and the bulk of the increase in GNP represented real growth. In constant prices GNP rose between 1959/60 and 1970/71 by 143 percent, or at a compound rate of nearly 8.5 percent per annum; allowing for an annual population growth of nearly 3 percent, the rate of increase in real per capita income stood at 5.5 percent, a very high figure. In the period 1971/72-1974/75 real income rose by 188 percent, or at a compound rate of 30 percent per annum. This is, of course, an abnormal increase, caused mainly by the sharp rise in oil prices in 1973 and 1974 which raised real GNP by 34 percent in 1973/74 and 42 percent in 1974/75, and cannot serve as an indicator of future growth. The Fifth Plan (March 21, 1973—March 20, 1978) foresaw an annual real growth of 25.9 percent, raising GNP (in 1972/73 prices) from 1,165 billion rials to 3,686 billion rials and per capita income from 37,523 rials to 102,665 rials, i.e. from $556 to $1,521.[17] It is highly probable that, in the sixth and subsequent plans, per capita growth will have to proceed at a much slower rate—say 10 percent per annum. But, as pointed out later in this chapter, a per annum increase of 10 percent represents a rate of growth that is almost unmatched.

Table 4.6 shows the sectoral composition of GNP and brings out the changes that have occurred in it in the last fifteen years. The most striking feature of the table is the increase in the share of oil in gross domestic product

(GDP), at first relatively slowly, from 11 percent in 1959/60 to 19 percent in 1971/72, and then very rapidly, to 51 percent in 1974/75. Leaving aside this drastic shift, which was peculiar to Iran and the other oil-producing countries, table 4.6 shows the usual structural transformation accompanying economic development: the slow growth and relative decline of agriculture and the rapid growth, in both absolute and relative terms, of industry and, to a lesser extent, the services. Taking the nonoil sector alone, agriculture accounted for 36 percent in 1959/60 and 19 percent in 1974/75, industry for 19 percent and 29 percent, and services for 45 percent and 52 percent.

Table 4.6
GNP by Main Economic Groups, at Current Prices
(Billion Rials, at Factor Cost)

	1959/60	1962/63	1968/69	1971/72	1974/75
Agriculture[a]	85	97	140	172	305
Industry[b]	45	58	130	205	464
Services[c]	108	130	243	375	826
Non-oil sector	238	285	513	752	1,595
Oil[d]	28	38	83	180	1,635
Gross domestic product	266	323	596	933	3,229
Net factor income from abroad[e]	-0.4	-3	-12	-19	-300
GNP	266	320	584	914	2,929
Indirect taxes	18	20	46	65	45
GNP at market prices	284	340	629	979	2,975

Source: Bank Markazi, op. cit.

a.   Includes farming, animal husbandry, forestry, fishing, and hunting.
b.   Includes manufacturing, mining, construction, water, and electricity.
c.   Includes transport, communications, banking, insurance, brokerage, domestic trade, house rents, private and public services.
d.   Includes income accruing to Iranian factors of production (value added in national oil).
e.   Excludes oil.

Another way of studying the relative changes in the various sectors is to calculate their average annual rate of growth in constant prices. For the period 1960/61-1971/72, which stops short of the sharp rise in oil prices and represents a "normal period" during which real GDP grew at 9.2 percent and real GNP grew at 8.8 percent per annum, the main branches rose as follows: agriculture at 3.2 percent per annum; oil at 13.8 percent; manufacturing and mining at 11.8 percent; construction at 7.8 percent; banking, insurance and brokerage at 16.6 percent; government services at 12.6 percent; and private services at 9.5 percent. Looking at it from another viewpoint, of the average annual increase of 9.2 percent in GDP, just under three-fifths (5.4 percentage points) came from the production of goods and just over two-fifths (3.8 points) from services—a happy contrast to most developing countries where the services sector has grown more rapidly than the goods sector. In the services sector the fastest growing branch was government, with an average annual contribution of 1.6 percentage points; this may be attributed to high and rising defense costs, growing bureaucracy (the number of government officials rose from 248,000 in 1956 to 474,000 in 1966 and 640,000 in 1972) and increasing expenditure on education, health, and welfare. In the goods sector, the bulk of the increase came from industry, with 2.4 points, followed by oil with 2.2 points; agriculture made the very small contribution of 0.8 percentage points to the total growth.

Table 4.7
GNP BY FINAL USE
(BILLION RIALS, AT MARKET PRICES)

	1959/60	1962/63	1968/69	1971/72	1974/75
Private consumption	209	252	423	572	1,128
Government consumption	30	35	101	189	586
Gross domestic fixed capital formation	53	47	137	216	559
Net export of goods and services	12	34	28	118 ⎫	702
Net factor income from abroad	-20	-29	-59	-116 ⎭	
Gross national expenditure = GNP	284	340	629	979	2,975

SOURCE: Bank Markazi, op. cit.

The final uses to which GNP has been put are shown in table 4.7. Over the period 1959/60-1971/72 preceding the sharp rise in oil prices, private consumption accounted for 65.8 percent of the total, government consumption for 14.6 percent, and gross domestic fixed capital formation for 20.0 percent. Net export of goods and services, at 10.4 percent, fell just short of net payments to factors abroad, 10.8 percent; this means, first, that the Iranian economy was practically self-sustaining, drawing on foreign resources for the insignificant fraction of 0.4 percent of GNP; and secondly, that national savings covered nine-tenths of the high rate of gross domestic investment of 20 percent. There were, however, some important shifts during that period. Capital formation increased markedly, from an average of 17.1 percent in the period 1960/61-1962/63 to 21.7 percent in the period 1968/69-1971/72 and consumption declined correspondingly, since Iran's drawing on foreign resources showed no significant change. A further breakdown indicates that the share of private consumption declined appreciably, from 72.8 to 65.8 percent, while that of government consumption rose rapidly from 10.3 to 14.6 percent. But although there was a relative decline in private consumption, it registered a large absolute increase—at an average annual rate of 6.6 percent, in real terms, over the whole period. This took place at both the mass level, as indicated by the consumption of such staples as sugar, textiles, shoes, radios, and bicycles, and in the form of luxury consumption. Two sets of figures illustrate the trends: between 1963 and 1972 Iran's consumption of sugar rose from 413,000 to 870,000 tons and the number of registered passenger vehicles from 108,000 to 394,000.

The trend in Iran's balance of payments may be briefly reviewed at this point. In the 1950s United States aid played a crucial part in meeting Iran's foreign exchange needs, but by the 1960s this had tapered off and been replaced by oil revenues. By and large, the value of merchandise exports, of which oil (subsequently supplemented by gas) constituted three-quarters or over, more than covered the cost of merchandise imports. But the remittance abroad of the profits of the oil companies operating in Iran and of the interest on government debt, as well as other invisible items, resulted in a fairly large overall deficit on current account. This, however, was more than made up by the influx of new capital, and until 1972 Iran drew on foreign resources.

The sharp rise in oil prices in recent years drastically changed this situation. In both 1973/74 and 1974/75 the value of exports greatly exceeded that of imports and other payments—by $8.2 billion in the latter year. Table 4.7 shows that in 1974/75 the surplus in the balance of payments amounted to nearly a quarter of GNP, a ratio that had hitherto been recorded only in very small countries with a large oil production and a strictly limited domestic market, like Kuwait or Libya. Iran has used this surplus to repay its foreign debts, increase its foreign exchange reserves, provide aid to several countries, and invest large sums abroad. (Probable developments in the balance of payments are discussed at the end of this chapter.)

Lastly there is the question of the distribution of national income. In Iran, as in practically all countries that have experienced fairly rapid development—whether under a capitalist or a socialist system—the rise in average income has been accompanied by an increase in income inequality. This is clearly shown by a study based on the surveys of household expenditure periodically carried out by the Central Bank and the Statistical Center of Iran.[18] According to the center, between 1959/60 and 1970/71 the Gini coefficient (an index commonly used to measure inequality) rose from 0.4188 to 0.4545, indicating an increase in inequality; this is confirmed by the fact that the share of the top 20 percent of households rose from 50 to 52 percent of total expenditure, while that of the bottom 40 percent fell from 17 to 14 percent. However, the period 1970/71 to 1972/73 saw a reversal of this trend, the Gini coefficient falling to 0.4228 and the share of the top 20 percent to 49 percent of the total, while that of the bottom 20 percent rose to 15. In 1972/73 the top 10 percent accounted for 34 percent of total expenditure and the bottom 10 percent for only 2 percent and, since the figures did not cover savings, the spread of incomes must have been even wider. It should be added that this distribution is roughly similar to that prevailing in the great majority of developing countries for which data are available. It should also be added that Iran's middle class is growing very rapidly.

The Statistical Center's study shows that in rural areas incomes are somewhat less unequally distributed than in urban areas. This is explained partly by the equalizing effects of the land reform and partly by the fact that in the modern sectors of the urban economy (oil, banking, large factories) incomes are closely aligned on those of the advanced parts of the world while in the traditional sectors (handicraftsmen, petty traders, unskilled workers) they are closer to those prevailing in agriculture. Money incomes are far higher in the towns, and especially in the capital, than in the country, and so are real incomes when adjustments have been made for differences in the cost of living. This is shown by the distribution of consumption expenditure: in 1971/72 Tehran, with a little over 10 percent of Iran's population, accounted for 33 percent of total expenditure and other urban areas, with slightly under one-third of the population, for 36 percent, while rural areas with almost 60 percent of the population had only 32 percent of the total. Moreover the differential between town and country seems to be widening. Between 1959/60 and 1971/72 consumption, at constant prices, rose by 206 percent in Tehran, 152 percent in large cities, 101 percent in small towns, and 45 percent in rural areas.[19] Urban per capita consumption, which in the period 1959/61 was twice as high as rural, by the period 1971/73 was over three times as high.[20]

Lastly, there is the question of inequality between the more prosperous northern regions and the poorer southern ones. In 1971/72 average monthly household expenditure in East Azarbayjan was 8,711 rials and in Gilan 8,329, but in Kerman only 3,845 rials and in Sistan and Baluchistan 5,012 rials.[21] No data are available to show whether the gap between the regions is growing, but the experience of other countries suggests that this too is a normal feature of development.

It is clear that inequality of incomes is one of the most serious problems facing Iran, and it will be discussed further at the end of this chapter.

AGRICULTURE

In Iran, as in the vast majority of developing countries, agriculture has been the most sluggish sector of the economy—only here its rate of growth looks even lower when contrasted with the very rapid progress of the other branches. Officially, the average annual rate of growth during the Fourth Plan was put at 4 percent.[22] However—again as in other developing countries—agricultural statistics are unreliable, and both lower and higher figures have been given. Nevertheless, it can be stated with some confidence that, from the early 1960s onwards, Iran's agricultural output kept somewhat ahead of the population growth—a performance better than that of most developing countries—but that it fell far short of meeting the huge increase in demand for food and raw materials on the part of the booming economy. Hence, Iran has been importing rapidly growing amounts of foodstuffs, and is likely to import far more in the future.

Unlike the governments of most developing countries, the Iranian one has for at least twenty years been fully aware of the vital importance of agriculture, and has sought to promote it in many ways. The most important single measure has undoubtedly been the Land Reform Law of 1962, discussed in chapter 7, which has completely transformed the land tenure system. Whereas the bulk of the land was previously held by a small number of landlords, by 1975 only 12 percent of the farm area (19 percent of irrigated and 8 percent of dry-farmed land) was in properties of over 100 hectares. Another 50 percent of land (39 and 57 percent, respectively) was in medium farms of 10 to 100 hectares, owned by some 400,000 families, and the remaining 38 percent (43 and 35 percent) was in some 2,500,000 small farms of under 10 hectares.[23] It was in the hope of increasing output, and more particularly the marketable surplus, that the government had experimented with other forms of organization: production cooperatives, farm corporations—in which individual farmers in a village transfer their holdings to a corporation in return for shares—and highly capitalized agribusinesses. It was still too early in 1976 to judge the success of these various forms of production, but their scope was to be extended under the Fifth Plan.

In addition to fundamentally altering the tenurial system, the government has done much to improve the organizational framework within which agriculture operates. Thousands of miles of feeder roads have been built and thousands more improved (see below), and for the first time in their history most Iranian villages have been put within reach of wider markets. Some modern storage has been provided, to eliminate the huge crop losses that have been a feature of Iranian agriculture, as of Middle Eastern agriculture in general. In 1972, silo capacity aggregated 392,000 tons and this was to rise to 900,000 in 1978; however, even the latter figure would still fall far short of needs and a more distant objective was 2 million tons. In addition, temporary storage, cold storage, and warehouses were to be built.[24] The number of credit cooperatives increased very rapidly after the 1962 land reform and was then reduced by consolidation to 2,800 in March 1975; membership had steadily risen to 2.5 million, thus covering the enormous majority of the farm population. Loans by the Agricultural Cooperative Bank of Iran multiplied many times, to reach 31.1 billion rials ($464 million) in 1974/75.[25] Thus, for the first time, Iranian farmers were obtaining the greater part of their needs through institutional credit sources, rather than from moneylenders or landlords.

Action on the technical front had also been far-reaching and the capital inputs of Iranian agriculture—water, fertilizers, improved seeds, pesticides, machinery and modern implements—had greatly increased.

Shortage of water has always been the main constraint on Iranian agriculture and substantial irrigation works have been carried out for at least three thousand years. In the years 1957/58 to 1966/67, twelve major dams were begun and had come into operation by 1972; their utilizable storage capacity is 7.8 million cubic meters, they generate some 3 billion kilowatt-hours of electricity a year, and have made it theoretically possible to expand the irrigated area by 290,000 hectares and to improve another 336,000.[26] In addition much irrigation was provided by means of deep wells and *qanats*. However, far from full use has been made of the water stored in the dams, owing to inadequate systems of distribution, and it is estimated that whereas under the Third Plan an additional 145,000 hectares were put under irrigation and another 240,000 provided with improved facilities—figures above, and close to target, respectively—in the Fourth Plan only 130,000 hectares were put under irrigation (or one-third of target) and only 74,000 were improved, or one-seventh of target. In 1972, the total irrigated area was about 3.6 million hectares compared to 2.8 million in 1960.[27] The Fifth Plan aimed at raising this to 4 million. Another 500,000 hectares may be brought under irrigation during the Sixth Plan, ending in 1983. In the meantime, successful experiments have been made with "drip irrigation," from pipes laid out in orchards and vegetable fields. This method, which saves some 25 to 30 percent of water, was in 1975 used on some 2,000 hectares, and was to be extended to another 2,000 in 1976.[28]

Along with irrigation, fertilizers are essential for Iran's agricultural progress and here the expansion has been spectacular. As late as 1956, total consumption of chemical fertilizers was only 2,000 tons and even by 1962 it was only 47,000. The vast increase in local production after 1963, and much higher imports, raised total consumption to 225,000 tons in 1970 and 615,000 in 1974, of which more than two-thirds were domestically produced; the forecast for 1975 was 850,000 and for 1976 about 1,000,000 tons, making of Iran one of the three main users of chemical fertilizers in the Middle East. In 1975, about one-half of total local production of fertilizer was being applied to wheat, one-fifth to rice, and one-seventh to cotton.[29]

Thanks to her natural resources and developed petrochemical industry, Iran now produces several basic fertilizers at prices far below the landed cost of imports; thus for urea and ammonium sulphate the ratio was under one-third. Prices charged to farmers for both local and foreign fertilizers have, so far, been well below domestic costs, and represent a heavy subsidy. This is surely justified if the official estimate is at all accurate: that whereas in 1974 the total cost of fertilizers used was 12 billion rials, the increment in agricultural output attributable to them was 33 billion, or six times the amount of subsidy.[30]

Starting with the Fourth Plan, an intensive effort has been made to supply selected seeds, mainly in wheat and rice. Both imported varieties, such as the Mexican "miracle wheat," and improved local strains have been used. By 1975, nearly 700,000 hectares of wheat and 100,000 hectares of rice had been planted to selected seeds.[31] Quite rightly in a country with as much rural underemployment as Iran, less stress has been put on mechanization, and the number of tractors rose only from 4,500 in 1960 to 22,000 in 1972.[32] However, attempts have been made to supply improved agricultural tools.

That all these programs and inputs have had an effect on agricultural yields and output is undeniable, and over the last fifteen years, some crops, such as beets, sugarcane, cotton, and rice, have registered a large expansion. But the unreliability of most agricultural statistics, and the fact that rainfall fluctuations are still the most important determinant of production, make it very difficult to reach any overall quantitative results. Table 4.8 presents recent figures on the main crops, along with the target for the end of the Fifth Plan.

Food consumption in Iran has been insufficient in quantity—the estimated daily intake of 2,300 calories per capita being still below physiological requirements—and inadequate in quality.[33] However, it accounts for nearly one-half of rural family expenditure and three-sevenths of urban, and because of a high-income elasticity of demand, food consumption per capita is increasing rapidly with rising incomes. Until very recently, Iran was almost self-sufficient in practically all basic foodstuffs, and the cost of production of many staples—notably wheat, barley, sugar, fruits and vegetables, cotton and

Table 4.8
OUTPUT OF MAIN CROPS (000 TONS)

CROPS	AVERAGE 1968/9-1972/3	1972/3	1973/4	1974/5	TARGET FOR 1977/78
Wheat	4,201	4,546	4,600	4,700	5,640
Rice	1,061	1,200	1,334	1,313	1,400
Barley	1,058	1,009	923	863	1,154
Sugar beets	3,733	3,918	4,240	4,300	5,610
Sugar cane	559	700	1,050	1,100	2,000
Oilseeds	40	54	57	79	160
Cotton (unginned)	525	600	615	715	615
Tobacco	19	24	15	14	25
Tea	77	88	93	96	91

SOURCE: Vizarati Kashavurzi va Manabii Tabii, "Baravard Mizani Tavlidi va Rushdi Mahsulati Kashavurzi dar Sal 1353" (Aban: 1354).

some varieties of meat—compared favorably with the landed price of imports. This relation is, however, rapidly changing as greater demand and higher wages and other costs drive up the price of Iranian produce; indeed there are signs that such a traditional export item as cotton is losing ground in foreign markets.[34] Hence in 1974/75 food and agricultural imports rose to almost 100 billion rials ($1,500 million) and were estimated to increase almost threefold (in constant prices) by the mid-1980s, unless efforts were made to increase Iran's production and concentrate on the mix best suited to her resources. In the late 1970s, two constraints were evident. First, Iran's pastures were judged adequate for only half the then size of herds, hence the low yields and high cost of red meat products; this called for both improvement of ranges and herds and drastic reduction of numbers. Second, even if all of Iran's estimated 120,000 million cubic meters of available water were used (85 to 90 million surface and 30,000 million groundwater) and her 5.5 million hectares of irrigable land fully cropped—providing over four-fifths of agricultural production—an attempt had to be made to concentrate on products that provide most calories and proteins per cubic meter of water.

Various studies show that this may be best attained by reducing local production of red meats. It has been calculated that by 1992 Iran could be self-sufficient, or slightly more than self-sufficient, in such essential and highly nutritive crops as wheat, rice, pulses, vegetables, poultry, and eggs; that it would have a small deficit in oil and oilseeds, sugar, fruit, and cotton; and that it would cover only about one-third of its needs of red meat and milk.[35] Such a product mix would provide a daily calorie intake of 2,700-2,800, which is well above physiological requirements, and at the same time assure self-sufficiency in the basic foodstuffs in which no nation can afford to be too dependent on outside sources.

Given reasonable progress and the necessary adaptations, Iranian agriculture can provide the country with an adequate food supply to meet its growing needs. It is however doubtful whether it can ensure to the farmer an income that can be regarded as adequate when compared to that of the urban sector. All projections of the value of Iranian agricultural output agree that, although the real income of farmers will rise very considerably over the next two decades, it will do so at a rate that falls far below that of the growth in such sectors as manufacturing, transport, commerce, finance, and services. Hence the gap between rural and urban incomes may be expected to widen greatly. Two developments could reverse this trend and narrow the gap. First, a rise in the price of foodstuffs and agricultural materials relative to that of manufactured goods; this is desirable since the price of such produce has been kept artificially low but, beyond a certain point, it does not represent a real solution. Second, a sharp decline in farm population, mainly through accelerated migration to the cities; but this too raises grave social problems. It is therefore essential that means be sought to raise rural incomes through nonagricultural activities, e.g. by locating more large-scale industries in the countryside and by promoting small-scale industries, handicrafts, and services like tourism in villages, and it is encouraging that attempts are being made in this direction. This, together with the provision of many more social services by the government, could help to keep the economic progress of the villages more in line with that of the rest of the country.

INDUSTRY

As in other developing countries manufacturing and mining, in sharp contrast with agriculture, have grown much faster than GNP. But in Iran the rate of industrial growth after 1960 has been of a magnitude almost unmatched in history. During the Third Plan period the value added in industry increased at a rate of 12.7 percent per annum, as against a planned growth of 10 percent, and during the Fourth Plan at 15.2 percent, against 12.8 percent.[36] As of mid-1976, performance had met expectations in the Fifth Plan: gross industrial output was planned to rise from 509 billion rials ($7.6 billion) in 1972/73 to 1,130 billion ($16.9 billion) in 1977/78, or at an annual average of

Table 4.9
OUTPUT OF SOME LEADING INDUSTRIES

UNIT	1338 1959/60	1344 1965/66	1349 1970/71	1350 1971/72	1351 1972/73	1352 1973/74	1353 1974/75
Sugar (000 tons)	147	225	567	581	579	514	527
Beer (million liters)	6	13	26	30	32	39	43
Biscuits (000 tons)	2	14	24	26	24	20	28
Vegetable oils (000 tons)	33	101	167	185	194	183	242
Cigarettes (billion)	7.4	9.7	12.3	12.7	13.1	13.4	14.4
Cement (000 tons)	679	1,417	2,415	2,820	3,392	3,300	4,300
Window glass (000 tons)	—	—	22	30	49	87	79
Cotton and synthetic cloth (million meters)	169	350	450	450	465	483	533
Steel and aluminum— sheets and shapes (000 tons)	—	29	124	183	246	246	275
Writing paper (000 tons)	—	—	9	17	26	31	36
Paints (000 tons)	1	7	20	24	26	22	33
Urea (000 tons)	—	—	56	115	179	201	201
Fertilizers (000 tons)	—	27	79	196	322	408	414
DDB (000 tons)	—	—	4	10	10	8	9
PVC (000 tons)	—	—	11	11	17	18	19
Tractors (000 units)	—	0.1	2.5	3.8	4.5	7.1	7.7
Passenger cars (000 units)	—	2	30	39	49	50	71
Trucks & buses (000 units)	1	5	14	15	21	28	38
Television sets (000 units)	—	12	13	15	19	22	31
Telephones (000 units)	—	—	60	91	66	113	186
Gas ovens (000 units)	—	87	190	177	209	190	220
Water heaters (000 units)	13	23	44	56	61	61	82
Electricity (billion kwh)	0.4	3.1	6.8	8.1	9.6	12.1	14.0
Coal (000 tons)	237	285	530	600	550	845	900
Iron ore (000 tons)	58	2	10	150	800	895	900
Lead (000 tons)	131	82	200	210	220	. .	. .
Chromite (000 tons)	66	241	180	180	180	. .	. .

SOURCE: Ministry of Industry, Department of Statistics.

17 percent, and value added from 164 billion rials ($2.4 billion) to 408 billion rials ($6.1 billion), or at 20 percent per annum.[37] In fact, value added increased by 18 percent in 1973/74 and by 22 percent in 1974/75.[38]

This rapid growth has, naturally, been accompanied by a marked change in the composition of Iranian industry. Like that of other countries, it was, for a long time, dominated by the three groups that minister to man's basic needs of food, clothing, and shelter: food and drink, textiles and wearing apparel, and nonmetallic minerals, i.e., mainly building materials. In 1962, these three groups accounted for no less than 73.6 percent of industrial output, but with the growth of new industries this figure had fallen to 64.9 percent by 1973. Conversely, the share of capital-intensive and technologically advanced industries, which become dominant only in the later stages of industrialization, rose sharply: chemicals from 4.6 to 6.2 percent, basic metals from 0.8 to 4.9 percent, machinery from 0.6 to 5.8 percent, and motor vehicles from 4.4 (a misleadingly high figure, accounted for largely by repair work) to 7.6 percent. Table 4.9, in which industries have been divided into broad groups, shows both the general increase and the much faster growth of the chemical, metal, mechanical, and electrical branches.

This structural change was accompanied by another that may be described as a gradual shift from import substitution to export promotion, and backward integration from assembly to production, with the aim of passing on to design and development technology. All Iranian industries were set up to replace imports and survived only thanks to very high protection. Again, all but the simplest industries relied heavily on imports of intermediate products and many were little more than assembly plants for foreign components. In the mid-1970s, these conditions still prevailed in many industries, but others had become competitive and several were exporting their products. Moreover, most industries were by then getting the bulk of their inputs from local sources. An example was provided by the automobile industry. In 1975, 65 percent of the value was locally produced and it was hoped to raise this figure to between 80 and 85 within a few years. Cars and buses were being exported to fifteen countries, including several in Eastern Europe, and plans called for the production of one million passenger cars and over one hundred thousand trucks and buses by the early 1980s, of which a quarter were for export. Moreover work was proceeding on designs for cheap cars, suited to the rough roads and exacting climate of developing countries.

More generally, Iran was aiming at large-scale export of industrial products based on its natural resources. Its huge gas reserves—believed to be the third largest in the world—provide the raw materials for fertilizers and various petrochemicals; a constant effort is being made to increase the value added per unit of raw material. Gas and other forms of cheap power—to include, eventually, atomic—have also given rise to energy-intensive industries such as aluminum, copper, and steel, which are exporting or are expected to do so soon.[39] The electronics industry is receiving special attention, for economic and military reasons, and it is hoped to export some of its simpler products such as television sets and telephone equipment. Thus whereas such countries as Japan, India, and Brazil began by exporting very simple manufactured goods and only gradually moved to more complex ones, in Iran the process may be compressed into one decade.

The great increase in industrial production was made possible by much greater inputs of labor and capital. Employment in manufacturing rose from 816,000 in 1956 and 1,298,000 in 1966 to 1,543,000 in 1970 and 2,013,000 in 1974.[40] The proportional increase in factory employment must have been far greater since the number working in modern industry, including oil, was little over 100,000 in 1956 and some 200,000 in 1966 whereas by the mid-1970s it may have been over 400,000. The quality of the labor force also rose markedly, because of the spread of education, vocational training in schools and on the job, and improved health, nutrition, and living conditions of workers. So did that of the managerial sector, which had absorbed thousands of graduates of foreign universities and of such Iranian institutions as the Industrial Management Institute and the Iran Center for Management Studies. Thanks to these factors, and above all to the very high rate of capital investment, per capita output, in *constant* prices, in selected manufacturing industries rose by 53 percent between 1969/70 and 1974/75, i.e. by 9 percent per annum, while per capita wages and fringe benefits rose by 108 percent in *current* prices, or, dividing by the cost of living index, by some 43 percent in real terms, i.e. by 7.5 percent per annum.[41]

Capital investment in manufacturing and mining has been massive and accelerating. During the Third Plan 65 billion rials were invested (34.5 billion rials by the government and 30.5 billion rials by the private sector) and during the Fourth Plan 300 billion rials (116.4 rials and 183.6 billion rials, respectively). The Fifth Plan provided for a fixed capital formation of 780 billion rials in manufacturing (277 billion rials public and 503 billion rials private) and 66.5 billion rials (61.8 billion rials public and 4.7 billion rials private) in mining; a further amount of 624 billion rials (536 billion rials public and 88 billion rials private) was allocated to oil, 168 billion (120 billion rials public and 48 billion rials private) to gas, and 311 billion (all public) to electricity.[42] The result was to raise the capital stock of manufacturing and mining from some 120 to 140 billion rials (in 1972/73 constant prices) in 1964/65 to some 400 to 420 billion rials in 1973/74, or about threefold.[43]

This breakdown of investment brings out a very important characteristic of Iran's industrial development, the happy mix of public and private enterprise. Unlike the governments of so many developing countries, the Iranian one quickly realized that it had neither the capital nor the administrative and managerial skills to undertake more than a limited amount of industrial development, and left the rest to the private sector, which it sought to regulate, guide, and encourage. The latter responded at first cautiously, then with increasing boldness, as the advantages of industrial investment compared to such traditional outlets as moneylending, commerce, or agriculture (temporarily discouraged by the land reform) became evident. By now it has produced a breed of captains of industry to whom, in the words of perhaps the most knowledgeable authority on the subject, the following description of the Englishmen who started the Industrial Revolution applies: "They were self-made, half-educated, vigorous, bullying, irrepressible men of ambition, always pushing, always grasping, edging ever more insistently into a society dominated till then by men of gentler breeding."[44] The enterprise of this new bourgeoisie may be judged by the scope of some of its ventures. The government has reserved to itself such industries as oil, steel, and copper smeltpng, and has set up huge plants like the steel mill in Isfahan, the Shahpur petrochemical plant, the machine-tool factory in Arak, the tractor factory in Tabriz, and the aluminum smelter near Ahwaz—all of them, incidentally, built with the help of United States or Soviet capital. But these factories are matched by some of the privately owned giants: the Shahriar metal plants in Ahwaz, the man-made fiber factory (in partnership with Du Pont) in Isfahan, the Karun paper plant, the automobile plants, the Karun sugar company, and others.[45]

Unlike the English and American pioneers of industrialization, however, the Iranian ones have received an enormous amount of help and guidance from their government, through licensing, trade policy, taxation, and credit.

Licensing has been used to direct private investment to the industries regarded as most desirable (first consumer goods and then intermediate and capital goods) and to the provinces rather than Tehran, in order to secure economies of scale by preventing the proliferation of an excessive number of small plants, and for ensuring a certain degree of competition.[46] It should be noted that a license entitles the holder to receive "water, electricity, etc., at advantageous industrial rates as well as financing from industrial development banks."[47]

Trade policy has been used to provide protection through tariffs and other duties and quotas and to promote exports. Tax rebates or exemptions have encouraged industrial investment and given it an inducement to move away from Tehran; they have also increased the attraction of Iran's rapidly expanding economy for foreign investment, and by 1975 some "193 joint-ventures had been set up with firms from 18 countries."[48]

Lastly, the government has been lavish in its supply of credit to private industry, establishing several specialized banks for this purpose: the Industrial Credit Bank in 1957, the Industrial and Mining Development Bank of Iran

(IMDBI) in 1959, the Industrial Guarantee Fund to help small-scale industries, and, in 1973, the Development and Investment Bank of Iran. The investments and loans made by these banks run into billions of dollars, and additional billions have been advanced to industry, in the form of working capital, by Bank Melli and the commercial banks. In 1974/75 the IMDBI alone made loans of 19.5 billion rials ($291 million) and investments of 3.3 billion rials ($49 million); for the period March 1959—March 1975 the figures were 61.1 billion rials (about $873 million) and 8.1 billion rials (about $116 million).[49] These advances have stimulated a huge and rapidly increasing private investment. Thus whereas until around 1970 the IMDBI's assistance represented nearly one-half of the total cost of the projects launched with its help, in the following five years this ratio fell rapidly, to less than a quarter in 1973/74 and 1974/75.[50] It may therefore be said that the government has succeeded in one of its principal objectives: to produce a vigorous and resilient private sector that can carry the main burden of industrialization.

In addition, presumably because of its confidence in the strength of industry, the government has felt it safe to embark on a far-reaching social experiment and reform by seeking to diffuse the ownership of industrial capital, which up to now has been heavily concentrated in a few family groups. A few years ago, businessmen were advised to divest themselves of between 33 and 49 percent of their shares, first to their own workers and then to the public at large, and by the beginning of 1975 some thirty-nine companies were implementing such a program. At this point a law was passed on this subject and plans were made for 320 large companies to distribute 49 percent of their shares within three years, and for the government to sell to the public 99 percent of its holdings in certain industries. This program, if successfully implemented, was expected to do much to ensure a wider distribution of share capital, a fairer distribution of income, and more harmonious relations in Iran's industry.

TRANSPORT

In a land as vast and rugged as Iran, with her shortage of internal waterways and with her population scattered in over 60,000 towns and villages, inadequate transport constitutes an even more serious obstacle to economic development than in most countries. It was only under Reza Shah that a serious attempt was made to provide Iran with railways and roads and not until the last fifteen years or so that the effort deployed in this field became commensurate with the country's needs. Between the middle of 1955 and the end of 1958 a total of 12.8 billion rials ($171 million) was spent by the government on transport and communications, or 35 percent of its total development expenditure. In the Second Plan, which extended from 1959 to mid-1962, and the Third Plan, transport and communications again received the largest allocation, with 17.5 billion rials ($233 million) and 53.8 billion rials ($717 million), or 18 percent and 26 percent of the total, respectively.[51] In the Fourth Plan the share of transport and communications was reduced to 21 percent of total allocations, but expenditure on those branches continued its steep rise, to 100.3 billion rials ($1,337 million).

The results of this massive investment appear clearly in table 4.10, which shows the great increase in the capacity and utilization of the transport system. By 1972 Iran's transport system had become more or less adequate for the country's needs. The railway system inherited from Reza Shah's reign and expanded and extended during World War II had been greatly developed and improved. In the northeast, the Tehran-Mashhad line was completed and opened in April 1957 and a branch from Bandar Shah to Gorgan was opened in October 1960. In the northwest, the Tehran-Tabriz railway was opened in April 1958 and a branch from Sharaf Khaneh to the Turkish border in

Table 4.10
TRANSPORT

	1328 (1949/50)	1338 (1959/60)	1348 (1969/70)	1352 (1973/74)	1353 (1974/75)
Railway track (kms)	2,561	3,539	3,966	4,519	. .
Railway freight (million ton-kilometers)	756	2,327	2,585	4,874	. .
Road network (thousand kms)	. .	25[a]	41	50	55
Automobiles (thousand)	16	80	267	469	. .
Trucks (thousand)	14	32	40	72	. .
Freight unloaded at ports (thousand tons)	742	1,301	2,361	5,257	7,972
Freight loaded at ports[b] (thousand tons)	87	362	708	1,265	1,189

SOURCE: Ministry of Transport.
a. 1961/62.
b. Excluding oil.

September 1971; these two lines link Iran, respectively, with the Soviet and Turkish railway systems and thus provide an important channel for overland trade with Europe. In the southeast, a line has been laid down from Qom to Isfahan and Rez Lenjan, the site of the steel mill; in a more easterly direction, the railway has been continued to reach Kerman and will eventually be extended to Zahedan, where it will link up with the Pakistan railways.[52] The road network had been improved and expanded to a still greater degree during the four national development plans, nearly 25,000 kilometers of roads had been added to the 17,000 classified as serviceable before the implementation of the plans, and a great amount of widening, straightening, and resurfacing of roads had taken place.[53] The ports and airports had been enlarged and improved and the traffic flowing through them had increased severalfold.

However, the great increase in economic activity registered in the period 1973-75, and more particularly the enormous expansion in imports, once more put the transport system under strain. An unfavorable characteristic of Iran's transport system should be noted at this point. By far the greater part of Iran's exports, measured by volume, consists of oil, which is discharged by pipelines into tankers. Hence her land transport system is mainly devoted to the carrying of imports, which means that traffic flows overwhelmingly in one direction: from the periphery to the center, and more particularly to Tehran. During the summer of 1975, it was reported that ships had had to wait up to 120 days before they could find a berth at Khorramshahr, which handled some 44 percent of cargo, and once goods had been landed there were not enough trucks or trains to carry them inland.[54]

Attempts to deal with this situation, which was seriously impeding the country's development, included both short-term emergency measures and the implementation of long-term plans. Among the former were various efforts to speed up the transit of goods in the main ports by technical improvements and administrative reorganization. Several thousand trucks had been imported, many of them with foreign drivers (Indians, Pakistanis, Koreans) to operate them until such time as sufficient trained Iranian drivers were available. Schools for drivers, mechanics, and maintenance men had been set up, with foreign instructors.[55] These measures decreased the congestion in the main ports and highways.

Long-term plans were drawn up for all branches of transport. The annual capacity of the ports was to be increased from 7 million tons in 1972 to 29 million tons at the end of the Fifth Plan, while facilities for overland transport across Iran's frontiers were to be raised to 4 million tons in cooperation with Turkey and other countries. Specific projects included the completion or construction of jetties at Bandar Shahpur, the improvement of Khorramshahr, the expansion of Bushire, Bandar Pahlavi, and Nowshahr, and the construction of a new commercial port at Chah Bahar:[56] To increase their efficiency, ports were to be granted wide administrative and management powers and authorized "to enter into contracts with qualified private firms for the execution of all or part of the port's internal operations and services." The setting up of some "dry ports" in the interior, for customs clearance, was also being considered. Total allocations for port construction and expansion under the Fifth Plan amount to 62 billion rials ($925 million). In addition, the capacity of the Iranian merchant marine was to be raised from 1.2 million tons to 8 million tons by the end of the plan; it was hoped that this would further ease the importation of goods to Iran.

Airport construction and improvement had been allocated 25.5 billion rials ($381 billion) under the Fifth Plan; the most important single item was the Tehran International Airport, scheduled for 1981/82; sixteen airplanes were to be purchased to expand the international services of Iran Air.

Railway projects had been allocated 80 billion rials ($1,194 million) in the Fifth Plan. The most important new line was the electrified line connecting Bandar 'Abbas with Sirjan and on to the Yazd-Kerman railway at Bafq. This was about to open up a vast tract of territory previously almost denuded of modern transport facilities, and in particular promote the export of copper and other minerals; in addition it promised to divert traffic from the overloaded northern ports of the Persian Gulf (especially Khorramshahr and Bandar Shahpur) to Bandar 'Abbas. The other main projects were the doubling and electrification of the old lines: between Tehran, Ahwaz, and Bandar Shahpur; between Tehran and Mashhad; and between Tehran and Qazvin and Tabriz. The Tabriz-Julfa line was also to be electrified.

Road building and maintenance were to receive an amount roughly equal to that allocated to. railways. Under the Fifth Plan, 1,730 kilometers of highways were to be begun, of which the longest single stretches were the Qom—Ahwaz—Bandar Shahpur highway (855 kilometers) and the Qom-Kashan highway (300 kilometers). It was hoped to complete a total of 455 kilometers by the end of the Fifth Plan and the balance during the Sixth Plan. As for Iran's main roads, in 1972 the total length of asphalted roads open to traffic was 12,500 kilometers. The first task of the Fifth Plan was to complete 2,400 kilometers of main roads started under the Fourth Plan. New main roads to be started and completed under the Fifth Plan totaled 3,668 kilometers; an additional 3,830 kilometers were to be started under the Fifth Plan and completed under the Sixth.

Highways and main roads can meet most of the needs of the cities and main industries, but the greater part of the country has to rely on feeder roads. In 1972 the total length of Iran's completed feeder roads was 12,000 kilometers, a figure still far too low in relation to the country's vast size. In the Fifth Plan, 3,500 kilometers of feeder roads started under the Fourth Plan were to be completed. Work was also to begin on a further 15,500 kilometers of feeder roads, all of which were to be asphalted; it was hoped to complete 8,000 of these during the Fifth Plan and the balance during the Sixth.

Under the strain of modern transport, roads deteriorate very fast and adequate maintenance and repair is at least as important as new construction. The Fifth Plan allocates 25 billion rials ($373 million) for road maintenance and reconstruction, to be spent on the purchase of machinery, the resurfacing of 3,000 kilometers of main roads, and the asphalting of 10,000 kilometers of gravel roads.

As mentioned earlier, by 1972 Iran's transport system was beginning to be nearly adequate for its needs. During the following three years the capacity of that system was subjected to an enormous strain, with most unfortunate results. If the projects provided for in the Fifth Plan are carried out, however, by the end of the 1970s Iran's transport—already greatly expanded and improved—should be once more able to serve the needs of a much larger economy and, one can hope, will have ceased to act as a constraint on the country's development.

FINANCE

The huge expansion of Iran's economy necessitated, and was accompanied by, a corresponding development of the financial system.[57] At the end of World War II Iran was served by a handful of government and foreign banks, headed by the Bank Melli which issued notes, kept the deposits of the government and advanced loans to it, and performed some other functions of central banks as well as carrying out the usual private commercial operations. After 1950 however, and more particularly after 1958, numerous private, foreign, and government banks were founded; among them was the IMDBI, established jointly by the government, the private sector, and foreign banks and institutions. By 1960/61, ten government and seventeen private banks were operating in Iran.

This rapid expansion of the banking system led to the mobilization of large amounts of savings and the expansion of credit, which greatly stimulated economic activity, including investment and trade. However, uncontrolled credit expansion was one of the causes of the inflationary pressures experienced in the late 1950s. Hence the need was felt for more control over the financial system and the government-owned Bank Markazi Iran was founded and began operations in July 1960. Bank Markazi took over the central bank functions of Bank Melli and has, since its inception, served as the country's central bank. Its powers were further enlarged and defined by a law passed in 1972.

The upsurge of the economy after 1963 brought with it a spate of new banks, including several founded jointly by Iranians together with U.S., Japanese, European, Arab and other foreign capital. By 1975 the number of banks operating in Iran was thirty-five, of which twenty-five were commercial banks; seven specialized development banks set up with government help to assist in the financing of industry and mining, agriculture, and construction; and three regional development banks designed specifically to promote the development of the Caspian, Azarbayjan, and Khuzistan regions. Whereas in 1962 the total number of bank branches had been 1,240, by 1975 there were more than 7,200 branches in operation and several banks had established branches abroad.[58] The capital of these banks rose from 17 billion rials to 120 billion rials during this period.

Bank deposits by the private sector increased more than correspondingly, from 49 billion rials in March 1963 to 699 billion rials in March 1975, a fourteen-fold increase, and bank loans and credits to the private sector rose from 61.5 billion rials to 698 billion, or almost twelve times. A breakdown shows that industry received a rising share of the total—21 percent in 1974/75—while the proportions going to agriculture and construction—9 and 12 percent, respectively—remained relatively unchanged. Trade and financial activities still absorbed a large share of total bank credit, the proportion going to import trade having risen sharply with the great increase in imports, to 16 percent in 1974/75.

Other financial institutions have also developed, including fifteen insurance companies with a combined capital of 8 billion rials, savings and loans associations for housing and, since the beginning of 1968, the Tehran Stock Market. At first the activity of the stock market was very limited, owing to the small number of government bonds or company shares available for exchange, but by the mid-1970s its scope had considerably widened. In 1968/69, share transactions totaled only 31 million rials, but by 1973/74 they had risen to 1,333 million rials ($200 million) to which should be added 1,451 million rials ($220 million) in government bonds.[59] In 1975 the nominal value of the forty-three companies listed was over 45 billion rials ($650 million) and the total number of shareholders was over 45,000.[60] The volume of transactions was to be greatly widened by a law of 1975 requiring businesses to offer up to 49 percent of their shares to their workers and the public. A large fund had been established by the government to advance the money needed to purchase these shares by the workers, to be repaid from future profits, and it was expected that "over the next three years shares with a nominal value of Rls. 120 billion from some 320 qualified companies should be taken up by small investors."[61]

Another aspect of the widening of the capital market in Iran was the increase in savings and time deposits—from 38 billion rials in 1964 to 503 billion rials ($7.5 billion) in 1974. The number of savings accounts in Bank Melli alone rose from 2 million to 4.6 million, of which 3 million were outside Tehran.[62] Yet another important source of capital was the rapidly increasing investment by the pension funds and other institutional funds.

Since its inception, Bank Markazi sought to use its power and influence to provide an adequate money supply and offset the inflationary or deflationary pressures that alternately made themselves felt. Using the instruments available to it—the discount rate, the maximum interest rate payable on bank deposits, the reserve requirements (i.e., the proportion of deposits that banks are required to hold with the central bank), and the credit advanced to the private sector—the bank, in cooperation with the government, pursued a restrictive policy in the period 1959-62, an expansionary one in the period 1963-65, a restrictive policy followed by an expansionary one in the period

Table 4.11
CONSUMER PRICE INDEX AND WHOLESALE PRICE INDEX

	CPI		WPI	
	1959/60 = 100	1969/70 = 100	1959/60 = 100	1969/70 = 100
1960/61	108.0		102.0	
1961/62	109.6		102.2	
1962/63	110.6		103.6	
1963/64	111.7		104.0	
1964/65	116.7		109.6	
1965/66	117.0		110.6	
1966/67	117.9		110.2	
1967/68	118.9	95.1	110.2	
1968/69	120.7	96.6	110.9	96.2
1969/70	125.0	100.0	114.7	100.0
1970/71		101.5		103.4
1971/72		107.1		110.7
1972/73		113.8		117.0
1973/74		126.5		132.3
1974/75		146.1		153.4

SOURCE: Bank Markazi, *Annual Reports.*

1965-67, and once more a restrictive policy in the period 1968-70. The high degree of success of the monetary and fiscal policies pursued during these years may be judged from three facts. First, the money supply and credit facilities provided were sufficient to produce a rapid growth in real GNP. Second, this was achieved without running down Iran's foreign exchange to a dangerously low level. Lastly, until 1971 Iran enjoyed a remarkable degree of price stability, as is shown in table 4.11.

After 1971, however, the large rise in oil revenues and the very rapid growth in GNP greatly reinforced the inflationary pressures to which the country was subjected by the rise in its import prices.[63] In such circumstances, monetary policy by itself can do little, and the burden of price stability must be borne by the government, acting through the budget. But where, as in Iran, the bulk of government revenue comes from outside the country, taxation—as distinct from the increase or decrease of government expenditures—is not a very effective tool of policy. In recent years the yield of Iran's taxes has greatly risen—that of indirect taxes from 28.0 billion rials in 1967/68 to 103.2 billion rials in 1974/75 and that of direct taxes still more rapidly, from 10.1 billion rials to 67.8 billion rials.[64] However, there seems little doubt that the burden of taxation in Iran is still too low, particularly that of direct taxes on upper and middle brackets.[65] In addition to promoting social justice, a strengthening of the fiscal system could achieve a doubly beneficial purpose: to increase Iran's savings rate and thus lay a wider basis for future growth when oil revenues begin to decline (see below); and to give the government a powerful tool for achieving price stability in the stormy financial times that lie ahead.

AN EVALUATION

The performance of the Iranian economy in the last fifteen or twenty years may be appraised under the following headings: growth, structural development, employment, stability, protection of environment, social justice and international balance, and future viability.[66]

Growth

Iran's growth in both GNP and per capita income compares favorably with that of other countries. The International Bank for Reconstruction and Development has computed worldwide figures and its tables provide a good basis for comparison.[67] In the period 1960-72, Iran's annual growth of 9.4 percent in GNP was exceeded only by Libya and Taiwan, and equaled by Japan. Owing to its high rate of population increase, however, Iran's growth in per capita income was relatively lower, its rate of 6.3 percent being exceeded by eight countries, in the following order: Libya, Japan, Romania, Greece, Saudi Arabia, Singapore, Taiwan, and South Korea. In the period 1965-72 Iran did even better. Its growth rate of 10.4 percent in GNP was exceeded by Singapore, Libya, and Japan, and equaled by South Korea, while its per capita rate of 7.2 percent was exceeded only by Singapore, Japan, South Korea, Libya, and Greece. In other words, even before the upsurge caused by the recent rise in oil prices, Iran was among the fastest-growing countries in the world.

The question immediately arises as to whether this rapid growth can be attributed to oil. It is clear that without its oil revenues Iran could not have hoped to advance at anything like its recent speed. But the role of oil can easily be exaggerated. First, the direct contribution of oil was not very great: its share in gross domestic product (GDP) was only one-tenth in 1960 and still below one-fifth in 1972; its contribution to growth of GDP was under one-quarter (see above); and its foreign exchange contribution was not very large when measured against GNP or population.[68] Second, the fact that oil is not a sufficient condition of growth is shown by the relatively poor performance of all other OPEC countries except Libya and Saudi Arabia, and in those two growth was overwhelmingly attributable to oil. It may be added that large exporters of other minerals, such as diamonds, copper, or tin, have also had relatively low growth rates.

In the mid-1970s Iran's growth was definitely excessive, and was straining its social fabric and administrative capacity. Within a few years, it would have to slow down to a rate much closer to that of the 1965-72 period than to the level of the following three years.

Structural Development

The concept of structural development is qualitative rather than quantitative. It implies the reform of existing economic and social institutions and the creation of others that bring into being new forms of economic and social activities. The preceding pages have shown the far-reaching development that has taken place in Iran's economic and social structure during the last fifteen years. Its human resources have been developed by the expansion of schools and extension of medical services. Its stock of technical, managerial, and administrative personnel has greatly increased in quantity and quality. Its infrastructure—particularly transport and energy—has been vastly expanded. In agriculture, the system of ownership and tenure has been revolutionized by the land reform; the technical basis has been strengthened by irrigation and much greater use of fertilizers; credit, transport, and storage facilities have improved; and there has been an intensification of production and a shift to more valuable cash crops. But much remains to be done, and agriculture remains the weakest and most sluggish sector of the economy. In industry, by contrast, the change has been immense. Not only has output multiplied severalfold but many new, more complex, industries have come into being and the linkages between the various industries have been greatly strengthened. Iran now provides a significant part of the intermediate and capital goods it requires, and the proportion should rise steeply during the next few years. Lastly, the banking system has been vastly expanded, many new specialized institutions have been created, and a capital market has begun to develop. All these developments are reflected in the changing composition of GNP and in the rise in the investment and savings rates to levels that assure continued growth.

Employment

One of society's main tasks is to ensure gainful employment for all its members. Judged by this exacting standard, Iran may be faulted since, until the early 1970s, even its rapid growth failed to create enough jobs for its burgeoning population. More should have been done to provide useful work for the unemployed and underemployed in construction, rural development projects, and other public works.[69] In 1975, the labor market was very tight and seemed likely to remain so for some years. But as growth falls back to more normal levels, a labor surplus may reemerge and thought should be given to long-term plans for dealing with it.

Stability

The relation of the value of money to its obverse, the price level, is characterized by more or less stability. In the short run, high stability may be sacrificed to other objectives judged more important, such as fuller employment, faster growth or higher investment. But, as the experience of the last few years has shown only too clearly, the imbalances and distortions produced by inflation—both internally and in the balance of payments—soon become intolerable and require the harshest and most painful of corrective measures.

Until 1972, Iran had a degree of stability that was matched by very few countries. The rise in its price indices was well within the limits of tolerance and distinctly below that of the vast majority of countries, whether advanced or developing.[70] In the following three years, due partly to the upsurge in import prices and partly to the expansion of internal demand and liquidity, Iran's rate of inflation rose sharply—though even in 1975 it did not compare too badly with that of other countries. The authorities were aware of the dangers posed by this situation, and in that year took stern corrective measures, but it was not clear whether a country like Iran, by itself, could do much to bring under control an inflation that was worldwide.

Environment

Here one can be brief. In common with every other country in the world, Iran has been negligent in protecting its environment. Air pollution in Tehran and other large cities is only the most visible sign of this neglect, and to it must be added water pollution, deforestation, and soil erosion. Awareness is, however, increasing and attempts are being made to reforest and to site industrial—and more particularly power—plants in areas removed from the main population centers.

Social Justice

In a country like Iran in the 1950s, where the bulk of the land was held by a few hundred families, where wealth and income were highly concentrated, where the literacy rate was 15 percent (the female rate being only 8 percent), where medical services were practically confined to the towns and only a small fraction of city dwellers enjoyed modern amenities, the imperatives of social justice were clear: first and foremost, to raise the level of the masses; and second, to reduce the inequality of distribution of wealth and income. Progress towards the first objective has been rapid, through the great increase in private consumption, the expansion of health and educational services—particularly noteworthy being the work of the Health Corps and Literacy Corps in the villages—the extension of such amenities as electricity and drinking water to the towns and many villages and the successful efforts to improve the condition of women. A good index of social progress is the rise in the overall literacy rate to 43 percent in 1975 (30 percent for women) and in the urban rate to 66 percent (55 percent for women).[71]

As regards the second objective, the most important steps have been the land reform—one of the most radical outside the communist countries, and one of the most successful—and, more recently, the profit-sharing measures in industry. Nevertheless, as pointed out earlier, income distribution is if anything becoming more unequal. This seems to be a normal concomitant of rapid economic growth, as the history of the advanced countries of Europe and America and the more recent experience of those non-Western countries that have achieved rapid growth shows only too clearly.[72] It is, nonetheless, a deplorable and socially dangerous trend. To check it one can only suggest still more rapid increase in social services, a greater effort to upgrade the labor force and raise its earning power, and the application of more progressive taxation.

Viability

The question here is whether Iran's modern sector and its agriculture can be made self-sustaining by the time oil production and revenues begin to decline sharply, say by the end of the 1980s. Two powerful potential constraints on growth will be ignored here: skills, because the domestic supply has been increasing very rapidly and can be supplemented by hiring foreigners; and internal savings, because Iran had reached a very high savings ratio—approaching 20 percent of GNP—before the recent rise in oil revenues. Attention will therefore be focused on the balance-of-payments constraints, i.e., on whether foreign exchange earnings can be expanded to meet anticipated disbursements.

Until recently, Iran's export of goods other than oil and gas was increasing somewhat more rapidly than her imports—in the period 1968/69-1972/73 the average rates were 19.9 and 16.7 percent, respectively—but since they covered less than one-fifth of imports the deficit was also growing fast, at 16 percent.[73] A breakdown shows that by 1972 consumer goods accounted for less than 13 percent of total imports, capital goods taking 25 percent and intermediate goods 62 percent. As for exports, traditional goods (carpets, agricultural produce, etc.) formed three-quarters of the total and new industrial goods only one-quarter, but the rate of growth of the latter, 45 percent per annum, was three times as high as that of traditional goods.

In the following three years, however, imports shot up, by 45 percent in 1973/74 and 77 percent in 1974/75, while exports, after rising by 44 percent in 1973/74, fell by 8 percent in 1974/75. Such a rise in the import surplus is perfectly normal and desirable at a time of rapidly expanding oil revenues. But it serves as one more warning that Iran must pursue a policy designed to optimize the use of her future oil revenues. For the period 1973/74-1992/93, these have been estimated, on various assumptions, at $312 billion to $528 billion, with gas contributing another $57 billion.[74] This means that, until about the end of the 1980s, Iran can count on substantial annual flows of oil revenues to ease the pains of transition. In the interval strenuous efforts must be made to raise the productivity of agriculture, to make industry produce a far larger proportion of the intermediate goods it is using, and to increase its competitiveness in world markets. The growth rate will have to be brought down from its recent abnormally high level and imports, investment, and defense expenditures will have to be reduced. Such an adjustment will not be easy but, in view of Iran's fortunate financial position and its recent economic performance, there is every reason to envisage the future with confidence.

I should like gratefully to acknowledge the help I have received in preparing this chapter from various officials in the Ministries of Agriculture, Industry, and Transport, the Plan Organization, the Industrial and Mining Development Bank and, above all, the Central Bank of Iran.

HARALD MEHNER

5

Development and Planning in Iran after World War II

The history of planning in Iran is an exciting chapter in Iranian national development. To understand the present economic situation in the country—not only the tremendous growth in all economic and social sectors, but also the resulting tensions and shortcomings—one must examine the last five development periods and the executive agencies responsible for planning during this time.

PLANNING IN MODERN IRAN: AN OVERVIEW

During the reign of Reza Shah the Great the first steps were taken to modernize the medieval economic and social sectors of the country. However, the private economic sector continued to be restricted to traditional handicrafts and trade, both on a small scale; the only carrier of modernization was the government. Many infrastructural projects and industrial investments were assumed by the public sector which, for example, established textile, cement, tobacco and sugar factories. The planning and implementation of these projects were done by various ministries that, between 1926 and 1938, invested almost 35 percent of the regular budget in these industries and mining.

At this time, when there existed no economic plan and no government planning institution, officials took the initiative by drawing up a memorandum in November 1939 to the prime minister, Dr. Ahmad Matin-Daftari. This memorandum, which postulated the necessity of an economic plan and the establishment of a planning center for Iran, recommended better use of the country's limited economic resources, the fixing of priorities, and the establishment of economic coordination. These proposals were designed to rectify an incoherent economic situation that was characterized by various inefficiencies. For example, there was a law enabling government monopolization of foreign trade; but at the same time there was no responsible agency that could channel the expenditure of foreign exchange in accordance with the necessities of the entire economy. In the balance of its lateral trade with Germany, Iran had a surplus, and yet did not use this currency properly in spite of an urgent need to do so. In another example, several public sugar-beet factories were constructed and started production without qualified supervision—supervision that could also have promoted seed production and successful methods of cultivation, regulated prices, and solved other problems related to the new program. Almost forty years later, some aspects of this program were still waiting for optimal solutions.

In February 1946, a second memorandum was published by officials.[1] This memo was based on the same facts as the first one, only the political, economic, and social situation in Iran had become more critical because of the disastrous consequences of World War II. The memorandum pointed out that Iran's lack of experience in economic reconstruction did not permit a laissez-faire policy, as in the industrialized countries. These proposals, with the support of Mohammad Reza Shah Pahlavi, led to the creation of the High Planning Commission and a Planning Board, as well as to the first preparations for an Iranian national development plan.

As a consequence of closer cooperation between Iran and the United States and on the recommendation of the U.S. State Department the American construction company of Morrison Knudsen was commissioned in 1947 to draft Iran's First National Development Plan. Shortly thereafter, Iran asked the International Bank for Reconstruction and Development in Washington (the World Bank) to participate in Iranian development by giving loans. At the World Bank's request the drafting of the plan was transferred to the American consulting company Overseas Consultants. American experts analyzed the economic and social situation of Iran in five volumes that included proposals for the organization and functions of a planning administration, as well as for public investments and development programs in different sectors.[2] At that time the Iranian economy was fundamentally agricultural and underdeveloped except for a small number of mostly light consumer industries. The majority of the country's active work force was engaged in agriculture, which was based on an antiquated, feudalistic system of landlord and peasant. Per capita income was less than $120, equivalent to that of today's least-developed countries, and the majority of the Iranian population was living at subsistence level.[3]

The First Development Plan, with an expected length of seven years, began in September 1949. Several budget calculations were made, accompanied by negotiations with potential national and international creditors. Finally, the planning budget was fixed at 21 billion rials, or $100 million per year (a modest amount as compared with over $6,000 million in 1974/75, the second year of the Fifth Plan). The 60-fold increase of the annual planning budget within a generation dramatically indicates the demands and stresses under which development in Iran was carried out and in what dimensions progress was achieved. With 9 billion rials earmarked for projects and programs already started but not completed, only 4.179 billion more of the above-mentioned 21 billion rials were available for development spending in the First Plan. Because of political and financial disturbances, especially during the Mosaddegh period (1951-53), the First Plan had to be terminated prematurely in September 1955.[4] In spite of these problems, the foundations were laid for the activity of the Seven Year Plan Administration as the country's first planning agency. Some public investments were made in different sectors under this plan. Industries that had been established during the reign of Reza Shah the Great were in a pitiful state because of overexploitation and lack of proper maintenance. These units were reorganized and some new factories constructed. The agricultural and infrastructural projects that were carried out under the First Plan constituted the first steps towards the physical and social foundation of the country's economic growth—the modernization of agriculture and the mobilization of manpower.

After the new oil agreement of 1954 and the resumption of oil income, the law for the Second Development Plan was enacted in March 1956. Its total projected budget amounted to 84 billion rials of which 68 billion rials were actually spent. In 1955 the Iranian currency was devalued to 75.75 rials for $1, which meant an expected expenditure of $1.1 billion during the Second Plan. In this plan the main infrastructural systems for future economic transformation of the country were launched. The result was a general reactivation of the Iranian economy that led to a decline in unemployment and an increase in income and purchasing power.

The Second Development Plan (1956-62) was scheduled with the same framework as the first one but was implemented on a broader scale. Development in some industries achieved remarkable results. For example, textile factory production was increased from 60 million meters to 480 million meters, cement production from 100,000 tons to 1.2 million tons, and sugar production from 85,000 tons to 227,000 tons during this period. The successful construction of three big dams introduced modern irrigation and hydroelectric power to Iran. These included the Amir Kabir Dam on the Karaj River, the Farah Pahlavi Dam on the Sefid Rud River, and the Mohammad Reza Shah Pahlavi Dam on the Dez River; together, they had a storage capacity of 9.3 billion cubic meters of water and a generating capacity of 692 megawatts. Agricultural projects were successfully implemented; these dealt with the use of improved seed, farm mechanization, more fertilizers, and the cultivation of sugarcane. Private investment, which had previously been far smaller than public, was increased by the granting of loans from Bank Melli to private investors and by the establishment of the specialized Industrial Credit Bank by the Seven Year Plan Administration to make loans available to the private sector.

The rapid changes during a development period required the shortening of the plans' duration from seven to five years. The Third Development Plan (1962-68) was extended over a period of 5½ years to adapt it to the Iranian calendar year. At the same time the name of Seven Year Plan Administration was changed to Plan Organization.

The Third Plan was prepared during a recession period in Iran, when high government expenditures led to inflationary price increases and deficits in the foreign exchange balance. Development expenditures had therefore to be limited to 140 billion rials in the early stages of the plan; however, after the increase in oil income and the improvement of the economic situation during the second half of the plan they were raised to 230 billion rials. Of this amount, 204 billion rials were expended for development projects, with especially large allotments for transport and communications (26 percent) and fuel and energy (16 percent). Basic industrial projects, such as plants for steel, petrochemicals, machine tools, tractors, pipes, and aluminum smelting were started, but could not be completed as projected in this plan. Agriculture and irrigation received, as in former plans, 23 percent of the total budget, but because of bad climatic conditions and infrastructural and administrative difficulties, the growth rate of this sector could not reach the planned target.

Beginning with the Third Plan, national economic and social goals such as equitable income distribution and manpower and employment mobilization, as well as protection of the country's natural wealth—water, forests, and other such resources—were all made part of development planning. These development objectives, financed by the Development Budget and implemented by special programs, were politically supported by the proclamation of the White Revolution by Mohammad Reza Shah Pahlavi. The Third Plan coincided with a series of major social transformations that consisted in the implementation of a land reform program; the sharing of industrial workers in the profit of the enterprises in which they worked; and the establishment of the three rural corps. The Literacy Corps was formed to fight illiteracy, the Reconstruction and Development Corps to support village development activities and modern agricultural cultivation, and the Health Corps to combat diseases and establish a rural health system. The first six principles of Iran's White Revolution, of which three were mentioned above, were increased to twelve by 1967 and to sixteen by 1975. These first six principles aimed at improvement and promotion of the standard of living and welfare of the entire population, especially the low-income groups.

In the Third Plan, the private economic sector was for the first time treated as a whole for planning purposes, and was promoted by guidelines, incentive programs, a favorable credit policy, etc. The expected annual rate of economic growth of 6 percent in the country's gross national product (GNP) was surpassed by 2.8 percent for a final figure of 8.8 percent. Per capita income rose from 12,800 rials to 17,200 rials, which moved Iran out of the group of least-developed countries. During the first half of this plan private sector activities replaced missing public sector investments which were restricted because of low government revenues resulting from economic stagnation and recession. However, in the last two years of the same plan oil income increased and total domestic investment reached 430 billion rials, of which 57 percent came from the public sector. The investment proportion of the gross domestic product (GDP) increased from 13 percent in the first plan year to 18.5 percent in the last plan year.

The Fourth Development Plan (1968-73), enacted in March 1968, was the turning point in terms of annual economic growth and social welfare. Particular attention was paid to public welfare and to the extension of social services, especially for the low-income groups. A more equitable distribution of income as well as the development of social services, welfare, housing, and environmental sanitation got priorities.

The Fourth Plan was prepared in a period of economic growth and large public production investments. The target for public sector development investments was a volume of 480 billion rials, with another 370 billion rials for the private sector. Because of increasing oil income during this plan, the target for public development expenditure alone was surpassed by 98 billion rials, for a total of 578 billion rials. The introduction of modern technology, not only in industry and other productive activities, but also in social activities, was another means by which it was hoped the Fourth Plan would speed up the rate of economic growth. The expenditure for industry and mining was increased by 14 billion rials to 20 percent of the Plan Budget, while the expenditure for oil and gas investments was doubled to 10.7 percent. Industrialization, especially in heavy industry, received priority in this plan, whereas agriculture and water and irrigation projects were reduced to 16.7 percent of the total expenditure. The annual consumption of electricity rose from 4.5 billion kilowatt-hours to 12 billion kilowatt-hours and the per capita consumption from 175 kilowatt-hours to 400 kilowatt-hours. Many communication and transportation projects, including construction of roads and railways, ports and airports, and in the field of telecommunications were started or completed. The Fourth Plan included large-scale housing projects especially for government employees. Education also received special attention because 1.6 million children entered primary schools.

The level of investment and development expenditure of the public sector and the corresponding investments in the private sector led to an annual growth rate of 9.5 percent, which is unique among Asian countries except Japan. Per capita income increased from 23,300 rials to 32,000 rials. At the end of the Fourth Plan, with this per capita income, Iran became one of the Third World's "take-off countries."

At the end of this plan the National Plan and Budget Act was enacted and the name of the Plan Organization changed to Plan and Budget Organization, denoting its new organizational structure and expanded tasks.[5]

AIMS AND OBJECTS OF PLANNING IN IRAN

As mentioned above, in the first two plans development expenditures were appropriated to three sectors: agriculture and irrigation; industry and mining; and the physical and social infrastructure. In subsequent plans subsectors like tourism, public sanitation, and preservation of national culture and arts became objects of planning and received appropriations from the Development Budget. With the introduction of comprehensive and integrated planning, a growing range of government activities became subject to the planning process.

Starting with the Fifth Plan, military and civil defense were included in the planning budget, of which it consumed 33 percent. In this sector administrative experiments and innovations were introduced through the so-called detailed inspections and testing examinations to determine administrative standards and qualifications. These methods were initially used in the military sector, to be later extended to civilian administration and private business enterprises.

The activities of Iranian planners included the establishment of a planning and budgeting system; exercising the necessary supervision to ensure rapid, comprehensive, and coordinated development in all social and economic fields; drawing up the necessary technical standards and criteria for the implementation of development projects; and notifying the relevant bodies. Other main objectives of the Plan and Budget Organization were to carry out and expand social and economic studies and surveys, as well as to develop activities of a statistical nature including the establishment of a national data system.[6] Further objectives were to facilitate and increase the productivity of government agencies through continuous evaluation of projects and activities executed by the government and—finally—to cooperate with other agencies of the government to carry out the policy of decentralization and regional development. The Plan and Budget Organization was expected to inform the public about the importance of development, with its possibilities and advantages for the whole nation. This task was often taken up by the Shah in his speeches and proclamations to different bodies of the government and in nationwide addresses.

In the beginning, development efforts were concentrated on the main economic subsectors and on small units in sections such as mining and rural industry. Reforms needed as a base for development on a broad scale—land reform, for example, and the nationalization of forests, pastures, and water resources—were not initiated. Inefficient infrastructure and lack of qualified personnel were other major obstacles to any nationwide program. Thus big investments in mining, forestry, and fishery projects, and in modernizing the traditional animal husbandry, as well as programs in rural industry, could be included in the planning activities only after the above-mentioned reforms were executed and the gaps filled. Projects of this type were taken up in the Fourth Plan for the first time but later on a much broader scale in the Fifth Plan (1973-78).

National planning objectives can be formulated only after analysis of the country's economic and social situation. The First Plan was based on such an analysis, but with only rough estimates; subsequent plans contained much more detailed and explicit data. These analyses uncovered many economic and social shortcomings. Since the feudal system prevented the farmers from investing in agriculture, increases in production were limited and antiquated production methods were seldom replaced. There was a scarcity of skilled labor. Many difficulties hampered the transfer of the technical "know-how" essential for profitable modern production. Other major obstacles to develop ment included the differences between towns and villages and the "dual economy"—i.e., the disparity between the so-called traditional sector, with primitive working and living conditions for the majority of the people, and the occasional enclaves of modern capitalism in industry and in the service sector. There were also huge disparities between the different regions of the country in income levels, health standards, productivity, and education. The overriding object of planning, at least during the first three plans, was the removal of these obstacles.[7]

Beginning with the Third Plan, the Iranian planners' quantitative goals played an increasingly important part in setting the framework of economic activities for the country's public and private sectors. The GNP and its average annual growth rates offered a base for other economic calculations such as annual income per capita.

The overall ratio of consumer expenditure to GNP serves as an indicator for evaluating a nation's living standards and quality of life. The public's consumption expenditure serves to indicate how hard the government is trying to improve the general welfare and the social services related to it. The gross domestic fixed capital formation of the public and private sector in relationship to GNP is another quantitative objective of planning with wide consequences. It is of a special importance to ensure continuity of growth in long-term planning. In comparing the five development plans, the rate of public investment in Iran was always higher than that of private investment. This also applied to the annual growth rates of both the public and private sectors. In the Fifth Plan, two-thirds of the expected investments were to be made by the public sector and the rest by the private, with expected annual growth rates of 38 percent and 18 percent respectively. The elimination of bottlenecks and shortcomings in the economic infrastructure, the establishment and expansion of mother industries, and the extension of social activities made such a rate of growth possible.

Increase in GDP is another quantitative objective. Knowledge of its sectoral value and its per capita terms facilitates decisions about urgent production investment and information, production capacities, and various interrelationships. The actual contribution by the major economic sectors to the GDP indicates the present and future importance of these sectors. The sectoral annual growth rates provide guidelines for the possible investments in these sectors and for the credits that must be made available to private investors. For example, the contribution of agriculture at constant prices decreased from 24.5 percent at the end of the Third Plan to 18.1 percent at the end of the Fourth Plan, and was expected to reach 8 percent at the end of the Fifth Plan. In contrast, the contribution from the oil sector during the same period had increased from 13.8 percent to 19.5 percent and was expected to reach 48.7 percent.

Beginning with the Fourth Plan and extending to the Fifth Plan, qualitative targets were introduced for every sector and subsector of the planning program while the basic objectives, policy strategies and general guidelines were formulated. They constituted a supplement to the quantitative goals and provided information to all government agencies in explaining in detail the aims of the planners. Specific policies were drawn up about the proper utilization of that part of the country's foreign exchange earnings that could not be absorbed domestically in the short term. Among these were investing part of the country's oil revenues abroad, granting commercial loans, participating in foreign economic projects, and acquiring shareholdings in foreign industrial enterprises. Other parts of foreign exchange could also be used to meet domestic needs by importation, and by increasing the facilities, organizations, and systems necessary for such trade. Moreover, inflationary pressures could be controlled and benefits from the advantages of greater competition between domestic and foreign industry maximized by reducing restrictions on imports—especially of consumer goods, which had been in short supply on the domestic market.

Another qualitative objective of the Fifth Plan was to raise the quality of life for all social groups, and especially to develop systems of participation, to establish a healthy environment for growth, and to support democratic organizations such as producers' and consumers' cooperatives as well as village, city, and provincial councils. Measures had to be taken for the growth and development of individuals in society by selecting talented persons in every sphere of social endeavor and assisting their progress in fields suited to their talents. It seemed likely that rapid, balanced, and sustained economic growth together with minimum price increases could be obtained by encouraging private sector savings and investment in productive activities, by strengthening the capital market, and by ensuring greater cooperation between the public and private sectors.

All-round expansion of social, economic, political, and cultural justice, with particular emphasis on the equitable distribution of services among all social classes and groups, could be achieved by, for instance, ensuring proper nutrition and health standards for urban and rural children.[8] Other such measures were organizing an integrated regional medical and health network; training the auxiliary medical and health personnel required to provide such services in rural and depressed areas; and offering free health service through expansion of welfare services to low-income groups in urban and rural areas. By expanding educational programs illiteracy could be eradicated rapidly, the quality of educational services improved, and the maximum use of educational technology applied. Suitable housing for all social classes and groups could be ensured by expanding the activities of housing cooperatives, providing housing loans as well as the necessary materials and manpower for construction, and seeing that housing received an appropriate share in total credit and the allocation of scarce resources.

Development of science and technology as well as creativity and initiative could be promoted by reorienting the educational system to encourage scientific and independent thinking. This could be achieved by promoting greater cooperation between the higher educational institutions and the productive and nonproductive sectors of the economy, by increasing contact with foreign scientific and research institutions, and by upgrading statistical methods and other infrastructural services necessary for research work.

Relative competitiveness in the production and export of industrial goods at the international level could be established by giving priority to investment in capital-intensive heavy industry, particularly through the public sector, and by protecting these newly established industries. Grants could be given to the profitable public enterprises concerned, and direct government investment and protective import tariffs of limited duration at decreasing rates could be established. Investments could be made abroad in strategic industries whose products are import items of special importance for Iran and that, at the same time, could help expand Iranian exports and ensure the country's presence in international markets.

Promotion of research and teaching and participation in cultural and artistic fields, establishment of facilities for artistic and literary creation, and development of cultural relations could become vital activities maintained by taking the necessary measures to preserve the nation's valuable cultural heritage.

In order to preserve cultural purity and national identity, measures necessary for the cultural and artistic education of all social classes and groups could be taken to strengthen and establish cultural links within the geographic region influenced by the Iranian culture and the Persian language.

Other general guidelines of the Fifth Plan dealt with taxation policy, monetary and banking strategy, national defense policy, and the administrative system. Similar to the first part, which contained general guidelines under the heading of "Social and Economic Generalities," each of the following four parts—"General Administration and Defense Affairs," "Productive Programs," "Infrastructure Programs," and "Social Affairs"—had its own qualitative goals in the form of overall objectives, basic guidelines, and executive policies. For example, steps were to be taken in the field of agriculture to ensure that within areas irrigated by dams or series of deep wells already built or to be built by government investment, separate or irregular parcels of land would be acquired from individuals owning or possessing them. They would be converted into integrated plots of a size appropriate for the irrigation network and service roads, and utilized by integrated economic units of a size to be determined on the basis of master plans that would be announced for each region. Such units would be used individually or in the form of jointly owned farms, cooperative farms, agroindustrial corporations, meat and dairy complexes, or any other kind of legal corporation, with emphasis on a very high degree of efficiency and the use of advanced agricultural technology.

Qualitative objectives in the field of transportation and communication consisted of the expansion and revitalization of the country's rail network through electrification, doubling the track of some existing lines and increasing the capacity and speed of trains. By encouraging, supporting, and instructing the private sector in the proper and rapid utilization of road transport, the maximum utilization of round trips, particularly on routes serving import and export gateways, would be achieved. With regard to telecommunications, telephone systems and other networks were to be selected with due regard for economy and technical programs by utilizing modern management methods, and by supervising the implementation of projects to achieve economy in costs and to shorten the time between investment and utilization.

In the field of social affairs, the qualitative objectives for education were listed as a basic revision of the goals, raison d'être, structure, and teaching methods of secondary education, a revision that would involve large-scale participation on the part of experts and would be inspired by the long-term needs of Iranian society. It would also involve a fight against the quest for diplomas being considered more important among young people than the quest for knowledge, competence, and specialized skills. Revisions had therefore to be made in the Civil Service Code, both in its implementation and in creating the necessary legal authority to grant certificates equivalent to academic credentials for skills acquired through experience in appropriate fields.

For social security and welfare, appropriate support was to be provided to uninsured low-income groups by expanding social insurance, creating productive employment, and adjusting family incomes. At the same time, however, the government was to assume responsibility for providing such groups with support in the short term. Multifunction centers were to be established to provide the services needed to attain the objectives of the program.

One main goal of Iranian planners has been the most profitable use of the country's raw materials, manpower, and other domestic resources. In spite of Iran's enormous production and reserves of oil and gas, this topic has been a dominant concern in all the past planning periods. The responsible Iranian authorities have been aware that, after one or two generations, oil and gas will lose their role as financial backbone of the country's social and economic development. Other economic activities will have to replace this function. For this reason, value-added production of local raw materials and semimanufactured goods has been promoted in order to create employment and to improve the foreign exchange balance with more valuable exports. The vast gap between foreign exchange income from nonoil exports—$585 million in 1975—and foreign exchange expenditure for importing consumer and capital goods—almost $19 billion—has been of permanent concern to Iranian planners, who have given this item special attention. By the mid-1970s, many efforts were being made to change the structure of Iranian exports, to diversify nonoil exports, and to promote value-added production in petrochemicals. As in many other developing countries, the export of industrialized goods was considered an important factor in accelerating economic growth. During all five plans many steps were taken to stimulate the export business by tax relief, decrease of port and other fees, setting up of an export guarantee fund, credit facilities for export financing, etc.

DECISION MAKING IN THE PLANNING PROCESS

In the formative period of the Plan Organization—corresponding to the first two Iranian plans—the Shah entrusted its directorship to Abol Hassan Ebtehaj. Known for his tendency to increase the power of his organization in

the direction of actual implementation of planned projects, Ebtehaj encountered resistance in various ministries intent on preserving their jurisdictions.
He was followed in his position consecutively by Khosrow Hedayat, Safi
Asfia, Khodadad Farmanfarmayan, and 'Abdol Majid Majidi.[9] During their
terms of office, in the 1960s and 1970s, the scope of planning was both
expanded and defined with greater precision. Regardless of who headed the
Plan Organization, the Shah consistently took great interest in its activities
and, from the late 1950s onwards, his earlier supervision of the development
planning changed to direct guidance and personal intervention.

The procedures for enacting the Fifth Plan reveal the decisive influence of
the Shah in this field. At the session of the Plan Organization on December 29,
1970, the monarch gave the outlines for the new five year plan in an address
lasting more than one hour. He bluntly criticized the bottlenecks, shortcomings, and failures of the past plans and covered many details, especially in
agriculture.

Almost two years later, at the historic conference in Persepolis in autumn
1972, the draft of the Fifth National Development Plan was discussed in
detail. In three days of meetings, general directors from the Plan Organization
and the heads of the various ministries involved conferred under the chairmanship of the Shah. The advantages and problems of the different programs
of the future plan were discussed and the final appropriations and policies
were set. This conference was held in a candid and relaxed manner reminiscent of the teamwork found in a modern Western economy. Defense expenditure, for example, was one of the items included in the budget of the Fifth
Plan. The direct involvement of the Shah at this session strengthened the Plan
Organization's position and the eventual efficient implementation of the
defense program. In his speeches at the conferences as well as on other
occasions, the monarch advised that not only rationality and activity but
emotional and moral involvement were essential for the success of planning in
Iran. With his White Revolution as a basic philosophy for political, economic,
and social progress, the Shah became the preacher of the "Great Civilization"
as a final stage of Iranian national life for the end of the century.

The Shah's strong involvement in long-term planning has been constructive
and successful. Although his direct interventions in the execution of the plans
occasionally upset the tidy schedules that obtained at the start, such interventions provided the necessary flexibility—necessary because it was based on
changing political and economic circumstances that he, as active head of state,
was in the best position to see and understand. For example, during the Third
and Fourth Plans, private industry was promoted on a large scale with
astonishing results. In this period of prosperity, the Shah had continually
requested the private sector to accept its social obligation to raise the general
standard of living by producing quality goods at reasonable prices. After

realizing that, to the detriment of economic and social stability, his appeals were being neglected, the Shah launched an antiprofiteering campaign and enacted strong and severe edicts against price increases.

The authority for conceiving, supervising, and executing the five plans was unequally divided in the different periods. In Iran it is common for several competitive institutions to handle public affairs. Thus, in planning, not only the Plan Organization but also the various ministries and the Central Bank were involved. In the first two plans the managing director of the Plan Organization was also its representative on the Council of Ministers and in the Planning Committee of the Majles. During the Third Plan, while the head of Plan Organization became deputy prime minister, the prime minister himself exercised the organization's executive authority. At the beginning of the Fifth Plan the head of the Plan Organization was given the rank of minister of state and eight different sections were created, each led by an undersecretary.

Thus, while the Plan Organization had less power during the end of the Second Plan and during the Fourth Plan, institutionally it became more and more established over the last thirty years, and reached its peak of influence during the Fifth Plan after enactment of the National Plan and Budget Act in March 1973. Conflicts about the competence of the Plan Organization's supervision and the distribution of development expenditures arose during the periods when the organization's power was on the decrease. These conflicts were resolved, however, by the above-mentioned law of 1973, which formalized the procedures and functions of the organization.

The effectiveness of planning in Iran has always been limited by Tehran's decisive role as Iran's political and economic center. Not only administration, but also business, banking, and industry have been concentrated in Tehran and its environs. More than 60 percent of Iran's industrial production in the mid-1970s emanated from the capital, in which more than 65 percent of the country's one million automobiles, buses, and trucks were concentrated. Efforts were therefore made during the decade 1965-75 to decentralize economic development and to regionalize administrative power. Planning decisions and the implementation of programs were to be shifted henceforth to a certain extent from the center to lower levels. In the Fifth Plan 16.4 billion rials were appropriated for regional projects. Closer attention was to be paid to the balanced and coordinated development of the provinces. Their development would be based on the potential, the resources, and the specific needs of each region. Authority had already been delegated to local organizations for the implementation of specific regional projects. Decision making in regional affairs through public participation and through councils at the provincial, district, town, and village levels was to be promoted; and economic mobility was being encouraged in remote regions of the country to ensure a more balanced development of regions with low growth rates.[10]

Legislative participation in the creation and supervision of the first four development plans consisted more or less of a formal approval by the Majles and its Planning Committee. Members of the Majles and the Senate were approached to influence programs so as to favor the sectoral and local interests through personal contacts with the responsible individuals.[11]

In the 1970s the standard procedure for the government was to submit the budget bill to the Majles, which immediately referred it to its Budget Committee for study. After completing its review, the Budget Committee was expected to submit its report to the full Majles. Any views that the Senate might have with regard to the budget were to be communicated to the Majles in the form of advice and recommendations, and the final vote on the budget bill was to be taken after it had been returned by the Senate.

Decisions about development plans and their implementation were to be taken to the newly organized Economic Council, the former High Planning Council, under the directorship of the prime minister and composed of selected ministers and the governor of the Central Bank of Iran. The council provided another opportunity for the ministers concerned to influence the planning decisions. Similarly, influence could be exerted by the members of the High Social Council, which under the leadership of Shahbanou Farah Pahlavi, released decisions regarding social projects within the development plan.

As mentioned above, foreign consulting companies and experts were mainly responsible for the drafting of the first two plans, but had very little supervising or executive power. One exception was an American consulting company, the New York-based Resources and Development Corporation, which was under contract to the Iranian government to act as consultant on the Khuzistan Water and Power Authority as well as direct the general social and economic development in that province. Managers of this company also had executive power in some aspects of the projects while the company itself partly financed them.

With the first loan of $75 million in 1956, as mentioned above, the World Bank became involved in the decision-making process for Iranian development plans. During the Second Development Plan programs were directly influenced by advice and guidance given at the meetings of the bank's board of directors and on other occasions. Later on, the reports of the bank, made singly or by a team, affected Iranian planners, especially in financial and monetary matters, until the end of the Fourth Plan.[12]

METHODS OF PLANNING

In their planning methods Iranian planners have always had to realize that time is a very important factor and that development has to be implemented in only a few years, whereas in Western countries much longer periods, sometimes a whole generation, are necessary. As already mentioned, above, the first two development plans consisted of a chain of isolated projects and independent programs without national integration. This partial planning was applied to the most important sectors of economy and to selected regions. Limited capital and resources left the first two plans with few good opportunities for investment and forced an unbalanced growth policy. Inefficient infrastructure and administration as well as lack of trained personnel were other reasons why these plans were so limited, concentrating on a few capital-intensive projects instead of on many small and labor-intensive ones. At that time, since there was no possibility of using benefit-cost analysis for the different projects, many failures occurred. The private sector was promoted only by an expensive loan and credit policy that led to inflation and foreign exchange deficits. This situation was later offset by a restrictive money and credit policy that forced the Iranian economy into a recession.

Regional planning and development had already been introduced in the first two plans, but implemented only on a small scale. Nevertheless, this first Iranian model of regional planning influenced the conception and implementation of planning in other developing countries. This early experience was used in the foundation of development authorities in the Third and Fourth Plans and especially in the broad regionalization of development—a process that, in the Fifth Plan, received its own special budget.

After having realized the shortcomings of the first two plans, the Plan Organization inaugurated a more comprehensive program in the Third Plan by including the private economic sector and foreign private investment as objects of planning. To attract investment, these two sectors received special treatment in the form of guidelines and regulations for tax relief and credit facilities.

Methods of planning under the first two plans depended very much on the level of the available statistical data and other records. In the beginning, however, there were only estimates. For example, the First National Census was completed in 1956 with inaccurate figures, and was not rectified until 1966 when the second one produced more reliable data. The general difficulty in gathering statistical data and records, as well as in calculating statistical interrelationships, was compounded by the fact that the methods used by industrialized countries for data processing could be applied only partially in Iran. Thus new methods had to be developed. Steady improvement in the statistical services led to more exact methods of planning and more precise evaluation of development policies. Since the general director of the Iranian Statistical Center was automatically appointed as undersecretary for statistics and information in the Plan and Budget Organization, efficient cooperation between both agencies was guaranteed.

In the Third Plan, GDP was included as a target. Goals were also set for the major sectors, such as industry, agriculture, oil production, and construction, and each sector was further subdivided with goals for consumption, investment, and net export. Wherever possible the roles of the public and private sectors were separated. The total expected investment, including the net capital influx from abroad, was compared with the estimate of domestic savings. A program with additional savings possibilities was expected to be created if necessary. Manpower calculations were also made for all planned investments.

In the Fourth Plan, integrated planning was applied. This included political, economic, social, and regional aspects, and was based on a policy of balanced growth. In spite of these goals, the one-sided promotion of big industrial investments during this plan resulted in unbalanced growth. The old problems of inefficient infrastructure and administration and lack of trained personnel were further impediments to planned, balanced growth.

In the Fifth Plan, the above-mentioned policy and goals were more thorough in every respect. In this plan, planning objectives were based not only on economic analysis, with fixed goals, priorities, and quantifiable results, but also on noneconomic conditions and their feedback to the economic sector. Accordingly, programs were being implemented with the participation of the local population, taking into account the expected changes in family, class, and tribal structure, and with the growth effects of resources and structures in the provinces. Continuous and systematic collection of data on national income and national production, as well as detailed statistics about manpower development, foreign trade, and public revenues and expenditures were also needed. The annual evaluation, as a basis for the coming budget year, initiated a new phase of planning in Iran. With this method, contradictions between middle-term and yearly budget planning were eliminated.

At the beginning, planning methods in Iran had to be simple. They contained primitive instruments, because the counterparts of the Plan Organization in the respective ministries would not have understood complicated planning objectives or the interdependence of the various planning goals. At that time, qualified experts with experience in interdisciplinary teamwork, who would have been indispensable, were not available. In subsequent plans these instruments and methods could be extended, refined, and used more effectively. New planning programs were first introduced on a small scale and later extended, on the basis of experience. For example, in the Fifth Plan, welfare goals such as social security and unemployment insurance, promotion of low-income housing, and upgrading underdeveloped regions received large-scale priority treatment, while in the Fourth Plan only the first experiments in these sectors were made.

In order to use up-to-date mathematical methods for planning, the under-secretary of statistics and information in the Plan and Budget Organization was equipped with the most modern data-processing equipment. With the help of this office it was possible to calculate alternative development models in a short time and to procure the data necessary for the annual economic report, the yearly budget, and the Budget Settlement Bill.[13] This bill, published within thirteen months after the end of the fiscal year, was in effect an evaluation of the implementation of the improved, previous budget. A General Directorate of Planimetrics was established in the office of the undersecretary for planning in the Plan and Budget Organization. It was to use the national data to calculate the effects of development plans with respect to alternatives and to evaluate past development policies.

The Fifth Plan was presented to the decision makers in the form of three sets of alternatives, allowing for various economic growth rates, changes in prices, and other factors, and a host of social and economic observations. The effects of selecting any of the sets of alternatives were analyzed in detail. The set selected for the Fifth Plan was the one that, in the light of estimates of available resources, would create the fewest difficulties. This set was subjected to detailed scrutiny in final meetings before its final text was prepared by the Plan and Budget Organization.

FINANCING OF PLANNING

Iran's oil income established the basis for the financing of past development plans and was regarded as the guarantee for international and foreign loans. Since the beginning of planned development, the annual income from oil increased from $100 million in 1947 to almost $20 billion in 1975. Therefore, except during the First Plan and some periods of the Second and Third Plans, money and foreign exchange have not been long-term bottlenecks in develop-ment. The nationalization of the oil industry in 1951, with the resulting cutoff of oil income, destroyed all financial calculations of the First Plan; in fact, only one-fifth of the planned projects materialized. As a consequence of the oil crisis and the international boycott of Iran, the expected 50 percent financing of this plan by national and foreign loans could not be achieved, and the proposed sales of public factories and installations to the private sector had to be postponed. Later, during the Third Plan, the sales of public enterprises partly financed the costs of agrarian reform. In all periods, though, the sale of these government enterprises, especially factories, was difficult, and did not achieve the expected results.

The law legalizing a quota of 80 percent of the oil income for the development budget and only 20 percent for the ordinary budget was enacted for the first time as a part of the Second Seven Year Plan. A weakening position of the Plan Organization among the government agencies, increasing deficits in the ordinary budget, and a growing stagnation at the end of the Second Plan and the beginning of the Third Plan, gravely impeded the financing of the development budget for these periods. The portion of the revenues from oil income for the development budgets had been increased from 64.5 percent in the Second Plan to 66.2 percent in the Third Plan and 78.3 percent in the Fourth Plan. After the ordinary and development budgets had been amalgamated in March 1973, oil revenues for the Fifth Plan covered 80 percent of the state general budget and, in comparison with former budgets, 100 percent of the development expenditures.

In the last three years of the Third Plan, the bonus payments for new oil concessions from five foreign oil companies had a great effect, as a special income, on financing this development plan. The budget for this plan was increased from the original 150 billion rials to 230 billion rials, of which 204 billion rials were spent on development investments. In the Fourth Plan, the development expenditures were set at 480 billion rials, an amount that was increased during the plan period to 621 billion rials as a result of the constantly growing income from oil exports.

The development budget of the public sector for the Fifth Plan amounted to 3.118 billion rials, almost five times more than in the Fourth Plan. The amount of money available in the Fifth Plan was three times more than the combined development expenses of the four preceding plans. These figures demonstrate in what proportion development had been accomplished, and what enormous tasks planners in Iran had to solve. Critics outside Iran evaluating the results of planning in that country would have been well advised to keep in mind the circumstances, the extent, and the growth rates of development in Iran during the postwar period.

The first loan of $75 million from the World Bank to Iran in 1956 was of decisive importance for subsequent development plans and for Iranian financial policy. In fact, this loan also greatly influenced the further credit policy of the bank towards developing countries, because it was the first decision of its kind and of such a magnitude.[14]

In the Second Plan, then, already 27 percent of development expenditure could be financed by foreign loans but only 4.5 percent by domestic ones. The figures in the Third Plan showed an increase of domestic credits to 15 percent while foreign loans constituted 13 percent. When payments for interest and for amortization were deducted, the net figure was only 7.7 percent. Similarly, the corresponding figures in the Fourth Plan were 12.5 percent for domestic loans and 14.4 percent for foreign ones, both as net account.

With these public and private foreign loans, not only had the financing of development taken place, but, more importantly, the participation of foreign creditors and profits of the financed projects had been established. An example of successful participation was the already mentioned activity of the Resources and Development Corporation in Khuzistan Province for nearly twenty years. With the help of this corporation, such infrastructural projects as road building, electrification, and training facilities were executed, and productive sectors were promoted. For example, experimental farms were established. Sugar cane was introduced in Iran to attain yields of more than 100,000 tons of sugar from a 12,000-hectare plantation. This figure represented almost one-seventh of national consumption.

A proposal for participation by German companies in a steel mill at Azna in 1961 failed because the Germans lacked understanding of the situation. In a letter to Ludwig Erhard, then the German minister of economics, Abol Hassan Ebtehaj invited German participation. Because Iran lacked experience, the foreign partner was asked to undertake the type of joint venture that would assure his interest in the successful and profitable conduct of this enterprise during a reasonable period of commercial operation. To this end, the Iranian government was willing to guarantee protection against losses and decreasing profits arising from changes in the prices of raw materials and wages that were not reflected in sales prices. Iran also agreed to protect the German partners against losses in profits even if such losses arose from actions over which the Germans had no control.[15]

In spite of the enormous oil income, Iran in 1975 again reverted to the policy of seeking foreign loans to secure participation from foreign suppliers and more profits from all her investments. Amid the national enthusiasm stemming from the tremendous increase in oil income, Iran concluded many contracts with foreign companies for development projects with cash payments. After reviewing the results of this financing strategy the responsible authorities returned to the former procedures of buying and partial crediting.[16] In the revised Fifth Plan, enacted on May 28, 1975, foreign credits of 115 billion rials, or 5 percent of the development budget income, were projected. The strategy of encouraging foreign investments in heavy industry was expected to result in an influx of $2.5 billion of long-term private foreign capital into Iran during the Fifth Plan. This sum was 8.3 times the corresponding total of the preceding plan. Due to the high amount of Iran's foreign exchange reserves in the 1970s, foreign loans were returned ahead of schedule. The expected total repayment of $6 billion during the Fifth Plan was 4.5 times the corresponding figure under the Fourth Plan. This comparison demonstrates how the financial and foreign exchange situation of Iran had changed in the course of the successive five plans. During the Fifth Plan, Iran also expected payments of 135 billion rials as revenue from public sector investment in and commercial loans to other countries. These receipts were included in the development budget of this plan. As mentioned above, the promotion of foreign exchange income by exports other than oil had high priority in all development plans, but especially in the Fifth Plan.

By creating a single budget institution in 1973, the Plan and Budget Organization vastly improved the government's budget policy and development financing. For the first time the resources of the ordinary budget and the development budget were merged. Development plan revenues, separated into income from oil, foreign and domestic loans, and other sources, disappeared from the budget. A single source of revenue—general revenue— became the basis of the country's budgetary system. All disbursements were centralized in the Ministry of Finance, later renamed the Ministry of Economic Affairs and Finance.

Starting with the Fifth Plan, the state general budget was prepared annually but at the same time assumed a biannual character. During a given budget year forecasts were made for the following budget year, forecasts that at the same time revised the appropriations of the current year. Then both were presented in one volume to the National Assembly. From then onwards, this overall budget consisted of three main parts: (1) the government general budget, including the ordinary budget of the ministries and government agencies, and the development budget for the implementation of development projects; (2) the budget of public enterprises; (3) the budget of other agencies not falling into either of the above categories.

The development budget was concerned with income and expenditure relating to the government's investment operations. These were mainly nonrecurrent and formed part of government functions for a limited period only. Thus the construction of a road, a school, or a hospital was considered a development-and-investment operation. Once a construction project was completed, its maintenance became a current government expenditure, which had to be funded from the ordinary budget. Distribution of the funds by the development budget into different programs had served as an important indication of the choice of priorities, especially in the first three plans.

In the Fifth Plan, especially, the annual budget processing and its stages of preparation opened possibilities for setting priorities in the various sectors within the limits of the five-year planning period. The role of the Plan and Budget Organization also increased during the Fifth Plan, because previously budget implementation agreements related to projects mentioned in the development budget had to be signed and exchanged. These agreements included a description of the work involved in each activity of the project, the relevant appropriation, any special conditions, and an estimate of progress.

IMPLEMENTATION OF THE PLAN

Development planning means orderly and sustained efforts, carried out in an intelligent and well-informed manner to achieve specific objectives. It is an organized activity with its own continuity, backed by the determination to create an effective relationship between the resources available and the objectives held. The Iranian planners intended to mobilize the resources and potential inherent in their society to meet the nation's material needs and ensure its social welfare. Planning should improve the state of a nation's economy, but at the same time it has to introduce the necessary social changes. One objective of planning is a proper and scientific implementation of social and economic development programs designed to meet the needs of the public. Iranian planners were convinced that their country's low rates of economic growth could be increased by means of planning and that deficiencies could be overcome to realize its full potential. For this purpose, strict observance of planning and financial discipline had to be introduced.

The Plan Organization in the first stages of development in Iran was limited mostly to planning and its supervision. Later, it also received an executive capacity. As mentioned above, within the various plan periods, the Plan Organization and respective ministries differed in their relative power to supervise the implementation of development plans. Especially during the Third Plan there was little cooperation between the Plan Organization and the respective ministries involved. Projects were implemented according to the ideas and guidelines proffered by the various institutions.

Under the first three plans, the Plan Organization was mostly responsible for the economic programming and the preparation and supervision of the development budget's implementation. In 1965, the functions of planning and programming were centralized and coordinated with those of budgeting. Both activities were entrusted to a single agency, the Plan Organization, while the government's budgeting system was changed to that of "program budgeting." In order to avoid dissension between the head of the Plan Organization and the heads of the different ministries involved, the prime minister received executive responsibility for the state general budget, which was then formulated by the Central Bureau of the Budget within the Plan Organization. In his capacity as chairman of the High Planning Council, the prime minister was also responsible for decisions regarding development planning and its implementation. Due to these structural and functional changes, the activity and efficiency of the Plan Organization considerably improved. After some years of the new system's operation, the authorities became convinced that there were still obstacles that prevented optimal financing and implementation of development. Therefore, as mentioned above, with the National Plan and Budget Act of March 1973, the ordinary and development budgets were merged. The Plan Organization was renamed Plan and Budget Organization to establish the complete integration of planning and budgeting.

The structure of the former High Planning Council, which was founded in 1947, was revised and reorganized as the Economic Council. Under the directorship of the prime minister, this council consisted of a selected group of ministers and the governor of Central Bank of Iran. With the instructions of the Shah, the Economic Council has had to establish the major development policies and make final decisions about projects with large investments.

As previously mentioned, the Economic Council was involved in the formulation of the Fifth Plan at different stages during the time between the two important conferences—in December 1970 at the Plan Organization in Tehran, and in autumn 1972 in Persepolis.

In the budgetary system of the mid-1970s, the government organizations were divided into four main groups: ministries and government agencies; government corporations such as the National Iranian Oil Company or Iran Air; noncorporate government enterprises such as the Ports and Shipping Organization; and other agencies that dealt mainly with public welfare activities.

All government operations and functions were classified into several "affairs," each "affair" into several "chapters," and each "chapter" into several "activities" and/or "projects." "Activities" and "projects" were clearly defined, the former indicating items funded from current appropriations and the latter those from capital appropriations. Furthermore, new procedures were worked out for operational and financial control. A "development project" consisted of a number of specific operations to be carried out by an executive agency. They were created on the basis of technical, economic, and social feasibility studies within a definite period of time; a specific allocation of funds was made in order to attain the objective of the plan in question. All or part of the expenditures involved in the implementation were funded from development appropriations.

Projects of this kind were classified into profit-making, non-profit-making, and research projects. A profit-making project was to produce and appropriate profit in line with government policies within a reasonable period after becoming operational. A non-profit-making project was to facilitate the overall functions of the government. A research project was based on a contract in order to carry out clearly defined studies for specific purposes. The Plan and Budget Organization was to execute the planning down to the "program" level. The division of "programs" into "activities" and "projects" was made within the executive agencies.

The implementation of planning by the Plan and Budget Organization included both preparation of long-term plans in conjunction with the executive agencies for submission to the Economic Council, and preparation of five year development plans according to the Plan and Budget Act. It also included: ongoing supervision of the country's statistical processes; formulation of social and economic surveys and studies to formulate plans and budgets; and evaluation of the productivity and performance of executive agencies, together with submission of these reports to the prime minister.

Other basic functions of the Plan and Budget Organization were: to present biannual progress reports in conjunction with development projects; to submit annual economic and operational reports for each planning period; and to determine in conjunction with the executive agencies the debts and claims relating to previous development plans, after which the Ministry of Economic Affairs and Finance was to be informed accordingly. Finally, the organization had to carry out any other functions entrusted to it by virtue of legislation and regulations other than the above-mentioned Plan and Budget Act.

In order to fulfill all these functions, the Plan and Budget Organization was given in March 1973 the following structure. A minister of state was head of the Plan and Budget Organization, and was also a member of the Council of Ministers and of the Economic Council. Both councils were presided over by the prime minister. Furthermore, a Civil Evaluation Review Committee was established in order to support both institutions with regard to the efficiency and the results of planning and development in Iran.

The Plan and Budget Organization consisted of eight undersecretaries, executing the many functions concentrated in this organization. The undersecretary for regionalization established four provincial Plan and Budget Bureaus in the largest and most important provinces in Iran to improve planning and supervision of regional development. Other sections included Finance and Administration, Civil Evaluation, Statistics and Information, Planning, Budgeting, and Coordination and Supervision. The last was placed under an undersecretary who supervised fifteen special General Directorates such as Power and Fuel, Industry and Mining, Water Resources, and Agriculture and Livestock. These General Directorates were the counterparts of the respective ministries for all development projects. The eighth undersecretary, for technical affairs, was responsible for the cooperation with consulting companies, domestic and foreign contractors, and foreign experts.

The founding of independent organizations for special activities was another way in which the Plan Organization could carry out its objectives. Among such organizations were the Bureau of Standards, the Institute for Agricultural Mechanization, the Industrial Credit Bank, and the Cartographic Center. After a period of independent operation, most were transferred to the corresponding ministries.

Another way of implementing the plans was by regional development through the agency of independent "authorities." As mentioned above, the first one was founded in 1956 as the Khuzistan Water and Power Authority. This model was copied and applied to five other regional development projects created only during the Third Plan. Two of them, Kuhkiluyeh Development Authority in the Bouyer Ahmadi region and Jiroft Development Authority in the Minab region, were situated in the southern part of

Iran. The activities of these two authorities included the improvement of small infrastructural projects; the implementation of experimental programs for the introduction and improvement of forage crops and of tropical fruits; combating plant pests and diseases; and an examination of the development potential of animal husbandry in both regions.

Thanks to the establishment of similar development authorities during the Third Plan, agricultural production increased in three of Iran's most fertile plains.[17] The Gorgan and Dasht Regional Development Authority, in northeastern Iran, made an appraisal of the region to evaluate its potential for agriculture, irrigation, and animal husbandry, while ways were developed to encourage dry-farming methods. In northwestern Iran, near the border with the Soviet Union, several development units for the cultivation and irrigation of more than 100,000 hectares of fertile land and the settlement of more than 50,000 families were combined by Plan Organization into a development authority that was later transferred to the Ministry of Agriculture. Under the Fifth Plan this project was expected to be completed after investments of more than $200 million.

The third independent agency, the Qazvin Development Authority, was established after the earthquake of fall 1962. This project consisted of a series of studies and extensive measures concerned with developing agriculture, animal husbandry, and groundwater resources. Almost 100 villages, with more than 8,000 families, were supported by agricultural extension and training programs; more than 150 deep wells were dug and the stock breeding of sheep and cattle was improved.

During the Fourth Plan, the activity of these development authorities was continued, but the administrative responsibility was transferred from the Plan Organization to the respective ministries. The largest one, the Khuzistan Water and Power Authority, was transferred to the Ministry of Water and Power, while some agricultural functions went to the Ministry of Agriculture. During the Fifth Plan, specific provincial development programs were introduced. From their budget of 16.4 billion rials, one-third was appropriated for the comprehensive development of tribal regions and one-third for regional development credits. Fifty tribal complexes were to be established in Luristan, Sistan, Baluchistan, Fars, West Azarbayjan, and other regions, each with a capacity of 2,000 families. During this plan six provincial banks were to be established to attract and safeguard small savings, provide the capital needed to best utilize local potential, and supply the technical services needed for the preparation of economically sound projects.

In retrospect, while basically successful, the performance of the Plan Organization was hindered by the limited number of experts in each of its General Directorates, which had to handle the projects of an entire ministry.

Under all five plans, implementation of development planning by regional organizations was highly rated. Past experience was used to improve both the methods and the structure of the development authorities. With the exception of the Development and Resources Corporation in Khuzistan, foreign consulting companies and foreign experts were always limited to an advisory capacity. The number of these companies continuously decreased until, under the Fifth Plan, only two small groups of foreign experts remained as consultants for such special items as social security, which was included in planning for the first time. During each planning period, Iranian experts cooperated very efficiently with their foreign colleagues and were successful in adapting the proposals and recommended models to Iranian conditions.

PROBLEMS IN THE IMPLEMENTATION
OF DEVELOPMENT PLANS

Iranian people are individualists, and their mentality and virtues were not easy to reconcile with the requirements of planning. The introduction of planning in Iran was only made possible by gradual acceptance, at all levels of the administration, of "planning discipline" designed to overcome mental and traditional habits. Iranian planners had also to overcome the Iranian people's lack of confidence in corporate organizations. For example, the people thought the published accounts of the industrial corporations did not reflect their true profits. They therefore hesitated to invest in economic enterprises.[18] The realistic quantitative objectives of the Third and Fourth Plans and their fulfillment contributed to overcoming these difficulties. Thus Iran joined the group of those few developing countries with investment rates of more than 19 percent of GDP.

During the first five plans there were never enough experts at various levels to guarantee achievement of the development planners' full expectations. Under the Fourth Plan, the capital formation of the public sector for education amounted to 3.2 percent of GNP; with the private sector added, the rate was 3.6 percent. In comparison to other developing countries and in spite of many declarations about the importance of all stages of education, the results of this program did not attain the stated goals. In vocational training, for which the first facilities were already established in the 1930s, only 31,000 places were available at centers for skilled and semiskilled labor at the end of the Fourth Plan. Most of the 90,000 students of the country's eight universities were getting an education that did not match professional activities after graduation. Links between higher education and the economic and business sector were missing, the educational system in Iran having few connections with reality. The vastness of the country and its infrastructural difficulties hindered attainment of the goals of primary education. The program for the eradication of illiteracy that was carried out jointly by the Ministry of Education and the Literacy Corps had been partly successful, but in the mid-1970s 68 percent of those aged 10-40 were still illiterate. Kindergarten education was only rudimentary—20,000 places, mostly for well-to-do families. So the output of the educational system in Iran could not match the demand, especially after the tremendous budget increases of the Fifth Plan, which could only be accomplished with 20,000 to 30,000 foreign personnel, ranging from truck drivers to top management officials.

According to Iranian planners, sufficient portions of the development budgets were appropriated for construction of the country's infrastructure during the Second through Fifth Plans, which improved this sector more rapidly and on a broader scale than it was being improved in most other developing countries. At the end of the Fourth Plan the total length of asphalted roads open to traffic amounted to about 12,500 kilometers. At the same time, about 12,000 kilometers of feeder roads (non-asphalted) were completed. In a large country such as Iran, where the main centers of population and consumption are widely separated from the main regions of production, the feeder-road program has been of great importance. This system links agricultural, industrial, and mining regions, enables forest resources to be developed, and gives remote regions access to large towns, thus raising rural standards of health and culture. However, maximum weights for trucks were not controlled very carefully and so in many parts of the country the road system was damaged by overloading. The normal annual capacity of the country's ports was increased to 7 million tons, excluding oil cargo. The country's rail network was expanded, but much of the system in the mid-1970s still consisted of single-line tracks. In addition the capacity and speed of trains remained unchanged.

From their beginnings, transportation and communication were mostly a matter of government administration. Consulting engineers and contractors of the private sector were not used and experience of international research was not applied in this field. At the province level, large construction companies capable of carrying out regional transportation and communication projects were not available. In view of the tremendous increase in oil income for internal investment since 1973, the infrastructure proved too weak to accomplish the aims of the Fifth Plan. Many industrial, agricultural, and tourism projects representing heavy investment by both the private and the public sectors were being completed in the mid-1970s, but the communication facilities required for them to be fully utilized were still inadequate.

Foreign investments in Iran were of great significance for the construction of the domestic economy during the various plans. The zenith of foreign investment was reached during the Third Plan, in which many industrial plans were begun with foreign participation. In spite of the optimistic expectations for the Fifth Plan, with numerous international investment conferences in Iran and exuberant commentaries in local newspapers, foreign investors have held back; neither the number of investors nor the volume of investment has fulfilled expectations. Inefficiency in the respective Iranian administrations, as well as potential investors' misconceptions about Iran's internal affairs and lack of understanding of the local people were the main reasons for this unsatisfactory situation.

Especially in the first two years of the Fifth Plan, opportunities were neglected for the elimination of domestic shortages and the reduction of inflationary pressure by the import of consumer, capital, and intermediate goods on the most favorable terms possible. The relatively competitive position of the export of industrial goods, especially by the petrochemical and heavy industries, was not fully utilized. Marketing opportunities for industrial goods in the Persian Gulf and other neighboring countries were tried on a very limited scale and often with inefficient methods.

EVALUATION OF PLANNING RESULTS

Because of the 1951-53 oil crisis, the goals of the First Plan—but also, in part, those of the Second—were not attained. In the Third Plan, quantitative aims including the growth of GNP, of the ratio of consumer to nonconsumer expenditures, of per capita income, and of gross domestic capital formation were accomplished and even considerably surpassed, except in agriculture and some minor subsectors. Reliable data about these increases were gathered by the Statistical Center and by the Economic Department of the Central Bank. The public sector was informed about the government's decisions and the private sector received the guidelines on which incentives and supporting legislation such as customs and import regulations were based.

However, analysis and evaluation of qualitative aims revealed larger problems. These aims were not attained according to the expectations of the first four plans. In the Fifth Plan, therefore, much more attention was paid to the formulation of qualitative goals and to detailed information about the way to execute development programs. For example, manpower, employment, and professional training received special emphasis during the Third and Fourth Plans but deficiencies in these programs were not solved. Similar results affected administrative reform, rural development, improvement of roads and transportation, etc. The instruments for planning were not refined and flexible enough for the realization of qualitative planning objectives.

In his speech of December 29, 1970, at the Plan Organization, the Shah complained about the "heaviness" of the administration: "Now with our checklists and inspections we will see whether our officials are light or heavy.

We need heavyweights in wrestling and weightlifting but our administrators should be light and always on their toes." For the industrial sector he postulated:

> Our production units must attain levels of output that, in terms of quantity and technological achievement, including automation, as well as the availability of engineers, skilled workmen, and specialists, enable them to compete in price with the products of the industrialized countries. This can only be achieved when our production units reach the same standard as those of the developed countries, which is far from being the present situation. There are two other important points in this connection. The first, on which we cannot place too much stress, is the question of management. The second point is the importance of marketing, the question of packaging and the way products are presented and advertised. This should not be done by making extravagant claims but by producing high-quality goods that the public ultimately comes to know.

Another example of failure to achieve a plan objective was the continued existence of a wide income gap between different classes and between the urban and rural populations. In spite of the general increases in income among the rural population after the land reform, the differences between the income levels of town and village people increased during the Third and Fourth Plans. The traditional dualism in the Iranian economy, together with the population increase and various infrastructural problems, were the main causes for this situation.

Wrong decisions and mistakes during the first five plans, however, could not diminish the overall success of development planning in Iran during the postwar period. Only through planning could waste of resources and capital, disorderly growth of the private sector, stagnation of employment, and chaos in the infrastructure and other public sectors be prevented or at least limited.

For example, the construction of eleven dams with a storage capacity of 9 billion cubic meters of water to irrigate 500,000 hectares and with a generating capacity of 820,000 kilowatts was criticized severely because 81 percent of the irrigation sector expenditure was spent during the Third Plan for dam construction and a further 85 percent during the Fourth Plan. Yet the decision to construct these dams was correct! Water is of vital importance in an arid country like Iran and is one of the main production factors for agriculture. Irrigation is also a main condition for introducing modern agricultural production, especially the profitable application of fertilizer and mechanization. The generation of hydroelectricity was another aim of Iranian planners in order to best utilize domestic resources and save the precious oil reserves for other purposes.

Due to the low level of administrative ability and infrastructure, Iranian planners could afford only the implementation of locally limited projects, not of regional or nationwide ones. Because of these obstacles, even in these projects with deliberately limited targets, the necessary supplementary work, such as construction of the irrigation network, the power line, and other small infrastructural programs, was not completed on time. For the same reason, regional development programs could be executed only over long periods and at tremendous administrative and managerial cost. From the standpoint of benefit-cost analysis, the results of these programs were certainly not better than those of dam construction. For example, in the first eight years after the establishment of the Mohammad Reza Shah Pahlavi Dam on the Dez River, 300 million tons of silt piled up behind the dam as the result of rains and floods. If this were allowed to continue for another twenty or thirty years, the dam would be completely silted up. This was a result of the failure to prevent soil erosion on the banks of the river above the dam.

Frequent criticism that the so-called green revolution has not taken place in Iran is incorrect. The methods of this revolution, such as the introduction of high-yield grain varieties and the application of artificial fertilizers and modern agricultural technology, were utilized in irrigated regions of Iran, especially in the runoff areas of the dams. The green revolution raised yields for wheat, sugar beets, sugarcane, cotton, and rice with enormous production increases—but only in the limited area where improved irrigation was possible. Iran's main agricultural production areas have been in the arid zones with rain-fed cultivation. Production in these areas could be increased only slowly, since they were subjected to frequent climatic hardships such as dry periods or cold winters. The dry-farming sector and the less-developed irrigation regions were improved by various other programs of agrarian reform, including cooperative movements and extension services; however, their success, too, was limited by the above-mentioned structural obstacles.

The importance of the promotion of the private sector, which dated from the beginning of the Third Plan, became evident when the goals of this sector were surpassed in this plan and the ones that followed it. Private enterprises proved to be more flexible and elastic in overcoming economic bottlenecks and meeting consumer demands than enterprises run by the government. The tremendous increase in oil income during the Fifth Plan, however, strained the private sector, since business administration, training, production, and construction were available only in limited amounts. Skilled labor became scarce and building materials were subject to enormous price increases, which led to a partly justified rise in the prices of industrial goods, as well as to a general inflation because of their scarcity.

The integration of the private sector in planning was helped when a policy of reasonable interest rates was launched. For many generations Iran's private economy had been accustomed to annual interest rates of 12 percent to 30 percent, mostly for short-term business loans. These unusually high rates of interest, which were marked by extreme risks for every creditor, had become the standard fare of traditional trades and businesses. Iranian planners formulated credit guidelines for private investments with an annual interest rate between 6 percent and 8 percent for medium- and long-term credits, thus initiating a new economic era. As a result, the traditional class of merchants, landowners, and other "capitalists" of the private sector gained access to cheap commercial and industrial credit in modern enterprises.

Especially before the advent of large oil revenues, customs receipts were a major revenue source of the regular budget. At that time, freedom from duty was often granted for the import of capital goods and—in part—for half-finished goods, a policy that efficiently supported private sector activities. Training of manpower and expansion of employment were two of the main objectives for Iranian planners. So in each plan mention was made of the number of jobs to be created. The Fourth Plan provided for 400,000 new jobs while the aim of the Fifth Plan was 1.1 million new jobs.

The official statistics of unemployment in Iran are only rough estimates. At the end of the Fourth Plan, according to this source, only 1 percent of the work force was unemployed. This may have been correct for the cities. In agriculture during the Fifth Plan, according to a study of the International Labor Organization, 40 percent of the rural work force of 3.6 million laborers was working less than 42 hours per week and 15 percent not more than 28 hours.[19] The agricultural output in 1976 could have been produced by 2.6 million laborers. Thus in the rural areas there was disguised unemployment of some one million people. Increases in rural employment opportunities have become possible only with the extension of the dry-farmed areas and with more intensive cultivation and better irrigation. In 1976, it seemed that only after these objectives had been achieved would the aggregate economic aims be reached and equitable income distribution achieved. In the past, industrial labor was favored with wage increases and public social programs while the situation of the peasants continued to stagnate. Agricultural production per capita increased from the Second Plan to the Fourth Plan by 49 percent, whereas industrial production per capita increased by 140 percent—another indication of the dualism in income distribution. Annual per capita income for agricultural labor was $130 at the end of the Fourth Plan compared with the average per capita income of $367.

Another achievement of Iranian planners was the small rate of price increases during the Third and Fourth Plans, with fluctuations between 0.3 percent and 5 percent per year. The average in these two periods was 2.3 percent, a very low figure in comparison to other developing countries. After the increase in oil income inflation occurred because annual investments were tremendously expanded. As mentioned above, a number of countervailing measures were taken to prevent not only this inflation but speculation and price increases.

Another result of the activity of the Plan Organization was its influence on the reshaping and redesigning of various ministries and government agencies. What little administrative reform was accomplished received substantial help from the Plan Organization. The conversion of some of the above-mentioned public corporations, created by the Plan Organization, to departments of the respective ministries marked stages of this reform and brought new encouragement to these government agencies. The transfer of personnel from the Plan Organization to various ministries had the same beneficial effect.

The Plan Organization played the most important part in creating a proper system of public tender, so that many private companies were established as efficient contractors for government-sponsored development. The Plan Organization also played an important role in promoting and licensing the activities of private consulting companies in Iran. The organization not only rated the competence of consulting engineers and contractors but also formulated the standards, general principles, and conditions relating to their work.

Interim Statement on the Fifth Plan and Long-Term Estimates

The more than tenfold increase in income from oil during the Fifth Plan, in comparison with the Fourth Plan, marked the beginning of a complete transformation in Iranian society. Income from oil under this plan was greater than the absorptive capacity of the Iranian economy and administration. The quantitative objectives of the plan, with average annual growth rates of 26 percent of GNP, were extraordinary and without precedent in international development. The enormous income from oil was also responsible for the unusually low ratio of consumer expenditure—an estimated 66 percent of GNP—to the extremely high annual increases for investment—an estimated 17.7 percent for the private and 38.1 percent for the public sector above the levels of the Fourth Plan.

The Fifth Plan cited the need for international cooperation in light of the greater suitability of Iranian industrial goods for exports, the need for importing labor and energy from abroad, and the need for better utilization of the infrastructure, especially by transportation through the neighboring states. Other objectives of this period were the development of agriculture to raise the productivity and purchasing power of the farmers, and the development of industry based on native Iranian technology. Furthermore, development of education was stressed to supply the demand for trained manpower.

In the first year of the Fifth Plan, the Iranian economy grew at a rate of 35 percent and in the second year at a rate of 42 percent. These rates of growth could not be sustained indefinitely, but the goals of an average of 28 percent annually could be achieved. The budget of the first year of the Fifth Plan was 170 percent larger than the budget for the previous year. The budget of the second year constituted a 26 percent increase over its predecessor. Subsequently, Iranian planners aimed at a less dramatic rate of growth. The increase in the size of the state general budget for the third year was expected to be only 15 percent more than the second, and increases in the budgets of individual ministries and agencies were to be more modest than in the previous two years. The rate of growth of oil revenues had slowed down. The sudden increase in investment yielded results but also inevitably led to bottlenecks. A breathing spell was needed to allow these bottlenecks to sort themselves out. For the third year, no increase in the budget was expected, which Iranian planners have described as part of the process of returning to normalcy. The annual budget became a reflection of the government's operational plans for the year and was to be more strictly adhered to. The imposition of greater budget discipline was also evident in the Plan and Budget Organization's efforts to reduce costs. Two examples were the directive that went out to the state-owned companies instructing them to begin operating at a profit, and the active role outlined for the committee, established at the Shah's instruction, to supervise detailed implementation of the various projects.

The private sector was also expected to play a larger role in the development of the economy and mobilization of resources. The government could not be expected to carry the burden of providing all investments and services. Thus it was looking to the private sector to play a major part in industrial and agricultural development. In the housing sector, the government was not to engage in large-scale construction itself. It was to create, however, a favorable climate by providing technical assistance and credits while leaving the main work to the private sector. The private sector was also expected to return to international money markets, particularly for credits from foreign suppliers. Government credit for the specialized banks was decreased from 20 billion rials in the second year to 10 billion rials in the third year of the Fifth Plan.

The goals and strategies for long-term planning were proclaimed on several occasions by Mohammad Reza Shah Pahlavi and Prime Minister Hoveyda. At the session of December 29, 1970, these objectives were stated as follows: in the next twenty-two years as in the past twenty-two, per capita income should increase five times its original level. Obviously, continuation of this growth and development would require greater efforts on the part of the government and the public. In addition to increasing savings and investments, plans had to be adopted for the implementation of projects that were economically feasible. Maximum effort had to be made to increase the return on capital and the productivity of such investments. The rapid increase in per capita income would also necessitate the implementation of a rational population policy, including family planning, so that the rate of population increase would decline to a suitable level.

During the forthcoming two decades Iran was expected to undergo rapid and large-scale industrialization. One of the most important tasks the country was expected to face was the need to expand into world markets and meet the challenge of strong international competition. In the domestic sector, elimination of the gap between urban and rural areas and the narrowing of income disparity between farmers and city dwellers was to be an urgent priority.

Saadabad Palace

Mohammad Reza Shah and Empress Farah at the opening of Parliament.
Court Minister Assadollah Alam stands behind the Shah.

Mohammad Reza Shah at the graduation
ceremony in the Military Academy

Mohammad Reza Shah at his desk in the Saadabad Palace

Mohammad Reza Shah at a public function. Prime Minister Amir Abbas Hoveyda, second from left, Court Minister Assadollah Alam (with arms crossed) between Hoveyda and the Shah.

Mohammad Reza Shah at the educational conference in Ramsar. To his right, Premier Hoveyda. To his (far) left, Court Minister Alam.

Mohammad Reza Shah in a public school classroom

A cartography workshop in the State Geographic Organization

The Empress Farah Dam on Sefid Rud River

Shaikh Lutfullah Mosque in Isfahan

The Shahanshahi Freeway in Tehran

The Peacock Throne in Golestan Palace. The throne was made during the reign of Fath Ali Shah (1798-1834). The original Peacock Throne, brought from India by Nader Shah (1736-1747), was demolished after his death.

Carpet-making

Girls of the Qashqai tribe

Mohammad Reza Shah distributing deeds of property to the villagers of his Crown Lands. To his right, Assadollah Alam.

Reza Shah, accompanied by Crown Prince Mohammad Reza (in cadet's uniform), on a military inspection.

Reza Shah and his children. Crown Prince Mohammad Reza second from left, Princess Ashraf third from left, Princess Shams second from right.

Reza Shah surrounded by officers and dignitaries of the Ministry of War

A commissioned policewoman directing traffic

Girl-cadets

Volunteers of Iranian Red Lion and Sun Society

Mohammad Reza Shah, Empress Farah, and Crown Prince Reza at the coronation ceremony, 1967

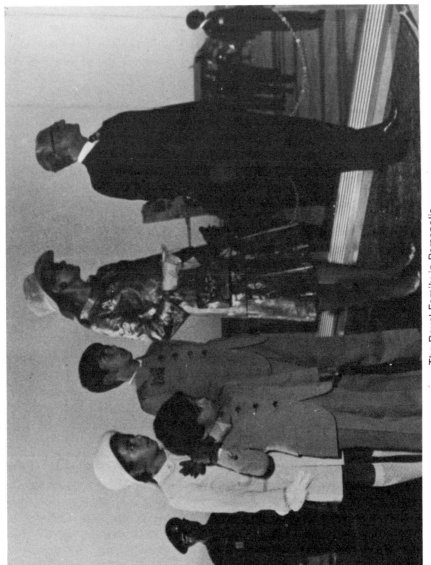

The Royal Family in Persepolis

Mohammad Reza Shah and Empress Farah at the coronation ceremony

Mohammad Reza Shah, Empress Farah, and Crown Prince Reza
at the coronation ceremony

Mohammad Reza Shah and Empress Farah at the opening of Parliament

Mohammad Reza Shah receiving Sheikh Issa ben Salman Al-Khalifa, Emir of Bahrain, in Persepolis, 1971

Mohammad Reza Shah meeting Soviet President
Podgorny on his arrival in Persepolis, 1971

Parade before reviewing stand in Persepolis at the 2500-year
celebration of the Iranian Empire

ROBERT B. STOBAUGH

6

The Evolution of Iranian Oil Policy, 1925-1975

From 1925 through 1975, Iranian leaders, in setting oil policies, sought two goals: *(1)* independence from domination by foreign companies; *(2)* higher revenues. To be sure, these goals often were intertwined, impinging on one another. But I shall discuss them separately; for the complicated picture that unfolded during these fifty years must be simplified in order to discover the rationale for Iranian actions.[1]

THE QUEST FOR INDEPENDENCE

It is seldom easy to shake off the yoke of foreign domination. Iran certainly did not find it so. The nation had to fight every step of the way—and hard fights they were, bringing retreats as well as advances, losses as well as gains. The battles, of course, were not fought with guns. The weapons were legal, political, and economic actions, used in a variety of innovative ways.

The early battles were against Britain and Russia, which dominated the Persian oil scene in those days.[2] This dominance was not surprising, for these two nations had been rivals in Persia since the mid-1800s. The rivalry had been eased by the Anglo-Russian Agreement of 1907, which carved Persia into three zones: the northern, in which only Russian nationals could seek political and commercial concessions; the southern, reserved for British nationals; and a neutral zone separating the two. Nationals of either country could seek concessions in the neutral zone.

Both the British and the Russians had the right to explore for oil. The British found it in large quantity on May 26, 1908. The Russians found none. The British discovery took place at Masjed-e Solayman, in the southern zone, on a concession that William D'Arcy had obtained in 1901 with the aid of the

British government. D'Arcy's company went through several corporate reorganizations in order to bring in more capital. Finally, in 1909, came the formation of the Anglo-Persian Oil Company, later known as the Anglo-Iranian Oil Company and still later as British Petroleum. In 1914, the British government, mainly through the efforts of Winston Churchill, then first lord of the Admiralty, bought 52.5 percent of Anglo-Persian's stock to ensure that the navy would have an inexpensive and secure source of oil. In 1920 the company and the Persian government concluded an agreement that was intended to settle all disputes that had arisen over the D'Arcy concession. During the negotiations leading to this 1920 agreement, Sir Sydney Armitage-Smith, a British Treasury official sent to Tehran by the British government, represented the Persians!

By 1925, the Anglo-Persian Oil Company still had complete control over the oil produced in Persia. The company owned and operated the oil fields, transportation networks, and refinery. The managers, of course, were British, not Persian. The company determined export destinations, quantities, and prices. It used a complicated set of formulas to determine profits derived from Persian oil and to set prices on oil sales to the British navy. The Persians believed that through these formulas the company had a large degree of control over the revenues that the Persian government received from oil, for Persia's oil revenues were calculated as a percentage of the company's profits. The oil fields were located down on the Persian Gulf, far from domestic population centers, and internal transportation facilities were inadequate; so the British had little interest in supplying Persian oil for Tehran and the Persian market. This task was left to the Russians, and the oil they sold was produced in the Soviet Union.

The apparent stability of these arrangements was more illusion than reality. The British were sleeping on a volcano, which soon erupted.

Weakening the Company's Ability to Determine Government Revenues

The chain of events leading Persia from subjugation to independence began to be forged soon after Reza Khan became Shah in 1925.[3] He hired the London solicitors Lumely and Lumely to evaluate the legal status of the 1920 agreement. They gave an opinion that the agreement was a modification and not an interpretation of the D'Arcy concession. Therefore, in the eyes of the Persians, the agreement was not valid since it had not been approved by the Majles (the Persian parliament), a requirement for modifications. After rejecting the 1920 agreement as invalid, the Persian government began to raise questions about the amount of oil revenues received. In 1929, it undertook new negotiations with the company on the issue. These negotiations ended in August 1931 without agreement.

On November 28, 1932, the Persian Council of Ministers, at a meeting presided over by the Shah, canceled Anglo-Persian's oil concession. The *New York Times* reported, "The Persian Government today hurled a sudden challenge at Great Britain," and a special edition of the Tehran newspaper *Ettela'at* proclaimed that "the last foothold of foreigners on Persia's soil" had finally been removed—a claim that proved quite premature. In fact, the Persian finance minister stated a willingness to negotiate a new concession with the company. In the meantime, the company's activities were permitted to continue uninterrupted.

No single explanation was generally accepted as to why Persia canceled the concession. The British view was that the Persians resented the decline in oil revenues, a decline that was inevitable because of the fall in oil prices during the worldwide depression. Indeed, Persia's oil revenues had fallen by 76 percent from 1930 to 1931, a fall much greater than the 36 percent decline in

Table 6.1
OIL REVENUES OF PERSIAN GOVERNMENT AND NET PROFITS
OF ANGLO-IRANIAN OIL COMPANY, 1924-1931
(thousands of pounds sterling)

YEAR	OIL REVENUES OF PERSIAN GOVERNMENT	NET PROFITS OF ANGLO-IRANIAN
1924-25[a]	831	4,067
1925-26	1,054	4,397
1926-27	1,400	4,800
1927-28	502	4,106
1928 (9 months)[b]	529	3,686
1929	1,437	4,247
1930	1,288	3,785
1931	307[c]	2,413

SOURCE: Zuhayr Mikdashi, *A Financial Analysis of Middle Eastern Oil Concessions: 1901-65* (New York: Praeger, 1966), pp. 45-46. Mikdashi's sources were: Anglo-Iranian Oil Company, *Annual Reports;* and International Court of Justice, *Pleadings, Oral Arguments, Documents: Anglo-Iranian Oil Co. Case* (The Hague: 1952).

a.   Twelve months ending March 31; for example 1924-25 figures are for the fiscal year April 1, 1924, through March 31, 1925.

b.   April 1, 1928, through December 31, 1928.

c.   Revised to £1,339 by the 1933 agreement between government and company.

company profits (table 6.1). True, the payment of such a small sum was resented by the Persian government, which immediately protested that it was beneath the dignity of a company like Anglo-Persian to offer it. But the Persians flatly denied that diminishing royalties in the depression provoked them to annul the concession. They pointed out that the Persian budget was balanced easily, and that they had financial reserves of £4 million in London. Furthermore, Persian income had experienced some large drops in prior years—a 64 percent drop in the period 1927-28, for example—without cancellation. Rather, the concession was canceled, they said, because Anglo-Persian had exploited the country, paying the government only £10 million between 1919 and 1930, a sum far less than that to which Persia was entitled. Also, the Persians were frustrated by the lack of response to their prior questions on oil revenues. In addition, they charged that Anglo-Iranian had manipulated its 1931 financial statements in order to reduce its payments to the Persian government.[4]

The press offered a variety of other explanations for the cancellation. Iraq had obtained better terms from British oil interests than had Persia; the Shah was a bit "irked" at the British because of a change in an Imperial Airways route, which deprived him of money, and Great Britain's refusal to relinquish her protectorate over Bahrain, which the Shah claimed; Russian influence was responsible; or it was the fault of the United States—but not of the American oil companies, which had assured Anglo-Persian that they would maintain a "hands-off" policy.

Whatever the reasons for the cancellation, the battle was joined, with the British government rushing to defend the company. Persia was the world's fifth largest producer of oil and the British navy depended to a large extent upon Persian oil for fuel. Furthermore, Persia lay in a strategic position on the road to India.

As the controversy unfolded, it was clear that Britain thought of itself more as the lord of the manor than a paying guest. The *New York Times* reported that "the British regard their monopoly as firmly established and can be expected to resist to the utmost any attempt to deprive them of it." The company's attitude was straightforward. There was no provision for cancellation of the contract, and consequently it could not accept the notification received from the Persian government.

In one sense the picture was that of a dramatic duel between Anthony Eden and Reza Shah. The young Englishman, then undersecretary for foreign affairs, announced in the House of Commons that Britain would not tolerate any damage to the company's interests or any interference with its premises or business activity in Persia. The Shah, in turn, warned the British against sending a single soldier or marine to guard the oil fields and reminded them that only a couple of Persian shells or a single well-aimed bomb would be needed to send millions of barrels of British oil up in smoke. Simultaneously, the Persian War Office purchased from Italy gunboats manned by Italian seamen and placed an order in Germany for military airplanes.

In another, larger sense the rivalry embodied an age-old conflict over the rights of foreigners in Persia. The British denounced Persia's action as a repudiation of a solemn contract, and the Persians claimed complete authority to annul any concession in their territory and challenged the British government's right to intervene in an internal Persian question. Yet both sides wanted to settle, and indeed, it was said at that time that the Shah was well-disposed toward the company and very friendly with Sir John Cadman, its chairman.

Britain and Persia both went to the League of Nations, Britain to obtain a judgment as to the rightness of the Persian government's actions, and Persia to complain against Britain's "illegitimate interference" in a question that "must be settled according to internal laws in the Persian courts." Before the League could reach a decision, the company and Persia compromised and a new concession was signed on April 29, 1933.

Persia won a new method of determining her oil revenues, a method that was more straightforward than the old one.[5] Royalties were to be based on the volume of oil produced and the amount of dividends paid by the company to its stockholders, with a guaranteed minimum payment to Persia of £975,000 annually regardless of output or dividends. The payments were to be calculated in terms of gold, thus maintaining Persia's purchasing power in case of changes in the value of sterling. Also, the company made a lump sum payment in settlement of all past claims. Whether the Persian government would get larger payments than under the old contract depended on estimates about the company's production and profits.

In addition to the financial settlements, Persia won other benefits that were intended over the long run to give her more independence from foreign domination. The company relinquished 80 percent of the land in its concession, thereby reducing its total concession area to 100,000 square miles. Persia was allowed to appoint a delegate who would have access to all information to which the stockholders of the company were entitled. (In 1919 the British foreign secretary had turned down a Persian government request to be allowed to purchase a few shares out of a new issue of £7.5 million to be made in 1920, though presumably any Persian could have purchased shares on the London Stock Exchange.) The company was to recruit its technical and commercial staff, as well as its artisans, from among Persian nationals to the extent that it found any such persons possessing the requisite competence and experience. Finally, the company was to develop the Naft-e Shah oil field and to process its output for Persia's domestic consumption, thereby eliminating Persia's dependence on imports from Russia.

The British won an extension of their concession to 1993 instead of 1961—a gain that in retrospect had little significance. The settlement of 1933 resulted in relatively calm relations between Iran and the company until after the end of World War II.* Other actions, however, affected the nation's freedom to achieve control over its oil industry.[6] Iran became the artery through which Allied military supplies moved to Russia; as a result, British and Russian troops occupied the country in August 1941. Within a month Reza Shah abdicated; his son, Mohammad Reza Pahlavi, succeeded him.

In accord with a 1942 treaty between Iran, Britain, and Russia, British troops were withdrawn after the war. The Russians first refused to withdraw, then extracted from Iran a fifty-year oil concession in exchange for their exit. U.S. pressure, however, was needed to remove Soviet troops by mid-1946. Freed from coercion, the Majles declared the concession "null and void."

Yet the problem of foreign domination of the oil industry remained—the British were still in charge.

Loosening the British Grip

After the Russians left, there began spreading little by little in the minds of the Iranians ideas that would not merely change this or that detail of the agreement, or substitute one agreement with Anglo-Iranian for another, but would overthrow the company itself and shatter the bases on which it stood.[7] The Iranians gradually began saying to themselves that foreign ownership of Iranian oil rested upon foundations that were not just. As the Shah was reported to have said in an interview some twenty-five years later, "We were hearing that the oil company was creating puppets—people just clicking their heels to the orders of the oil company—so it was becoming in our eyes a kind of monster—almost a kind of government within the Iranian government."[8] As Alexis de Tocqueville had remarked in 1848, a wind of revolution was blowing and the storm was on the horizon.[9]

The British failed to see what was going on in the hearts and minds of the Iranians. As a result, the British attitude was wholly inappropriate to the new age that was dawning. They believed that the Iranians should have been grateful to Anglo-Iranian for providing things that they could not have provided for themselves—employment, houses, schools, and hospitals, as well as a solid income. The British believed that the company had given Iran "a half-century of generous and enlightened treatment."[10] Furthermore, Anglo-Iranian had no intention of giving up Iran, the cornerstone of its empire—a cornerstone that provided 76 percent of the company's crude oil

---

* In 1935, when Persia changed its name to Iran, the Anglo-Persian Oil Company became the Anglo-Iranian Oil Company.

production in 1950 in spite of the company's giant oil fields in Iraq and Kuwait.

The resulting confrontation for control over the Iranian oil industry stands as one of the great political and economic battles between a developing country and a multinational enterprise with its important allies. In this case, the company had the active support of the British government, which still owned more than half of its stock, and the silent but crucial support of the six other major oil companies. Before the confrontation was resolved, there were killings, riots, untold economic hardships, and changes in the Iranian government. An understanding of the confrontation is necessary for an understanding of Iran's long-term goals.

Iran fired an opening salvo in the late 1940s with a request that the company increase her revenues *and* give her a voice in the management of the Iranian oil industry. At first the British were slow to respond, but the company eventually signed an agreement with the Iranian finance minister on July 17, 1949, to increase Iran's oil revenues substantially. Then, on January 11, 1951, the Majles refused to ratify the 1949 agreement. Their oil committee, under the chairmanship of Dr. Mohammad Mosaddegh, had recommended against it. The company then brought forth some sweeteners: a cash advance plus an offer to reopen negotiations for a 50/50 profit-sharing settlement, presumably along the lines of agreements that had been reached in Venezuela in 1947 and Saudi Arabia at the end of 1950. Negotiations were never reopened. The Iranians chose a more daring course.

The nationalization and shutdown. On February 19, 1951, Dr. Mosaddegh proposed to the oil committee of the Majles that the industry be nationalized, a proposal that brought forth a deluge of extraordinary events.[11] On March 3, a member of a nationalistic religious group, the *feda'iyyan-e eslam,* assassinated Prime Minister General 'Ali Razmara when he opposed the nationalization plan. On March 8, the oil committee adopted the nationalization proposal. One week later, the Majles voted unanimously in favor of nationalization, following which a crowd of two thousand carried the deputies on their shoulders. On March 20, the Senate also approved. Following royal assent (the Shah did not have the right of veto), nationalization became a legal fact. On March 20, the Shah appointed Hosayn 'Ala, former ambassador to Washington, as prime minister. But growing tension in Iran caused Ala to resign in April. He was replaced by Dr. Mosaddegh, whom the Majles had voted to request the Shah to appoint.

In contrast to the popular frenzy within the country, the Iranian government took a more conciliatory stance toward the outside world. They explained that the nationalization was necessary to avert new Russian pressure for oil concessions in Iran. Furthermore, the Iranians explained that they were not confiscating the properties but would compensate the company for them. They said they were exercising their sovereign right to nationalize, as the ruling British Labour Party had recently done over parts of British industry. The Iranians would continue to supply Britain with oil.

The British attitude started out as one of smugness; they believed that Iran was dependent on Anglo-Iranian. Reports like this filtered out of London: the size and complexity of Anglo-Iranian's operations were "almost beyond the comprehension of a primitive country such as Iran"; the Iranians would "come crying back to the company for help in a very short time" after trying to run the refineries themselves; even if they could run them, they still could not get the oil transported, for the company owned more than 160 tankers and chartered others, while Iran owned "exactly none." Furthermore, Iran could not stand the grave economic consequences, because the Iranian government—according to a leak from London—had not been able to pay its civil servants for the last two months. This British optimism that Iran would not take drastic action continued in the face of overwhelming evidence to the contrary. For example, in June 1951, as Iranian political leaders were producing documents showing the company to be, in their eyes, a detestable influence that must be extirpated once and for all, reports from London were indicating that "the Iranians are beginning to realize that they have bitten off more than they can chew."

Although the Iranians insisted that nationalization was an issue between the Iranian government and the Anglo-Iranian Oil Company, the British government actively entered the fray on the company's side. The British justified this intervention on the grounds that the government was the majority stockholder in the company. There was consternation within the government about Anglo-Iranian's handling of the dispute. Minister of State Kenneth Younger, in a memorandum unpublished until 1975, stated that Anglo-Iranian never tried to make a proper political assessment of the situation and that Sir William Fraser, head of the company, had on many occasions explicitly stated in Younger's presence that he did not think politics concerned him at all.[12] According to Younger, Fraser appeared "to have all the contempt of a Glasgow accountant for anything which cannot be shown on a balance sheet." The Labour government nevertheless continued to support the company, and government support continued when Churchill and the Conservatives came to power in October 1951.

The British responded at two levels. On one level they took, in the words of one newspaper correspondent, a "legalistic attitude" involving "tenuous points of law." Their fundamental theorem was simple: their concession until 1993 was chiseled in granite. To be sure, any nation could nationalize its industries, as Britain itself had done, but Iran's actions were not a legitimate exercise of sovereign rights. The 1933 agreement, which had been concluded under the auspices of the League of Nations and ratified by the Iranian Parliament, contained two important provisions: *(1)* the agreement should not be altered by law; *(2)* any conflict between the parties should be referred to arbitration. The real issue, the British explained in a note to Iran, was the wrong done if a sovereign state broke a contract that it had deliberately made. True, Britain eventually expressed a willingness to consider some form of nationalization. But British concessions continued to run behind Iranian demands.

Britain's other approach was to carry on a war of nerves. The British government warned that it would take "all possible steps" to protect such a major British enterprise and hinted that it would "resist by force any effort to take over the Anglo-Iranian Oil Company." To back up such threats, it dispatched 4,000 British paratroopers to the Mediterranean and reinforced its Mediterranean fleet with seven additional warships. Behind the scenes, the British continued to argue among themselves over the question of military intervention. Foreign Secretary Herbert Morrison, although he had been a pacifist in World War I, was hawkish on Iran. On September 27, 1951, at a crucial cabinet meeting, he expounded the case for military intervention. He was cut short by Prime Minister Clement Attlee, who insisted that force was out of the question. The British attitude continued to be: "Just wait until the beggars need the money badly enough—that will bring them to their knees."[13]

The Iranians responded with a barrage of words. Prime Minister Mosaddegh declared that Iran would "fight to the end." Hosayn Makki, secretary of the parliamentary oil committee and secretary-general of Dr. Mosaddegh's National Front Party, proclaimed, "We are going to nationalize our oil if it takes the last drop of our blood." Iran was a "powder keg," and Britain had better not approach with the match lest both countries be burned together.

No doubt popular feelings in Iran supported such statements. An Iranian religious leader, declaring that Britain had looted Iran's God-given riches and despoiled her people, proclaimed that all Iranians were "ready to die for their objectives, for a better life."[14] Prime Minister Mosaddegh easily won votes of confidence in the Majles. True, in June 1951, several deputies were incensed over the tactics that Mosaddegh used to force a vote, but no one was prepared to face the odium of a public nay on an issue as popular as nationalization. And in Baharestan Square before 6,000 persons, nationalist orators one after another called for unlimited sacrifices to extirpate Anglo-Iranian "root and branch, and, with it, foreign domination."

Perhaps part of the reason for the Iranian adamancy was the widespread belief in Tehran that at the last moment the United States would come to the aid of the Iranians to prevent a shutdown of their oil industry.[15] The Iranians had compiled a simple equation for themselves: the United States could not afford the risk that the Iranians might be driven to ask for Soviet help in running their oil facilities. "The West has far more to lose than Iran" was a belief held strongly in Iran because of prior U.S. and British emphasis on the vital importance of Iranian oil to the Western world.

The Americans, surrounded by this thunder of combat, were making a special effort to keep out of the third-power position once occupied by Germany. To be sure, the U.S. ambassador to Iran, Henry F. Grady, described Iran as a "companion state in the assembly of free nations" and Iranian oil as "one of the invaluable assets of the free world in the present critical times."[16] Yet the United States did not help Iran against Britain, and later in the crisis expressed disappointment that Iran had summarily rejected without any study a British offer to negotiate. Clearly, the United States was worried that the Iranian oil crisis might produce a chain reaction in other major producing countries of the world.[17]

The major oil companies, including the five U.S. majors, were even more adamant than the U.S. government about not helping the Iranians. The oil executives deplored the Iranian action as an illegal repudiation of a valid concession. In fact, no major oil company was likely to purchase oil from the nationalized concession of another company for fear of setting a precedent that might rebound against itself. And without the help of at least some of the majors, Iran was helpless in her fight with Anglo-Iranian. For at that time, the seven majors controlled virtually all of the production and most of the refining and marketing outside North America and Russia; in fact, they controlled some 98 percent of the so-called "world oil market" (see table 6.2).

In spite of this lack of support, Iran moved to take over the physical assets of the company. June 11, 1951, was the day when the Iranian government's mission to take over the oil facilities had its first meeting with Anglo-Iranian officials. Across the river from Abadan's bright metal storage tanks and massive towers, the mission raised the Iranian flag over the general manager's office, while the Iranian navy band played the national anthem. A few days later talks between the Iranian government and Anglo-Iranian opened in Tehran, but within a week they had broken down.

The British made the physical move that eventually caused the Iranian oil industry to shut down. At the end of June 1951, the British suspended loadings of oil tankers in the face of Iranian insistence that the tankers' masters sign receipts acknowledging unconditional Iranian title to all the oil loaded. Operations at Abadan began to be cut back as the oil began to pile up in the limited storage capacity. And so the Iranian oil industry ground creakingly to a halt.

To be sure, the Iranians attempted to export oil, but few foreign buyers were willing to face Anglo-Iranian's threats to sue any purchaser of oil that it considered to be "hot." And, indeed, the company made good its threats. A British court in Aden ruled that a cargo of Iranian oil that had come into its

Table 6.2

CRUDE OIL PRODUCTION OF PRINCIPAL COMPANIES AND PRODUCING COUNTRIES IN THE WORLD OIL MARKET, 1950 [a]

(thousands of barrels a day)

	Exxon	Mobil	Socal	Texaco	Gulf	Total U.S.	Royal Dutch/ Shell	Anglo-Iranian	Subtotal Previous Seven	Other Companies	Grand Totals	Seven Majors as Percentage Grand Total
Iran	—	—	—	—	—	—	—	665	665	—	665	100
Kuwait	—	—	—	—	172	172	—	172	345	—	345	100
Iraq	16	16	—	—	—	32	32	32	96	40	136	71
Qatar	4	4	—	—	—	8	8	8	24	10	34	71
Saudi Arabia	174	58	174	174	—	579	—	—	579	—	579	100
Indonesia [b]	3	3	16	16	—	38	41	—	79	—	79	100
Venezuela	818	48	15	—	231	1,112	378	—	1,490	10	1,500	99
TOTAL	1,015	129	205	190	403	1,942	459	877	3,278	60	3,338	98

SOURCE: Adapted from M.A. Adelman, *The World Petroleum Market* (Baltimore: Johns Hopkins University Press, 1972). p. 80.

NOTE: Because of rounding some columns and rows do not add to the total.

a. World Oil Market defined as the world excluding those countries whose production is used primarily for internal consumption, that is, excluding the Communist blocs; North America; South America and the Caribbean outside Venezuela; Western Europe; Africa (but in later years Algeria, Libya, and Nigeria began large-scale production and were therefore included as part of the world oil market); and the Middle East outside the Persian Gulf.

b. Includes Brunei and Sarawak.

jurisdiction remained the property of Anglo-Iranian even though an Italian company had purchased it from the National Iranian Oil Company (NIOC), the state-owned company that had been formed to operate the Iranian oil industry. But not all oil shipped from Iran came into the jurisdiction of a British court; some did arrive at the buyers. Yet the quantities were miniscule compared with shipments before the nationalization. Thus, other than provide oil for the small domestic market, the Iranian oil industry was practically idle for three years.

Within Iran, the contrast between ambitious dreams and harsh reality became evident as the crisis pursued its course. The majors had no difficulty in increasing production elsewhere in the Middle East to replace Iranian oil in the world's markets (see table 6-3), and the profits of Anglo-Iranian, which had extensive holdings elsewhere, did not suffer disastrously. They dropped from £34 million in 1950 to about £24 million in each of the three subsequent years. Iran was the main sufferer, and domestic opposition to Mosaddegh began to mount.[18] He countered by increasing his powers and attempting to destroy his opponents politically. When many in the Majles turned against him for challenging the authority of the Shah, he ordered a plebiscite in August 1953 to dissolve the Majles. When the Shah appointed a new prime minister,

Table 6.3
WORLD PRODUCTION OF CRUDE OIL, 1950-54
(thousands of barrels a day rounded to nearest ten thousand)

	1950	1951	1952	1953	1954
Iran	660	340	20	30	60
Saudi Arabia	550	760	820	840	950
Kuwait	340	560	750	860	950
Iraq	140	180	390	580	630
Other Middle East	60	80	100	120	150
Total Middle East	1,750	1,920	2,080	2,430	2,740
United States	5,410	6,160	6,260	6,460	6,340
Rest of world	3,730	4,210	4,650	4,910	5,350
World total[a]	10,890	12,290	12,990	13,800	14,430

SOURCE: *B.P. Statistical Review, 1960,* p. 19.

[a] This is the entire world and not the "world oil market" defined in table 6.2.

General Fazlollah Zahedi, Mosaddegh refused to recognize him and took control of the army, which had traditionally been under the direct control of the Shah. The Shah then left the country. The internal dispute reached a climax. After riots, Mosaddegh was ousted and General Zahedi assumed control. The Shah returned, having been out of Iran only a few days.

The settlement. By the time Mosaddegh had fallen, the British had begun to realize that they could no longer retain the monopoly on Iranian oil that they had enjoyed for forty years [19] In the meantime, U.S. leaders also concluded that any solution satisfactory to Iran must involve non-British companies. Iranian resentment against the British was too strong and the future security of Iran rested more with the Americans than the British. Thus in December 1953 Sir William Fraser, still chairman of BP, called a meeting in London to which he invited the five U.S. majors along with Royal Dutch/Shell and Compagnic Française des Pétroles (CFP). All companies accepted the invitation, although the American companies first checked with the U.S. government.[20] So negotiations began between the majors and Iran.

The diplomacy leading up to these negotiations was largely in American hands. Herbert Hoover, Jr., acting as a special representative of the United States within the Department of State, flew between Tehran, Washington, and London to mediate. The negotiations themselves showed even more clearly the extent to which the British had lost their position in Iran. The head of the negotiating team for the international group of companies was Exxon's Howard Page. He was joined by Shell's John Loudon, and by BP's Harold Snow, whom one author called "too silent to give offense."[21] Their bargaining with the Iranian finance minister 'Ali Amini was long and difficult, but an agreement was reached in August 1954 and was soon afterward approved by the Majles and the Shah. On October 30, 1954, oil exports were begun by the group of companies, commonly known as the Consortium, and formally as Iranian Oil Participants, Ltd., incorporated in London.

The oil companies still had plenty of power and influence. The Consortium, as contract agent for the NIOC, operated the facilities and exported the crude oil and products. Consortium operations were conducted by two companies, the Iranian Oil Exploration and Producing Company in association with Iranian Oil Refining. The exports were handled by trading companies established by individual members of the Consortium. Despite all this, Iran emerged with unquestionable ownership. The year 1954 stands as one of the great turning points in the history of oil-exporting nations. For the first time ownership by foreigners, so tightly woven into the fabric of the past, began to unravel. The heart of the agreement between the Consortium and Iran was that the entire assets belonged to Iran—a concept that was to become widely accepted over the next several decades in the other oil-exporting nations.

Table 6.4

PARTICIPANTS IN THE IRANIAN CONSORTIUM, 1955

COMPANY	NATIONALITY	SHARE (PERCENT)
British Petroleum	British	40
Royal Dutch/Shell	60/40, Dutch/British	14
Exxon	U.S.	7
Socal	U.S.	7
Texaco	U.S.	7
Mobil	U.S.	7
Gulf	U.S.	7
CFP	French	6
Iricon Group[a]	U.S.	5
		100

SOURCE: United States Senate, Ninety-Third Congress, "Multinational Petroleum Companies and Foreign Policy," *Hearings Before the Subcommittee on Multinational Corporations of the Committee on Foreign Relations* (Washington, D.C.: U.S. Government Printing Office, 1975), part 7, pp. 245, 246.

[a]   The Iricon group was added in 1955 and consisted of American Independent (American Independent, in turn, was owned by ten independent oil companies) with 2/3 percent, Richfield Oil Corporation with 25 percent, and Standard of Ohio, Getty Oil Company, Signal Oil and Gas Company, Atlantic Refining, Hancock Oil Company, Tidewater Oil Company, and San Jacinto Petroleum Company, each with 8 1/3 percent. The Iricon group subsequently changed membership somewhat.

These other nations also followed Iran's lead in establishing a national oil company.

The agreement also contained a number of other clauses that moved Iran along the road toward oil independence. First, dependence on the British was lessened, for BP's share was reduced to 40 percent and American companies were brought in (table 6.4 shows the shares). Second, long-run dependence on the majors was lessened because independent oil companies, which were allowed to own 5 percent of the Consortium as window dressing in response to antitrust complaints in the United States, got a taste of cheap foreign oil and their appetites were whetted for future international activities. Third, two of the seven directors of each of the two operating companies were Iranians. Fourth, financial and technical information about the operations was to be made readily available to NIOC. Fifth, the Consortium agreed to assist NIOC in training Iranians to replace foreign personnel. Sixth, NIOC kept the local distribution facilities along with the Naft-e Shah oil field and Kermanshah refinery used to supply the local market. And, seventh, NIOC was to carry out non-basic operations, such as those related to housing, public roads, medical, canteens, clothing stores, education, and similar services.

The exact financial settlement has been reported in detail elsewhere.[22] The highlights were: the agreement was to last until 1979, with the Consortium having renewal rights until 1994; Iran's share of the profits was to approximate the 50/50 split in profits between nations and companies that had become commonplace in the oil world; the Consortium guaranteed to produce at specified levels from 1955 through 1957; British Petroleum was paid for its loss by the other Consortium members and Iran, and in addition obtained a tax benefit from the British government.

To many observers, from Iran's viewpoint the most obvious word to be associated with the 1951 nationalization and the 1954 settlement is failure. They argue that because of the power given the Consortium, the British won the struggle. Such arguments are based primarily on the fact that Iran's financial gains in the 1954 settlement were essentially nothing more than could have been achieved three years earlier without nationalization and without the enormous costs to the nation. However, these arguments overlook Iran's nonmonetary gains. Yet it is possible that even these gains could have been made at less cost to Iran had Dr. Mosaddegh adopted a more flexible bargaining position. And, to be sure, Iran was still wholly dependent on the Consortium for exports and for operating the domestic industry.

Lessening Dependence on the Consortium

Shortly after the dust of the 1951-54 conflict settled, Iran's leaders, with the Shah playing an ever more active role, moved to lessen the nation's dependence on the Consortium. They did this not by reducing the Consortium's absolute importance, but rather by reducing its relative importance through bringing in more foreign companies and expanding the activities of the National Iranian Oil Company. The Iran Petroleum Act of 1957 was a key document in this thrust because it opened up new territories for exploration and allowed NIOC to enter into new types of contract.[23]

Bringing in more foreign companies. The period following passage of the Petroleum Act is full of interest, for Iran began to experiment with new types of agreement that would allow foreign companies to explore for Iranian oil.[24] The experiment attracted international attention; President Eisenhower heard much about it when he stopped in Tehran on a goodwill tour in December 1959. Perhaps more important, the Arab nations were fascinated because the new agreements enabled NIOC both to share in management and to obtain a bigger percentage of the profits—twin goals of all the oil-rich nations. The *Wall Street Journal* reported on December 8, 1959, that the experiment might "do much to influence oil's future in the entire Middle East—and in other major producing areas as well." NIOC, as representative of the Iranian government, introduced two new types of agreement. In one type, the foreign company was in a joint venture with NIOC; in the other, the foreigner provided exploration service to NIOC under a contract.

NIOC had begun to make joint venture agreements almost before the ink was dry on the 1957 Petroleum Act. In August 1957, just a few weeks after the act was ratified, NIOC signed an agreement with Italy's state-owned oil company, Ente Nazionale Idrocarburi (ENI), to form an Iranian-Italian Oil Company, known as SIRIP. At the time, this deal was quite controversial. Although technically the profit split between the company and government was to be 50/50, in practice the Iranians would get 75 percent; for half of the profits would go to the Iranian government and half to the joint venture, which in turn would pay NIOC 50 percent of *its* profits without NIOC's putting up capital until oil had been discovered. The majors, which had a number of 50/50 deals elsewhere, were unwilling to go beyond the 50 percent mark. The majors were angered by the ENI deal and called it "blackmail." Furthermore, the majors expressed doubt about the ability of the Italian company to do the job, because it had had no experience with the kind of terrain it would encounter in Iran. In addition, the U.S. State Department was worried that the deal might "upset the Middle East oil apple cart." Accordingly, it made representations to Rome and Tehran at various times, but to no avail.

As the ENI arrangement approached consummation, the majors downplayed its importance. The *New York Times,* echoing the majors, reported that if the deal should be approved, "it would not set a pattern for other oil-producing countries, since it would be simply an arrangement between governments." Most governments of oil-importing nations, the *Times* continued, would rather deal with private companies than with governments in oil operations; except for the fact that both Iran and Italy were anxious to increase the government's share of oil revenues, it was hardly likely that the deal would go through."[25] The deal was said by unnamed U.S. oil companies to be unattractive to private oil companies from a commercial standpoint—the 25 percent share was far too small.

In spite of such warnings, Iran proceeded to make joint ventures with numerous companies, including state-owned ones. Although the basic terms remained unchanged, the agreements became increasingly favorable to Iran. The government not only received cash bonuses but also gained more control over the operations, made the ventures more subject to Iranian law and arbitration, and gave fewer years for exploration and exploitation.

Less than one year after the ENI contract was signed, the Standard Oil Company of Indiana—a large U.S. oil company, but not one of the "majors," since it did not operate much abroad—offered Iran terms that startled both the oil industry and the Iranians. In addition to the 75/25 deal that ENI had granted NIOC, Standard of Indiana also offered a cash bonus of $25 million to the Iranian government. The Iranians were amazed by the terms. But George Jenkinson, who handled the Indiana company's bidding, said that it was no "stiffer" than some oil deals he had made in the United States.[26] Thus, Iran's second joint venture, named Iran Pan-American Oil Company (IPAC), was born on June 5, 1958.

Later, two other batches of joint ventures were established. In 1965, six were formed. These agreements were established on the basis of bids made by 29 foreign companies, individually, or as part of a group, that had financed a seismic survey of certain offshore areas that were open for bids. Again the independent oil companies took the lead: only three members of the Consortium bid—Royal Dutch/Shell, Mobil, and Compagnie Française des Pétroles—and only Shell was a successful bidder. There were five other successful groups of companies, and these groups included twelve American independents, six German independents, and three government groups (Italian, French, and Indian). Six years later, in 1971, NIOC approved three more joint ventures. In addition to one major (Mobil) and one American independent, the successful bidders for the first time included Japanese companies.

In contrast to these joint ventures, the second form of agreement under which foreign companies had the right to find and produce oil in Iran was the so-called service contract. Such agreements called for the foreign company to be a contractor working for NIOC and to be remunerated in oil for its services—no oil, no renumeration. The first such contract came in 1966 with Entreprise de Recherches et d'Activités Pétrolières (ERAP), the French state-owned company. Iran was to get 90 percent of the profits, which at the time was heralded as a "revolution." Thus the first two non-Iranian signatories of the innovative agreements were state-owned companies of two European nations that long had been frustrated at their exclusion by the majors, and by the home governments of the majors, from most of the world's major oil fields. Three years later, NIOC awarded two additional service contracts, one to an American independent and the other to a group consisting primarily of state-owned companies of European nations—again ENI and ERAP, plus Hispanoil of Spain, Österreichische Mineralölwerke (OMW) of Austria, and Petrofina of Belgium.

More recently, in 1974, NIOC granted a different type of service contract, under which it undertook to assume responsibility for production operations as soon as commercial production started. The foreign partner would then obtain a contract to purchase 35 to 50 percent of the crude oil at prevailing market prices less a 3-to-5-percent discount and less an additional discount for the recovery of exploration and development expenses. NIOC signed six such agreements, again with a mixture of independent oil companies and European state-owned companies.

A number of persons have made comparisons of Iran's revenues under the various types of agreement. As with all economic analyses, the results depend on the assumptions. For example, one analysis, based on 1971 prices, indicated a profit split of 78/22 in favor of Iran for the Consortium agreement rather than one of 50/50, because of the difference between the posted price on which Iran's profit share was calculated and the lower market price, and because of royalty payments (I discuss the complexities of oil pricing later).[27] The same analysis indicated a 79/21 split for the typical joint-venture agreement, though the 79 would be higher if a bonus payment were taken into account. Estimates of the Iranian share under the service contracts ranged from 91 percent down to 45 percent, depending on assumptions concerning realized market prices, the time value of money, and how Iran marketed her share of the oil. As of 1975, however, the discussion over revenues from service contracts was still largely of theoretical interest, since no oil of commercial quantities had been found under those arrangements.

Thus, in the nineteen-year period 1957 through 1975, Iran obtained a remarkable diversity of new entrants in the Iranian oil industry (figure 1). In all, NIOC made twenty separate agreements involving thirty-four foreign companies of nine different nationalities. Only two of the thirty-four were major oil companies.

Yet these agreements contributed little towards lessening Iran's dependence on the Consortium. By 1975 only four of the joint ventures and none of the service contracts had resulted in commercial production, and together they were responsible for less than 10 percent of Iranian output. Still, the cash bonuses received from the agreements had enriched Iran's treasury by some $300 million, a sum equivalent to about one year of revenues from the Consortium in the 1960-62 period.

Other NIOC activities. Iran did not rely on foreign companies alone to lessen her dependence on the Consortium, for NIOC proceeded to attack the problem in four main areas: *(1)* domestic oil facilities; *(2)* oil exports; *(3)* gas exports; *(4)* petrochemical manufacture.[28]

(1) Domestic oil facilities: NIOC's first task after the Consortium settlement was to manage the domestic operations assigned to it. These consisted in the

Figure 1

ENTRANTS OTHER THAN CONSORTIUM IN THE SEARCH
FOR OIL IN IRAN, 1955-1975

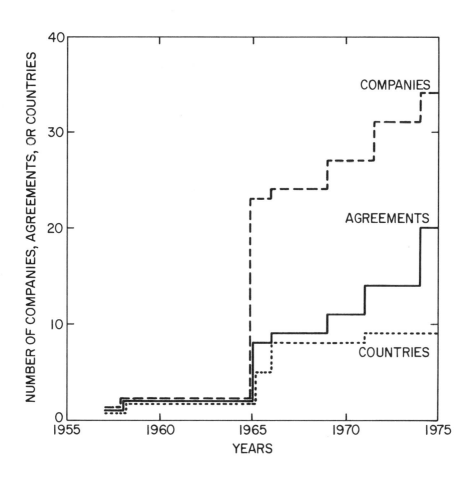

Source: Summarized from information in various issues of
Iran Oil Mirror and from NIOC, Details of New Contracts
(Tehran: NIOC Public Relations Office, 1974), as tabulated in
Fesharaki, op. cit., pp. 74-75, 81, and 83.

nonbasic operations of the oil industry and the supply of domestic oil and gas products.

By the end of 1961, the transfer of all nonbasic operations from the Consortium to NIOC was complete. In 1963, NIOC organized the Non-Basic Operations Organization, a new group with some 12,000 employees, to care for the social and welfare needs of the oil workers.

Between 1955 and 1975, Iran's domestic consumption of petroleum products ranged from a mere 4 to 7 percent of her total oil production. Yet the rapid growth in domestic consumption caused NIOC to take increasing amounts of products from the Abadan refinery and also to add new refinery capacity, pipelines, and marketing facilities. For example, NIOC expanded the Kermanshah refinery, added a new refinery at Tehran in 1968, expanded it in 1975, and added a new refinery at Shiraz in 1974.

But Iran's big step forward in gaining control over operations came in 1973. On January 6 of that year, the Shah presented to the Consortium two options: either to continue its existing agreement till its expiration in 1979, after which its member companies would be treated as other ordinary buyers, or to sign a new agreement ceding to Iran full control of her oil industry in return for a long-term pledge of specified supplies of oil at preferential, specially discounted prices. The Shah, speaking to 5,000 farmers and workers later in the month, accused the Consortium of mishandling operations under the 1954 agreement: Iran had been pressed with orders from international buyers, but the Consortium had not provided adequate capacity to meet these. A spokesman for the oil companies disputed the Shah's legal right to terminate their contract in 1979, saying that they had the option of renewing it. The United States and Britain, in actions reminiscent of bygone days, rushed to express diplomatic concern to the Shah over his announcement. However, there was to be no turning back the pages of history. The advantage was now with the oil producers, and such legal arguments, as the *New York Times* pointed out, were given "little political weight."

At the end of February 1973, the Consortium announced that it had reached an understanding with the Shah at talks in St. Moritz; and on March 16 the Shah, addressing a huge crowd of steel mill workers in Isfahan, announced that Western oil companies had "surrendered totally" and "handed over to us total and real operation of the oil industry of Iran with the ownership of all installations."[29] On March 24, Iran and the companies signed the new agreement, which according to the *New York Times* was "the most far-reaching agreement ever amicably worked out between the government of an oil-producing country and the international oil industry." On July 31, the Shah ratified a new bill encompassing the agreement, thereby ending seventy-two years of foreign control of the operations of the Iranian oil industry—and the *Iran Oil Journal* reported that "after signing the 100-page document the Shahanshah with a victorious smile declared 'a new day in Iranian history.' "[30] The signing was telecast live across the nation and Iranians stopped working briefly to watch the historic event. The agreement in effect handed the operations of the industry over to NIOC, although the Consortium formed the Oil Services Company of Iran (OSCO) to handle the exploration and drilling for NIOC for a period of five years.[31] NIOC had the right to an agreed amount of Iranian crude to sell itself, as well as control over the reserves formerly controlled by the Consortium. In exchange, the Consortium received the right to purchase oil for twenty years at a discount from the prices posted by the Organization of Petroleum Exporting Countries (OPEC). Thus NIOC was to receive no less revenue, in terms of dollars per barrel, than its Arab neighbors.

This takeover of the Iranian industry by NIOC was paralleled by an increase in the relative number of Iranians in the management of the oil industry. In 1951, non-Iranians constituted some 40 percent of the staff (management, technical, clerical, and other "white collar" employees). By the early 1970s, this figure had dropped to less than 10 percent.[32]

During the mid-1960s, NIOC even began to export "know-how," providing petroleum specialists, mostly on a short-term basis, to a number of less-developed countries. And the extensive NIOC training programs used to train Iranians were made available to foreigners; from 1964 through 1971, for example, NIOC provided training at Iranian oil facilities and the Abadan Institute of Technology for over 150 foreign personnel.

In spite of extensive training facilities in Iran, NIOC was willing to reach far afield to educate its own personnel and sent a number of persons abroad for study. In 1972, NIOC formed a joint venture with BP to explore for oil and gas in the North Sea and, in 1975, with BP, Socal, and SAGA to explore offshore western Greenland. Although NIOC undoubtedly hoped to earn a profit from the investments, my judgment is that NIOC's primary motivation was to gain experience in the world oil industry in general and in offshore operations in particular.

(2) Oil exports: the second undertaking of NIOC—and one likely to have significant implications for the future—was to sell oil in the export market. This activity bore Iran's characteristic stamp of not putting all her eggs in one basket. It included direct sales, barter, and downstream investments.

In the mid-1950s NIOC began to sell very small quantities of bunker oil for ships, but it was not until the 1960s that NIOC's exports assumed importance. Under the joint venture agreements NIOC was entitled to take up to 50 percent of the output. As NIOC gained experience, it took increasing amounts of its entitlement.

In 1967, under a Supplemental Agreement, the Consortium began to supply limited quantities of crude to NIOC for export. But the crude could be exported only to markets where the Consortium members were not operating. So, in practice, other than a small barter with Argentina, this meant Eastern Europe—initially Romania and later Bulgaria and Czechoslavakia. And, in practice, this meant barter. Most of the payment received by Iran for these exports consisted of machinery and goods for Iran's development; little cash was involved. The deals with Eastern Europe were important because they enabled Iran to make incremental sales without any noticeable impact on world oil markets and gave NIOC experience as well. Yet the volumes were quite small in the overall scheme of things, averaging about 40,000 barrels a day by the early 1970s, or less than 1 percent of Iran's total oil production. And until 1973, crude from joint ventures continued to represent NIOC's major supply for the export market. When the 1973 agreement with the Consortium gave NIOC access to more crude oil, the Consortium became NIOC's chief source of crude; indeed, NIOC liftings from the Consortium increased sixfold between 1972 and 1974. The main market for NIOC's direct sales was Europe, both the state-owned oil companies and the large spot market.

In addition to direct sales and barters, NIOC had invested in three processing plants in other countries: in India, a refinery in 1969 and a fertilizer plant in 1971; and in South Africa, a refinery in 1971. These investments gave NIOC "captive" outlets for some crude oil, and in 1974 it exported about 60,000 barrels a day of oil to the two refineries.

The perceived world shortage of crude oil in the period 1973-74 caused a flurry of negotiations about possible additional barters and downstream investments. In 1974 and 1975, Iran made long-term barter deals with several foreign governments, including France, Britain, and India. All were complex arrangements scheduled to last many years. For example, Iran was to provide India with crude oil, capital for an expansion of the Indian refinery partly owned by NIOC, and capital to improve India's mining interests. In exchange, India gave Iran cash—some immediately and some in five years—for some of the crude oil and eventually was to supply iron ore and aluminum ore to Iran.

In addition to less-developed nations, the proposed downstream investments also included industrial ones such as West Germany, the United States, and Belgium. Some of these investments were to contain a new element in that NIOC for the first time would own part interest in service stations in foreign countries. But as the perceived world shortage of crude oil turned into a surplus, most of these negotiations broke down. In late 1975, however, NIOC was concluding an agreement with BP to purchase its service station chain in Senegal and another with the Senegalese government to enter into a joint venture to build a refinery in Dakar. This latter agreement also had an element of barter in that Senegal was expected to provide phosphates at some future time for use in NIOC fertilizer plants in Iran.

In another activity related to its oil export program, NIOC entered the shipping business. Starting with its first two tankers, *Reza Shah the Great* in 1958 and *Mohammad Reza Shah* a year later, the fleet was expanded slowly. But in 1975 NIOC increased its capacity threefold and at the end of 1975 was completing negotiations to increase it yet again, by forming a tanker company owned jointly with its old adversary, British Petroleum.[33] But even this deal, if it went through, would have brought NIOC's total tanker capacity up to only 1.4 million tons, which was sufficient to transport only 5 to 10 percent of Iran's oil exports.[34] Over the long run this NIOC-owned tonnage was likely to be integrated with NIOC's oil export program; in the short run most of the tonnage was being chartered to foreign companies.

In spite of all this activity, NIOC exports of crude oil in 1974 had climbed to only 421,000 barrels daily—a sizable quantity but still only 7.4 percent of Iran's total exports of oil. NIOC exports were less in 1975, in both quantity and percentage, because of a drop in world consumption. And NIOC had yet to enter the export market for refined products, except for very small quantities of aviation fuel sold to Afghanistan.

(3) Gas exports: the third prong of NIOC's attack consisted of exports of natural gas. The Soviet Union was the obvious target because of its proximity. Iran, after establishing the National Iranian Gas Company (NIGC) in 1965 as a subsidiary of NIOC, laid a gas pipeline to Russia. Gas exports began in 1970 and reached 879 million cubic feet daily in 1974 (the energy equivalent of 157,000 barrels a day of oil), bringing revenues of $180 million for the year.

This was just the start. In November 1975, NIGC, in what was headlined "the world's largest natural gas deal," signed a five-nation agreement under which Iran was scheduled to deliver, starting in 1981, additional gas to the Soviet Union for use in its southern industrial regions. The Soviet Union, in turn, would deliver gas for Iran's account to West Germany, France, and Austria. The price of the natural gas would fluctuate in accordance with European market prices and competitive rates for fuel, with a floor price. On the basis of prices existing at the end of 1975, Iran would receive for the delivery of 1,300 million cubic feet daily about $450 million annually, approximately 80 percent of which would be paid in goods and the remainder in cash. In addition, NIGC signed agreements with two foreign groups to export liquefied natural gas to Japan, Europe, and the United States, though initial deliveries were some years away. The volumes involved in these two projects were a little more than the exports via pipeline to the Soviet Union.

Natural gas began to play two other important roles in Iran. First, Iran used gas to make more oil available for export. It did so by increasing the output of oil fields through gas injection in those fields, and by employing gas for part of the primary energy used domestically—16 percent of domestic energy in 1974. It announced plans to convert 1,500 taxis and 500 private cars to operate on natural gas. The gas for such uses was scheduled to come from recently found gas fields and from greater utilization of gas "associated" with oil—some 44 percent of Iran's natural gas production was "flared" (i.e., burned off at or near the wellhead) in 1974. Second, Iran used gas as a feedstock to its petrochemical industry.

(4) Petrochemical manufacture: the petrochemical industry added a high value to each unit of natural gas and oil used as a feedstock. NIOC's petrochemical sales, through its wholly-owned subsidiary, the National Petrochemical Company (NPC) reached $184 million in 1974. According to NIOC reports, the figure would have been $86 million higher had the firm not sold fertilizer products at subsidized prices to the Iranian market in order to contribute to the nation's agricultural development.

Up to 1975, the petrochemical industry had served primarily the domestic market and had used mainly natural gas. But plans were being made to change both these situations, with two major export-oriented projects actively under consideration. One, to be wholly owned by NIOC, was to produce aromatics from petroleum fractions obtained from the Abadan refinery. The other was to be a $1-billion joint venture between NIOC's petrochemical subsidiary and a group of Japanese companies; the object was to produce olefins from ethane, which were to be extracted from Iranian natural gas. The olefins, in turn, were to be used to manufacture a variety of intermediate petrochemical products that could be more readily exported than olefins, on which transport costs were high because of the need to liquefy them. Startup was scheduled in the early 1980s, with 19,000 persons involved in construction and 3,500 technicians in the actual operation. Iran had allocated over $1 billion in her Fifth National Development Plan, ending in 1978, for the development of her petrochemical industry, and expected an additional $1 billion from the private sector.[35]

But, struggle as she might, Iran at the end of 1975 still found herself relying on the Consortium for the overwhelming portion of her oil and gas exports. As figure 2 shows, NIOC's exports of natural gas and petrochemicals were not about to change this basic picture. And the undesirability of heavy reliance on one entity was brought home once again when the Consortium's purchases of Iranian oil for export in 1975 were some 740,000 barrels a day, or 15 percent lower than it had indicated in the previous year to NIOC that they would be. The disparity presumably was caused by the decline in industrial production in Europe, since demand for the heavier-than-average Iranian crude, which is used to make fuel oil, is correlated closely with industrial production. But

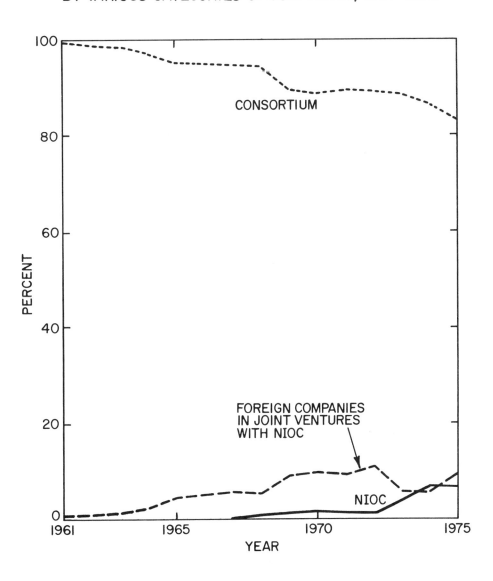

Figure 2
EXPORTS OF IRANIAN OIL
BY VARIOUS CATEGORIES OF COMPANIES, 1961-1975

Source: Unpublished table from National Iranian Oil Company.

whatever the reason for the decline, it was an embarrassment to Iran, costing it some $3 billion and causing a budgetary deficit. Obviously, then, a crucial item on the agenda continued to be how to lessen reliance on the Consortium.

THE QUEST FOR HIGHER REVENUES

One hardly needs to say that the possible ways of obtaining higher revenues are to raise the quantity sold, or to raise the unit price, or both. After the 1954 settlement, Iran's leaders chose to raise both quantity and price. This task required a balancing act, for sometimes attempts to expand output conflicted with attempts to obtain higher prices. Despite this conflict, I shall discuss the subjects separately for ease of exposition, an approach facilitated by several factors. First, during the early parts of the 1955-75 period Iran emphasized expanded output, whereas during the latter part the emphasis changed to price. Second, Iran acted alone on the output question and her actions can be discussed with little reference to the actions of other producing nations, whereas she fully cooperated with other oil-exporting nations to obtain higher prices. Thus, a discussion of price must inevitably include a discussion of the actions of a number of oil-exporting nations.

Boosting the Consortium's Output

The reason for Iran's go-it-alone policy to obtain higher output seems clear: since the major oil companies typically used Middle Eastern production as a "swing area" or "surge pot" to meet the world's needs for oil that remained after other sources had been used, any increase in Iranian output came at the expense of increases in other Middle Eastern countries.[36] Thus the Middle Eastern nations, including Iran, saw the level of production as a zero-sum game in which a gain by one country had to cause a loss elsewhere.

Stuck in the memory of the Iranians was the fact that other Middle Eastern nations had profited substantially from Iran's 1951-54 shutdown and that Iran had a right to regain her position as the largest producer in the Middle East. The Shah's words describe the Iranian needs: "By increasing production we hope to raise our standard of living and to ensure the welfare and prosperity of the people."[37] Other oil-rich nations, in turn, wanted criteria—such as size of reserves—that favored their own needs for increased output and increased revenues.

Iran moved relentlessly ahead to obtain higher output. Of course, some of the actions taken by the Iranians to lessen dependence on the Consortium—in particular, allowing additional companies to explore for and produce Iranian oil—also resulted in increased output. But since Iran continued to depend heavily on the Consortium for oil exports, any drive for higher output naturally had to focus on the Consortium.

Yet most of the Consortium members had a fundamental problem. Not only did they have access to more crude than they could profitably sell, but they were under pressure from other Middle Eastern countries to increase output there. That is why at least one of the U.S. majors, at the time the Consortium was being formed, stated that it had no interest in joining for commercial reasons but would join to help U.S. national interests. Indeed the five U.S. majors—Exxon, Mobil, Socal, Texaco and Gulf—at the time of joining the Consortium had to persuade the pro-Western rulers in Saudi Arabia, Kuwait, and Iraq that the production there should be held back to make room for Iranian oil as a necessary sacrifice to help Iran, and possibly the whole Middle East, avoid falling within the Soviet orbit. But the rulers of these countries did not want the majors to lift more Iranian oil than they were obligated to do in order to satisfy the requirements of restoring Iran's production. Thus, the Consortium members, in increasing their offtake of Iranian oil during the 1950s and 1960, always had to keep one eye on their other oil operations. As Howard Page of Exxon testified before a Senate subcommittee some twenty years later: "If we hadn't played ball with him [King Ibn Saud], we could have lost the Aramco concession, which is not something to lose. It is the biggest concession in the world, and we [Exxon] had 30 percent of it as against a concession one-quarter as big in which we had a 7 percent [share]."[38]

The Consortium's mechanism to control output. At the time the Consortium was formed, its members wanted to restrict the output of Iranian oil to a level that could be sold within the framework of the existing world price system. For this purpose, they relied on a mechanism known as the Aggregate Programmed Quantity (APQ) system. The system, in fact, was not only used to set production levels but also to allocate supply among members. Briefly, under the system the holding company of the Consortium would estimate the total Consortium production needed to give each participant the quantity it requested for the coming year. E.L. Shafer, a Continental Oil executive, explained the system to a U.S. Senate subcommittee in 1974. He said the participating companies were listed in descending order of the magnitude of their requests, or "nominations." The nomination of the company "whose listing fell at or above a cumulative total of 70 percent of equity" became the APQ.[39] Table 6.5 illustrates this system for the year 1966; the total Consortium equity of the top five companies in the list just exceeded the 70-percent mark. Hence, the APQ was the nomination of CFP, the fifth company— 1,945,000 barrels a day. And each company received a proportion of the total APQ equal to its equity share of the Consortium.

Table 6.5
DETERMINATION OF OUTPUT OF
IRANIAN OIL BY CONSORTIUM, 1966

COMPANY	EQUITY SHARE (percent)	CUMULATIVE EQUITY SHARE (percent)	NOMINATION (thousands of barrels a day)
Iricon[a]	5	5	2,030
BP	40	45	2,027
Shell	14	59	2,027
Mobil	7	66	1,964
CFP	6	72	1,945
Exxon	7	79	1,890
Texaco	7	86	1,712
Gulf	7	93	1,700
Socal	7	100	1,644

SOURCE: United States Senate, "Multinational Petroleum Companies . . . ," part 7, p. 254.

a.   See table 6.4 for list of companies in Iricon.

Three companies consistently wanted more oil than they were allowed: the Iricon group of independents, because Iran was their primary (and in some cases only) source of foreign oil; BP, because of the important role that Iran played in its overall supply picture; and Shell, because it traditionally had been short of crude. As would be expected, four companies consistently were the lowest in their requests: Gulf, because of its large share of Kuwait output; and Socal, Texaco, and Exxon, because of their ownership of 30 percent each in Aramco, which was the holder of the concession in Saudi Arabia. The other two companies, CFP and Mobil, were in between the high and low nominators, and their nomination often turned out to be the actual level of production; in fact, one or the other's nomination set the production level for eleven of the twelve years from 1960 through 1971.

Pressure on the Consortium. As part of the 1954 settlement, the Consortium had guaranteed to Iran to produce 302 thousand barrels a day in 1955, 439 in 1956, and 603 in 1957. The Iranians had wanted a guaranteed growth rate after these first three years, but the Consortium agreed only to increase Iranian production in line with average annual growth in the Middle East.

The members further promised, although in an additional letter, to keep the Consortium's annual growth at the same pace as their own Middle Eastern growth. Iranian oil was absorbed into world markets without much difficulty, and the Consortium exceeded the guaranteed production rates for the 1955-57 period, passing the 1950 peak in 1957. Both the Iranian government and the oil companies seem to have been well pleased with the agreement.

Such indications of stability must be set against the pattern of pressure developed by Iran. In early 1956, the Iranian government made overtures to the Consortium for a rise in production above the goals set for 1955-57. On May 31, 1956, in a five-minute speech from the throne to the Majles, the Shah outlined the attainment of a significant increase in oil income as one of three main national obligations. This proved to be an omen of demands to come. After a while, in fact, the *New York Times* headlined an Iranian demand for higher output as "It Could Happen Every Spring."

A minor skirmish took place in 1961 and major skirmishes in 1966 and 1968.

The 1961 matter was relatively straightforward. Iran demanded that the Consortium raise its production capacity by expanding its facilities and installations. An Iranian team led by 'Abdollah Entezam, chairman of NIOC, met with the Consortium in London during September 1961. The meeting ended on a friendly note and reached some measure of agreement, although the details of the agreement were not made public. The 1966 skirmish proved to be more serious. The Consortium had increased its output since 1957 by more than had been promised to Iran, but in 1965 had let its yearly increase slip to 8.8 percent, a figure below the growth in Middle Eastern output and far below Aramco's boost of 17.9 percent. The Iranian government, dissatisfied, launched a concentrated attack to obtain a big boost in output by the Consortium. Explicitly, the Iranians demanded an increase of 17 percent for 1966 over 1965. The Consortium responded that, because of a combination of market conditions and limited production capacity, 9 percent was the likely growth rate for 1966. The Shah then complained about Western inflation and threatened that Iran would have to turn to the Communist countries for cheaper imports. Consortium output actually went up 12.8 percent in 1966.

In October 1966, in addition to repeating the demand for a 17 percent increase in output, Iran made two new demands to the Consortium: *(1)* relinquish part of its concession, so that the government could raise extra revenue through competitive bids and more development; *(2)* sell some oil at cost to NIOC to market on its own at a profit.

These demands ricocheted among the U.S. and U.K. governments and the majors in a series of meetings. The British Foreign Office complained to the U.S. State Department that the U.S. majors were not taking their maximum allowable share of Consortium production. The State Department turned to the American majors, which were armed with their own analysis showing that they had responded more positively than BP or Shell.

At a meeting between the American members of the Consortium and the State Department on October 24, 1966, one company executive, noting that the United States was providing Iran with military aid, agricultural products under Public Law 480, development loans from the Agency for International Development, and loans from the Export-Import Bank, raised the question of invoking the Hickenlooper Amendment if Iran took action against the Consortium.[40] This amendment, authored by Senator Bourke B. Hickenlooper (R., Iowa), called for cessation of U.S. aid to countries expropriating U.S.-owned property without adequate compensation. By this time the Shah had firmly assumed personal supervision of Iran's oil policy; yet at this meeting a company executive questioned whether or not the Iranian pressure came directly from the Shah and also whether the Shah might be "misinformed again." Specifically, the companies questioned whether the real issue was an Iranian desire to get NIOC into the business of marketing oil, and wondered whether Dr. Eqbal, chairman of NIOC, "was trying to carve out something on his own initiative." The companies said that they would appreciate anything that the U.S. and U.K. ambassadors in Tehran could do to "keep the lid on" and find out what was really going on in Tehran. In turn, the companies would try to find "some way of skinning the cat."

Both the U.K. and U.S. governments urged the companies to do their best to meet Iranian demands. But in the end the companies were left to themselves to solve their differences and to negotiate with Iran. The companies, however did manage not to argue in public and thus presented a united front to Iran—in line with Acting Secretary of State George Ball's instructions to the American Embassy in Tehran that the sensitive subject of intercompany agreements "should not become part of the argument with the Iranians."[41]

The companies, feeling threatened by the revolutionary type of agreement that Iran had concluded with ERAP in August 1966, indeed, found a way to skin the cat. On December 10, 1966, the Iranian government and the Consortium reached an agreement. The Consortium would increase production by 11 percent in both 1967 and 1968 and relinquish about 25 percent of its concession. Furthermore, as indicated earlier in this chapter, the Consortium made available oil to NIOC for export. This was done by allowing NIOC to buy any oil taken in lieu of royalty payments for export during the period 1967-71 to certain Eastern European countries at a price halfway between the cost of the oil (including taxes paid to the Iranian government) and the posted price. The posted price was the price from which the government's share of profits was calculated, and, of course, was much higher than the cost.

Within a year the Shah was pressing the Consortium for even greater output. The occasion that triggered the chain of events leading up to this pressure was the 1967 Middle East War. This war caused the Consortium to increase Iranian output by 22 percent during 1967 to offset the Arab oil embargo, but when the embargo ended, Arab output was restored to its former level. This drop irritated the Shah, who told both the Consortium and the home governments of its parent companies that he expected to be rewarded with increased output for the political risk involved in supplying the West during the embargo. The brushing aside of his complaints and the restoration of production in Saudi Arabia heightened Iran's suspicions that Aramco's parents (Exxon, Mobil, Socal, and Texaco) favored Saudi Arabia over Iran.

Evidence was shortly forthcoming that tended to confirm Iran's deepest suspicions about discrimination. The Shah found allies in the crude-short companies, that is, those Consortium companies that lacked large supplies of crude oil. One company, widely believed to be the French firm, CFP, gave the Iranians a copy of the Consortium's secret Participants' Agreement; and Shell, Mobil, and the American independents were suspected by their crude-long Consortium partners of leaking secret details about the offtake rules, which had the effect of rationing low-cost Iranian oil to the crude-short members. Also, the U.S. State Department suspected that the French and British encouraged the Iranians to blame Aramco's parents for output limitations. The issue was highly sensitive. A year earlier Walter Levy, an international oil consultant, had advised Undersecretary of State Eugene Rostow that the disparity between the Aramco offtake rules and the Consortium offtake rules was potentially "political dynamite," because the Aramco rules made it more attractive for a company to lift oil beyond its equity share than did the Consortium rules. The State Department duly noted that "it would be to the Consortium's advantage if it could see its way clear to giving the Iranians the same advantage as the Saudis now enjoy."[42]

To quiet internal squabbling and to reduce pressure from the Shah, the Consortium changed its offtake rules in September 1967 and again in January 1968 to bring its rules in line with Aramco's. A Consortium member now could purchase limited quantities of oil beyond its equity share of total liftings at a price one-quarter of the way between the cost of the oil (including taxes paid to the Iranian government) and the much higher posted price. But the entire squabble turned out to be much ado about nothing. In spite of the great reluctance of the crude-long companies to change the rules, the change, when finally made, did little to increase output. This, indeed, had been predicted by one of Mobil's experts, who, according to a secret report of the American Embassy in London, thought that the new formula was "not going to bring about any increase in offtake."[43]

Having won a hollow victory, the Shah then changed his tactics to win a real one. On February 3, 1968, NIOC presented the Consortium with a formal letter demanding that it meet the annual revenue requirements of Iran's Fourth National Development Plan, which covered the years 1968 through 1972. As the *New York Times* reported, the government in effect told the Consortium, "We need the money." And if the Consortium's output was insufficient to meet Iran's revenue needs, then the Consortium would have to provide the difference, since the Iranian government's budget would no longer be held hostage to the Consortium's production programs. During this 1968 confrontation, described in the press at various times as "a giant poker game" and "a wrestling match," the Iranians had the U.S. State Department as well as the crude-short Consortium members for allies.

On March 28, 1968, Undersecretary of State Rostow met with President J.K. Jamieson of Exxon and other senior officials of the American companies of the Consortium. Rostow's message was not unexpected: the department did not normally interfere in commercial matters, but in the current problem with Iran, the Consortium members had to put the country's interest above their own. "State expects Russia to encourage and support the Arabs hoping to gain control of the Middle East oil that Europe is dependent on. As Iran is the strongest state in the area, it is very important to the U.S. in maintaining influence."[44] Another Arab-Israeli war could erupt at any moment and the Shah might support an Arab embargo to punish the American companies for their unwillingness to meet his revenue demands. The State Department also asked the British government to request BP to shift some of its production away from Abu Dhabi and Oman to help Iran.

The crude-short Consortium members pressed for the right to buy additional oil at cost. In making this argument, the American independents cloaked themselves with the American flag. For example, in February 1968, Frank Lortcher of Signal (Iricon group) in a private conversation with a State Department official said that although he didn't want to "get into a hassle with the big boys," he thought that when the Shah asked them questions they had "often ducked or tried to confuse the issue, believing that the Shah was not fully informed."[45] Lortcher believed that the State Department had a duty to tell the U.S. majors to allocate their Middle Eastern production on the basis of American national interests, that is, favor Iran because it was a more reliable long-run source of oil that the Arab sheikhdoms.

The crude-long majors saw things differently; they held that the crude-short Consortium members wanted to take away established markets of the crude-long companies at lower prices.[46] The crude-long companies fought to maintain the status quo. Thus Socal, in pushing its rationale for not making a promise to the Shah of large increases in output, produced a study for the State Department showing that a growing rate of increase in production from other parts of the world might leave only a 5 percent residual growth rate in Middle Eastern production. (In fact, from 1968 through 1973, the Consortium's Iranian production and Middle Eastern total production approximately doubled, growing at annual compounded rates of 14 percent and 16 percent, respectively.)

And in another attempt to maintain the status quo, the Consortium members, at an audience with the Shah on April 20, 1968, informed him that his five-year revenue targets were very unrealistic. The Shah's view was that oil company predictions of world oil demand had always been wrong and, he hoped, would continue to be wrong. The Shah was adamant, threatening that if the Consortium could not provide the required revenue, he would seize one of its oil fields, put his own company on the Consortium's board, or get "quarter-price" oil to sell in Eastern Europe.[47]

The Shah, issuing an ultimatum that the matter must be solved by May 10, 1969, eventually won the hassle—at least as far as that year was concerned. The Consortium, through a combination of increased output and an advance on future oil payments, which the Shah said Iran would repay "when we have the money available," did agree to pay Iran the $1.01 billion required for the Iranian budget.[48] On May 14, the two negotiating teams, led by Dr. Eqbal on one side and David Steel of BP on the other, signed the agreement. The Shah expressed only qualified satisfaction because the oil companies still had not given specific commitments on output and earnings beyond March 1970. Iran wanted long-range assurances that would enable the country to proceed in a planned way with its economic development.[49]

Yet the agreement disturbed Saudi Arabia, Kuwait, and Iraq, all of whom complained to the majors operating within their borders. These complaints came as no surprise. During the negotiations, one oil executive warned the press that "the sheiks" were "not going to stand" for a cutback in the growth of their oil output to allow the Shah's goals to be met. Shaykh Zaki Yamani, oil minister of Saudi Arabia, said that he would act quickly to protect his country's interests if pressures from Iran were to interfere with Saudi Arabia's normal growth rate; Kuwait's prime minister gave a similar warning.

There were Iranian arguments, developed in the late 1950s and elaborated on in the 1960s, that remained the backbone of their requests for maximum production. Iran had a large population and thus needed the income; she recycled the money for purchases, thereby putting no strain on the balance of payments of the oil purchasers; she offered security of supply; and she needed money to purchase arms to fill the military and political vacuum in the Middle East. Used by Iran to differentiate itself from the Arabs, these arguments were laid aside for a while as the output issue faded into the background to be supplanted, in 1973, by the issue that shook the world: higher oil prices.

As shown in figure 3, from the mid-1950s onwards the increase in Iranian oil output was substantial, from 720 thousand barrels daily in 1957 to 5.4 million in 1975, an annual growth rate of 12 percent. And the Consortium did indeed keep to its 1954 understanding with the Shah: Consortium output increased at a higher rate than that of either the Middle East as a whole or the Consortium members' output in other Middle Eastern countries.

Yet Consortium output still remained as an unfinished agenda item. Iranian leaders were unhappy about the Consortium's purchases in 1975 being 740,000 barrels daily less than it had indicated. And Iran still had ample capacity for growth. Her 1975 production was almost 2 million barrels a day lower than the capacity goal of 7.2 million included in the Fifth National Development Plan (1973-1978).

Raising Prices

Oil pricing is a complicated subject, so a word or two is in order. There is no one world price of oil, but rather a structure of prices. The price of crude oil from each of hundreds of different oil fields varies according to quality, quantity, location, and length of contract. For example, throughout 1955, the posted prices for three crude oils well known within the industry were as follows: $1.91 a barrel for Iran 34° API, f.o.b. Bandar Mahshahr (an Iranian port); $1.93 for Arabian 34°, f.o.b. Ras Tanura (a Saudi Arabian port); and $2.55 for Venezuelan Tia Juana 31°, f.o.b. Amuay Bay (a Venezuelan port). The price of each crude was "posted" by an oil company and represented the price at which the company was willing to sell the oil. If more than one company had access to identical oil at the same location, then the posted prices for all companies typically would be identical. In other words, the prices posted for Arabian 34°, f.o.b. Ras Tanura, typically were identical at any one time for all of the Aramco parents that chose to offer this type of oil for sale.

Because the shares of the profits that the governments of the oil-exporting nations received were calculated from posted prices, these governments wanted such prices to be as high as possible. The oil companies faced a different picture. Because of competition, they often had to discount posted prices in order to make sales. These discounts took various forms: such as the sale of crude oil f.o.b. at an actual discount; the sale of crude oil delivered, with part of the transportation costs absorbed by the seller; or the sale of refined products, with part of the transportation and refining costs absorbed by the seller. During much of the time between the end of World War II and the early part of the 1970s, the posted prices for crude oils from the major exporting nations were higher than the so-called market prices—that is, higher than the prices that the companies actually received for crude oil.[50]

In the years immediately following the Iranian settlement of 1954, the price scene was tranquil. As far as one can tell, market prices were about the same as posted prices. The companies raised world oil prices—both market and

Figure 3
PRODUCTION OF CRUDE OIL IN IRAN
1955–1975

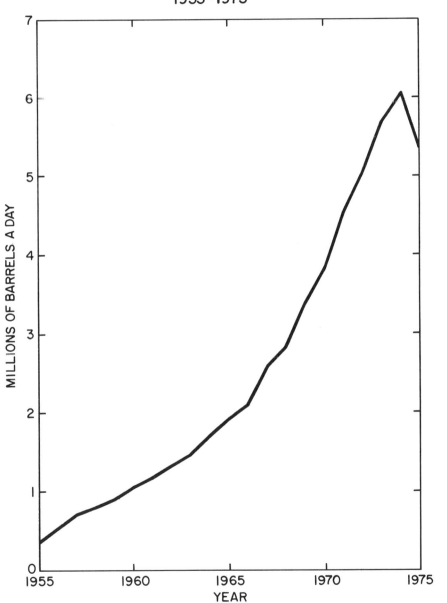

Source: <u>BP Statistical Review</u>, various issues.

posted—in 1957, following a price rise in the United States related to the 1956 Suez Crisis. But, from this zenith, market prices began to drift downward. The companies maintained steady posted prices, at least for a while. Thus, the per-barrel taxes of the oil-producing nations, being based on posted prices, remained constant, while the companies' per-barrel profits were declining. The governments of oil-exporting nations, therefore, began to receive more than 50 percent of the actual profits. This situation was not to last forever.

OPEC's birth and infancy. Cuts at two different times in posted prices triggered the formation of OPEC. In February 1959, the major oil companies reduced posted prices by 18 cents a barrel, a move that cost the four major producing nations in the Middle East somewhat over $100 million yearly. Iranian 34° crude, f.o.b. Bandar Mahshahr, was cut from $2.04 a barrel to $1.86 a barrel; cuts in posted prices on other crude oils varied depending upon quality and location.[51] This move was not a great surprise because it restored the price approximately to the level that had existed prior to the Suez Crisis. But market prices continued to be below the posted prices. For example, Italy made a deal to purchase Russian oil at 60 cents below the Middle East price and Japanese firms were purchasing oil from some major oil companies at huge discounts. Faced with such pressures on profits, Exxon announced on August 8, 1960, that its posted prices on Middle East crude would be reduced by an average 10 cents a barrel. After a short time, the majors made adjustments to equalize their posted prices for crude of similar quality and location. The fall in the posted price of Iranian crude was 8 cents a barrel; thus, the posted price of Iranian 34° fell to $1.78.

The second price cut and the fear of additional cuts prodded the oil-exporting nations into action. On September 9, 1960, representatives from five nations met in Baghdad and the Organization of Petroleum Exporting Countries was formed. The five nations were: Iran, Iraq, Kuwait, Saudi Arabia, and Venezuela. The Saudis and the Venezuelans generally are credited with being prime movers in the formation of OPEC.[52] Given Iran's experience in dealing with foreign oil companies, however, it was not surprising that an Iranian, Dr. Fuad Rouhani, became OPEC's first secretary-general.

In retrospect, OPEC's first pronouncement seems quite modest. OPEC announced the immediate goal of restoring "present prices to the levels prevailing before the reductions." OPEC members, it continued for the record, required a steady source of income to balance their budgets; oil was a wasting asset, which they must replace with other assets; price fluctuations were undesirable, not only for producers but also for consumers; and oil companies should not unilaterally control oil prices, which in turn determined the income of the OPEC members. OPEC's defensive posture was made necessary at the time because of the existence of a buyer's market and the dominant position of the major oil companies.

A number of OPEC members subscribed, at least in principle, to the idea of controlling the oil output of the OPEC nations in order to support the price. In practice, the scheme foundered on one shoal: On what basis should production quotas be allocated? Each nation wanted criteria that favored its own needs for increased output and increased revenues. And a variety of criteria were brought forward: population, ability to utilize revenues, security of supply, size of proven reserves, current output, current capacity, amount of investment, costs of operation, and ratio of nonoil exports to oil exports.

After much discussion in the early 1960s, OPEC took its first positive step toward proration in 1965 when it established a permanent Economic Commission and instructed it to work on a "regulatory production program" and on how to implement it. But when the Economic Commission proposed growth rates in production for the various nations in mid-1965, the reaction was so unfavorable that some OPEC officials dismissed the figures as "mathematical exercises."[53] Iran dissented because she wanted to be free to regain her role as the largest producer in the Middle East.

Not surprisingly, the proration scheme failed: OPEC had no means to force either the member states or the oil companies to comply with the proration schedule. No mention was made of the subject at the Eleventh Conference of OPEC, held in Vienna in April 1966, and as of 1976 it had never again been given serious consideration. In fact, as of 1976, OPEC still had not operated as a classic cartel. Instead, it had served more as a meeting ground and information clearinghouse. To be sure, decisions were taken at OPEC meetings; but compliance with the decisions was voluntary on the part of the member countries.

Although OPEC failed to implement a prorationing scheme, OPEC not only helped to prevent further erosion of the posted price of oil but managed to increase government "take" during the 1960s. This was no easy feat, for market prices were declining during the period. OPEC, with Dr. Fuad Rouhani in charge of negotiations and Saudi Arabia offering strong support, managed to get the companies in 1964 to agree to change the accounting treatment of royalties. Until that time, under the 50/50 profit-sharing agreements, royalties had not actually resulted in revenues to the oil-exporting nations. In effect, a portion of a host government's oil revenues was called a royalty in order to satisfy the U.S. tax collectors, because royalties paid to a host government were treated less favorably under U.S. tax laws than were income taxes.[54] Royalty payments to host governments were less than income taxes due the host governments. Furthermore, companies could subtract any royalties paid to a host government from any income tax owed that government.

In 1964, the system was changed so that royalties were treated as an expense before calculation of the profits that determined income taxes. The producing government's income tax of 50 percent was then calculated on profits after the royalties had been deducted from them.

A simple example of a hypothetical crude oil illustrates the point: in the table opposite, Situation A shows the split of profits if market prices had equaled posted prices, and Situation B shows the split of profits with market prices lower than posted prices, as was generally the case. But this gain of OPEC's was moderated by the fact that the companies were allowed certain discounts in calculating payments to governments. During the next few years, however, these discounts were gradually eliminated.

Thus, government revenues per barrel climbed ten to twenty cents a barrel during the decade of the 1960s, a decade during which company earnings per barrel were declining because of weakening market prices. The Eastern Hemisphere earnings of the seven majors dropped from 54 cents a barrel in 1961 to 33 cents in 1970. During this same period, the per-barrel revenues of the host governments climbed from 70 cents to 86.5 cents; albeit, after being corrected for inflation, the per-barrel revenues of the governments stayed about level.[55]

The capitulation of the West in 1971. By 1970, conditions in the world oil industry were dramatically different from the conditions of ten years earlier.[56] The so-called independent oil companies, many of which would have been considered large in other industries, had entered the world oil scene en masse. Over 300 firms, both U.S. and foreign, had entered the international oil business between 1953 and 1970. Oil had been found in a number of additional countries and OPEC's membership increased to ten, including Libya. The impact of the independents in Libya was especially important. They were instrumental in causing a sharp increase in Libya's output, an increase that contributed importantly both to the decline in market price and to the decline in the market shares of the majors in the world oil industry. The production shares of the seven majors dropped from 98 percent of the world oil market (as defined in table 6.2) in 1950 to 76 percent in 1969, and proportionate falls took place in their shares of refining and marketing activities.[57]

Several unexpected events occurred in 1970 to increase the value of Libyan oil. Libya demanded higher posted prices and, in July 1970, forced Occidental, an American independent heavily dependent on Libyan oil, to cut its production. Occidental capitulated and gave Libya higher per-barrel revenues. It was followed quickly by the other companies operating in Libya, including the majors. Thereupon oil prices began to bounce between two walls—the North African nations and the Persian Gulf nations—like a

Before 1964 Agreement	After 1964 Agreement
Royalties treated as a credit against income taxes	Royalties treated as an expense before income taxes calculated

Posted price	$2.00	Posted price	$2.00
Production costs	.20	Production costs	.20
Taxable profits	$1.80	Taxable profits	$1.80
Government revenues ($)	.90	Royalties	.25
of which:		Profits after	
royalties ... .25		royalties	$1.55
income taxes .65		Government income tax ($) ..	.775

Situation A: Market price same as posted price $2.00

Situation A: Market price same as posted price $2.00

Before 1964 Agreement (continued)

Situation A: Market
price same as
posted price $2.00

Company profits .... .90

Government share
of profits 50%

Situation B: Market
price lower than
posted price

Market price $1.60

Company profits .... .50

Government share
of profits 64%

After 1964 Agreement (continued)

Government revenues ($) 1.025
of which:
royalties .... .25
income taxes .775

Situation A: Market
price same as
posted price $2.00

Company profits .... .775

Government share
of profits 57%

Situation B: Market
price lower than
posted price

Market price $1.60

Company profits .... .375

Government share
of profits 73%

ping-pong ball pushed steadily upward by a jet of air. The posted prices on shipments of Persian Gulf oil from Mediterranean ports were immediately brought into line with the Libyan price. OPEC, however, saw the opportunity for even more money. In December 1970 it passed a resolution directing the nations in the Persian Gulf area to begin a separate negotiation with the companies. The Shah, with the approval of the other gulf states, personally led the negotiations, which began in early 1971.

The negotiators of both sides mounted an impressive group of arguments, but in the end a combination of economic and political power triumphed over the private firms. The nations argued that *(1)* the rich countries (that is, the industrialized nations) should pay more to the poor countries (such as OPEC members) by increasing prices paid for raw materials, especially since prices of manufactured goods purchased by poor countries had been rising; *(2)* the taxes levied on oil, especially gasoline, by consumer governments were many times those received by the producing governments; *(3)* rises in price of oil products in the consuming countries had not been passed along to the oil-exporting nations.*

The companies argued that *(1)* the concession terms must be respected according to international law; *(2)* they were responsible neither for the tax policies of the consumer governments nor the rises in price of manufactured goods; *(3)* the price increases reflected increases in their operating expenses. Then, remembering Occidental's experience of July 1970, they proceeded to erect a set of formidable barriers against OPEC in order to avoid, in the words of Sir David Barran of Shell, being "picked off one by one in any country."[58] The American companies obtained a letter from the U.S. Assistant Attorney General for Antitrust, Richard McLaren, allowing them to form with the European firms a united front against OPEC. The letter gave antitrust clearance for the companies to send a joint "Message to OPEC" and form a "Libyan Producers' Agreement." The message, sent on January 13, 1971, made plain the companies' conclusion that they could not further negotiate the development of claims by member countries of OPEC "on any other basis than one which reaches a settlement simultaneously with all producing governments concerned." It therefore proposed that a group representing the companies should begin negotiations with OPEC, representing all its member countries, so that an "overall and durable settlement could be achieved."[59] The agreement provided that if one company were forced by the Libyan government to cut production as a consequence of its resisting Libyan demands, the other companies producing in Libya would replace the shut-in production with crude oil from other countries (including those in the Persian Gulf) at cost or near cost.

---

* With regard to *(2)*, the producing governments neglected to mention that consumer levies do not represent a cost to the consuming nation as a whole, because these levies represent a transfer of wealth within a country rather than from one country to another. As for *(3)*, the producers did not know the exact cause of these price rises—whether higher taxes in consuming countries, higher profits by the companies, or higher costs of the companies.

In addition, the companies organized the London Policy Group and a support group in New York to carry out the terms of both the message and the agreement. Finally—and this was to prove a fatal flaw in the companies' armor—the U.S. companies requested the U.S. State Department to send a representative on a mission to the OPEC countries, a mission whose general objectives would be to *(1)* prevent an interruption of oil supplies by preventing an impasse between the companies and the OPEC nations; *(2)* explain why the U.S. government had granted antitrust clearance exemption to enable the oil companies to negotiate jointly; *(3)* seek assurance from the Persian Gulf states that they would continue to supply oil to the free world at reasonable prices. The U.S. Secretary of State, William Rogers, with President Nixon's approval, decided to send Undersecretary of State John Irwin II.

How Irwin got selected for the assignment is not clear. Irwin himself thought that he was suggested to the secretary of state by John J. McCloy, the highly influential lawyer, who for quite a while had represented the companies in Washington. McCloy, however, later said that he had not requested Irwin explicitly, and only specified "a person of dignity, with clout."[60] Irwin had joined the State Department four months previously, and in the words of Senator Clifford P. Case (R., New Jersey), was "just a bright young man from a big New York law firm."[61] Irwin had not been in the oil business nor had he been an oil lawyer. In fact, he testified in 1974 that he was "certainly not" an expert in the oil business.[62] Irwin did not have much time to prepare for the trip. The secretary of state called Irwin into his office on January 15, 1971, to inform him of the assignment. Irwin left the very next day for Tehran.

Irwin arrived in Tehran on January 17, 1971, two days ahead of the companies' negotiating team, which was led by George Piercy of Exxon and Lord Strathalmond of BP. The Shah proceeded immediately to sink the companies' constructed dreadnought. He informed Irwin that "any attempt by the companies to say that they would not sign the agreement unless other OPEC members signed it" would be taken by the Shah, the Iranian finance minister, and OPEC as a whole as "a sign of bad faith."[63] On the other hand, if the companies dealt with the Persian Gulf producers as a separate group, those nations were prepared to sign an agreement even though producers in other areas obtained better terms from the companies. Irwin was impressed by the Shah's arguments that an area agreement for the Persian Gulf was desirable so that Libya would not be able to force up gulf prices. He also accepted the Shah's assurance that the gulf countries would not be influenced by any subsequent deal with Libya. Without waiting until the company representatives arrived so that he could talk with them, Irwin immediately cabled his recommendation to the State Department that it encourage the companies to negotiate with the gulf countries separately unless the companies had good reasons to the contrary.[64]

Piercy, shortly after arriving in Tehran, met with U.S. Ambassador Douglas MacArthur and questioned "whether there was anything in the record from dealings in this area that would give us any confidence that these gulf countries would be able to keep an agreement if we subsequently made a preposterous settlement in Libya."[65] But Secretary of State Rogers endorsed Irwin's recommendations, and sent them to McCloy, who immediately relayed the message to the chief executive officers of the companies. According to Henry Schuler, the representative of an American independent oilman, Bunker Hunt, in the London Policy Group, "the momentum had shifted to OPEC" after the failure of the U.S. government to back the companies.[66]

The companies tried several tactics to avoid the "leapfrogging" of prices from one negotiation to another. First, they split the industry team into two parts—Piercy was sent to Tripoli and Strathalmond remained in Tehran—with an understanding that, in order to reach an agreement on "separate but necessarily connected" formulas for pricing Mediterranean and Persian Gulf oil," neither half of the team should be prepared to negotiate on the proposals or counter-proposals."[67] This tactic failed when the gulf producing nations demanded immediate negotiations until agreement was reached. So the company team next tried to get the gulf states to include, as part of the gulf agreement, the portion of their oil that was delivered to the Mediterranean via pipeline (corrected for freight). Such a clause would have tied down the bulk of the world's oil in one agreement, and the gulf countries refused to include this oil in the Tehran negotiations.

In addition to the failure of the U.S. government to back the companies, the decline in spare capacity of oil was a decisive factor in OPEC's favor. Although there was some spare capacity left, it was all concentrated in OPEC countries. In the United States, spare capacity had declined to almost zero. During the negotiations, Saudi Oil Minister Yamani observed to Piercy, "George, you know the supply situation better than I. You know you cannot take a shutdown."[68]

After heated negotiations, which appeared deadlocked on several occasions and brought forth a flow of charges and countercharges, the companies and the gulf countries signed an agreement on February 14, 1971. The companies, in exchange for a "binding agreement" for five years through December 31, 1975, for the purpose of establishing security of supply and price stability, agreed to make what were characterized by McCloy as "extremely high" financial payments to the producers.[69] The agreement called for an immediate increase in income taxes, which raised government revenues an average of 30 cents a barrel, rising to 50 cents by 1975. The added payments to the gulf producing governments in 1971 were estimated to be $1.4 billion and the total added payments for the five-year period were $11.7 billion. Although the agreement did not limit product prices set by the companies, the Shah did not want the increase in crude oil prices to be reflected immediately in the marketing of products.[70]

Some five weeks later, on March 20, 1971, the companies agreed to grant the Libyan government an immediate increase in revenues of approximately 65 cents a barrel above the increases already obtained in Libya in September and October of 1970. Thus Libya leapfrogged the gulf nations and, according to McCloy, "Iranian officials expressed with increasing vigor the resentment of Iran at the outcome of the Libyan negotiations."[71]

Over the next two years the revenues received per barrel of oil by the producing governments continued to bounce even higher. The stated reasons varied. Because of the devaluation of the dollar, the companies and OPEC agreed to increase posted prices twice—by 8.49 percent in January 1972, and another 11 percent in June 1973. And agreements on "participation," i.e. a partial takeover of oil properties by the governments, had the effect of increasing the governments' revenues. In October 1972, the companies and the five producing governments in the Persian Gulf reached an agreement in New York providing for participation by each government in the ownership of the established producing concessions within its boundaries, beginning with an immediate share of 25 percent, rising to 30 percent in 1979, and to 51 percent in 1983. Although the agreement left negotiations of the details of the transfer of ownership to each set of concessionaires and each government, it was clear that the agreement would result in higher per-barrel revenues to the government. With participation, the companies would be allowed to take the oil from their share of the oil fields under regular terms (this was called "equity oil" because the volumes were proportional to the share of ownership still held by a company). The oil that the nations received for their share of ownership could be sold to the concessionaire holders. The oil sold to the concessionaire holders was called "buyback oil." According to then-existing formulas, the companies paid the governments much less for "equity oil" than for "buyback oil," which was priced by the governments to the companies as 93 percent of posted prices for 1973 (and less than the average price of the government's sale of oil to third parties for 1974 and beyond).

The July 1973 agreement, under which the Consortium handed over its entire interest to the NIOC in return for 20 years of preferred access to Iranian crude oil, also carried a price clause: NIOC was to sell oil to the Consortium on terms equivalent to those negotiated by Aramco with Saudi Minister Yamani.

By the summer of 1973, the stage was set for one of the most profound international economic revolutions in history—the great escalation of oil prices.[72] By this time virtually the entire world oil industry was operating at full capacity. Only Saudi Arabia had the capability of substantial increases in the short run. Independents were snapping up any oil offered by the OPEC governments, and some U.S. companies were ignoring the State Department's urgings not to buy oil produced from the properties that the Libyan government had obtained by expropriating certain U.S. companies.

The Saudis knew that they were in a pivotal spot. Yamani was dictatorial in dealing with Aramco; on August 23, 1973, he told Aramco that he would not bargain on the price of buyback oil, but that the price would be set by the third-party sales of Petromin (Saudi Arabia's national oil company). He added, "Don't be surprised if at any moment, I pick up the phone and instruct Brock [Powers, chairman of the board of Aramco] or Frank [Jungers, president of Aramco] to cut production to seven million barrels a day."[73] The then current rate was 8.4 million barrels.

The war clouds, which had been gathering all during 1973, dropped their rain in October.

The "Great Fear" of 1973. The Israeli-Arab War of 1973 began on October 6 of that year. On October 16, in anticipation of an oil cutback, announcement of which was imminent, a ministerial council of six OPEC members from the Persian Gulf unilaterally raised the posted price of Saudi light crude oil by 70 percent, from $3.011 to $5.119 a barrel (this Saudi light crude 34° API had become the "marker crude," so named because it was used as a reference point for pricing other crudes). This was the first time that oil-exporting nations rather than oil companies had set posted prices.

There was never a serious question as to whether this increased price would hold; an announcement the very next day settled the issue. On October 17, at a meeting in Kuwait, the Arab oil ministers decided to use the "oil weapon" to support the Arab cause. Within a few days, the Arabs began to reduce oil output and embargo certain nations, principally the United States and the Netherlands.[74]

The embargoes caused little economic dislocation because the oil companies were able to deliver non-Arab oil to embargoed countries as a substitute for Arab oil, which in turn was channeled to the nonembargoed nations.[75] The cutback, however, had far-reaching consequences. It reduced the availability of Arab oil from 20.8 million barrels a day in October 1973 to 15.8 million by December. However, this cut of 5 million barrels was partially offset by slight increases in production in other countries, including Iran. The December low for the world was therefore only 7 percent, or 4.4 million barrels, below the

October high of 59.2 million. In terms of international trade in crude oil, the net loss was relatively larger—about 14 percent.

According to the philosophy of romanticism, man is governed more by emotion than by reason. And, indeed, this time the romanticists were correct. These cuts on top of the tight supply already existing caused a number of independents to panic. The reason is obvious: they were desperate. The competition for crude was described by many refiners as "not so much bidding for crude, but bidding for survival."[76] Prices rose rapidly. OPEC members began to sell increasing quantities of oil directly, rather than through the foreign companies that had concessions. The sales of this state-owned oil were not well coordinated; each country charged as much as possible.

In November 1973, an independent U.S. company bid $12.64 a barrel for 80,000 tons of Tunisian crude oil auctioned by Sitep, a company owned jointly by Tunisia and ENI.[77] Iran (NIOC) held an auction on December 10, 1973, allowing 64 companies, primarily independents, to bid on 470,000 barrels a day for the first six months of 1974. The companies bid as high as $17.34 per barrel. NIOC awarded five contracts on December 11 and ten more on December 14; they ranged in price from $9.00 a barrel to $17.34, depending on quantity and quality. All the winners were companies from the United States, Japan, or Europe. As the trade press reported, "The prices confirmed that some crude-short buyers would pay anything to get nonembargoed oil in the current supply crunch." About the same time, Italian buyers bought cargoes of Algerian crude at $14 to $16 a barrel.

Thus the stage was set for the meeting of OPEC's Persian Gulf members that took place in Tehran on December 22 and 23, 1973, a meeting that was to become the great turning point of oil history.

At this meeting the cleavage between those seeking high prices and those desiring not-so-high prices soon emerged. The Shah, having a sense of the future that caused him to steer and not to drift, was determined to raise prices sufficiently to originate a new society of nations, a society in which the oil exporters would begin to receive a fair price for their wasting asset. Moreover, he had done his homework well. He was supported by two studies indicating that oil prices should be much higher. One had been prepared by a team sent by him to investigate the cost of alternative fuels. One of their important conclusions was that "no one in the West was worrying about what would happen when the oil ran out, and the communists could easily take advantage."[78] This enabled the Shah to argue that expensive oil was in the best interests of the West. A second study, by OPEC's Economic Commission, indicated that the price should be around $17.00 a barrel, considering the cost of alternative energy sources. The Shah also argued that a price rise was justified to compensate for the depressed price levels of prior times. He pushed for a posted price of $14—less than some wanted, but a lot more than the $7 that King Faisal had told Yamani not to exceed.

Just prior to the meeting Yamani had warned that the $17 price realized in Iran's auction should not be taken as a basis for determining new prices because the bids to a large extent reflected "the effects of the oil embargo and cutback measures taken by the Arab oil producing countries." Since these measures were of a political nature, he continued, they should not have an economic impact; a price of $17 would ruin the economic structure of the industrialized and developing countries.[79]

The negotiating sessions were stormy; at one point the Saudis threatened to walk out. Yamani was faced with what he considered to be one of the critical moments of his life.[80] He telephoned Riyadh, the capital of Saudi Arabia, and got approval from Prince Fahd, deputy prime minister, to agree to a compromise figure.[81] Thus OPEC solidarity was maintained.

The next morning, on December 23, 1973, the Shah announced at a press conference that the new posted price was to be $11.65 a barrel, a figure that would result in revenues to the host governments of about $7.00 a barrel. This was about four to five times more per barrel than before the 1973 war. The Shah had dramatically demonstrated his leadership within OPEC, although according to some reports he created some Arab resentment over his upstaging the oil ministers, since they were the ones who had decided on the price increase.[82]

With one shattering blow, the new price level was to bring down the ancient system under which the West had enjoyed cheap oil. The oil revenue of the OPEC nations was to jump from $20 billion annually to $100 billion, with the bulk going to the Persian Gulf area.

Yamani later announced that in the opinion of Saudi Arabia, a "lower price would have been more equitable and reasonable." But the OPEC communiqué announcing the new price level called the government take of $7 a barrel "moderate," and concluded with the hope that the consuming countries would "refrain from further increases of their export prices." As for the consuming countries, an unnamed Western oil expert captured the West's feelings when he said, "I'm shocked and appalled."[83]

The oil-exporting nations had no problem in collecting the higher taxes that resulted from the increase in posted prices. Indeed, such payments to the governments seemed like a bargain compared with subsequent open-market bids for crude oil (although not all of the accepted bids were consummated as sales). On the very day on which the price increase was announced, a Japanese firm and two other independents bid $22.60 a barrel for Nigerian crude oil. And well into 1974, independents were bidding $14.00 or more a barrel.

The continued demands of the independents for state-owned oil, the high market prices, and the higher-than-usual profit margins of the majors were all

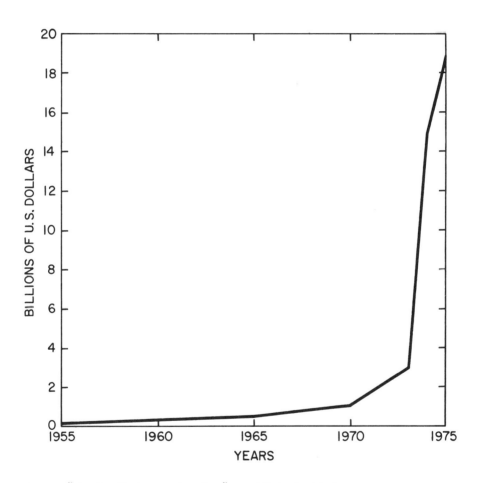

Figure 4

OIL REVENUES OF IRAN, 1955-1975

Source: "Foreign Exchange Receipts" unpublished table from Bank Markazi, Iran.

instrumental in encouraging a further increase in government take. Royalties were increased from 12.5 percent of posted price to 14.5 percent at an OPEC meeting in June 1974, and to 16.67 percent at an OPEC meeting in September. Also at the September meeting, the income tax rate used by OPEC members to calculate payments due from concession holders was increased from 55 percent to 65.75 percent. Meanwhile, the countries were increasing their participation in the ownership of the oil facilities on their soil, thereby effectively raising their revenues by lowering the amount of equity oil and increasing the portion of buyback oil. At a meeting of the six Persian Gulf OPEC members in Abu Dhabi on November 10, 1974, Saudi Arabia, with the support of Qatar and the United Arab Emirates, effectively increased government take again. They announced a decrease in posted price, but another increase in royalty and income taxes so that the government take was increased to about $10.00 a barrel. The Saudis took this action independently of OPEC, perhaps to reinstate some of the leadership position that they felt they had lost in December 1973. The other OPEC nations, given the opportunity for higher revenues, followed suit willingly. In December 1974 the Shah proposed, and OPEC adopted with minor changes, a unified price system to ensure a government take of $10.12 a barrel for marker crude oil, with about 22 cents a barrel allowed for oil company profit.

The price remained frozen until the OPEC meeting in October 1975, at which time prices were boosted approximately 10 percent, depending on the particular crude oil. During the rest of 1975 and early 1976, various OPEC members made adjustments to certain of their prices. These adjustments were necessary because changes in market conditions caused the inherent market value of some crude oils to get out of line with the inherent value of the marker crude. In some cases the adjustments resulted in price increases and in others decreases, with such factors as industrial activity, freight rates, and weather causing variations in the value of different crude oils. But these adjustments, which typically were less than 2 percent of market price, were of no important consequence in terms of OPEC revenues.[84]

The increase in Iranian oil revenues during the period 1957 to 1975 hardly seems believable. From the platform of about $200 million provided by the Consortium in 1957, the combination of greater output and higher prices expanded Iran's oil income *100 times* to nearly $20 billion (figure 4). In round numbers, both output and price had each gone up about tenfold.

OUTLOOK

What does a nation do for an encore after it has increased its oil income 100-fold in less than two decades? That was the question facing the Shah and other

Iranian leaders in 1976. To be sure, Iran's goals—independence and higher revenues—would likely remain the same, but the emphasis placed on each would shift. Thus it looked as if Iran would turn heavily to petrochemicals, which represented the brightest light along the road to greater revenues for the nation. One dollar's worth of oil or gas could be converted into petrochemicals worth five to ten dollars in the export market. Of course, petrochemical facilities were expensive to build. And, of course, markets were not unlimited, so no one suggested that Iran would convert $20 billion of oil and gas into $100 to $200 billion of petrochemicals a year. But a more modest target over a number of years of converting enough oil and gas to produce, say, $20 billion a year in petrochemicals seemed plausible—not to shut down existing petrochemical capacity in Europe, Japan, and the United States, but rather to provide some of the new capacity that would be needed for growth in world consumption. Moreover, the relatively low freight costs per unit of product and the standardized nature of many products would facilitate the export of petrochemicals.[85]

The fact that high export revenues were to be gained from petrochemicals was quite important. The outlook for increases in oil revenues was different from what it had been during much of Iran's history as an oil-producing nation. A definite ceiling on production seemed in sight because of the physical characteristics of the oil fields. Oil output was expected to grow only about 40 percent above the 1975 production level of 5.4 million barrels a day to a new total of 7.5 million barrels. Furthermore, with proven reserves of some 70 billion barrels, Iran would be drained dry in 35 years if the 1975 rate were continued or in a mere 25 years at a rate of 7.5 million barrels daily— unless, of course, more reserves were found. To be sure, more reserves were likely to be found, although how much, when, or where was difficult to foretell. Furthermore, production would not continue at a high rate throughout the life of the fields but likely would be tapered off gradually so as to save oil for the domestic market and for "high-value" uses, such as petrochemicals. Still, 25, 35, or even 50 years are short periods in the history of a nation. But what about increased income from higher oil *prices?* Such income seemed closer to an absolute ceiling than it had during much of the past. Not even the most rabid fan of higher oil prices was expecting another tenfold increase.

In addition to providing foreign exchange revenues for the country, petrochemicals offered other advantages. Each petrochemical product was almost a separate industry, with its own markets and sources of technology. True, there was some overlap: Monsanto, for example, manufactured both styrene monomer and acrylonitrile. However, not all manufacturers of styrene monomer manufactured acrylonitrile—and vice versa. In fact, it was rare that a list of manufacturers of two different petrochemicals would be identical. This diversity would mean less dependence on any one foreign company, whether its role was as a joint venture partner of NIOC, a purchaser of the petrochemical product, a supplier of technology, or some combination of these three. Furthermore, it offered Iran the opportunity to do business with chemical companies in order to lessen dependence on the major oil companies.

In addition, petrochemical manufacture would make an important contribution to Iran's domestic economy. The availability of a variety of products would encourage the construction of plants domestically to upgrade the petrochemicals into consumer goods for the domestic market, such as tires, synthetic fabrics and innumerable plastic products. Furthermore, the petrochemical industry requires higher skills than oil refining and thereby would provide long-term opportunities for Iran to move up a technological ladder— a ladder whose first rung is the importation of technology. There are many higher rungs, including the development of process improvements and new processes for export. Also, the industry would offer the opportunity for a parallel development of factories to supply materials and equipment, at first for Iran and later for export.

Iran had a special advantage in petrochemical manufacture because of its large supplies of gas and gas liquids, an advantage not available to many new plants in the industrialized nations—and petrochemicals could be shipped more cheaply than the gas and gas liquids. Furthermore, Iran had a more secure supply of oil than most industrial nations, which reduced the risk in building a petrochemical facility. Yet Iran would have to be willing to receive less than the world price for the gas or oil used in the first, and perhaps second, petrochemical export facility. After a major Iranian petrochemical industry had been established, complete with infrastructure of all kinds, then the price received by Iran for the raw materials used in additional ventures would rise.

Development of a petrochemical industry would also be consistent with the Shah's belief that oil was a noble substance, too valuable to be burned as a fuel.[86] Overall, oil's economic advantage over coal is much greater as a petrochemical feedstock than as a fuel.

Besides petrochemicals, natural gas was another bright light on the revenue scene. It was important not only as a raw material for petrochemicals but as an export commodity and a source of domestic energy. Discoveries in the 1970s suggested that Iran's gas reserves were greater than anybody had thought. In terms of energy content, they might even approximate the oil reserves. However, the domestic uses of gas were likely to get priority over gas exports. Even though gas was considered to be a cleaner and hence more valuable fuel than oil, Iran would obtain less revenue per unit of energy content because the cost of transportation to the consumer (either by pipeline through the Soviet Union or in liquid form by ship) was greater for exported gas than for oil. The domestic fuel markets for gas would include homes, transportation, and energy-intensive industries—aluminum, steel, and copper. Developing such industries was a natural activity for Iran to aspire to in the last quarter of the century.

In spite of the increased emphasis on petrochemicals, natural gas, and energy-intensive industries, Iran was not about to neglect oil. In many ways, her future actions were bound to be a continuation of the past. Much was left to do in lessening her dependence on the Consortium, which through its oil purchases still provided over 80 percent of her oil revenues in 1975—revenues that in turn provided the bulk of her foreign exchange. This nibbling away at the Consortium's importance to Iran was likely to take a long time and require many actions.

The central performer in this pageant had to be NIOC surrounded by its affiliates, such as those involved with petrochemicals, gas, and tankers. Yet these companies would still be subjected to the strong checks and balances inherent in Iran's governmental organization, especially on matters of strategy. It seemed unlikely that NIOC would be able to take the kind of autonomous action, independent of other government agencies, open to state-controlled companies in some other nations.[87] As one Iranian government official told me, "His Imperial Majesty *makes* the policy. The executives in the government and NIOC *execute* the policy."

NIOC was likely to continue making "downstream" investments in refineries and marketing operations in consuming countries. Such investments not only would help to get outlets and thereby provide increased sales of Iranian oil, but also would provide stability for such sales. Hence, the very reasons that led the majors and other oil companies into being integrated chains would likely cause NIOC to do the same, albeit on a smaller scale downstream. Rather, NIOC's downstream investments would be made on a selective, judicious basis in response to specific opportunities, not as part of a grand strategy to become a multinational oil company, which seemed NIOC's probable fate at one time.[88] For NIOC could not but give priority to the Iranian economy, with its needs for industrial development.

Iranian refineries to make oil products for export were on NIOC's list, but they were being delayed by the surplus of refining capacity that existed outside Iran. It looked as if Iran would have to absorb some of the difference between the cost of shipping refinery products and the lower cost of shipping crude oil. However, this would be worthwhile for Iran for at least some projects, because of the greater diversification of markets and contribution to domestic industrial activity that they would provide. Yet product exports by NIOC would certainly be small in terms of Iran's overall revenue from the oil and gas industries.

As in the past, many actions taken to lessen dependence on the Consortium also would contribute to the goal of increasing output. One such activity that

Iran would continue would be the search for barters—Iranian oil for goods that Iran lacks. The barters could be with companies or nations. Many of the deals were likely to be with less-developed nations that lacked cash to pay.

As Iran's oil production approached its ceiling, the government would be likely to feel an increasing need to raise oil prices for Iranian consumers—prices that traditionally had been lower than those in most countries. And in addition to substituting gas for oil, nuclear power also would be substituted for some domestic oil uses.

In the meantime whatever efforts Iran made to increase total oil output would continue to be taken independently of other OPEC members. In contrast, price action would continue to be taken through OPEC, by necessity. Closer relations were likely to be sought with Saudi Arabia, especially, because of the latter's key role in affecting world oil prices. As of 1976, the Saudis in the short run could vary their production within a range of 3 to 11 million barrels a day, and in the long run the upper figure could go to 20 million. This was a very broad range indeed, considering that OPEC's production level in early 1976 was about 30 million barrels daily, of which 8 was Saudi.

The Shah was likely to continue emphasizing whatever argument he thought necessary to increase oil prices. Yet OPEC was like a mountain climber: the higher up the revenue peak one got, the greater the risk from a fall. The first order of business, therefore, would be to preserve the price gains made during the 1973-75 period. Thus, the price strategy would likely be reminiscent of OPEC's early days, defensive for a while until the world made an economic recovery that caused some of OPEC's spare production capacity to be used. At that time a more aggressive price stand could be taken.

Meanwhile, the Shah was willing to sign a bilateral deal with any nation to sell oil for a price indexed to a representative sample of manufactured goods.[89] This was a defensive strategy, designed to maintain the purchasing power of Iran's oil sales. In contrast, the Shah's argument that oil should be priced on the basis of alternative energy sources, such as coal, oil shale, tar sands, nuclear power, and solar power represented a somewhat more aggressive stand. True, it was difficult to determine exactly how aggressive, because as of early 1976 experts were still unsure about the prices of these alternative energy forms. The most aggressive price stance would be based on the "noble substance" argument: oil shouldn't be burned. This could justify a very high oil price indeed, because of oil's substantial economic advantage over coal as a raw material for petrochemicals.

Whatever the exact policies chosen, it seemed entirely likely that Iranian actions in the face of changing circumstances would continue to reflect two characteristics of Iranian policy in the past—innovation and flexibility.

7

Land Reforms of Shah and People

The chronology of all land reforms is uncertain. The years of decisive action follow preliminaries and lead on to a lengthening sequence of consequences. The start, not infrequently, is as obscure as the end is unknowable. Land reform in Iran is no exception. The concentrated events of the twenty years 1951-71, the time of the central drama, are wholly inexplicable apart from the fortunes of the House of Pahlavi in the days of Reza Shah the Great. And none can judge the purport of those years in isolation from the events that followed the formal ending of land reform in 1971. We live too close to the central events to tell in every respect what the outcome of the land reforms may eventually be.

Of the events themselves, especially those of the last ten years, there can be no doubt: in dispatch and scope they have no equivalent in other modern societies that, because they have escaped the turbulence of totalitarian revolution, can be classified as stable. Elsewhere, part reforms and parochial affairs might match the Iranian achievements in terms of accomplishment, but none can do so in scale and completeness. Pace, scale, and completeness put the Iranian land reforms in a class of their own. Even more remarkable is the political authority behind the reforms. Where else in the modern world is there recorded a land reform instigated, pursued, and established at the instance of a supreme power destined to sacrifice in some measure its own potency in the very reforms it promotes and authorizes? In nothing are the Iranian land reforms more remarkable than in the provenance of the power that directed them. Usually, reforms follow the cry from the fields. In Iran they answered the command from the throne.

FORTUITOUS PREPARATION

The Iranian land reforms were in obedience to a supreme royal command, but they also followed precepts based on practical demonstration and success. Neither command nor precepts would have been possible had not the throne been strengthened and the country unified between the two world wars under the genius of Reza Shah the Great. In progress and culmination, the land reforms had been a national movement—a movement no country divided against itself could have sustained. Although the transformation of the rural scene could not have been in the forefront of his mind, it is to the founder of the Pahlavi Dynasty that we must revert to find in his idealism, strength of purpose, and victory the foundations on which it has been possible for an illustrious son to build. "Land reform" had been one of many slogans used by left-wing militants, notably Mirza Kuchek Khan and his partisans, who occupied the dense forests of Gilan in 1921. And the end of the practices of granting lands to tax gatherers and making grants to curry the favor and support of the private forces of the armed *khans* have been reforms in their own way, making for the redistribution of power and land from the days of the new constitution onwards. In these changes and aspirations there was nothing radical and universal. There could not have been: the country lacked a single mind and common purpose, and suffered a government at variance with turbulent local *shaykhs, sardars,* and *khans,* sovereign as some were over petty, breakaway kingdoms.

The tear and strain of the present day rob the memory of the past in whose records lie strength, inspiration, and the praise of famous men. Well should we remember that between the days of Ahmad Shah and the third decade of Mohammad Reza Shah Pahlavi an inspired nation has been brought to spiritual, political, and administrative rebirth. Reza Shah the Great, the first of the Pahlavi kings, was the founder of it all. But it is not for the one who would lay the foundations of a great edifice to bother his mind too much with the superstructures. In those days, even if land reforms on the early scale could have been conceived, there were neither administrative facilities nor experience to mount them. To the lasting credit of Reza Shah, some order was brought into the registration of land holdings for tax purposes, and in his later years preparations were made for tenancy reforms between landlords and rural tenants. More definite in character were two extensive moves, one in Khuzistan and the other in Sistan, to do something with *khaleseh,* the lands of the public domain. The lip service of the laws also spoke of land distribution to the cultivators, but in the event these allotments and leasings of public domain found their way into the hands of local men of prominence, the *shoyukh* of Khuzistan and the *sardars* of Sistan. Later in Luristan more successful attempts were made to settle the nomads by granting public domain lands to any who would improve them, and by exchanging tracts in one province for tribal lands in another.

These sporadic activities were too brief to be valuable lessons for the future policy makers. In this sense they were unpremeditated preparations for what was to come, but never more markedly so as an event of special and personal purport to the reigning family of Pahlavi. To take a first-hand interest in the improvement of the living conditions of the villagers and to court the latest ideas in farming and rural pursuits, Reza Shah made a practice of acquiring villages as crown lands in many provinces. As might be expected, he was accused wrongly by his critics of being avaricious. Neither he nor they could have foreseen the time and place in the history of Iran's rural affairs that those royal estates were destined to occupy. The Pahlavi lands were to become, in the hands of his son and successor Mohammad Reza Shah Pahlavi, an inheritance from which the whole nation has benefited. But for those lands of Pahlavi and what was to be done on and with them, it is reasonable to postulate that the modern land reforms of Iran would never have taken place. Reza Shah the Great welded together a nation and an inheritance in lands. In the nation's and the Pahlavi lands lay the seminal promise of a reformed countryside.

OWNERSHIP AND SOCIAL ORDER

Mohammad Reza Shah Pahlavi, the present Shahanshah of Iran, came to the throne at a time most unpropitious for his own or any other country whose leaders were given to the pursuit of peaceful progress and the betterment of mankind. In 1941 the nations of the world were locked in mortal conflict and his own country was the barracks of uninvited foreign armies. Yet this young Prince, now King, brought with him to the throne a conviction that for him and his people the unified Persia passed to him by his father could and would become a nation vocal in the world's councils. And in a green corner of his vision of the future were the villages, the mountains, and the watercourses of an emancipated countryside, the lure and the love and the latitude of which had inspired the determination of the Shahanshah from his student days.

The cause of the concern that the Shahanshah had for the plight of his rural folk lay in the unchanged and unchanging land tenure system. The administrative reforms, the exchange of estates here and there, and the buildup of the crown lands had not affected in any material sense the ancient proprietary structure and tenurial relationships. We can draw parallels with the state of affairs as they then were in rural Iran and the agrarian and land tenure patterns in other places and at other times. One parallel however we should not make, lest we fall into the trap of certain ill-informed commentators: we should not liken the traditional land tenure of Iran to feudalism. Half of the cultivable land of the country was in the hands of the *khans* and great land proprietors, held absolutely as private property, *melk*. Under feudalism these men of power and land wealth would themselves have been tenants holding their estates of the king or some other seigneur and of them, in turn, other freemen high in social stature would have held derivative tenure. Feudal tenure was free tenure. In Iran the free landowners owned their land in absolute title. They did not hold it of the Shah to owe him personal fealty, homage, or services.

The domains of these landowners could be vast, extending to twenty, thirty, or forty villages. For the most part the villagers, especially those who cultivated the soil, were serfs, *ra'aya*. A serf is a bondman, not a free feudal tenant. To understand the emancipation of the Iranian countryside that the land reforms have achieved, we must see the land before reform as the habitation of a people resembling in their social status the bondmen and serfs of medieval Europe. To draw parallels with feudalism is to belittle what the Revolution of Shah and People has done for the well-being of rural Iran. Besides the vast holdings of the great landowners, some 20 percent of the cultivable land was owned absolutely by men of a modest way of life, the *khordehmalekin*, who nonetheless would have cultivators working on their small holdings. One-tenth of the cultivable land was shared between the 2,000 villages or so that made up the crown lands, *amlak*, and the lands of the public domain, *khaleseh*. In the villages the *zare'in*, as the cultivators with customary rights of cultivation were called, would work the fields. The remaining one-fifth of the cultivable land was held in a kind of fiduciary ownership, either in ways that resembled a private trust, *vaqf-e khass*, or for religious and public purposes, *vaqf-e 'amm*. Besides the cultivators of the village arable land, *nasaq*, there would be found in rural settlements landless folk. Some of these would have no relationship with the farming and husbandry of the village; grouped together as *khoshneshin*, they would be artisans, traders, workers of various kinds, or unemployed and unemployable. Counterparts with them as having no land right at all would be the *kargar-e keshavarzi*, whose place was on the land as farm workers. Variations were found on these main types: the *barzegar*, for example would hold an inferior position among those with customary rights over the village *nasaq*—inferior because in exchange for the use of the land and unlike the *zare'* he had no implements or animals to bring to the fields. Again, there was the *gavband*, the middleman who would provide oxen and implements to the cultivators but did no work himself in the fields. In many parts the *zare'in* would join together in groups known as *boneh* or *harasseh* to work the land. As in so many other open field systems of the world in the past and present, the unit of division was the plowland, the *joft* of the Iranian village. Cultivators in one village would have use rights under custom in severalty; and in other villages would hold them in common with their neighbors (a type of property known as *mosha'*). A not infrequent occurrence was the plot or field, *mazra'eh,* detached and lying away from the *nasaq.* And associated with many villages were extensive areas of barren or neglected land, *ba'er,* and the dead no-man's-land, the *mavat.*

The Iranian land reforms have been single of purpose: to free the village cultivators of their bondage. Socially and politically the consequences have been immediate, and rightly handled the economic outcome could revolutionize Iranian village agriculture. So much can be said looking back over the quarter-century since the accession of the Shahanshah, but to weigh correctly what has been accomplished we must start with the uncertainties of the immediate postwar years.

Land reform takes the land right from one sector, the landlords, and gives it wholly or in part to another, the tenants, whose tenurial hold on the land has always been dependent upon the sanction of the landlord.* The possibilities are many and can involve land distribution to the landless. In Iran the cultivators, the *zare'in,* had by dint of long use, which in places had hardened into recognized custom, an expectancy over the village *nasaq* and the pasture lands. Such cultivators were to be the main beneficiaries of the land reforms, but in those far-off days the way forward was blocked by tradition, ignorance, vested interests, lack of finance, and sheer incredulity that such changes could take place. These obstacles made it certain that no moves would be made voluntarily towards the emancipation of the cultivators. Meanwhile, the prospects of the law of the land being fashioned to equip either cultivators or government with coercive powers against the landlords were darkened by the frowns of the vested interests of the delegates to the Majles, the legislative chamber. Someone had to take a lead where freedom of action was possible and at a prominence none could overlook. There was one such: the Shah himself.

A ROYAL PRECEDENT

At this juncture in the rural affairs of Iran, the immense land wealth accumulated by Reza Shah the Great and now in the title of his son was the key by which the royal hand could unlock the door to the future for the rural peoples. Despite postwar problems of political and constitutional gravity, the Shah took action. That he did so at such a time is a measure of his determination to see to the better ordering of life in the villages. There were

---

*Definitions of land reform are not standard; some are much wider than others and include tenancy reform. See D.R. Denman, *Rural Land Systems* (London: FIG/RICS, 1968).

no precedents, no guideposts. At first, in the late winter of 1949 (1328)* the king's thought was to constitute the royal estates as a public *vaqf* and hand them to the government to manage in the best interests of the villagers. Bureaucracy took such a toll of the income that little was left to benefit the true recipients of the Shah's intentions. A year later the lands were taken back into the Pahlavi title and a royal *farman* of February 3, 1950 (1328) announced the Shah's intention to distribute his village lands to the cultivators. A Council for the Distribution and Sale of the Pahlavi Crown Lands was set up and in January of 1951 (1329) the royal assent was given to its regulations governing procedures and distribution policy. But in April that year elements hostile to the royal prerogative of the House of Pahlavi assumed ascendancy in the Majles. The Shah's purpose to distribute the crown lands and benefit the people was opposed by this faction. Everything was held in abeyance until August 1953 (1332) when as a result of the Mordad 28 Rising, the Shah regained power and initiative.

The Shah's action was not a hollow philanthropy. From the start the aim was to help the farmers to help themselves, above all to engender in them a sense of responsibility for their own affairs. Never for a moment was there an intention to transfer the crown lands gratis to the villagers; indeed, to have done so could have been held to be a breach of the sacred principles of the *vaqf* already created at the instance of the King. Payment was to be made for the land in easy installments spread over twenty-five years, and eased in the first instance by a 20 percent discount deducted from the assessed value of the land. Priorities of distribution were necessary as there was not enough land to go round all the villagers including the *khoshneshin*. First claim was given to the *zare'in* and to the *gavbands* who had implements and animals for the practice of their husbandry. What was left was allocated to the farm workers of the village, and to those of neighboring villages if the land supply permitted.

There were two ways of allocation: the clean sheet method and the customary. Both methods restricted an individual family's allotment to a maximum of 20 hectares. The former of the two methods was neat and logical. After land had been set aside for common purposes—roads, open spaces, schools, mosques, and so on—the village land was distributed by lot among the claimants deemed eligible by a body of commissioners responsible to the land distribution council. The other method recognized a kind of tenant right in the land, locally known as "root-right," which had been won by the cultivators clearing virgin forest land and planting perennial crops. Naturally

---

*Important dates in this text will be given with reference both to the Western (Gregorian) calendar and to the solar Persian calendar, with the latter in parentheses.

this custom was found more in the hill country of the Caspian area than in the open plains. On a similar principle, plantations and gardens established by the tenants were not reallocated under the lottery but were secured to the creators of them.

To have transferred land to a village people in whom the past had imposed little or no responsibility would have been akin to a mockery. The Shah accepted the need to support his land distribution by the provision of funds to promote credit facilities and finance the provision of roads, water supplies, health clinics, and other public services in the villages. Installments of the purchase price for the land were to be plowed back into an improvement fund to help provide these collateral facilities. What was required was a financing agency to handle the inflow and outflow of monies. Thus as an integral feature of the Pahlavi distribution program a special bank, the Bank Omran, was established, and in 1957 (1336) took over from the Council for the Distribution and Sale of Pahlavi Crown Lands. Full administrative responsibility was assigned to the bank. Some indication of the monies involved is found in a calculation made by the Bank Omran in 1960 (1339) that the credit requirements of the newly created peasantry amounted to 750 million rials. Credit on this scale was advanced to support rural credit cooperatives in Pahlavi villages. Through careful supervision success was achieved; by 1970 (1349) the cooperatives were in capital funds to a tune of 200 million rials, and the bank's loans to them totaled 1,444 million rials. These monies are no measure of the financial commitment involved in the royal distribution of the village lands. When all the repayments for the land have been gathered in, the sum will be no more than 940 million rials. By 1972 (1351), the accumulated payments had reached 510 million rials, but in the meantime the bank had funded 5,200 million rials worth of development operations.

Twelve years after the royal *farman* of February 1950, in April 1962 (1341), the directors of the Bank Omran at a special celebration announced to the Shah the completion of the distribution program. Although scattered over the country, for the most part the crown land villages were concentrated in three main areas: to the west of Kermanshah; along the Caspian from Babol westward to Rasht and south beyond Tehran; and in the far northeast from Gorgan to Bojnurd. Pockets of villages were also located south of Mashhad at Fariman and at Jiroft in the far south. Distribution had started at Varamin in 1952 (1331) as a pioneer venture. After the setbacks of that time the movement advanced quickly and by 1961 (1340) the entire 517 Pahlavi crown land villages had been distributed and some 729 rural cooperative societies established to serve their needs. Ultimately the entire responsibility for the administration of the Pahlavi villages, the collection of installments of the land prices, and the affairs of the rural cooperative societies became the responsibility of the Ministry of Cooperation and Rural Affairs.* The funds of the cooperative societies came under the benign eye of the Agricultural Cooperative Bank of Iran. The Ministry of Cooperation and Rural Affairs took on sundry debts incurred by the Bank Omran and owing to the Plan and Budget Organization. By 1976 the treasurer was in the process of paying back to the Bank Omran some part of the expenditures incurred, notably the sum of the outstanding repayments.

ACTION WITH PUBLIC DOMAIN

Five years after the royal *farman* directing the distribution of the Pahlavi crown lands, the government legislated for the wholesale distribution of the *khaleseh* in the Sale of Public Domain Law of 1955 (1334). As previously remarked, attempts to do something with the *khaleseh,* especially in Khuzistan, Sistan, and Luristan, had already had a relatively lengthy history running back to the land policy of Reza Shah the Great. And as recently as 1944 (1323), a Public Domains Office had been added to the Ministry of Finance in order to oversee, among other tasks, the transfer of the *khaleseh* to the peasants. In those days of war, administration of the crown lands and the *khaleseh* was entirely concentrated in the Ministry of Finance. Despite the sporadic but numerous attempts to handle the public domain, to leave it to improvers, grant concessions in it, and even distribute it to the cultivators, nothing worthy of note had been achieved. It was a tale of lost causes and lost records, a chain of disappointments that could well have influenced the Shah to take personal charge of the Pahlavi lands at the end of the war.

We now know from what has proved to be a successful distribution of the *khaleseh* villages among the *zare'in* and other villagers that there were throughout Iran some 1,535 "entire" *(shesh-dang) khaleseh* villages, and 247 others in which the public domain titles were shared with the owners of private lands and the guardians of *vaqf* endowments. Of these villages no fewer than 92 percent were clustered in Azarbayjan, Kermanshahan, Khuzistan, and Fars; and 63 percent of the total were in Khuzistan itself. So large a share doubtless accounts for the constant attention paid by the government to the province of Khuzistan and its *khaleseh* lands. One would have supposed from the way in which the government had been taken up with the *khaleseh* in Sistan that that province would have had, like Khuzistan, a concentration of *khaleseh* villages for distribution. According to the official statistics, however,

---

* Prior to the spring of 1970 this ministry had been the Ministry of Land Reform and Rural Cooperation. In the text that follows, its designation is sometimes the one and sometimes the other title, according to the context.

of all the *khaleseh* villages distributed, only 13 percent were found in Sistan. There is some ground for supposing that the earlier policies had been so mishandled by officialdom in league with the local *sardars* that the cultivators, far from being settled, were dislodged from the villages; hence the scarcity of numbers when, in the late 1950s, the comprehensive distribution policy for the *khaleseh* got under way.

The distribution of the *khaleseh* villages eventually was caught up in the national land reforms of the private estates. For many years however the *khaleseh* land reforms were a thing apart, unrelated to the actions taking place on the crown lands and well before the advent of the nationwide reforms of the private estates. Although the law giving authority to a newly created Public Domains Board, or *bongah,* had been passed in 1955 (1334), it was not until three years later that action seriously started. Delay was inevitable. There was no clear evidence as to where the boundaries lay between public domain and other lands. Immediate ad hoc surveys were essential and had not the King ordered the army to lend a hand, the requisite preparations would probably never have forerun the greater reforms of the 1960s. Legal disputes referable to special courts further held up progress. Added to all this, the distribution of the *nasaq* of the *Khaleseh* villages among the cultivators was but one of a number of land management responsibilities ascribed to the new board. In fact the new board was nothing short of a development corporation, responsible for all the public domains, the cultivable lands, the pasture and forest lands, and urban areas developed and ripe for development; it was specifically charged with duties of sale, transfer, and management. The new powers and the new board were in extent and purpose an administrative reform designed to achieve specific land reforms of the *khaleseh* whose previous policies had failed. Of no small consequence was the requirement that the Public Domains Board should lease lands on conditions favorable to the improvement of them, should make concessions in marsh and salt lands for the rehabilitation and reclamation of them, and should operate a lottery for the allocation of small plots of land to the lower-paid officials in government departments.

All these actions belong in character and purpose to the land reform story of modern Iran. But the distribution of village lands on the Pahlavi model by the Public Domains Board is an accomplishment that links the Shah's action on the crown estates with what was to come on a national scale. Nothing in the *khaleseh* villages resembled the granting of land to cultivators according to root-rights. Each village in the early days was the subject of a survey, a population count, land valuation, an allotment plan, and the casting and supervision of lots—all by a local Distribution and Sales Committee. Maxima were fixed at 10 hectares of irrigated land and 15 hectares of dry farming *(daym).* In tribal areas and national borderlands, settlement was baited by offering as much as 100 hectares to anyone who would run the risk of living and farming where rifle shots spoke louder than the law.

The local Distribution and Sales Committee reported all details pertaining to a village to a committee at *ostan* (province) level. This higher committee used the evidence to decide on the size of the allocations to be made and the value of them. Although selection of actual plots was by lottery, as with the Pahlavi villages the cultivators with implements and animals were granted prior claims; even so, where land was available the *khoshneshin* were not excluded.

The average value of the allotment greatly varied from province to province. Overall values averaged out at 18,097 rials ($240) per family allotment.* This average ranged from 45,385 rials ($600) per allotment in Khorasan to 4,283 ($60) in Kuhkiluyeh and Bouyer Ahmadi. At the higher extremes were lands in the provinces of East and West Azarbayjan, Sistan, Tehran, Gilan, and Gorgan. The values in Khuzistan, although it was the province with the greatest percentage of *khaleseh* villages, were well below average at 11,633 rials ($150) per family allotment. The official grand total for *khaleseh* distribution was a land value of 1,357 million rials ($18 million) allocated to 94,181 families. In the two provinces of Isfahan and Hamadan there is no record of a *khaleseh* village having been distributed.

By 1960 (1339) the distribution of the Pahlavi crown lands was more or less complete and the *khaleseh* program was off to a promising start. In themselves they were outstanding, something undoubtedly novel in Iran. But against the vast measure of rural Iran they were lone stars in a barren night. Both programs when completed would account for no more than 2,000 villages out of a sum of 55,000 villages. He who would countenance a national land reform had to take the measure of it by this ratio. And having done so, he would find that the figures belied the true magnitude of the task. For the crown land villages and the public domain were the estates of monopolies whose decisions chimed with their desires. No third power was needed to authorize their command. Numerically the emancipated villages were but 4 percent of the national total—a mere token of what might be done, and wholly unrepresentative of what had to be done to overcome the obstacles on the pathway to a truly national land reform.

NATIONWIDE REFORMS

The national land reform that was to encompass in its sweep the 55,000 or so villages and detached farms is associated in the annals of modern Iran with the events that have become known as the Revolution of Shah and People.

---

* Here and elsewhere in this chapter, U.S. dollar equivalents of rials are given in round numbers.

The referendum of January 26, 1963 (Bahman 6, 1341), turned the tide in favor of the Shah's aspirations. Against the opposition of the landowners, the obscurantism of cautious religious opinion, and the obstruction of left-wing Tudeh extremists, the Shah pitted his own convictions and referred them to the people's vote. Of a six-point program of practical purpose, the intended land reform was the primary goal.

The outcome of the referendum could thus be seen as the culmination of a struggle of wills, those of the King and those of the majority of the deputies to the Majles of three years earlier. In 1960 (1339) the Majles had played havoc with a bill introduced by the King that would have authorized and set afoot a land reform to touch every corner of the land. The measure was not rejected outright. Sophistry and cunning whittled down the initial shape of it. Amendment followed amendment until the text became a wide variation from the original. Looking back in the light of what was to come, it would have paid the landowners to have accepted in 1960 the moderate proposals of the Shah. As it was, they tried to drive too hard a bargain and so precipitated a national crisis. Where the presented text gave the landowner a year to make up his mind to sell out to the cultivators, the amendments extended the time to two years and doubled the amount of land to be retained in possession by the landowner. The amendments also would have permitted a voluntary sale of the land to the cultivators on the landlord's terms, avoiding government acquisition of the surplus; they likewise required no more than a notification from the landowner of his intention to get on with land reform, and so bypassed government supervision. The presented text imposed a fine for contravention of six times the amount required by the amendments. Where a landowner undertook to cultivate dry land, the amendments gave him four years' grace against a proposal of three years. Under the original text the landowner was to be repaid by fifteen yearly installments, but under the amendments repayment was to be in ten years. The amendments left the upkeep and hence the control of *qanats* (underground water channels) and watercourses with the landowner. A "favored persons" clause in the amended text would have enabled the richer landowners to buy themselves out of all obligations to participate in the land reform by payment of a "development charge" on all land retained and that otherwise would have been distributed. In sympathy and intention the Majles was for the landowners, although in all fairness it must be noted that the deputies were prepared to support a national land reform and were not unconditionally hostile; in one or two respects, the terms of the amendments appeared to be more favorable to the cultivators than those of the original bill had been.

The land reform issue eventually went to the heart of the constitution. New elections were due in 1961 (1340). In these, the landowners' lobby and others opposing the Shah's land reforms overplayed their hand. Undue influence biased the result in favor of the landlords and the Shah declined to convene the Assembly. For a year the Shah, assisted by his cabinet, conducted the affairs of state by royal *farman*. Criticism and dissension were rife, and were generated on every pretext. The Shah and ministers disregarded them. Acting with remarkable swiftness, they amended the text of the land reform proposals again, in a manner that went far beyond the draft law, inasmuch as the new version stood to hasten the distribution of village lands to the cultivators. The now twice-amended law, dated January 9, 1962 (Dey 19, 1340), was immediately effective. One feature stood out, new, radical and destined to be decisive: in place of the great village landowners, the law insisted on the establishment of rural cooperative societies. Membership of a local cooperative society was to be incumbent upon any who wished to have a share in the *nasaq*. Through the cooperative societies the peasants, endowed by the distribution of the lands to them, emerged as a new force in the land. Through them the Shah spoke to the nation at large at a remarkable and unprecedented congress in Tehran. To this Peasant Congress he put his proposals for the six-point national reforms, with land reform topping the list, and declared his intention to call upon the people to condemn or to uphold them. The congress was held on January 9, 1963—one year to the day after the passage of the Land Reform Law. The referendum that followed on January 26 began a new era for Iran: an overwhelming assent ratified the Shah's action. Strengthened by the people's vote the Shah recalled the Majles to implement with him and his government the land reform law of twelve months earlier, with sundry changes that the experience of the past year had required.

The retrospect of fourteen years from 1976 presents an orderly succession of phases that proceeds by logical steps to the present day. But little if anything in the retrospect indicates that these phases were the consequence of forethought. Rather, the reverse appears true—that is, if the assurances given in the earlier stages by the government to the smaller landowners are compared with what in later events the government felt bound to do. The face of the evidence suggests that the ministers who, in January 1962, legislated for land reform in compliance with the royal *farman* had their attention primarily, if not solely, directed towards the large landowners and the political power and social power traditionally vested in them, powers so overwhelming as to exclude the free exercise of a peasant's will, to say nothing of excluding his person from the legislative assembly.

The First Phase

The first phase of the nationwide land reform was consequently directed to breaking up the large estates and distributing the village lands to the cultivators. Many of the lessons learned from the previous attempts at framing policy were heeded. Permitting a maximum amount of land to be retained and requiring the distribution of the surplus was a basic principle, but the definition of the maximum was practical this time—one entire village. The concept of an entire village was an abstract one; a landowner could retain either a full, actual *(shesh-dang)* village or he could select parts from a number of villages owned by him so as to make up the equivalent of such a village. So straightforward a measure was commendable for its simplicity. In application, however, difficulties arose. It became necessary to put a precise legal meaning to the word "village." An explanation of the seemingly contradictory statistics, published from time to time, on the progress of land reform lies in the early difficulties encountered in defining a village. As the law settled down and was applied, a standard but relative formula was recognized. Even so, none could say with any certainty just how many villages (within the legal meaning) existed in rural Iran. Early official estimates were as low as 35,000, a figure short of the facts by about 20,000. Even by 1976, over four years after the official completion of the land reform program, there was no agreed figure. In 1972 the statistics of the then Ministry of Cooperation and Rural Affairs put the grand total at 55,030, a figure that shrank in 1976 to 54,575. The reason for the changes, especially the decline in the mid-1970s, was the settlement of disputes between government and landowners. A place that the government would rank as a village, and hence as the maximum of land to be retained, the landowner would claim as a cluster of outlying fields that, when put together with an adjacent habitation, would constitute a single village. A habitation, if registered by name on the land registry, would be proof paramount of its identity as a village; registration by itself, however, was insufficient. A residential center associated with *nasaq*, varied though the pattern or the association may be, was the fundamental morphology of the village. The only attempt at an absolute standard was the requirement of the Land Reform Organization that by no interpretation was a village to be less than 60 hectares.

Although the scope and direction of the land reform policy changed with circumstances and needs as one stage succeeded another, its inspiration and intent had never been other than fulfilling the Shah's vision of a better life in the villages. It was not devised as a policy for the redistribution of wealth. Care had to be taken and was taken to see that the reforms were not harmful to the advance of Iranian agriculture. For this reason, all lands planted as orchards and gardens and land being farmed by modern mechanical means were excluded from the sweep of the land reform laws. Lands privately endowed, the *vaqf-e khass*, were distributed, but the trusts were respected and the compensation money handed over to the trustees. For the time being publicly endowed lands, *vaqf-e 'amm*, were excluded. By an oversight the earliest text of the law had omitted water rights from the definition of land, and this caused trouble in the first phase of the reforms.

Action was first taken at Maragheh in East Azarbayjan, an experimental thrust, testing ways and means and reactions, carried out by senior men from the Ministry of Agriculture. Evidence from the test was propitious and gave no signs of the trouble that at a later stage the government had to encounter in other parts of the country, notably in the region of Qom and in Fars. Opposition only energized the government's advance and in the trouble spots villages were acquired at a faster rate than elsewhere; in Fars as many as two to three villages a day were being acquired. By the end of the first year the highest proportion of acquisitions among the villages was in the region of Arak and the highest number of villages acquired was in East Azarbayjan, with Khuzistan a close second. At the time it was not possible to measure the pace of the first phase of the reform in terms of what had to be done. Nobody knew how many eligible villages there were to be acquired. Now that we can look back over the entire span of progress, the rate of advance can be calculated and is given in table 7.1 Within the first four years well over 75 percent of the eligible villages had been acquired; and by 1968 (1346) only 10 percent remained to be dealt with. By 1976 a hard core of 13 entire villages and 39 acquisitions of part villages remained outstanding, an insignificant fraction but nonetheless real.

Table 7.1
PERCENTAGE OF ELIGIBLE VILLAGES
PURCHASED YEAR BY YEAR IN FIRST PHASE

DATE	NO. OF VILLAGES PURCHASED	% OF ELIGIBLE VILLAGES
1962/63 (1341)	3,888	23
1963/64 (1342)	8,707	52
1964/65 (1343)	10,312	61
1965/66 (1344)	13,303	79
1966/67 (1345)	14,878	88
1967/68 (1346)	15,014	89
1968/69 (1347)	15,461	92
1969/70 (1348)	16,000	95
1970/71 (1349)	16,292	97
1971/72 (1350)	16,426	98
1975 (1354)	16,817	100

Source: Ministry of Cooperation and Rural Affairs. Other tables in this chapter are from the same source unless otherwise indicated.

The regional pattern of acquisitions of all villages of the first phase of land reform excluding the *khaleseh* villages is given in table 7.2.

In the first phase of the land reform, titles to the surplus villages and lands passed to the Ministry of Agriculture and later to the Ministry of Land Reform and Rural Cooperation. Sale was compulsory but the terms were not ungenerous. There was no rural land market in Iran, no market price of land or villages to which compensation could be related. Values for compensation purposes were based on the landowners' tax returns and assessments of income made upon them. Incomes were multiplied by coefficients that took into account differences in situation, soil, market, the date of the current assessment, and other factors; they ranged from 100 to 180. The lowest coefficients were found in Gilan and Mazandaran and the highest in East and West Azarbayjan. Such discrepancies bore no relationship to the average price paid for a village in the provinces. In Gilan, for example, where the average coefficient was the lowest, the average price paid for a village was 1,583,426 rials ($21,000) compared with 275,057 rials ($3,670) per village in Fars, with coefficients as high as 150. Rounded figures give an average price per village on a national scale of 700,000 rials ($9,300).

Landowners were paid in cash and by payment order. A payment order is negotiable and carries the right to a 6 percent per annum interest payment. The government's debt to the landowners is in theory to be discharged in fifteen yearly cash installments, payable against the presentation of the payment orders. Under this arrangement, the first installment of the purchase price was paid in cash on completion of the purchase by the government, and the balance made up in payment orders. By the mid-1970s, it seemed from the most recent official figures that more than the original intended 10 percent of the purchase price had been paid as a first installment in cash.* Over the country as a whole, 29.8 percent of the purchase price had been paid in cash in the first instance. What was also curious is the apparent irregularity of the percentage of the purchase price represented by the first cash payment among the provinces—in East Azarbayjan it was as high as 41 percent while in Khuzistan it was not more than 12 percent. Taking purchase price and interest together, the total government commitment to the landowners paid out in the first phase lay somewhere between 12,000 and 13,000 million rials.

At the distribution end of the operation, policy was directed to the dispersal of the *nasaq* among those who in the law were eligible to receive it and in accordance with standard priorities. Patterns of privilege followed closely what we have already seen happening with the crown lands and *khaleseh* distribution: the *gavband* and the *khoshneshin* were excluded while the farm

---

* The first installment payable in cash was 10 percent because in the early laws the repayment period was ten years and not 15 percent per year as later.

Table 7.2
COMPLETION OF FIRST PHASE AS AT DECEMBER 1975

REGION	LANDS BOUGHT				LANDS DISTRIBUTED			
	6-Dang		Less than 6-Dang		6-Dang		Less than 6-Dang	
	Villages	Farms	Villages	Farms	Villages	Farms	Villages	Farms
Tehran	221	—	617	434	221	—	617	434
Gilan	57	—	690	—	57	—	681	—
Mazandaran	174	71	537	39	174	70	527	38
East Azarbayjan	510	—	1,317	—	510	—	1,316	—
West Azarbayjan	422	—	435	—	422	—	435	—
Kermanshah	487	—	1,215	—	487	—	1,213	—
Khuzistan	256	4	452	297	256	4	452	297
Fars	247		1,405	—	234	—	1,398	—
Kerman	97	—	254	—	97	—	454	—
Khorasan	222	—	1,069	—	222	—	1,068	—
Isfahan	60	—	338	—	60	—	338	—
Sistan & Baluchistan	1	—	3	—	1	—	3	—
Kurdistan	166	—	511	—	166	—	503	—
Luristan	99	—	449	—	99	—	448	—
Hamadan	189	—	648	—	189	—	648	—
Ports & Oman Coastal Area	3	—	13	—	3	—	13	—
Persian Gulf	49	—	132	—	—	—	—	—
Chahar Mahal Bakhtiari	6	—	102	—	6	—	102	—
Yazd	—	—	15	—	—	—	15	—
Zanjan	169	3	429	—	169	3	429	—
Ilam	210	—	89	—	210	—	89	—
Semnan	10	—	59	—	10	—	59	—
Gorgan & Gonbad	2	—	21	—	2	—	21	—
Kuhkiluyeh & Buyer Ahmadi	335	26	43	—	335	26	43	—
TOTAL	3,992	104	10,843	770	3,979	103	11,004	769

Table 7.2
COMPLETION OF FIRST PHASE AS AT DECEMBER 1975

OUTSTANDING				NUMBER OF PEASANT FAMILIES	COST OF LANDS (Rials)	PAYMENT OF 1ST INSTALLMENT TO LANDOWNERS (Rials)
6-Dang		Less than 6-Dang				
Villages	Farms	Villages	Farms			
—	—	—	—	50,504	1,164,255,024	344,903,276
—	—	9	—	41,213	1,182,819,827	311,798,083
—	1	10	1	69,767	840,555,773	87,907,818
—	—	1	—	123,138	1,740,050,683	773,618,485
—	—	—	—	34,681	819,669,368	195,141,853
—	—	2	—	59,013	715,557,248	150,663,507
				22,464	287,425,911	37,757,964
13	—	7	—	63,307	454,394,509	57,383,750
—	—	—	—	6,219	168,447,972	38,206,861
—	—	1	—	26,343	515,258,072	144,372,683
—	—	—	—	22,192	191,686,270	43,118,844
—	—	—	—	45	1,872,130	124,951
—	—	8	—	32,145	291,830,971	59,009,624
—	—	1	—	16,602	227,580,838	79,439,111
—	—	—	—	80,906	1,177,290,270	613,644,259
—	—	—	—	219	4,681,994	387,260
—	—	—	—	6,111	54,269,250	5,779,138
—	—	—	—	5,978	39,450,582	1,014,339
—	—	—	—	82	609,085	39,565
—	—	—	—	20,141	356,480,295	147,571,311
—	—	—	—	9,547	117,346,001	9,072,104
—	—	—	—	698	28,699,861	6,231,051
—	—	—	—	5,990	42,221,894	3,354,352
—	—	—	—	12,413	30,705,473	2,048,899
13	1	39	1	709,718	10,453,159,306	3,112,589,088

worker, the man without customary rights in the *nasaq,* came last among the eligible recipients. Excluded also was anyone who at the time of distribution was not a member of the village rural cooperative society.

As a general rule each recipient would have conveyed to him a right to a stated proportion of the village lands, a conveyance that would not specify by detailed description and plan a specific allotment. This rule did not pertain everywhere; in some places specific allotments were made. A rough-and-ready valuation passed on the purchase price paid by the government to the village recipients. Repayment was demanded over a fifteen-year period, but the new peasant proprietors did not have to bear the cost of the 6 percent interest on the outstanding payment orders. Towards the peasants the government had been most patient and lenient; by 1976, the sum of the repayments received measured only 20 percent of what was due. Payment was made to the Agricultural Cooperative Bank, an institution that operated as a finance house between the Treasury, the Plan and Budget Organization, and the Ministry of Cooperation and Rural Affairs.*

The Second Phase

That the land reform, at what by the passage of events is now seen as the first phase of a three-stage policy, was in the first instance meant to be a national, all-embracing reform, is reflected in those provisions of the law of January 9, 1962, designed to deal with the relationship of landowner and *zare'* in those villages whose lands were not distributed to the cultivators. Perhaps with too sanguine a trust in its own authority, the law in effect executed a universal tenancy reform. No longer were the *zare'in* to be the occupiers more or less at will of the landowner and *khan.* They were by the law and by implication converted into tenants of a kind, tenants with rights of security, with claims to compensation for improvements, who could invoke the law to require a landowner to provide and maintain water supplies and irrigation facilities, and to share the harvest and land products more generously than custom had ordained.

On paper it looked well, but in the villages it was little understood. The landowners were still masters except in those villages where land distribution was no longer fancy but fact. Great estates were being broken up, but when all had been accomplished nearly three-quarters of all the Iranian villages would not have witnessed land distribution. Long before events could demonstrate this truth, a year to the day after the passage of the first effective land reform law, the Shah addressed the Peasant Congress in Tehran and called on the

---

*In its earlier form and before 1969 the Agricultural Cooperative Bank had been first the Agriculture Bank and then the Agricultural Credit Bank.

people to support him in his reforms. Clearly, a policy more radical than the dispersal of the large estates supplemented by tenancy reform was required, and nine days before the national referendum of Bahman 6, 1341, new measures were taken on which the second phase of the land reform policy went forward. A way had to be found that would give the cultivators of the villages retained under the existing law a sense of participation in the national land reform movement and at the same time lessen the grievances of the small landowners, which undoubtedly and justifiably would have caused widespread unrest had a ruthless extension of the compulsory distribution law been made at that time.

A somewhat paradoxical expedient was seized upon. Landowners in the villages were made to face a compulsory choice, a choice to be made between themselves and the cultivators. Government did not in a general way intervene, although the officials of the Ministry of Land Reform and Rural Cooperation were at hand to act as advisers, adjudicators, and assessors as occasion required. Three choices were open: to lease, sell, or divide the land. Later, in 1964, the range of choice was widened by the addition of two other options: the landowner could buy out the root-rights and other items of tenant right now vesting in the tenant under the tenancy reforms of January 1962; or the parties in the village, including the landowners, could get together in a formal joint enterprise scheme. Initiative in most places lay with the landowners; socially prominent as they were, local opinion would expect it of them, although it would mean opening discussions with the traditionally subservient on how to share the village land resources. Ultimately the consensus of the cultivators could decide the outcome. In default of agreement and action the officials of the Ministry of Land Reform and Rural Cooperation would assess the rental value of the land and require their figures to be used in letting it.

Prices under the sale arrangements were left to open bargaining; the formula of a proportion of the landowner's tax income multiplied by a coefficient may have been used as a basis, but this method was not mandatory. Compared with the other options, outright sale was the neatest and left the cultivators in unencumbered possession of all the land to the exclusion of the erstwhile landowner. But put side by side with the terms of acquisition operative in the compulsorily acquired villages, voluntary purchase in the second phase appears to have favored the landowner. Whatever the price might be, the purchaser was required by law to pay two-fifths in cash at once and the remainder in yearly installments over ten years. Loans were available to assist purchasers from funds subscribed by the Agricultural Cooperative Bank to the Ministry of Land Reform and Rural Cooperation. There was one exception to the full bargaining principle: where the subject of transfer was paddy fields under rice cultivation, voluntary bargaining was limited to 30 hectares and any excess could be bought by the cultivators on the price formally adopted for the acquisition of villages by the government under the first-phase distribution.

A similar areal limitation was imposed to control the acquisition of tenant right where the landowners chose the option and bought out the cultivators. Limits varied from region to region. In Gilan, for example, the maximum area of paddy fields allowed to the acquiring landowner was 20 hectares; while in Khuzistan and Sistan a landowner could acquire tenant right over 50 hectares no matter what the type of land use and cropping.

Division of the land between landowner and cultivators was patterned on the customary sharing of the main crop at harvest. Beyond the enunciation of this principle the law gave no guidance on how the division was to be made. If one ratio has become more generally accepted than others, it is a division of three-fifths to the landowner and two-fifths to the cultivator. Apart from taking a proportion of the land there was a price to pay; the cultivator had to find two-fifths of the value of the share in the land that came to him from the landowner. Arrangements under this option often meant prolonged negotiations over price and the actual partitioning of the land. Division of the land was a less risky business for the landowner than the outright sale. It seems that apart from providing credit to assist the outright purchase, the government did nothing to facilitate the sale operation, but where the land was divided the landowner received in cash from the government one-third of the money due to him and also enjoyed the benefit of a government guarantee of the payment of the remainder in yearly installments over ten years.

Under the second-phase law, letting the land was a formal matter. The terms and the relationship between the parties were not left to the vagaries of the tenancy reform of an earlier year. Cultivators assumed a status equivalent to a tenant's under a contractual tenancy and were secured by the terms of the agreement for a thirty-year term. Rents were cash payments calculated by reference to the landlord's income from the land over the years 1961-63 (1340-42) and were subject to revision every five years.

The joint enterprise option was an attempt to coax the village parties to cooperate in extensive farming under conditions suitable for modern agricultural techniques. The legal text makes reference to shareholders and to the participation of the villagers in an initial vote of establishment. One can see in this idea the adumbration of the farm corporations that were to follow. Constitutional and political questions were provoked, particularly over those villagers who were opposed to the idea but outvoted. History allowed no time for the answers to be found to the questions raised before the joint enterprise policy was overtaken by the finality of the third phase.

During the second phase further attention was paid to endowment lands, to the public and private *vaqf*. Cultivators whose villages were on endowment land, especially public endowment land, were no longer to be deprived of the benefits and choices of land distribution. The public *vaqf* however was not to be acquired outright by the government nor by the cultivators. The latter were given ninety-nine-year leases in the land at rents comparable with those reserved under the thirty-year leases granted as one of the normal five options. The government could, if necessity required, buy out the private *vaqf* and see that the proceeds of the sales went to support the aims and purposes of the trust or endowment. By the end of 1975 some 6,200 public endowment villages had been distributed along with 685 held as private endowment.

Table 7.3

CHOICE DISTRIBUTION UNDER SECOND PHASE

OF LAND REFORM AS AT DECEMBER 1975 (AZAR 30, 1354)

CHOICE	LANDOWNERS		CULTIVATORS	
	No.	%	No.	%
Letting land on 30-year lease	233,334	74.70	1,263,961	80.62
Sale of land to cultivators	3,111	1.00	51,531	3.30
Cultivators selling root-rights	8,989	2.90	13,374	0.85
Joint enterprise villages	41,615	13.30	81,292	5.18
Divided villages	25,359	8.10	157,597	10.05
TOTAL	312,408	100.00	1,567,755	100.00

We can now stand back from the operation of the second phase and review its overall performance. An analysis of the figures as at the end of December 1975 (Azar 30, 1354) is given in table 7.3. The percentage distribution of the choices made differs slightly between the landowners and the cultivators over the country as a whole. With both, the letting of land was an obvious first preference, predominant over all others: with the landowners, letting accounted for 74.7 percent of the choices made, while the corresponding figure with the cultivators was 80.62 percent. Second preferences differed: of the landowners, 13.3 percent opted for the joint enterprise idea, but the cultivators preferred the division of the land as a second option, a choice made by 10.05 percent of them. More cultivators than landowners wanted to buy the land outright—3.3 percent compared with 1.0 percent. There were more landowners who showed an interest in buying out the cultivators (2.9 percent) than vice versa (0.85 percent). The patterns of preference varied with the regions. The thirty-year leases were relatively of less consequence in Kerman and Khorasan, both provinces in which the joint enterprise idea was more readily carried out in the early years of the policy. Selling land outright was more noticeable in the provinces of Azarbayjan, Gilan, and Tehran than elsewhere. And the sale of tenant right had quite a vogue in the south and east in Kerman, Bandar 'Abbas, Sistan, and Baluchistan. But a remarkable feature of the interregional distribution was the concentration in Fars of 50 percent of all the arrangements made for dividing the land between landowners and cultivators. The thirty-year leases excluded all other transactions in Ilam and Yazd, and accounted for over 95 percent of all transactions in Gilan, Mazandaran, Khuzistan, and Kuhkiluyeh and Bouyer Ahmadi.

The Final Phase

Because the land reform policy in its second phase left so much to choice, to discussion and decision among the parties concerned, the rate and extent of progress could never be exactly determined. Final statistics can never be better than the field returns that supply them, and in the second phase the officials of the Ministry of Land Reform and Rural Cooperation were more referees than the directors of operations they had been in the first phase. The Shah had promised emancipation from serfdom and this had been accomplished—either through the distribution, sale, and division of land, or through tenancy reform. Nevertheless there was discontent; the peasants to whom the land had been distributed in the acquired villages, the crown land villages, and the *khaleseh* appeared favored above the run of their fellows in the more numerous retained villages or in public endowments. Cultivators had not been prepared to buy out the landowners on open bargain terms and had opted to take leases at rents that had to be fixed by government officials. On the evidence of the final figures for the second-phase transactions, no less than 56.4 percent of the 2.5 million village families benefiting from the nationwide land reforms and the *khaleseh* distribution were occupying their *nasaq* as tenants, either holding a thirty-year formal agreement or as tenants under *vaqf* leases. This percentage, high though it is, is probably on the low side; it does not reflect those uncertain relationships in which landowners and tenants had not come to an understanding within the choice range of the second phase. Information obtained in the process of the third phase suggests that at the start of the third phase no less than one in five of the landowners had not declared their hand under the second phase. The prolongation of uncertainty under the second phase added to the growing dissatisfaction of cultivators who found a formal tenancy held from a traditional landlord difficult to distinguish from the practicalities of the old one. The government acted in December 1968 to bring in the Law for the Redistribution and Sale of Rented Farms to Farmers (Azar 24, 1347). Action would doubtless have been taken earlier if the government had found some other way of resolving the dilemma of keeping faith with the small landowners, who had been promised security, and with the cultivator who was expecting ownership.

The new law required the leasing arrangements and the joint enterprise schemes to be put back into the melting pot. Lands that had been subject to these arrangements and all lands still under dispute within the second-phase options had either to be divided between the landowner and tenants or sold to the tenants. Initiative was left with the landowners, but in the interests of expediency the issue was to be decided by a majority vote of the landowners of the village or other area involved. Asked for their preferences in an inquiry conducted by the Ministry of Land Reform and Rural Cooperation, 88 percent of the 222,360 landowners approached opted for the division of the land. This pluralist attitude delayed progress, as it appears that the cultivators were of an opposite mind. Three years went by until the spring of 1971 (1350). The government was determined to bring matters to a head and the Shah ratified by royal *farman* a law that sealed the end of the land reform program on a given day at a given hour. The terminus was the close of working hours on September 22, 1971 (1350). The next day was Farmers' Day. As from that day all land that was not the subject of an agreement to divide was deemed to have been sold to the tenants; the rental payment next due and the subsequent payments were treated as installments of the purchase price.

Where the land was sold, the tenant either paid in cash ten times the rental figure fixed by the officials of the Ministry of Land Reform and Rural Cooperation, or twelve times the rent over a period of twelve years. On division, the tenants' share was sold to them at two-fifths its value less a 15 percent discount. Where the purchase price was paid in installments the landowners were given promissory notes guaranteed by the government.

Termination of the land reform program in this arbitrary way inevitably left numerous titles to be investigated and transactions settled. At the end of 1975 the process was still going on. By then, however, it was little more than a mopping-up operation. Official figures recorded a total of 358,932 landowners who were either selling their land or dividing it under the third-phase law. This total was 78,000 more than the aggregate number of landowners recorded under the second phase as having let land or entered into joint enterprise schemes. The additional numbers were 21.7 percent of the total and were the basis for the earlier statement that one in five landowners had not decided what to do under the second phase by the time events had caught up with them and the third-phase law took over. As a postscript to this grand finale the Shah announced his intention of granting full ownership to the cultivators of public *vaqf* lands—and this was duly done, to the benefit of some 6,995 villages and separate farm lands.

BARREN AND DEAD LAND

At the traditional heart of rural Iran lay the *nasaq* of her thousands of villages. It was towards this that the spearhead of land reform had been directed and among its cultivators that the spectacular social and proprietary changes were wrought. In areal magnitude however the totality of the village *nasaq* accounted for a relatively small proportion of the vast expanse of the land mass running beyond the cities and the towns. Measured in the aggregate, land under cultivation occupied no more than 12 percent of the country's land area and this included the mechanized farms, gardens, and orchards that were excluded from the land reform distribution and lay alongside, but were not part of, the village *nasaq*. Some 6 percent of the land area of the country was made up of natural pasture and another 11 to 12 percent of natural forests. Over half the nation's land was uncultivable, but much potential lay in some 19 percent of the total that in the mid-1970s was uncultivated yet held out promise of reclamation and development. Within the great sweep of the reforms of Shah and people, endorsed and set in motion by the referendum of Bahman 6, 1341, was the bringing under public title of the far-ranging natural pastures and forests. These occupied a special category within the land use pattern and the reform laws. In this sense they lay outside the great expanses of deserts, mountains, scrub lands, and swamps that took up 70 percent of the total, and that included the 19 percent of potential development land. Of these, some had fallen into neglect after being cultivated in the past and others held out promise of fertility and yield not yet tested. Both categories of these neglected yet cultivable lands were referred to as *ba'er*. The remainder were the dead lands, *mavat*. At law, *ba'er* is distinct from *mavat* as land that although in possession of an owner is neglected; *mavat* is unclaimed in any formal sense. Although they concentrated on the distribution of the village *nasaq*, the land reforms, including the ones that transformed the Pahlavi villages and the ones that dealt especially with the *khaleseh*, were not unmindful of the *ba'er* and *mavat*. In the Pahlavi villages the peasants-to-be were not prepared to give a thank-you for grants of *ba'er* and *mavat;* these lands remained a reserve to be caught up in the national policies of later days. When in 1960 (1339) the Majles redrafted the proposed land reform law, it intended that landowners should be permitted to retain as much barren land as they were able and willing to mechanize and work.

The operative law of January 9, 1962 (1341), dealt with the outlying lands in a preemptory yet comprehensive manner. Little thought was given to this aspect of reform policy at the time, but the very inclusion of the barren and dead lands in the reform law proved with the passage of events to have been an act of conception from which sprang one of the major finance houses of modern Iran—the Agricultural Development Bank. The story had its parallel in the history of the idea and growth of the Bank Omran. If successful achievement means ratifying steps taken in the hour of necessity, then the story of the *ba'er* and *mavat* lands and the growth of credit and banking facilities related to their development is an outstanding example of such achievement. None could have foreseen the outcome who first read the simple provisions of the 1962 law.

With a rough-and-ready embrace, the law of January 9, 1962 (1341), included the *ba'er* and *mavat*, the uncultivated and barren lands of the villages, among those lands, along with the village *nasaq*, that were to be acquired. No distinction was drawn between the lands of the villages acquired and those of the villages retained; all *ba'er* and *mavat* was to be acquired and distributed. It was a tidying-up gesture to which at the time neither official-dom nor laity paid much attention. The law was too vague for action, but its vacuity was no embarrassment as no one was interested one way or the other. Three years passed before the government paid serious attention to these hinterlands and wider domains. In January 1965 (1343) the government sharpened up the law. There was to be a vesting procedure handled by a special interministry commission. At the instance of the commission, area by area was brought under action and the *ba'er* and *mavat* transferred to the Ministry of Agriculture. As the lands passed into government title, so and simultaneously were they offered to individual persons, companies, and other institutions willing and able to develop them. Nothing happened for a further three years, mainly because the government set too high a price on these problem hectares. By 1967 (1346) the government had got round to offering the barren and neglected land freely to any who would farm it, or had settled nomadic tribesmen on it. Lack of money was proving to be the stumbling block. Not until the Agricultural Development Fund was established in 1968 (1347), with authority to make adequate loans, was any movement seen; and even then the government had to lower its sights from an original minimum loan of 5 million rials to 1 million. Grants of land were conditional on an agreed policy of cultivation and sometimes of improvement being pursued satisfactorily and, where a loan had been made, on the loan being repaid. As and when these conditions were met the title to the land would be conveyed by the government to the grantee. The Agricultural Development Fund eventually became the Agricultural Development Bank of Iran with widened responsibilities, including finance for the new and extensive agribusiness enterprises. Year by year the ramifications of the Agricultural Development

Bank proliferated, and it is difficult to trace from the public accounts and policy statements just how far the bank's activities in the mid-1970s were financing the improvement and reclamation of *ba'er* and *mavat*—the original ideal and purpose. If we exclude the agribusinesses and what are called "other" loans, and restrict the records to loans for cultivation projects, livestock, husbandry, poultry, and fruit plantations, the official figures point to ever-rising commitments: from six projects in 1968 (1347) representing a total investment of 264 million rials, to 449 projects in 1975 (1353) and a corresponding investment of 15,126 million rials.

FORESTS AND NATURAL PASTURES

A reform complementary to the ownership of *ba'er* and *mavat* by the government was the nationalization of forests and natural pastures. In size the operation was a lesser affair involving 10 million hectares of pastures and 19 million hectares of forests. Socially and politically, it was the more significant; indeed, it ranked with the land reform itself as an aspect of the Revolution of Shah and People. It differed again from the treatment of the barren and idle lands and the land reform itself in that its justification was found deep in Islam's understanding of God and nature. As the Shah himself so persuasively argued, the forests were "a divine gift for which no one has labored except nature." It was therefore perfectly logical that "something which nature has bestowed on a country should belong equally to all the inhabitants."

Historically the referendum of January 26, 1963 (Bahman 6, 1342), was a ratification of the government's intention to nationalize the forests and pastures, since the operative law was dated January 17, 1963 (Dey 28, 1342). For sylvicultural purposes the state took over the title and management of the natural forests, but the law was flexible. There were borders and patches where the forests were impoverished or stunted by scrub and overgrown thicket—areas better cleared, leveled and turned to pasture or something better. These places were offered to landowners to exploit and improve. For a year or two they would be occupied by the improvers or lessees who, if and when successful, would have the full *melk* title conveyed to them. And there were exceptions to the general law; among these were woodland areas within the ring boundary of farms, as also were plantations and gardens and other occupied and developed lands lying in the natural forest. The bulk of the vast naturally wooded areas, the highlands of the Elborz and Zagros Ranges, were to be systematically managed to make good the long years of neglect and indifferent exploitation; felling programs were to be matched with nursery extension and planting policies. Time, knowledge, and lack of skilled manpower were limiting factors which the policy makers had to contend with and overcome.

Here and there the forests blended into the natural grazing grounds. The new forest law permitted the Forest Department, under whose authority the forests were managed, to grant grazing rights, freely yet with limits on the number of beasts grazed, to families living in the forest; and similar rights were given to villagers to take timber for repairs to buildings and implements and to meet other rural needs.

Pasture lands are natural resources in the agrarian economy of Iran, which is unaccustomed to the grassland husbandry of the more temperate countries. Nonetheless there are domestic and remote pasture lands and in the pattern of land reform the difference has a meaning. Each village, as a general rule, would have some ground where the flocks and herds and plough beasts would graze. These domestic pastures are grazed in common by the *zare'in* and others according to the customs that regulate the cultivation and cropping of the *nasaq*. These are the village pastures. Title to them passed to the government under the first phase of the land reform on those occasions when the village itself was acquired; and remained with the villagers when the village was retained. In some places individual farmers were able to substantiate titles to private pastures and these, like the other domestic pastures, were exempt from the nationalization procedures.

The remote pasture lands that for the most part run over the hills and higher contours were, like the natural forests, to be managed by the government department responsible for natural resources. For centuries some nomadic peoples had claimed what to them appeared as indisputable rights of tracking and grazing over the mountain pastures. The drove lands were theirs, and the sophisticated laws of townsmen meant little to them. The government's answer was to encourage these people to settle so that their grazing habits and demands could be controlled. Better management of the wider pastures, especially where they march with hard-pressed domestic pastures, could prove to be an issue of first consequence for the future development of agriculture in Iran, whose stall-fed dairy cattle are so costly to breed and rear.

COOPERATIVES REPLACE THE LANDLORDS

Of the many lessons that, by the distribution of his own villages, the Shah had taught the policy makers who were to frame and guide policies for the nationwide reforms, the most profound was the need to find a substitute for the traditional landowner once he had left the village scene. To the cultivators of the village lands, he had always been there; good or bad, he was under God their patron. Nowhere was this more obvious than in the villages that enjoyed the royal patronage. From the very outset the Shah was aware of the hollowness that would follow a simple carving up of the village lands and the assignment of the operations to the new peasantry. Always there had been someone to account to, someone to ask, someone to blame. Whether on the royal lands or elsewhere, the peasant standing alone with no authority beyond himself to guide his thinking and direct his actions would be lost. Who or what could replace the lord of lands?

With nothing of any validity to help them, the Shah and his administrators of the Bank Omran pioneered in hope to set up cooperative societies in the emancipated villages. Properly organized and instructed, the new peasantry could help itself—what stronger, what more reliable than self-help? The ideal would be a multipurpose cooperative, or a set of cooperatives, to serve each village in production, marketing, consumption, and credit. Foreign experts were called in and an elaborate program embarked upon in the royal villages. The instructors learned more lessons than they imparted. A fully functional cooperative society is a complex enterprise of administrative skill, technical wisdom, and social judgment; and the more its functions the greater its complexity. Multipurpose cooperatives were simply beyond the ability of the rustic folk of the Pahlavi villages to comprehend or wish to understand. There was much enthusiasm to start with, as when in 1952 some 600 villagers stormed into Varamin to elect directors of the proposed multipurpose Varamin Rural Cooperative Society. Failure pruned the ideals down to what was practical and possible—the setting up and operating of rural credit cooperatives to bring funds and credit facilities to the villages and loosen the grip of the money lenders. The Bank Omran became the central finance house; it opened branches and encouraged cooperatives to be formed in the villages and to be organized in regional groups. Loans were made more frequently in kind than in cash. Success bred success. By the time the royal distribution of lands was complete no less than 729 rural cooperatives were fully functional. These had handled some 1,500 million rials in loans, had a credit balance of 200 million rials, and had no serious debts to mar the picture. A pattern had emerged and been established.

The policy makers in 1962 (1341) could want no better precedent. With a bland presumption, the law ordering the first phase of the land reform carried a mere footnote to the effect that "only persons who are members of the cooperative of the village in which the land is being distributed shall be eligible to receive the land." A simple logic was to rule the distribution: no cooperative, no distributed land. In the event, the law operated more in hope than actuality. Although the text of the law referred to "the cooperative of the village," it was soon patent that in the wake of the rapid advance of the first phase of the land reform, cooperative societies were not being set up in each village and in many their provision was for some time a notional idea, a mere willingness to join a cooperative if and when it was possible to organize one.

At no time throughout the conduct of the first phase did the number of village cooperatives match the number of villages acquired and distributed. By September 1963 (1342) only 927 rural cooperatives were functioning to serve 8,042 acquired and distributed villages, and the highest number of rural cooperatives ever to be recorded in the country was 8,652 in 1967 (1346), by which date 15,014 villages had been caught up in the advance of land reform. To the credit of the government, it was not blind to the realities and in the early days made provision for regional development organizations to plan ahead of actual land distribution so as to be on the spot with credit facilities and aids to marketing and production. Only two of these stop-gap institutions ever existed, the first and most successful at Maragheh and the other at Qazvin. Regional development organizations were multipurpose in aim and did not multiply in numbers because the rural cooperatives as they were set up were incapable of taking over the many-sided functions of these directly government-financed and staffed complex organizations. As the Bank Omran had found, a credit cooperative was as much as the normal village folk could master.

Experience of the regional development organizations was not entirely abortive. Although they asked too much of the rural cooperatives as successors to them, they had demonstrated the futility of peppering the countryside with hundreds of tiny cooperative societies without a coordinating authority to give each a sense of belonging and a framework of reference. The government acted on the evidence and in the summer of 1963 (1342) called into being the Central Organization of Rural Cooperatives (CORC). This was to be an autonomous body, a commercial house, through which the village cooperatives and the local unions into which they were formed could apply for funds and generally keep in touch with rural affairs. Shares in CORC were to be held mainly by the Ministry of Land Reform and Rural Cooperation, but the ideal was for the unions of cooperatives to become the main shareholders and then to control the affairs of this central clearing house. CORC started life with 1,000 million rials to dispose of. At the time, at least two-and-a-half times that amount was needed to finance the cooperatives springing up in the wake of the first phase of the land reform. Ideally, however, the village cooperative was for each and every village, not only for the distributed villages. To answer the needs of all the villages, whether emancipated or not, called for 4,400 million rials, and if all engaged in farming in the villages were to join the cooperatives, CORC would need 9,000 million rials.

The rural cooperative movement did not play the full integrating role in the villages that had been hoped for. Within the limits of its specific function, as a channel to relieve the countryside's financial drought, it was, however, self-

Table 7.4
PROGRESS OF COOPERATIVES 1961-70
(1340-53)

	1961 (1340)	1962 (1341)	1963 (1342)	1964 (1343)	1965 (1344)
Cooperatives	960	1,292	2,722	3,846	6,067
Members	351,973	403,929	542,118	644,926	791,807
Capital (millions of rials)	199	249	369	512	686
Loans granted	157,869	71,012	151,385	328,993	391,119
Loans granted (millions of rials)	449	211	504	1,434	1,883
Loans per head (rials)	2,844	2,971	3,329	4,359	4,814
Value of shares per member (rials)	565	616	681	794	866

	1966 (1345)	1967 (1346)	1968 (1347)	1969 (1348)	1970 (1349)
Cooperatives	7,685	8,652	8,644	8,377	8,298
Members	967,428	1,105,402	1,278,402	1,430,653	1,606,083
Capital (millions of rials)	952	1,281	1,648	1,995	2,379
Loans granted	558,751	673,062	738,500	837,553	901,712
Loans granted (millions of rials)	3,024	4,077	5,041	5,753	6,314
Loan per head (rials)	5,412	6,058	6,826	6,869	7,002
Value of shares per member (rials)	984	1,159	1,289	1,394	1,481

irrigating. Numbers grew, but not without practical help from CORC both as the obvious supplier of credit and as teacher; training courses for cooperative managers were funded and area courses for the general members held at provincial centers. CORC, the central headquarters, had much itself to learn. Experience taught its officials to refuse cash loans to individual members and

Table 7.4
PROGRESS OF COOPERATIVES 1961-70
(1340-53)

	1971 (1350)	1972 (1351)	1973 (1352)	1974 (1353)
Cooperatives	8,450	8,361	2,717	2,847
Members	1,853,860	2,065,202	2,263,135	2,487,882
Capital (millions of rials)	2,769	3,329	3,857	4,678
Loans granted	876,356	1,152,297	1,175,554	1,363,377
Loans granted (millions of rials)	6,812	10,072	12,372	19,744
Loan per head (rials)	7,773	8,688	10,524	14,481
Value of shares per member (rials)	1,494	1,611	1,704	1,800

to offer productive assets instead. Productive assets, however, were not cared for if owned by the cooperative as a whole and loans would be provided only if members, either individually or in groups, took personal responsibility; CORC had learned the old Aristotelian truth that that which is most common has the least care spent upon it. Initially the expansion programs went for small societies of 200 members. These proved too weak to be effective and from 1967 (1346) larger concerns were demanded, a change of direction that checked the rate of growth in the number of societies. From 1972 (1352) a drastic policy of merger was followed and the number of rural cooperatives dropped by nearly 70 percent.

A profile of the progress of the cooperative movement in the villages is given in table 7.4. The changes in the number of societies just mentioned is clearly shown, with numbers rising to a maximum of 8,652 in 1967 (1346) and dropping to 2,217 in 1973 (1352). Since then there has been a slow trend towards an increased number of new, relatively large, concerns. Where steady growth has been sustained however is in the size of total membership—from one-third of a million when land reform began to nearly two-and-three-quarters million in 1976 (1354). A similar story is told of the accumulation of capital; from 200 million rials the sum has grown to give a 25-fold increase. Loans multiplied in numbers and in amount; from 157,869 loans distributed among 351,973 members to 1,066,538 loans among 2,663,085 members. On

average the size of loan advanced from 2,844 rials in 1961 (1341) to 14,425 rials
by the end of 1975.*

What is not apparent from the profile given in table 7.4 is the fundamental
change in constitutional and administrative policy in 1969. CORC ceased to
be the central distributor and handed its functions over to the transformed
Agricultural Credit Bank, which now became the Agricultural Cooperative
Bank of Iran. Hope was in its name—the hope that one day the representative
cooperative societies grouped into unions would be successful and rich
enough to buy out the government as chief shareholder and hold the bank
themselves. Although the 1975 register showed 113 unions as shareholders the
day of cooperative ownership seemed a long way off. Paradoxically, the more
successful the movement, the more difficult it was for the unions to catch up
and find the necessary finance; for with success the government's proportion
of cash tended to enlarge, although the total contribution from the unions also
grew in absolute terms.

The Agricultural Cooperative Bank of Iran was soon extending its credit
facilities to borrowers who were not members of the cooperative societies. In
1974-75 (1353) some 1,309 million rials were advanced in loans to nonunion
members. As the finance house responsible for land reform and associated
matters, the bank handled the payment orders issued to the dispossessed
landowners and collected the installments of the purchase price of land from
the peasants. A special function of the bank was the purchase of stock in
government-owned factories for landowners who used their compensation
credit to that purpose. By 1974 (1352) shares to a total of 3,700 million rials
had been bought in twenty factories scattered throughout the country—a sum
that equaled 37.5 percent of the total compensation payable to landowners
under the first phase of the land reform. It did not however follow that all the
purchasers of stock were landowners using payment orders. Nevertheless, the
figures give some indication of the extent to which the Shah's policy had gone
of offering shares in government factories as a means of financing land
reform—the third of the six objectives put before the nation in the referendum
of January 1963 (1342).

A FIVE-YEAR EXPERIMENT WITH SIZE

Land reform could lead to complacency, to the view that the nation's
following in the steps of the Shah had lifted Iranian agriculture out of its
ancient order on to a modern plain, there to be left without further ado to

*The final figures given here are as at the end of 1975 and are not shown in table 7.4 which gives
the statistics for each full solar year of the Iranian calendar to 1353.

serve the economy and meet the people's need for food and primary products. Again it was the Shah who, two years after the start of the second phase of the land reform program, alerted the Economic High Council to the stark realities. Amelioration of the peasants' lot was not a substitute for the pursuit of modern technology which alone could gain the maximum output from the sparse acres of irrigated land and from the latent potential of the improvable terrain. Focus hitherto had been on the social and political aims of land reform. The stabilizing benefits were made available to an agriculture highly fragmented in structure and proprietary pattern. The Shah had concern for the future productivity of the land, for the reliance that the urban dweller was to place upon the rural agriculture, and for the living standards of the emancipated villages. He wanted to find ways and means of bringing the advantages of large-scale agriculture and the employment of the massed machinery associated with it to rural Iran, and especially to the villages now free of the suzerainty of the landlords. Thus it was that, five years to the day from the beginning of the second phase of land reform, the government embarked upon a five-year experiment to set up what came to be known as farm corporations. Villages were to be knit together in single corporate enterprises capable of large-scale unified action.

The five years were up in 1973 (1352) but the experiment went on. In 1968 (1347) the Ministry of Land Reform and Rural Cooperation, which was responsible for the farm corporation program, established a Rural Research Center under the farm corporation legislation to monitor and assess the experiment. Never did the government see the farm corporation as a universal feature of Iranian agriculture. The emphasis on experimentation was indicative of the caution expressed at the time. The policy had its ups and downs. From an initial spurt of fourteen farm corporations in 1968 (1347) the pace slackened and over the following two years only another five corporations were added to the total. From 1970 to the autumn of 1975 (Mehr 1354), sixty-six new corporations were founded, making eighty-five in all.

Behind the farm corporation expedient was a sound and informed reasoning. A convincing case for the corporations could be argued on the grounds of improved incomes for the participating villagers; of the facilities to be afforded by large-scale enterprise for the employment of modern agricultural equipment; of the promise held out for improving the man-land ratio in the use of resources; of the focus a farm corporation could give to local planning; of the need to remove fragmentation; and of the better use that farm corporations could make of the neglected *ba'er* and *mavat*. All these points were plus signs. But there were two contrary factors: the lack of managerial skill and—more serious—social aspects. These factors moved in a vicious circle. If the farm corporations were successful, their very success could prove the best advocacy against the suspicions of the ignorant; but success depended on sound management.

The social problem was the more intractable of the two. On the morrow of their emancipation, a liberty unprecedented and undreamed of and now real, the peasant proprietors were required to hand over their lands, so it seemed to them, to officials and a committee of management in exchange for shares in a venture that, even to the most intelligent, must have been very difficult to understand. And as the law had it, the farm corporation possessed wider arms than the beneficent distributive policies of the land reform. Landowners, the new peasantry, even tenants holding thirty-year leases, the *barzegaran* cultivating gardens and plantations, and *vaqf* holders were all eligible for membership; only the *khoshneshin* were left out. The *zare'in,* who had been the darlings, the privileged above all others in the land distributions, were expected to join hands with the *khordehmalekin* and other landowners. To those peasants and landowners of long standing who had land, the demands of the farm corporation must have smacked of land expropriation. They were required to grant to the farm corporation the full use-right of the land; the law was vague on the question of landownership. For all practical purposes the farm corporation took possession of the plots and holdings. It was this apparent arbitrary appropriation of the land rights, rights that in many instances had been so recently granted to the peasants, that in some places set the farm corporations off to an indifferent start.

Siting a farm corporation was the responsibility of the minister for land reform and rural cooperation. But however propitious he might consider time and terrain to be, a corporation was not set up without sounding out local opinion; a vote was taken of all who in the villages affected were eligible to join a corporation, and only if a majority, however slender, was in favor did the minister proceed. Care was taken to explain the objectives and to describe how the farm corporation would be set up and how it would operate; but the formation of the early farm corporations, unlike the founding of the later ones with precedents and examples to follow, must have been an act of faith.

Geographic and other evidence suggests that the minister chose the first twenty sites with strategic skill. Initial success was vital to the entire policy. The sites were relatively near large towns and tended to be in the north and west of the country on the more fertile lands. On average the first nineteen sites were within 40 km. of a main town; while three years later corporations were being sited in places over 400 km. from main urban centers. The general siting strategy is exemplified in the placing of the first and most prodigious of the farm corporations, the Aryamehr Farm Corporation, under the shadow of Persepolis and joined to Shiraz, 60 km. distant, by a first-class motorway. Another difficulty that undermined the case for the founding of farm corporations in the early days was, ironically, the threat of unemployment in the villages consequent upon the success of mechanized farming; for this reason the oldest corporations had a deliberately arranged lower tractor-land ratio than did the later ones.

A shareholder, once a farm corporation is formed, has only his shares to dispose of and not his land. Allotment of shares followed a valuation of the use-rights. Where the corporation was relatively small, as was the Aryamehr Farm Corporation, and the *nasaq* shareholders were proprietors holding equal portions of the cultivable land, the apportionment of shares was simple. Problems arose where the village shares were not equal and where landowners, *barzegaran,* and tenants came into the corporation. Assessment was further complicated by shareholders offering cattle and farm implements to the corporation along with their land. Valuation of the use-rights was undertaken by a special committee appointed for the purpose by the shareholders, who elected two members, and by the minister for land reform and rural cooperation, who chose a third. Values were based upon evidence of income from the land and, where they were available, the values used under the land reform laws for the compensation of the landowners and the distribution of the land.

Financing the farm corporations was a three-way process: the farming activities themselves, if successful, would be profitable and provide the shareholders with dividends after meeting wages, running costs, and overheads; loans were raised by the corporations from the Agricultural Cooperative Bank of Iran; and the government gave the corporations generous grants to meet the cost of improvements of various kinds—mosques, clinics, sports grounds, and sundry incidental expenses of a technical and social nature that fell outside the range of normal farm activities. In 1968 (1347) the government's total outlay in grants and aid was 214 million rials, an annual burden that by 1975 (1352) had become 2,005 million rials. From the inception of the farm corporation program to 1975, contributions from the state totaled 4,791 million rials.

Justification for this skyrocketing expenditure must presumably be made in terms of the national welfare. Table 7.5 shows how the shareholders of the farm corporations improved their incomes and living standard by joining them. The average Iranian taxpayer might well argue that the manifest benefits are in large measure the result of the government's generous grants-in-aid, without which the farm corporations could not have been equipped to produce the highly remunerative dividends and wages. Against this it can be urged that the farm corporations have been more efficient in the use of labor, land, and investments generally than the small holdings of traditional agriculture. Nevertheless it is reasonable to ask whether, if so large a sum of

Table 7.5
Income of Shareholders of Farm Corporations As in 1974 (1353)

Sequence	Name of Farm Corporation	No. of Share-holders	Dividend per Shareholder Before Corporation	Dividend per Shareholder 1974 (1353)	Wages	Dividend and Wages Dividend	Dividend and Wages Total
1	Aryamehr	86	11,803.5	181,508.32	19,263.36	181,508.32	200,771.68
2	Farah	563	3,293.5	22,197.18	9,306.30	22,197.18	31,503.48
3	Reza Pahlavi	334	5,376.0	65,918.96	15,750.68	65,918.76	81,669.44
4	Shahnaz	213	14,641.1	85,603.21	12,738.93	85,603.21	98,342.14
5	Farahnaz	96	9,525.3	90,777.41	52,669.85	90,777.41	143,447.26
6	Dargazin	422	2,112.8	26,287.43	20,580.64	26,287.43	46,868.07
7	Golpayegan	136	7,462.3	97,259.00	111,173.29	97,259.00	208,432.29
8	Khashan	60	6,782.2	30,652.64	40,149.05	30,652.64	70,801.69
9	Shiravan	297	9,606.8	74,091.54	4,084.76	74,091.54	78,176.30
10	Baghein	116	22,325.0	103,757.09	77,115.01	103,757.09	180,872.10
11	Garmsar	640	13,798.9	133,021.39	80,743.87	133,021.39	213,764.26
12	Shahabad Ghaenat	1,248	6,075.5	14,258.97	20,192.26	14,258.97	34,451.23
13	Roudpish	164	25,601.4	57,616.09	92,517.26	57,616.09	150,133.35
14	Semeskandeh	338	11,902.2	77,220.37	94,963.42	77,220.37	172,183.79
15	Torbat-e Jam	276	11,740.0	73,490.43	56,134.28	73,490.43	129,624.71

Sequence	Name of Farm Corporation	No. of Share- holders	Dividend per Shareholder Before Corporation	1974 (1353)	Wages	Dividend and Wages	
						Dividend	Total
16	Mahabad	446	6,038.0	55,563.40	4,852.95	55,563.40	60,416.35
17	Dariush Kabir	148	12,950.0	157,204.27	5,092.53	157,204.27	162,296.80
18	Adl	351	12,550.5	60,355.25	16,338.21	60,355.25	76,693.46
19	Edalat	364	40.9	49,349.00	46,701.59	49,349.00	96,050.59
20	Shapoore Aval	374	6,186.6	121,310.81	11,721.12	121,310.81	133,031.93
21	Ranansar	197	10,592.2	44,804.86	3,597.16	44,804.86	48,402.02
22	Moghan	274	36,124.0	114,360.98	58,005.41	114,360.98	172,366.39
23	Bampoor	783	4,000.0	8,503.84	8,528.06	8,503.84	17,031.90
24	Kamyaran	134	6,978.0	48,081.01	15,344.00	48,081.01	63,425.01
25	Rostamabad	225	19,700.0	57,292.13	22,209.73	57,292.13	79,501.86
26	Azna	301	7,506.0	71,139.57	18,800.34	71,139.57	89,939.91
27	Dez	222	10,528.0	94,618.19	32,919.72	94,618.19	127,537.91
28	Firoozabad	137	21,000.0	56,919.55	20,261.97	56,919.55	77,181.52
29	Eligovdarz	505	11,707.0	44,235.29	10,019.68	44,235.29	54,254.97
30	Aras	374	34,602.0	147,510.12	95,738.95	147,510.12	243,249.07
31	Sabalan	399	26,912.0	126,991.77	60,895.07	126,991.77	187,886.84
32	Nader	419	18,654.0	92,030.00	49,379.35	92,030.00	141,409.35

Table 7.5
Income of Shareholders of Farm Corporations As in 1974 (1353)

Sequence	Name of Farm Corporation	No. of Share-holders	Dividend per Shareholder Before Corporation	Dividend per Shareholder 1974 (1353)	Dividend and Wages Wages	Dividend and Wages Dividend	Dividend and Wages Total
33	Koorosh	272	8,622.7	39,804.94	15,476.41	39,804.94	55,281.35
34	Syroos	295	9,072.8	20,743.60	12,230.66	20,743.60	32,974.26
35	Ghir	451	13,000.0	9,795.64	4,750.45	9,795.64	14,546.09
36	Afzar	438	9,500.0	8,891.98	8,469.96	8,891.89	17,361.85
37	Karzin	831	8,000.0	16,619.00	11,732.10	16,619.00	28,351.10
38	Shamsabad	235	13,920.0	40,067.77	38,929.48	40,067.77	78,997.25
39	Shoosh	357	10,482.0	77,234.20	38,362.99	77,234.20	115,597.19
40	Shoostar	244	13,407.0	12,328.57	24,927.63	12,328.57	37,256.20
41	Foomen	414	19,925.0	60,898.07	64,819.32	60,898.07	125,717.39
42	Dezful	269	9,777.0	44,988.88	14,187.57	44,988.88	59,176.45
43	Tiroft	979	13,170.0	15,383.54	13,055.16	15,383.54	28,438.70
44	Aslandooz	350	7,634.0	26,659.68	25,509.76	26,659.68	52,169.44
45	Hasankhanloo	294	59,702.0	135,362.43	66,264.06	135,362.43	201,626.49
46	Shahsonan	286	—	169,813.14	86,997.66	169,813.14	256,810.80
47	Zahab	682	11,437.0	38,094.93	8,579.40	38,094.93	46,674.33

| Sequence | Name of Farm Corporation | No. of Share-holders | Dividend per Shareholder | | Wages | Dividend and Wages | |
			Before Corporation	1974 (1353)		Dividend	Total
48	Nahavand	293	36,567.0	61,621.95	57,943.78	61,621.95	119,565.73
49	Khorramabad	245	7,833.0	21,599.15	14,432.22	21,599.15	36,031.37
50	Marndasht	221	26,225.0	63,574.78	19,002.97	63,574.78	82,577.75
51	Ramjerd	247	20,545.0	95,583.36	26,789.24	95,583.36	122,372.60
52	Soltanieh	308	—	(13,331.15)	14,349.94	(13,331.15)	1,018.79
53	Doroodzan	252	27,720.0	80,084.15	21,193.58	80,084.15	101,277.73
	AVERAGE		13,742.4	50,509.00	31,862.52	13,742.4	82,371.52

Source: Agricultural Cooperative Bank of Iran

money had been spent in the improvement of public services, roads, water supplies, market facilities, and so on to the villages as they stood, the results would have been equally impressive or perhaps more so.

Judged simply as a way to improve the living standards of the shareholders, the farm corporations must undoubtedly score high marks. On the average, as table 7.5 shows, the dividends and wages from fifty-three corporations had lifted the income of the shareholder from 13,742 rials a year before joining the corporation to 82,371 rials in 1974 (1353)—a six-fold increase. The pull and counterpull of dividends and wages has always been one of the managerial complications of farm corporations. Investment in machinery has tended to raise dividends and reduce the opportunities for wage earning; while reliance on hand labor has employed more wage earners only at the expense of dividends. Taken separately, the average dividend in 1974 was 267 percent higher than the prefarm corporation income and the average wage was 132 percent higher. Whatever the emphasis, the shareholder stood to gain—and gain handsomely.

The farm corporation program aimed to have 140 establishments and to reach that goal by the end of the Fifth National Development Plan in 1978 (1357). By the precedents already set, this final target represented a national investment of land and capital that could well equal the full cost of land acquisition under the first phase of land reform. But looked at village by village, 140 farm corporations would only account for between 500 and 700 villages, or somewhere in the neighborhood of 1.5 percent of the total number of villages in Iran. Other experiments were afoot, as will be explained later. But when all was taken into account, it seemed that the future of the Iranian villages would in large measure depend upon the long-term outcome of land reform and the emancipated villagers' understanding of the opportunities given to them by that reform.

The farm corporations had an immediate continuity with the land reforms. They were set up and administered by the minister of cooperation and rural affairs, as a feature of the post-land reform policies aimed at attempting to solve the problems of petty agriculture and scattered plots that the land reform itself aggravated. Because of their link with the land reforms, farm corporations should not be confused with the extensive agribusiness complexes that the Iranian government set going below the national dams. In the mid-1970s, these highly complex and capital-intensive enterprises were relatively few in number and in the main were situated in Khuzistan. The agribusiness schemes had been a magnet for foreign capital and management, with results seesawing between success and failure. They did not come within the purview of land reform proper, although it seemed possible that the movement towards détente between agriculture and land reform referred to later in this chapter might in the future in some way bridge the gap that past policies had intentionally accepted.

SOCIAL POLICIES TO BUTTRESS
LAND REFORM

Right from the start and with his own crown villages in mind, the Shah always saw the land reforms as a facet—the most important one, but nonetheless a facet—of the complete image of what he wanted for his rural people. Land reform by itself was not a whole message of hope. Time was needed to cultivate a new generation to take full advantage of what had been done to break the age-old yoke that had harnessed the cultivator to the land. But the task was not a future one; the present would be parent to the generations to come. In the present, preparations had to be made and made without delay. Many villagers were illiterate, well grounded in the arts of traditional farming but lacking a modern science; to this toll of ignorance ill-health as fact and risk added its burden to life. Land reform would be isolated as a desert rose unless its benign prospects were brightened by the removal of illiteracy, by the improvement of health, by the expansion of farm knowledge, and by the introduction of stabilizing influences such as insurance and justice. There was needed also a widened culture to open the windows of village lives upon the world beyond. Provision of such necessary collaterals became part and parcel of the land reform policy.

A national attack on illiteracy had been implicit among the six points of the Revolution of Shah and People of Bahman 6, 1341, and, like many other reforms, it had by that date already been embarked upon by the government. "Attacked" would not be too strong a word. There are more ways than one to serve king and country, even for a military man. It was national policy to conscript high school graduates for service in the army. The most immediate threat to the promise of a fuller rural life after land reform was the entrenched illiteracy of rural areas. Only 24 percent of children went to school in 1963 (1341) in the country districts, compared with 74 percent of town children. Conscripts to the militia, if able to pass an intelligence test, were therefore given the option of joining the Literacy Corps and serving in the villages. The policy was a tactic of great acumen and served the Shah's ideals well. As experience was gained the Literacy Corps lost its pioneer general functions, became more hierarchical with officer grades, and in 1968 (1347) inspired the foundation of a sister force, the Women's Education Corps. Both corps were imbued with a crusading spirit and did not balk at hardships and primitive conditions. Much was accomplished: apart from the teaching service new schools were rigged up, old ones renovated, mosques and other public buildings erected, wells dug, and secondary village roads constructed. And there were side benefits besides the primary ones of combating illiteracy in children and adults: public relations between the rural folk and the army were much improved. Costs per pupil were reduced and the young militia men and women of the corps became permanent recruits to the teaching profession. The primary and frontal attack on illiteracy won a cumulative victory as the pupils passed on their acquired skill and knowledge to contemporaries and looked forward to teaching succeeding generations. Without this assault on illiteracy, the full benefits of land reform and the opportunity that the reform gave to practice new farming techniques would have been lost to the present generation and denied to successive ones.

In its early days the Literacy Corps stopped at nothing to open up the emancipated villages to a better use and development of resources. The corps pioneered the way for similarly specialized corps to take over the many tasks that were not immediately educational and that stood in the way of the corpsman devoting his full time to teaching and the attack on illiteracy. Prominent among these specialist corps was the Extension and Development Corps set up in September 1964 (1343). A period of training was necessary for the initiated corpsman and once in the field he was assisted by specialists in highly technical matters. In general, however, he worked to a strict regimen. Set schedules were adhered to that required the men of the Extension and Development Corps to accomplish specified and clearly defined tasks, such as organizing demonstration plots, instructing in the maintenance of buildings and water conduits and in the construction of simple types of new equipment, vaccinating cattle, and even helping out the Literacy Corps on occasion. Like his colleague in the Literacy Corps, the corpsman in the Extension and Development Corps reaped benefits beyond the satisfaction of seeing his years as a conscript put to practical use; the Extension and Development Corps was an open door to the university for the highly intelligent and a guaranteed qualification for the permanent civil service.

Disease and chronic illness, even more than illiteracy, inhibited progress in the rural areas. The establishment of a Health Corps took precedence over the formation of the Extension and Development Corps. From the outset the structure of the Health Corps was more complicated than that of the Literacy Corps. Qualified doctors, dentists, surgeons, and nurses were required from the start to spearhead the movement and instruct the conscripts in the skills of auxiliary medicine. A network of mobile field units was woven to serve groups of villages and link them to a health center equipped with a medical laboratory, dental surgery, and public health department. In two years, over 4 million patients had received treatment of some kind or other—a figure that of itself speaks of the crying need for medical and first aid care. The Health

Corps was charged not only with providing curative medicine but was required to take preventive measures also. A systematic field survey was made in 1970 of the corps' activities. The findings of the survey spoke of the conquest of disease and of ignorance of health measures, facts and benefits that in themselves commend the work of the corps. The Health Corps was not alone in its work among the villages; the Red Lion and Sun Society was looking after 9,000 villages in 1971 (1350) and as many villages again were within access of medical care in the towns. The Health Corps network at the time was reaching 14,000 villages. By the mid-1970s the corps had extended its activities, but some villages still remained beyond its reach and care.

Under the old order villagers had known little of the dispensation of justice between neighbor and neighbor. Such justice as there was depended more on a truncheon tyranny under the gendarmerie than on the weighing of issues with impartial, judicial wisdom. Again from the early days of the nationwide land reform and to promote its success provision was made to bring an elementary justice to the villages through Houses of Equity. These resembled somewhat the customary courts of the European medieval rural culture. The parallel was not exact, as each local juridical assembly was elected by the villagers and supervised by a nearby formal court that sent an official to act as judge and president of the village House of Equity. Assembly days were regular and weekly. Judicial business was limited to petty issues, where the theft, fraud, default or other malfeasance was of the order of 1,000 tuman or less. As the years passed, these village courts began to devise their own procedures, set their own bodies of precedents, and become the guardians of local customs that were accepted by the law-abiding and controlled the unruly.

Concomitant with land reform the rudiments of civil order had been introduced into the emancipated villages to aid literacy, health, technical knowledge, and the dispensation of justice. These were of the first order of necessities. Some seven years after the start of land reform, the Shah formed a National Association of Rural Cultural Houses under the honorary presidency of the Crown Prince. A village cultural house was a social benefit above what was essential to the health and ordering of society. Its concern was with the leisure time of the rural man and his family rather than with his work-a-day life. Nonetheless, the cultural houses have developed an industrial and commercial interest. At first they were to be the eyes and ears of the village society, to keep it in touch with the wider world outside its boundaries, especially with the modern progressive Iran—in short, to help the villagers see and find themselves in the general picture of a revived nation. Later, however, it was through the cultural houses that the Ministry of Cooperation and Rural Affairs was able to help the villages develop nonfarming communal crafts— crafts that had a special significance for farm corporations where alternative employment had to be found for the displaced field workers. The ministry organized an advisory service and a scheme for giving financial aid where necessary. The rural cultural houses have proved to be most valuable observation posts, watching over the life of the villages and keeping both them in touch with departments of government and the latter in touch with them.

By 1976, the Ministry of Cooperation and Rural Affairs, through its Department of Social Insurance for the Rural Population, had provided the beginnings of a social insurance scheme. Difficulties abounded and the first objective was limited to insurance coverage for medical care. Premiums had to be very low and the cost of collecting them in the rural areas often turned out to be more than the premiums themselves. The insurance scheme, which required its own clinics, was confined to villages where the facilities of a farm corporation could assist with the collection of premiums and with the administration of the scheme.

Production and Property

That rural welfare should be associated with land reform was all of a piece with the idealism and principles that had inspired the Shah in his youth and throughout the distribution of the Pahlavi villages. Welfare and productive efficiency stand in mutual relationship; social contentment and welfare are conducive to physical and mental effort and the more productive the land, the less the risk to nutrition, shelter, and clothing. At the same time an undue emphasis one way or the other can upset the reciprocal benefits. The farm corporation program singled out production as its primary concern. Improvement in earnings was a telling but secondary boon and in its way contributed to the welfare of the shareholders. But also on the welfare side there was a discount in that the farm corporations unavoidably diminished the sense of proprietorship in the land that the land reforms had promoted. The government was not unmindful of this and experimented in the spring of 1971 (Esfand 24, 1349) with a compromise. Attention was turned back upon the rural cooperatives as institutions through which communal production programs could be engineered and promoted in a manner that would not deprive the participants of ownership in the land by substituting shares in a corporation for the land itself, as the farm corporations were doing. "Production cooperatives" were promoted and made the responsibility of the Minister of Cooperation and Rural Affairs.

The new program called to its assistance the traditional communal husbandry inherent in the *mosha'* activities of the villagers, the ubiquitous rural cooperatives, and the peasants' concern for a proprietary identification with the land. Participants in a production cooperative each held on to their respective land titles; there was nothing approaching land consolidation or the restructuring of proprietary boundaries. What the peasant surrendered to his fellow members in the cooperative was a freedom to indulge in a cropping program of his own; there was postulated, as it were, an agreement between the members to determine a common cropping and production policy, and to abide by it. The fundamental difference between the production cooperative and the farm corporation was in the status of the members; in the former they remained landowners and landholders, while in the latter they became shareholders in a corporation. Nevertheless a similarity prevailed in the subjugation of each member of a production cooperative to the dictates of the communal voice. A villager was free to leave or refrain from joining the production cooperative, but such a course could lead to the forfeiture of his land. There were gains to induce voluntary response, for the government could and did provide generous funds for the improvement of village facilities, roads and water supplies, as with the farm corporations. In the mid-1970s, it seemed as if there might still be too great an element of coercion in this alternative to the farm corporation. Time would tell, for as with the farm corporation program the government was regarding this alternative as a five-year experiment.

Production cooperatives were in the vanguard of the government's drive to utilize more effectively the benefits deriving from the building of dams and other irrigation works. Only villages in what were termed development areas could be so organized. A development area was the subject of a development plan drawn up by the minister of cooperation and rural affairs. It was he who linked the production cooperatives into the plans. At the outset he took his cue from the provision and planning of the minister of water and power, on whose instigation the irrigation and water supply projects were conceived and financed. The development plans included within their anatomy designs for small rural towns, based upon villages or associated with them. At village level the law required cultivation and production plans, the blueprints and schedules for the cropping and marketing programs. At this level the actions of the members of the production cooperative were controlled by their representatives in committee working with experts from the Ministry of Cooperation and Rural Affairs. Priorities governed procedures. First came the development plan and then the execution of an improvement program. Not until the ground plan and infrastructure stages were complete was it permissible for the field and cropping programs to be made. Unlike the farm corporations, the production cooperatives were not relying on ambitious mechanization. The entire endeavor was based upon and built up from the traditional *boneh* system, the working of cultivators in small groups, especially so with the working of the land, the sowing, and the harvest. The full cooperative acted at marketing levels in the interests of the groups. Financial support was in kind and in cash. Production cooperatives within the develop-

ment area benefited from ministerial investment made during the preparatory
stages of opening up the area and bringing facilities of various kinds to the
villages. Among the specific obligations imposed by the law on the Ministry of
Cooperation and Rural Affairs were the building of feeder roads linking
villages and fields to communication arteries, the construction and maintenance of administrative buildings, the setting up of repair shops and the like,
and the provision of public facilities—schools, clinics, cultural houses and
telegraphic services. Needless to say, the linking of villages to the regional
irrigation system and water supplies held a special place in this list of statutory
obligations. On the cash side, production cooperatives were expressly empowered to borrow from the Agricultural Cooperative Bank of Iran monies
for expenditures more immediately related to farming the land—that is, for
field drainage, trackways, and the purchasing of implements and livestock.

AGRICULTURE AND LAND REFORM:
A NEW DÉTENTE

The wholesale approach of the production cooperative policy gave to the
minister of cooperation and rural affairs some authority over a development
area together with what, on the face of it, appeared to be a prior obligation to
expend funds on the opening up of the area for the benefit of all who, by
accident of history, were eligible to join a rural cooperative society. Inevitably, implementation of the program tended to be one-sided and to provoke
antagonism among farmers and agriculturalists who came off second best in
the development areas. A stage was reached when the Ministry of Agriculture
and Natural Resources and the Ministry of Cooperation and Rural Affairs
were to seek a new détente over development plans. Events were reminiscent
of the early days of land reform, when the question of overall authority for
rural affairs had to be settled between the then minister of agriculture, the
minister of the interior, and others. By 1975, the production cooperatives had
pointed the way to a more comprehensive treatment of the irrigated regions
and that way had led to a new departure in agrarian policy: the legislation for
agricultural development in agricultural zones of June 3 that year (Khordad
13, 1354).

Like that of the production cooperatives, this policy was directed to the
better development of the lands watered by the dams and irrigation schemes.
The law was more direct: it specifically designated twenty project areas that
ranged in extent from 8,000 hectares at Golpayegan to 295,000 hectares at Lar
in Mazandaran, with an average size of 91,000 hectares. Lying for the most
part within the project areas were agricultural zones, localities where the land,

through the irrigation works of the area, was fitted for advanced agricultural exploitation and livestock husbandry.

The maestro of this latest development program was the minister for agriculture and natural resources. Farm corporations, production coopera tives, and rural cooperative societies could still be established by the minister of cooperation and rural affairs, but if any such fell within an agricultural zone as defined by the new law, the operations and development plans had to be in accord with the wishes of the minister of agriculture as well as what the minister of cooperation wanted. The focus of policy was upon the preparation of integrated development projects within the agricultural zones by government agencies in agreement with the Ministry of Agriculture and Natural Resources and by persons and companies engaged in agriculture within the zones, in conformity with models prepared by the minister of agriculture and approved by him. A novelty of vital consequence was the authority given by the law to the minister of agriculture to make plans for restructuring the proprietary patterns of the agricultural holdings in these zones. This was in every respect orthodox land consolidation, and it was curious that so fundamental a reform had not been entrusted entirely to the minister of cooperation; although the land consolidation plans needed the approval of zonal committees representative of both agricultural ministries and of the Ministry of Energy. Power was given to the minister of agriculture to buy out the holdings or parts of holdings that did not fit into his restructuring plans. No minimum size of holding or agricultural unit was laid down except indirectly, where the law prohibited the splitting of holdings so as to make fragments of less than 20 hectares.

Farmers and landowners within the project areas could not escape the requirements of the new law. They had to indicate their willingness to conform with the plans and ideas of the Ministry of Agriculture and Natural Resources, to prepare their own proposals for farming, restructuring, and improving their lands, and amend these as the minister might wish. Refusal to conform placed their holdings at risk; they could be compulsorily acquired by the minister of agriculture, and the landowners and farmers compensated. The minister of cooperation had a special responsibility for two kinds of ownership unit: those held by peasants taking their lands under the land reform laws; and those held by the *khordehmalekin* where the units were less than 10 hectares and were held by the present landowners at the time of land reform, or had been retained by them after the division of the *nasaq* between landowner and cultivators. Only two courses were open to the minister; he had either to absorb these holdings into farm corporations or organize them as production cooperatives.

A special feature of the law was the provision made for valuing the holdings and land where adjustment of boundaries was made or the land was compulsorily acquired. Two bases of value emerged: the value of the land before the provision of water under the irrigation network of the project area; and the value of the land in consequence of the irrigation. The former value governed the assessment of holdings prior to consolidation, and the latter the assessments of the values of the new holdings. A special board representing the agricultural ministries, the authorities for energy, and others was set up to make the assessments and determine compensation. Experts were to be called to advise the board. No provisions were made for appeals from the board to a higher or to an alternative authority, and the decision of the minister of agriculture and natural resources on the restructuring of holdings was also final and obligatory.

FUTURE HORIZONS

Land reform in Iran is the story of the peasant in Iran. Within the mosaic of farms and land holdings, the small peasant holding of 10 hectares and less, the prize of the long and sweeping land reforms accounts for over 80 percent of all holdings. In 1976, the bulk of the rural population, 60 percent and more, dwelt on these holdings; and yet they contributed no more than 20 percent of the marketed output of the agricultural sector of the economy. A government like Iran's, concerned as it is with improving agricultural performance, cannot evade the message of these percentages: the extensive array of tiny holdings needs to be restructured, if to do nothing more than to bring the percentage of small holdings into parity with the percentage of the rural population that lives on them.

The ensign of land reform is liberty. Throughout the tens of thousands of rural villages the cultivators of the *nasaq,* the *zare'in,* were freed by it from the bondage of serfdom. But they continued to be cramped and cajoled in other ways. Hope for the future must surely lie in finding ways and means of putting a firmer trust in the village farmer and gradually freeing him to take part in a more competitive and effective market economy.

Admittedly, the law requires that proposals for farm corporations and cooperatives be put to the vote. But a bare majority, a majority of one, can carry the decision. The chances are, therefore, that many peasants have been required to join the farm corporations and production cooperatives who would rather have cultivated their own newly acquired holdings according to their own values and ways. Under the agricultural development law that obtained in the mid-1970s, the recipients of land under the land reforms and other small landowners were going to be controlled and directed either into farm corporations or production cooperatives. Eventually, such policies will deny good land, the land irrigated from the great dams and reservoirs, to the peasant proprietor; he will have no chance to show what he can do with such irrigated hectares as he may call his own.

At the same time, the new law was indicative of a wholesome judgment that accepted the need to consolidate the fragmented holdings and aimed at a minimum holding of 20 hectares. It was curious that the policy makers had not yet attempted to marry liberty with production incentive and initiate a policy designed to encourage the peasants to restructure the proprietary pattern of the villages voluntarily In the early days of land reform the principle of nonalienation was adopted as fundamental. The recipients of land under the distribution policy were debarred from selling their holdings freely among members and on a wider market. There may well have been a reason for this at the outset. Once again, however, the crown estates showed a better way, and before the administration of the Pahlavi villages passed to the Ministry of Cooperation and Rural Affairs the peasant farmers were permitted to sell their holdings; the more able among them enlarged their farms so as to make them more productive and profitable.

Surely hope for the future was bound to lie in some such policy promoted and supported universally. The pace would inevitably be slow. Guidance and credit would be needed and in many places investment in an improved infrastructure. The evidence of history and of the contemporary international scene suggests the outcome would be rewarding in terms of social stability and agricultural productivity. Such a policy could, as with others, be experimental to start with. Once set in motion, the incentive of the small landowner and farmer and the mobility of the market would increase the proportion of medium-sized holdings without the compulsory dislodgment of rural families. A variant on a free-market adjustment could be made by using the village cooperative to sound out the majority opinion concerning land consolidation, meanwhile using coercion to bring the minority into line. Where necessary this would be far less arbitrary than the enforcement of the land consolidation procedure as provided for in the agricultural development zones. Indeed the general tenor of the law seems to be too rigid and to give no room for individual initiative, maneuver and enterprise.

Bureaucrats are never the best of farmers. The path of land reform in Iran has been the highway to liberty. Too great a bureaucratic interference with the liberties given and inspired so long ago by the Shah could rob a newborn countryside of its hopes. Success in the future will lie in finding a balance between the liberties inherent in ownership and the touch of public control that is inspired by the pursuit of the common good.

8

Educational and Cultural Development in Iran during the Pahlavi Era

Being the son of a high school headmaster and later launched upon an academic career myself, I took advantage of my first stay in Iran in 1933 to obtain information about its educational system. At Shiraz, only twenty-six years old but holding the title of Doctor Juris, I was admitted with all respect to visiting Persian schools. There was one incident that I did not forget. It was after Nowruz 1933, when I had just arrived in Fars, that the amiable headmaster of a high school *(madrase-ye motavasseteh)*, after showing me the school buildings, had kindly invited me to see his home. There I found two ladies with their faces unveiled, one being headmistress of a girls' high school, the other a teacher in it. Enjoying tea and lettuce with oxymel *(kahu ba sekanjebin)*, we spoke about the scheduling of classes, the goals of the school, and the number of pupils. As if it were today, I still can see before me at the table the two pretty and youthful faces and hear them speaking vivaciously on the subjects that interested them both. Suddenly we heard someone knocking at the door, and the houseservant, after letting the new arrival in, rushed to our room upstairs and stammered the name of a high-ranking officer. With a suppressed shriek the two ladies disappeared into a side room, and returned clad in their *chadors* when the unexpected guest came in and greeted us with dignity. All the informality of our free conversation was gone and the ladies kept a reserved silence.

I still imagine how shocking this situation must have been for my hosts. Their intention had been to show me the lack of prejudice of the new generation in matters of school training and the national importance of an unrestricted education for girls. Here in Shiraz, so they had hinted to me, sound liberalism prevailed. From now on, women would not stand back behind men in knowledge and education. Yet an unannounced visit from a tradition-minded military officer wrecked all these good intentions.

Some years afterward I went again to Iran. By then no woman or girl wore the veil, at least not in the larger towns. Reza Shah had flatly forbidden the *chador*. There were stories, not devoid of a comic flavor, of how policemen, equipped with big scissors, were instructed in case of noncompliance to cut asunder the veils of reluctant women.

Since then much time has passed and things have changed radically and rapidly. Once we spoke of a *madrase-ye ebteda'i* and *madrase-ye mota-vasseteh;* later we noticed plenty of *dabestans* (elementary schools) and *dab-irestans* (secondary schools). Beside the boys' schools *(pesaraneh),* girls' schools *(dokhtaraneh)* had become common and taken for granted. In Tehran the female veil had almost totally disappeared, but it continued to be worn in provincial centers.

From Qajar Stagnation to Pahlavi Reforms

How are the numerous and profound changes of the last forty years to be explained? Where do they begin and to where do they lead? These are historical questions. To find answers we have to turn back to the situation a century earlier, to the Iran of Naser ad-Din Shah and his successors. Reports of contemporary observers of the Qajar era—Iranian, European, and American—expressed one common lament: the gap between the mental gifts and high education of the upper stratum of Iranian society, and the ignorance, backwardness, and moral indolence of the masses. The best-educated men were proud and convinced of their cultural superiority, especially in matters of poetry and philosophy. Moreover, a comparison with neighboring countries such as India and Turkey or Central Asia served well to enhance the awareness of their own abilities. In these regions, Islamic culture was almost identical with Iranian culture. Foreign observers and travelers have always noticed these facts. In spite of the backwardness of the cultural scene, a good number of these observers never concealed their belief in the Iranian nation and its future. It was not, however, until the Pahlavi era that Iran was to experience impressive cultural resurgence.

Still, most shocking for a contemporary friend of Iran has been the exorbitant number of illiterates, contrasting with the high mental and artistic gifts of the nation. Official estimates in the 1970s set the rate of illiteracy between 60 and 70 percent. Against the background of the general national renaissance, above all considering the great technical and economic progress, this deficiency appeared shocking. Under the Qajars illiteracy was one of the striking features of Iran, all the more so as the physical state of the country was an unrelieved image of decay. There were no real roads, bridges and caravanserais lay in ruins, towns were filthy, and the villages were run down because the dilapidated *qanats* (subterranean aqueducts) kept them short of water.[1] With all this one cannot deny that there were individual rulers who possessed vigor and initiative. Yet the domination of Persia by the world powers and the internal resistance to change annihilated all endeavors at reform. The clergy, a dangerously obstructionist power already in Sassanian times, strove to maintain their hold over the people's souls and misused their religious position for political aims. Under Naser ad-Din Shah (1848-1896) his enlightened grand vizier Amir Kabir (Mirza-Taqi Khan-e Farahani) fell victim to a court and harem intrigue after three years of beneficial work.[2] He was murdered before his program of wise reforms could be realized. It was he who founded the first public university in Tehran, the Dar al-Fonun (House of Sciences), adding foreign scholars to the teaching staff. He sent a number of young men to Europe for studies. The Dar al-Fonun included the sciences of medicine, technology, and jurisprudence.[3] For a long time its name remained virtually synonymous with the law school, until the latter was converted to the Faculty of Law *(daneshkadeh-ye hoquq)* during the Pahlavi era.

Otherwise—if we disregard schools of foreign missions among Jews and Christians—the old-fashioned schools remained untouched. General instruction lay entirely in the hands of the *mollas' madrase-ye akhundi;* teaching took place in the mosques.

Still, there existed already the first newspapers, and translations of foreign—mostly French—books into Persian were promoted. But it was not before the finally successful struggle for the constitution (*mashrutiyyat,* August 5, 1906) that the press and journalism came into vogue.[4] The newspapers, which were generally printed by lithographic methods, included *Sur-e Esrafil* (The Trumpet of the Angel of Resurrection), *Mosavat* (Equity), *Ruh al-Qodos* (The Holy Spirit), *Majles* (Parliament), *Neda-ye Vatan* (The Voice of the Fatherland), *Kashkul-e Zaban-e Mellat* (The Beggar's Cup of Nation's Tongue). Their tone tended to be moralizing. A firm grip on reality was not their forte.

The weakness of the country was starkly revealed by the British-Russian Agreement of 1907 which divided Iran into two spheres of interest and influence, assigning the south to England and the north to Russia.[5] Only with the coup d'état of Reza Khan on February 21, 1921, did things undergo a drastic change. The first concern of this new statesman (and later Shah) was to restore peace and order, which the country had not seen for so long a time.

However, it was not until the coronation of Reza Shah Pahlavi, in 1925 after the last Qajar Shah had been removed, that his hands were free for comprehensive reform. It was a testimony to the wide horizons of the new ruler—a man who had never traveled abroad—that without delay he began to convert Iran's backward school system to Western patterns. His first move was to wrest control of the schools from the clergy and, more broadly, to curb their influence. He devised an ingenious way to counter superstition and misuse of the clerical position: together with a group of enlightened and loyal *mollas,* possessed of the necessary erudition, he created a theological faculty endowed with official authority and housed in the Sepahsalar Mosque in Tehran *(Madrase-ye 'Ali-ye Ma'qul va Manqul).* Now all young clerics had to present themselves to this board of learned theologians and undergo an examination if they wanted to obtain official license for their spiritual vocation. At that time the country was inundated with poorly trained and often spurious *mollas.* Their level was so low that 90 percent of the candidates failed their tests and had to choose other professions. Towns and villages were thus freed from the stifling grip of clerical charlatans.

By the mid-1930s many improvements had been introduced in the field of education. Reza Shah's primary concern, however, seemed to focus on higher education, followed by interest in secondary schools. Elementary education appeared to receive the lowest priority. This was perhaps the expression of the Shah's eagerness, bordering on impatience, to produce as fast as possible a highly trained cadre of competent civil servants and army officers who would carry out the ambitious task of transforming the country into a modern state.

HIGHER EDUCATION

Higher education in Iran under Reza Shah generally followed Western patterns. The old Darulfunun with its six departments had declined already under Qajar rule and by the time of Reza's advent to power it was clear that a new start had to be made. The first step, taken in 1928, was to create an Arts and Sciences Faculty, first called *Dar al-Mo'allemin-e 'Ali* and later renamed *Daneshsara-ye 'Ali.* In 1934 a final law was issued creating an autonomous University of Tehran *(Daneshgah-e Tehran)* with six faculties. The grounds for it were chosen on the western edge of the city, but erection of the buildings was delayed until 1951-52, when the entire university, until then housed in provisional lodgings, was moved to its new site.

A predominantly secular institution, the University of Tehran underwent various phases in its development. In the early postwar period, it comprised eight major departments and schools: philosophy, medicine (including pharmacology and dentistry), law, veterinary medicine, natural sciences, agriculture, fine arts, and theology.

In spite of endeavors to concentrate its activities on one site, the university soon outgrew its premises and many of its new institutes, laboratories, and research centers became scattered in the huge capital city of four million inhabitants. In subsequent years the university was enlarged by creating new departments or incorporating some previously independent schools. These additions included the Institute of Administration and Commerce, the departments of economics, hygiene, and forestry, as well as special institutes for sociology, atomic studies, Iranian culture and civilization, psychology, and cooperatives. By the mid-1970s the university counted fifteen distinct units.

In 1967 an Administrative Council was created to guarantee financial and administrative independence. At the same time plans were afoot to construct a University City that would provide an integrated complex of grounds and facilities for students and professors alike. Catering to the needs of well over 20,000 students by the early 1970s, the university grew in size and steadily developed its resources under the leadership of its chancellor, Dr. Hushang Nahavandi. Yet soon it appeared that its facilities did not suffice to satisfy the growing needs of the country.

In consequence a new university arose in 1960, organized on a private basis, the National University *(Daneshgah-e Melli)* situated in the region of Ayvin, northwest of Tehran. In 1970 it had 3,000 students and their number was increasing. Its departments included architecture, economics and political science, law, medicine, literature, humanities, dentistry, and natural sciences. In the mid-1970s its chancellor was Seyyed Hosayn Nasr, a noted Sufi philosopher.[6]

In 1966 the Aryamehr University, with a preponderantly technological character, was founded by imperial decree. Initially it was planned to move it to Isfahan, but eventually it was established in Tehran and from the beginning it drew to itself large numbers of students (the goal, according to the national development plans, was 10,000). Instruction was offered in electricity, mechanics, chemistry, metallurgy, natural sciences, and industrial management.

To counteract excessive centralization of government and education in the capital, steps were taken to develop educational institutions in the provinces. This was comparatively easy in the western parts of the country but difficult in the south and east, where deserts hindered communication. Tabriz, the largest city after Tehran, had its university, the *Daneshgah-e Azarbayjan,* founded soon after the war in 1946. The journal of its philosophy faculty, *Nashriyyeh-ye daneshkadeh-ye adabiyyat va 'olum-e ensani,* established high standards of scholarship. Beside this faculty the university comprised the departments of agriculture, engineering, medicine, pharmacology, natural sciences, and dentistry. Attached to it were a polytechnic institute and an institute of animal breeding. Also offered were courses in electromechanics and astrophysics, as well as instruction for nurses that included obstetrics, hygiene, and nutrition.

The University of Mashhad *(Daneshgah-e Ferdowsi)* became known for its emphasis on philosophy and for its journal, *Majalleh-ye daneshkadeh-ye adabiyyat va 'olum-e ensani.* Famous for its holy shrine of Reza, the eighth

Imam, Mashhad developed excellence in theological studies under the direction of the dean of the theological faculty, Dr. Mojtahedzadeh.

In 1962 a new development took place: the Pahlavi University *(Daneshgah-e Pahlavi)* was created in Shiraz along American lines. It offered many courses in English and its teaching staff included a number of foreigners. Instruction was given in literature, natural sciences, medicine, agriculture, and engineering. An institute of agricultural technology formed part of the university, as well as a college for nurses. Other units included the Sa'di Hospital, the Khalili Clinic for Ophthalmology, and the great Namazi Hospital with its section for nuclear medicine. A big boarding house lodged 8,000 students. The American-educated Senator Isa Sadiq A'lam, formerly minister of education, provided much of the early guidance in the establishment of this university.[7]

In the southwest, the University of Ahwaz was founded in 1956. It aimed at a revival of intellectual life in the province of Khuzistan, famous in the remote past for its medieval University of Gondishapur.

In the mid-1970s a new school, the University of Isfahan *(Daneshgah-e Shah 'Abbas-Kabir)* was still in process of being organized, with the Shah's sister, Princess Fatima, serving as honorary president of its board. Tastefully landscaped amidst well-watered groves, the buildings were situated above the imperial gardens, Hazarjarib, at the foot of the mountain, Kuh-e Suffa, with a beautiful view over the city. Its curriculum included, among other disciplines, the humanities *('olum-e ensani)* and foreign languages, the latter offered in a separate center *(Markaz-e Zabanha-ye Khareji).* Following the tradition of Safavid Isfahan, where Shah 'Abbas had given domicile to the Armenian immigrants from Julfa, Isfahan University developed its own Center of Armenian Studies, endowed by generous private bequests.

An Institute of Horticulture *(Anstitu-ye Baghbani),* found nowhere but at Isfahan with its old tradition of gardening, was established in 1971. In fact, botany has enjoyed a privileged position in Isfahan. The Medical School was provided with a big hospital. Interest in this field was underlined by the appointment in the 1970s of a epidemiologist as chancellor of the university. Progress in developing the university was especially accelerated in the 1970s. The primary goal was to promote research work; it aimed at a capacity of 3,000 students.

Further academic institutions were planned for Zanjan, Rezayeh, Hamadan, and Rasht, where thus far lower-ranking colleges were located. Concerning Rasht, the plans called for the establishment of a university of a prevailingly scientific-technological character. Its site was expected to be in the south of the town on the slopes of the Elborz Mountains. Until Iranians had achieved the necessary skills, this university was to be staffed with German teachers and apply German teaching methods and organization.

Considering this rapid development in higher education, fears were expressed that too many universities, particularly if brought into being too quickly, would not be able to keep the intended high standards, for intellectual quality could not be produced ad libitum. This held equally true of academic teachers and of students. Moreover, genuine research was likely to trail behind teaching, a situation that had undoubtedly developed in the mid-1970s. In this respect Iran was no exception to the general development all over the world, including the West, where advances in higher learning came gradually and were interwoven with the general progress of society. A visitor to the campus of an Iranian university was likely to be impressed by students walking alone, sometimes stopping, holding a book in their hands, looking into it and glancing afar with moving lips. These were the industrious students who would learn the subject matter word by word from the book. However, at the academic level of instruction, thoughtful pondering on the subjects studied should have been given preference to mere learning by heart and intellectual appreciation should have replaced mechanically acquired knowledge. What could be noticed here was a parallel with the behavior of Asian students at universities in Europe. Industry usually took the place of intellectual independence. Knowing by heart is certainly no vice, but a good memory could never compensate for systematic understanding and logical formulation of ideas. Yet even in this respect some progress was noticeable. The generation of the 1970s was remarkably more free and critical than the preceding one. For any Western scholar with teaching experience in Iran, it was a source of gratification to find his former students in their new role of professional colleagues capable of joining in learned discussions even in the fields that were methodologically remote from the traditional Eastern focus on linguistics and ethnology. This was undoubtedly the result of systematic exposure to the methods of research and the influence of European and American scholars. Interestingly enough, absorption of Western methods in the area of humanities seemed to create more difficulties than training in natural sciences and technology.

Elementary and Secondary Schools

Difficulties for an Iranian university student usually began with the end of secondary school, which was expected to lay the groundwork necessary for academic study. Perhaps even more important, therefore, than university education was the condition of secondary and elementary education. Consequently, it is important that this phase of educational development during the Pahlavi era now be reviewed.

Elementary education as introduced by Reza Shah and continued ever since comprised six years of *madrase-ye ebteda'i,* later renamed *dabestan.*

After graduating from this school the pupil entered the *madrase-ye mota-vasseteh (dabirestan)*, which consisted of six years culminating in matriculation for university study. Elementary schools were supposed to be under a headmaster with a secondary school certificate, while secondary schools were to have a university-educated headmaster (a goal not always attained). The pupil at the secondary level, according to his inclination and natural gifts, could choose between the literary-historical side *(adabiyyat)* or the mathematical-scientific side *('olum-e tabi'i va riyaziyyat)*.

This system underwent a complete change in 1974. Instead of the former division of the school curriculum into two six-year categories, a new organization was introduced. An elementary school from now on was to consist of only five grades, above which a new type of school, *dowre-ye rahnama'i* (guidance school) was established. It was the task of these guidance schools to orient the students toward their future occupations and develop the talents that one day would be the basis of their careers. The new guidance plan was being executed seriously and could compare with experiments made in Western Germany with the *Gesamtschule* (comprehensive school) and its *Förderstufe* (advancement grade).

Through the introduction of the guidance school, elementary education was extended from six to eight years, and a ninth year was contemplated. Secondary education as a result became limited to four years. As before, students had to attend school for a total of twelve years if they intended to go to higher training colleges or universities. This latest reform was given a good start and was expected to provide the young people with good vocational guidance. The secondary-level curriculum embraced three main concentrations: literature *(adabiyyat)*, mathematics *(riyaziyyat)*, and natural sciences *(tabi'iyyat)*. Religious instruction became compulsory for all Moslems, who represent the vast majority of the population. It could be given by a lay teacher who had the ability and felt so inclined, not necessarily by a *molla* with a license in theology *(lisans-e elahiyyat)*. School books offered a Persian translation of Arabic passages.

Schools founded and maintained by non-Moslem groups of the nation had not ceased to exist, but were thoroughly subordinated to government regulations. A major Zoroastrian school continued to function in Kerman. Interestingly, it was attended by many more Moslem than Zoroastrian pupils, the latter accounting for only one-sixth to one-fourth of the student body. The name of the boys' school was *Dabirestan-e Pesaraneh-ye Iranshahr* (Iranshahr Boys' High School); the girls' school, named *Dabirestan-e Dokhtaraneh-ye Kaykhosrow Shahrokh* (Kaykhosrow Shahrokh Girls' High School), was headed by a Zoroastrian lady. Boys and girls were instructed separately.

However, coeducation *(tarbiyat-e mokhtalet)*, at first sight a strange notion in a Moslem country, had existed throughout, particularly in rural districts and almost everywhere on the elementary school level. Similarly, at universities both sexes mixed freely. But on the secondary level, in the high schools, corresponding to the period of adolescence, boys and girls were educated separately. On the other hand, coeducation on a private basis had been practiced as early as the Middle Ages, but it seems only occasionally. The literary episode of Laila and Majnun is a case in point: miniatures show us that the two young people are sitting side by side at the feet of their teacher. In the schools for girls, besides theoretical education, special value was attached to such practical arts as housekeeping, cooking, dressmaking, needlework, child care, and the like.[8] Middle Eastern women and girls were often clumsy and inexperienced in these arts, and practical instruction in them was indeed badly needed. Formerly, many women were not even able to mend textiles *(rofukardan)*; they only drew together *(vasleh kardan)* instead of darning them carefully *(rofugari)*.

After a period of turmoil caused by the foreign invasion of Iran, free instruction for elementary schools was promptly resumed by the young Shah together with compulsory education (1941). A serious drawback, however, was the insufficient number of qualified teachers as well as school buildings. There was also a great need for teachers' training colleges. As an incentive, teachers' salaries, until then very low, were substantially raised. The instructional materials could not be procured in time, and free distribution of primers, readers, and similar books encountered many difficulties. Effective relief did not come until the budget for education had been suitably increased; later the oil boom greatly helped the government in this area. Since 1974 free training of all pupils on the *dabestan* and *rahnameh'i* level has been guaranteed by imperial decree.[9]

The government also undertook to provide free meals for school children through the eighth-grade level *(taghziyeh-ye rayegan dar madares)*. At ten o'clock in the morning boys and girls were given fruit, milk, and biscuits, i.e., food rich in calories and proteins. This of course was no substitute for a complete meal, but it helped parents to give their children adequate nutrition. The great new program of school meals was to start in autumn 1976.

FOREIGN AND SPECIAL SCHOOLS

The government allowed the operation of foreign schools (English, American, and French, known collectively as *madares-e duzabani va khareji)* on condition that they conform to the principles of Iranian education. Naturally, attendance at such private schools cost money. They were adapted to the reforming ideas of the Shah. Outwardly the change could be recognized by the change of names. The American College, famous through its former headmaster, Professor Jordan, was renamed *Dabirestan-e Elborz.* In the same manner the French schools were adapted to national forms: Jeanne d'Arc became *Dabirestan-e Razi,* most attractively endowed with modern landscaping. Similarly in Isfahan the Ecole Jeanne d'Arc, though still run by Catholic sisters (Soeurs de la Charité, St. Vincent de Paul), was changed into a *Kudakestan-e, Dabestan-e,* and *Dabirestan-e Rudabeh.* The German School, which before the war existed as "private class" *(kelas-e makhsus),* developed into two sections, one with Persian as an optional subject for German children, the other with a preponderantly Iranian program. The English College in Isfahan, founded and led by Methodists, was closed. It was transformed into a *Debastan-e Dokhtaraneh-ye Melli-ye Rahmat,* i.e., an elementary boarding school for girls, with a British headmistress. In these schools, insofar as they kept their original character of providing instruction for the children of foreign citizens, the Persian language was optional *(entekhabi);* otherwise it was compulsory *(ejbari).* All Persian schools had their own individual names.

Built upon the general school training of eight years was the curriculum of technical schools *(honarestan).* Reza Shah had furthered them long before the war; they were supported by German technological teachers and headmasters. Before the war such schools existed at Tabriz, Isfahan, Mashhad, and Shiraz. In the meantime their number had increased several times more. Iran needed qualified technicians in addition to engineers of academic grade if modernization and industrialization were to spread all over the country. To train such technology teachers, special schools were instituted, such as the one at Babul (Caspian Sea), the *Danesh sara-ye Fanni-ye 'Ali.* A technology teacher *(mo'allem-e herfeh'i)* had to attend this school four years to obtain a license. The Technical School at Tehran *(Madrase-ye San'ati)* which after World War I had replaced the German *Oberrealschule* under the name *honarestan,* was raised to the rank of a higher technical school *(Honarestan-e 'Ali-ye Tehran).* Technical schools of a lower rank *(amuzeshgah)* were instituted everywhere after the war.

Vocational schools, especially of the technical and agricultural type, were established in Tehran and other parts of the country, in the north and west more densely than in the desertlike areas in the east and south. In the mid-1970s these schools had over 133,000 pupils (out of nearly 7 million pupils in Iran), of whom over 26,000 were girls. For graduates from this type of school the way was open to the *Anstitu-ye Teknolozhi,* but not to the university.

The kindergarten *(kudakestan)* was not formally included in the years of schooling. There had already been kindergartens under Reza Shah mostly privately owned. In the postwar period kindergartens became government institutions, not compulsory but enjoying popularity. Nearly 90,000 children, almost half of them girls, attended them in the 1970s.

For adults who had not attended school when young, training courses and evening classes were instituted as early as Reza Shah's reign, in the thirties. Under Mohammad Reza Shah, adult education became part of his broader campaign against illiteracy. The Shah put substantial funds, deducted from the military budget, at the disposal of UNESCO to combat illiteracy.

THE STRUGGLE AGAINST ILLITERACY

In spite of considerable progress achieved since the end of the Qajar era, illiteracy was being eradicated at a slow pace. In 1966 it stood at the rate of 80 percent and by 1975 it was still showing an alarming rate of more than 60 percent. Under Reza Shah primary schools were declared to be free of charge *(rayagan)*.[10] However, the number of children going to school increased only gradually. Especially among the villagers and tribesmen the number of illiterates remained at a constant level. However, many positive measures had been taken during his reign. Even small hamlets were provided with school-houses. Similarly, adult education was introduced, and special manuals were prepared for it. However, as was only natural, few individuals were eager to serve as schoolmasters in poor villages. The most active teachers shied away from the country, favoring bigger towns and in particular Tehran. Raising the number of teachers by increasing the size of teachers' training colleges certainly contributed to a common raising of the educational level. But the problem of illiteracy seemed likely to plague Iran for a long time.

The ministry concerned (in due time a separate *Vezarat-e Amuzesh va Parvaresh,* or Ministry of Education, had been created) started from the premise that the founding of a school among peasants required the presence of at least 200 souls, and among nomads at least 300. The question remained, how to manage scattered settlements whose parts were separated by miles of desert from each other? This question was sometimes difficult to answer even in more developed regions of the earth. Moreover, in Iran introduction of compulsory education was bound to depend on a number of prerequisites. First of all, practicable roads *(rahha-ye mashinrow)* had to be constructed to replace the existing camel or mule tracks *(rahha-ye malrow)*. Once this was done, a "flying teacher" could be installed who would travel by car from community to community to instruct people on certain days of the week. Excessive heat in the summer and freezing cold in the winter, together with many other hardships, required much idealism from prospective teachers and made recruitment difficult.

Such young teachers and, later, members of the Literacy Corps, had to cope not only with hindrances of this sort. The real difficulties to be overcome lay even deeper. In a village there was usually a *molla* or some other person who had usurped the spiritual leadership of the inhabitants. The simple and mostly illiterate people would tend to follow his word and his superficial thinking. By instinct he would be against any sort of enlightenment. He might also be old and enjoying high status in the village. Would the adults who by tradition followed such a leader entrust their children to the new arrival, a young man who came from outside uninvited? He had to criticize a lot; it was his duty to change and improve the customs and conditions of the village. This could not make him very popular. He arrived, it is true, commissioned by the government and even though there might not be any doubt as to the loyalty of the people toward the Shah, he was compelled to act cautiously. He had to find the decisive word and do the right thing in the decisive moment if he did not wish to be boycotted from the very beginning. He had to be tactful with the *molla* of the place and be on reasonable terms with him, be this man as he be. If quarrel was unavoidable he had to get through even with compulsion and see that obstinate people leave the place. There were villages where the children simply did not appear at school. Children were looked upon as hands and helpers for their parents; thus occasionally attendance at school had to be paid for in rials.

One of the most urgent problems was the education of the girls. Religious custom did not allow fathers and mothers to hand over their daughters to a man for education. Female teachers were required. This might be done by assigning a married teacher to a village, a young man whose wife took over the teaching of girls. In similar fashion a young member of the Literacy Corps, if married, might or was even expected to take along his young wife to the village for support. Then both of them, as an up-to-date young couple, might set the peasants an example to follow.

Similarly, girls who wished to study had to submit themselves to a year of public service. In 1968 the Literacy Corps was supplemented by a corps of women.[11] By 1970, of 2,800 girls with high school certificates and female university students, 1,920 joined the Literacy Corps, 820 the Housekeeping Corps, and 60 the Health Corps. As a result, 321,239 children between seven and thirteen, among them many girls, were provided by the government with basic school education.

The aforementioned Literacy Corps was certainly among the most successful reforming measures of the Shah and his "White Revolution." The creation of this brigade of young people was one of his most noteworthy achievements, beside such other social and political innovations as land reform, nationalization of natural resources, and the sharing of profits by industrial workers. Creation of the Literacy Corps was followed by that of the Health Corps and later the Development Corps.

The idea of the Literacy Corps and the two other corps modeled after it could be described as follows.[12] Men with high school certificates, especially those aiming at academic studies, did not need to devote their entire period of military service to army training; they were permitted to do service for their country in other ways, by bringing education to peasants and tribal people, to rural regions and the tents of nomads who up till then had not seen educational institutions. Precondition for entry into the Literacy Corps was four months basic training in the army, where the young teachers would also receive the necessary instructions to guide them in their task. On principle they were to be sent to rural districts other than those of their home and origin, to regions that were new to them. Thus at least they could learn to know their country. An exception was made to this principle only in tribal areas, where tribal teachers, trained in the army, had great success. This was especially so in the southwest of Iran, among the Qashqa'is in Fars (e.g., in the environs of Firuzabad).

The teaching objectives were the basic elements of reading, writing, and arithmetic. Beyond that the corpsmen might teach the pupils (or adults) matters that were close to their own taste and interest, connected with personal experience. Classrooms often had to be improvised, although where feasible new school buildings were to be built. General hygiene was taught; baths and toilets were being introduced.

At the time of Reza Shah the ancient type of bath, consisting of a big common basin, was replaced in towns and hamlets by modern shower rooms *(hammam-e dush)*. This innovation, naturally, was difficult to introduce in villages where water supply was scanty and no pipeline system existed. Public cleanliness after World War II increased remarkably. Privies, however, were unhygienic and sometimes nonexistent. The demonstration of the relation between cleanliness and disease had been most beneficial. Moreover, in the field of hygiene, a special domain of the Health Corps, teachers had the opportunity to invoke the Islamic rules of cleanliness based on the Qor'an. The task of the teachers was to give these rules appropriate interpretation. Indeed, the adage *ab-e ravan pak ast* ("Running water is clean") could hold true only of a desertlike region void of people.

In addition to their cultural tasks, the young people sent to the villages were expected to settle quarrels among the peasants, of course only in simple cases. Otherwise the White Revolution had brought to the rural districts courts of arbitration, the Houses of Equity, in order to unburden the city law courts.

Stimulated by the great success of this tripartite "Army of Revolution," the Shah, on the occasion of the award of an honorary doctorate at Harvard, initiated the creation of a Universal Welfare Legion within the United Nations. In Iran, the legion became active in the underdeveloped south, where the Shul project, especially, proved a success; it was carried out by volunteers in a coordinated campaign against poverty, hunger, and social injustice. The project was continued in the rural districts of Jam and Rez (near Bushire on the Persian Gulf).[13]

By founding these youth organizations, in particular the Literacy Corps, Mohammad Reza Shah had accomplished what at the time of his father would have remained pure theory. In those days certainly nobody would have thought it possible to raise educational standards through grassroots action. The idea, it should be pointed out, originated in the Shah's own mind. It was implemented with energy and resolution. It set an example for other countries to emulate. In fact, Israel subsequently adopted similar measures. By 1976 the Literacy Corps could boast of thirteen years of successful operation. Its related organizations had also acquired considerable experience.

The Shah considered this campaign for improvement in his own country as part of a global struggle against illiteracy and backwardness. Prompted by him, UNESCO held its first International Congress against Illiteracy in Tehran, in 1965. Although children were the first and foremost object of these endeavors, one should not overlook the success achieved in elevating the level of adults by special adult courses *(tarbiyat-e akaber, parvaresh-e bozorgsalan),* given by ordinary teachers as well as by members of the Literacy Corps. Every year thousands of adult students in rural districts and towns were becoming literate.

SPORTS AND YOUTH ORGANIZATIONS

During the Pahlavi era sports became a special branch of instruction in all schools. As early as 1921 playing fields and gymnasia were organized. Gymnastic halls, *varzeshkhaneh* had to replace the old-fashioned *zurkhaneh,* frowned upon under Reza Shah. The *zurkhaneh* (houses of strength) were not only athletic clubs. They were also social centers attracting respectable bazaar people, tradesmen, and workmen of religious and moral qualities whose customs and rites carried a symbolic link with the glory of the heroic age of Iran as expressed in the *Shahnameh.* Members were thoughtful of ritual purity and bodily cleanliness. The athletes *(pahlavans)* invoked *hazrat-e 'Ali,* the first *imam,* before jumping into the small arena for their rhythmic exercises and dances. Perhaps the extremely religious-Islamic orientation and the danger of conspiracy had been the reason Reza Shah disliked the *zurkhaneh* and their members. Athletic qualities were particularly esteemed among the populace and photographs of *pahlavans* were displayed in the bazaars and smaller shops. Like the old bathhouses *(hammam),* which had to give way to modern bathrooms with showers and tubs, the *zurkhaneh* were destined to yield to modern gymnastics and sports. Although under Reza Shah the *zurkhaneh* were a dying institution, in the era following World War II they experienced a revival. This time the *zurkhaneh* emerged as an attraction for tourists. Whole groups of foreigners and even official guests of the government were invited to the shows given by the members of a *zurkhaneh*. Thus the *zurkhanehs*, now in a new secularized shape but considered a reminder of half-mythical times, of Rustam and his knightly ideals, were not only kept alive but even officially promoted. They were placed under the control of the department called *Sazeman-e Tarbiyat-e Badani* (Organization for Physical Education), while a special office in the Ministry of Education, the *Edareh-ye Koll-e Tarbiyat-e Badani Baraye Daneshamuzan* (General Administration of Physical Education for Secondary School Children), watched over the sports activities in schools.

This is perhaps the place to say a word about the Boy Scouts *(pishahang)*, which in the days of Reza Shah had played an important role in the education of youth beyond the school.[14] Iranian boy scouts, as everywhere, were a part of the general youth movement, though in somewhat different environmental circumstances due to the arid landscape and southern sky. The boy scout movement before the war was led by an American and influenced by American patterns, but adapted to Eastern Moslem conditions. The *Sazman-e Pishahangi* continued after the war, with its leadership in the 1970s in the hands of Dr. Banna'i and under the honorary presidency of the Shah himself. The hills and slopes of the Elborz Mountains, in the immediate neighborhood of Tehran, became a favored place for boy scout camping.

Distinct from the Boy Scouts were the mountaineering clubs of adults founded after the war. Their activities are recognized by signboards and marked mountain paths in the environs of Darband and elsewhere. They were distinctly a postwar phenomenon.

EDUCATIONAL ADMINISTRATION

The burden of these reforms had to be borne by an educational administration that was expected to be active and incorruptible. Removals and transfers of higher officials were a frequent occurrence in the administration, testifying to the alertness of the Shah to possible abuses and deficiencies and the need to eliminate them.

In 1966 the original Ministry of Education *(Vezarat-e Farhang,* old *Vezarat-e Ma'aref)* had been split into three new ministries. Most important was the ministry of education proper, i.e., the Ministry of Schools *(Vezarat-e Amuzesh va Parvaresh)*, headed in the mid-1970s by Dr. Ahmad Hushang Sharifi. Academic instruction and research became the province of the Ministry of Science and Higher Education *(Vezarat-e 'Olum va Amuzesh-e 'Ali)*, established in 1967 and in the mid-1970s headed by Dr. Abdol Hosayn Sami'i. The third institution that emerged from this reorganization was the Ministry of Culture and Art *(Vezarat-e Farhang va Honar)*, responsible for the wide area of cultural endeavors. In the mid-1970s its head was Mehrdad Pahlbod, brother-in-law of the Shah.

Besides these three departments, two other institutions were concerned with the problems of education, namely, the Ministry of War and the Women's Organization of Iran (WOI). The WOI was headed in the 1970s by Dr. Mahnaz Afkhami, a young American-educated woman who in 1976 became the first female member of the cabinet as minister for women's affairs. The Iranian school administration followed the principle of strict centralization. The Ministry of Education had its subordinate offices *(edareh)* in the provincial capitals and sometimes local branches in smaller towns. This system paralleled the early Achaemenid and Sassanian patterns of highly centralized and pyramidal government. It left little initiative or authority to local officials and headmasters.

The growth of the school system with its big administrative overhead was reflected in the steadily growing budgetary allocations, which showed substantial increase in the 1970s. In that period more attention began to be paid to teachers' salaries, previously very low but gradually improving. In the 1960s and 1970s the old disparity between salaries in Iran and those that Iranians could secure if they stayed abroad appeared to be gradually vanishing. Similarly, the pay difference between Iranians and foreigners working in Iran was being narrowed down. Bitter feelings had been aroused in the past when a graduate returning from his studies abroad received only a fraction of the salary that was paid to his European or American colleagues employed in comparable positions in Iran. Moreover, in the 1970s Iranians were increasingly filling the vacancies created by foreigners leaving Iran.

THE BRAIN DRAIN

But there remained a serious problem. Of thousands of students who had obtained their degrees abroad, many were not returning to Iran. Thus their costly education abroad was lost to the country. Moreover, the young people who studied abroad were often the most capable students. Among them were holders of national scholarships as well as those who studied at their own expense. There were different reasons for their deciding to remain abroad. Many of them married daughters of the countries in which they studied, because of attributes and expectations that could not be met by Iranian girls. In a number of countries, for example West Germany, marriage with a local girl helped them acquire citizenship—a change in status that was much coveted on account of the greater opportunities it gave of finding employment and exercising a profession without leaving. On the other hand, the low income and lower living standards in Iran deterred them from returning there.

Last but not least, there were individual Iranians who, having concluded their studies abroad with distinction and qualifying as eminent specialists, had made an attempt to return and accept positions offered to them. But apart from grossly inadequate pay, they found above them in a supervisory capacity men who had never been abroad and who had little or no knowledge of their specialty. Yet these less-qualified persons were often given preferential treatment because they possessed better connections. Under the circumstances, much talent was wasted, the disappointed specialists either going abroad in search of better opportunities or settling down in Iran to engage in work unrelated to their specialized education.

In certain sectors this brain drain caused serious problems. This was particularly true in the field of hygiene and health where the lack of doctors was so acute that Iran was compelled to bring in foreign physicians. The pattern was set in 1945 after the end of World War II, when fifty Austrian doctors were engaged to work in rural districts. In the 1960s and 1970s the prevalent trend was to hire physicians from India and Pakistan.

To secure the return of Iranian students after completion of their studies, the government sent special missions abroad, headed by important officials. A mission directed by Khoda'dad Farmanfarmayan and Dean Ahmad Ghoreichi of the National University of Law School was sent to Europe and the United States in the later 1960s. To encourage the students to return to Iran, the government offered them university positions and high salaries. To maximize the benefits for the country, it was important to direct the flow of the returnees away from Tehran to the provincial centers and rural areas. This was not an easy task in a country with a centralized system of administration.

To achieve a balanced development, the government had to resist the tide of immigration to Tehran and prevent the provinces from gradually being depopulated. In the 1970s government-sponsored decentralization was beginning slowly to take place. Creation of provincial universities and limitation of industrial settlements in Tehran marked hopeful steps in this direction. Intensive development of roads and communications was expected to help in this process and to ensure a better equilibrium between country and capital. By the 1970s the Iranian student population had substantially increased, partly as a result of a generous scholarship policy that provided free higher education to those students who pledged to be available for public service after completion of their studies. In the mid-1970s there were more than 125,000 students in the institutions of higher learning, as compared to 25,000 in the period 1962-63. In 1975 the number of applicants for admission to the universities rose to 240,000. This obviously caused a serious strain on the government's financial, administrative, and manpower resources.

Yet, with all the crowding of the institutions of higher learning, Iran faced a paradox. While on the one hand the universities were awarding ever-increasing numbers of B.A. and M.A. diplomas, the country suffered from the shortage of skilled manpower in a number of fields where a particular specialized skill was needed. In terms of the requirements of the growing economy and developing society, it might have been more useful to develop two-year colleges which would have prepared students for more practical pursuits.

There was no doubt, however, that mass education was definitely being introduced in Iran. By 1976 Iran's preuniversity student population had attained 7 million (of which girls accounted for more than half), as compared with 5,700,000 in the 1972-73 period. There was even hope that before long the need for adult education would be obviated through stricter implementation of compulsory school attendance by children all over the country. While many dedicated men were active in developing Iran's educational system, the efforts of two ministers of education in the postwar period, 'Ali Asghar Hekmat and *Isa Sadiq,* were particularly praiseworthy.

An important opportunity for self-criticism and reform planning was provided by the annual meetings of educators at Ramsar, on the Caspian Sea. They were regularly attended by the Shah and the Shahbanou, who in 1968 made scathing attacks on the slow humdrum ways and routines of the universities, and on the numerous unworthy holders of chairs who were droning their old-fashioned lectures while seeking financial gains outside the university and neglecting research. Thereupon the chancellors of all the universities resigned and many posts were filled by active young men with a better academic background. In 1972, again, bitter remarks were directed at low educational standards and the "diplomas of ignorance." Most important were the resolutions taken in 1975. These included the takeover of private elementary schools by the state; raising teachers' salaries; setting standards of minimum education for elementary school teachers (a high school diploma) and secondary school teachers (a university or teachers' college degree); a possible abrogation of the university entrance examination and its replacement by annual examinations in secondary schools; elevation of teachers' training colleges to the rank of universities; free university education for those who would undertake to serve the government or the private sector in Iran (two years of service for each year of university training); price reductions for university textbooks and manuals; promotion of women's and girls' education; and other improvements.[15]

THE LANGUAGE ACADEMY AND SPECIAL INSTITUTES

The picture of cultural life in Iran would be incomplete without a glance at other institutions whose task was to promote cooperation with the Western world. First to be mentioned in this sector is the Farhangestan, or Iranian Academy, founded by Reza Shah as an academy of the Persian language and literature more or less after the French pattern. A particular aim of this academy had been to purify the Persian language from the overlay of Arabic words that it had acquired after the Islamization of Iran in the Middle Ages. Removal of linguistic loans has never been an easy task and full success could not be assured. In the 1930s the Ministry of Finances (renamed from the Arabic *Vezarat-e Maliyyat* to the Persian *Vezarat-e Dara'i*) published a booklet under the title *Daftarcheh-ye vazhehha-ye pazirofteh shodeh dar Farhangestan-e Iran* which was intended to help officials and interested persons in the Iranization of their language. As a result, many proposed expressions were accepted and entered the common usage of the people: *amar* (statistics), *bakhsh* (district), *bazargan* (merchant), *parvandeh* (file), among others. Such words were partly forgotten ones that had now been resurrected, often with changed meanings, and partly new-coined. Not all were happily chosen and in some cases they did not correspond to the laws of language. Still they became common language. In this respect, the Persian language is no exception: European languages also contain many an artifically formed word that survives although it has been wrongly derived. Such words as automobile, television, and homosexuality constitute Greco-Latin deformities, yet they have been firmly adopted and widely used.

The Farhangestan was also engaged in renaming localities so that their current names were replaced by their ancient ones. Thus Nosratabad was changed to Zabol, Salehabad to Andimeshk, Shah 'Abdol 'Azim to Ray, etc. Similarly, names of vulgar sound and meaning were abolished and replaced by new ones. Furthermore, the academy changed a number of Arabic and Turkish geographic names into Persian ones: thus Mohammara became Khorramshahr and Qamishle was converted to Nayistan. On the other hand, some localities were renamed for the express purpose of honoring the memory of Reza Shah.

If one were to compare these moderate and in most cases successful endeavors with the chauvinism of European countries, which have tended to "nationalize" place names with any change of borders, the Iranian name changes would not appear in an unfavorable light. To sum up, the existence of the Farhangestan did to some extent put limits to the barbarization of the language and irresponsible play with neologisms. The restraint and prudence of the academy's members in this respect deserved full acknowledgment.

The government had also furthered the nationalization of personal and family names. Family names, mostly unknown in the past, had to be invented while first names of Iranian origin were being introduced. Here the registrars' offices played a major role: the new fashion induced many parents to give their children historical names that had earlier been limited to the Zoroastrian community and tribal groups. Ancient names taken from the rich legacy of Iranian history and legend—names such as Ardashir, Gudarz, Goshtasb, and Rustam, which had almost disappeared from common usage—reemerged with considerable popularity among townsfolk and peasants.*

In the postwar period, the academy was reorganized under the name *Farhangestan-e Zaban-e Iran* (Iranian Academy of Language). Headed in the 1970s by Professor Sadeq-e Kiya, the Farhangestan had among its prominent members Dr. Isa Sadiq and Professor Mahyar Navvabi. It became part of the *Bonyad-e Shahanshi-ye Farhangestanha-ye Iran* (Imperial Foundation of Iranian Academies). Under the motto *"Pishnehad-e shoma chist?"* (What is your suggestion?), it regularly distributed its pamphlets, expecting literate laymen and philologists to voice their opinion on the modern scientific terminology and neologisms suggested by its members. Its guiding principle was that Iranians themselves would have to decide in which way their language should be purified and preserved. Learned scholars were expected to exercise their authority with circumspection. This cautious approach contrasted with the boldness of the language reform in neighboring Turkey, the latter being viewed with considerable criticism in Iran.

Since 1961 a major role in Iran's cultural life has been played by the Pahlavi Foundation, established under the Shah's personal patronage. Members of its board included the prime minister, minister of the court, chief justice of the Supreme Court, president of the Senate, and speaker of the Majles. Well endowed financially, the foundation was a philanthropic organization with a broadly cultural orientation. It granted scholarships to able and needy students and assisted student hostels. In 1974 nearly 8,000 students, of whom 1,000 were studying abroad, were its beneficiaries. Affiliated with it was the Pahlavi Library headed by the vice-minister of court, Dr. Shoja'ad-Din Shafa. Its name, however, was something of a misnomer. The Pahlavi Library was not a library in the ordinary sense of the word and was not commonly accessible to scholars and the public the way the Parliament Library was; rather, it was a separate department of the Pahlavi Foundation in charge of cultural exchange, awarding prizes for books and itself publishing books, the latter through the Translation and Publishing Institute, which was attached to

---

*Friends working in the Statistical Office, which in Iran has also the function of a registrar's office *(edareh-ye amar va sabt-e ahval),* were amused to tell me, in the days before the war, that peasants and lower-class people, when announcing the birth of their child, asked whether the official wished to hear "the name into his right ear" or "the name into his left ear." For the inner circle of family they kept a Shi'ite name such as Hasan, Hosayn, 'Abbas, or Fatima, but for official use they chose names like Bizhan, Dara, Firuz, Siyavush, Shapur, and for their daughters names like Farangis, Rudabeh, Sudabeh, etc., even if the roles these ancestors once played in the *Shahnameh* had been a tragic one. We have experienced similar phenomena in Europe and America at various periods.

it. In 1975 alone nearly 400 new titles were published. Preservation of national relics, especially old shrines, was another task of the Pahlavi Foundation.

Intellectual life, particularly in the capital, comprised a number of associations of an artistic, literary, or scientific nature, among them the Bonyad-e Mowlavi. This association, founded in 1974, was headed by Professor Zabihollah Safa, historian of Persian literature.[16] It was devoted to research and propagation of the works of Jalal ad-Din Rumi—his *Masnavi-ye ma'navi,* for instance, and the *Divan-e Shams-e Tabrizi*—as well as the books influenced by his School of Dervishes.[17] One of the greatest mystics of the past, Jalal ad-Din left a deep imprint on the world and his Sufism became the guiding philosophy of Iran, permeating many aspects of its culture. To judge by his own writings, especially *Mission for My Country,* Mohammad Reza Shah could be considered one of its followers. The great poetry of Iran was imbued by Sufism and would lack depth without it. Many members of higher society quite openly confessed to belonging to one of the existing dervish orders.

Certain institutions of international character were established in Iran by the course of political events. They comprised the Asian Cultural Documentation Center, for UNESCO, and the Regional Cultural Institute in Tehran. The latter was an agency of the Regional Cooperation for Development (RCD), an organization that, since 1965, had embraced Iran, Pakistan, and Turkey—three countries bound together by geographic and cultural proximity. The Tehran branch of this international organization had among its members in the 1970s Professor S. H. Nasr, philosopher and chancellor of the Aryamehr University, and Dr. M. Forugh, dean of the Faculty of Dramatic Art. It published a journal containing excerpts in English of articles written in Persian, Urdu, and Turkish.

PUBLICATIONS AND LIBRARIES

Another manifestation of Iran's cultural life was the existence of a number of literary-aesthetic journals. These included *Sokhan* (The Word), a periodical dedicated to culture, knowledge, and the arts, and providing information about new publications in Europe and America.

Another notable publication was *Rahnama-ye Ketab* (Book Guide), a monthly edited by Professor Ehsan Yar-Shater and concentrating on language, literature, and Iranology. Of scholarly significance was also *Farhang-e Iranzamin* (Culture of the Land of Iran), a literary monthly, edited by the head of the Central Library and Documentation Center *(Ketabkhaneh-ye Markazi va Markaz-e Asnad),* Professor Iraj Afshar.

Barrasiha-ye tarikhi (Historical Studies of Iran published by Supreme

Commander's Staff) focused on historically important documents, especially from the recent past, reproducing many facsimiles. It was an official publication created by imperial *farman*. Of a more popular character was *Honar va Mardom* (Art and People), a richly illustrated monthly published under the auspices of the Ministry of Culture and Arts by Dr. Khodabandalu. The articles in it covered not only general subjects of cultural or historical interest but also folklore and dialects. More specialized studies of an ethnological and linguistic nature were the subject of a periodical named *Folklor,* under the editorship of 'Abdol Hosayn Nayyeri. The above list of journals is selective; many more periodicals published in Iran often contained valuable works of poetry and literature.

Mention should also be made of periodicals issued by religious communities, such as the Shi'ite journal in Arabic, *al-Hadi,* published in Qom; a Zoroastrian monthly, *Hukht;* and an Assyrian organ, *Ashur.* Important information of financial and economic facts were regularly given by the reports of the National Bank of Iran. Not less important were the economic statistics published by the Central Bank of Iran.

Good books have always been highly esteemed by Iranians and the art of printing had early entered their country. In the 1930s lithography *(chap-e sangi),* because of the cheaper reproduction, still prevailed over other printing methods. Even the Persian reading manuals were printed this way, having the advantage of being written in an attractive *nasta'liq* script developed by the Iranians from Arabic cursive script in the Middle Ages and thus providing an excellent calligraphic model for the students. Linotype machines were in those days found only in two or three newspaper offices in Tehran. It was noteworthy that even provincial towns had the ambition to print their own books and papers. In spite of the general trend toward centralization, towns like Isfahan, Shiraz, Tabriz, and Mashhad possessed and preserved their printing and publishing establishments. Provincial towns *(shahrestanha)* cultivated pride in their historical past. This local patriotism expressed itself in the multitude of books on the history of single towns and provinces, on Fars, Qom, Shiraz, Yazd, etc. There was a long tradition behind this, as attested by the fact that even the renowned history of literature compiled in post-Safavid time, the *Atashkadeh* (Firetemple), had been arranged alphabetically according to the names of towns, not of authors or titles. Many poets and scholars were generally known only by the name of their home town— Kazaruni, Qazvini, Razi, and so forth.

The pleasure that Orientals traditionally take in writing and calligraphy has not died out in Iran. Every year there have appeared new authors whose names, it is true, have usually fallen back into oblivion. In the postwar period the government published and supported an impressive number of serial publications which contained valuable new editions of old manuscripts, sometimes completely unknown before. A good example of this activity was provided by the University of Tehran Press *(Entesharat-e Daneshgah-e Tehran),* which published several thousands of volumes.[18] Many other books came from the press of the aforementioned *Bonyad-e Farhang-e Iran.* Noteworthy among them was a masterly work of scholarship, the *Loghatnameh* by Dehkhoda, a huge encyclopedia of Persian literature and history, the volumes of which continued to appear after its compiler's death under the editorship of a university-based team of writers.

Scientific and literary creativity is invariably linked with the existence of good libraries. There were in Iran valuable private libraries, but only the presence of well-stocked libraries accessible to the public could guarantee the success of literary and scholarly endeavors. As early as the Middle Ages there existed prominent libraries in Iran. In modern times this function has been exercised to some extent by the Parliament Library, pending the full activation of the National Library, which was still being organized in the postwar period. Rich bequests of internal and external organizations enabled the Parliament Library to become an important place for study and research, possessing a wealth of Iranian as well as European and American books and publications.

For their part, the universities, led by the University of Tehran, have provided their share of well-equipped libraries. On the other hand, real treasures of manuscripts and ancient prints are preserved in the library of the Astan-e Quds, the Holy Shrine at Mashhad.

Iran's national temper has been characterized by a proneness to quick response to ideas and events that sometimes borders on inflammability and excess of zeal, to be followed by frustration and cynicism. These characteristics have often been reflected in Iranian journalism. Many newspapers were started at one time or another, to face an early demise and oblivion as the circumstances changed. A widely read newspaper before the war was *Iran,* but it has long since ceased publication. In the postwar period the leading papers could be listed as *Ettela'at* (continuing its prewar tradition), *Kayhan,* and *Ayandagan.* In addition, two political party organs, *Iran-e Novin* and *Mardom,* enjoyed substantial circulation in the 1960s and the early 1970s as long as the parties they represented were in existence. Moreover, four foreign language newspapers, the English *Kayhan International* and the *Tehran Journal,* the French *Journal de Téhéran,* and the German *Die Post* (a weekly) catered to the needs of foreign communities in Iran. The level of professional journalism was considerably enhanced by the creation, on the initiative of Senator Dr. Mostafa Mesbahzadeh, president of the *Kayhan* organization, of the College of Communications (with its press, radio, television, and public relations sections), under the directorship of Dr. 'Ali Gholi Ardalan, former ambassador and foreign minister.

The Iranian press was subject to supervision by the Ministry of Information and Tourism *(Vezarat-e Ettela'at va Jahangardi)*. According to the directives of the Shah, the function of newspapers was to criticize within the framework of national interests, uncover and expose irregularities, and play their part in enlightening the public. As such the newspapers were not expected to function as an extension of the government's propaganda apparatus. Their role was clearly different. However, while positive criticism was welcome there was no room for foreign ideologies. Revelation of official secrets was punishable by military tribunals if it involved espionage or other offenses.

To sum up, journalism and journalists have tended to flourish in Iran. Writing books is always in vogue. Artistic printing is greatly appreciated. In a country of widespread illiteracy, the scribe and the scholar are much honored. Of these, in conformance with national tradition, poets have always enjoyed special prestige and distinction.

MUSEUMS, MONUMENTS, AND EXCAVATIONS

Because of the emphasis on modernization under Pahlavi rule, the authorities did not initially encourage interest in and studies of folklore and tribal customs, viewing them as backward and filled with superstition. With the passage of time, however, the growth of national self-confidence produced a change in these attitudes. In the postwar period, especially, much attention began to be paid to the museums dedicated to the preservation and enhancement of folk culture. A major role in this respect was played by the Ethnographic Museum *(Muze-ye Mardom Shenasi)* lodged in the old palace of Mukhtarussaltana and organized by a Hungarian ethnologist, Hannibal.

However, an undisputed place of honor was reserved for the Tehran Archaeological Museum *(Muze-ye Iran-e Bastan)*, designed and directed for many years by a French scholar, André Godard. Housed in a building reminiscent of the Parthian style, the museum gained considerable fame through its unique collection of pre-Islamic Iranian antiquities. It was continuously being enriched by additional exhibits from the excavations conducted by various archaeological expeditions.

In 1971, the year celebrating twenty-five centuries of the Iranian Empire, Mohammad Reza Shah opened another museum of Iranian history: the modern Shahyad Monument, straddling the main avenue that leads from the airport to the capital. As for the memorabilia of the Qajar era, they were concentrated in the Golestan Palace. Iran's high artistic culture was further propagated through the Museum of Decorative Arts and the Tehran Carpet Museum. Moreover, beginning with Reza Shah, the government had steadily supported annual exhibitions of Iran's industrial products and traditional crafts; these exhibitions grew in size and variety in the postwar era, proving a major attraction to Iranians and foreigners alike.

This brief account would be incomplete without mentioning the provincial museums. Foremost among these should be listed the Safavid Chehel Sotun Palace, in Isfahan, and the Muze-ye Pars, in Shiraz. Exhibits of the ancient East could be admired in Susa (Shush) and in the neighboring Haft Tappeh Museum, opened in the 1970s by the Empress. These museums and exhibits tended to enjoy considerable popularity among the local inhabitants, for whom visits to them became a favored pastime. Mention should also be made of the Holy Tomb of Fatima in Qom, converted to a museum by Reza Shah (reserved for Moslems only), and the Museum and Library of the Holy Threshold (rich in precious manuscripts) in Mashhad.

There were no official excavations undertaken by the Iranian government before the Pahlavi era. Clandestine diggings, made or instigated by greedy dealers of antiquities, continued to pose serious danger to legitimate archaeological research and the preservation of the ancestral heritage. Persepolis and Pasargadae in Fars and, already in the past century, Susa in Khuzistan, being famous residences of the Achaemenid kings, had been the object of European and American expeditions. Since the 1930s many new archaeological sites had been discovered.

After World War II, the Iranians themselves, often with the support of foreign specialists, began excavations with excellent results. This activity enjoyed the support of the imperial couple, who showed personal interest in the work of the various expeditions. A good antiquities law had put the excavation sites as well as the remains of medieval and later edifices under government protection. The Shahbanou in particular showed concern to preserve older buildings of secular character, insofar as they were characteristic of Iranian artistic skills or connected with Iranian history, that were threatened with demolition to make place for new streets. The haste with which, under Reza Shah, the gates of Tehran erected in Qajar times were sacrificed to modern traffic, and similar precipitate acts, were later regretted. Motivated by the new spirit of conservation, the authorities left intact one of the spectacular pigeon towers on the university grounds in Isfahan.

In the time of Reza Shah some famous sepulchers had been designated as national commemorative sites *(yadgah-e melli)*. This was notably the case with the tomb of the great poet Hafez at Shiraz, which was stripped of its pretentious iron fence from the era of Naser ad-Din, attractively landscaped, and provided with striking colonnades.

Reza Shah likewise ordered that a worthy monument should be erected for the great cosmographer Hamdollah Mostowfi Qazvini (eighth century A.H., or fourteenth century A.D.) at Qazvin. Instead of the original brickwork building a new cupola with green tiles was constructed in the surrounding garden.

Under Reza Shah the once paltry tomb of Sa'di *(Sa'diyya)* near Shiraz was replaced by a somewhat modernistic mausoleum situated in a superb garden. Also modernistic and inspired by European architecture was the peculiar tomb- or tower-like edifice in memory of the philosopher Avicenna (Ibn Sina) at Hamadan. Last but not least, Ferdowsi, master of the Iranian national epic, was honored with a grandiose monument at Tus near Mashhad, with a huge stone pedestal covered with verses from the *Shahnameh*. This monument was inaugurated by the old Shah on the occasion of the millenary of Ferdowsi internationally celebrated in 1934.

Pasargadae with the tomb of Cyrus the Great, where the celebrations of the twenty-fifth centenary festival were inaugurated in 1971, was provided with an extended grove of trees. Before the war one had to cross the Pulvar River on horseback to reach it; later it was made easily accessible from the main road linking Shiraz with Isfahan.

Another great national monument, the Achaemenid residence of Persepolis, was given its own administration, housed on the site and headed by an Iranian archaeologist. Under the supervision of this office a team of Italians, noted for their skill in restoration work, was engaged to preserve the venerable remainders of this grandiose site with its palaces.

In Chehel Sotun, the graceful palace of Shah 'Abbas and his Safavid successors, the Department of Antiquities *(Edareh-ye Bastanshenasi)* of the province of Isfahan carried out the costly work of restoration for a number of years. Another major project, the reconstruction of the Hasht Behesht Palace, was nearing completion in the 1970s. Most happily, the old Iranian art of tile mosaic *(kashitarashi),* seen on the cupolas and walls of the mosques, was being revived and assiduously cultivated in the restoration of these and other ancient buildings.

The religious sanctuaries, which could be entered by foreigners with special permission under Reza Shah, became closed to non-Moslem visitors after the war, with the exception of those mosques and shrines that had been registered as historical monuments, especially the ones in Isfahan and Shiraz. All other religious places were henceforth to be reserved exclusively for divine worship, the great mosques of Imam Reza at Mashhad and Fatima in Qom being conspicuous in this respect.

The manifold cultural activities supported by the state were placed under the jurisdiction of the High Council of Culture and Arts *(Showra-ye 'Ali-ye Farhang)* operating in conjunction with the Center of Research and Cultural Coordination. Composed of members distinguished in the arts and literature and of other prominent persons, the council, under the management of its secretary-general, Professor Zabihollah Safa, was also responsible for the development of dramatic art and music.

THEATER, ARTS AND MUSIC

Early plans under Reza Shah had called for the establishment of an opera. Except for the construction of a building on Tehran's Ferdowsi Avenue, the project never materialized. It was not until the late 1960s that a big concert and theater hall, the Talar-e Rudaki, was established. Before long the Rudaki Hall gained distinction for its excellent concerts and theatrical productions. After the war, the theater arts took a new and liberal turn. In the past, Iran knew only the Shi'ite passion plays *(ta'ziyeh)*, introduced in the Safavid epoch.[19] They were forbidden by Reza Shah because of their fanatical religious overtones. In the postwar period theatrical companies of a secular type sprang up in several places, most successfully in Isfahan. Many plays were translated from foreign languages. The popular preference was for comedies. From 1969 onwards the *Kargah e Namayesh,* an experimental theater workshop, operated in Tehran; its purpose was to promote young talent, to train actors, and to encourage playwrights.

Films have always had a great attraction for Iran's public. Especially popular were open-air performances, frequently in attractive garden settings. Most of the films were imported, especially from India and the United States. The first Iranian film writer had been a poet, 'Abdol Hosayn Spanta, a native of Isfahan. His *Dokhtar-e Lur* ("The Luri Girl") was the first Persian film produced in Iran; it brought great success to the author. Much criticism was directed against the importation of poor quality films, especially those of a pornographic character or that glorified violence. On the popular level this opposition was expressed in the destruction at Qom of a movie theater by a fanatical mob acting under the influence of *mollas.*

In the past, European music was little appreciated in the East. Naser ad-Din Shah is reported to have declared after a performance that what he had liked most was the tuning of the orchestra. This has changed radically. Along with Johann Sebastian Bach and the composers of the baroque, the Viennese classics and romantic composers have begun to appeal to Iranians long trained in a different tradition. The language of Islamic music (which has been essentially Iranian since Sassanid times) is based on a multitude of scales, many of them having quarter-tone steps, and on a polyrhythmic movement. But there is no harmony produced as a consonance of several voices, as is the way of Western music. One may call it linear music as against vertical music in the West, hence similar to the linear music of the ancient Greeks. For Europeans, music of this type is rather difficult to understand and learn. The ability of Iranian musicians to transcend these limitations commands respect. Among such "bilingual" musicians, Colonel 'Ali-Naqi Vaziri, director of the Tehran Conservatory of Music, achieved prominence. A master of the *tar*

(Iranian lute), he was also at home with European music. His major contribution was to compile a book of theory that described all the Iranian keys with their quarter-tones, in Western musical notation.[20] He also published his own compositions.

The phonograph record and tape recorder, radio, and television produced a revolution in the Iranian world of music. Bastardized music, oscillating between East and West, began to be heard more frequently. In the 1970s Tehran was being visited by foreign musicians several times a year; these included soloists, chamber music ensembles, and big orchestras led by renowned conductors. Although such performances were heavily patronized by Westerners resident in Iran, fashion and social pressures led many Iranians to attend as well. There was no doubt that this invasion of Western music threatened the survival of traditional Iranian music, unless conscious endeavors were made to preserve the old heritage.

In this context one should also mention a major role Iran began to play in the 1970s as host to artistic festivals and scholarly congresses. Of these, the annual Shiraz Art Festivals featuring films, drama, and dance gained fame as major international events under the patronage of Empress Farah. Similarly, Iran initiated the convocation of the first International Congress of Iranologists in 1966, to be followed by sponsorship of conferences and symposia on special subjects (such as the congress on Mithraicism in 1975).

CONCLUSION

On the basis of the foregoing review, we believe we have truly convincing evidence of the great strides in the field of education and culture that Iran has made during the Pahlavi era. This progress has been, in the first place, quantitative: the institutions of higher learning grew from one old-fashioned college to eight full-fledged modern universities with at least four others being planned or founded. The number of university students increased one hundredfold. A similarly impressive growth could be seen on the secondary and elementary levels of instruction, making education for the first time in Iran's history accessible to the masses. Equally impressive has been the record of the sustained struggle against illiteracy, particularly during the reign of the second Pahlavi ruler. There was also a healthy proliferation of institutions and activities dedicated to the promotion of culture in such fields as drama, music, the visual arts, archaeology, and ethnography.

But, beside the impressive statistics there was also a consistent striving for quality. This undoubtedly was a more subtle endeavor whose results could not be easily measured and where setbacks and slowdowns were apt to occur. The Shah, seconded by Empress Farah, was not only fully aware of the dangers of mediocrity in the educational field but actually took the lead, especially at the Ramsar conferences in the 1970s, in prodding the academic community to make the maximum possible effort to keep the standards of instruction high, to concentrate on teaching rather than profitable extracurricular activities, and to engage in original research.

One thing was certain: during the Pahlavi era Iran decisively broke away from the lethargy and backwardness of Qajar rule. Thanks to the persistent efforts of the government and the guidance of enlightened pioneers in modern education, Iranians were rediscovering their ancient heritage while aiming at the achievement of higher cultural levels.

It is perhaps appropriate to end this chapter by quoting Cyrus from Xenophon's *Cyropaedia* (7.5):

> If it is no small merit to acquire an empire, it is certainly much more important to remain in its possession. Whilst sometimes only courage was necessary to win the power, it was not possible without prudence and self-control, without courage and great care, to keep the gain.

9

The Literary Genres in Modern Iran

At the time Reza Khan, later Reza Shah, came to power, two seemingly unrelated events took place on the scene of Persian literature: the publication of a collection of short stories, *Yeki Bud, Yeki Nabud* ("Once Upon a Time"), by the novelist and essay writer Jamalzadeh; and the publication of a poem by Nima Yushij entitled *Afsaneh* ("Legend"). The significance of Reza Shah's takeover of the reins of the country as necessary in the establishment of a modern state is well understood in Iran as well as in the other countries of the world. The above-mentioned Persian publications, one in prose and one in poetry, must similarly be considered as a turning point in the establishment of a modern literary idiom in Iran.

Reza Shah, in order to set a new course, tried to break with the old system, which had not only forced a bankrupt Iran into economic and political dependence on foreign powers, but had kept her in ignorance and illiteracy. He knew that the half-measures applied to Iran during and after the Constitutional Revolution of 1905-1911 had not cured the illness of the nation and the country and that the only solution lay in applying drastic and decisive reformatory measures.

The publication of this collection of short stories by Jamalzadeh should be considered as the application of such a complete remedy to prose writing in Iran. As we shall see later, the prologue to *Once Upon a Time* should be considered not only as the literary manifesto of the author, but also as a Magna Carta for the written word in the Persian language.

The appearance of a poem written in free verse by Nima Yushij should be thought of as a point of departure from the centuries-old domination and despotic rule of *'aruz* (classical prosody) over Persian poetry. It is notable that these three events took place independently and at the same time without being in any way orchestrated. It was Iran's destiny.

All three—the statesman, the story writer, and the poet—were trying to find a way to discard certain values of the past that were hindering Iran's political, social, cultural, and literary development. At the same time, however, they were striving to preserve and if possible adapt some of the old values to the new circumstances of a society that, they hoped, was rapidly changing. The common goal of these three men was to build a new Iran with a better future but, at the same time, to preserve those still vital elements of the past. It is also notable that it took more than thirty years for the seeds sown by the three to fructify.

The question at stake was how to leap forward without destroying the internal equilibrium that had kept Iran alive for almost twenty-five centuries despite the constant inroads of enemies and migrating peoples descending upon the Iranian plateau from all corners. Even the most significant invasion of Iran—the Arab-Islamic conquest—could not wipe out the language of the country as it did elsewhere, but, on the contrary, it gave the old language a new vital infusion, saving it from stagnation. Later the Turks, Mongols, and Tartars became the patrons of Persian literature, from which they, in turn, derived the benefits. The court poets were coveted by competitive patrons who looked upon poets as their best public relations men.

Before we come to the discussion of the literature of Iran of the last fifty years, it is of vital importance to say a few words about the role that literature has played in Iran for centuries.

It is no exaggeration to say that there is a poet in every Iranian and that almost every Iranian is familiar with the great poetic tradition of his country to a degree that is rare among people of other cultures. In the long history of the Iranian nation, the language and its literary idiom have played a pivotal role around which the nation and the culture have revolved. Age-old values do find expression in poetry even in today's context. Poetry has been a reference system, a mirror of Iran's history and heroic myth, an expression of national identity. This is why, for example, despite the total commitment of Reza Shah and his son Mohammad Reza Shah to bring Iran into the community of the world's advanced modern nations, the Arabic script of the Persian language has not been replaced by the Latin one as has been the case with Turkish. Rather, the script has been actively safeguarded as an ongoing proof that the Persian language and the Persian literary corpus of modern times are connected to and descended from the great national literature of the past.

THE EARLIER PATTERNS

In this survey of Persian literature we shall concentrate on the last fifty years of its development, but for the sake of clarity we will draw some outlines of its development, especially during the years preceding the ascension to the throne of the Pahlavi dynasty. We will attempt to look at the three major genres of modern literature—poetry, prose and drama—with a special eye towards their similarities and interrelationships. Through this approach, the Persian literature of today can be judiciously and honestly evaluated as an expression of national artistic sensibilities.

The academic study of modern Persian literature suffers from a historical outlook inherited from the Arabic and Persian writers themselves and adopted by many contemporary scholars in the West as well. This will provide us with our second point of observation, an evolutionary one. The title of E.G. Browne's classic work, *A Literary History of Persia,* is indicative of a trend in analysis and literary criticism somewhat unfair to the work itself. Persian literature is there discussed as a linear history of genres and as a biographical history of its authors. To be sure, political and social considerations play a major role in this literature, and we will have occasion to examine historical as well as biographical data. However, since the sociopolitical setting is covered extensively by the other authors of this volume, we will limit our observations to a minimum. Indeed, to treat literature exclusively in its relation to history is to belittle individual creativity and deny any power of autonomous development to an art form that is, by definition, cumulative and derivative.

The accepted mode has been to divide modern Persian literature into three historical units: *(1)* the preconstitutional and constitutional periods, until the time of Reza Khan in 1921; *(2)* the period of Reza Shah; *(3)* the period beginning in 1941, when Mohammad Reza Shah ascended the throne. The fault does not lie in these chronological demarcations, as they are most operative, and we often will have recourse to them. The issue is the apparent disregard of a self-propelled literary development. Therefore, we will look at Persian literature within an important historical framework, as not only being influenced by and influencing history, but—with another eye to its natural and internal literary evolution—as far more than a radical reaction to outside stimuli.

In the middle and late decades of the nineteenth century, Iran was increasingly opened to Western economic expansion, and along with it came Western military realities, educational systems, and cultural influences. Teachers were recruited from Europe and, in addition to bringing Western education to Iran, influenced many Iranian students to study abroad. It has often been proposed that the return of these students (or their publications) from abroad was the impetus for the nationalistic and social yearnings of modern Iran. This is not surprising, as they were maturing in a European cultural milieu that reveled in the romantic expression and national determination exemplified by their musical contemporaries, Wagner and Verdi. A simple glance at the first works translated into Persian (excluding, of course, technical manuals) reveals the source of these students' rage at the shortcomings of their fatherland. They were enthralled by the romantic, patriotic and passionate heroes in the works of Dumas, Cervantes, Verne, and Hugo, by the drama of Molière, and by the poetry of Keats and Byron. They had a new goal for Iran. Comparing their new lives to the backward system dominating Iran, they were determined to effect reform. Their medium was the word.

Within this context, the need for a new form of expression became apparent. The translations of Western works, the plans of editors, and, in the mushrooming press, even the reporting of daily events required a new prose style; the verse of reform and social agitation also demanded a new poetic idiom. The reaction and resistance of the established literati and the public to those innovations gave the Persian language and its literary genres much of their modern direction.

In many respects, the creative concept of Islam in general, and of Iran in particular, had been governed by what has been termed a homeostatic dynamic, that is, an active refusal to innovate and an appreciation of the perfect paradigm of the past. Thus, throughout history, the movements of reform and innovation, whether religious, political, or social, have been the ones that looked to a purer and more illustrious past for their norms and directives. The arts are no exception to this rule. The goal of art, as was the goal of jurisprudence or government, was to reach the most perfect form possible. Having reached it, the goal was to copy it—to embellish it, but without intrinsic development—effectively stifling the creative urge.

Classical Persian poetry had long ago become a staid and rigid system. Once the perfect form seemed to have been attained, no new interpretations were tolerated; the 'aruz acquired a prestige demanding total obedience. The systems of the monorhyme, the semi-independent distich (bayt) consisting of two equally metered hemi-stichs (comparable in form and in execution to the heroic couplet in English), became the only accepted poetic vehicle. Poetic diction also solidified at the expense of ideas. The great fourteenth century Moslem thinker and social historian, Ibn Khaldun, discussed the importance of language (to poetry and prose):

> The ideas are secondary to the words. The words are basic . . . everyone may have ideas. . . . Speech is the mold for ideas. The vessels in which water is drawn from the sea may be of gold, silver, of shells, glass or clay. But the water is one and the same. In the same way, the quality of language, and the eloquence of its use, differ according to the different levels of execution in the composition of speech, depending on the manner in which an utterance conforms to what it wants to express. But the ideas are the same.[1]

While the harmonic and sonorous beauty of Persian poetry was maintained, its soul was exorcised. Image and emotional response were also conventionalized. For example, the cypress was a frozen metaphor for the slender delicacy of the beloved; or, the rose was a symbol for the ephemeral and transient nature of beauty and love. Both are indeed images of some power, but they came to have, as did thousands of other such images, this specific and invariable association, an association and interpretation whose understanding was imperative for either the composition or the comprehension of poetry. In short, the images of thirteenth-century Persian poetry, as well as its form, were not renovated until the turn of the twentieth century. When change did occur, it was not, as it is often portrayed, a sharp break with the past and the creation of a new literary outlook. On the contrary, there was a difficult and determined evolutionary transition, and although much of the poetry of the early decades of this century may now seem quite unimpressive, at the time it was innovative and vital.

We have seen that these poets, no longer absorbed in the "eternals" of the classical past, were motivated primarily by constitutional aspirations and desire for social reforms such as the emancipation of women. Their poetry reflected this; it was critical, satirical, and often oppressively didactic. The poetic idiom also began to change somewhat to serve its new master. While there was no overall reorientation of stylistic formalities (some attempted it, but theirs was a premature effort), the idea was elevated above the form. If there was a revolution in poetry in the twentieth century, this, then, was its essence: the ascendancy of theme and the relegation of form to a subsidiary position.

POETRY DURING THE PAHLAVI ERA

When Reza Khan came to power, the literary scene was divided into two general trends: the Modernists (*nowparastan*, literally "worshipers of the new") and the Conservatives (*kohneparastan*, "worshipers of the ancient"). Their positions and debates, essays and rebuttals were argued in the pages of the literary journals. The Modernists were those who felt an aversion to any of the classical elements of poetry, be they stylistic or thematic. They were concerned primarily with the destruction of the old literary order. Their poetry, emotional and personal to the point of obscurity, illustrated and demanded reform. The hard-line conservative position, and one that has not disappeared even today, was held by those educated men in all walks of life who continued to write in the rigid classical tradition.

A more moderate conservative reaction, and perhaps a more traditionally Iranian one, was the growing movement on the part of some poets to return to and emulate an older and purer poetic style. They saw an unavoidable correlation between the changes in Persian language and literature during their lifetime and the historical rebirth of Persian in Arabic script during the early centuries after Iran had been inundated by the Arab-Islamic conquests. Iranian-Persian literature had sprung up again in the ninth and tenth centuries in the eastern provinces of Khorasan; hence the stylistic title "Khorasani." This style reached its peak in the tenth- to eleventh-century epic of Ferdowsi, whose nationalism these men revered. Simultaneous with this rebirth of Persian language were their efforts to simplify and modernize Persian and especially to purge it of its abundant Arabic vocabulary. What is significant is that these "Returnists," adopting a simpler and more common language and holding steadfastly to the *'aruz* of the Khorasani style, were able to accept the modernist assertion of thematic superiority; it was precisely this combination that insured their ascendancy.

The Returnist Movement was actively encouraged and supported by the government of Reza Shah. They were the eloquent spokesmen for the folk-pride and patriotic affiliation that the government sought so earnestly to develop. The Returnist poetry, with its historical and epic allegory, its gentle social criticism and supportive calls for government-sponsored reforms, and its abuse of the foreign pressure on Iran, coincided with government design.

On a symbolic level, this poetry also reflected the current political milieu; it was new and innovative in conception, but still bound to traditional restraints and dogmatics. Its acknowledged master was Bahar.

Bahar (d. 1951) has been called the "father of modern Persian poetry," and in a very real sense this is a valid estimation. Bahar's personality and his superior literary output represented the beginning of poetry's independent development. Without his contribution, substantial change could not have developed from within. He was the guiding light of poetry and also the culmination of this movement to assimilate old form and new purpose. Bahar's neoclassical poetry, bound to Khorasani *'aruz,* is seldom adulterated by Western influence. The important element is content: "Bahar remained faithful until the end of his life to the classical poetic art (*'aruz*) as the external form. . . . In spite of this, Bahar is one of the greatest renovators of Iranian poetry. He attired new contents derived from the current life of the nation in a classical garb."[2] His were the most successful attempts at uniting modern notions and classical stylistics. In so doing, he was able to awaken emotion, by carefully calculated artistic means, to new and progressive ideas.

As a journalist and poet, Bahar was outspoken in his support of progressive elements in the country. He bitterly satirized both the government red tape and the religious institutions, and he condemned the growing cult of the West. "The fact that nearly every representation of nature is connected with reflexions and remarks on social and generally human themes is an original feature of Bahar."[3]

One of his primary objections regarded the radical Modernist Movement.

He saw nothing but detrimental effects to Iran in the present generation's turning away from its ancestral literary heritage. He condemned without hesitation those Modernists who would destroy the old in an undiscriminating fashion. He was angered because he believed that they had no design other than blind annihilation of everything from the "grand tradition" and an equally myopic imitation of everything Western. Though he wrote many essays and critiques, his most eloquent argument is his own poetry.

Bahar was one of the first poets in Persian literature to speak about his private life. In his poetry he portrays his family, his work, his associates, the atmosphere in his office, and the city he lives in, with its streets, public bathhouses, bazaars, mosques, squares, and people. He was also one of the first poets to introduce a simplified vocabulary and common expressions into his poetry.

Considering Bahar's poetry in chronological order, we observe his development from classical poetry in the strictest sense to the innovations here described. Even in his descriptions of nature, he gradually deviates from the classical convention and liberates himself from the bounds of traditional clichés.

F. Machalski observes that the break from the traditional conventional metaphors to new and original natural imagery of a more realistic kind appears in Bahar's poetry around the year 1922.[4] This is yet another manifestation of the very spirit of change enveloping all facets of Iranian life in the early 1920s that we have taken as a point of departure for this deliberation. This period, with its educational possibilities and broader cultural contacts, also created a more discerning literate class. As a result, poetry became more introspective and critical of its own aesthetics. The subject and, to a smaller extent, the form of poetry had changed, but the classical forms had retained their supremacy. It was during this period of incubation, compelled by government policies and by internal artistic concerns, that the ground was laid for formalistic readjustments.

NEGATION OF CLASSICAL FORMS: NIMA YUSHIJ

The revolution in Persian poetry evolved through arguments carried out by poets and critics within the confines of literary journals. Not since the literary journal appeared in Iran had it played so important a role. There always had been great, often pompous, discussions about the direction of poetry, and these included serious evaluation of the role played by the poet in society. But never before had it been used as an instrument of literary innovation. It was a development carried on within the belletristic world while the public was still absorbed in historical novels, neoclassical poetry, and a myriad of Western pulp translations. The first glimmer of this development was the publication, in 1921, of *Afsaneh* by Nima Yushij. Although roughly contemporary with Bahar's, Nima's poetry is, in a sense, derivative. The poetry of Nima Yushij unequivocally negates the classical form. However, without the transitional steps taken by Bahar and his followers—without their new hopes and new standards cast in established forms, and largely revived idioms—Nima's poetry would have been unacceptable. The earliest reformists combined new style with new themes. Experience of Europe had destroyed their faith in concepts they had been brought up to regard as eternal and divinely invariable. They simply rushed too quickly to overturn centuries of poetic tradition. That they essentially failed to create a new style is not surprising. They were productive contributors to the linguistic reform of Persian, but stylistic and formalistic modernization had to wait for another generation to develop these changes from within. The changes had to keep pace with the development of an appreciative audience. Their poetry had jumped ahead of what was to become its natural growth process; audiences found it often incomprehensible—and most horribly un-Iranian.

In the decade of the fifties the Modernists, who now had a clear theoretical orientation, a more organic approach to poetry, and a growing audience, successfully assailed the poetic bastions. Nima Yushij represents the beginning of this new, strictly Persian poetry and its release from theoretics. The magnitude of his contribution demands careful analysis.

Nima Yushij (d. 1959) was the pioneer of Persian free verse. During his early years as a journalist, he was a militant reformist and, like his associates, propagandized in didactic and patriotic journals for social and constitutional reform. His early poetry showed a strong predilection for the great Romantic poets; it is possible to interpret his later development in terms of the self-dissatisfaction of a Romantic artist. As the Romantic Movement in Europe destroyed the last vestiges of neoclassicism, so did Nima destroy the strongest and longest-surviving element of classical poetry: its form—meter and rhyme.

Nima realized that the traditional rhyming system, even when handled with the expertise of Bahar, was detrimental to the sense and the flow of ideas. It was an artificial and detractive element that demanded of the author a reorganization of his thought pattern and diction to fit a dysfunctional system. It was a development similar to the one that grew out of Romantic poetry in Europe. Nima represents this change within a Persian poetic tradition that was ready to accept it. One should not, however, condemn this seemingly simplistic evaluation of rhyme. Nima was concerned with the obligatory nature of a particular method of poetic construction. He did not abandon rhyme altogether; in fact, he realized that it can be an effective and desirable poetic device. His accomplishment was to show that the use of rhyme (or the lack of rhyme) to augment the purpose of the metaphor could be more effectively realized by a freer interpretation of style and with the abolition of rhyme as a compulsory element. Congruent with this idea, he was willing to accept as rhyme a much looser form of consonance and assonance than the classical *'aruz* demanded.

To this revolution of rhyme Nima added his attack on standardized rhythm which, like metaphor, had come to represent certain aspects of a poem. In much the same manner, he submitted that meter was indeed an important tool in the poet's repertoire, but that the strict classical meters, with their unyielding regularity, had to be altered to carry the new emotional expression of rhyme and theme. Nima understood the intrinsic connection between sound and sense. In his desire to give a new sound to the newer senses of Persian poetry, he saw the need to readjust the symbiotic elements of rhyme and rhythm commensurately. His poetry tried to convey the rhythmic and intonational diversity of life in the modern world. Thus, the new sense of unity between idea and emotion was maintained by means of the harmonic combination of images in common language with these new elements of sound. In Nima's own words:

> I try to impart meter and rhyme to Persian poetry. It is the traditional poem that is void of meter and rhyme, even though the opposite seems to be the case. But I believe that metrically a hemistich or a line cannot be a complete verse because it cannot reproduce the natural rhythms of speech. Rhyme acts as the organizer of the rhythm; it separates the melodious sentences; it is like the conductor of an orchestra.[5]

At the First Congress of Iranian Writers, Nima publicly argued his position as follows:

> In my free verse, rhyme and meter are another matter. The length of a hemistich is not determined by fancy or whim. My disorder has a kind of order. Each word is related to the rest according to a rule. It is more difficult to write in free verse than in classical.

> My suffering is the source of my poetry. Any poet should possess that source. It is for my suffering that I write. Form and diction, or rhyme and meter are only tools that I change to suit the expression of my suffering and the sufferings of others.[6]

MODERN FREE-VERSE POETS

Nima saw the restrictions of classical *'aruz* as limitations on creativity. His essays on this point contributed far more to poetic development than did his poetry, which is considered by some to be second-rate. Accordingly, we have chosen other examples of modern free-verse poets. In the following two stanzas from "Sad Love," by Faridun Tavallali, it is evident that metrical irregularity, staggered rhyme, and organized yet unconventional linear pattern all interact and emphasize the feeling and expression of the poet's solitude and desperation.

> Below the ancient plane
> That since so long ago,
> > Head lifted so,
> > Solitary
> > Stands in the plain
> > A lonely tree,
> Love, too worn out to weep
> > For Fate,
> Too sad, too desolate,
> > Love lies asleep.
> . . . .
> Anon out of the heart
> Of some black, lowering cloud
> > That caps a proud
> > Far mountain-head
> > Quick lightnings dark,
> > Sudden and red.
> From a dark corner bathed
> > In gloom
> A spirit from the tomb
> > Stirs, shadow-swathed.[7]

The purpose here is not to become involved in any complex textual analysis. A simple consideration of the words, "solitary," "Fate," and "gloom" indicates the complex of relationships that this poet has set up between the linear arrangement and the word itself. These words are so placed in each stanza as to define their inherent meanings as well as their relationships to the rest of the sentence. "Solitary" is isolated physically as well as conceptually from the rest of the stanza.

The following excerpts, from a long poem by Bamdad, epitomize the flowering sophistication of Persian free verse. Further—and for our purposes this is doubly fortunate—this very verse is used to discuss the responsibilities and motivations of the modern poet.

> . . . .
> The subject of
> > today's poetry is
> > > another thing . . .
> Today, poetry is the people's weapon
> For poets are branches from the same jungle forest

Not jasmine
Nor hyacinth of another man's garden.
Today's poet is not a stranger
He shares people's pains.
He smiles with people's lips,
He grafts people's hopes and aches
With his bones,
Today,
The poet
  Has to get dressed up
  Has to wear gleaming shoes
  Walking amidst the crowd
  He must pick
  His rhyme, meter, and subject
    (One by one, all with care all his own)
From the passers by in the street
"—Come with me, dear friend!
I have searched for you three full days
  Vagrant
  Everywhere!"
"—For me?
  I wonder
  Sir, maybe you have mistaken me for someone else."
. . . .
He writes poems,
Which means
He cries out the pain of his city and his country
Which means
With his song,
  He fortifies
    Tired souls.
He writes poems,
Which means
He fills the empty hearts
    With joy.
Which means
He awakens the eyes
    To the rising sun.
He writes poems,
Which means
He explains the pride
    Of men.
Which means
He recites
  The glory
    Of his time.[8]

The development of poetry within the last fifty years has been particularly hard to assess because all of the essential change has happened within the span of one lifetime. Most of the poets involved wrote with different motives and norms at different junctures in their personal lives and in the turbulent life of Iran, and although Modernist free verse became well established as an accepted form, the classical model of the Conservatives is still potent.

A good resource tool in this respect is the volume of poems collected by Forugh Farrokhzad, and recently edited and published as *Az Nima ta Ba'd* ("From Nima On").[9] It is an anthology of some 112 poems by thirteen modern poets. For the first time it brings together these artists and their work to be considered as a whole, not as individual masters. Beyond this, its special significance is that each chapter is introduced by that poet's own explanation of what his art means to him and his estimation of the role and future of poetry in modern Iran. It is rare that a poet is willing to commit himself to any serious prose analysis of his own work, and for that reason we have here reproduced excerpts from four of those introductory notes:

ATESHI (from the introduction to *Another Tune*)

I would like to say that my poems are my words. I express the most profound and deepest thoughts which arise from moments of solitude. I always try to relate stories about unknown lands, people and objects, from yet a different point of view. The problem is just that. Undoubtedly, people see and learn differently, and thus they describe what they see differently.

Some readers look for a special result or a specific purpose when reading a poem. They don't pay attention to the parts of the poem. The subject matter permeates the entire poem in each and every word. Every word is a flower which cannot be discarded without being smelled. But the whole idea is to contemplate life. One should look at everything, free his mind from abstruse logic and look across the horizon of knowledge and observe that life, like a pilgrim's caravan, is dispatched towards the aimless or purposeful Ka'bah which is the life and the permanence of humanity, and then paint that beautiful view.[10]

FORUGH FARROKHZAD (interview)

One of the reasons for indulgence in artistic work is the subconscious need to combat decadence. Artists are people who like life. They know life and death. Art is a kind of struggle for the preservation of "self." It is a kind of defiance of death. Sometimes, I think it is true that death is a law of nature, and that man feels weak and humble before that law. The problem is not soluble. One cannot even combat it. There is no use. That's the way it is. And it is good.

This, of course, may be a general and ridiculous explanation. Yet, poetry for me is like a friend to whom I can open my heart freely and easily. It is the complementary part of me. It satisfies me, it does not harm me. Most people cure their shortcomings by taking refuge with one another. But nothing can cure those shortcomings. If it could, wouldn't human relationship be the greatest poem ever told? Human relationship cannot be complete or complementary— especially in these times. Some people, however, try to get along and they lack nothing. For me, poetry is like a window. Whenever I approach that window, it automatically opens. I sit at its edge, I look out, sing out, cry out, and weep. I blend with the shadows of the trees. I know that beyond that window, there exists a space and there exists an individual who listens. He may come into being 200 years from now or may have existed 300 years ago. It doesn't really matter. That is the means by which I can relate to life and existence in its broadest sense. The advantage is that when one writes poems, he can assert: "I am" or "I was." Otherwise, how can one say: "I am" or "I was"?[11]

A. BAMDAD

Poetry is conceived in my subconscious, taking shape, maturing, and then falling as a ripe fruit. I never "plan" on what to write. I only feel the need for writing. I feel the need when a poem has "ripened" within me. If it has a rhyme and form, at the time of its picking, I write it in rhyme and form. Otherwise, I write it without any.

The whole idea revolves about this simple fact: I ought to be a trustworthy medium between my feelings and the reader. My poems should convey my feelings. I must not alter that message.

I am not an artisan who suffers only for his lot. My suffering is my life. My suffering is our lives. And that suffering suffices me. I am a medium between poetry and logic. My verses are slits through which you can sense strong sentiments. They describe a more hidden and a more organic life.[12]

FORUGH FARROKHZAD

When I want to talk about an alley that reeks with the odor of urine, I cannot list the names of perfumes and choose the best of these to describe that odor. That would be a vicious lie, both to myself and to others. One has to have, at least, some knowledge about his work. I didn't learn poetry from books, or else I would have been writing panegyric today. I learned it from life. As a child, lost in the forest, I turned in each direction looking at everything, contemplating it all, until I reached a spring in which I found myself.[13]

It is interesting to note that in this same volume devoted to the "New Wave," the poetry of Naderpour is included, despite his predilection for classical diction. In a sense, he represents an important link to the past, binding modern poetry to its great tradition. Such recent developments in poetry, if they can honestly be considered at such proximity, show a parallel development with Western counterparts in their abandonment and condemnation of modern systems, on the grounds that they are as restrictive as the older systems, and therefore no less odious.

The New Wave: Forugh Farrokhzad

The poets of the New Wave insist that while perseverance against the resurgence of classical norms must continue, poetry must free itself from all conscious norms. Nima was wrong, they contend, in attributing even minor importance to form and structure. They argue that the idea must be served by unencumbered expression. They are perhaps the final step in the modern artistic trend toward the expression of personal emotion freely and without conscious intent. They are the pure expressionists, shunning logical progression of ideas or intentional symbolic representation in favor of pure and uncensored personal communication. The poetess Farrokhzad, killed in an accident in 1967, stands at the beginning of and overshadows this movement of young poets:

. . . .

Dear Stars
Dear Cardboard Stars
When lies billow in the sky
Then how is it possible to rely on the surahs of
    disgraced prophets?
We, like corpses dead a thousand years, will gather together;
    and then
The Sun shall judge the rottenness of our dead bodies

. . . .

Fortunate corpses
Dejected corpses
Quiet and reflective corpses
Well-countenanced, well-dressed, well-fed corpses.
In the stations of certain times
And in the doubtful field of temporary lights
And the lust of buying the rotten fruits of vanity
Oh,
What people at the crossroad are looking for accidents
And the sound of the stop whistle
In the moment that a man must, must, must
    be smashed under the wheel of time
A man who is passing by the wet trees.[14]

The four volumes of her poetry, published before her death, provide us with a guide for analyzing Farrokhzad's development until just before her fatal accident. In her simple and clear poetic style, these poems reflect a transition, both personal and artistic; as for her, art was inextricably bound to personal growth. It is a movement of independence from the bonds of tradition to a yearning for and attainment of freedom, and, ultimately, to a new self and a purer art.

The titles of the collections alone indicate this progression: *The Prisoner, The Wall, The Revolt,* and *Another Birth* reflect a move, on the one hand, away from the restrictions of traditional poetry, and in this she is a close follower of the doctrines of Nima Yushij. The first two titles represent the poet's understanding and assessment of those bonds; the second two, the struggle against them and the emergence, from their destruction, of a new poetic form.

On a much deeper plane, however, it represents the struggle of the individual. In social life and in personal contacts, the soul is bound and baffled by appearances, never really grasping a complete truth. Taking her impetus from the classical mystic poets of Iran, she submits love as the means and the ultimate goal of escape:

> Yes, this is the beginning of love
>   though the path's end is not in sight.
> I no longer think about the end,
>   for 'loving' itself is beautiful.[15]

She takes many of her best images from the mystical repertoire, particularly in her use of light versus dark and her concentration on shadows (which is also influenced by Hedayat's treatment), but her most consistent appeal is to love, love that ranges from the contentment felt among the company of friends to the devotion of religious activity or the passion of human sensuality:

> Sin smiled in his two eyes,
>   upon his face the light of the moon.
> In the passage between his lips
>   an infinite flame smiled.
> Bashful and filled with dumb need
>   with a look tinged with intoxication
> I looked into his eyes. He said:
>   The crop of love should be harvested.[16]

Another Birth is Farrokhzad's personal as well as artistic climax. Faced with the inexplicable power of evil and ugliness, she fights to overcome the alienation, fear, and frustration portrayed in the poem "Couple," an alienation made all the more poignant by the intimacy of the physical situation:

> Night comes
> And after night, darkness.
> After darkness,
> Eyes.
> Hands.
> And breathing breathing breaths . . .
> And the sound of water
> Which falls deep, drop, by drop, by drop, from the tap.
> And then two red points
> Of two lit cigarettes.
> Tick-tock of the clock.
> And two hearts.
> And two lonelinesses.[17]

These poems are also her best mechanically. For as she becomes ready to accept a more limited goal than the understanding of perfect, universal love and union, so too does her poetry achieve a new understanding of itself. It is the most economical of all her works, yet at the same time the most precise and articulate. There is a reorientation, indeed, a rebirth toward a more possible and perhaps more important goal: the value of each image and experience in and of itself. In the poem from which this final volume takes its title, "Another Birth," she accepts the fleeting transience of all human experience and cherishes those experiences as the only possible glimpse of a more perfect love.

ANOTHER BIRTH

> My whole being is a dark chant
> which will carry you
> intoning you
> again and again in itself
> to the dawn of eternal blossoming and growth.
> I sighed you in this chant
> I sighed
> in this chant I grafted you
> to the tree to water to fire
>
> Life is perhaps
> a long street down which a woman goes every day
> with a basket
> life is perhaps
> the rope with which a man hangs himself from a bough
> life is perhaps a kid on his way home from school

Life is perhaps
lighting up a cigarette
in the drugged pause
before making love again
or the abstracted look of one passer-by
who doffs his hat to another passer-by
with a meaningless smile and a good-morning.

Life is perhaps
that blocked moment
when my gaze wrecks itself
in the pupils of your eyes
and in this there is a feeling
that I shall blend
with my understanding of the moon
my perception of the dark.

In a room the size of loneliness
my heart which is the size of love
looks at the simple pretexts of its happiness
at the fading beauty of flowers in a vase
at the sapling you planted
in our little garden
the canaries
which fill the window with their song.

This is my fate
this is my fate
a sky taken from me at the fall of a curtain
my fate is to go down a disused flight of stairs
and meet with something
amid alienation and decay.

My fate is to wander sadly in the garden of memory
to die in the sadness of a voice which tells me
"I love your hands" . . .

I shall plant my hands in the garden
I shall grow, I am sure, I am sure . . .
the swallows will lay eggs
between my ink-stained fingers
my ear-rings shall be
a pair of scarlet cherries
and I shall fasten dahlia-petals to my finger-nails.

There is a lane where
the boys who were in love with me
still with the same tousled hair
thin necks and legs

wonder about the simple smiles of a little girl
whom the wind one night
carried off.

There is a lane
which my heart has stolen from
the haunts of my childhood.

The journey of a form along a line of time
and the barren line of time
impregnated by the form
the form of conscious image
returning from being a guest
in a mirror.

And this is why
someone dies
someone lives on.

No pearl fisher will find a pearl
in a miserable little stream
which flows into a hollow.

I know a sad little fairy
who lives in an ocean
and who plays her heart out
into a wooden flute
softly, gently,
a sad little fairy
who dies from a kiss each night
and is born with a kiss each dawn.[18]

MODERN PROSE: THE NOVEL

While the partisans of one poetic tradition, to debate the direction of poesy
and defend the validity of their own position, summon those of others to
combat on the pages of the numerous literary periodicals, the partisans of
prose have won their battle, and the Iranian reading public is enjoying the
fruits.

During the upheaval of the constitutional period, which provided much of
the impetus for change in the poetic tradition, prose was introduced in great
quantity from the West. Prose writing was not unknown in Iran, but in the
previous centuries it had been limited to the fields of theology, philosophy,
and history, or to short moralistic and anecdotal fables. Moreover, the most
admired form of that prose was a style that included metered and rhymed

elements. This rhymed prose, *saj'*, is an illustration of the strong hold poetic *'aruz* had on all artistic sensibilities. Even so, it was restricted primarily to history, and there was no tradition of creative fiction. The introduction of the latter was received on the one hand by an eager public conscious of its entertainment value, and on the other hand, by sharply critical conservative literati who felt responsible, as defenders of the old faith, to be a bulwark against its contaminating influence.

Classical prosody had become an ornate but empty husk—convoluted, obscure, and incomprehensible to those uninitiated in its intricacies. As in poetry, rhetorical consideration had become the object, the goal rather than the vehicle. Laudable according to the standards of Ibn Khaldun, this situation was an unacceptable tool for translating into Persian the great Western prose works with which the young generation had come in contact. Luckily, and due largely to the journalistic efforts of their predecessors and the requirements of a prose idiom for technical purposes, they had an adequate foundation. By the time of the constitutional period, many of the epic and romantic novels of the nineteenth century had been translated with a fair degree of competence.

There were, however, severe internal problems with original prose works— problems more significant than opposition to them by the literary establishment. While a purely prose idiom was still evolving and indirect, complex, logical narrative patterns were still ingrained, most attempts at longer works were aesthetically unsuccessful. Original Persian novels were unpalatable to the Western tastes they were imitating. Adventure was staid, love had no fervor, and patriotism was of a mundane nature. The writers of prose fiction had chosen the historical novel as the vehicle for their social and political comments, but these drawbacks rendered their writing sterile. Part of the problem lay in the nature of their attempts: loath or unable to be really bold, enamored with the historical-romantic novels of the Dumases, Hugo, and Verne, they adopted a form that was beyond the capacities of their fledgling talents.

One of the best and most successful of these attempts was Badi's *An Old Legend or the History of Cyrus.* Having studied Achaemenid history in Western sources, his novel is historically accurate, which in itself was an innovative accomplishment. More than that, through this honest but glorified adventure, set in an Iranian golden age, he hoped to elicit a subliminal patriotic identification, and with it to develop a nascent national pride. Badi' stands above others of this period, such as Zaynal-Abedin Mo'taman and Kamal, through his relatively deep characterization and the unification of plot that he managed to produce.

In contrast, *The Heroes of Tangestan* by Hosayn Roknzadeh Adamiyat can by no standards be called creative literature or even competently composed.

What it is, however, is a strong patriotic statement couched in a narrative that deals with an uprising against the British and Russian occupation of Iran during World War I. The prose is overbearing and unimaginative. The narrative is often interrupted with long and dry excerpts from official documents. It was critically acclaimed, nonetheless, for its allegorical condemnation of England and for its suspicion of European influences in Iran.

MODERN PROSE: THE SHORT STORY

By far the most vibrant genre of modern Persian prose, the one in which issues and art are equally served, is the short story. There are exceptions, and a work like *Aku Khanom's Husband* by 'Ali Mohammed Afghani proves that as a form of art, as a form of social criticism, and as a vehicle for naturalistic expression, the novel has an important future. But the truly great Persian prose works to date have been the short story and the novella.

In the short story, the Persian author found his reprieve from keeping up the suspense or the dialogue and from the stringencies of developmental plot and characterization. He could make powerful use of stereotypical characters and common institutions, particularly in satires, without belaboring them or being required to examine them more closely. The author need only provide minimal plot and significant, effective, terse dialogue. Indeed, one of the greatest advances in modern Persian prose, and incidentally drama, is the adoption of colloquial and socially distinctive dialogue. However, given the skill and the impetus, deep characterization and psychological motivations were also accommodated. Stylistically, the short, straightforward syntax, prized by the journalistic reformers of prose, was of perfect adaptability for the short story.

The Persian short story, particularly in the twenties and thirties, should not be isolated from the world scene, as it owes most of its development to the short stories and novellas of the West. The interwar decades, when Jamalzadeh, who was educated in the West, was publishing, and Hedayat was a student in France, was the period par excellence of the short story; Hemingway, Fitzgerald, Maugham, and Sartre were its demigods.

Jamalzadeh

Within this world literary scene, the publication in 1921 of the first book of Jamalzadeh's stories, *Once Upon a Time,* was of minor import. Within the literate circles of Iran it was a revolution and an abomination. Jamalzadeh was educated in the European tradition. Schooled as a boy in the French Academy in Beirut and then in France and Switzerland, he grew up with the literature of the West. The effect of his great appreciation and understanding of prose is evident in his style and in the tasks to which he addresses himself. The conclusion of World War I prompted his move to Berlin, in many respects a portent of Iran's changing political affections, which were now veering from France to Germany. There he worked on a progressive Persian publication and wrote the six stories that comprise the first volume of *Once Upon a Time.*

With a strong background in history and social science, and gifted with acute literary perception, he was able to elevate Persian prose from the historical and the pedantic to the universal and humorous. This small volume of stories represents the first artistically successful attempt at social comment in Persian prose. The fact that it elicited such anger and hostility—directed toward its author as well—testifies to the convincing nature of its accusations. Biting critical satire and abuse are not met with hostility if their accusations are spurious and their method unsuccessful. Jamalzadeh portrayed not simply the corrupt religious and governmental systems; they had been condemned and satirized before. The rights of women and the need for social reform had also long been topics of critical poetry and historical novels. Rather, he interpreted these signs in contemporary life as indications of a decayed system and condemned the men who propagated them. As a "tenacious militant" and malcontent, he opened the floodgates to the Persian short story as an artistic and effective tool. Jamalzadeh's style is an extricable element of his design. He discusses current injustices in current and lucid language. While he treats his themes as ominous obstacles in the path of Iranian progress, his salvation from the deeply depressing and the moribund is his superb manipulation of Iranian humor, especially his flair for hyperbolic descriptions and caricatures of the common life.

As a novelist and essayist, the figure of Jamalzadeh also requires serious examination. His most prolific literary productions are novels, novels that are witty, philosophical, and deal with the same social ills and cultural stagnation as do his short stories. But it is those few stories that captured the spirit of the Persian audience and the talents of its future authors. *Once Upon a Time* had to overcome sincere opposition from the established religious, government, and belletristic circles, but it guaranteed, by the very nature of that opposition, the survival of literary prose and the supremacy of the short story. In his own essay introducing *Once Upon a Time,* Jamalzadeh discusses his feelings toward the future of prose. He argues that as well as being informative and entertaining, prose is the natural mode of expression of progress and democracy. Prose, he maintains in a prescient manner, is the future of Iran, because the tradition-bound writer

when he takes pen in hand, is interested only in the opinion of a group of literary scholars and ignores those who have the ability only to read simple writing, unadorned with difficult embellishments. Our writers do not accept the principle of literary democracy. There is no doubt that this condition is extremely regrettable, particularly in a country like Iran where the ignorance of the majority of the people is the main obstacle in the way of progress.[19]

Jamalzadeh's opposition to conservatism in government and in literature assured his canonization as the guiding spirit for the next generation of Persian writers who felt an impulse toward fiction, a generation whose pinnacle was Sadeq Hedayat.

Sadeq Hedayat

In many respects, Hedayat represents the confluence of foreign influence and the evolution of Iranian prose. The language was by this time more malleable, the audience more aware and receptive. The personality, goals, and yearnings of Hedayat, influenced by European standards between the wars, were nonetheless characteristically Iranian.

Hedayat was born in 1903 in Tehran, and being from a well-placed and affluent family, was sent to study abroad. It was in Paris that, after having considered numerous scientific and academic professions, he committed himself to writing. It is abundantly clear that Hedayat was involved in the artistic realities of the post-World War I period in Europe and America. Perhaps, after a trial-and-error period, he would have gravitated to the short story in any event, but from the outset he showed a decided predilection for it. The prose works of Stefan Zweig, Poe, Maupassant, Chekhov, and contemporary philosophers captured his imagination. Having the social sensitivities of Iranian art as a heritage, and having adopted the educated convictions of Sartre and of Kafka, whose "In the Penal Colony" he translated into Persian with extensive notes, Hedayat was confronted with existential torment.

Throughout Hedayat's work, one can follow the thread of his obsession with man's veiled search, culminating in his despair at his unfulfilled yearnings in the face of an absurd universe. The subverting of temporal and spatial time and plot in his novella, *The Blind Owl,* creates a surreal atmosphere in which the allegorically unenlightened, unseeing owl (an animal of human wisdom in Persian) searches, questions, and entreats, only to discover terror and frenzy with the realization that he will find only silence. From *The Blind Owl:*

Generally speaking, it is ordinary stupid conduct that makes one laugh, but this laughter of mine arose from a deeper cause. The vast stupidity that I saw before me was a part of the general inability of mankind to unravel the central problems of existence, and that thing, which was shrouded in impenetrable darkness, was a gesture of death itself.[20]

It is this lack of chronological plot that has often relegated some of Hedayat's less penetrating works to second-class status, but when he is at his best, plot is irrelevant. Like contemporary Western writers, Hedayat is concerned with the psychological implications of man's existence and of his interactions with his fellows. He probes constantly into the unseen forces that govern life's unrelieved misery, irrespective of social class, and finds them, for the most part, malevolent. This was, unfortunately, his final conclusion, one he seemed constantly striving to overturn by wit, by satire, and by serious discussion. It was this conclusion of the silent and malign which he could not bear. In the end, addicted to opium and alcohol, he yielded to the only possible release from the unresolved dilemma of Kafka: he committed suicide, alone, in a hotel room in Paris in 1951.

There are sores which slowly erode the mind in solitude like a kind of canker....

It is impossible to convey a just idea of the agony which this disease can inflict. . . . Relief from it is to be found only in the oblivion brought about by wine and in the artificial sleep induced by opium and similar narcotics. Alas, the effects of such medicines are only temporary. After a certain point, instead of alleviating the pain, they only intensify it. . . . The solitude that surrounded me was like the deep, dense night of eternity. That night of dense, clinging, contagious darkness which awaits the moment when it will descend upon silent cities full of dreams of lust and rancour.

Only death does not lie. The presence of death annihilates all superstitions. We are the children of death and it is death that rescues us from the deceptions of life. In the midst of life he calls us and summons us to him.[21]

In the stories themselves, Hedayat displays two basic and specifically Iranian trends that are central to understanding his complex personality. For his whole life, Hedayat was an ardent patriot. He was an expert on Persian folklore, which he studied on grants from the Reza Shah government, and his writing is full of the expressions and reflections of folk culture. During the great nationalistic projects of the thirties, he set about collecting folk tales and songs from rural Iran. He studied Sassanian history (itself an action of Irano-nationalism) and gained such a degree of competence in Middle Persian that he translated a few Sassanian texts into Modern Persian. This love for Iran and for her heritage is an important element in his work. We are constantly confronted with the displaced Iranian adrift in the West as an allegory of the eternal conflict of East and West, a conflict which he was also subject to.

Tied to this love for the land and its history of greatness was an indelible love for the people. As had the Naturalists of the West, Hedayat abandons the upper classes of Iranian society as sources for his material and turns instead to the seamy elements of Iranian street life. His stories are of the gutters and slums as well as of the students and minor officials. His characters include: the slang-speaking, boisterous mule attendant, or laborer, who is a local hero among the poor by virtue of his bullish strength; the brooding scullery maid; and the sullen streetwalker, to whom the measure of a man's love is the stoutness of the blows with which he pummels her. This full, well-developed psychological insight into urban low life might have engendered in him the aloof and simon-pure attitudes of the Western-educated intellectual or literate bourgeoisie, but it did not. It was his affection and compassionate response, borne out by his undeniable technical skill, that allowed him to revel gently in his compatriots' daily disappointments, while he was rejecting life itself. Ironically, that consumptive weakness of compassion, which makes his literature truly great, must have made even more painful his alienation and his anguish over the realization of human frailty and the futility of hope. Hope abandoned as a causal motive for life, suicide is inevitable. Again, from *The Blind Owl:*

> As I look into the mirror I said to myself. "Your pain is so profound that it has settled in the depths of your eyes . . . and if you weep the tears will come from the very depths of your eyes or they will not come at all." Then I said, "You are a fool. Why don't you put an end to yourself here and now? What are you waiting for? What have you to hope for now?"[22]

With Hedayat, Persian prose at last earned a place in the body of world literature. He was a universal writer, and the Persian author of today is subject to the influences of the modern literary ethos and modern artistic alienation simply by reading Hedayat's works. Despite the unevenness of his work, he has compelled Iranian authors to look further than politics and sociology without abandoning them, and he has compelled recognition by the world community of the universal capacities of Persian prose. He has acquired, in our view, status as the most important Iranian author of the twentieth century. He followed a young and militant movement, but it was the work of Hedayat that signaled the victory of prose in the face of serious claims that Persian had no merit when used to adorn nonpoetic expression. In a sense, this ascension of prose finally brought Iran out of the old oral tradition into the written.

Sadeq Chubak

One of the short story writers who represents the new tradition is Sadeq Chubak. His brief sentences paint pictures with the skill and perfection of detail of the Persian miniaturist. Every word is designed to bring about a unified effect. He presents a story from an angle that both limits and illuminates the action. Although Chubak is a follower of Hedayat, his own style differs from that of Hedayat, who intertwined personal confessions with character development. Chubak's stories are made up of characters who act in a total physical, social, and psychological setting, and though he stresses only the aspects of his characters that the situation requires, they are as real as the ones of flesh and blood we meet daily. To illustrate social problems, Chubak lets events follow their own course; thus the story develops its own outcome internally. He strips characters of their moral, religious, and social pretensions, exposing their instinctual lives by introducing speech patterns used by all classes throughout Iran.

Chubak brings his characters to life by what in modern terms might be called an accompanying sound track. Hedayat and Jamalzadeh also employed the language of the streets, but with Chubak this becomes an artistic means of reproducing realistic pictures of the Iranian locale and people. Reaching down into the meanest levels of society, he utilizes the phonology and grammar of the common people to confront the reader face to face with the universality of the human struggle. He reproduces the "language of the people" with such vigor that, despite his sensitive and often poetic prose style, he seems sometimes aggressive and vulgarly obscene. However, Chubak's exploitation of crude and explosively offensive language is an integral part of his own interpretation of the human condition.

"The Hubcap Thief" is a very short story. It is like a snapshot of an event, but it has a distressing emotional and intellectual impact. It proceeds single-mindedly to its climax unencumbered by compound sentences, peripheral descriptions, or inconsequential dialogue. Chubak has exploited here certain common social stereotypes and colloquial language, triggering predetermined images and emotional reactions that render lengthy exposition unnecessary. A full range of stock characters and behavioral patterns of varying complexity are thus utilized in a matter of sentences.

The Hubcap Thief

They caught the thief while he was loosening the second hubcap. One hubcap was hidden under his arm. He was struggling to pry loose the second with a screwdriver, when a vicious blow on the head threw him to the ground. A kick in the side sent a sharp pain through his stomach and blurred his vision; he retched and pissed on himself.

A crowd gathered around him. The hubcap fell from under his arm, rolled on the ground, and settled a few feet away. Someone took him by the arms and pulled him to his feet. His hands were still clutching his stomach. He couldn't stand straight. Another heavy blow on the head, followed by several slaps, again flung him to the ground. His face was contorted with pain and tears. He was convulsed in agony. He was thirteen and barefoot.

A shiny black Cadillac slept like a churchyard beetle in the midst of the crowd, not giving a damn that its hubcap had been wrenched off. And the little boy, like a swatted fly, encircled by the web of afflicted, sick legs around him, was writhing about. The sinister, bitter words that reached his ear only increased his pain.

"You m. . . . .f. . . .! Stealing—and in broad daylight at that!"

"Then it must have been you who swiped our pitcher the other day!"

"Well, tell me, who the hell ever led you to this neighborhood?"

"And a few days ago a bowl was stolen from our house."

"Nobody can remember petty thievery going on in this street."

"Now whose car is it anyway?"

"The car? Don't you recognize it? It belongs to Mr. Haji Ahmad, the chief of the butchers union."

"Well, let's call the cop."

"There's no cop around. Let's take him to the precinct ourselves."

"When they throw him in jail and he rots there, he won't take a fancy to stealing anymore."

The thief's tongue had dried up in his mouth. He felt as though a heavy load had fallen on him and he was unable to move from under it. Again, somebody grabbed hold of his shoulders, pulled him up, and spat in his face, shouting:

"Tell me, who the hell led you to this neighborhood?"

He was a bulky man with glaring eyes and open collar and a rough unshaven beard that seemed to have coagulated on his skin.

The little boy wanted to straighten up, but his legs kept giving way. Each time, the ground seemed to disappear from under his feet. The pain was exasperating him. Struggling between convulsions, he finally managed to say:

"In the name of the Hidden Imam don't hit me. I'm poor."

Again they beat him, punched him, kicked him, and covered his face with spit. He tried to protect his body with his hands, but it was impossible to cover it all. A groan died at the base of his throat, blood oozed out of his mouth and nose, mixing with his tears.

"Now let's call the hajji himself to let the kid have just what he deserves."

This suggestion came from a passing fruit vendor who knew the hajji well. He spat on the ground and sneered.

They knocked, and the hajji came to the door in his floppy, sweat-stained undershirt and underpants. He looked like a peasant. He was bald. The bags under his eyes were like saddlebags swollen with wrinkles. His belly was bloated. His little son, dressed up as an American cowboy, pistol in hand, appeared on the doorstep in front of his father. He peered at the crowd with curious eyes while leaning against his father. He was about the same age as the young boy who, clutching his stomach, writhed in agony—blood and tears mixing into one.

The mob made way for the hajji to walk up to the little boy who was clutching his belly and whose blood and urine had soaked the pavement. On reaching him a kick in the crotch was dealt by the hajji that left the boy gasping for breath, his face blue, and body in spasms.

"He's pretending to be dead."

"He's got seven lives, like a dog."

"If they'd just hang one of them, we wouldn't have any more thieves."

"They should cut off his hand and put it in hot oil. And now he's playing dead."

The little boy was hunched up on the ground, blood and froth oozing out of the corner of his mouth onto the pavement glistening and warm with blood and piss.[23]

Certainly, various stylistic elements of "The Hubcap Thief," as well as its social comment and overall artistic merit, survive well in translation. What is not translatable, and this is lamentable, is the intricate counterplay between the lyric and the macabre, the poetic and the horrible, which is decidedly Chubak.

In Chubak, prose strives for poetic expression; like poetry, it is meant to be read aloud, not from the page. His control of language is strict and precise, caressing and pampering the reader only to bring him to a surprising and dissonant climax. The effect is startling, for it is the music of the pastoral and of the lover applied to the squalor of a child, beaten and reviled, dying in a pool of blood and urine; and it is precisely this ecstatic lyricism put to the service of the terrifying that, while allowing him to remain personally uninvolved, is Chubak's most effective and distinctive mark.

Most of Chubak's short stories deal with this kind of "slice-of-life" situation; they include vignettes not only of human life, but of animals as well.

Although the literary content, symbolism, and setting of Chubak's stories may be characterized as Iranian, they never lose their universal appeal. Whether he is utilizing a tightly plotted story, a story employing a specific Iranian locale, or a story with a surprise ending, one discerns, in the end, Chubak's compulsion to say something significant.

Chubak lives in a revolutionary period in Iranian history, one in which traditional values are breaking down and there is a corresponding search for new ones. In his trust and hope in the ultimate victory of good over evil, he is the opposite of Hedayat. Even when he describes life at its most depressing, we sense a very strong subcurrent of optimism. When this optimism is not readily visible, the reader is at least offered a sense of human dignity, and he is invited to replace ugliness with the beautiful.

It is not only by analogy with the title that we can compare "The Hubcap Thief" with Vittorio De Sica's film, *The Bicycle Thief,* and the postwar neorealism of Italian cinematography. Chubak's treatment of segments of human life has the power of observation of the zoom lens, and his short-sentence technique the impact of the use of black-and-white film.

We have spent a great deal of space discussing the last fifty years of prose development, from the historical novel—a basically European genre in

Persian dress—to a body of literature that is a vital and important segment of the Iranian artistic constellation. Quite aptly, this period extending from Jamalzadeh and his followers until today has been termed the "Age of Prose"; it has been adopted and assimilated and has matured in the last five decades. It fought with poetry for its existence as a valid art form, and has now equaled it in expression and popularity. The great stress on universal literacy during this period is equally as important, for the development of a specifically Iranian prose required a literate Iranian audience.

THE DRAMA

Until now, we have conscientiously avoided the topic of drama. The reasons for our trepidation in discussing drama revolve around the deceptively simple assertion by students of Persian that there was no dramatic tradition in Iran previous to this century, and that it is only in the last fifteen years that any plays of literary significance have been penned and produced. On the surface this thesis is quite correct: there is no established corpus of Persian creative drama. Even Goethe, the great admirer of Persian literature, regrets that there is no Persian drama to match the Persian epics and lyrics.[24] But one cannot reduce the *ta'ziyeh-khani* of Iran to such a negligible position in such an offhanded manner. The *ta'ziyeh* is the only indigenous drama by the world of Islam; it is ritual theater, and derives its form and content from deep-rooted religious traditions. But although it is Islamic in appearance, it is strongly Persian, drawing vital inspiration from its special political and cultural heritage. Its genius is that it combines immediacy and flexibility with universality. Uniting rural folk art with urban, royal entertainment, it admits no barriers between the archetype and the human, the wealthy and the poor, the sophisticated and the simple, the spectator and the actor. Each participates with and enriches the other.

This epic passion play of Iran had prepared a public to deal with modern drama. In some of its aspects, it represents the early English-Latin "mystery" and "miracle" cycles, from which modern Western drama evolved. Indeed, by the end of the nineteenth century it was on the brink of giving birth to a secular Iranian theater. This does not mean that the religious theater would have disappeared; rather, it would have paralleled the newly emerged secular theater, grown from the *ta'ziyeh*. Unfortunately, the native intellectual elite that had resisted other Western-motivated innovations in literature joined in the campaign against the *ta'ziyeh* as merely a backward and superstition-ridden ritual. The production of Western-style dramas was encouraged and praised by the whole spectrum of the literate public as well as by the government. However, their superficial understanding of the forms and situations of Western drama, and their ignorance of the technique of its inner workings, rendered their attempts critically poor, while at the same time blinding them to the high drama and pure comedy contained within the *ta'ziyeh*. The dramatic climax of the Passion itself was to them less noble than the passions of Western tragedies. They seem to have misunderstood the cathartic effect of the mounting climax that is consummated by the martyrdom of Hussein, a climax heightened all the more by an audience involvement that ranges from wailing to self-mutilation.

The 1960s saw the beginning of new and serious research that was crowned with a symposium on the *ta'ziyeh* during the 1976 Shiraz Arts Festival. Perhaps the contemporary fashion of producing the *ta'ziyeh* as a strictly secular dramatic piece has helped to uncover some of its strange significance, for it is in this period that secular Persian drama has matured into a potent and appreciable artistic genre. Significantly, Iranian participation in the worldwide dramatic movement toward impromptu and unpremeditated dramatic form has initiated a revival of the *ruhowzi*.

The *ruhowzi* is a type of folk drama, staged in private parties and festivals. Using certain stock farcical characters, the actors improvise upon current local gossip, historical or political events, and Iranian lifestyles in general. It was with the notion that this nostalgic revival of the *ruhowzi* would provide a fresh impetus to the world avant-garde theater that it was included in the Shiraz Arts Festival in 1974.

The great popularity of radio programs and plays, begun in the fifties, has given a new dimension to the dramatic arts in Iran. Complex plot and perception of insight have no part in radio drama, where, on the contrary, humor, farce, and the maudlin abound. It is radio, and later television, that have had the greatest possible popular access and appeal. Thus, it was only in the 1960s, with the creation of drama schools by the Ministry of Fine Arts, the proliferation of theaters, and the establishment of the Shiraz Arts Festival (which in 1976 celebrated its tenth anniversary) that drama was free to explore its own directions.

Dramatic style in Iran has masterminded one of the major innovations of all Persian writing. Drama has been the forerunner in adapting colloquial speech and its phonetic spelling to literary expression. Original Persian comedy, written as far back as the late twenties, has attempted to portray people speaking as they do in daily intercourse. Its influences are everywhere. Phonetic colloquial dialogue is used in fiction as well as in poetry and has been advanced to the stage where even regional and class distinctions are discernible and are used skillfully in the service of characterization. It seems clear, moreover, that the theater was a natural breeding ground for this development. It is essentially an aural innovation, one that is meant to be heard, and while it can be effective in a text, it is more so on stage. The adoption of this style by the other genres on such a large scale, with its universal appeal, is an internal development that is just now reaching its peak.

CONTINUITY AND CHANGE

Throughout this discussion we have tried to maintain the attitude of the literary critic and analyst rather than the historian, and we have tried to argue for a strong element of native direction, particularly in the last thirty years, guiding the trends of Persian literature.

Certainly, contact with Europe was essential, but contact with Europe alone did not initiate literary change. Rather, it was the reaction of those Iranian students to what and how European artistic and national ideals were saying by inference about their homeland, where feudalism was just then entering its death throes—a social and economic feudalism that sustained itself by class immobility, religious intransigence, and economic repression, reflected in a literature that had canonized its own rigidity. Unable to manipulate political and social forces for change, the pen was their only weapon. They immediately discovered, however, that a new literate social order required a new literary idiom, and they were determined to create one. Tied as they were to their past, they molded not from nothing but from what was at hand.

Of critical pertinence was the realization that purely social and patriotic themes were important, but that they severely limited the elaboration of universal literary themes. This realization of an artistic responsibility as well as a social one, which arose in the twenties and is reflected in the literary debate, is the jump that brought Iran into the modern literary fold. The literary forms had themselves evolved to a point from which greater sophistication was unattainable without their internal evolution and readjustment.

Furthermore, once exposed to new possibilities and types of stylistic devices and contrivances, the Iranian authors, through painstaking elimination and alteration, evolved styles that today are both independent and self-determined, and share rather than follow international direction. Contemporary poetry has developed, paralleling the poetry of the rest of the world, as has the contemporary short story. While both participate in a literary aesthetic that transcends national boundaries, their development and their expression is unquestionably Persian.

As a closing note, in order not to close, it is necessary to emphasize that our discussion represents an early and perhaps premature analysis of an ongoing and vital literature. Persian literature is a living and constantly changing entity, unlike its late-medieval ancestor, which was stagnant and obtuse. However, the strong pivotal connection to that ancestor is kept alive through poetry no matter how modern. There remains, amidst great contemporary short stories and plays, a national passion for the poetry and its centuries-long tradition. The works of the old and the new masters are treasured and recited daily in streets, homes, and teahouses, as well as on the Iranian radio and television, against musical backgrounds. With the spread of the transistor radio, literary programs and poetry recitations are savored as much by country peasants as by the most sophisticated residents of the capital. The quantity and quality of radio-disseminated poetry is not only remarkable, it is without parallel anywhere else in the world.

Each morning before he goes off to work, an Iranian listener may be cheered and heartened by poetry. As he falls asleep at night he may listen to the rhythmic chant of poetry against a tasteful musical background. If the radio does not suffice, the Iranian poetry lover may go to a teahouse where a traditional storyteller stages recitations of national epics in a one-man show. Nowadays, "Palaces of Poetry" are extant in central cities as meeting places for both poets and the public. Literary societies are training grounds for ambitious young poets, immersed from childhood in the lore of their culture. Once or twice a week many of these societies offer programs where young poets may recite their original works in free or classical versification, or even prose, before an audience of colleagues and masters. Statesmen and politicians, university professors and students, shopkeepers and laborers—all attempt to compose poetry, and much of this is enjoyed by young and old, literate and uneducated. The elemental and universal feeling for poetry permeates the entire fabric of Persian society.

The *mosha'ereh,* or traditional poetry recitation contest, is one of the most popular forms of competition in all Iran. It is eagerly watched on television and listened to on radio by many millions. This contest is also traditional party entertainment, following or accompanying dinner or other feasts and festivities. Cheap paperback editions of poetry and prose are widely distributed throughout the country. According to UNESCO, almost half of the titles published in Iran are fiction, poetry, and literary criticism, and about 25 percent of the content of the primary school textbooks is poetry. The *Divan* poetry collection of Hafez is described in one of these textbooks as the book nearest the heart of every Iranian next to the sacred Qor'an. The same *Divan* is used even today for traditional fortune-telling: a passage is picked at random by an individual, then its meaning is interpreted by the fortune-teller.

Great poets of the past are given the most transcendant titles, such as *hakim* (learned doctor), or *shaykh* (venerable chief), or *mawlana* (lord and master). Their wise sayings in verse lend zest and color to everyday conversation and often settle disagreements.

Graphically, this bridge of the past, present, and future is best seen on the Iranian banknotes, which are, no doubt, the symbol of Iranian economic stability and industrial aspiration. On these banknotes are pictures of great modern dams, petrochemical complexes—and the tombs of the venerated poets. These last are architecturally and spiritually imposing, and are still popular pilgrimage sites.

Even though in the 1970s there was an almost total devotion to progress and Iran was fast moving into an impressive industrial era, this feeling for and dedication to poetry seemed likely to endure, creating a balance between a respected and loved classical past and a modern society increasingly encumbered by the uniformity of computer printouts.

Thanks must be given to Mr. William Shpall for his invaluable assistance in preparing this chapter.

10

Iran's Foreign Policy in the Pahlavi Era

In the beginning was the Persian Empire.[1] In its Achaemenid glory in the sixth and fifth centuries B.C. it bestrode much of the civilized world. Indeed, what most of the West still thinks of as its greatest defeats—by the Greeks, at Thermopylae and Marathon—were probably viewed in its great capitals, Susa and Persepolis, as irritating frontier problems at most. But after its conquest in the fourth century B.C. Persia suffered the humiliation of being overrun by a series of foreign conquerors, by Alexander the Great, the Arabs, the Seljuk Turks, then—worst of all—the Mongols, then (briefly) the Afghans.[2] In the nineteenth century she was increasingly dominated by the British and the Russians.

Iran's recent revival, therefore, is in the minds of her ruler and of many of her citizens a revival of lost glories. Like China and Japan, Iran today is that rare phenomenon in modern history, a reviving empire. In one sense Iranian continuity is greater, for unlike China it still has a monarchy, and unlike the emperor of Meiji and post-Meiji Japan (one of the best parallels to contemporary Iran), the Shah not only reigns but rules. Moreover, the Iranians, like both the Chinese and the Japanese, treasure their language and culture as a national heritage—a heritage with an influence that, like the Chinese, has gone and still goes beyond the nation's borders, playing a great role in Iran's successful adjustment to and absorption of all her conquerors.

Like China and Japan also, contemporary Iran is an example of rapid, forced modernization of a hitherto underdeveloped country. In this respect, however, a better parallel is Ataturk's Turkey. Like Iran, Turkey is a Moslem but not an Arab country, and both had to grapple with two obstacles to modernization: the Moslem mollas as well as the traditionalist landowners. And like Ataturk's Turkey (and Meiji Japan), Iran under the Pahlavi dynasty has adopted a model of modernization that is primarily Western. For it was the West that brought modernization as well as humiliation to Turkey, Iran, and Japan, and all three have tried to profit from the West's technological achievements while retaining and cultivating their own ancient cultural traditions.

Alone among these states Iran is multilingual, in which the Persian-speaking inhabitants are a majority and Persian is the official, cultural, and administrative language but in which large minorities speak other languages—Kurdish (an Iranian tongue), Azarbayjani (Turkic), Arabic (in Khuzistan in the south), and Baluchi (also a branch of Iranian, in the east). Because these linguistic groups extend into Soviet Azarbayjan, Turkey (Kurdish), Iraq (Arabic), and Pakistan (Baluchi), some of the neighboring states have at one time or another tried to disrupt Iran's unity by encouraging irredentist movements among them. This potential for disruption has, for example in the case of Baluchis, helped to explain Iran's consistent policy of support for the unity of Pakistan (apart from other fundamental considerations), a country threatened with dismemberment along ethnic lines, especially after the separation of its eastern part, since known as Bangladesh, in 1971.

The two great modern threats to Iran's independence and territorial integrity have come from Russia and Great Britain. Of these two the Russian threat has been the more serious and the more lasting: indeed, to this day it is the major single concern of Iranian foreign policy. In the nineteenth century Russia annexed, and still holds, considerable Iranian territory in Central Asia and the Caucasus. She tried twice, in 1921 and 1946, to annex or at least to dominate Iranian Azarbayjan. Finally, her Soviet incarnation added an ideological and internal subversive threat: the Soviet-controlled Iranian Communist Party, the Tudeh, dedicated to the overthrow of the Shah and the Sovietization of Iran.[3]

British policy, until the 1951 nationalization of the Anglo-Iranian Oil Company, was less hostile to Iran's independence. London viewed Iran from the viewpoint of its Indian empire, as a buffer between India and Russia, and after the early 1900s also as a major source of its oil. Both considerations required, from the British viewpoint, that Iran be stable and viable, although not strong. They also required that Russia not conquer it, and for this reason, but only for this reason, British policy was not as total a threat to Iranian independence as Russian policy was.

The result was a degree of foreign penetration of the Iranian polity and society that may perhaps best be compared with that in pre-Communist China. It was aided in Iran, as in China, by the close ties that the Iranian political and commercial elites developed with foreigners, and by the opportunities that Iran (unlike China) gave to foreign interference and intervention because of her multiethnic nature. This foreign penetration was one of the factors—corruption, incompetence, and stagnation were the others—that discredited the Qajar dynasty, the predecessor of the Pahlavi, gave rise to the modern Iranian nationalist movement, and made the main thrust of Pahlavi foreign policy the end of foreign penetration and the recovery of national independence. As in other states in the same geopolitical, military, and economic situation, surrounded by foreign enemies, foreign penetration also greatly strengthened the traditional Iranian tendency toward a strong, autocratic central government and toward primacy for foreign policy and for Iranian nationalism. Finally, given the Anglo-Russian competition for influence in and domination over Iran, it caused a search for a counterbalancing "third force" to protect the country's independence against these two major foreign threats.[4]

THE SAFAVID AND QAJAR PERIODS

Eighteenth- and nineteenth-century Iranian foreign policy was characterized by alternation between unrealistic and unsuccessful Iranian irredentism and defeat (including conquest) by Turkey, Russia, and Afghanistan. This resulted in declining social cohesion, tempered by traditional Persian absolutism but increased by dynastic weakness. The end of the eighteenth century also saw the beginning of the Iranian third force tradition. Napoleon attempted to interest Iran and Russia in assisting him to conquer India. Iran responded favorably at first because she thought that France could counterbalance the intrusion of Russia and Great Britain. But Napoleon's invasion of Russia and his subsequent defeat ended these hopes. The nineteenth century saw constantly increasing Russian and British economic and political penetration in Iran. This did give some impulse to economic development, but also to the growth of a xenophobic, unrealistically maximalist Iranian nationalism that was often self-defeating. Indeed, the first major outbreak of this nationalism, the wresting from the Shah of the 1906 constitution, strengthened the determination of the Russians and the British, once they had become reconciled in the Triple Entente, to bend Iran to their will. The result was the 1907 partition of Iran into Russian and British spheres of influence. The Russian sphere, which included Tehran, was greater than the British, and Russian interference in Iranian politics was more direct and brutal. Thus Iran became the victim of détente between her two principal foreign enemies, and her nationalism became all the stronger because it was more frustrated. Moreover, because the democratic nationalism of the 1906 constitution had been so rapidly proven helpless before the foreign threat, integral Iranian nationalism, as in interwar Eastern Europe, took priority over democracy. Modernizing absolutism soon came to be seen by much of the political elite as the best, perhaps the only, means of the recovery of Iranian independence.

Initially, however, the Russian presence became greater and more humiliating, and rising British reliance on Iranian oil, particularly for the Royal Navy, made London also more inclined to strengthen its influence in Iran. The Iranian reponse was to look for a third force. Her hopes rested in Germany, which was hostile to Russia and Great Britain, and in the United States, because it seemed disinterested and might at least influence the British to Iran's benefit.

Both calculations turned out to be unrealistic. Iran was neutral and pro-German in World War I, but ineffectively so. Realistically it should have been pro-Entente, for the United States was indeed far too disinterested. The first American financial adviser, W. Morgan Shuster, appointed by Iran primarily in the hope of getting U.S. diplomatic support, tried after 1911 to reorganize Iranian finances. He was frustrated and in the end ineffective. Indeed, World War I and Iran's unrealistic, ineffective and in some respects pro-German neutrality brought only more disruption to the Iranian polity.

World War I also brought Bolshevism to power in Russia and thereby revived Anglo-Russian antagonism, including its traditional manifestations in Iran. Although this could have been used by Iran to balance one against the other, it became less important, by the beginning of the 1920s, than Soviet expansionism—a combination of the traditional Russian drive south with the Bolshevik attempt to found and favor indigenous Communist parties, particularly around her borders. In addition, Moscow believed that Iran was the gateway to India and thus to revolution in Asia. Once the Soviets had pushed back the British intervention against them through Iran and Baku, they invaded northern Iran and set up a separatist puppet regime there. These developments further strengthened Iranian nationalism, as did the propaganda of Wilson and Lenin for self-determination.

Since Moscow, not London, seemed to be the overwhelming threat to Iranian independence, in 1919 the Iranian Premier Vosuq ad-Dowleh made an agreement with the United Kingdom that would have meant British economic and political domination of the country. However, Iranian nationalism made the Majles reject it. Thereupon the new premier, Moshir ad-Dowleh, successfully used conciliation without appeasement to negotiate the Soviets out of northern Iran. (The parallel to the similar events in 1946 is striking.)

REZA SHAH

The Qajar dynasty fell after Reza Khan, a successful officer, had come to power by a coup d'état in 1921. He came to the throne as Reza Shah in 1925 for primarily internal political reasons: weakness, indecision, corruption, and failure to respond to the challenge of modernization.[5] Yet, as we have seen,

His Imperial Majesty Mohammad Reza Shah Pahlavi Shahanshah Aryamehr

Iran's internal problems, then and since, have been intimately interrelated with her foreign policy and have interacted with it: the Qajars fell, and Reza Shah came to power, also because of the humiliating penetration of the Iranian polity by foreign powers, particularly by the Russians and the British.

The first point to make about the foreign policy of Reza Shah is that it was nationalist in both politics and economics. The second is that it was essentially the heir of the nationalist policy of the constitutionalists of 1906. The third, and for the purpose of this essay the most important, is that it foreshadowed not only in general but also in many details the policy of the present Shah.

Nor is this at all surprising. In our century all underdeveloped, colonialized or semicolonialized nations have been obsessed—and why not?—with nationalism. Iran was the more so because her nominal sovereignty and monarchical tradition had been maintained despite foreign penetration, and because of her collective memories of past imperial glory.

Reza Shah knew well, as did his son, that Iranian independence could only be recovered by making Iran once again internally strong. Thus the primary thrust of his policy, like that of Ataturk, was to aim at modernization, with the help of the oil revenues and nationalist protection for Iran's economy, by first building a modern infrastructure (notably the Trans-Iranian Railway), and above all a modern army, which the Qajar dynasty had never possessed. He also tried to modernize Iranian society, in the same fashion, although hardly as radically as Ataturk and Turkey, and in particular to decrease the power of the *mollas.*

His second priority was to diminish as much as possible the influence in Iran of Moscow and, secondarily, London.

Reza Khan's first foreign policy achievement was his maneuvering the British and Russians out of Iranian territory. Soviet troops had returned to Iran in 1920, ostensibly to combat British intervention against the Soviet Union, and a Soviet-sponsored Communist republic of Gilan had been set up in northern Iran, out of control of Tehran. In the same year, before Reza Khan came to power, Premier Moshir ad-Dowleh, realizing that cold war with the Russians promised nothing, had begun negotiations with Moscow on troop evacuation and a trade agreement, which was signed immediately after Reza Khan's February 1921 coup.

The treaty abolished the tsarist privileges in Iran and provided for the resumption of Soviet-Iranian trade, but it did allow, under certain specified conditions (essentially, Iranian refusal to stop a third power menacing the Soviet Union through Iran), the Soviets to send troops into Iran. Thereupon the new Prime Minister Seyyed Ziya, Reza Khan's principal associate in the coup, managed by a combination of persuasion and pressure (delaying the Majles' ratification of the treaty) to get Moscow to withdraw its troops. Thereafter, Moscow having shown its disinterest, Reza crushed by force the

Gilan regime. Only then did the Majles ratify the Soviet-Iranian treaty, and trade between the two began to increase. (Again, the parallel to Iranian policy in Azarbayjan in 1946 is almost complete.)

Meanwhile, the British had acquired practically complete control of the southern, partly-Arabic-speaking province of Khuzistan, become the protectors of its tribal chieftain, Shaykh Khaz'al, and thus consolidated their hold on Iran's oil production. Indeed, in 1919 Iranian Premier Vosuq ad-Dowleh underestimating the force of Iranian nationalism, and in order to counteract domestic disorder and Soviet pressure, had made a treaty with Britain that would have made Britain predominant in all aspects of Iranian policy—only to have his successor, Moshir ad-Dowleh, suspend it. After the coup Seyyed Ziya cancelled the treaty and the Majles formally refused to ratify it. Reza Shah eventually occupied Khuzistan by force and reimposed central control over it. The British accepted this with what good grace they could summon up, and thereafter both Moscow and London ostensibly adopted a policy of noninterference in Iran's affairs, which enabled the Shah the more easily to reestablish Iranian independence.

Reza Shah's foreign policy also included an attempt to find a third force to counterbalance Moscow and London. At first, because of the weakness of Weimar Germany, the disinterest of Britain, and the British alliance with France, he tried, as had his predecessors, to turn to Washington. He offered oil concessions to U.S. companies and invited a U.S. financial adviser, Arthur C. Millspaugh, to reorganize Iran's fiscal system. Neither attempt, however, succeeded, and indeed Reza Shah in 1927 dismissed Millspaugh because he resented his powers. A German adviser, Dr. Lindenblatt, subsequently became governor of the national bank.

The Shah's other attempt to counterbalance Russian and British pressure was to bring about reconciliation with his neighbors, notably with Turkey, British-dominated Iraq, and Afghanistan. (The 1937 treaty with Iraq, however, gave Iran a boundary in the Shatt al-Arab, which for most of its course was on its eastern [Iranian] bank and for the rest in its deepest channel, the *thalweg*.) These measures contributed to Iranian security, and foreshadowed his son's similar and more successful policy in the 1970s.

Reza Shah also gradually gained more economic independence, especially from the Soviet Union. He cancelled all the foreign capitulations in 1928 and the major British concession (D'Arcy's) in 1932.

Reza Shah's third and eventually disastrous move, in 1941, was to overestimate his ability to hold out against Russia and Britain. His policy toward Germany was primarily conditioned by his overriding nationalism. In this respect, his attitude toward Germany did not differ in essence from his attitude toward the United States as exemplified by his earlier mentioned engagement of Dr. Millspaugh. It was an attitude that entailed using certain foreign powers, rather than being used by them, to achieve his nationalist objectives. This was, indeed, his one failure in foreign policy. Otherwise, the final verdict of history is likely to be that Reza Shah was a successful nationalist modernizer of Iran. Certainly until 1941, he greatly increased Iran's degree of independence from its two major foreign threats. Moreover, he began, as his son has continued, the modernization and westernization of Iran, without which it is difficult to see how the country could have recovered independence and power. Above all, he accomplished what Chiang Kai-shek did not in China: the reestablishment of effective central control over the country.

Thus until 1941 Reza Shah's foreign policy must be judged as successful from the point of the recovery of Iranian national independence. How and why, then, did it collapse in 1941? The main reason was that, with his imperfect knowledge of foreign countries, he overestimated the power of the Germans and underestimated that of their opponents. Above all, he underestimated the Anglo-Soviet determination to control the supply route through Iran to Russia, an objective for the attainment of which the presence of German technicians in Iran served more as pretext than a real cause.

Thus regardless of Reza Shah's actual stance toward Germany (which was not that of unrestricted friendship, if we consider that German broadcasts were strongly attacking him for his alleged subservience to the British), it is at least questionable whether or not he could have retained Iran's independence during World War II. For basically Iran was once again the victim of her geopolitical position and, ironically enough, of Reza Shah's greatest achievement, the Trans-Iranian Railway. For the latter was the most effective way of getting U.S. supplies to the Soviet Union during the war. It was therefore essential for Russia, Britain, and the United States that this railway be absolutely secure and operate with maximum efficiency. But given Iranian nationalism and anti-Russian and anti-British feelings, it is very questionable if Reza Shah could have given to the Russians and British, even if he had wanted to, the kind of extraterritorial control over the railway that they would have thought sufficient. One must therefore doubt whether even if he had been less nationalistic and xenophobic, Reza Shah could have solved this dilemma. In any case, once again Iranian independence became the victim of Great Power politics. Reza Shah, in order to preserve the dynasty, abdicated and died a lonely death in South Africa in 1944, and his young son Mohammad Reza succeeded to the throne.

MOHAMMAD REZA SHAH: THE RECOVERY OF INDEPENDENCE (1941-1953)

In 1941 the new, young Shah confronted a situation even more menacing to Iran's independence than the one his father had faced in 1921. For in 1941 the Soviet Union was much stronger than in 1921 and, with Britain, she occupied the whole country. Moreover, one obvious third force, the United States, was their wartime ally, while the other, Nazi Germany, had been forced out of Iran by the Anglo-Russian invasion. Finally, the new Shah's personal position was initially very weak, and he did not dominate Iranian foreign policy. Even so, he and his advisers managed to use the partially competitive situation between the Russians and the British. They also used the goodwill of the United States, which they tried in every way to involve in Iranian affairs (including reappointment of the American financial adviser, Arthur C. Millspaugh). Iran profited from both the competitive situation and the goodwill to maintain the appearance, if not the reality, of an independent state.

When World War II ended, the main task of Iranian foreign policy was to gain independence by ending the Soviet and British presence and domination. Except for the pro-Soviet Tudeh party there was a national consensus on this aim, which was shared not only by the new Shah and his advisers but also by his great opponent, Dr. Mosaddegh. Where they differed was not as to whether but how to recover Iranian independence. The Shah, like his father, regarded the Soviet Union, not Britain, as the principal danger, while Mosaddegh saw the British in that role. Mosaddegh, like the constitutional-ists of 1906 and indeed like Reza Shah in 1941, believed that Iran should and could follow a foreign policy of neutralism or "negative equilibrium," while the Shah and his principal advisers believed that such a policy, even if theoretically desirable, was no longer possible, for Iran was too weak and the international system had become too polarized between Washington and Moscow. The Shah therefore believed that Iran must align herself with the United States in order to contain the Soviet danger to her independence and territorial integrity, as well as to grow strong and become modern enough so that eventually she could recover her independence from Washington as well. To the Shah's opponents, such as Dr. Mosaddegh, this meant capitulation to a foreign power, and to the Tudeh party to the chief imperialist power as well.

In retrospect, the Shah's strategy was more realistic and more in accord with Iranian national interests. Mosaddegh neglected three facts: the postwar weakness of Great Britain (which, it is true, was not expected in Washington either); the weakness of Iran but also her potential strength in the long run (because of her oil resources); and the necessity of rapid modernization if she were soon to become strong enough to recover complete independence. (Contrary to a common impression, Dr. Mosaddegh was not as much of a modernizer as the Shah. Rather, he represented a combination of feudal landowners and the nationalist intelligentsia, and his lack of realism was typical of irredentist, integralist Iranian nationalism.)

The first task for Iran was to get the Soviets out of her northern provinces. Soviet and Iranian policies in this respect were remarkably parallel to those after World War I. By 1945, the Soviets set up puppet separatist regimes in Iranian Azarbayjan and Kurdistan, and seemed determined to detach them effectively from Tehran's control and to force Iran to grant Moscow major oil concessions. The Iranian Prime Minister Qavam used much the same tactics as he had in 1921. During the war he delayed, tried to get United States help, and used the Majles to avoid concessions. After the war he got the Soviets to evacuate their troops from northern Iran in return for the promise of a major oil concession. In this he was greatly aided by U.S. pressure on the Soviet Union for evacuation—pressure that had been conspicuously lacking in 1921. Indeed, the 1946 Soviet-American crisis over this issue was in retrospect the beginning of the Cold War. Thereupon the Shah and his government crushed the two separatist regimes by military force; first postponed and then had the Majles refuse to ratify the oil concession; and finally crushed and banned the Tudeh party.

Thus began the period of rapid, massive United States involvement in Iran and the Soviet-Iranian cold war. Basically, they occurred because both had a common enemy, the Soviet Union, and the United States wanted to strengthen Iran for that reason. Washington sent to Iran large numbers of economic, financial, military, and policy advisers, and granted some credits—although never as much as Tehran wanted. However, the Shah and his advisers had a second aim in their involvement with the United States, an aim that Washington only partly shared: to use it to strengthen their own position against their domestic enemies on the Left and the Right. Washington, on the other hand, concentrated its attention in the immediate postwar period on Western Europe, and tended to apply primarily economic criteria to economic aid: it wanted to allocate the aid directly to agriculture, education, and health rather than to grant it as a lump sum and rely entirely upon the Iranian government to allocate it.

The conflict between the Shah and Mosaddegh broke out in earnest when the Shah reluctantly named him prime minister in April 1951, just after the Majles had nationalized the British-owned Anglo-Iranian Oil Company. Mosaddegh gave high priority to maintaining this nationalization than to land reform—not surprisingly, since many of his supporters were feudal landowners. Mosaddegh was, from the Shah's viewpoint, so serious a threat because of the major policy differences between them and because Mosaddegh was determined that at most the Shah should reign, but certainly not rule. (In 1925 Mosaddegh had voted against Reza Khan becoming Shah.) Thus the struggle between the two was not only over foreign or even domestic policy, but essentially over the political system of Iran. For although in the immediate postwar period the Shah had reigned more than ruled, and his prime ministers represented more the shifting majorities in the Majles than his personal choices, he was determined to return to the traditional Iranian system of monarchical absolutism. Like Mosaddegh he wanted to nationalize Iran's oil resources, but he was also determined to carry out a drastic program of land reform that would break the power of the feudal landowners and *mollas* and thus establish a popular peasant base for his rule.

On these issues there could be no compromise, in or outside of Iran. The British were determined to block and, after the event, to reverse the nationalization of their oil. As political polarization went forward within Iran, Mosaddegh was inevitably pushed toward the Soviets and the Tudeh party, despite all his distrust of them and his desire for neutralism. The Soviets and the Tudeh party played along with Mosaddegh in order, they hoped, to get rid first of the Shah and then of him. The United States was inevitably pushed more toward the Shah and the British and against Mosaddegh. The denouement, in 1953, was the Shah's initial unsuccessful attempt to remove Mosaddegh, his flight to Rome, and then his return as a result of a rebellion against Mosaddegh led by General Zahedi with United States encouragement and support.* The result was the establishment of the Shah's supreme rule and the cementing, for the time being, of alignment with the United States (but not, it should be noted, the denationalization of the oil fields), plus the end of effective Soviet influence in Iran.

"POSITIVE NATIONALISM"
(FROM 1953 TO THE EARLY 1960s)

The Shah's post-1953 policy was one of tactical, temporary alignment with the United States, in order to maximize Iranian security against the Soviet Union, to get a breathing space to consolidate his personal rule, and to acquire a broader social base among the peasantry, not as a result of United States pressure but of his own strategic calculations. This policy also involved a rapid military buildup, especially of the Iranian army. In regional politics, it included adherence in 1955 to the U.S.-sponsored Baghdad Pact (later CENTO). The overthrow of the Iraqi monarchy in 1958 and the establishment there of a radical, pro-Soviet regime together with the Egyptian President Gamal Abdel Nasser's pan-Arab radicalism and his alignment with the Soviets, produced a new danger for the Shah: pro-Soviet Arab radicalism on his western borders, in Egypt, and potentially in the neighboring gulf states too. This perceived danger tended initially to tie the Shah closer to the United States. It also moved him to establish close if informal relations with Israel, which later led to Iranian-Israeli cooperation, with United States support, in supporting intermittent Kurdish rebellions in

---

* For further discussion of this event, see chapter 12, below.

Iraq. Once again, Iran was befriending her enemy's enemy.[6]

After Stalin's successors turned toward international détente, the Shah engaged in intermittent negotiations with them, in part to make the United States more likely to give him what he wanted in aid. Not until 1962, however, did the Soviets give up their demand that he cut his ties with the United States in return for détente with them. His most important move in that year was to agree that United States missiles would not be stationed in Iran. That any such medium-range U.S. missiles were in any case being gradually replaced by land- and sea-based intercontinental nuclear missiles made it easy for the United States not to oppose this move. Moreover, the Soviets had really been using the issue to force Iran and the United States apart, and their acceptance of the Shah's statement showed that they had not succeeded.

The policy of "positive nationalism" should in my view be considered quite successful in terms of the Shah's objectives.* It enabled him to stabilize his personalist regime; increase and modernize his army; crush the Tudeh party; settle the oil nationalization problem by setting up an international consortium in which the United States and the United Kingdom each had 40 percent, to produce and market the oil; provide the stability that enabled him to begin his massive land reform program; and assure himself of sufficient United States economic and military aid so that he could gradually free his country from what he saw as an increasingly unnecessary degree of U.S. penetration into Iranian affairs, and thus begin to cut the ground out from under his opponents. It also gave him the base he needed to adjust to the changes in international politics that began with the death of Stalin in 1953.

"INDEPENDENT NATIONAL POLICY"
(FROM THE EARLY 1960s ONWARDS)

The Global Dimension

The first of these new developments was the Soviet-United States détente. The Shah viewed it—as did General de Gaulle, whom he greatly admired—as both a danger and an opportunity. It was a danger because it could mean that matters involving what he saw as Iran's vital interests would be settled by a Soviet-United States *double hégémonie,* over his head and without his being consulted. It was an opportunity because it meant that the immediate Soviet threat to Iranian security would decline and that therefore Iran would be more secure and need not have such close ties with the United States. The second development, which the Shah perceived early along, was the Sino-Soviet split, which enabled Iran, as it did the United States, to improve relations with

---

* For the concept of "positive nationalism," see chapter 12, below.

China and therefore to make herself more interesting to and thereby less threatened by the Soviet Union. The third was the involvement of the United States in the Vietnam War, which from the Shah's viewpoint distracted U.S. attention from his region and, by its final denouement, gravely weakened the will of the American public and Congress to fulfill the country's foreign policy commitments. The fourth was U.S. inaction and lack of support for Pakistan, a CENTO ally, in the 1965 and 1971 Indo-Pakistani wars, which increased the Shah's doubts about the reliability of the U.S. commitment to Iran's security, and the brief, unsuccessful U.S. attempt during the Kennedy and Johnson administrations to pressure the Shah into economic reforms. The fifth was the rising strength of the Iranian economy and military establishment, primarily because of the higher prices of her oil exports but also as a result of increased economic development and political stability. The sixth was the Soviet desire for détente not only with the United States but also, in an interrelated fashion, with her neighbors to the south, Turkey, Iran, and Pakistan. The seventh was the technological development of the arms race, which enabled the United States to rely more on sea-based nuclear deterrence and therefore made it much easier for the Shah in 1962 to promise Moscow that he would not allow U.S. land-based missiles in Iran. This concession for the first time made Moscow agree to a Soviet-Iranian détente without Iran having to abandon her alignment with the United States. Moscow ceased most of its subversive activities in Iran, increased Soviet-Iranian trade, gave Iran some economic aid, and even sold her some arms. There followed until 1968 a period of Soviet-Iranian détente. Thereafter, because of greater Soviet support for Iraq and for the Dhofar Rebellion and increasing Soviet naval presence in the Indian Ocean, relations worsened somewhat again but did not return to the pre-1962 cold war situation. This, added to Nixon's cessation of pressure on Iran and increased weapons sales to her, reintensified the Iran-United States alignment. However, the end of U.S. military and economic aid, primarily because of Iran's rising oil revenues, greatly diminished Washington's ability to influence the Shah.

All these factors convinced the Shah, as the 1960s went on, that Iran must normalize her relations with the Soviet Union and, later, with China because of the Soviet Union. At the same time, he wanted to maintain a primary but less close alignment with the United States, and above all develop his own country's military power as rapidly as possible, in order to achieve the maximum possible degree of military self-reliance. This would involve a diversification of contacts, notably with Western Europe, and regionally a détente with as many Arab states as possible. Moreover, such an independent national policy, and in particular diminished alignment with the United States, would take the wind out of the sails of his nationalist opposition and thereby give him an even more stable domestic base on which to carry out the White Revolution.

The Regional Dimension

All these global and domestic factors also enabled the Shah to respond in the early 1970s to two major regional developments: the trend away from radicalism and Soviet influence in the Arab world, and the withdrawal of the British from the Gulf shaykhdoms in 1971.

The decline of Arab radicalism and Soviet influence. As has already been pointed out, the radicalism and pro-Soviet policies of Nasser and the Syrian and Iraqi Ba'th regimes were seen in the late 1950s and 1960s by the Shah as a major new threat to Iranian security, and in particular as an opportunity for the Soviets to encircle Iran from the west and south as well as from the north. These tendencies were also a domestic threat insofar as they might reactivate the Tudeh party and any other pro-Soviet elements in Iran. Finally, Arab radicalism could well turn into irrendentism with respect to the partially Arabic-speaking Khuzistan province in southern Iran. Until the 1967 Middle East war, the Shah saw the most serious expression of this danger in the Egyptian and Soviet support for the republican side in the civil war in the Yemen. Also serious was the support that both they and Iraq were giving to subversive movements such as the People's Front for the Liberation of the Occupied Arab Gulf (PFLOAG), in the Sultanate of Muscat and Oman and the gulf shaykhdoms.

In retrospect, Nasser's catastrophic defeat by Israel in the 1967 war and his consequent abandonment of his operations in the Yemen marked the point at which the danger to Iran of Arab radicalism began to decline. Nasser's death in 1970 and his replacement as president by the moderate and increasingly anti-Soviet Anwar Sadat greatly intensified this trend. Sadat concentrated on revival of the Egyptian domestic economy, whose crisis-ridden state was due in large part to the failure of Nasser's so-called Arab socialism, and on getting United States support to pressure Israel out of its occupied territories. Both aims required a rapprochement with the conservative Arab oil states, notably Saudi Arabia, as well as with the United States, and a drastic cutting back of Nasser's close relations with the Soviet Union. The result was a *bouleversement des alliances* in Arab politics, which since then have centered on the close relations between Egypt and Saudi Arabia.

The Shah was quick to take advantage of this development. Desirous of improving his relations with the Arab states in order to diminish Soviet influence among them, further domestic political moderation in their politics, and gain their support in his oil diplomacy and his grasp for hegemony in the

Persian Gulf (of which more below), he moved rapidly, with United States encouragement, to improve his relations with Sadat and with the Saudis. Indeed, given the traditional rivalries between Egypt and Saudi Arabia and between Iran and Saudi Arabia, both perhaps only temporarily papered over by common enmity toward Israel, Arab radicalism, and the Soviets, it is not surprising that Sadat's relations with the Shah have been and remain closer than either's with the Saudis. All these tendencies were strengthened by the 1973 Israeli-Arab War, which gave the Shah the opportunity to press successfully, with Arab cooperation, for much higher oil prices.

The establishment of Iranian hegemony in the Persian Gulf.   The second major regional development that affected the Shah's "independent national policy" was the 1971 British withdrawal from the Persian Gulf shaykhdoms. This had been decided upon several years previously, and had then given rise to gloomy predictions in the West of a power vacuum in the Gulf that the Soviets and Arab radicals, notably the Iraqi Ba'th regime, would fill. By 1976 these predictions had still not come true, in considerable part because the Shah had filled the power vacuum himself.

Historically Persia was always concerned with the southern shore of the Persian Gulf. By the 1960s many Iranians lived in the shaykhdoms, notably in Bahrain, to which Iran had an old claim. Moreover, the gulf, and notably the narrow exit from it through the Straits of Hormuz into the Arabian Sea and the Indian Ocean, had become much more important for Iran because through it was shipped the Iranian oil that was the base of rising Iranian prosperity and power. The Shah and probably the overwhelming majority of the Iranian political class considered it essential that the Arab side of the gulf, and particularly the shores of the Straits of Hormuz, which were partly Omani territory on the Arab side, should not fall under actually or potentially hostile control.

To attain this objective, Iran tried to encourage the British and the shaykhdoms to set up a stable federation after British departure; to solve her long-time dispute with Bahrain over sovereignty in that island; to prevent the growth of subversion in, or the overthrow of, the gulf shaykhdoms; to lessen and, if possible, end the threat from Iraq; and to establish and consolidate Iranian military predominance in the gulf area. The Shah therefore in 1971 acknowledged Bahraini independence (after a facesaving United Nations report), but took over three small but strategically located islands in the gulf, Abu Musa and the Great and Little Tunbs, with minimal use of military force. Even so, this was a blow to Arab pride, and Libya used the occasion to break off diplomatic relations with both Tehran and London, and to nationalize the holdings of the British Petroleum Company (BP) on its territory. Iraq also denounced the Iranian moves.

FOREIGN POLICY IMPLICATIONS
OF THE 1973 OIL PRICE INCREASE

Iran's greatest single leap forward in foreign policy during the period 1970-76 was the quadrupling, in 1973, of her oil prices.[7] The Shah and the Venezuelans had long taken the lead in attempting to push the prices up. This was not surprising, for of all the major oil producers Iran and Venezuela combine experience and sophistication on the international political and economic scene with large populations capable of absorbing massive capital investments. Moreover, the oil reserves of both were much less than Saudi Arabia's, so they needed as much money as possible to build an industrial base before the oil ran out. Finally, both felt in need of more power because of much larger neighbors: the Soviet Union for Iran and the United States and Brazil for Venezuela. The 1973 Israeli-Arab War and the resultant Arab oil production cutbacks and boycott of the United States offered both countries their opportunity, for they removed the inhibitions on raising the price of oil that had long been felt by such pro-U.S. Arab oil producers as Saudi Arabia. Thus in late 1973 the sale price of Iranian oil was effectively quadrupled, and the Shah therefore had at his disposal massive new oil revenues for economic development and military purposes. (Iran also that same year took over complete control of her oil from the Consortium.) The result was a major increase in Iranian national development—economic, educational, etc.—as well as massive arms purchases intended to strengthen the thrust of Iranian foreign policy, to consolidate domestic political stability, and ideologically to disarm the nationalist intelligentsia. They also had the effect of cementing the Shah's personal domination of Iranian foreign and domestic policy.

Needless to say, the Shah's participation in quadrupling oil prices brought him much criticism in the oil-consuming countries, notably in the United States, where Secretary of the Treasury William Simon's denunciations were characterized more by violence of language than by diplomatic tact. Indeed, United States-Iranian relations were strained by this development more than they had been at any time since Dr. Mosaddegh's premiership in the early 1950s. Yet on balance the Shah's relations with Washington continued good, for several reasons. He had long and carefully cultivated the U.S. defense and foreign policy bureaucracies, which now stood him in good stead, for they supported him or at least did not fully share the fury of the U.S. economic bureaucracy against his oil price increase. This was the more so because it was in the early 1970s that the United States began to perceive the Soviet naval buildup in the Indian Ocean as a danger to American interests. Given the hostility of India, the weakness of Pakistan, and the looming defeat in Indochina, the Shah was the obvious regional ally of the United States against this new danger—the more so because, as we shall see, the Shah himself perceived it as a greater threat than the United States did. Finally, and ironically, the Shah profited from fury of the U.S. government and public at the Arab oil boycott, for most Americans apparently blamed the Arabs rather than (as they should have) the Shah and the Venezuelans for the oil price increases. Moreover, as of mid-1976 the Shah had remained firm in refusing, despite all U.S. pressure, to lower oil prices, and had indeed constantly tried to increase them further.

Iran, Oman, and the Dhofar Rebellion

The first major indication of the extent to which the Shah intended to project Iranian military power was the dispatch in 1973 of an Iranian expeditionary force of several thousand ground troops and helicopters to the Sultanate of Oman. Here Qabus ibn Sa'id, the new Sultan, was attempting with British support—to which the Shah's was now joined—to suppress the Dhofar Rebellion in the sultanate's western part, which bordered on the People's Democratic Republic of the Yemen (Aden). The rebellion, led by PFLOAG and supported by the Aden regime, had been going on for nearly a decade. Its roots were partly tribal, partly personal—the medieval despotism of the new Sultan's deposed father—and partly ideological, since both the radical, Marxist-oriented pro-Soviet government in Aden and (to a lesser degree) the government of Iraq were providing the rebels with Soviet arms. The Shah's primary motives in complying with Oman's request (after all Arab states had refused similar ones) were two: to prevent Oman, and therefore its enclave of territory on the south side of the Straits of Hormuz, from falling into radical, pro-Soviet hands; and second, to counteract PFLOAG attempts to subvert the gulf shaykhdoms, where in the early 1970s some PFLOAG cells were uncovered. After several years of fighting, and despite Arab uneasiness about Iranian presence so far south and west of her borders, the rebellion seemed by early 1976 to be nearly crushed. To this the Iranian military presence had contributed significantly—not, perhaps, as much as Tehran liked to think, but more than the Sultan's British officers were willing to admit. Thus the Shah had demonstrated his ability to project Iranian military power far from its shores. His troops had acquired some combat experience and he had demonstrated to the Arabs that he was a force to be reckoned with in the region. Finally, he had from his own point of view, as well as that of the United States, contributed significantly to containing and pushing back a Soviet-armed, anti-Western radical guerrilla movement.[8]

The Iranian-Iraqi Rapprochement

Of all the recent developments in Iranian foreign policy, the Shah's 1975 rapprochement with Iraq was the most unexpected. It remains one of the most important because, as long as it lasts, it removes the threat to Iranian security from her western neighbor and contributes toward decreasing Soviet influence in Iraq.

The hostility between Baghdad and Persia has such a long history that the rapprochement was all the more surprising. Arab versus Persian; Sunni versus Shi'a; overlapping religious sects and languages—neither ever lacked reason to fight the other. The main shrines of the Persian Shi'a are in Iraq. Tehran has always feared Iraqi subversion among its Arab-speaking population in the southern province of Khuzistan. Iraq has always, from Iran's viewpoint, been under the influence of her enemies: the Omayyad and Abbasid Caliphates; the Ottoman Empire; in the interwar period the British; and, after the overthrow of the Hashemites there in 1958, the Soviets—to Iran the most dangerous of all. Moreover, as we have seen, Reza Shah had felt compelled in 1937, because of British pressure at the time, to recognize Iraqi territorial sovereignty over part of the Shatt al-Arab. As a result, the boundary came close to the Iranian oil refineries at Abadan, instead of remaining in the deepest channel (*thalweg*) of the river. From the Shah's viewpoint, his father had left him two legacies of Iranian humiliation to overcome: foreign control of the country's oil, which ended in 1973, and the Iraqi domination of most of the Shatt al-Arab. By the early 1970s, Iran had in effect forced Iraq to recognize her free access to her main refinery, Abadan, up to the Shatt al-Arab, but the legal situation still rankled with the Shah and many other Iranians.

Finally, there was the Kurdish Rebellion. The Kurds, who, as the saying goes, "have no friends," are largely spread among Iran, Iraq, and Turkey. Their desire for autonomy or independence was used by the Soviets in setting up their puppet Kurdish regime in Iran at the end of World War II. The centralizing and radical tendencies of the Iraqi Ba'th, with the covert aid from Iran, Israel, and the United States, aided the rebellion in Iraq. The fortunes of the rebels rose and fell during the late 1960s and early 1970s, depending on the concessions that Baghdad seemed willing to offer and the external aid that the Kurds received.

By late 1974, however, the situation had from the point of view of Iran and of Iraq become critical. With large-scale, although reluctant, Soviet material aid, the Iraqi army had inflicted heavy losses on the Kurdish rebels, but Iranian artillery fire from across the border had also inflicted serious casualties on the Iraqis. Tehran realized that it was faced with the choice of either much more engagement on the side of the Kurds, including probably the use of Iranian ground troops, or a settlement. Iraq, on the other hand, did not want to run the risk of a war with Iran, which would inevitably have reversed the new line of policy that the Baghdad regime's strong man, Saddam Hussein al-Takriti, had designed. The policy involved using the money from nationalized oil and quadrupled oil prices to buy Western technology; to become less dependent on the Soviet Union's economic and military aid (which, inter alia, the Kurdish war had forced it to become); and to emerge from isolation in the Middle East and improve Iraq's relations with the predominant "conservative" trend led by Sadat, the Saudis, and the Shah.[9]

In retrospect, therefore, the world should not have been as surprised as it was when the Shah and Saddam Hussein, on March 5, 1975, at an OPEC summit meeting in Algiers, signed an agreement whose main provisions were that Iran would abandon support of the Kurdish Rebellion in return for Iraq abandoning support of subversive movements against Iran or its allies and granting to Iran the *thalweg* boundary for the whole length of the Shatt al-Arab. Since then the agreement has been working remarkably well. The Kurdish Rebellion, having no more friends, ended precipitously, as apparently did Iraqi support of anti-Iranian subversive organizations. Soviet influence in Baghdad reportedly also declined, while Western economic and technological presence dramatically increased. From the Shah's viewpoint, then, the rapprochement with Baghdad not only removed a serious danger from Iraq but also greatly diminished what he perceived as a threat to Iran of Soviet encirclement.[10]

Iran's Foreign Policy Toward the East

The Shah also perceived another such threat, this time from the East—from Soviet influence in India and Afghanistan and from the weakness of Pakistan. Western observers have all too often thought of Iran as essentially the farthest east of the Middle Eastern states. Yet historically she could often have been thought of as concerned as much with the territories to her east as with her northern neighbor. In 1722 the Afghans conquered Isfahan and brought down the Safavid dynasty. In 1738 the great Iranian ruler Nader Shah conquered Delhi and brought the Peacock Throne back with him to Tehran. The language of the Moghul court in Delhi was long Persian.

The Shah's concern about the lands to his east was the result of his perception of danger and opportunity coming from them. He saw danger because of the Indian victories over and partition of Pakistan in 1965 and 1971, the rise of Soviet influence in India and Afghanistan, and his fear that Pakistan would be dismembered or subverted by Soviet and Indian moves. Moreover, he then had to fear that a dismembered Pakistan would produce independent states in Pushtunistan and Baluchistan, under Soviet influence, and thus a Soviet-controlled outlet to the Indian Ocean, with subsequent Soviet support for a "Greater Baluchistan" that would include the 750,000 Baluchis in eastern Iran. (The outside observer may regard such considerations as "worst-case analysis" carried to the extreme, but the history of Soviet attempts to detach Iran's northern provinces hardly demonstrates that a similar Soviet attempt in Baluchistan, if the possibility existed there, should have been excluded as unrealistic.) He saw opportunity, because Iran's rising power could be used to expand her influence east and south, into Pakistan and the Indian Ocean. The Iranian plan to construct a major naval base close to the border of Pakistan indicated that both were intended. The Shah's visit to Australia in September 1974, and his close relations with South Africa, of whom Iran is the major oil supplier, showed his concern lest the Soviet Navy become dominant in the Indian Ocean. His reiterated proposal that the Persian Gulf be closed to nonlittoral powers' naval forces, while it would mean that the U.S. Navy would have to abandon its facilities in Bahrain, was primarily intended to deny the Soviet Navy access to the Iraqi port of Umm Qasr. Significantly, the Shah seemed not to oppose the construction of U.S. naval facilities on the Indian Ocean island of Diego Garcia.

To return to the subcontinent. Pakistan was, with Iran and Turkey, a member of CENTO, which the United States had sponsored but not formally adhered to. It is not surprising, therefore, that the Shah had drawn his conclusions from what he perceived as insufficient support by the United States to Pakistan in her 1965 and 1971 wars with India. True, U.S. policy had in neither instance been pro-Indian, and in the latter one had tilted against New Delhi, but for Tehran the issue was whether after such limited U.S. support for Pakistan, Iran could any longer rely so much on the United States. Fortunately for the Iranian decision, she no longer needed so much to do so. It seems clear, however, that the two wars in the subcontinent significantly speeded up Tehran's decision to become as self-reliant as possible in the military field. This decision was, not surprisingly, further speeded up by the debacle of the United States in Southeast Asia and its impact on U.S. public and congressional opinion.

Tehran's concern was further strengthened by internal developments in Pakistan, Afghanistan, and India. In Pakistan, the 1971 war led to the replacement of Yahya Kahn's military regime by 'Ali Bhutto's civilian one. But the shock to the Pakistan policy of its defeat and partition was such that there was a rise in autonomist and separatist agitation in the Northwest Frontier Province, inhabited in part by Pushtuns (as was much of Afghanistan), and Baluchistan (bordering on the 750,000 Baluchis in Iran). Moreover, the 1973 overthrow of the Afghan monarchy by Mohammad Daud was initially seen in Tehran, as elsewhere, as a victory for a pro-Soviet "Greater Afghanistan" regime committed to a "Greater Pushtunistan" that would include the Northwest Frontier Province of Pakistan. Another portent for Iran was the discovery in Karachi that the Iraqi Embassy was importing large numbers of weapons, presumably for the tribal insurgents, through its diplomatic pouch.

Finally, after the 1971 war and the United States tilt toward Pakistan, Soviet-Indian relations became increasingly close, and Tehran seems to have been convinced that the Indians were actively involved, with the Soviets, in working toward the breakup of Pakistan into a group of pro-Soviet and pro-Indian successor ministates.

Iranian tactics in dealing with this situation were a combination of carrots and sticks. The sticks were perhaps more important. The Shah made clear publicly that so far from tolerating the dismemberment of Pakistan, he would immediately intervene militarily to prevent it. (Indeed, in 1973 he briefly sent some helicopters to aid the Pakistanis in quelling a Baluchi tribal insurgency.) Secondly, his military and naval buildup in eastern and southern Iran increasingly made this threat a credible one. On the other hand, the Shah provided India and the Soviet Union with inducements to end what he saw as their subversive activities. Those to India were more substantial: the Indians, who had been very hard hit by the 1973 quadrupling of oil prices, were given a long-term, low-interest loan of some $300 million to purchase Iranian oil. With the Soviets he continued his policies, already a decade old, of increasing and institutionalizing economic ties. Moscow was presumably also attracted, as Tehran must have known, by the declining dependence of Iran on the United States, and worried lest Iran's ties with China become too close.[11]

WESTERN EUROPE AND JAPAN: ANOTHER "THIRD FORCE"?

Iran's policy since the early 1960s has been one of maximizing independence and military self-reliance and diversifying her alliances and economic ties, while retaining a primary but not confining alignment with the United States. Historically, however, Persia's ties with Western Europe were always much closer than this. Moreover, Iran was by the early 1970s one of Japan's biggest sources of petroleum. It would have been surprising, therefore, had Iran not used the twofold opportunity of Western European economic recovery and Japanese prosperity to cement economic and political ties with both areas.

Of course, Western Europe was given priority. Tradition, geographic proximity, common concern with the Soviet threat, common desire to diversify foreign ties and thus lower dependence on the United States—all these factors combined to produce strong mutual interests in improving relations. This was particularly true of France and the German Federal Republic: of the former because of her desire, like Iran's to improve her position in the Arab world and her massive arms sales capability (France is now the world's third largest exporter of arms, second only to the United

States and the Soviet Union), and also because the Shah and General de Gaulle admired each other and to some extent followed parallel policies; of the latter, because of the country's great economic potential, the long history of German-Persian friendship, the prestige of German technology in Iran, and a mutual fear of expanding Soviet power. Great Britain also was a source of arms and of military and economic diversification, and by the early 1970s the memories of past Anglo-Persian enmity had faded somewhat.

Once her oil revenues were quadrupled, Iran increased her ties with Western Europe. Arms were imported from Britain and France as well as from the United States, although the latter, for political and technological reasons, remained the main Iranian arms supplier. Extensive economic contracts were entered into with Western European countries. French- and German- as well as English-speaking universities and institutes of technology were to be set up. A triangular contract was entered into with the Soviet Union and the German Federal Republic, whereby Iran would export natural gas to the former, in return for which the former would export it to the latter. (Thus Iran and West Germany profited mutually from their policies of détente with the Soviet Union.) While taking the side of the raw-material-producing countries in the North-South dialogue, Iran has also tried to play a mediating role between them and the OECD countries.

INSTITUTIONS AND STYLE

The Shah *is* Iranian foreign policy, has been so since 1953, and will in all likelihood remain so as long as he reigns. Such personalization of any nation's foreign policy has both advantages and disadvantages. As to the former, assuming the statesman's ability and devotion to his national interest, which the Shah certainly has, it enables a complex, sophisticated, balancing policy of *Realpolitik,* using but not being used by popular emotions, and thus maximizing the independence and security of a geopolitically menaced middle power such as Iran. In my view the Shah has used this opportunity and achieved these goals. Moreover, since he has now reigned for thirty-five years and ruled supremely for twenty-three, in a period when Iran's foreign relations were continually presenting new challenges, he has acquired almost unparalleled experience in the conduct of foreign policy. Finally, Iran, like the Persian Empire before it, has historically been characterized by absolute monarchical rule and extreme personalization of power. The Shah has benefited from and used this heritage. Moreover, even more than his father, he has combined traditional kingship, Iranian nationalism, and rapid modernization. (It is as though Ataturk had become Sultan and ruled as long.) The Shah has thus, by now, effectively deprived his opponents, on the

Right and Left, of issues in foreign (and largely indeed in domestic) policy.

There are, of course, also disadvantages in such extreme personalization. The main one is, historically, the problem of succession—an unpredictable issue. One might add, however, that it is not only monarchs who have this problem: it has been rightly said that Bismarck set up a foreign policy that only a genius like himself could have successfully carried out. Personalization also often leads to extreme sensitivity on issues of personal and national prestige. Finally, it inhibits institutionalization and therefore the installation of any built-in corrective mechanism for errors by the monarch (or foreign minister), and because of the latter's tendency not to ask for or to disregard advice or opinions contrary to one's own, it tends to attract conformists rather than independent officials.

Since Iranian foreign policy is so much *le secret de l'empereur,* it is difficult if not impossible to get a clear picture of the extent to which these theoretical disadvantages present themselves in Iran. It would be surprising, however, if they did not exist. Yet the Shah does, of course, have advisers, and the outsider is impressed by their knowledge and sophistication.

On balance, then, in my view the Shah's foreign policies through 1976 had fulfilled his aims: security, independence, domestic stability, and supreme power. All four had been characteristic of all strong rulers of Iran and of the Persian Empire. Moreover, Iran's foreign policy had been greatly aided by domestic modernization and economic growth. One could argue, as many of the Shah's critics did, that domestic repression was at a level that threatened to become, or already was, counterproductive with respect to these goals. Others could argue that the extent of the external threat and the dislocations of rapid modernization required, as they did in Ataturk's Turkey, Meiji Japan, and, for that matter, in all Communist states, a centralized, personalized, authoritarian system of rule.[12] It is not the purpose of this essay to attempt to answer this domestic question, but it should be pointed out that the answer, whatever it may be, has considerable implications for the future of Iranian foreign policy.

PROBLEMS AND PROSPECTS

Iran has three other looming domestic problems which overlap into foreign policy. The first, the succession, has already been mentioned, and since it is basically unpredictable nothing more can usefully be said about it. The second is to some extent predictable but falls outside the scope of this essay: the future of Iran's oil revenues. (In 1976, diminished oil sales were forcing Iran to cut back on some economic and military projects.) How long will Iranian oil last? How will OPEC pricing policy develop and how successful will it be? Will Iran succeed in building an industrial base sufficient to continue her economic and military development and safeguard her independence and security before the oil runs out? Perhaps most important of all, will Iran be able to train enough people, and rapidly enough, to make her new industrial infrastructure and military power efficient? And will the enormous number of foreign personnel required to bridge the gap produce a revival of nationalist xenophobia in Iran, directed against the Shah's domestic and foreign policy? These are issues treated elsewhere in this volume; suffice it to say here that the way in which they are handled, along with the succession, will in my view be the three major determining domestic factors in Iran's future foreign policy.

Modern Iran has always been characterized by a Russian threat to her independence and territorial integrity and by Iranian attempts to counterbalance and contain this threat. Despite Iran's developing ties with Western Europe and Japan, the main potential counterbalance for the Russians remains the United States. Iran's leaders today perceive a double future threat in this context: rising Soviet military and naval power and declining United States will to project its power abroad and so help defend the security of its allies, such as Iran. This double problem, in my view, will be for the decade ahead, and perhaps longer, the main international problem that Iran will confront. That Soviet power will continue to rise and attempt to expand seems probable. Whether, when, and how the present semiparalysis of U.S. foreign policy will give way to a more selective but also a more determined posture is far more difficult to predict. In my view the present crisis of U.S. foreign policy is largely due to specific historical events, notably Vietnam, Watergate, and a weak presidency combined with the opposition party in control of a weakly led Congress. It seems on balance probable, therefore, that from Iran's viewpoint her concern about U.S. policy is likely to be somewhat alleviated in the next few years as the memories of these events fade in U.S. public opinion and a stronger administration and congressional leadership come to power.

Yet only somewhat. For Iran must assume that complete U.S. recovery of its foreign policy thrust will come later if at all, and that in the meantime Soviet power will continue to grow. Indeed, it is this reasonable calculation above all else that has made the Shah place such high priority on as much Iranian military self-reliance as possible. He is likely to continue this policy in the future.

Regional Problems

Iran's regional problems intersect directly with her international ones, for the Soviet-American conflict of interest in the Middle East is by far the most serious remaining regional crisis area between the two superpowers. Unless another Arab-Israeli war can be averted, which seems (to many Iranian leaders, among others) increasingly doubtful, Iran may well be confronted with the resultant major weakening or even overthrow of some or all of the moderate Arab leaders—notably President Sadat, King Hussein, and the Saudis—on whose close relations with Iran the Shah's regional policy in 1976 was based.[13] Iran could thus again face revived Arab radicalism and Soviet influence in the Arab East comparable to, or even greater than, Nasser's pan-Arab and pro-Soviet policies. Moreover, whether or not such a development occurs is something on which Iran herself can have at best peripheral influence.

To the east Iran's major regional problem will remain that of safeguarding the independence and territorial integrity of Pakistan and helping to prevent Afghanistan from falling under Soviet domination. Neither danger seemed very great in 1976, but the ethnic tensions in Pakistan and the opposition to Bhutto's increasingly authoritarian rule did not bode well for the future. Here, as in the Persian Gulf, it looked as if the potential or actual projection of Iranian military and naval force might be critical. This, in turn, seemed likely to depend at least as much on the level of competence and training of Iranian personnel as on any cutbacks in weapons procurement that lower oil revenues might continue to demand.

Finally, Iran's relations with Iraq, although remarkably good in 1976, could not be forecast with any certainty. Tension and hostility had usually characterized them in the past, the 1975 rapprochement was so much the personal achievement, on the Iraqi side, of Saddam Hussein al-Takriti, and Iraqi regimes since the late 1960s had been so unstable, that one could be anything but sure that Iranian-Iraqi relations would remain as good. Again, it seemed as if the future course of Arab-Israeli relations might well be the deciding element.

It would be incorrect, however, to conclude only with a list of problems and dangers. They exist, but the Shah and his senior officials know that they do. Indeed, his massive weapons purchases and his attempt to train personnel rapidly to man them are for him the most logical and important insurance policy against these dangers threatening Iranian security. It is, after all, the same policy as was followed by Ataturk's Turkey and by Meiji Japan.

Despite the problems and the dangers, if the foreign policy record of the Pahlavi dynasty by 1976 was any guide to Iran's foreign policy future, pessimism seemed out of place. Iran in 1921 was weak, divided, largely under Russian and British control, underdeveloped, and deeply penetrated by foreign influence. Iran in the mid-1970s was united, much stronger, much more developed, and basically independent of foreign influence. When one surveys the underdeveloped world, and particularly when one thinks of Iran's perilous geopolitical position, Pahlavi foreign policy must on balance be judged successful indeed.

ALVIN J. COTTRELL

11

Iran's Armed Forces under the Pahlavi Dynasty

The military history of the Pahlavi dynasty, the legator of 2,500 years of Persian identity, is integral to an understanding, not only of that dynasty's origins, but of the modern Iranian state's evolution and role in its regional and global setting. Reza Shah Pahlavi, the founder of both the dynasty and the state, was a military man. He focused upon the Persian army, once it had been purged of foreign influence, not only as the symbol of Iran's independence and integrity, but also as the principal instrument of his country's administrative centralization and viability. His son, the present Shah, has been sensitive to this legacy one that has become all the more precious in the face of the manifold new challenges that confront the security of his country.

THE REZA SHAH RENAISSANCE

Under the Qajar dynasty in the nineteenth century several attempts were made to reform the Persian army along European lines. The first such attempt came from France in the context of Napoleon's plans to invade the British territories in India by way of Persia. The first French military mission arrived in Persia in 1807 and was headed by General Gardanne in 1807. Virtually all these attempts—and experts later came from Great Britain, Italy, Austria, Russia, and Sweden—concentrated on the creation of good infantry forces. Almost no effort was made until the very end of the century to modernize that arm of the military—the cavalry—that had given Iran so many military victories in earlier centuries.

None of these nineteenth-century attempts to modernize the army were at all successful. This was basically because the reforms were intermittent and none of them was sustained for the necessary length of time. The Qajar administration was also very poor, taxation revenues were low, and the bureaucratic machine was unable to implement any serious policy of far-reaching change.

The one exception to this sad state of affairs was the Cossack Brigade. This brigade was founded in 1879, after Naser ad-Din Shah had visited Russia the previous year. It became the elite unit in the Persian army. By the end of the century, it was the only source of military strength on which the King could rely—and its officers were Russian. It operated largely in the northern provinces of the country and it was this unit that Reza Shah joined about 1892 or 1893. Originally created at regiment strength, the unit was later enlarged to a brigade, and finally—by 1920—to a division of some eight thousand men.

At the end of the nineteenth century all other units in the Persian army were very weak, often far below their nominal strength, very poorly clothed and equipped, and often badly in arrears with their pay. They received little or no regular training, and many travelers to Persia reported seeing poverty-stricken soldiers trying to earn a living by taking additional jobs.

In 1911, however, a new unit was created: a gendarmerie, officered by Swedish experts and charged with the task of maintaining security on the roads. It was a useful force and by 1916 contained some eighty-five hundred men.

In that year the British created a further unit of some six thousand men, the South Persia Rifles, which was designed to deal with tribal unrest and internal insecurity in the provinces bordering the Persian Gulf. It must be noted that although Persia therefore had relatively effective forces of some twenty-two to twenty-three thousand men by 1920, there was no central control of these three separate units, and no central means of coordination in recruitment, training, or disposition of the forces. In effect, Iran had three separate armies.[1]

This was a situation that Reza Khan, the future Shah, was determined to remedy. By 1920 he had become colonel of the Cossack Brigade (the last White Russian commander had left the unit the previous year). Mohammad Reza Shah Pahlavi has recounted his father's attitude at this time as follows:

At the beginning of 1920, Russian officers still commanded the Persian Cossack Brigade. They were nominally White Russians but some of them had sold out to the Bolsheviks . . . . My father's nationalism convinced him that he must get rid of all Russians in the brigade. In August of 1920, my father acted as his conscience required. He engineered the dismissal of the Russians in the brigade and he himself became Commander.[2]

On February 21, 1921, Reza Khan marched from Qazvin with the units of the Cossack Brigade to Tehran and so staged the coup d'état that ultimately led to the formation of the Pahlavi dynasty in Iran. In the capital they met with weak resistance and were supported by local police and the gendarmerie. Reza Khan immediately took the post of war minister, and two years later he became prime minister. In December 1925 he was proclaimed Shah.

One of the first decisions taken by the new minister of war in 1921 was to disband the South Persia Rifles, which controlled the southern area of the country. Behind this decision lay Reza Khan's resolve to free the Iranian armed forces of all foreign influence. He then proceeded as minister of war and commander-in-chief to integrate the Cossack Brigade, the Persian Rifles, and other paramilitary forces into one Persian military force.

The nucleus of the new army was to be drawn from the Cossack Division, and many of Reza Shah's fellow Persian officers in that unit were to receive high military posts. The men from the gendarmerie were also brought into a new army. Although many of the most important reforms had to wait until Reza Khan became Shah in 1925, the new pattern had already begun to emerge in 1921. A year later Reza Khan received the support of the legislature to send officer candidates to military schools in Western Europe, especially France. In all, approximately three hundred Iranian officers were trained in France and Germany. Reza Shah understood that in a divided country such as Persia a large loyal officer corps was absolutely vital. He apparently deemed it imperative to place heavy emphasis on the training of officers so that if the mobilization of larger forces should become necessary, an adequate officer reserve would be available to meet this expansion.[3]

The military force grew rapidly. By the early 1930s, counting both regular forces and gendarmerie, the military force totaled just over one hundred thousand. About eighty thousand were regular army troops and the remainder consisted of the gendarmerie. This combined force had grown to an estimated one hundred and twenty-five thousand at the time of Reza Shah's abdication in 1941.[4]

What the new minister of war had seen very clearly was that a much more modern, capable, and centrally controlled army was needed if the political fragmentation of Persia was to be prevented. Various tribal leaders were beginning to assert their authority in the more remote provinces; from 1921 to 1925 Reza Khan devoted much energy to suppressing such rebellions.

In the spring of 1921 a revolt in Khorasan led by Colonel Mohammad Taqi was put down, and in October of that year the pro-Bolshevik guerrilla forces of Kuchek Khan in the Caspian provinces were defeated. In the summer of 1922 the Kurdish forces of Isma'il Aqa Simitqu were crushed by the central government after the former had occupied the important northern town of Maragheh. Also in that year a revolt in Tabriz was suppressed by the gendarmerie garrison in Tabriz, as was an uprising of the Shah Sevan tribe.

In 1924 the army was initially defeated in a confrontation with the wild tribes of Luristan, but after some bitter fighting Tehran was able to reassert its control of this turbulent area. By the end of 1925 the shaykh of Mohammara, who was the de facto ruler of much of southwestern Persia—including most of the oil field areas—had been compelled to submit to orders from Tehran, and in April 1925 he was removed to the capital for a period of house arrest. In 1925 the powerful Bakhtiari and Qashqa'i tribes were largely disarmed, and a revolt by Turcoman tribesmen on the eastern shores of the Caspian was also quickly crushed.[5]

These military victories were essential for the continued existence of central government in Persia, and Reza Shah recognized that a powerful and unified army was the key to the rebuilding of his country. As early as 1922 Persian officers were being sent to France for modern training, and six years later the first Persians were sent to Russia for flying instruction. Reza Shah had been quick to perceive the advantage of using aircraft to control the tribes and to ensure safe and speedy communications in so large and diverse a country. The air force had been created in 1924 (it remained a part of the army until 1955).

In 1925 Reza Shah introduced a new law that allowed for the conscription of all fit males over the age of 21 into the army for a two-year period. Thereafter conscripts were liable for duty in the reserves until the age of 45. In order to make trained manpower available for his other ambitious economic projects, those who had received a high school or university education served in the army for shorter periods.

The new Shah had already realized that conscription could be an agent of considerable social change for recruits, who could be taught literacy and other useful social skills while undergoing military training. Reza Shah, in fact, endeavored to raise the prestige of a career in the army and to give the Persian army something it had lacked for over a century and a half, namely, a sense of pride. He took a close interest in all aspects of military affairs—recruitment, training, equipment, and morale. He paid regular visits to military units in all parts of the country and dealt harshly with many cases of corruption and lack of loyalty.

In 1927 money began to be spent on the navy—in the early stages this too was treated as a department of the army—and in 1932 two frigates and four smaller gunboats arrived from Italy. These ships were used in the Persian Gulf to help stamp out smuggling, an activity that had grown greatly as a result of high taxes on tea, sugar, and cloth. Reza Shah had imposed these taxes to pay for the construction of the 861-mile Trans-Iranian Railway, which ran from the Persian Gulf via Tehran to the Caspian Sea. (This line was much used by the Allies after 1941 for the transportation of American and British war materials to Russia.) When he embarked on the project, Reza Shah was determined not to contract foreign loans to pay for the railway, as he had seen the disastrous impact of such loans on Persia's finances during the latter years of the Qajar dynasty.

Iran also began to develop her own small-arms industry: the Tehran City Arsenal was inaugurated in 1924, and a machine-gun factory was opened in the 1930s. At the same time, aircraft repair facilities were created at Tehran and a naval base opened at Khorramshahr (formerly Mohammara). Two officer training schools were built in Tehran.[6] To demonstrate the importance Reza Shah attached to military service, it is worth quoting from an address he made in 1931 to Iranian students going abroad to study:

> You will render full service to your country only when you have served in the army. Military service is one of the essential duties as a patriot, especially of the student class. Military service strengthens the spirit and prepares the mind for work. It is my opinion that students completing the middle schools and even those finishing the higher courses should serve in the army for a time, even though for a shorter period than is ordinarily required. Thus, they will be able to render more satisfactory service and prove more useful to the country and to the protection of its interests. Then you and the Crown Prince will be equal in my sight.[7]

This dedication of Reza Shah to the role and mission of the military services was obviously transmitted to his son. General Hassan Arfa, as well acquainted with the present Shah as with his father, states in his important book *Under Five Shahs:* "No military chief's prestige in the army equals that of the Shah [i.e., Mohammad Reza Pahlavi] who is cherished by the rank and file."[8] He also writes of the care the incumbent Shah took to secure the well-being of the young officers and the NCOs.[9]

In 1935 the recruitment system was improved, the system of promotion was regularized, and levels of pay were increased. By 1941 Iran for the first time seemed to have a modern and unified standing army. Yet in that year the Iranian armed forces collapsed in the face of the Anglo-Russian invasion.

Much criticism has been leveled at the Persian Army (at that time numbering one hundred thousand men) for failing to put up stiffer resistance in August 1941. Yet it should be remembered that the new army of Persia hardly had been created for the contingency of repelling a determined invasion by two of the world's strongest military powers. Rather, it had been created out of a military shambles by Reza Shah to cope with the urgent needs of internal security. It was charged with a strictly domestic task: the pacification and political reunification of Persia. It had performed this task very capably, enabling Persia to survive as an independent entity at a time when her very existence was threatened by a series of serious internal revolts. To condemn the Iranian army for failing to repel the Allied invasion of 1941 is to misunderstand the nature of the Iranian armed forces at that time, and to deprecate the considerable achievement of Reza Shah in creating a powerful security force out of the military chaos that he inherited in 1921.

Reza Shah's contribution to modern Persia was enormous in many areas, but from a national security standpoint his great achievement was the Persian military force he created and that he used in order to leave his son, the present Shah, a centralized administrative system at the time of his abdication in 1941. It remained for his son to improve upon the great asset he had been bequeathed. Nevertheless, the legacy also included an effective centralized administrative system that had been made possible by Reza Shah's adroit use of the army, and that continues to distinguish Iran from her Arab neighbors of the Persian Gulf region. The legacy stands in stark contrast with that of all other royal or traditional rulers of the Persian Gulf-Arabian Peninsula area, who have been forced in one way or another to build their countries' administrative systems practically from the ground up.

Iran proclaimed her neutrality in World War II, as she had done in World War I. Reza Shah's ostensible affinity for Nazi Germany was initially related to his concern over Soviet and British pressures on Iran, and was undoubtedly enhanced by the rapidly developing trading relationship between Iran and Germany. By 1940 approximately half of the foreign trade of Iran was with Germany, and a great deal of German technical assistance and equipment was provided to Iran. Air service between Berlin and Tehran was inaugurated by Junkers Airlines, and many German tourists visited Iran.[10]

Germany's invasion of Russia in June of 1941 abruptly altered the political and military picture for Iran. Reza Shah refused to bow to joint British and Russian diplomatic pressures calling for the eviction of German personnel from Iran. On grounds that the large number of Germans in Iran constituted a threat that must be removed, British and Russian forces occupied Iran in August 1941.[11]

THE NEW SHAH AND THE POSTWAR SETTING

When the British and Soviet forces entered Iran in the fall of 1941, Reza Shah abdicated on September 16 in favor of his son, the present Mohammad Reza Shah Pahlavi. The latter has stated that, contrary to the belief of some historians and observers of this critical juncture in Iran's history, Reza Shah did not abdicate primarily to save the dynasty but because he could not accept the idea, given his pride for his country, of seeing foreign forces occupying Iran and interfering in her internal affairs. He writes that his father told him "it was humanly impossible for him who had such prestige and hold over his people, to act as the nominal ruler of an occupied country."[12]

Reza Shah made certain that his son would appreciate the value of military discipline in personal behavior as well as the role of the armed forces in the future of the country. He created a special elementary military school for the education of his son in the company of the children of certain carefully selected senior army officers. The Shah has reminisced that his early youth was preoccupied with military studies and military drilling.[13] One of his companions at the military school, General Hosayn Fardust, still remains a trusted adviser, responsible for security matters. He is today head of the Office of the Inspectorate General, perhaps the most important security position in the Iranian government.

The Shah left the military school at the age of twelve in May 1931, to study in Switzerland until he was seventeen. He then returned to Iran in 1937, entered the Military College, and graduated as second lieutenant two years later. He was made an instructor in the army and traveled widely, observing various military establishments. He could always be seen attending annual army maneuvers with his father. At the age of 21 he succeeded to the throne.

When Mohammad Reza Shah Pahlavi assumed the throne and, more specifically, after he had survived the difficult years of World War II and the Anglo-Russian occupation, he faced several tasks: *(1)* to rebuild the army in men and equipment; *(2)* to restore army morale; *(3)* to restore the prestige of the military. These were all extremely difficult tasks in time of war and under conditions of foreign occupation, especially for so young a ruler. Moreover, initially at least, these tasks had to be undertaken in an environment of Anglo-Russian occupation.

Barely years after he ascended the throne, the new Shah's will was tested in a military challenge that threatened the integrity of his country. Six months after the end of World War II, Russian forces remained in their occupation zone despite an agreement for mutual withdrawals—an agreement that had been observed by the Western allies.[14] The deadline for evacuation was March 2—a date very close to the Iranian New Year. The Soviets not only refused to comply with demands that they withdraw, but they actually increased the size of their forces, and prevented approximately two thousand Iranian troops from entering Azarbayjan province. On the very eve of the deadline a Soviet news broadcast from Radio Moscow announced that the forces of the Soviet Union would be withdrawn only partially and that "Soviet troops in other areas of Persia will remain until the situation becomes more clear."[15] This crisis marked the real beginning of Iranian-American military alliance and cooperation.

While Iranian military capabilities and strategy will be treated below, a note of irony seems in order here. The United States gave strong diplomatic support to Iran in this postwar crisis. This support was in no small measure based on the belief that Iran, by remaining an integral entity, could contribute to the security and stability of the Persian Gulf region specifically, and of the Middle East in general. At that time Iran was poor economically and weak militarily. Yet, in the context of the late 1970s, many of Iran's critics in the

West had not brought themselves to accept that a more prosperous and militarily strong Iran could play a key role in a region of even greater importance to the West—and at a time when the United States was retrenching militarily in the wake of Vietnam.

In any event, under pressures from Iran, the United Nations, and the United States, the Soviets evacuated their forces in May 1946. Nevertheless, they attempted to retain indirect control of some northern parts of Iran by supporting a puppet government in Azarbayjan and a Kurdish government centered in the city of Mahabad. When the government of Azarbayjan failed to call for new elections, the young Shah ordered Iranian forces into the area. Iranian forces marched into Tabriz in December 1946, and the Kurdish Republic dissolved quickly thereafter.

This show of force represented the first use by the young Shah of Iranian armed forces to protect the integrity of his country. It reinforced him in the conviction that Iran, in order to resist the encroachments of the Great Powers, would have to construct the kind of modern military establishment that would be equal to the task.

It seems fair to conclude in retrospect that the aborted Soviet move in Azarbayjan signaled the first chilly wind of the global Cold War. For U.S. President Harry S. Truman the incident represented handwriting on the wall of Soviet ambitions. The American president had done his homework: he had studied Russian history and that country's time-hallowed drive toward the warm-water ports to the south of the Russian landmass. Truman concluded that "it all seemed to add up to a planned move on the part of the Russians to get at least northern Iran under their control. Together with the threat of a Communist coup in Greece, this began to look like a giant pincers movement against the oil-rich areas of the Near East and the warm-water ports of the Mediterranean."[16]

These fears in Washington sharpened in early 1947 when an accelerated Communist offensive in Greece and Soviet pressures against Turkey coincided with Great Britain's decision to shed her defense burdens in the Mediterranean. Although the Truman Doctrine of March 1947 focused on U.S. aid to Greece and Turkey, nevertheless Iran figured prominently in the evolving U.S. strategy of containment of the Soviet Union. Thus, a definitive account of the decision-making process in Washington that culminated in the Truman Doctrine describes a critical meeting in the State Department chaired by George F. Kennan on February 21, 1947:

> Everyone was aware that what was involved was the commitment of American power in Greece and the Middle East. The members of the [State Department] Office of Near Eastern and African Affairs were quite openly elated over the

possibility that the United States might now take action on a broad enough scale to prevent the Soviet Union from breaking through the Greece-Turkey-Iran barrier into the Middle East, South Asia, and North Africa.[17]

IRAN'S ALLIANCE WITH THE UNITED STATES

This early notion of a "barrier" was the precursor of the "Northern Tier" concept that animated the Middle East policies of Secretary of State John Foster Dulles in the Eisenhower administration. In April 1954 Turkey, fearful of being outflanked by the Soviet Union to the east, concluded a mutual assistance pact with Pakistan. Ankara followed this up with a treaty with Iraq in February 1955, which became the basis for a regional alliance known as the Baghdad Pact. During 1955 Great Britain, Pakistan, and Iran acceded to the pact, thus establishing the Middle East Treaty Organization (METO).[18] The alliance assumed its present name of Central Treaty Organization (CENTO) following the antimonarchical revolution in Iraq in 1958 and that country's defection from the pact.

The Shah's decision in favor of close ties with the United States was motivated by several major considerations. First of all, he recognized in the United States the "third power" that could countervail against both residual British interests and reasserted Russian expansionism. Already in 1943, in an audience with American officials, the Shah "two or three times spoke of his conviction that the United States was completely disinterested, having no contiguous frontiers and no selfish ends to serve in Iran."[19]

Second, the Shah attached the highest priority to the strengthening of the Iranian armed forces as the necessary guardians of Iran's security. He believed that countries like Iran "must strive for the security which is their first essential for advancement. Freedom-loving peoples forget—but the Communist powers never forget—that most of the world's economically underdeveloped countries are also militarily underdeveloped."[20]

Finally, the Shah in the late 1950s discerned the global sweep of forces, and concluded that a neutralist course no longer was feasible. To him, although abidingly suspicious of British and Western imperialist impulses, the question was one of the immediate danger. He explained: "In our experience it is the new imperialism—the new totalitarian imperialism—that the world's less developed countries have most to fear. . . . It concentrates on negative, destructive nationalism and thrives on the chaos that follows. . . . We all saw this happening in our country, right under our noses, in Mosaddegh's time."[21]

There was disappointment in Iran at America's failure to join the Baghdad Pact. Nonetheless, the 1950s witnessed a tightening of bilateral ties between

Iran and the United States. The flow of American aid to Iran, suspended during the Mosaddegh period, resumed. In March 1957, Tehran and Washington signed an agreement for cooperation in civil uses of atomic energy.

The pace of cooperation quickened after the overthrow of the monarchy in Iraq in 1958 and the establishment of the radical Kassem regime in Baghdad. To the Shah, who had observed with growing apprehension the incipient tides of radical Arab nationalism-socialism in the Middle East, the shocking events in Baghdad conveyed a compound of dangers. First of all, the fall of the Iraqi monarchy portended a potential domino pattern of rebellion against traditional rule in the Arab world—a pattern that would also give encouragement (and possibly direct assistance) to antiroyalist forces in Iran. Second, the defection of Iraq from the Baghdad Pact meant a crack through the center of the Northern Tier. Third, this crack seemed all the more ominous with the rapid Soviet political ensconcement in Baghdad, along with substantial Soviet military assistance to the new regime. The portent was of a Soviet pincer, backed by radical Arab forces, around Iran and of a beleaguerment in which the Iranian monarchy would have to fend not only against multiplying external threats, but also growing domestic unrest.

Against this somber background, Iran entered into negotiations with the United States toward a bilateral agreement, which was signed on March 5, 1959. In this agreement, it was stated that the United States deemed Iran's independence vital to its own national interest and undertook to furnish Iran military assistance. The agreement also included the resolve by the United States to come to Iran's assistance in case of aggression. It was, however, couched in cautious and qualified language that merely stated appropriate action would be taken when mutually agreed upon.[22]

In general, as one analyst puts it, from 1953 to 1970 the international attitude of Iran had gone "from a form of neutralism to participantship and back to neutralism."[23] The "neutralism" presumably refers to the policies pursued by Premier Mosaddegh until his overthrow in August 1953 and the return of full decision-making power to the Shah. The army—or at least the major units in Tehran—demonstrated its loyalty to the Shah during the crisis in August 1953 by clearing the streets of dissident elements and pro-Communist mobs demonstrating in favor of Mosaddegh; at the same time, the soldiers refused to fire on the Shah's supporters.

After 1953, the Shah was strengthened in his belief that the principal threat to the integrity of his country stemmed no longer from British policies and interests (as Mosaddegh had assumed), but rather from the expanding power and ambitions of the Soviet Union. Indeed, the Shah's view was conditioned not least by Communist infiltration of the Iranian army during the Mosaddegh period. As the Shah was to reminisce later, "even the commander of the most trusted battalion of my Imperial Guard was a hard-core Communist.

The testimony of these men revealed their plan to kill Mosaddegh as soon as he had overthrown the Pahlavi dynasty, then to establish their own Communist regime following the pattern in other countries."[24]

The Strategic Context of the 1960s

In order to gauge the full measure of Iranian strategy and policy, it is necessary to review the events over the decade of the 1960s.

In the late 1960s, a significant change marked both the pace and scope of Iran's national defense and security policies. Tempting economic incentives and a mellowing of the previously harsh Soviet propaganda offensive against Iran gradually brought about a thaw in Soviet-Iranian relations. On the Iranian side, several factors encouraged this change. The Shah took cognizance of a growing domestic security that followed the reforms of the "White Revolution," and of the popular support that was evoked by these policies. Ensuring the stability of the home base in Iran was a vital precondition before Iran could seek an effective military posture in defense of her interests in the Persian Gulf. In the Shah's view, in order to safeguard these interests, Iran would eventually have to become the paramount power in the gulf. The White Revolution was thus a key prerequisite to his security policy and enabled him to begin planning a broader foreign and military policy for the Persian Gulf and, eventually, beyond. In turn, the feeling of confidence that redounded from the success of his domestic policies encouraged him to exercise greater initiative in foreign affairs, particularly within the gulf area.

The Shah continued to evince his belief that CENTO provided some measure of guarantee against a serious global Soviet threat, but he did not hide his concern that the treaty would be of questionable value to Iran if his country ever became involved in local conflicts. This faith in the treaty was badly shaken when the CENTO powers did not come to Pakistan's aid at the time of that country's war with India in 1965, and when Iran was prevented from offering to Pakistan some of the weapons that had been provided to Iran under U.S. military assistance programs. His doubts were accentuated by Washington's speedy recognition of the republican regime in Yemen and by what he deemed parsimonious levels of American economic aid for Iran at a time when oil revenues were still very low.

Under the circumstances, the Shah decided that Iran would have to take steps to defend her own interests. In this context, he saw a potential easing of Iranian-Soviet tensions as a welcome means of giving Tehran broader freedom for diplomatic maneuver in the Persian Gulf. At this time, moreover, the Shah was becoming increasingly concerned about the Pan-Arabism emanating from Cairo under President Nasser's leadership. Egypt broke off diplomatic relations with Iran abruptly in 1960, allegedly over Iran's close relations with Israel, but this act was perceived by the Shah as evidence that Nasser's expansionist aims now extended to the Persian Gulf region. It was at this historic juncture, on September 15, 1962, that Iran gave her pledge to Russia that no foreign rocket bases would be permitted on Iranian soil.

Without detailing possible reasons for the Iranian decision, it seems clear that paramount was the desire for freedom of action to confront threats to traditional rule in the Persian Gulf region against revolutionary Arab threats emanating from Cairo and Baghdad. In rendering this "concession" to Moscow, Iran relinquished no real strategic assets, extant or potential. There is no evidence that Iran was ever seriously considered by the United States as a site for the deployment of the Jupiter missile, which by that time had become clearly obsolete. The Shah was undoubtedly aware of this fact, as well as of the deployment of the A-1 Polaris missile in the Mediterranean in 1961 and of the A-2 in the summer of 1962. The A-1 was capable of striking the principal Soviet population centers, e.g., Leningrad and Moscow, and the A-2 could target just about all the key industrial complexes and other installations in Russia.[25]

Iran's incipient fear of regional isolation and lack of ability to deal with local disputes was exacerbated by an awareness that her increasing oil interests needed to be protected with respect to both the exploitation of resources and their unimpeded export. Unlike Iraq and Saudi Arabia, Iran had no pipeline leading directly to a Mediterranean export terminal; oil from the provinces of southwestern Iran and from potential offshore fields had to be transported through the Persian Gulf. One of the most important of the Shah's decisions—based on the recognition that détente increasingly permeated superpower relations—was that the focus of Iran's military and diplomatic activity should be moved from the northern frontier to the Persian Gulf.

Iran's Growing Interest in the Persian Gulf/Gulf of Oman Region and Beyond

Two developments prompted Iran's involvement in the Persian Gulf to intensify sharply in the 1960s. The first was the exploitation of offshore oil fields. The existence of these resources had long been known, but the technology necessary for their exploitation did not become available until the late 1950s, and the first explorations in Iranian waters began only in 1957. The second major magnet to quickened Iranian interest in the gulf was the construction of the immense oil-exporting terminal on Kharg Island, a rocky outcrop some thirty miles from the Iranian mainland. This port was developed because the old terminal at Abadan suffered from two serious defects:

the shallowness of the approach channel in the Shatt al-Arab, and the fact that this waterway was nominally under exclusive Iraqi control. Indeed, Abadan itself is within easy range of mortars emplaced on Iraqi territory. For both economic and strategic reasons, Iran needed to free herself from dependence on Abadan as her major oil-exporting terminal.

While the Iranian government's concern with the direct Soviet threat began to ease in the early 1960s, a more immediate and potentially powerful antagonist emerged to the south in the person of President Nasser. The Shah saw in the Egyptian president's prestige and his ability to inspire the masses a significant spur to the antimonarchical threat represented by the radical doctrines of Arab nationalism and Arab socialism. The scale of Egyptian military activity in Yemen, together with the possibility of a British withdrawal from Aden, raised the specter of Egyptian forces ensconced on the southern fringes of the Arabian Peninsula, whence subversion could be directed into Oman prior to threatening the Arab countries of the gulf itself. Arab radicals could thus be in a position to imperil Iran's economic lifeline— her oil exports.

In response, and against the background of reduced confidence in CENTO, the Shah declared in March 1965 that Iran's military preparations would henceforth be focused on the Persian Gulf. The joint American-Iranian military exercise of April 1964 (Operation Delaware) had only partially reassured him of sustained U.S. interest in the Persian Gulf; and in the autumn of 1965, the Iranian legislature passed a bill to strengthen the armed forces at a cost of some $400 million.[26]

A large part of this sum—and of later allocations—was devoted to the creation of a modernized Iranian navy and air force. Iran's specific procurements toward that end will be detailed below.

It is important here to note that the schedule of these procurements bore a direct relation to significant events pertinent to Iran's security: thus, Great Britain's decision in 1968 to put an end to her presence east of Suez prompted the Shah to accelerate the delivery of the American F-4 fighter-bomber aircraft, and the 1973 Israeli-Arab War accelerated purchases of the F-4 and other weapons systems.

The Shah's intent to provide Iran with a modern and sophisticated defense force to cope with future responsibilities in the region was clearly enunciated in a speech he made to the graduating officers of the Command and Staff College as early as September 1971—about three months before Britain carried out her decision to withdraw from the Persian Gulf. He stated that the experience of World War II when Iran was invaded would never recur, for three reasons. "First, we are procuring all the equipment necessary for the defense of this realm." Second, "[we have] the determination to resist" so that "in case our force fall short, we shall not abandon this country intact to the invaders" and "they shall get nothing but rubble." Then "Third, our independent national policy has enabled us to have very good relations with all countries except one. And where we face those who intend to inherit the role of dead or moribund colonialism . . . we have, thank God, the power to counter their policies. Moreover," stressed the Shah, "our program for the buildup of the Imperial Armed Forces will, in five years, turn Iran into a regional pillar of stability, peace, and progress."[27]

Persons skeptical about the need for the Iranian arms buildup often ask, "What threat is Iran aiming so massively to counter?" On the assumption that a direct threat from the Soviet Union had receded, a superficial look at Iran's immediate security environment generally tends to identify only Iraq as a plausible antagonist of Iran. The argument is advanced that Iraq is no potential match for the armed power that Iran already has amassed. That point may be debated—especially to the extent that Iraq functions not only by dint of her own indigenous resources, but as the client of a superpower that directly adjoins Iran. The argument in any event mistakes the real nature of the threat that Iraq has represented from the vantage point of Tehran, a threat that relates not so much to Baghdad's intrinsic military power as it does to the fragile political-ideological structure of the gulf region.

In terms of the prevalent nature of rulership, the Persian Gulf is truly a unique area in the world. Of a total of fourteen states (counting all the sheikhdoms) ringing the gulf, only one is nonroyal or "nontraditional" in its form of government: Iraq. The overthrow of the monarchy in Iraq in 1958 has thus far been the only break in the chain of ruling tradition that links the littoral states of the Persian Gulf. Moreover, since 1958 Iraq has been an energetic exporter of her own radical brand of Arab socialism throughout the region, and has given direct support to those elements and movements that seek to overthrow kingly or sheikhly rule. It remains to be seen whether the Iranian-Iraqi agreement of March 1975 will have the effect of dampening this Iraqi campaign. In any event, while Iraq has been Iran's principal antagonist, Tehran sees the source of future conflict in the gulf primarily in terms of swift and unpredictable changes in political leadership in the gulf and the Arabian Sea area—changes that could spread contagiously through the region.

This is the concern, incidentally, that, notwithstanding historical differences and mistrust, continues to link Iran and Saudi Arabia. The transition of royal rule in Saudi Arabia in the wake of King Faisal's assassination was carried out smoothly. Nevertheless, developments in Riyadh continued to be watched closely by Tehran. Should a coup or rebellion, remote as it seemed in the mid-1970s, place radical socialist elements in power in Saudi Arabia, they would then gain not only a strategic promontory whence to press their offensive into the entire Persian Gulf-Arabian Sea area, but they would also grasp the enormous oil wealth of the country with which to finance military assistance.

In November 1970, the striking power of the augmented Iranian forces was demonstrated in a major military exercise held near the island of Beni Farur, a Persian possession in the gulf. The maneuvers, which involved units from all three services, were praised in the Tehran press as showing that Iran's military planning had begun to bear fruit and that the country would be in a position to exercise undisputed leadership in the gulf after the British withdrawal. There is little question that Iran is today the strongest regional military power in the Persian Gulf.

It is important to note here that Iran's increasing concern with events in and relative to the Persian Gulf was manifested before Britain's announcement in January 1968 of the intended withdrawal of her residual military power from that region. Nevertheless, there can be no doubt that the Shah's decision to accelerate arms purchases to present levels was prodded significantly by his apprehensions of a potential power vacuum that was certain to emerge in the gulf region.

It is necessary, however, to draw up specific scenarios for documenting Iranian fears. The sources of potential instability in the gulf region are manifold. They not only inhere in the weaknesses of some regimes and issues of contention within the region itself, but they are also a function of the broader instability of adjacent areas. The Persian Gulf is subject to the spillover effects of the Arab-Israeli conflict to the west and of the Indian-Pakistani-Afghan tensions to the east. It may also not be possible to insulate the Persian Gulf from the possible repercussions of intensified conflict in the Horn of Africa.

The arms buildup in Iran is taking place against this background. By the mid-1970s, the broader geographic considerations and Iran's proliferating economic interests had led the Shah to the conviction that his country needed military capabilities that could reach beyond the Straits of Hormuz.

One other point needs to be considered with respect to Iran's military programs. Iran's military capability is frequently compared to that of the nations of Western Europe. Not only need the European states not key their military expenditures to comparable dangers of instability immediately around them, but they can still take ultimate recourse to the proximate protective power of the United States. The Shah has expressed his appreciation of America's friendship and military assistance. He has supported an American naval presence in the Indian Ocean area. But he is also a realist who discerns the global tides of events and the trends on the American domestic scene. He recognizes that in any conflict in the area, the contingency may well arise in which Iran will have to fend strictly for herself. It is within this broad and indeed ever-widening context of Iranian policy that Tehran feels that its arms purchases must be judged. The Iranian ruler believes that if we would only assess his arms purchases against the background of Iran's commitment, we would find the much-criticized Iranian military program a modest one.

It was not by mere coincidence that the Shah began to procure the F-4 aircraft from the United States in the last week of December 1968, the year in which Britain's Labour government announced its decision to pull back all forces east of Suez before the end of 1971. The Shah had earlier warning of ultimate British intentions. He had discerned quite accurately that the British decision to withdraw from the Aden Protectorate in 1967 was the harbinger of a more general British departure from the Persian Gulf. By anticipating British policy, he was able to take the necessary precautionary steps to strengthen Iran's defense capabilities for the tasks they would have to face in the event of a British evacuation of the area. To be sure, the Conservative Party led by Edward Heath campaigned on a platform of modifying the categorical decision by Wilson's Labour government to abandon the last major vestige of Britain's erstwhile global empire. Nonetheless, the Shah believed that Britain's economic problems would block any real prospect of deviating from the decision. His view proved correct. Indeed, he told this writer at an audience in St. Moritz, Switzerland, in March 1971 that even if a Conservative government should come to power and reverse or modify Labour's decision in regard to the Persian Gulf, as the author suggested might happen, this would not change his plans. He indicated that Britain's chronic economic state would lead to a rapid return of Labour to power and thus to a return to the Labour policy of withdrawal from the Persian Gulf.

The Shah's fears of a political-military vacuum in the Persian Gulf were comprehensible. There was a multitude of territorial disputes and claims among the littoral states of the gulf and these claims would certainly be strongly reasserted once the major restraining force, which the British had traditionally wielded in the region, was retracted. Armed with this recognition, he moved quickly on the diplomatic as well as military front. In a demonstration of skillful statesmanship, he relinquished Iran's claim to Bahrain, which had been considered by many Iranians as the fourteenth province of Iran. At the same time, however, he consistently and steadfastly denied any intent to abandon Iran's historical claim to the Great and Little Tunb Islands and to Abu Musa, all of which are located so strategically close to the narrow (21-mile-wide) entrance to the Straits of Hormuz.

It was rumored at the time, but discounted by British authorities, that Iran believed she had obtained a tacit understanding from Britain whereby Iran's historic claim to these islands was to be satisfied as a compromise for Iran, permitting the people of Bahrain to decide their own political future. There was a significant difference between Bahrain and the islands, since Bahrain's population totaled over two hundred thousand, and the islands were almost devoid of inhabitants (Abu Musa's population was not more than 500 people). Thus the Iranian government believed that, given the great difference in population size, the issues were completely different in a substantive political sense. Also, in the case of the three islands, the strategic issue was critical as seen from Tehran, since the islands in question were located astride the vital sea lanes that pass through the Straits of Hormuz.

In any event, on November 30, 1971, one day before the expiration of the British treaties that had given Britain control of the external relations of the gulf sheikhdoms, the Shah occupied all three islands. The forces of Iran landed on Abu Musa under a "memorandum of understanding" among Iran, Britain, and Sharjah, which also claimed sovereignty over the island. The settlement included a provision that "one half of the oil revenues from the island and its continental shelf should be allocated, under special arrangements, for the welfare of the people of Sharjah." The people of Sharjah were also granted fishing rights and a guarantee of Iranian assistance for economic development. No agreement, however, was reached with regard to the Tunb Islands, which the British had treated as being under the sovereignty of Ras al-Khaymah, but to which the Iranians had held a claim that dated to the era of the Persian Empire.

The Shah's decisive moves served to demonstrate that he considered the Persian Gulf to be within Iran's security purview and that he would act quickly in pursuit of his country's interest in the stability of the region. The move also served to demonstrate dramatically and with considerable psychological and political impact, coming as it did just one day before the treaties giving Britain control of the external affairs of the Trucial Sheikhdoms were to expire, that Iran was preparing to assume Britain's role as protector of the Persian Gulf. In short, a local monarchy was to replace a foreign one.

THE EXPANSION OF IRANIAN SECURITY HORIZONS

The Shah began to think in terms of an Iranian policy that would be projected energetically beyond the Straits of Hormuz to encompass the regions of the Gulf of Oman and the wider reaches of the Indian Ocean. These regions had borne directly on the vital interests of Iran's "lifeline" even before the Tehran OPEC conference of 1971. Already at that time discussions were taking place with the young new ruler of Oman, Sultan Qabus, who had overthrown his father in 1970, and the possibilities of joint naval defense and other projects were under active consideration.

This broader security horizon and the need for a modern navy have been consistent themes in the Shah's pronouncements. Thus, at ceremonies marking the occasion of the forty-second anniversary of the establishment of the Imperial Iranian Navy in November 1974, the Shah declared that "in building up a modern navy our aim has not been confined to leadership in the Persian Gulf or Iran's territorial waters . . . because in the world today Iran enjoys a position which gives its duties regional dimensions."[28] He was articulating, in other words, his view that Iran's defenses depended upon the stability of the Arabian Peninsula and the security of the approaches to the Persian Gulf, including the Indian Ocean.

Even earlier, in November 1972, at ceremonies celebrating the founding of the navy he referred to the need for Iran to consider a policy that would encompass an area beyond its southern boundaries. He stated: "We are not merely concerned with the protection of Jask and Chah Bahar: it is the inviolability of the security of Iran that is the object of our attention. In this respect we do not say how many kilometers are involved, because anyone who is familiar with geography and strategic capabilities—and especially with world air and naval capabilities—knows how far removed from Chah Bahar this frontier can be. We are now taking steps to meet this situation, but for the present I shall refrain from mentioning them in detail."[29]

The Iranian navy has also acquired port facilities on the island of Mauritius. The fact that "the ocean knows no frontiers" has begun to be as appreciated in Tehran as it was in London during the nineteenth century.

The Shah's interest in the Indian Ocean has always been closely related to the protection of the sea routes for the transportation of oil from the Persian Gulf, especially against the disquieting background of an expanding Soviet naval presence in the Indian Ocean. In various conversations with this writer during the 1970s, the Shah consistently and forcefully elaborated his view that Iran's vital interest in maintaining her shipments of oil to the rest of the world did not stop at the Straits of Hormuz. He did not believe in the willingness and ability of the larger powers to protect these sea lines of communication. He had discounted for some time—before Britain's withdrawal from the Persian Gulf—Great Britain's ability to contribute significantly to the security of the routes, given the attitudes in the British Labour Party and the multiplying economic ills in that country. In his view, the popular mood in Washington in the wake of the Vietnam war also rendered it impossible for the United States despite its military power to shoulder this role. In the case of Japan, which had imported about 43 percent of its oil from Iran alone and a total of 90 percent from the gulf states, the Shah saw that country as too remote and as incapable of protecting the routes for its oil supply even as far as the Malacca Straits, let alone into the gulf region. He was thus led to the hard conclusion that Iran would have to assume a significant role in protecting the sea routes and maintaining security and stability for a considerable portion of the area to the east and south of the Straits of Hormuz—the area frequently referred to as the northwestern quadrant of the ocean. This area extends from the Persian Gulf to the Horn of Africa and the general region of the Indian subcontinent, at approximately ten degrees north latitude.

A more narrow but still vital concern of the Shah in the Indian Ocean focused on the security of the approaches to the Persian Gulf from the Gulf of Oman. The Shah saw the Baluchistan issue as a strategic problem closely linked to the internal security problems of Pakistan—problems that directly concerned and disquieted Iran. A dissident movement in the Pakistani part of Baluchistan might easily have spilled over into Iran, and a hostile regime on the northern shore of the approaches to the Persian Gulf could then have threatened Iran's attempts at preserving the security of tanker routes in the area. In 1972 Iran announced that an attack upon Pakistan would be considered an attack on Iran herself and thus irrevocably committed herself to the territorial integrity of the Islamic Republic.[30]

The Shah's fear was magnified by the specter of a radical seizure of power in Oman, in which case the narrow strategic Straits of Hormuz would have been threatened from both shores. In regard to the strategic importance of Oman and her territory at Cape Musandum, which points into the straits, the Shah had often mentioned to the writer and others that Iran could not permit a hostile force to take over Oman on the other side of the strait. Since Hormuz was Iran's oil lifeline, it would have been intolerable for the Shah to accept Communist rule on the territory of Oman. For that matter, any form of hostile rule was to be considered a threat and therefore unacceptable to the Iranian monarch.

This concern impelled the Shah to support Pakistan, and also to respond to the sultan of Oman's request for help in his struggle against the Dhofar Rebellion. He achieved success in both endeavors. The Pakistanis, with some Iranian support, brought the Baluchistan issue largely under control, thus securing the eastern side of the Gulf of Oman. At the same time, the Shah's intervention with troops and helicopters in Oman, augmenting the sultan's forces, helped, with Jordanian assistance (which had been largely air support), to create the most satisfactory military situation in Oman since 1965.

IRANIAN INTERVENTION IN OMAN

The Dhofar Rebellion merits attention because it illuminates both the tinder of instability in the region and the nature of Iranian security interests. More importantly, it also represents the key example of a part of Iran's modern military forces in action. Iranian military intervention in the Dhofar fighting, which began in 1973, may be seen as clear evidence of the Shah's consistently articulated policy of preventing any change in the status quo along the littoral of the Persian Gulf. Iran intervened in Oman at the request of Sultan Qabus. It is uncertain what Iran would do if the other minisheikhdoms were threatened and if Iran's assistance were not requested. Clearly, however, Iran's intervention in Oman signaled a significant clue with respect to the Shah's perceptions, and to his likely future actions in regard to other threats to traditional rule in the gulf.

It is quite evident that Iran's military and economic support made an indispensable contribution toward turning the tide in Oman. As Ray Vicker of the *Wall Street Journal* reported from Muscat:

> There is no doubt that Iran's assistance is vital to Oman. Such aid from a non-Arab country irritates many in the Arab world and Sultan Qaboos is condemned by the more radical countries as a traitor to the Arab cause. . . .But Sultan Qaboos is getting little help from brother Arabs in checkmating the radical ploy in Dhofar, even though all of the oil states in the Persian Gulf would have much to lose were Dhofar to swing Communist.[31]

It is quite clear, as he indicates, that if it had not been for the Iranian forces, the sultan's forces would have waged the military conflict practically alone.

The Dhofar Rebellion was the expression of a twelve-year-old movement that had as its aim the overthrow of the royal or quasi-royal states of the Persian Gulf. The insurgency used the People's Democratic Republic of South Yemen as a sanctuary. The movement changed its name in 1973 from PFLOAG, the "People's Front for the Liberation of the Occupied Arab Gulf," to PFLO, the "People's Front for the Liberation of Oman." The name change was undertaken in an obvious effort to gain the tolerance of other traditional rulers in the region. Nevertheless, in the mid-1970s the objective of the movement remained unchanged: namely, the toppling of traditional rule in the entire gulf area. The movement had received doctrinal and material support from both Russia and China, but by 1976 the Soviet Union had moved to the fore in supplying military assistance and influence. The decrease of Chinese support was in no small measure due to Iran's successful effort to improve relations with China.

To give some of the background: in 1970 the sultan of Oman, Sa'id ibn Taymur, was overthrown by his Sandhurst-educated son, Sultan Qabus. Ibn Taymur had endeavored to perpetuate his rule through the standard formula of shielding his some seven hundred thousand largely illiterate subjects from comparing their poverty with the outside world. Incidentally, he was so very introverted that the Shah's dialogue with him was very limited. In contrast, as soon as the new sultan came to power in 1970 talks immediately began on the security of the Straits of Hormuz, the Gulf of Oman, and the region in general.

Despite the more progressive outlook of the new sultan, a man in his early thirties, Oman still had much to do in order to make the transition to the twentieth century. The British, notwithstanding their 1968 decision to withdraw their forces from the Persian Gulf region, maintained their strong influence in the economic and military affairs of the sultanate. The commander of the Sultan's Defense Forces (SDF) was a British major general who was seconded to the Omani armed forces but remained on the active list of the British officers. The commander and other Britons were welcomed in Oman because of the lack of training of the Omani armed forces. They also served the purpose, however, of guarding against the danger of a potentially rebellious "Arabization" of the leadership of the Omani armed forces. The latter motive largely explains the continued engagement of British officers in key positions in various sheikhdoms of the southern gulf, and especially in the former Trucial Sheikhdoms, where pressures were mounting to replace them with Arab officers.

It was quite conceivable that, should the British eventually decide to end their military role in Oman, Iran might be asked by the sultan to supply the personnel to direct the Omani armed forces and thus protect the sultan against possible disloyalty from his troops. In 1976, there could be little doubt that the Iranian forces were very welcome in Oman, and there was certainly no question that they could stay for a very long time if the situation continued to require their presence. A good part of the reason for this had been Iran's circumspection and awareness of local sensitivities. Thus, Iranian forces had not "lived off" the local economy. Rather, they received direct supplies of water and food on a daily basis from Iran.[31] However, there was no evidence that Iran considered such a course of action, let alone pressed for it. Nevertheless, to the extent that the Shah quite consciously was moving Iranian power into the vacuum left by the British withdrawal, it seemed likely that he might in the future feel compelled to replace the British role even "on the ground" in areas deemed vital to Iranian interests.

In any event, the rebellion in the Dhofar Province of Oman had been flaring in an area that hosted less than 10 percent of the Omani population. Of this small population, some 90 percent of the Dhofar inhabitants were of non-Arab ethnic origin. Given this demographic disparity, some observers found it difficult to understand why the Shah committed such substantial military forces to defeat the Dhofar rebellion. There were many observations about the value of the Iranian effort in Dhofar in terms of training for the untried Iranian armed forces. There could be no doubt that Dhofar had been of great value to Iran from the standpoint of training. The principal training, however, had not dealt in any really serious sense with the more sophisticated weaponry, such as aircraft and naval vessels. Rather, it had focused largely on counterinsurgency operations involving special ground forces and helicopters. One engagement did take place in which several Iranian naval vessels shelled the Raysut area for two days with one to two thousand five- and six-inch shells. According to analysts, the sailors and gunners of the Iranian navy performed creditably in this operation.[33] But to suggest that training in sophisticated warfare was the prime rationale behind the Shah's commitment of Iranian forces is to misunderstand grievously his concept of the strategic importance of Oman within Iran's security perimeter.

The Shah deemed the rebellion in Dhofar a strategically significant conflict because of his fears that a victory there by the radical Arab forces of PFLO would be simply a prelude to the subversion and radicalization of all of Oman and, eventually, the Union of Arab Emirates. In other words, he faced the danger of a wildfire of radicalism in the gulf, and he was joined in this concern by Great Britain and Jordan. As has already been mentioned, Britain was in charge of the military operations against the insurgents, while Iran had intervened with a force reported as ranging between fifteen hundred and two thousand men supported by a substantial number of helicopters.

Some air and artillery support was provided to Oman by the Jordanian air force. The Jordanian role of supplying air support and aircraft to the Omani forces also provided Tehran with the benefit of a lowered profile in Oman. Had Iran been compelled to support directly the Omani forces with aircraft of the F-5 and F-4 type, she undoubtedly would have drawn more open and much harsher opposition from the Arab states. Indeed, Iran had used the Jordan connection adroitly. Thus, for example, she had provided about 12 modern F-5 aircraft to Jordan, which had enabled the latter to place her older Hawker Hunter planes at the disposal of the Omani forces for their own air support. All this had permitted the Iranian forces to concentrate their intervention where it counted most: namely, on the ground. Meanwhile, the minuscule Omani navy bought three modern patrol frigates from Britain and the sultan's navy was being trained in part by Pakistani naval officers (who, interestingly enough, replaced Indian naval personnel in this training role). In this way, the Iranian forces were able to pit their weight where it was most effective, while largely avoiding the negative image that inevitably attaches to those who introduce "sophisticated" weapons into an ostensibly "backward" conflict.

The sultan was under strong pressures from Arab elements in the area to "rid his land of British imperialists." The late King Faisal of Saudi Arabia, while he gave some financial assistance to the sultan, withheld fuller support, reportedly because of his displeasure at the high degree of Britain's military involvement in Oman. Faisal apparently took the view that the British primarily were after the financial gains from military assistance payments and equipment sales in Oman, and were thus hoping to protract the conflict as much as possible.

The Iranian forces generally gave a good account of themselves in the fighting in Dhofar. They suffered some losses—for example, in January 1975, when Iranian soldiers were reportedly killed in an ambush near Raysut—but flamboyant press accounts of such losses clearly were exaggerated. Indeed, the war had not been one of the large-scale casualties: reliable sources put the total number of dead by January 1976 at under 500.[34]

In any event, sporadic reports of engagements and casualties continued to obscure the basic military situation in Dhofar. The basic situation was that, by 1976, the Dhofar Rebellion was under more effective control than at any time during its twelve-year history. In 1976 the rebel forces were in dire straits. Many had been forced back into their sanctuary in the People's Democratic Republic of South Yemen, and several hundred more had defected. While some fragmented resistance remained, the sultan's announcement in December 1975 that the rebellion was defeated seemed to be supported by the facts. And the Iranian forces had played a significant role in this outcome. The British commander of the sultan's armed forces, Major General K. Perkins, paid them proper credit: "The war would certainly not have been won as quickly as it was without the Iranian assistance."[35]

Even before the sultan's announcement, D.L. Price wrote the following assessment of the situation in Oman: "Contrary to PFLO's propaganda the presence of the Iranians has had positive effects on Dhofar; the opening of the Midway road raised the morale of people in Salalah because it insured freedom of passage even if few people chose to or had the means to use it."[36] The Iranians had demonstrated uniform proficiency, particularly in their aircraft and helicopter operations. Moreover, they had apparently been well received by the Omanis, not least because they had brought money to the local economy. While they fought independently of the British, they adhered to a British strategic plan. This cooperative arrangement seems to have worked out very well; there were no reports of resentment by the Iranian forces at accepting a role under the overall direction of British military commanders. As was indicated earlier, by 1976 the Iranian military presence in Oman numbered between fifteen hundred and two thousand (not the eight thousand claimed by PFLO in their *Gulf Bulletins,* published in London, nor the absurd figure of ten thousand adduced by Fred Halliday in his book, *Arabia without Sultans.*[37] As was indicated above, the rotation of forces totaled between fifteen and seventeen thousand through 1976. Iranian forces were rotated about every three months.

Parallel with the border to the People's Republic of Yemen, the Iranian forces in Oman built up a defensive line called the Demavand Line, to prevent supplies from reaching the guerrillas from that sanctuary. Over twelve hundred defections from PFLO were reported since the beginning of 1974. It is worth noting that among the guerrillas captured several had been trained in the Soviet Union in the summer of 1974—and that their training reportedly included the operation of SAM missiles. Indeed, such Soviet weapons as the SAM 7 antiaircraft missiles, Katyusha rockets, and 82 mm mortars and heavy cannon with sophisticated fragmentation projectiles were introduced into Oman during 1975.

The influx of these weapons convinced Sultan Qabus in his belief that Iranian forces would be indispensable to Oman's security for some time to come. Iran made it known that she was prepared to withdraw or reduce her forces when and if the sultan so desired. In an interview with this writer in January 1976, the Shah evinced his pride in the effectiveness of the Iranian forces in Oman and his satisfaction at the current situation there, but he projected that it would be necessary for Iranian forces to remain in Oman for some time in order to keep the situation under control.[38] This projection was clearly influenced by the evidence of quickened and concerted Soviet and Cuban assistance to, and direct intervention in, "national liberation wars," such as the one in Angola in 1976. The possibility that the revolt in Oman could be fanned again into serious proportions by large-scale external assistance was not lost upon the Shah. The possibility was made all the more palpable by the presence of Soviet naval and air facilities, and more than fifty Cuban military "advisers," just across the Gulf of Aden.

The hard-core guerrilla force in Oman was said to number under eight hundred. Although the rebellion had been frustrated, it could not be completely stamped out so long as the rebel forces were able to use South Yemen as a sanctuary. In his firsthand account of the fighting, Ranulph Fiennes wrote: "There is hope that diplomatic lobbying within the Arab League will finally defeat PFLOAG by removing its lifeline. But should the British officers be withdrawn due to left wing pressures in Britain, or Iranian soldiers due to left wing pressures on Qaboos, the Marxists might yet succeed in Dhofar."[39] As Sultan Qabus himself explained during his visit to the United States in late 1974, it is always difficult to crush an insurgency in its entirety. The priority task was to contain the rebellion so as to permit the Omani government to shift its attention to the kinds of social and economic development programs that could ensure a longer-range stability.

The reasons for the Shah's interest in Oman, and indeed all of south Arabia, should be obvious to anyone who has looked at a map of the area. Omani sovereignty extends from Cape Musandum, jutting into the Straits of Hormuz through which 18 million barrels of oil pass each day, down along the coast to the rebel sanctuary of South Yemen—a distance of some one thousand miles. The narrow tanker lanes—approximately three to four miles wide in the straits—are within artillery range of Cape Musandum. The area of fighting in Dhofar is strategically close to the entrance to the Gulf of Aden, and not too far from the narrow twelve-mile-wide entrance to the Red Sea. These facts of geography amply explain the Shah's concern that Omani territory remain in friendly hands. The Shah himself, in order to convey the depth of Iranian security concerns involved, compared them to Western anxieties that Gibraltar remain under friendly sovereignty. He also concluded that his fears about threats to shipping in the approaches to Hormuz were hardly idle ones, recalling the June 1973 attack by Palestinian elements on an Israeli tanker in the even narrower Bab el-Mandeb at the southern entrance to the Red Sea.

When all these factors are drawn into account, the Shah's policies in the Persian Gulf and his military programs emerge not as the harbingers of an "Iranian imperialism," but as the endeavors of a ruler to protect the priority security interests of his country. Against a potential wildfire of Arab radicalism, he has seen the defense of those interests linked integrally to the survival of traditional rule in the Persian Gulf. In that respect, Iran's intervention in Oman served a psychological objective beyond its immediate military mission: it went a long way toward dispelling any lingering doubts in the region that the Shah would hesitate to resort to military force if he deemed Iran's vital interests at stake. This applied to developments not only in the gulf, but on the Indian subcontinent as well. A friendly Pakistan is vital to Iran's overall concept of security in the northwestern approaches of the Indian Ocean. If a dissident movement in Pakistan, such as the one in Baluchistan or in the Northwest Frontier Province, should gather momentum to the extent that it would clearly threaten the further dismemberment of that country, there is little question that Iran would go to Pakistan's aid.

IRANIAN-IRAQI RELATIONS: DISTRUSTFUL COEXISTENCE

To be sure, the ring of traditional rule around the littoral, deemed critical by the Shah to Iran's defense and security, no longer exists in its entirety: it was broken in 1958 when Colonel Kassem overthrew the Hashemite monarchy and established his own radical regime in Baghdad. Since that time, for over a decade and a half, Iraq and Iran have been antagonists in the Persian Gulf region. Kassem and his successors have pursued a policy fundamentally opposed to Iranian interests: they have sought to create a climate in the gulf conducive to the overthrow of traditional rulers and their replacement by revolutionary regimes. Against this background of fundamentally opposed objectives, Iran and Iraq have clashed over focal issues: the question of the Shatt al-Arab and the Kurdish rebellion. Both of these contentious issues ostensibly were resolved in the Algiers Agreement of March 1975. The agreement, however, did not bridge the more fundamental disparity in interests between the radical Arab leaders in Baghdad and the traditional Persian ruler in Tehran.

The Shatt al-Arab Dispute

A key dispute between Iran and Iraq has centered on the Shatt al-Arab, a narrow body of water formed by the confluence of the Tigris, Euphrates, and Karun rivers at the head of the Persian Gulf. Under the Iranian-Iraqi Treaty of 1937, which was written largely under British auspices, the waterway came under Iraqi sovereignty; no median line was drawn to give Iran control over the water adjoining Iranian soil. The treaty did contain a provision that permitted Iran and Iraq to share a three-mile section in the river near Abadan. Thus, the Iranian Abadan refinery, already within reach of artillery and mortar fire from Iraqi territory across the water, now fronted a waterway partly under Iraqi control.

Iran never fully recognized the 1937 treaty, which had been largely imposed upon her. So long as Iraq was under Hashemite rule, however, both Iran and Iraq were content to let the issue remain more or less dormant. Once General Kassem overthrew the pro-Western Hashemite monarchy and established a radical regime at Iran's doorstep in 1958, the situation changed drastically and the tacit understanding between the two nations over the Shatt al-Arab evaporated. The Shatt al-Arab issue flared up from time to time: it produced a serious crisis in early 1960, even though an armed confrontation was in the end avoided.

In the Algiers Agreement of March 1975, the two nations agreed to accept as the boundary line the deepest channel in the Shatt al-Arab, known as the *thalweg* line. To be sure, the agreement replaced an already nonexistent 1937 treaty, which Iran had openly flouted by sending her ships up the waterway flying the Iranian flag and escorted by Iranian naval vessels and aircraft. Still, this is not to belittle the concord. The Shah, as he emphasized to this writer in an interview on the Iranian Island of Kish in the Persian Gulf on March 27, 1975 (just as the settlement was being concluded), considered it very important that the matter was settled by an international diplomatic agreement.

The Kurdish Issue

Much more important than settling the border issue, the Algiers Agreement of 1975 in effect ended the Kurdish rebellion in northern Iraq and thereby averted a possible armed conflict between Iraq and Iran. Iran had long supported General Barzani's Kurdish forces, who sought autonomy from Baghdad. A major rationale behind Iranian arms aid to the Kurds was to keep the Iraqi forces engaged in the north and thus to prevent them from exerting pressure on Iran at the southern border. In the months leading up to the Algiers Agreement, Iraqi government forces had inflicted severe losses on the Kurdish guerrillas. Many Kurdish refugees had crossed into Iran—the number was estimated by Iranian sources at as high as one hundred and fifty thousand—and Tehran had provided them with shelter and food on a massive scale. Under the terms of the Algiers Agreement the Kurds were offered amnesty by Baghdad, and many of the guerrillas in Iraq accepted this offer. Those Kurds who had fled to Iran were given the option of returning to Iraq or remaining in Iran, and several thousands exercised the option of going back to Iraq. For her part, Iraq agreed to permit Kurds living in Iraq to return to Iran, and the Iranian government agreed to accept all who wished to do this.

In entering into the agreement with Iraq, Iran was criticized for "pulling the rug" from under General Molla Mostafa Barzani and his Kurdish followers.[40] This simplistic and emotional charge generally was made in ignorance of the predicament in which Iran had been placed by the Kurdish issue. Iran had been the principal military supporter of the Kurds up until the time the settlement was reached. The fighting between the Kurdish rebels and Iraqi forces had become very heavy in 1974 and was slowed only by the snows in the mountainous areas later in that year. While Iraqi military losses were heavy, they had been making progress in the fighting. Indeed, by late 1974 and early 1975, Barzani found the situation serious enough for him to appeal to Iran for additional military assistance. By that time the conflict was already escalating. The Iraqi forces had committed border violations as they pressed their military campaign against the Kurds, and there were several air clashes between Iraqi and Iranian forces. The fighting was certain to become more intense and the chances of escalation into a full-scale war between Iraq and Iran increased rapidly.

Avoidance of such a conflict was the principal motivation behind the Iranian signature on the Algiers Agreement. The Shah was confident that Iran would have emerged victorious from a war with Iraq, but at a price to Iran's economic development plans and oil production. As has been noted, the Abadan oil refinery is within easy range of Iraqi mortar and artillery. The great Iranian oil terminal on Kharg Island could have been damaged if even a few Iraqi aircraft had managed to penetrate to the facilities. The conflagration easily could have spilled over into other parts of the Persian Gulf.

In light of all this, there was a kind of irony to the charges advanced in the West to the effect that the Algiers Agreement represented a cynical sellout by the Shah of the Kurdish cause for the sake of strictly Iranian interests, whatever these were purported to be. Had the Shah protracted the confrontation with Iraq and a war been triggered—with disruption to the flow of oil and threats to other Western interests in the gulf—one can easily imagine the hue and cry that would have been directed at him from the West for alleged adventurism and imperialist designs.

The Algiers Agreement reflected the Shah's need to win time and his desire to defuse an extremely combustible issue of potential conflict—especially against the ominous background of prospects of a new Middle East war. The agreement also fitted coherently into the overall pattern of Iran's defense policy vis-à-vis the area beyond Hormuz. In order for the Shah to cast his policy southward into the Indian Ocean, he had first to make sure that Iran's flank would be relatively secured and that Iraq would not try to exacerbate the problems in the gulf region. The Algiers Agreement included a provision whereby each party pledged not to interfere in the domestic affairs of other gulf countries.[41]

The settlement of the Kurdish question also had subtle and generally unnoticed implications for Iran in Oman. By settling the Kurdish dispute with Iraq, Iran helped the effectiveness of her military position in Dhofar, since the agreement called for an end (or at least a truce) to subversive efforts to overthrow existing regimes in the area. Indeed, even in Oman Iraq had been assisting subversive cells in the northern part of the country while the insurgency was concentrated in Dhofar. Iraq was one of the prime sources of funds for the training and arms, as well as a base of operations, for the subversives in the north. With this support being cut off, the sizable Omani forces guarding the northern part of Oman were freed to assist with the fighting in Dhofar.

Soviet Ties to Iraq

As has already been noted, the Shah saw the Iraqi revolution of 1958 primarily as a magnification of the threat from the Soviet Union. By ensconcing their influence in Baghdad, the Soviets had found a springboard for infiltrating the gulf region as well as a proxy with which to disrupt the then prevailing pro-Western status quo. Iraq and Russia had clearly shared aims in the latter respect. The Shah's apprehensions were sharpened against the prior background of Soviet influence in and arms shipments to Nasser's Egypt. As was brought out earlier, he saw the revolt in Iraq and the subsequent defection of that country from the Baghdad Pact, not only as a crack through the Northern Tier, but as a potential wedge of Soviet power extending through the very center of the Middle East.

The Soviets did nothing to lessen the Shah's anxiety when they began to deliver MIG-15 aircraft and other weapons to Iraq in 1958 after the Kassem revolution. As of 1976, the Soviets had continued to supply Iraq with increasingly sophisticated weapons (e.g., the MIG-21 and MIG-23). Soviet military aid to Iraq from 1958 to 1976 totaled about $2 billion, and the Soviets had maintained between five hundred and a thousand military advisors in that country during the last few years of that period.

Iran's concern with the Soviet threat abated somewhat with the easing of Iranian-Soviet tensions from the 1960s onwards. Nevertheless, as late as April 1972, the concern was again heightened when the Soviets concluded a fifteen-year treaty of cooperation and friendship with Iraq. The treaty contained two clauses involving close military cooperation between the two countries, clauses replete with wording that suggested the quid to the Soviets for their quo of military assistance would be Soviet use of the Iraqi naval base at Umm Qasr, which had been built up with Soviet help well beyond the ostensible needs of the minuscule Iraqi navy.

The Shah voiced his worries in an interview with this writer in May 1972, one month after the treaty was signed. He stated: "I do not like especially clauses 8 and 9. The wording of these provisions troubles me."[42] The provisions he referred to read as follows:

> *Article 8.* In the event of the development of situations endangering the peace of either party or creating a threat to peace or a violation of peace, the High Contracting Parties shall contact each other without delay in order to agree their positions with a view to removing the threat that has arisen or reestablishing peace.
>
> *Article 9.* In the interests of the security of both countries, the High Contracting Parties will continue to develop cooperation in strengthening their defence capacity.[43]

Anticipating the Shah's concern, the Soviets attempted to explain to him that the treaty was not directed at Iran. Inasmuch as Iraq was Iran's principal antagonist at that time, however, and given the centuries of hostilities between Russia and Iran, the Shah was hardly reassured.

The Shah's concerns were eased somewhat with the Algiers Agreement. It remains to be seen, however, whether the agreement will have the effect of lessening Iraq's dependence on the Soviet Union for military aid. In concluding the agreement with the Iraqis, the Shah undoubtedly had in mind the fact that Baghdad already possessed very advanced aircraft of Soviet manufacture, such as the MIG-23s, whereas the American F-14 aircraft were not to be delivered to Iran before 1976 and, given the training lead-times, would not be fully operational for some time after that. The Shah's apprehensions about the superiority of Iraq's Soviet-supplied arms were reflected as early as in 1960 when he wrote:

> Iraq has only about a quarter of our population and a fifth of our land area, yet her air force is more powerful than ours. It includes many of the latest jet fighters that easily out-perform our earlier American ones, and unlike us she also possesses modern jet bombers—Iraq's armed forces as a whole are better equipped than ours. How does this happen? Iraq relies upon both the British and the Russians for equipment while since the Second World War ours has come almost entirely from the Americans. And although we are deeply grateful for what we have received, I must in candour point out that it fully meets neither our own needs nor those of the Free World in this sector.[44]

THE IRANIAN ARMED FORCES

The evolution of Iran's foreign policy has been mirrored in many respects in the growth of her military capabilities. The development of Iran's armed forces has kept pace with the Shah's broadening policy vistas. After the fall of the Mosaddegh government in 1953 and the Shah's firm grasp on the decision-making reins of his country, Iran's defense program focused on the modernization of the ground forces. The major upgrading and buildup of the air force did not begin until the mid-sixties, while the expansion of the navy began to gather momentum in the late sixties.

The Imperial Iranian Air Force (IIAF) underwent the most impressive changes. Between the mid-1960s and the mid-1970s the number of combat aircraft doubled to include the most sophisticated vintage of American fighters. The Imperial Iranian Ground Forces (IIGF) did not increase in numbers as the other services, but were transformed from a largely infantry-based force to an army built around armor and mechanized elements. The Imperial Iranian Navy (IIN), with its primarily coastal orientation, was being markedly upgraded and expanded to offer a deep-water capability.

Iran's growing defense establishment numbering approximately three hundred thousand men under arms represented clearly the largest as well as the most modern military force in the Persian Gulf area. Yet this was not an excessive number for a country with a population of 35 million, nor was the ratio at all high for the region. Iraq, Syria, Turkey, and Israel were all keeping a proportionately larger number of men under arms. Egypt retained a force of comparable size. Saudi Arabia, whose security problems were less serious than Iran's, could afford to keep a considerably smaller volunteer force. The Iranian conscription period of two years was less than that of Israel and Egypt (three years) or Syria (thirty months), and the same as Iraq's. Rather than relying upon the sheer number of military personnel, the Shah preferred to stress quality of personnel and weapons.

A developing country cannot modernize its military establishment without a good deal of technical training assistance from outside. The rapid acquisition of increasingly sophisticated weapons and other equipment therefore adds an additional dimension to the military problem. By 1976, the development and upgrading of Iran's armed forces was being supported by a large number of foreign military and civilian advisers. Most of these were Americans, but there were also some British and French. Since the Iranians had no sophisticated Soviet equipment, Russian technicians were not present. There were approximately 250 U.S. officers in the Military Assistance Advisory Group (MAAG). This was only about half the number in the MAAG a decade previously. There were, however, at least 2,000 additional American military and civilian technicians for training the Iranians in the use of complex new systems—aircraft, missiles, destroyers, communications, and other equipment. The level of foreign technicians seemed likely to remain high for several years, and even to increase as delivery was completed on all the sophisticated equipment purchased during that period. The Spruance-class destroyers alone were to require a number of American technicians aboard for an indeterminate period of time.

The Imperial Iranian Ground Forces

After the overthrow of the Mosaddegh regime, when the Iranian military rallied to the Shah, the Shah focused on strengthening Iran's ground forces. Deeply concerned about Iran's internal security problems and her vulnerability to pressures from the Soviet Union, with which Iran shares a 1,300-mile border, the Shah was determined to improve his country's military security. The ground forces were steadily upgraded until, in the mid-sixties, two basic developments combined to fuel a reexamination of Iran's strategic interests.

One event was the Indian-Pakistani War of 1965. It had not escaped the Shah that the United States had in effect abandoned her ally in favor of an even-handed policy. While Washington had frozen its arms shipments to both belligerents, the American action basically affected only Pakistan, whose armed forces largely depended on American equipment and spare parts. A second development was the growing influence of radical Arab movements along the periphery of the Arabian Peninsula. All these reasons help to explain the accelerated modernization of the Iranian armed forces from the mid-sixties onwards.

Grouped into three field armies, the combat forces by 1976 included three armored divisions, four infantry divisions, and one airborne and one special forces brigade. A small Aviation Command was also being established.

The infantry forces were equipped with modern rifles and machine guns, and had more than 2,000 armored personnel carriers at their disposal.[45] The artillery units comprised about 30 percent of the Army's personnel and had undergone a major upgrading. They were for the most part equipped with Soviet antiair guns and American surface-to-surface gun systems.[46]

In the armored divisions some of the M-47 and M-60 American tanks were being replaced with the newer and more advanced British Chieftain and Scorpion tanks. The medium-weight Chieftain, armed with 120 mm guns, was to be fitted with laser range finders. Iran in 1973 began to take delivery of her order of some 760 Chieftains.[47] In May 1975 Iran reportedly ordered another 1,200 Chieftains. Of the lighter Scorpion tanks some 250 were being acquired. Additional plans, then, called for a tank force approximately comparable in total number to the separate forces of Egypt and Israel, and about one-quarter or one-third larger than those of Syria and Iraq. Iran's projected tank force was just about equal to that of France, and double the size of the British tank force.[48]

To service and maintain the Chieftains, Iran had built a Military Industrial Complex (MIC). The MIC was to produce Chieftain spare parts and ammunition as well as replacement parts for Iran's armored vehicles, and thus was to complement the Royal Armaments Factories in northern Tehran, which produced small arms and ammunition.

Iran had also developed an airborne brigade as well as a special forces brigade along American lines for counterinsurgency operations. These forces offered a capability for suppressing insurgencies in the gulf region. To provide them with a rapid deployment capability, the army was developing its Aviation Command, with headquarters at Isfahan. The core of the Army Aviation Command was to be some 600 helicopters, which were to provide transport, command, and close fire support elements to the Sky Cavalry Brigade.[49]

Although at first mainly deployed in the northern section of Iran, the ground forces were for the most part stationed along the border with Iraq. Army troops were also deployed in the south, near the Pakistani frontier, to prevent the crossing of insurgents from Pakistan into Iran. Some fifteen hundred combat troops were deployed in Oman to help the sultan of Oman defeat the insurgency of the Dhofar Liberation Front. As has been mentioned, from the time the Shah began to support the sultan up to 1976, some fifteen to seventeen thousand troops had been rotated through Oman, and the process was to be continued as long as the situation seemed to require an Iranian presence.[50]

The equipment, training and discipline of the ground units pointed to a highly capable force. A soft spot, however, remained the limited education and technological skill of most of the troops. Another weakness was their lack of combat experience. Yet, when Iran deployed troops to Oman to fight against the Dhofari guerillas, several accounts indicated that the Persian troops performed creditably. There is no reason to assume that the ground forces could not ensure internal order to stop limited local conflicts elsewhere in the gulf region.

The Imperial Iranian Air Force

Although the Imperial Iranian Air Force did not receive separate service status until 1955, it had been organized as a branch of the army already before World War II.[51] After the war, and especially after Iran had joined the Baghdad Pact in 1955, the U.S. military aid program enabled Iran to develop her air force with the F-86 fighter as its workhorse. The primary mission of the air force was to provide air defense and close air support for the ground forces.

Still, it was not until 1965, when the government in Tehran allocated some $400 million to its defense buildup, that the expansion of the IIAF began to make rapid strides. Much of the impressive modernization of the air force bears the stamp of its former commander, General Mohammad Khatemi, by whose untimely death in 1975 the IIAF lost one of its most illustrious leaders.

With more than 60,000 personnel, the IIAF in the mid-1970s was patterned on the American model. It had a projected strength of approximately 500 combat aircraft, including F-4 Phantoms, F-5 Tiger fighter-bombers, and F-14 Tomcats, all of which were equipped with air-to-air missiles.[52] The most spectacular item among Iran's latest purchases, the swing-wing F-14 Tomcat, equipped with long-range Phoenix missiles, provided an effective counter to the Soviet MIG-23 or even, should the Iraqis acquire it, to the MIG-25. It also offered the capability to keep Iranian air space free from intruders.

In deciding to acquire the U.S. F-14 aircraft, the Shah was clearly concerned about Iraq's possession of the MIG-23, which was superior to Iran's F-4. The Shah's assessment of the superiority of Iraqi aircraft to those supplied by the United States, at least until the acquisition of the F-14 fighter-bomber, was correct. The F-14, however, is not just an aircraft for if judged only as an aircraft it could not be called superior to the MIG-23 aircraft in Iraq's possession. There are two versions of the MIG-23: a reconnaissance version and a fighter version. It is the latter that was delivered to Iraq in 1974 by the Soviets, as contrasted with the reconnaissance type that was deployed to Egypt in 1972 before the Soviets were requested by the Egyptian government to leave. One can determine whether the version is the fighter or reconnaissance one by the number of deployment: the fact that there were only six or so of the MIG-23s in Egypt marked them for a reconnaissance mission.

Since, by the mid-1970s, there were about thirty MIG-23s in Iraq, they clearly had a fighter mission. Where the U.S. F-14 really attained clear superiority over the MIG-23—or, indeed the MIG-25, were Iraq or others in the area to acquire this aircraft—was by dint of the fact that the F-14 was more appropriately characterized as a whole weapons system rather than a mere fighter aircraft. For one thing, it carried the Phoenix missile, which made it superior even to such aircraft as the advanced MIGs that had greater speed and altitude. The Phoenix missile system enabled the F-14 to destroy a MIG at higher altitudes. The F-14 could thus operate in the lower altitudes for which it was designed and in which it could outmaneuver a MIG-23 or MIG-25. Through the acquisition of the F-14 Iran had thus for the first time clearly established the superiority of her air force over that of Iraq.

For inflight fueling, the Iranian fighter-bomber force relied on a squadron of Boeing 707 tankers, which could increase the combat radiuses of the F-4s and F-5s to 1400 miles, thereby enabling them to cover the northwestern sector of the Indian Ocean region.[53] In fact, Iran's location in this vital area was militarily analogous to that of an aircraft carrier positioned for maximum effect. Iran had evinced some interest in carriers such as the recently launched Soviet Kiev class and a new British cruiser, both of which could employ vertical takeoff or short takeoff and landing aircraft. Even without carriers, however, Iran with her air force could cover a significant part of the Persian Gulf—Gulf of Oman—Indian Ocean region from home bases in Iran. The upgrading of Iran's fighter and bomber capabilities had been matched by the expansion of her transport forces.[54] Air-defense missiles had also been installed.[55]

In 1976, all air force training was conducted at the Air Force Training Center in Tehran. Instruction was in English; this facilitated further training, which usually occurred in the United States and occasionally in Pakistan.[56] The elite of the F-5 pilots were trained to fly the F-4 fighters; in turn, the best F-4 fliers were shifted to the F-14 program. Even more so than in the army, the air force placed a premium on skilled manpower. But as in the army, the acquisition of technically trained personnel posed a major problem. This did not mean, however, that Iran lacked qualified pilots. No less than other non-Arab Moslem countries, notably Turkey and Pakistan, Iran boasted excellent fliers. By Western standards, the IIAF might not have reached the status of a highly skilled and efficient force. But by criteria prevailing in the Persian Gulf—Middle East—Indian Ocean area, which was the environment in which the Iranian air force would have to be tested, the IIAF clearly ranked among the superior forces.

Iran's air force of 1976 consisted of approximately 300 combat aircraft. But Iran's projected air force of at least 500 or more combat aircraft already bought was expected to roughly equal the number and exceed in quality the air force of Egypt in the late 1970s (568, including 100 in storage) or to exceed that of Israel (466). It was expected to become more than twice as large as that of Iraq (218), and vastly superior to the Saudi Arabian combat force, which in 1976 numbered 90. Compared to West European air forces, Iran's was about to be numerically equal to the British (500), and as large as those of West Germany (468) and France (431). It was to be twice as large as those of Turkey (290) and Italy (279). These figures, of course, indicate only quantitative equivalents. If we consider qualitative equipment factors, we must conclude that the Shah's determination to purchase the most modern and sophisticated aircraft available was about to give Iran, on a selective basis, at least, technological superiority over those air forces mentioned above.

The Imperial Iranian Navy

The Imperial Iranian Navy (IIN) traces its origin to 1927, when the Ministry of War ordered two frigates for its recently established Southern Command.

The two gunboats delivered in 1932 were followed in subsequent years by several other ships until, in 1941, the Southern Command had four squadrons at its disposal. Each squadron included one frigate and at least two sloops.[57] In the years after the war Iran received a number of torpedo boats, minelayers, and minesweepers from the United States, and some reconditioned destroyers from Britain.

More recently the IIN has undergone a major modernization. While in terms of manpower still easily the smallest among Iran's armed services, nevertheless the navy has become a respectable ocean-going force. By 1976 it already constituted by far the most impressive fleet in the Persian Gulf; no combination of forces of the littoral states could offer the IIN a serious challenge.

In the mid-1970s the IIN included one former British Battle class destroyer, the 2,325-ton *Artemiz,* and two former U.S. 3,320-ton destroyers, the *Babr* and the *Palang.* They had been extensively modernized and armed with standard missiles. They were in good condition and manned by adequate crews. The navy also included four newly built fast frigates equipped with British surface-to-surface air missiles. Four U.S. patrol frigates supplement the larger units.[58]

To help protect the sea-lanes of communication through the Indian Ocean to the Persian Gulf, Iran had bought three Tang class diesel submarines from the United States. Four U.S. Spruance class destroyers, fitted with multiple missile launchers and a new U.S. Harpoon antiship missile, had also been purchased. It seemed possible that Iran might acquire another two of the Spruance class destroyers. Four of the destroyers already purchased, of the same tonnage as light Soviet cruisers, were scheduled for delivery by 1980.

The light naval forces included six large patrol craft; six 40-foot coastal patrol craft; and three 70-ton patrol boats.[59] The light forces underwrote the Iranian navy's mission of supporting the Iranian army in local interventions, when necessary. Important in this respect were the military hovercraft. In 1976, Iran operated the largest military hovercraft force in the world, and the Iranian navy had been the first in the world to acquire hovercraft for patrol purposes. The hovercraft were uniquely qualified for operations in the shallow waters of the Persian Gulf. The craft, first used when Iranian forces landed on Abu Musa and the Tunb Islands in November 1971, were based in the northern part of the gulf and were generally used for coastal defense and logistic missions.

There were more than a dozen other smaller British patrol craft, several of them fitted with surface-to-surface missiles, and twelve fast attack missile patrol boats of the Combattante type bought from France.[60]

The Iranian navy had an air arm of some forty operational aircraft of various types, fixed wing and helicopter, used principally for purposes of antisubmarine warfare and for the escort of tankers sailing through the Shatt al-Arab. They could also be employed to support amphibious landing operations.[61]

For maritime patrol duties, six long-range P-3 Orion aircraft had been purchased and delivered. The long-range Orion, which was to be operated by the air force, could stay aloft for seventeen hours, and thus could be used for maritime missions well beyond the gulf. Within the gulf, the antisubmarine warfare requirements were limited in light of the narrow choke points and shallow water. A number of support ships as well as three former U.S. coastal minesweepers and two U.S. inshore minesweepers further rounded out the Iranian naval capability.

To support the Iranian navy a network of bases was being built. Fleet headquarters were at Bandar 'Abbas, with Bushire and Chah Bahar to be the main subsidiary operating bases. The base at Chah Bahar was being built to accommodate the Spruance class destroyers and the diesel submarines purchased from the United States. This arm of the navy was to operate in deep water, patrolling the sea-lanes and routes of access and egress to and from choke points and other strategic passages east and south of the Persian Gulf. It was thus vital to Iran's Indian Ocean policy. It was near the Pakistani border on the Gulf of Oman, and less vulnerable than would have been the case if it had been situated inside the landlocked Persian Gulf. Chah Bahar was also to be provided with an excellent air base for giving air cover with F-4 Phantoms and for the antisubmarine warfare and surveillance capabilities made possible by Orion P-3 aircraft, ranging well out into the Indian Ocean.

The light naval forces were based at Khorramshahr. Bandar 'Abbas was also the site of the fleet maintenance unit. Bandar-Pahlavi, on the Caspian Sea, was the headquarters of the Northern Command, which had primarily a training mission.

The U.S. Spruance class destroyers, the diesel submarines, and the existing fleet of minesweepers and larger ships, of which almost all had antisubmarine capabilities and both antiair and antiship armament, combined to support the Shah's strategy for keeping the sea-lanes open. The Shah, moreover, was clearly determined to turn the IIN into a first-class force. His anxiety to upgrade the navy and to keep it free of domestic controversy was reflected in his decision to dismiss the Iranian naval commander-in-chief, Vice-Admiral R.H. 'Ata'i, whose professional skills were unquestionable, but who for reasons of impropriety could not be maintained in his position. Along with Attaie, and for the same reasons, went the vice-commander of the navy and a sizable number of other experienced naval officers. It was rumored that in all over forty were involved. The new commander-in-chief of the IIN was Admiral S. Habibelahy. It is worth noting—keeping in mind the strategic importance of the Persian Gulf–Indian Ocean area to Iran—that he was formerly in charge of the Persian Gulf–Sea of Oman Command.

The IIN was already patrolling Iran's nearly 2,000 miles of coastal waters, as well as islands over which she exercised sovereignty in the Persian Gulf, and also large portions of the northwestern Indian Ocean extending down to ten degrees north latitude. The U.S. Spruance class destroyers, it appeared, would enable Iran to extend her patrol of the sea-lanes as far down along the shipping route as South Africa. This potential underlay Iran's persistence—despite the sharp increase in unit costs—in procuring the Spruance class destroyer. It was the Shah's conviction that to purchase smaller ships, i.e., frigates, etc. as a substitute for the Spruance destroyers would not suffice for such extended deepwater missions.

The projected Imperial Iranian Navy of the late 1970s, with over 15,000 personnel and 30 principal combat vessels, was comparable to the Egyptian Navy (15,000 and 40, many of them older), somewhat larger than the Israeli (9,000 and 21), and much larger than the Iraqi (2,000 and about 20 smaller vessels, several of less than 100 tons). Iran was the only Middle Eastern country in possession of modern missile destroyers and missile frigates, and therefore enjoyed superiority in sophisticated naval equipment over the neighboring countries just mentioned. But the IIN was not on a par with the naval forces of several European NATO countries, such as Britain, France, West Germany, Italy, and Turkey. Even the Netherlands, with a population only two-fifths that of Iran, maintained an equivalent navy.

How Much Is Enough?

Since 1970 the development of Iranian military forces has become the subject of almost daily comment and analysis in the Western press. As one commentator has observed: "The statistics used to describe the build-up are themselves staggering. In 1966, Iran ranked twenty-ninth in the league of world arms expenditure: today it is the eighth largest spender on defence. . . . Seen in terms of European defence spending Iran's military budget is now approaching that of Britain, France, and Germany and by 1980 will exceed the $20,000 million mark."[62]

In commenting on the relative strength in the area in the wake of the British withdrawal, the International Institute for Strategic Studies (IISS) noted that among the local states Iran was "militarily much the strongest."[63] The IISS appraisal also pointed out that the Iranian air force was more than a match for the combined Arab air forces in the Persian Gulf, and that the Iranian navy, much improved though lacking experience, completely outclassed any Arab rival.[64]

Iran's weapons acquisitions have frequently drawn fire from observers who fear an arms race between Iran and its Arab neighbors, and who argue that Iran's resources could be better devoted to the country's development.[65]

Critics charge that the Shah has bought an unnecessarily large quantity of weapons systems. Moreover, much has been said, in the media and elsewhere, concerning a relationship between the increasing oil prices and the growth in arms sales to the Middle East, especially the Persian Gulf region. Certainly, the higher prices have enabled many of the oil-rich countries to purchase arms in much greater magnitude than would have been possible without such revenues.

It is important to recognize, however, that the dramatic expansion of Iran's role as a military power was not solely the function of the 1973 rise in the oil wealth of that country. Other oil-producing states have profited handsomely from their resources and from the global energy equation, without translating their newly amassed wealth into commensurate military and political power and influence. Furthermore, Iran's efforts to purchase very costly and highly sophisticated weapons began even before the Tehran oil agreement of February 1971—a fact that seems generally to have been overlooked in the Western media.

Had Britain stuck to her planned schedule for withdrawal from the Persian Gulf in the 1973-77 period rather than hastening the process, Iran's military development might not have been undertaken at the same pace and magnitude, but it would still have taken place. The stepped-up arms purchases by Iran have also reflected the realization in Tehran that the mere agreement to purchase such sophisticated weaponry does not automatically convert such capabilities into real military power. The need, as seen by Iran, to obtain the weapons quickly and in such large numbers has to do with the long lead-times between purchase and delivery, plus the time required for reaching an effective level of combat training for utilizing them.

There has also been sensitivity in Tehran to the sharp increase in costs the longer purchases are delayed. Thus, for example, in January 1976 the Shah told this writer that the unit costs had increased so sharply in the case of the Spruance class destroyer—from under $100 million to over $300 million—that he was in the process of reassessing his ability to buy them. He indicated that this sharp rise in the cost, along with an equally sharp deficit in oil revenues (about $3 billion), had forced him more generally to reconsider his strategy for the Indian Ocean region. The destroyers were the key weapon systems to support Iran's strategy of deployment beyond the Straits of Hormuz, and without them he could not seriously contemplate such a strategy. Indeed, he was also forced to consider stopping the development of the large naval and air base at Chah Bahar on the Gulf of Oman because, as he pointed out, there would be no need for such a large naval facility if he did not purchase the Spruance destroyer. The Shah sent his principal advisor for military procurement, Deputy Defense Minister General Hassan Toufanian, to the United States on January 16, 1976, to discuss the matter. A compromise was reached whereby Iran agreed to buy four Spruance destroyers at the same unit cost it would have paid for the six it had originally ordered. As a result of this compromise, Iran decided to adhere to her planned Indian Ocean strategy and policy, albeit initially with fewer ships of the Spruance class.

In any event, the spiraling costs of weapons systems inevitably have impinged upon Iranian military programs. Some critics point out that these cost increases have been fueled in large part by the rise in the price of oil. Be that as it may, in Iran's case the problem has been compounded by the earlier mentioned drop in oil revenues. The fact that he has pressed ahead with the substance of his military programs despite rising prices and lowered revenues emphasizes the priority that the Shah attaches to his country's security objectives.

The Shah's critics, who like to link his military programs to the "oil windfall," overlook the fact that the pivotal point in his military policies came in the wake of the Pakistani Indian conflict of 1965, long before the impact of the oil crisis. Noting that the CENTO powers, especially the United States, had not come to the aid of Pakistan, the Shah was confirmed in his conclusion that Iran must be prepared to defend her own vital national interests. It was during this period, in the mid-sixties, that Iran's drive to become a major power really was launched. It was then that the first serious discussions concerning the purchase of the F-4 Phantom aircraft were inaugurated.

The Shah's decision in favor of an independent Iranian military establishment has been strengthened by more recent events: he has witnessed the embargo on U.S. arms shipments to Turkey by the U.S. Congress with the clear intent of pressuring Turkey to withdraw her forces from Cyprus. Tehran has clearly opted for flexibility and seeks to have sufficient systems in reserve to minimize the impact of a potential arms cutoff by the U.S. Congress on the readiness and capability of the Iranian armed forces.

Finally, a consideration frequently ignored by critics of Iran's military buildup is the support U.S. companies derive from Iranian arms acquisitions, notably in times of declining U.S. purchases of military equipment. Litton Industries, which builds the Spruance class destroyers, Grumman with its F-14, Lockheed with its P-3 Orion and C-130 aircraft programs, and Hughes, which produces Tomcat aircraft missiles, are key U.S. defense contractors whose production and development capabilities have benefited through Iranian procurement programs.

Iran and Nuclear Weapons

The Iranian government has already bought nuclear power plants from European countries and in 1976 was scheduled to buy approximately eight nuclear power plants from the United States. Agreement had already been reached between Iran and France on the acquisition of nuclear reactors. The French agreements included the promise that France would supply at least two and perhaps as many as ten nuclear power plants. In all, Iran planned to establish 20 nuclear power plants and acquire 23,000 megawatts electric of nuclear power-generating plants by the late 1990s.

Much speculation has been triggered by these agreements in the Western media, especially in the United States, over possible Iranian military-nuclear ambitions. While it seemed much too early in the mid-1970s to prejudge eventual Iranian decisions—dependent as these were on the evolution of events in the Middle East-Indian Ocean region and the larger world scene—suffice it to say that the speculation seemed both premature and exaggerated. Not only is Iran a signatory to the Nuclear Non-Proliferation Treaty (NPT), but the decision to seek a nuclear energy capacity also seems to be economically justified. Iran's oil supplies are limited when compared, for example, with those of Saudi Arabia, which has to worry about a population of 5 million at the most. This is in sharp contrast with the domestic development tasks of Iran, which faces a soaring population growth of 3 percent per annum and will have 65 million people by the end of the century. As the Shah has said repeatedly: "How can we be compared to our neighboring oil producing countries? Iran must find 300,000 new jobs a year for those coming on to the work force."[66]

Iran's total possible oil reserve figures of some 80 billion barrels are often quoted, and these would give Iran an oil-export horizon of only some twenty-five to thirty years. Given this prospect, and Iran's ambitious drive for industrialization, the alternative of nuclear energy makes economic sense.

Iran is on record as favoring so-called free zones, i.e., zones free of nuclear weapons, in the Middle East. But the future of such proposals is uncertain, especially in light of the fact that one state in the region, India, already possesses a nuclear weapons option and, while as yet unconfirmed by official Israeli sources, that country was widely assumed to already possess some nuclear weapons. If India should implement her option with an actual development of nuclear weapons, Iran would logically be presented with the problem of reconsidering her own nuclear policy.

There is no evidence that the Shah is unduly concerned about the possibility of an Indian nuclear weapons development, even though such an Indian option could have the effect of offsetting Iran's costly conventional military capabilities and casting the shadow of Indian hegemony over large parts of the Indian Ocean area. Indeed, when this writer raised the question with the Iranian monarch in an audience in March 1975, he responded in a way that reflected a lack of concern over such a posible development.[67] The Shah emphasized that the large-scale conventional capability he was procuring should be seen as ample evidence that he intended and hoped to cope with defense problems in the Persian Gulf-Indian Ocean region on a nonnuclear basis. As he explained: "Why should I obtain so many conventional capabilities if I intended to go nuclear?" He has made this point many times. In a press conference in Australia in September 1974 he responded as follows to the question of whether Iran would opt for nuclear weapons:

> Our air force will be very well equipped in five years time. And this is needed because we just have a look around us and see what others have in order to equip [ourselves] with what we can. There is nothing more dangerous for a vitally important country geographically like mine to be unable to defend not only its borders but also its interests . . . . From those nuclear reactors we are not going to try to make bombs. And this is a cardinal point in our national policy.[68]

He averred that he was depending on the nuclear power of the United States to offset potential nuclear threats, arguing:

> First of all we have very close relations with the United States. Probably we could not do without them, because the present world is confronted with a problem of some countries possessing nuclear weapons and some not. We are among those who do not possess nuclear weapons so the friendship of a country such as the United States with their arsenal of nuclear weapons . . . is absolutely vital.[69]

While statements such as these reflect what is undoubtedly the Shah's present intent with respect to nuclear-military capabilities, they can by no means be interpreted as a permanent pledge to keep the door locked on a nuclear option. The Shah has already demonstrated amply his willingness to do everything in his power to safeguard the security of his country against all palpable contingencies. Should nuclear proliferation spill meaningfully into the region of Iran's security concerns, he would obviously be forced to reconsider his aversion to the nuclear path. It hardly needs to be pointed out that a key variable in this equation is the future role of the United States—and the credibility of that role—in the Middle East and the Indian Ocean.

CONCLUSIONS

The father of the Iranian armed forces was Reza Shah. From its humble origins in the Cossack Brigade, the Iranian military has been transformed into a force equipped with the most modern weapons. Regionally Iran is a military power to be reckoned with.

Questions have been raised about the credibility of the rapidly developing Iranian military forces and their ability to implement the strategy that has been described in this chapter. A related question has concerned the magnitude and quality of Iran's military procurement program: whether it is both too large and too sophisticated with respect to the likely security threats faced by Tehran.

In order to answer these questions, it might be well to consider a prime case in which the Shah has seen the role of Iran's military forces. One of the most important commitments Iran has undertaken is that of defending the approaches to the Straits of Hormuz from both north and south. The first and key problem for Iran in carrying out this commitment is to ensure that the Arabian side of the straits and the adjacent areas remain in friendly hands. The key problem is thus one of effective deterrence: of convincing radical movements bent upon overthrowing traditional rule in this area that Iran will move with speed and determination to frustrate their designs—and will do so at heavy cost to the offenders against the status quo. In the Middle East, Persian Gulf, and Indian Ocean areas, as elsewhere, military power casts a heavy political and psychological shadow. The Shah knows this, as do the radical and other antimonarchical elements in the region.

There is the chance, of course, that the mere existence of a potent military establishment will not suffice to discourage these forces. Changes could take place in the ruling constellations on the Arab side of the gulf that would imperil defense of the Straits of Hormuz and Iranian security interests as well. A new regime could take over in Baghdad, disavow the 1975 agreement with Iran, and mount a new confrontation. In either scenario, a serious military threat could be directed at the straits. It could be directed from the shores via artillery fire or missiles, or from small, fast patrol craft equipped with missile-launching platforms. In either situation, Iran would have to do it. There is every reason to believe that its weapons inventory will enable it to move decisively. Especially if Oman remained a hospitable base of operations, Iranian aircraft, helicopters, and antisubmarine warfare (ASW) capabilities could fan out from inside the gulf itself to fend against threats to the straits.

This brings us to the most dangerous threat to the sea-lanes on which Iranian security and well-being depend: the threat posed by submarines to tankers and other commercial vessels traveling outward beyond the Straits of Hormuz. This threat looms as a more logical one outside the straits because the shallowness of the gulf discourages combat submarine operations within it, except for surveillance or intelligence missions. Such a threat could be mounted by the Soviet Union itself—for example, in the larger context of a Middle East crisis—but one cannot rule out actions by such Soviet client states as Somalia. It is difficult to assign any measure of probability to such a threat, just as it is, for example, to adduce probability to the danger of an all-out nuclear war between the United States and the Soviet Union and therefore to a desirable level for U.S. strategic nuclear programs.

Nevertheless, as the guardian of his nation's ultimate security concerns, the Shah must give heed to such possible contingencies. This explains the existence in the Iranian inventory of Lockheed Orion P-3 maritime reconnaissance aircraft, with their ASW capabilities, as well as the Spruance class destroyers that Iran has purchased.

One could invoke any number of potential conflict scenarios in the region, with varying degrees of likelihood, that would directly impact on Iranian security concerns. As has been suggested, a future renewed Iranian-Iraqi confrontation is not beyond the pale of possibilities—a contingency in which the full panoply of sophisticated Iranian capabilities would have to come into play against an adversary directly supported by an adjacent superpower. The basic point to be made is that the Shah's security concerns, in behest of which he is pressing the armament of his country, can be understood only if one tries to gain a vicarious understanding of the multifaceted predicament confronting him.

The Shah's basic prodicament is that his country has been essentially a "loner" in a volatile region. This role is decreed by the ethnic factors that distinguish Iran from its Arab neighbors and the Indian subcontinent, as well as by the geopolitics of oil and power. In the wake of the retrenchment of Western power from the Persian Gulf and Indian Ocean—first Great Britain and now increasingly the United States—the Shah reached the inescapable conclusion that, in the final analysis, the survival of Iran will be a function of her own resources, particularly military resources. Indeed, underlying Iranian defense efforts is a strong sense of beleaguerment, and the determination to be prepared for a wide range of contingencies that could be spawned in an increasingly unstable regional environment.

It is all too easy for critics of the Shah to fault specific aspects of Iranian military programs and policies—especially if they fail to grasp the specific assumptions and fears that govern them. It is much more difficult, in any event, to argue with the fundamental premise that has sparked Iran's armament effort: namely, that in the evolving and increasingly complex global environment, each nation is likely to be the final arbiter of its own security.

12

Political Process and Institutions in Iran: the Second Pahlavi Kingship

In the political sense, the Pahlavi era in Iran has been one of ingenious blending of tradition and innovation. Profound political changes have occurred and yet certain time-honored institutions and customs have remained unaltered. The Pahlavi dynasty could be identified with certain major trends in modern Iran that set it apart from the experience of the country under the previous Qajar dynasty. The Qajar era was characterized by the weakness of the ruling institution combined with the despotism of the successive kings, by general backwardness, disorganization, encroachments of foreign powers, and the irresponsible behavior of egoistic and pleasure-seeking monarchs. By contrast, the new Pahlavi era ushered Iran to a new path of nationalism, jealous safeguarding of the state's sovereignty, centralization and strengthening of power of the government, and bold reforms aiming at modernization and development. Thus the Pahlavis brought about a real revolution in the life and status of a nation whose ancient and outstanding civilization had suffered serious deterioration, and that had reached a state of lethargy largely due to political weakness and repeated military defeats.

There is no doubt that politics have a primacy in the life of any nation. A nation may be highly developed economically; it may enjoy high cultural standards and progressive social institutions; but if it is politically and militarily weak, it may suffer subjugation by a foreign power and then, automatically, all the achievements and advantages in the nonpolitical sectors will follow the decline of the basic political environment. Czechoslovakia after World War II provides an instructive example in this respect. Frequently hailed in the West as an industrialized country of progress and democracy,

Czechoslovakia experienced first a Communist takeover, in 1948, and twenty years later an invasion of the Red Army supported by satellite troops when its national leadership, then at the helm of the state, tried to introduce "socialism with a human face." Similarly Iran, emerging in a state of chaos and anarchy from World War I, had to attend to her fundamental priorities, which were political, before serious and systematic thought could be given to problems of socioeconomic reform.

The Institutional Framework

In a formal sense, Iran's insitiutional framework rests on the Fundamental Laws (i.e., the constitution) of 1906, which was granted by Shah Mozaffar ad-Din in response to popular demands in the declining period of the Qajar dynasty. Based on Belgian models, the constitution was enlarged by the more elaborate Supplementary Fundamental Law of 1907.[1] Its main thrust was to establish a constitutional monarchy in Iran and thus put an end to the arbitrariness of the succession of weak kings who not only mismanaged the country's internal affairs but also became easy prey for the expansionist policies of czarist Russia and, to a lesser degree, the status quo imperial policies of Great Britain. The constitution introduced a strict separation of powers between the executive, legislative, and judicial branches of the government. It provided for the establishment of a two-chamber parliament composed of the National Consultative Assembly *(Majles-e Showra-ye Melli,* "Majles" for short) and the Senate. The Senate was to be composed of thirty representatives from Tehran and thirty from the provinces. In turn, half of the senators from each of these two constituencies were to be appointed by the Shah, while the other half were to be elected. While in principle deputies to the Majles were to be elected on the basis of territorial representation, the constitution made a provision for representation of national and religious minorities as well. Thus it assured the presence in the Majles of a Zoroastrian, an Armenian, an Assyrian, and a Jewish deputy.

Executive power was vested in the person of the Shah aided by the Council of Ministers, the latter chaired by the prime minister. Because of the principle of separation of powers, ministers were not permitted to serve in either of the two legislative chambers. The Shah's authority embraced the right to appoint and dismiss the prime minister and ministers, the right to appoint certain specified higher officials as well as officers of the army, and the right to sign the laws passed by the parliament. The constitution gave the Shah no explicit veto power, and article 49 of the Supplementary Law spoke of his duty to enact the laws passed by the parliament, thus implicitly denying him such power. The constitution also granted the Shah a conditional right to dissolve the parliament under very complicated procedures. The Shah was also vested with the authority of commander in chief of the armed forces.

The Supplementary Fundamental Law of 1907 included important provisions that could be broadly described as a bill of rights. It also contained a provision that a committee of learned theologians (*'olama* or *mojtaheds*) would be formed upon nomination of the religious functionaries and selection by the parliament. This committee of five would itself have the right to pronounce on the validity of the laws passed by the parliament in the light of religious precepts, since the Shi'a branch of Islam (in its version of twelve imamis, *Ethna 'Ashariyyeh*) was proclaimed to be the state religion of Iran.

Because of the reckless way in which the Qajar rulers incurred state debts with foreign powers or granted far-reaching economic concessions to foreign governments and citizens, the constitution expressly reserved to the parliament the right to give its consent to such agreements. Furthermore, it proclaimed equality of Iranians before the law. As for the judicial branch of the government, a hierarchy of courts was to be set up, with the Supreme Court (Court of Cassation) as the highest judicial body. This court, however, unlike the U.S. Supreme Court, was not given the right of judicial review. That right, presumably, was reserved for the earlier-mentioned committee of theologians.

Amendments to the Constitution

With the advent of the Pahlavi dynasty the constitution was amended on four occasions, in 1925, 1949, 1957, and 1967.

On December 12, 1925, a specially called Constituent Assembly formally proclaimed Reza Khan as Shah of Iran and in accordance with this decision amended articles 36, 37, and 38 of the Supplementary Law. The amended articles read as follows:

> *Article 36.* The constitutional monarchy of Persia is vested by the Constituent Assembly in his Imperial Majesty Reza Shah Pahlavi and his male descendants in succession.
> *Article 37.* The eldest son if born of a Persian mother, shall be the heir apparent to the throne. In the event of the Shah having no son, the heir to the throne shall be designated by His Imperial Majesty, subject to the approval of the Majles. No member of the Qajar family can, however, be so designated.
> *Article 38.* In the event of the throne becoming vacant, the Crown Prince cannot govern in person until he has reached the age of twenty. If he has not reached that age, a regent, who shall in no circumstances be a member of the Qajar family, shall be appointed by the Majles.[2]

Having thus legitimized his rule, Reza Shah saw no further need to effect changes in the constitution. Under his authoritarian tutelage, moreover, the real power of the Majles was considerably diminished. Nevertheless, Reza Shah maintained the parliamentary institution, seeing no reason to abolish it. While the center of decision making was certainly in the hands of the Shah during that period, the Majles continued to play a useful role as a school of political thought and experience. The least that could be said about its role was that it contributed to the political awareness and concern with public affairs of its members and those affiliated with them.

Furthermore, the decision of Reza Shah not to part with the institution of the Majles served as a safeguard for the continuity of the monarchical system. This became evident in 1941, when he was forced to abdicate under the impact of the dual occupation of his country by foreign powers, and when his son, Mohammad Reza, was proclaimed Shah of Iran by the parliament. In this difficult moment the Majles assured the continuity of the dynasty, provided for an orderly succession, and thus filled a gap that might have had very harmful consequences for the survival of Iran as an independent and sovereign state.

The war years and the immediate postwar period abounded in crises of an international nature and in domestic turmoil, both of which more than once placed in jeopardy the existence of Iran as an independent entity. The royal power was weakened while the power of the Majles was enhanced. Moreover, despite the explicit provision of the constitution of 1906, the upper chamber, the Senate, had not yet been set up. The new ruler, Mohammad Reza Shah, felt that his authority should be strengthened, and with this in view he undertook two initiatives. First, in June 1949, he caused the Senate to be established.[3] Because half the senators were to be appointed by him, it was bound automatically to strengthen his influence upon the governmental process. Second, he gave the initiative to the calling of a Constituent Assembly with an eye to amending certain provisions of the constitution affecting the relationship between the King and the parliament. Furthermore, paradoxically, neither the Fundamental Laws of 1906 nor the Supplementary Law of 1907 contained any provisions about the procedure of constitutional amendment. Faced with this situation, the Constituent Assembly passed on May 7, 1949, the "Additional Article" to the Fundamental Laws in which two procedures were established for constitutional amendments, one of a permanent nature and the other ad hoc. The permanent procedure was defined as follows:

> When the Assembly and the Senate separately vote by a two-thirds majority of both chambers, either on their own proposal or on a proposition of the government, the necessity of revising one or several specific Articles of the Constitution or its annex, and His Majesty the Shah confirms the opinion of the chambers, a Constituent Assembly shall be convened by Imperial Order.

The Constituent Assembly shall be composed of a number of members equal to the legal total of the Assembly and of the Senate. The elections to the Constituent Assembly shall take place according to a law which shall be limited to the revision of the Articles determined by the two chambers and confirmed by His Majesty the Shah. The decisions of the Constituent Assembly will require a two-thirds majority of the total number of members and they will be put into execution after approval by His Majesty the Shah.

This Article does not affect any of the Articles of the Constitution and its annex concerned with the Shi'ite rites of the Holy Religion of Islam, the national religion, or concerned with the constitutional monarchy of Iran which are unchanging and fixed for eternity.[4]

In its second part the Additional Article provided for an ad hoc procedure to revise articles 4, 5, 6, 7, and 8 of the Fundamental Laws as well as article 49 of the Supplementary Law. Articles 4-8 deal with the number of deputies to the Majles, the length of their term of service, the quorum, and the periods of session and recess. As for article 49 of the Supplementary Law, it implicitly denied the Shah the right of veto over the Majles-adopted laws by proclaiming that "the issue of decrees and orders for giving effect to the laws is the King's right, provided that under no circumstances shall he postpone or suspend the carrying out of such laws."[5] According to the Additional Article, however, the amending of the foregoing five articles of the basic constitution and the Supplementary Law was to be accomplished not by the regular process of calling a Constituent Assembly, but by calling a joint session of the Majles and the Senate under the chairmanship of the president of the Senate. The joint session was then to decide on the necessary revisions by a majority of two-thirds of their total membership.

Having thus adopted the Additional Article, the Constituent Assembly proceeded the next day, May 8, to amend article 48 of the Fundamental Law dealing with the dissolution of both houses of parliament and the reconciling of differences that might arise between the two in matters of legislation. As amended, article 48 proclaimed:

His Imperial Majesty may dissolve the Majles or the Senate both together or separately.

Whenever the Houses or any one of them are dissolved in compliance with a Royal Decree, the same Decree shall include both the reason for dissolution and the order for new elections. New elections shall take place not more than one month following the date of the decree; and the new House or Houses shall open their sessions not more than three months following that date.

The new House or Houses convoked after the dissolution of the preceding ones shall sit for a whole term and not only for the remainder of the term of the dissolved House or Houses.

The new House or Houses shall not be dissolved for the same reason.

Whenever a bill or proposal has twice been referred from one House to the other and returned with no agreement reached, a mixed committee shall be formed, composed of an equal number of representatives from both Houses, which shall consider the dispute between the Houses and submit its report to both the Majles and the Senate. If both the Majles and the Senate approve the report submitted by the mixed committee, the bill or proposal shall be submitted for Royal signature. If no agreement is reached by the two Houses on the report submitted by the mixed committee, the point or points of difference shall be referred to His Imperial Majesty who shall if he agrees with the view held by the Majles, order the enactment of the bill or, if he does not agree, consideration of the bill or proposal shall be suspended for a period of not less than six months, at the end of which time it may if necessary be resubmitted in either of the two Houses.

Article 48, or any of the Articles of the Constitution of Zigha'de 1324, Lunar Year, inconsistent with the provisions set forth herein, shall hereinafter be null and void.[6]

The next step in the history of constitutional revision was the convocation of the joint session of the Majles and the Senate in 1957—an ad hoc procedure, as provided by the Additional Article passed in 1949. The joint session amended articles 4, 5, 6, and 7 of the Fundamental Laws while leaving article 8—initially slated for revision—unaltered. According to these amendments, the number of deputies to the Majles was increased from 136 to a maximum of 200, the term of the Majles was extended from two years to four, and the quorum was determined as half of the membership of the Majles. Furthermore, article 49 of the Supplementary Law was amended to give the Shah a suspensive veto over any financial bills passed by the Majles. If he disapproved of such a bill, the Shah had the right to send it back to the Majles for reconsideration. Should, however, the Majles confirm the initial bill by a three-quarters majority of those present in the capital, the Shah was obliged to promulgate it.[7]

The fourth major revision occurred in 1967 when the Constituent Assembly, especially called for that purpose in September, amended article 38 of the Supplementary Law pertaining to regency. In its old version, article 38 stipulated that in case of the throne becoming vacant and the Crown Prince being a minor under twenty, a regent would be appointed by the Majles. Such a regent could under no circumstances be a member of the Qajar family.

In the amended version, article 38 said:

During the transfer of monarchy, the Crown Prince can only personally take over monarchical affairs if he is twenty years old by the Solar Year. If he has not reached this age, the Shahbanou, mother of the Crown Prince, will immediately take over regency affairs, unless another person has been appointed as regent by the monarch. The regent will form a Council consisting of the Prime Minister, the heads of the [two] Houses, and the President of the Supreme Court, as well as four other knowledgeable and enlightened individuals appointed by the regent. And [she] will execute her duties according to the constitutional law and with the consultation of the Council, until the Crown Prince completes twenty years.

In the event of the death or resignation of the regent, the said Council will temporarily execute the duties of the regent until a regent is appointed from other than the Qajar family by the Houses [of Parliament]. Marriage of the regent Shahbanou amounts to resignation.[8]

The change in the composition of the regency concluded a series of constitutional revisions. Side by side with this constitutional evolution went the revision of the electoral laws. Without going into detail, suffice it to say that these laws embraced two kinds of provisions: those pertaining to the number of members of the Majles and the Senate, and those dealing with the mechanics of elections. Beginning in the mid-1950s, the number of deputies was periodically augmented to keep pace with the growth in the size of the population. Thus by 1971, when the twenty-third session of the Majles was inaugurated, the number of deputies reached 268. As for the length of the session of the Majles and the Senate, it was subject to various changes through both the provisions of the constitution and the acts of the Majles. As mentioned earlier, in 1957 the term of the Majles was extended from two years to four. The term of the Senate was initially (i.e., in 1949) set at six years. On October 23, 1952, the Majles adopted a law limiting the term of the Senate to two years to make it run concurrently with its own two-year term. And in 1957 the Senate term was again extended, this time to four years to conform to the term of the Majles.[9] The postwar electoral laws, furthermore, brought greater order into the electoral process in Iran. Before and during World War II and as late as the early 1950s, elections in the country consumed much time, being spread over several weeks inasmuch as various districts were holding them on different dates. This process was unhealthy; it produced much uncertainty, and there was a risk that results of elections in one area might unduly influence those in another. Beginning in the mid-1950s, therefore, electoral legislation provided for elections on a single day in July or August.

THE CHANGING ROLE OF PARLIAMENT

In 1976 the parliament as an institution in Iran was seventy years old, out of which fifty years corresponded to the rule of the Pahlavi dynasty. An analysis of the role of the Iranian parliament must necessarily focus on the National Assembly—the Majles—for two reasons: first, it functioned for a much longer time than the Senate, which was called into being only in 1949; second, its formal powers and real political role definitely exceeded in importance those of the Senate. In the formal sense, the main differentiating features of the Majles are that it has exclusive competence over fiscal affairs and that it can regulate certain matters, for example the length of the term of the Senate, by its own decisions. Nevertheless, the introduction of the Senate in 1949 was intended to provide a balance in the legislative process in a dual sense, both by providing the nation with a more mature and experienced deliberative body, composed for the most part of former holders of important state positions, and also by ensuring that the Shah would exert greater influence upon the legislative process because he was empowered to appoint half the Senate membership.

The Majles as an institution was actually called into existence even before the Fundamental Law. This first Majles met in August 1906, whereas the constitution was granted only in December of that year. During this early era of parliamentary life, the general thrust of the Majles was to supervise the spending of the Crown and curb any activities of the Qajar kings that might result in further encroachment of Russia and Britain on Iran's internal affairs. Parliamentary debates were characterized by a certain primitive crudeness, exaggerated statements, mutual accusations, much oratory, and little work of legislation. Moreover, Mohammad 'Ali Shah, who succeeded the signer of the constitution, his father Mozaffar ad-Din, was clearly hostile to the parliament and did not hesitate to ally himself with Russia to destroy that institution. Between 1909 and 1911, the parliament was subjected to much turmoil and an actual molestation by the armed forces of the Shah and the Russians. The constitutional system was saved through the efforts of a rather improbable coalition of Western-oriented intelligentsia, tribal chiefs from the south, and the Shi'a clergy. Well-documented accounts of this tumultuous era can be found in Browne's *The Persian Revolution of 1905-1909* and in his subsequent report, *The Persian Crisis of December, 1911,* and I shall not try to improve on either.[10]

During World War I there was a virtual suspension of the parliamentary process in Iran as a result of the unhappy condition in which the country found herself. Despite her proclaimed neutrality, Iran experienced both invasions and occupation by Russian, Turkish, British, and German troops and agents. These events, coupled with tribal uprisings in the south and politically motivated rebellions in the north, brought the country to a state of chaos and anarchy. The situation was further aggravated by the formation of a dissident government in Qom, which in due course moved to Kermanshah to operate under the protective rule of the Turkish-German military contingent.

With the advent of the peace following World War I, the Majles resumed its normal activities and played a key role in electing Reza Shah to kingship and legitimizing his rule. This rule, however, gradually developed into that of an authoritarian system of tutelage dedicated to the strengthening of the government and to a broad program of reform. The parliament continued to be elected but gradually most members became nominees of the powerful Shah, thus reducing the importance of the parliamentary institution.

The rule of the parliament was revived after the abdication of Reza Shah in 1941. It was in fact the parliament that proclaimed the then Crown Prince Mohammad Reza as Shah of Iran. The change of rulers was effected as a result of the Soviet-British occupation of the country and, at least initially, resulted in substantial weakening of the King's authority. Under those circumstances the parliament assumed greater importance, but this new role was played at the least propitious time for the development of democracy due to the military control of the country by the two foreign powers. There is no doubt that the normal constitutional process in Iran was grossly vitiated by these abnormal circumstances of war and foreign occupation. The division of the country into two zones of occupation further aggravated the situation.

In the Soviet zone there was no question of maintaining or restoring any real freedoms. The heavy hand of the Russian military, secret police, and special political agents was felt throughout the northern provinces, and was to show itself in the conduct of deputies who were elected to the parliament from the north. Although only a small number of them represented the Soviet-sponsored Tudeh party, a number of others were subjected to varying degrees of Soviet pressure. As for the British policies in the central and southern part of Iran, they were much more tolerant and respectful of Iranian independence; nevertheless the British found themselves also compelled to exert influence upon the political process, partly in response to Soviet machinations and partly to ensure the undisturbed functioning of the oil fields in the south and the transit routes carrying military supplies to the hard-pressed Soviet allies.[11]

This was indeed a turbulent period in the history of the Iranian Majles. During that time, despite the constitutionally guaranteed right of the Shah to appoint and dismiss the prime ministers, a parliamentary custom developed whereby the Majles, by a majority vote, would indicate its "inclination" as to who the prime minister should be. The Majles also had some influence on the dismissals or resignations of the incumbent prime ministers, although this process was more complex due to repeated Soviet interference. One of the better known decisions of the Majles was to adopt in 1944 a law forbidding the government to negotiate or grant any oil concessions without prior approval and subsequent ratification of the parliament.

During the first five years following World War II the Majles continued to play a significant role in the political life of the country, with this difference, that now—that is, since the Soviet evacuation of Iran in May of 1946—the parliament could operate under conditions of freedom, free from coercion by a foreign occupying power. Among a number of debates and decisions taken by the Majles in these first postwar years, three stand out as positive achievements testifying to the patriotic inclination of the majority of deputies. The first of these was the decisive role of the Majles in repudiating by an almost unanimous vote (with the exception of two Communist deputies) in December 1947 an oil concession granted by Premier Qavam as-Saltaneh to the Soviet Union during his negotiations in Moscow in March of 1946. This decision was taken with American encouragement, expressed in public utterances of the American ambassador, George V. Allen, but it represented a genuine and free expression of the will of the Majles. The second major act was the role of the parliament in encouraging U.S. aid, particularly in the economic, financial, and technical sectors, to Iran. Thus the American offer to extend the so-called Point Four program of assistance to underdeveloped nations, inaugurated by President Truman, was fully approved and accepted by the Majles. As a result, an American Point Four administration was set up in Iran and proceeded to perform many constructive and useful tasks, not only significantly assisting Iran's economy but also establishing a closer political link between the two countries. The third positive measure undertaken by the Majles was the adoption of laws setting up development planning. By virtue of these decisions the first seven-year development plan, with appropriate allocations, mostly from oil revenues, was launched, to be followed by similar plans in the subsequent years.

THE MAJLES IN TRANSITION

Beginning in 1951, the record of the Majles became more ambivalent and controversial. In this second postwar period, which could broadly be described as stretching from 1951 to 1961, two trends could be discerned in the work of the parliament. The first was an emotion-charged nationalism that tended to reach irrational and therefore impractical proportions. This was perhaps best exemplified by the ease with which the parliamentary majority fell under the spell of a seven-man group of deputies led by Dr. Mohammad Mosaddegh, a group that strongly agitated for immediate nationalization of the Iranian oil industry with little regard for the economic consequences of such a move. While the measure could still be described as patriotically motivated, as were the postwar acts of the Majles described above, it nevertheless conveyed an idea of immaturity and proneness to succumb to demagogic slogans on the part of the majority of the deputies. While it would be hard to deny that in many underdeveloped nations, particularly those with a record of being dominated by foreign imperial powers, the desire to control one's own natural resources is understandable and legitimate, there is a vast difference between hasty and economically reckless decisions and ones based upon serious study and cool calculation of the benefits and disadvantages that would result from a given decision in this sector. Exaggerated nationalism and economic development do not necessarily go hand in hand; in fact, as pointed out in a perceptive study by Jahangir Amuzegar, the two often conflict with each other and an exaggerated emphasis on the nationalist aspects of certain economic moves defeats the ultimate long-range national purpose of developing the backward country's economy.[12] This is exactly what happened in Iran during the so-called Mosaddegh era, between 1951 and 1953. Nationalization of the Anglo-Iranian Oil Company brought the economy of the country to a grinding standstill, emptied the treasury, deprived the country of the opportunity to secure foreign credits, and unleashed many destructive forces that might have produced not only the overthrow of the monarchy but also subjection of Iran to the Soviet Union, making it a satellite state. It was only through the major exertions of a group of Iranians dedicated to preserving the existing political system and the country's independence that this dangerous alternative was avoided. In the meantime, however, Iran paid dearly for her repeated rejection of rational solutions to the crisis. There was tremendous turmoil in every sector of national life and the orderly development of the Iranian economy was set back by years.

The second manifestation of the parliament's ambivalent and on the whole negative role was in its approach to the land reform advocated by the Shah and some of his progressive-minded ministers. While the problem of land reform has been discussed in detail by other writers, our concern here is primarily with its political aspects. The Shah had realized for a long time that the antiquated semifeudal system of Iranian land tenure was politically untenable and dangerous. The largely destitute peasantry could become an easy prey for various kinds of subversive propaganda, and although the standard of living of the average citizen in the neighboring Soviet Union was still abysmally low even when compared with many underdeveloped countries, there was always the temptation for skillful agitators to contrast the ostensible equality in the state-run and collective farms of the Soviet Union with the inequalities of the Iranian agrarian system. Thus in his intelligent appraisal of the situation the Shah clearly saw the need for a substantial land reform in his country. He took the lead himself as early as 1950, by launching a program of distributing Imperial estates to the peasantry. This was conceived as a pilot project, to be emulated by more comprehensive legislation that would affect the majority of Iranian land holdings. When, however, the government introduced the first land reform bill to the Majles in 1959 it encountered much opposition, which gradually grew in intensity as the Shah and his ministers began to press for a firmer law.

This obstructionism in the face of land reform in particular and reform in general stemmed largely from the fact that the Majles was composed of deputies representing for the most part the privileged strata of the population. Some aristocratic or wealthy landowning families could easily sway the votes of the people living in their villages or of those dependent economically on their good will. Others represented entrenched tribal chieftains or conservative religious groups. Among the deputies one could also find former government officials, usually of a high rank and distrustful of social change, merchants, and certain professional men. In general, the cast of deputies had a conservative hue about it; furthermore, it was conservatism of an unimaginative, status quo type that clearly stood in the way of much-needed reforms in the country.

By the early 1960s, therefore, the lines of political division had been clearly drawn. On the one side, there was the Shah who, for understandable political reasons, clearly saw the need for far-reaching reforms in every sphere of national life, reforms that would not only make the general population more prosperous and satisfied and less prone to violent dissent but would also ensure the good will of those foreign quarters that were interested in the stability and strengthening of Iran as a bulwark against the southward Soviet expansion and subversion. Specifically, Washington was very much interested in the progress of reform in Iran and on more than one occasion intimated to the Shah and his ministers that the magnitude and availability of American aid was linked with the progress of reform in Iran. On the other side there was the parliament, dominated by elements primarily interested in the preservation of their own privileged position in the society. A clash between the two tendencies appeared inevitable and indeed it came to a head in the period 1960-1961.

Within a brief span of ten months, between July 1960 and May 1961, the parliament as an institution was twice subjected to the experience of being elected and shortly afterward dissolved. This paradoxical situation appeared to originate in a complex welter of factors. The Shah wanted to have a parliament that would steer a middle course between reaction and left-wing extremism, whether of a Communist or a Mosaddegh variety. His intention was to have a Majles peopled by deputies who would see the need for reform and at the same time cooperate with the ruler and his government. Such an objective, however, was not easy to achieve, for two reasons. First, the antireform landowning elements tried to pose as the only group that could effectively prevent the upsurge of left-wing extremism. Second, the prime minister, Dr. Manuchehr Eqbal, a man to whom any resurgence of the pro-Mosaddegh trend was an anathema, wanted to "play it safe" and thus make sure that candidates in any way linked to what remained of Mosaddegh's National Front or its ideology would not be elected. As a result, the summer elections of 1960 abounded in irregularities while also reflecting excess of zeal on the part of officialdom. Thus the composition of the Majles as it emerged in the early fall of 1960 was clearly contrary to the Shah's image of what it should be, not to speak of the aura of improper government interference that accompanied the electoral process. Dismayed at the result, the Shah, in exercise of his constitutional power as granted him by the amended article 48 of the Fundamental Laws, pronounced the dissolution of the Majles and called for new elections. These elections took place between January and March of 1961 and resulted in the formation of a Majles that, although elected with less abuse and interference than the preceding one, was nevertheless rather similar in terms of its political profile. It was clear that with this sort of parliament the Shah could not hope for a speedy and effective enactment of the much-needed land reform law and other progressive measures. In the meantime, an accumulation of economic woes and social discontent as expressed in sporadic strikes— one of them being that of teachers—called for decisive action to restore to the country its equilibrium and launch it on the path of progress.

On May 9 the Shah responded to the tense situation by dissolving the newly elected Majles and the Senate. For the next two years, until the fall of 1963, he ruled by *farman* (decree), submitting each one to the ratification of the parliament when it reconvened after the new elections of late summer 1963.

Although the constitutional process in Iran had thus been subjected to a temporary suspension, it was not altogether repudiated. The very ratification by subsequent Majles of the Shah's reformist decrees pointed to the desire of the Shah to have his acts fully legitimized by the legislative body. Furthermore, the Majles was still regarded by the Shah as a vital institution that could and did effect such constitutional revisions as the one in 1967 regarding the question of regency. In the formal sense, then, Iran experienced a return to constitutional rule. In reality, however, a profound change in the distribution of political power had occurred. During the two years that the Shah ruled by decree—for most of this period with a man he trusted, Assadollah Alam, as prime minister—a comprehensive program of reform was launched, first introduced by the land reform law of 1962 and then confirmed by the proclamation of the six-point reform program of January 26, 1963 (6 Bahman, 1341), which was approved by a referendum.[13] Resort to the device of a referendum inevitably brings to mind the methods of "plebiscitary democracy" frequently adopted by one-party states. There is no doubt that the Shah was fully aware of the political meaning of his act and that he deliberately chose to appeal to the people at large, particularly to the peasant masses, while bypassing the parliamentary procedure. It was not surprising under the circumstances that the verdict of the referendum was over 99 percent in favor of the proposed program of reform. These reforms were so obviously needed that the overwhelming approval thus voiced was certainly genuine and inevitable. While it is certain that entrenched landowning elements in the population were unhappy with the drastic solutions to the land problem thus proposed, they found themselves outmaneuvered and so gave up resistance that might otherwise have been reflected in somewhat lower percentage of approval in the referendum.

The referendum of January 1963 marked the conclusion of a ten-year period of entrenchment and consolidation of power by the Shah since the fall of Mosaddegh. While during those ten years his efforts had to be largely directed toward the overcoming of internal political obstacles and the safeguarding of Iran's external security (as exemplified by the signing of the Baghdad Pact in 1955 and the bilateral security agreement with the United States in 1959), from 1963 on the road was open for reform, development, and modernization under the royal tutelage. Clearly, the parliament, which during the war and in the postwar period had appeared to assume too much power relative to the authority of the Shah, was now relegated to a place of secondary importance, though not legislated out of existence. This was further reflected in the composition of the Majles in the 1960s and 1970s. The new deputies, elected with the government's encouragement, represented altogether new strata in the society, hitherto absent from the parliament. Thus a number of teachers, agricultural extension workers, labor officials, social welfare workers, and former government employees not necessarily of elevated rank, appeared as deputies in addition to engineers and other professional men, as well as a sprinkling of businessmen and landowners, the latter reconciled to their now diminished role in the system. As for the Senate, there was no discernible change in its composition: it continued to be filled with men of a higher age bracket, frequently former government dignitaries, generals, and similar men of distinction. More specifically, appointment to the Senate signified recognition by the Shah of a candidate's outstanding service to the country, bestowing upon him the status of an elder statesman, out of active service but with wisdom and experience that could still be utilized in the upper chamber.

PARTIES AND IDEOLOGIES

Ever since the granting of the constitution in 1906, a good many political parties were created in Iran. Their organizational strength, firmness of social foundation, objectives, and ideology varied a good deal according to the actual political circumstances of the period. At the time of Reza Shah, political parties went into disuse—a logical reflection of the authoritarian system then prevailing. As for the nonconventional forces (by which we mean groups questioning the legitimacy of the system and therefore placing themselves beyond its pale) the Communist party was banned in 1931 but reemerged in the mid-1930s as a small group, mostly clustering around the younger intellectuals educated in Europe. Led by a certain Dr. Erani, this "Marxist Circle" was outlawed in 1937 and fifty-two of its members suffered imprisonment until they were freed after the Soviet-British occupation of the country in 1941.[14]

During World War II these released Communists, their ranks swelled by certain left-leaning intellectuals, formed the Tudeh (Masses) party, which with active Soviet encouragement and assistance grew into a force capable of upsetting the existing system in Iran under propitious circumstances. That the circumstances were propitious toward the end of the war, especially in view of the Soviets' gross interference in their zone of occupation, in the country's internal affairs, and their not unsuccessful attempts to extend their influence to the center and the south, there was no doubt. The Tudeh was responsible for much unrest in the country during the closing stages of the war and immediately afterward, was active in mobilizing and indoctrinating industrial workers (including those in the British-controlled oil fields), and also extended its activities to the peasant sector. It possessed in Tehran three daily newspapers and succeeded in forming a coalition of about another twenty newspapers broadly sympathetic to its goals.[15]

The war period also witnessed the appearance of other political parties, including the Iran party, whose aims were broadly progressive and, on occasion, overlapping with those of the Tudeh. The skill and aggressiveness demonstrated by the Tudeh in particular produced a reaction on the part of those leaders who feared the communization of Iran and her eventual subjugation by the Soviet Union. This was why Seyyed Ziya ad-Din Taba-Taba'i, a former premier returned from exile, formed his own right-wing party, *Erade-ye Melli* (National Will), to counteract Tudeh activities and Soviet influence. He was unmistakably supported by the British, whose view coincided with his.

It was, however, an interesting feature of the Iranian political process that these political parties found only a weak reflection, if any, in the composition of the Majles. Most of the deputies continued to be elected as independents; only after becoming members of the Majles did they decide to affiliate themselves with a given political party or a parliamentary group to their liking. The most notable exception was the Tudeh party, which succeeded in electing a few deputies from the northern provinces under Russian control as well as from Tehran. Thus the internal political process in Iran functioned on two levels, the parliamentary and the extraparliamentary, of which the latter often appeared to be more important, at least in wartime.

The apogee of this extraparliamentary process was reached in late 1945 when the Tudeh party, adopting the name of "Democrat," seized power in the northwestern province of Azarbayjan with active support from the Soviet occupation authorities. On December 12, 1945, these Communist-dominated Democrats proclaimed an autonomous government of Azarbayjan, with the capital in Tabriz, and set up not just their own institutions but a separate army—commanded by a Soviet general. Simultaneously, a parallel development took place in the Kurdish area of western Azarbayjan, where an independent Kurdish Republic was proclaimed in the little township of Mahabad, also with active assistance from the Soviet military. The two insurgent governments, however, differed from each other in that while the one in Tabriz was clearly of a Communist hue, the Kurdish one in Mahabad was nationalist and tribal. It was supported by the Soviets not so much for its ideology as rather out of general Soviet strategic considerations in this part of the world. The Mahabad government was soon reinforced by a contingent of some two thousand tribal warriors who had come from neighboring Iraq under the command of their leader, Molla Mostafa Barzani. An important ingredient in this Kurdish national entity was the Komala party, which had nationalist and somewhat radical tendencies.[16]

The Azarbayjan and Kurdish episodes, although technically inside the boundaries of Iran, belong nevertheless more properly to the study of Iran's foreign policy inasmuch as they would not have occurred without the presence and active assistance of the Soviet forces. If they are mentioned here, it is with an eye to their impact in subsequent years upon the shaping of Iranian national consciousness and the policies of the Shah.

The two experiments came to an end by mid-December 1946 when, after the evacuation of Soviet forces from the Iranian territory (under American and U.N. pressure), the Iranian troops, on the Shah's orders, reentered Azarbayjan and its Kurdish districts and reestablished the central government's authority. The true nature of the leaders of the Azarbayjan regime was eloquently revealed by the fact that those who escaped capture by the Iranian forces fled to the Soviet Union which, anyway, was the original homeland for a number of them. This was certainly true of the self-styled president of the Azarbayjan Republic, Ja'far Pishevari, who had spent most of his adult life in the Soviet Union and who appeared in Iran in the early 1940s only with the advent of the Soviet troops.

For the Shah and those patriotic leaders who were anxious to preserve the independence and sovereignty of Iran, the dissident movements in Azarbayjan provided a lesson in the dangers of weakness and isolation. Furthermore, there was plentiful evidence to indicate that the true Soviet objective was not merely to detach these northwestern provinces from Iran but rather to use them as a lever of pressure to gain ascendancy in the central government of Iran and thus extend Soviet influence and possibly dominion over the entire country. The most dangerous point was reached probably in mid-year 1946 when succumbing to Soviet pressures, Prime Minister Qavam as-Saltaneh included three Communists and one Communist sympathizer in his cabinet.

Following an attempt on the life of the Shah by a Tudeh party member in 1949, the Tudeh was officially outlawed. It continued, however, to engage in clandestine or semiclandestine activities and, with the onset of the oil crisis in 1951, it virtually came into the open. Meanwhile other political parties, some formed during the war and others after it, pursued their activities. By 1951 a new grouping calling itself the National Front emerged under the leadership of Dr. Mohammad Mosaddegh, who as a deputy to the Majles gathered around himself six other like-minded deputies to whom the same party name was attached. Actually the National Front represented a coalition of which an important part was the former Iran party, and which included also certain leftist, nationalist, and even right-wing elements, particularly those associated with the well-known religious leader, Molla Abol-Qasem Kashani. That turbulent period witnessed also the rise of two other groups: the Iranian Workers party led by Dr. Mozaffar Baqa'i and the so-called Third Force of a former Tudeh member, Khalil Maleki. None of these parties could truly be termed conventional inasmuch as their attitude toward the legitimacy of the existing system was ambivalent and sometimes downright negative. On the periphery of this more-or-less open political spectrum we could find another group, the Fedayan Islam (*feda'iyyan-e eslam*, "fighters for Islam") whose leading member, Khalil Tahmassebi, killed, in March 1951, the prime minister, General 'Ali Razmara.

The events of this turbulent period having been amply described and analyzed elsewhere, suffice it to say that Dr. Mosaddegh, a prime mover in the Majles of the nationalization law, was appointed prime minister by the Shah following a brief interim period after the death of Razmara during which the premiership was assumed by Hosayn 'Ala. Although no admirer of Mosaddegh, the Shah found it advisable to appoint him as premier because he appeared to be a logical choice to undertake the implementation of the oil nationalization law for which he was mainly responsible. In terms of orderly government the Mosaddegh period may be described as its true antithesis. The premier neglected many aspects of administration to devote himself to the vindication of Iran's rights in the deepening oil controversy between his government on the one hand and the company and Great Britain on the other. He rejected the mediation of the United States, which was aiming at a compromise solution not dissimilar to the type of agreement established in the neighboring Arab countries between their respective governments and the foreign companies operating in them. This was the so-called 50/50 profit-sharing formula which after more than three years of crisis Iran agreed to adopt when it signed the consortium agreement referred to earlier. Although

Mosaddegh's dedication to achieve nationalist objectives seemed beyond doubt and he enjoyed a reputation of personal honesty, his behavior was erratic and unpredictable. The premier conducted much of his business either from bed because of recurrent illness or simply physical weakness, or from the balcony in Baharestan Square, where he frequently addressed large crowds gathered to demonstrate against Western imperialism. On such occasions, as well as during his rhetorical performances in the Majles, he was prone to cry and faint. While abetting and sponsoring these extremist and nationalist demonstrations, Mosaddegh tended to overlook the open return of the Tudeh party to an active role in politics, and, in his anxiety to exorcise the ghost of Western influence, he implicitly accepted its assistance.

Side by side with this emotionally charged campaign against the oil companies and the West, Mosaddegh began to question the rights and prerogatives of the Shah in more general terms, while asking and obtaining full powers from the Majles. In the name of the broader theory that "the Shah should reign but not rule," the premier tried to whittle down the Shah's influence, claiming that this was the right interpretation of the Iranian constitution.[17] Moreover, despite the explicit constitutional provision that the Shah is commander in chief of the army, the premier challenged the Shah's authority in this respect, dismissed a number of officers loyal to the Crown, filling vacant positions with his own partisans in the military establishment.

Without going into further detail, the struggle between the premier and the King was one of two mutually exclusive orientations. The premier tried to reduce the ruler to a position of nominal authority while, in the foreign sector, his emotional anti-Western nationalism and his acceptance of an unspoken alliance with the Tudeh party pointed to an alternative of growing Soviet influence and possible slippage into the Soviet orbit, particularly as the West refused to buy Iran's nationalized oil. As for the Shah, he saw things in a different light: he refused to satisfy himself with a merely nominal role, looking upon his person as indispensable to the preservation of national unity and sovereignty; and, by the same token, he rejected Mosaddegh's theory that Western imperialism represented a real danger to the country and that, instead of concentrating on such an imaginary threat, Iran should do her best to safeguard her independence and integrity against the frequently demonstrated Soviet ambitions in that part of the world.

The apogee of the crisis occurred in mid-August 1953, when Mosaddegh refused to accept the Shah's written order dismissing him from the position of prime minister and arrested Colonel Nasiri who personally brought to him the Shah's message. Moreover, he gave orders to arrest General Fazlollah Zahedi, who simultaneously was entrusted by the Shah with premiership. While Zahedi, forewarned in time, went into hiding, a campaign to overthrow the monarchy, encouraged and abetted by the premier, was unleashed by extremist elements both Tudeh and non-Communist. In the midst of this crisis the Shah, accompanied by Empress Soraya, flew to Baghdad and Rome where he found a temporary refuge. In the meantime royalist forces regrouped themselves in Tehran both among the civilian population and in the army. On August 19 these forces launched an attack on Mosaddegh's partisans, occupied the key government buildings, and secured control of the city. Emerging from hiding, General Zahedi assumed the reins of government and placed Mosaddegh under arrest. The road was open for the return of the Shah, who promptly regained his capital amid manifestations of loyalty to the throne.

Thus a new era opened, one during which the Shah relentlessly pursued the objective of strengthening his power and never allowing the internal situation in the country to slip again from his control. In terms of the freedom of political expression, it was certain that the Shah and his government would not tolerate a resurgence of the Communist movement, in whatever guise it might appear. This matter went clearly beyond the confines of domestic politics and touched upon the delicate issue of Soviet infiltration. Despite its formal outlawing, the Tudeh continued to engage in propaganda, print leaflets in its clandestine presses, and infiltrate various government organizations. Moreover, it was hard to draw the line between a "normal" party activity and Soviet espionage. In 1954 General Taymur Bakhtiar, chief of the security organization, discovered in the Iranian army a Soviet spy ring composed of six hundred officers of whom sixty held the rank of colonel or lieutenant-colonel. One can imagine what an uproar discovery of such a major espionage operation would produce in the United States, even if the number of people involved was ten times smaller than that in Iran. And yet here was a country directly adjacent to the Soviet Union discovering that her military establishment had been thoroughly infiltrated by agents in Soviet pay. The subsequent emphasis on the strengthening of the internal security organization generally known under the name of SAVAK *(Sazeman-e Ettela'at va Amniyat-e Keshvar)* appeared understandable under the circumstances.

The Shah did not view the country's political life entirely in terms of internal security. He was convinced that the proliferation of various political groups and parties, some inevitably associated with foreign interests, was harmful to the country, and that what was needed was to educate the people in orderly political debate and competition. With this in view he encouraged the formation in 1957 of a progovernment party, Mellioun, and of a loyal opposition party, Mardom. While the then prime minister, Dr. Manuchehr Eqbal, took charge of Mellioun, a statesman enjoying the Shah's special trust, Assadollah Alam, became leader of Mardom. In addition to these two, there were such minor peripheral groups as the pan-Iranist party and the Sumka party, but the scene was certainly preempted by the two major parties. In the meantime, the old National Front suffered a progressive disintegration, some of its leaders being tried for sedition and treason, some exiling themselves abroad, and others withdrawing from active political life.

THE GOVERNMENT-SPONSORED PARTIES

In 1963 the Shah felt that the progovernment Mellioun party, having played its useful role, should be replaced by a party whose composition and orientation would reflect more accurately the spirit of the reforms undertaken under the name of the White Revolution and inaugurated by the six-point program of January 1963. In conformance with these ideas, a new party called Iran-e Novin came into being under the leadership of 'Ali Mansur, who initially chaired a progressive group of young economists and social scientists and who, in 1964, became prime minister. In the meantime the opposition Mardom party continued in its previous form, although its leadership had changed, with Professor Yahya 'Adl replacing Assadollah Alam as its leader due to Alam's appointment as minister of the imperial court.

It is debatable whether the government-sponsored two-party system succeeded in performing its assigned task. With the growth of the royal tutelage, legitimate doubts were expressed not only as to the spontaneity of the party activity but also as to the importance of both parties under the existing system. In one way, however, the functioning of the two parties differed from the party system that had preceded it: both were represented by numerous deputies in the parliament, in contrast to the preceding era when most of the deputies were listed as independents and the existing parties conducted their activities largely outside the parliamentary arena. By the early 1970s a serious student of Iranian politics could not attach much importance to the Mellioun and Mardom parties; the central point in his studies should have been the administrative and decision-making process in the Iranian government under the Shah's supreme authority.

In the spring of 1975 the Shah himself recognized the artificiality of this situation. In a major speech delivered to the nation he declared that the system of two parties was no longer tenable and did not correspond to the current needs of national development. Instead he proposed the creation of a single party in which all politically aware elements would unite for the purpose of developing the country in the spirit of the principles of the White Revolution.[18] Thus a new party, Rastakhiz-e Iran (Resurrection of Iran) was formed to be chaired by Prime Minister 'Abbas Hoveyda. It was endowed with a formal structure including a central committee and within it a more select political bureau; there were also provincial and local branches. At the same time constructive political discussion was encouraged inside the party which, soon after its inception, developed two wings, the constructive wing under Hushang Ansari, minister of finance and national economy, and the progressive wing under Jamshid Amuzegar, minister of the interior. It was clear that the new party was conceived by the Shah as having a different role to play than the preceding two parties. It was to serve as a mobilizing agency in the modernization process; as a screening device in the search for talent to fill various high government positions; as a channel for educating the masses in the principles and priorities of the White Revolution; and as a system of communication with the people at large. Whereas some observers might be inclined to view the Rastakhiz party as a mere appendage to the existing power structure—a fact that neither the Shah nor his ministers were trying to deny—the Shah clearly preferred to have such an appendage than to do without it. Under the existing royal tutelage the only other alternative would have been to rely on bureaucracy, army, and police as props of the system. Such a formalistic solution was unacceptable to the ruler, who saw in his new party a very useful instrument not only for bolstering the existing system but also for ensuring maximum harmony among and cooperation from the people in the modernizing and nation-building process in which he was engaged.

This urge to unify the nation behind the throne, to mobilize national energies, and to direct the national effort toward the achievement of the reformist tasks as outlined by the White Revolution program was partly a response to the centrifugal and anarchistic tendencies frequently displayed in the recent history of Iran. Iranians are a highly individualistic people; they do not accept the notion of discipline easily. On the political level this was expressed on a number of occasions in the proliferation of political parties and groups, each seeking its own particular goals, and often representing no more than a cluster of followers behind some ambitious leader.[19] Furthermore, political dissent frequently overlapped with centrifugal movements that were chiefly tribal or territorial. In certain cases such movements had an additional ethnic or national connotation. Thus in the early 1900s and until Reza Shah came to power, Shaykh Khaz'al of Mohammara, district in Khuzistan with a numerous Arabic-speaking population, behaved like an independent prince, challenging the authority of the central government and entering into separate agreements with his British protectors. Similarly, the Qashaqa'i and Bakhtiari khans as well as other tribal chieftains frequently disregarded the existence and orders of the government in Tehran, to pursue policies of their own and use their armed tribesmen to achieve their objectives in open armed rebellions.[20] These had occurred not only during the early years of Reza Shah's reign but also during World War II and the immediate period following it. And it was not without significance that the Soviet occupation authorities chose the Turkic- and Kurdish-speaking areas of northwestern

Iran for their intrigues when sponsoring the creation of an autonomous Azarbayjan and an independent Kurdish Republic in 1945.

With this legacy of unrest based on anarchistic individualism or selfish pursuit of private aims by local potentates and warlords, it is not surprising that any Iranian ruler bent on modernizing the country had to set a high priority on the curbing of these disintegrative processes. There is a vast difference between a disorderly centrifugal process and an orderly decentralization. The former is harmful, the latter is desirable inasmuch as it helps reduce centralistic bureaucracy while developing a sense of local responsibility. However, before proceeding to decentralize, both Reza Shah and his son, Mohammad Reza Shah Pahlavi, had to make sure that the authority of the central government was unchallenged by any illegitimate center of power anywhere in the country.

The Second Pahlavi Kingship

While the consolidation of the central government's authority was thus of concern to both Pahlavi rulers, the emphasis of each was on different priorities, dictated by the time and circumstances. When he came to power in the 1920s, Reza Shah found his nation suffering from the effects of foreign military activities in his country, impoverished and disunited. His first concerns were to unify the country, strengthen the authority of the government, build a modern army, restore the rule of law, and assert full independence from foreign influence and interference. However, while he engaged in a bold process of modernization, his main motivation was the strengthening of the state rather than social justice. By curbing the influence of powerful families and introducing a system in which what counted most was service to the state based on merit, Reza Shah undoubtedly laid the foundations for a social evolution aiming at greater equality and the abolition of vested privileges. But it was not until his son came to power that social justice could become a focus of his systematic endeavors. To Mohammad Reza Shah it was clear that Iran could not take her rightful place in the community of nations without making major strides toward a general raising of economic, social, and cultural standards. Thus the major theme of his reign was the struggle between progress and the obsolete status quo. To enter this struggle on the side of progress appeared a necessity if Iran wanted to survive as a modern state bordering on Communist Russia.[21]

In the pursuit of survival, the Shah did not want to be hampered by strictly legalistic considerations. "We have refused to follow inexorable regulations," he declared in 1968, with an implicit reference to the restraining role of the official public law.[22] On another occasion he stated that heads of state should realize that political law, in modern society, was worthless unless it advanced in step with social as well as economic law. "Otherwise, such law cannot be useful except on paper. My country has in recent years engaged in social revolution which is in complete accord with these principles and concepts. Our social structure which was centuries old, was no longer adequate to cope with the real needs of our society. It needed a basic and complete change."[23] In amplifying these thoughts, he further distinguished between juridical justice and social justice. The former, although "totally indispensable," was "no longer sufficient, the present situation of the world being what it is. . . ." Legal principles alone, the Shah continued, could neither solve the real social problems nor ensure the happiness and well-being of the great mass of humanity; they could not even ensure that justice would be done, since without the support of social justice, the authority of legal principles would always remain incomplete.[24]

This need for action unhampered by constitutional restraints was felt most keenly by the Shah over the issue of land reform. Referring to the original bill that he presented to the parliament as early as 1959 (after the distribution among the peasants of his own estates), the Shah observed with bitterness:

> However, most of the members of parliament belonged to the ruling class of land owners and capitalists, and through the intervention of these irresponsible individuals who were unaware of the social advances going on in the world, the bill was rendered ineffective and meaningless.
>
> After this episode, it became quite clear to me that setting an example, giving advice and guidance, and recourse to *ordinary parliamentary methods* were not enough. In particular, the two opposing poles, black reaction and the red forces of destruction, whose aims were to prevent any real progress in the country, combined to paralyze my actions.[25]

Out of this frustration came a resolve that the Shah expressed as follows:

> I looked at Iranian society, recognizing its weaknesses, needs and potentialities; I studied the structure of other societies and saw how they had progressed; I analyzed the various philosophies and programs which had been advocated or implemented. The realization came to me that Iran needed a deep and fundamental revolution that could, at the same time, put an end to all the social inequality and all the factors which caused injustice, tyranny and exploitation, and all aspects of reaction which impeded progress and kept our society backward.[26]

It is in these thoughts of the Shah that we have to look for the genesis of his extraparliamentary action in launching the White Revolution during the early 1960s. The method employed was to bypass the parliament, which was suspended; to rule by decree (although, as mentioned earlier, subsequent formal ratification of these decrees was sought and obtained in the Majles); to resort to a plebiscitary method in seeking mass approval of the measures undertaken; to engage in central planning; and to revive and expand the concept of the monarchy as the supreme ruling institution in the country.

To overcome opposition from various vested interests and groups hostile to the regime, and to assure effective implementation of the reforms, the Shah felt that his and his cabinet's executive authority should be strengthened. Iran, in his mind, was a society on the march, bent upon achievement of difficult goals that required a high degree of discipline, coordination, and leadership. Such leadership was to be provided primarily by the King himself, and was to be enhanced by historical tradition, indoctrination of society in the sanctity and importance of the royal institution, and the maximum use of symbolism in confirming and glorifying the role of the monarch.[27] It is significant in this connection that the Shah had postponed for a long time the official act of coronation which, under normal circumstances, should have taken place shortly after his formal ascent to the throne. He felt that the coronation, while he was struggling for power and while the cause of reform was not yet assured of success, would be premature and perhaps even incongruous. For this reason he chose to celebrate the coronation ceremony only in 1967, more than a quarter of a century after he came to power, when he felt both that his power was well entrenched and that reform was securely launched. Moreover, in contrast to the previous kings, he introduced a new note into the ceremony by not only crowning himself but also by bestowing the crown upon his wife Empress Farah, thus inaugurating a new era in the annals of Iranian royalty.

Likewise, it was his desire to cultivate and enhance the status and image of the concept of kingship that led to the widely publicized celebrations, at Persepolis in 1971, of 2,500 years of the Iranian Empire.

The Concept of Tutelage: Modernizing Monarchy

Modern history provides a number of examples of political systems to which the term tutelage could apply. The term appears to have originated in Sun Yat Sen's China around 1910. It was subsequently used with reference to the reforms of Kemal Ataturk in Turkey, Reza Shah in Iran during the interwar period, and possibly in a few other cases. What clearly differentiates the Iranian type of tutelage under both Reza Shah and Mohammad Reza Shah is the monarchical principle on which it is based. Furthermore, the common characteristic of tutelage appears to be the notion of reform from above. Of course, in a strict technical sense, reformist legislation always comes from above, from the authorities that are actually in power. But there is a vast difference between the government that institutes reforms on the basis of well-considered long-range plans, in an atmosphere of order and tranquility, and a government carrying out major changes in an atmosphere of revolutionary effervescence, civil war, and emotion charged with vindictiveness born of the hatreds generated during the revolutionary upheaval. The latter type of change is usually more costly to society in the long run: there is, in other words, a price to be paid for the revolution. In Iran, the name "White Revolution" was deliberately chosen to emphasize the peaceful, nonviolent, nonvindictive type of reform. In the words of the Shah, "There is no hatred in it, no class hatred against anybody."[28]

The monarchy in Iran obtained its legitimacy from three sources: the historical tradition of kingship, which in its search for the ancient roots of the Achaemenian era emphasized its sacred character; the constitution of Iran of 1906 and 1907 with its subsequent amendments, especially those of 1925, which proclaimed the Pahlavi rule, and of 1967, which established an institution of regency under the Empress in case of the minority of the heir to the throne; and the third, more or less "populist" source, the reforms of the White Revolution aiming at social justice and modernization.[29]

These sources of legitimacy provided the fundamental base of support for the modernizing monarchy in Iranian society. Organizationally, the system had to rely on the army and the security apparatus, on the vast bureaucracy and, from 1963 onwards, on special semivoluntary organizations such as the Literacy Corps, the Health Corps, the Reconstruction Corps, and similar government-sponsored formations, membership in which, however, was voluntary for the young people directly concerned. As a result of the land reform, the peasantry began, for the first time in modern Iranian history, to provide the system with a major base of support. It became an important and perhaps truly vital sector for the regime, which through its reform policies had alienated some of the powerful groups in the former ruling establishment. To ensure peasant loyalty and devotion and identification of their interests with those of the system as a whole, a delicate psychological mechanism had to be operated. The main ingredient of it was to keep the peasant satisfied on two counts: first, that he was receiving his due share of wealth in the society, and second, that he was an independent owner of a piece of land. Both points deserved constant observation and study because, with the growing industrialization and concomitant inflation, it often happened that a gap began to develop between agricultural products and industrial goods, a gap in terms of widely differing prices to the consumer and earnings to the producer. Moreover, any scheme that aimed at increasing productivity in the land sector through coordination and supervision of the farmer's work ran the risk of making the farmer lose the sense of independence he had acquired when he first received his allotment of land under the reforms.

Another important sector of social support was the urban middle class.

This was a sector traditionally full of ambivalence, because it was among the urban middle class, particularly those with higher formal education and intellectual achievements or pretensions, that the greatest possibility of criticism and dissent existed. At the same time, however, the country's rapid economic progress, resulting in greater industrialization, more employment, higher levels of consumption, better housing and other amenities, a greater number of private cars, etc., was bound to find a reflection in the well-being and status of this very class. In addition, the growing bureaucracy, continuously more differentiated to carry out various aspects of the reform program, offered increasing opportunities for employment and advancement both in the formal and in a broader social sense. A visitor to the capital city and the major urban centers of the country in the mid-1970s could not fail to be impressed by the extensive and steadily growing number of private vehicles, the latter often producing monumental traffic jams. It was quite obvious that these vehicles were too numerous to be owned merely by a handful of wealthy people. By the mid-1970s a middle-grade government employee, a bank clerk, or a teacher was quite likely to possess a car and live in an apartment or house with modern plumbing and amenities. The combination of the higher oil revenues for which Iran had fought stubbornly and the White Revolution programs had not only increased the total wealth of the country but also contributed to its greater spread. As a result, an ever-increasing number of people, not only in the peasant sector but also in the cities, found a greater stake in the preservation of the newly created status quo. Last but not least, not only greater opportunities for industrial employment but also reform measures, particularly those enacted in 1975, that granted workers a share of the business profits, began to make a significant impact on the well-being and hence also on the identification of the industrial working class with the regime. It was precisely with an eye to the mobilization of these various social bases of support that, as mentioned, the Shah launched the Rastakhiz party.

Throughout his reign the Shah had to deal with various elements and expressions of opposition. The earlier struggles to assert his authority have already been recounted. They culminated in a major test of strength between the Shah and the forces supporting him and Dr. Mosaddegh and his allies. But even after Mosaddegh's downfall, elements hostile to the Shah manifested their opposition by legal or illegal means on a number of occasions. At the risk of some oversimplification, it is possible to state that after 1953 opposition to the Shah could be classified under four heads: the Communists, either identified with the Tudeh party or with its pro-Chinese wing (the Tudeh itself, whose leaders could be found partly in East Germany and partly in the Soviet Union, had split into pro-Soviet and pro-Chinese factions); the adherents, at least in the psychological sense, of the former National Front; the wealthy landowners, who opposed the reforms affecting their power and possessions;

and the segment of the religious functionaries, who viewed with hostility the Shah's modernizing efforts, particularly his striving to admit women to a fuller participation in the national life of the country. Of these four groups, the Communists operated definitely beyond the pale of legality. The segment of the intelligentsia inclined toward the National Front vacillated between outright denial of legitimacy to the regime and conditional acceptance of it provided it adopted more liberal attitudes. Landowners basically accepted the system but, so long as they could dominate and manipulate the Majles, tried to use the latter as an instrument of their influence to retard or derail the reforms initiated by the government. And the religious groups were ready to resort to violence, particularly by mobilizing the more conservative bazaar elements in Tehran and the provincial centers.

In responding to these dissident activities, the Shah did not hesitate to use his coercive apparatus, particularly in cases where an open challenge to law and order occurred. Thus the security organs were repeatedly discovering small clandestine centers of Communist activity and arresting such Communist militants as could be apprehended. Although on the whole Communism on a substantial organizational scale appeared to have been suppressed in Iran, sporadic cases of violence perpetrated by urban guerrilla groups in the 1960s and 1970s were a matter of public record, being publicized by the Iranian papers and condemned by the government. These activities resulted from time to time in the assassination of a high-ranking police officer, a judge, a member of the military, and even a foreign official or two, particularly among the American officers associated with the U.S. military advisory mission to Iran. Similarly, drastic measures were taken in the early summer of 1963 against the riots initiated by the religious opposition. These riots and their suppression took a number of lives and resulted in due time in the expulsion of a key figure in religious circles, Ayatollah Khomayni. It should be pointed out that the religious militants not only opposed the newly proclaimed rights of women but also the land reform which, according to some of their leaders, was contrary to the religious law. The latter aspect of their opposition indicated that there was an unwritten alliance between these religious groups and the wealthier landowners adversely affected by land reform.

The dissident intelligentsia, whose attitude could best be described as that of pro-Mosaddegh nostalgia, constituted perhaps the most intractable and complex element in the opposition. Accusing the regime of suppressing political liberties, persecuting the opposition, and applying crude police methods, these elements were vocal primarily abroad where, among the numerous Iranian student communities in the United States and Europe, they found many followers. These, in turn, were prone to engage in picketing events at which Iranian dignitaries were being honored in foreign schools; passing antigovernment resolutions; sometimes occupying Iranian embassies abroad; and on occasion throwing bombs and resorting to terrorist acts against Iranian official representations and the buildings in which they were housed. The more militant elements among them were either openly or implicitly acknowledging their allegiance to Communism, whether of the Soviet or the Chinese variety. There were indications that some of the dissidents had had, at the time of Nasser, some link with the revolutionary Egyptian regime, which at that time was very hostile to the government of Iran. Finally, there were others in the student groups who, intoxicated with the liberty and permissiveness of Western democracy and impressed by the protest movements in the United States and elsewhere, particularly in the 1960s, found encouragement in these manifestations of dissent and tried to emulate them.

The official Iranian response to these demonstrations of discontent was on the whole restrained. If it wanted to adopt a truly drastic measure, the Iranian government could have revoked the passports of those students who participated in open expressions of protest (their identity was probably known to the well-organized security services), or it could have banned altogether or made much more difficult study abroad for young Iranians. Yet it refused to resort to either of these measures, and the number of Iranian students abroad not only remained very high (about 40,000 by the mid-1970s) but was showing signs of growing. This discontent among various student groups was also partly responsible for the so-called brain drain: many Iranian graduates of Western universities chose to stay abroad and pursue careers there. In all fairness, however, it should be pointed out that the political motivation of such a choice was frequently secondary, if it existed at all, to the economic consideration. For example, a good many medical students studying abroad, particularly in the United States and Germany, preferred not to return to Iran inasmuch as they could pursue very lucrative medical careers overseas. This was also true of certain other professions, especially in engineering and the sciences, where opportunities for careers in technologically advanced Western countries were more abundant than in less-developed Iran. However, with the launching of ambitious five-year plans in the 1960s and 1970s, accompanied as they were by the dramatic influx of oil revenues, a growing number of young Iranians were choosing to pursue careers back at home in the fast-developing Iranian economy.

As for the Shah, his attitude, based on sad experience of Soviet interference, the Azarbayjan and Kurdish dissident movements, British meddling in the affairs of the south during the heyday of the Anglo-Iranian Oil Company, and the turbulence of the Mosaddegh period with its major Communist upsurge, led him to view all these opposition elements with suspicion that in many cases clandestine links existed between their dissent and foreign powers.

The Shah gave forceful expression to these views in his book *The White Revolution:*

For a period of more than 21 years until January 1963, my country and I were subject to frequent vicissitudes of fortune and witnessed artificial scenes played for our benefit by actors who, like puppets, were manipulated from the outside. These hypocrites chose to deceive their people and sought to avenge themselves on me and my family by secretly serving the cause of foreigners. They were incapable of rendering any real service to the country and were prepared to bring destruction and chaos upon Iran. Their behavior is suitably described by a Persian proverb which says, "Drown him, even if I drown too." . . . It was pathetic to see the credulous Persian people in their desperate efforts to seek reform and [liberation from] foreign influence, being deceived by these sham patriots whose political allegiances and objectives were known to me.

These agents of foreign influence in Iran formed several distinct groups. There were the so-called politicians whose aims were in some cases clearly apparent. Then there were other politicians who played a double game and betrayed their country in the guise of nationalists and liberals. A third category were the feudal lords who had created autonomous local governments and in order to protect their own interests competed among themselves to serve foreign designs. Finally, there were some self-styled religious leaders who, ever since the establishment of constitutional monarchy in Iran, were generally known to be at the beck and call of one foreign power in particular. All these groups acted as a deterrent to Iran's progress, for foreign interests depended on a permanent state of anarchy in the country to benefit fully.[30]

In a later passage of the same book the Shah contrasted his opponents with the peaceful and hard-working masses of Iran:

I was not the ruler only of a powerful class of corrupt reactionaries, feudal khans, and deluded or treacherous people who acted as a fifth column in the service of foreigners. First and foremost I was the sovereign of over twenty million hard-working, noble citizens who had placed all their hopes in me. I watched them toil, and saw the rewards of their ceaseless efforts slip through their fingers into the outstretched hands of a group of parasites, whose only abilities were in concluding illegal deals and serving foreign powers.[31]

By the 1970s opposition within Iran was dwindling to insignificant proportions and in an open, organized form was nonexistent. On the other hand, despite sporadic student protests abroad, there had been no major emigration comparable to that of the White Russians after the Bolshevik Revolution of 1917 or of the large numbers of citizens from Soviet satellites in eastern Europe. Some Iranians did choose to stay abroad, but they continued to enjoy the freedom to revisit their country and decide, if they wished, to resume their life and careers in Iran.

By the same token, there was an obvious contrast between the earlier uncertainties of the Shah's authority and his supreme power in the 1960s and 1970s. The Shah himself acknowledged this contrast in a number of eloquent passages in his earlier book, *Mission for My Country*. Thus, referring to his early years as King and the messages that he was exchanging with his exiled father, Reza Shah, the Shah wrote: "I think he realized that my colleagues and I were reorienting Iran's whole foreign and domestic policy and he did not want to prejudice our prospects of success."[32] In referring to the situation in the 1940s during the war and occupation, the Shah could indeed use the expression "my colleagues and I." In the 1970s, however, the use of such expression would have been obviously most inappropriate in depicting the reality of power in Iran. Similarly, when describing his first years as King, the Shah stated that "one of my first acts as King had been to affirm the rebirth of constitutional democracy. Yet such chaos had come to the country's political life that perhaps it would have been understandable if at that juncture, I had become permanently disillusioned with the democratic process."[33] In retrospect, it would be probably realistic to observe that the Shah had, in fact, become somewhat disillusioned with democratic processes, which in Iran were clearly associated either with foreign occupation and interference or, later, with domestic turmoil. In the past, the Shah also experienced moments of helplessness. In recounting the dramatic events following the nationalization of oil and in particular the fact that the loyal servant of the Crown, Prime Minister 'Ala, "was forced out after less than two months in office," the Shah wrote: "I appointed Mossadegh in his place; at that moment no one could stand against him."[34] And in another passage in which the Shah described his relationship to Premier Qavam during the Azarbayjan crisis of 1945-46, the Shah wrote: "Qavam displayed a peculiar attitude at this time. He seemed to be under the influence of the Russians. One day he told me that he wished I would either make all decisions or give him a completely free hand. It was obvious that he wanted the latter."[35]

These remarks pertain to the events of the 1940s and 1950s. They depict situations of weakness, confusion in the governmental process, uncertain authority, and danger. By the time the White Revolution was proclaimed in 1963 the situation had changed radically and the Shah had emerged as undisputed ruler of the country.

THE NATURE OF ROYAL AUTHORITY

While formally Iran was a constitutional monarchy, in substance it was a royal tutelary system that subordinated formal legality to the major goal of nation building and modernization. As such it became essentially authoritarian. In this respect the Iranian system has exhibited a remarkable continuity. Commenting on the type of government instituted by his father, Mohammad Reza Shah observed: "Oriental psychology in these matters differs from that of the West, and my father's methods for getting things done showed no little realism in the light of our authoritarian tradition."[36] And in another passage of the same book the Shah added that the "Persians were already accustomed to an authoritarian system."[37]

Modern liberal students of the Iranian political scene have tended to select this authoritarian principle as the main target of their criticisms, with a tendency to use the word "dictatorship" to describe the nature of the system.[38] Yet such an approach seems to constitute an oversimplification of a more complex picture. The Iranian system is authoritarian but is neither a dictatorship of totalitarian nature nor a despotic reactionary rule. A modern dictatorship is characterized by the lack of both tradition and formal legitimacy. Essentially it represents nothing more than an application of brute force or a political manipulation by a political group that, to maintain itself in power, is bound to promote the interference of the all-powerful state in every facet of the national life—including frequently the private lives of its citizens. Under a totalitarian system, the so-called "islands of separateness"—to use Friedrich's and Brzezinski's expression—are steadily reduced with the ultimate objective of obliterating them.[39] A totalitarian system confuses education with propaganda, encourages the rewriting of history to suit its own objectives, institutionalizes systemic purges as a way of assuring loyalty, engages in widespread terror and massive deportations—such as were inflicted on the kulaks in the Soviet Union during the 1930s—and as a matter of general policy confines hundreds of thousands if not millions of people in forced labor and concentration camps as documented in Solzhenitsyn's *Gulag Archipelago* and as practiced on a wide scale in Nazi Germany.

On the other hand, a despotic reactionary rule combines the essential weakness of the monarchy with abuse of power. In this respect, the Qajar era can provide a vivid contrast to the subsequent rule of the Pahlavis. The Qajars were weak to the point of degeneracy, pleasure-seeking, interested in expensive journeys to Europe with a large retinue of retainers, ready to mortgage Iran's treasury to foreign governments, particularly the Russian one, in exchange for loans to satisfy their immediate needs, reactionary in social and economic terms, and indifferent to building up the country's military strength. The modernizing revolution of both Pahlavi kings represented a deliberate rejection of this negative tradition.

Furthermore, historians tend to regard cases of strong rulers and the achievements brought about by them with a greater detachment, less emotion, and more profound understanding of the circumstances than do the modern-day critics of royalist authoritarianism. Louis XIV of France was certainly an authoritarian ruler whose phrase "L'état, c'est moi" symbolized his conception of absolute power. Peter the Great has been acclaimed as a great modernizer who "opened Russia's window to the West" and whose authoritarian methods are frequently justified in the light of the goals he pursued and results he obtained. Similarly, Napoleon emerged from the turmoil of the French Revolution to establish an absolute monarchy and empire and, although still a controversial figure in terms of his role in European history, is revered today in France as a great leader whose mausoleum at the Hôtel des Invalides in Paris displays the dramatic record of his achievements as a soldier, lawgiver, and stateman in golden letters engraved in marble and bronze.

Moreover, students of history and politics may point to instances where an undue reduction of executive authority by too much emphasis on parliamentarism has been definitely harmful to the state. The Kingdom of Poland presents an eloquent example in this respect. Developing its parliamentary institution to an absurd extent, the Polish-Lithuanian Commonwealth saw the power of its king so drastically reduced that it became an easy prey for the machinations and aggression of the neighboring powers. And it was precisely those powers—Russia, Prussia, and Austria—that developed royal absolutism in the seventeenth and eighteenth centuries, that jointly gave the *coup de grâce* to the Kingdom of Poland, successfully erasing what had once been the second largest state in Europe from its political map at the time of the American Revolution. A person with any sense of history cannot therefore blithely disregard the lessons of the past and expect that an artificial transplantation of Western democratic principles appropriate for the advanced industrial countries of the twentieth century can be accomplished in an altogether different social and psychological environment.

In contrast with his father, to whom other priorities of statesmanship and national security were more important, Mohammad Reza Shah, educated as he was in Europe, was not unaware of the issue of democracy. However, he refused to accept a one-sided interpretation of it. "In former times," he wrote, "free men thought of democracy as something primarily political."[40] Mohammad Reza Shah viewed democracy as expressed in three versions, political, economic, and social. To him, political democracy was meaningless if it was not accompanied by corresponding social and economic improvements. First of all, he believed that to practice true democracy, the people should possess an adequate level of education, that is, at least be literate. He stated:

> Effective political democracy needs intelligence. Voters must have some idea of the merits of candidates and issues. It needs maturity and tolerance; rich men must be content with the same single vote that the poor man possesses, and the party which loses at the polls (maybe by only a few votes) must peaceably bide its time and meanwhile furnish loyal rather than destructive opposition.[41]

All of this, in the eyes of the Shah, required a proper educational, social, and economic infrastructure. Thus political democracy, in his eyes, could not precede the social and economic democracy, but had to follow it. It is interesting to note in this respect that numerous Western writers have praised the Soviet, Chinese, or Cuban revolutionary achievements precisely because (they claimed) they represented social and economic advances in societies that had no tradition of democracy and in which establishment of a formal, Western-style democracy would have been meaningless.[42] And yet writers and observers from this broader group in the West were prone to show particular concern about the lack of Western-type democracy in Iran. The Shah and those participating with him in the work of modernization and development have felt under the circumstances that a double standard was being applied by certain Westerners in evaluating Iran's political reality.

Western critics have also tended to emphasize the assistance given by the West, especially the United States, to the Shah's government in building up national security, especially in the field of arms supplies and intelligence operations. In reality, the magnitude of these two types of assistance did not exceed the extent, either in absolute or in proportional terms, of American assistance to the state of Israel, a much smaller country, and one that was not linked to the United States by a formal alliance.

The United States stance at the time of Mosaddegh's attempt to overthrow the monarchy and the subsequent return of the Shah to power have been singled out by some Western writers to support the thesis that, without American help, the kingship would not have survived for lack of genuine social support at home. Putting aside the accuracy of such accounts—often sensationalized and magnified out of all proportion—two observations may be in order to give the matter a more balanced perspective. First, history has provided a number of instances in which, because of an alliance or community of interests, one government had assisted another in regaining or maintaining power. There appeared to be no such major outburst of criticism when, during World War II, President Roosevelt and Prime Minister Churchill lent their support to the Free French leader Charles de Gaulle and helped him install himself in liberated France although his formal, as contrasted with moral, claim to political legitimacy was subject to serious challenge. By the same token, the West accepted with equanimity an obvious show of American pressure to assure the victory of Alcide de Gasperi's anti-Communist coalition in the Italian elections of 1948. Second, there were no American forces in Iran in 1953, in contrast to the Soviet military intervention in Hungary in 1956 and Czechoslovakia in 1968, and it was the Iranians themselves—the army and the civilians—who fought their way to remove the dissident premier and restore the Shah to power.[43]

Western critics of Iran have frequently disregarded the fact that Iran was linked to the West through two instruments of alliance, the Baghdad Pact of 1955 and the bilateral security agreement with the United States of 1959. These alliances were formed in response to Iran's security needs and as an expression of the American policy of containment.[44] In describing the confused situation of his country in 1952 and 1953 the Shah stated that "even the commander of the most trusted battalion of my Imperial Guard was a hard-core Communist."[45] Under the circumstances, the Shah saw the need for an effective security organ. In particular, he observed that

> especially in a country as strategically placed as we are, there may be a need to act quickly and decisively to combat attempts to topple the government by unconstitutional means, particularly those which are foreign-inspired. Today every free country needs a political security agency which, in cooperation with other government departments, can detect and neutralize attempts of that kind. In present day conditions any other course would be reckless.[46]

The question of internal security controls is always a delicate one. The Shah in the above-quoted remarks has certainly put his finger on the true situation: in any modern state, security agencies are ubiquitous. The matter actually seems to be one of degree—the degree to which such institutions influence the political process in the country. The United States herself, although prone to set her own democratic system as an example for the world to follow, has not been free from perplexing problems in this respect. The internment of American citizens of Japanese extraction during World War II testifies to the readiness of President Franklin D. Roosevelt to disregard constitutional safeguards in order to achieve a higher national purpose, as he saw it, in time of war. He seems to have been guided by the old Roman adage *salus reipublicae suprema lex esto* ("Let the safety of the state be the supreme law"). Disclosures of widespread wiretapping, break-ins, and other acts of dubious legality by American internal and external security agencies in the 1960s and 1970s have pointed to the fact that even in democracies the government and the people face a continuous dilemma of where the line between the needs of security and the individual freedom should be drawn. Nor are the Western democracies, including the United States, free from the dilemma of undue concentration of power in the hands of the executive. There is ample evidence to suggest that, during World War II, the initial presidential promises to the electorate not to draw the United States into armed conflict were not made in good faith and that by various strategems, including executive agreements, the president was steadily committing the United States more and more towards participation in the war. The Vietnam conflict supplied another example of a democratic country being drawn into the war essentially on the basis of a presidential decision. It is not perhaps without cause that one of the standard treatises on the American political system bears the title *The Imperial Presidency.*[47]

It is worth noting in this connection that the Iranians did not cease to enjoy a number of freedoms inconceivable under a totalitarian Communist system. As we have seen, over 40,000 young Iranians were permitted to study abroad and were thus exposed to a free flow of ideas. This contrasted with a virtually complete ban on studies in foreign countries by the Soviet Union, the latter allowing a mere handful of more mature technical specialists to be trained abroad, usually with their families kept as hostages at home. Similarly, Iranians enjoyed complete freedom of religion, and the time-honored tolerance toward minorities and hospitality toward victims of persecution was fully maintained. Noteworthy in this respect was the prosperous status of the Armenian and Jewish communities, members of which frequently returned to Iran from countries, including Israel, to which they had initially emigrated. By the same token, Iran opened her gates to an influx of thousands of Polish citizens who, having been captured by the Red Army and secret police in 1939, were released from Soviet prisons and forced labor camps following the German invasion of Russia in World War II. To these victims of Soviet captivity Iran, even under the difficult wartime circumstances, appeared like a veritable land of promise and freedom starkly contrasting with a grim Soviet reality. Above all, unless heavily engaged in dissident political activities, the average Iranian was free to pursue his life and career without government interference in a country with a fundamentally private economy, in which the state was far from being the only employer. Even the fact that Iran was experiencing sporadic urban guerrilla violence seemed to place her closer to the Western world than to the totalitarian orbit. There were *no* urban guerrillas in the Soviet Union, China, and the satellite states. They did exist, however, in the United States, West Germany, and some other countries of the Free World precisely because these states abstained from total surveillance of their citizens.

These remarks are not made to suggest that the Iranian and American systems are alike or that any excess of zeal on the part of security agencies should be condoned. Their purpose is merely to point out that if a country with a seemingly well-entrenched democratic system is not free of dilemmas of this sort, one can understand that a country in a much more exposed strategic position, weaker, and a victim of recent foreign occupation and subversive attempts, may be understood to be more sensitive to the internal security issue than a state enjoying blessings of greater distance from the center of danger.

By the same token, the Shah's solicitude for the buildup of his military forces was understandable in the light of the country's recent history. Without creating a powerful army—powerful, that is, by regional standards—his father, Reza Shah, could not have moved Iran from a condition of anarchy and backwardness onto the path of modern reform. The challenges facing the Shah in the postwar period might have been different from those encountered by his father, but the need for a strong and reliable military power base remained the same.

Finally, it may be appropriate to conclude this discussion by pointing out that during the period 1951 to 1953, which is often presented as one of libertarian trends in contrast to the subsequent strong-man rule, Iran was exposed to a number of actions of dubious constitutionality and legality. These actions included pressuring the Majles into granting the then prime minister, Mosaddegh, full powers in early 1952; resort to mob violence to topple the legally appointed government of Premier Qavam in July 1952; the suspension of elections to the Majles once the early returns began to show a trend to the detriment of the prime minister; a rather Soviet-style method applied at the time of the referendum on the dissolution of the Majles, when electors were directed to separate booths marked yes and no and thus compelled to reveal their preferences; a constitutionally dubious dissolution of the Senate by the vote of the intimidated Majles in October 1952; the dissolution of the Supreme Court; the political manipulation of military appointments; and, finally, the refusal to accept dismissal from the prime-ministership although the right of dismissal was expressly guaranteed to the Shah by the constitution.[48]

Political Ideology

Enough has been said in the preceding sections to permit us to draw a broad outline of the Shah's ideology. It is essentially an ideology of nationalism and modernization. Although these two points follow the principles espoused by Reza Shah, the emphasis of each has changed not only with the coming of Mohammad Reza to power but also perhaps in the course of his own reign, which by 1976 had already been twice as long as his father's. While Reza Shah had simply to deal with the elimination of Soviet and British influence from his country, Mohammad Reza Shah had a more complex task to perform in terms of national emancipation and assertion of independence. For example, his father had to face the presence of foreign forces on Iran's territory, but this presence did not constitute a regular occupation as was the case later, during World War II. To be sure, both rulers faced Soviet armed intervention coupled with political subversion in the form of separatist regimes in the northern part of the country—the Gilan Communist Republic in 1920-21 and the Azarbayjan and Kurdish dissident political structures in 1945-46. However, in 1921 the Soviet Union was a weak country that had barely survived the travails of its own revolution, foreign intervention, and White counterrevolution. In 1945, by contrast, the Soviet Union, though greatly devastated in its western and southern areas, nevertheless emerged as one of the world's superpowers. Both rulers, similarly, faced the challenge of the British power, particularly in the oil sector. But the clash that Reza Shah had with the Anglo-Persian Oil Company in the early 1930s was simple as compared with the turmoil of the Mosaddegh era, 1951-52, following the nationalization of AIOC's assets and its ramifications and effects upon the very survival of the monarchy. Moreover, Mohammad Reza Shah did not rest after the conclusion of the oil consortium agreement in 1954, but with the passage of time adopted a strong assertive policy that twenty years later produced, on his initiative, the quadrupling of Middle East prices for crude oil. The result was to assure Iran of an influx of unprecedented wealth, which in turn his government was able to use for ambitious development programs.

Here again we are reminded of certain Western writers who assert that the Mosaddegh regime was par excellence nationalistic, with the implicit allegation that the Shah's regime was not. Nothing could be more removed from reality. It was the Shah's regime that was par excellence a nationalist one because the Shah tried to safeguard Iran's independence and integrity against what he saw as a greater danger, namely the very real threat of Soviet imperialism rather than the imaginary threat of American or British imperialism. In fact, already at the time of the oil nationalization showdown, it was clear that Britain was virtually an *ex*-imperial power rather than an actual one. She had abandoned her dominion over India, Egypt, and many other overseas possessions, and was soon to follow this up with withdrawal from the Persian Gulf. By the same token, although the United States emerged as a major military and political power in the Free World, i.e., all those areas of the globe outside the Sino-Soviet orbit, she neither coveted nor conquered any territory from Iran and, instead of engaging in classic colonial exploitation, was extending economic and technical aid and assistance to many countries in the world including Iran. In order to contrast his own approach to these matters with Mosaddegh's negativism, the Shah called his own philosophy that of "positive nationalism," which he defined as "a policy of maximum political and economic independence consistent with the interest of one's country."[49] This did not mean nonalignment; rather, he reserved the right to make any agreement in the country's interest, regardless of the wishes or policies of others. He continued:

> At the same time my country enjoys the added protection of mutual defense agreements with powerful and vigilant friends; and these agreements are completely in harmony with the spirit and letter of the United Nations charter. So you can see that our foreign policy has evolved in the light of very practical experience. In two world wars we learned the fallacy of neutrality for a country

so strategically located as Iran, for in neither case did it keep us from being overrun and after both great conflicts we became a happy hunting ground for foreign interests.[50]

Another aspect of the Shah's nationalism has been his struggle to reduce the gap between the advanced and the underdeveloped nations. He has given numerous expressions to his concern over this discrepancy, believing it to be a great source of danger.[51] His struggle for international equality has thus become linked with the second major aspect of his ideology, that of developing and modernizing his country. But again, although Reza Shah was already known as a revolutionary modernizer, the emphasis of Mohammad Reza Shah has been different, because it was he who tackled for the first time the agrarian question in his country and it was he who has been much more conscious than his father of the complex questions that can broadly be described as concern for social justice. "The war of today's society," declared the Shah at the World Congress of Iranian Studies in 1966, "is a holy war waged by man to eliminate discrimination, social injustice, differences, prejudice and selfishness, qualities shared by all mankind which release hatred under the pretext of unreasonable principles."[52] And in a major address at Harvard two years later he proclaimed:

> I want today to make a suggestion to all the people who are prepared to enter into a holy struggle for rendering real service to humanity. . . . I propose the creation of an international organization to be known by some such name as the Universal Welfare Legion in which individuals irrespective of country, class, race, religion, sex, age, economic level, or social status will render service.[53]

In concluding this section on the main thrust of the Shah's political thought, it is perhaps appropriate to refer to his attitude toward the problem of egalitarianism. It was rather natural for him to see the Iranian state and society as a pyramid with himself at its apex. To climb upward in this hierarchical structure, a person needed to demonstrate ability, competence, and loyalty. Otherwise the road was open for everybody to compete. The system thus designed was not geared to establish artificial equality of status and income for everybody. It was, however, a system that definitely rejected inherited privileges and opened the gates of opportunity for everybody. Persians, as the Shah himself pointed out, had never tolerated rigid systems of caste or class, and many of Persia's great kings, soldiers, and statesmen arose from humble origins.

> Our society has always been sufficiently open and flexible for men of humblest backgrounds to be able to aspire to positions of leadership. They might face severe economic and educational handicaps, but at least our political and social

structure never relegated them permanently to the bottom rung of the ladder. One has always been able to find a sort of elemental democratic spirit in Persia. I find it hard to put into words, yet it is very real.[54]

Similarly, in an interview with a foreign visitor, when queried about social mobility in Iran, the Shah replied: "Social mobility? Look at the career of my father."[55]

Style of Leadership

In *Mission For My Country,* the Shah gave an account of the religious visions he had had as a child and of instances of miraculous rescue from danger, including attempts on his life—rescue that he ascribed to divine providence. "From the time I was six or seven, I have felt that perhaps there is a supreme being who is guiding me," wrote the Shah in the above-mentioned book.[56] He reiterated this theme in his second book, *The White Revolution,* in the following words:

> I will frankly confess that I was convinced that God had ordained me to do certain things for the service of my nation, things that perhaps could not be done by anyone else. In whatever I have done, and in whatever I do in the future, I consider myself merely as an agent of the will of God and I pray that He may guide me in the fulfillment of His will and keep me from error.[57]

While thus revealing his deep religiosity and a strain of mysticism, the Shah has not followed a conventional pattern of religious observance. Commenting to a foreign visitor on the public prayers performed in a mosque by one of the well-known Arab revolutionary leaders—prayers that were invariably recorded in press photographs and newsfilms—the Shah stated that he considered such displays of religious fervor as insincere propaganda devices. His own approach to religion, he continued, had a deeper motivation.[58]

In spite of his belief in the divine guidance, Mohammad Reza Shah has always been convinced of the need for hard work and personal exertion. This conviction is linked with his devotion to the idea of a king's special mission and responsibility. In his own words, "with the growth of education . . . in Iran, a good king will be able to serve his country more effectively than ever before; but a mediocre or bad king would no longer have the means to cause damage, for the enlightened people of this country would not tolerate it."[59] This sentiment has caused the Shah to adopt what we may call an activist attitude with regard to his role in Iran. He has felt that it was his duty not only to reign but also to rule. He has developed hard-working habits exemplified in his daily routine, which begins with perusal of the newspapers at 8:00 A.M., to be followed by conferences with the minister of court, prime minister,

members of the cabinet, chiefs of the army and other high officials, not to
mention audiences with foreign ambassadors and visitors and the chairing of
various meetings. His day ends only between 6:00 and 7:00 P.M. Having a
highly developed work ethic, the Shah has taken the trouble to acquire special
expertise in three sectors: military affairs, foreign policy, and the international
petroleum industry. Visitors discussing these matters with him have frequently acknowledged his detailed knowledge of types of weaponry, facts and
figures regarding the distribution of armed forces throughout the world, and
the production, pricing and marketing of oil, not to speak of his more obvious
intimate acquaintance with international relations and what could broadly be
described as comparative politics.

The Shah has made a point of stressing that he was trained as a soldier and
that military affairs have always remained of special interest to him.

The problem of how much a head of state should rely on the information
and advice tendered him by those in his immediate proximity has been a
leading dilemma of government throughout the ages. Mohammad Reza
Shah, while acknowledging the tremendous influence that his father exerted on his formation and thinking, has nevertheless stressed the difference
in this respect between the latter and himself. Relying upon a small circle of
advisers, the Shah has written, was "one of the few mistakes my father made."

> Fearing Reza Shah, they flattered him rather than telling him the truth; and I am
> sorry to say they were by no means always incorruptible. My system is entirely
> different. I know that advisors, no matter how technically competent they may
> be, sometimes make the national interest subservient to their own. Furthermore,
> they are prone to try to funnel all information through themselves and to seal off
> independent intelligence channels. So in lieu of advisors I obtain information
> from many quarters and then try to strike my own balance sincerely and solely in
> the light of public interest.[60]

The Shah's system of assuring the flow of information and advice to himself
through various channels has naturally resulted in a degree of rivalry among
those who provide such services. According to one student of Iranian politics,
rivalry and tension between individuals and groups have been the essential
political reality in Iran.[61] While this is undoubtedly true, the phenomenon of
competition in political life and individual careers is not unique to Iran and
could rather be considered as universal, albeit expressed in different ways in
different societies. There are reasons to believe that the Shah has been
encouraging this spirit of competition to draw out, for the benefit of the state,
the maximum effort from competing individuals and groups.

According to his own testimony, the Shah has been exposed to contacts
with an impressively wide range of individuals and groups. One of his major
problems as King has been to be able to differentiate between flattery and

sound advice. In his position he has inevitably experienced a degree of loneliness known by other leaders and heads of state—a loneliness accentuated by the Iranian tradition of royalty.

> Although I am much more accessible and much less forbidding in demeanor than was Reza Shah, inevitably my role keeps me at arm's length from other people. During meetings of the Council of Ministers or in the course of private audiences I may laugh and joke, but everybody knows that such mutual understanding is in a true sense purely superficial. My isolation is accentuated by my reluctance to employ advisors and by my habit—which indeed is common among heads of state—of bearing the final decision-making burden. Except in trivial terms I do not even discuss affairs of state with my closest relatives.[62]

Inevitably, then, a distance has existed between him and even the highest state dignitaries. Nevertheless, the Shah has exposed himself to a wide range of contacts. He has made frequent inspection tours in the provinces of Iran, particularly when some new project was being launched, developed, or completed. He has personally distributed deeds of land to countless peasants under the land reform laws. He has attended army maneuvers and air force exercises, and taken special interest in the development of the navy and maritime facilities in the Persian Gulf. In fact, by his personal presence, which included occasional vacationing on the gulf island of Kish, the Shah may be said to have "opened the window" of Iran on the Persian Gulf more than any other ruler of his country in her recent history.

In the mid-1970s, the Shah was regularly devoting several hours a day to audiences not only with his high officials but also with private visitors, including foreigners. He was in the habit of granting interviews to representatives of the press, television, and radio, as well as to foreign scholars and writers. This availability to foreign visitors contrasted with the habits of his father who rarely, if ever, would grant interviews to non-Iranians. The fact that Mohammad Reza Shah was Western-educated and impeccably fluent in both English and French, languages that he knew how to use with great precision, was a material factor in this respect. However, above all, it was his willingness to see the visitors, learn from their remarks and questions various points of view, and articulate his own policies and attitudes that really mattered.

Similarly, the Shah had traveled widely both on state visits and in an unofficial capacity. Again, in contrast to Reza Shah, whose only official foreign trip was to Turkey in the 1930s, Mohammad Reza Shah visited the United States on a number of occasions, getting to know every American president since World War II and in turn receiving most of them in Tehran. There was virtually no continent and no major state in the world that he would not have visited either to discuss matters of policy and economic cooperation or as a gesture of good will. This included several visits to the Soviet Union and the reciprocal visits of Soviet leaders beginning with Nikita Khrushchev in Tehran. While many accounts, including the Shah's own, agree that the personality of his father, a man with penetrating eyes, tended to inspire fear in those who were dealing with him, Mohammad Reza Shah's behavior and manners were geared to inspire visitors with confidence and ease tempered by respect. According to his own testimony, he rarely would lose his temper and, to convey his feelings whether of approval or disapproval, he would effectively use the tone of his voice, facial expression, and his eyes.[63]

The Shah tended to pay special attention to major gatherings of his citizens at which he would rarely miss an opportunity to make an address exhorting those present to further endeavors, exposing the weaknesses of a given situation or organization, and calling for the achievement of specific goals. In doing this he showed that he understood the public functions of political leadership.

A major innovation was the substantial role assigned to his wife, Empress Farah, in performing a number of state functions and serving as an initiator and guide of a number of activities in which the people's voluntary participation was essential. In fact, the Shahbanou could probably be ranked among the best-educated and most socially conscious of the wives of heads of state in the 1960s and 1970s. Paris-trained, endowed with artistic talents and appreciation for intellectual pursuits, the Empress paid special attention to matters of social welfare, arts, and culture. Notable were her appearances at the annual educational conferences at Ramsar, her activities aiming at the elevation of the position of women, and especially her initiative in promoting the annual art festivals in Shiraz, which gradually attracted the participation of world-renowned talent. Similarly, the Shah encouraged and relied frequently on the public services performed by his royal sisters, Princesses Ashraf and Shams. Princess Ashraf in particular represented him on a number of important diplomatic missions while also serving as delegate of Iran on the U.N. Human Rights Commission and at various conferences concerned with the advancement of women.

In the mid-1970s a new feature was added to the Shah's style of leadership, namely, the increasingly frequent appearances of Crown Prince Reza, born in 1960, at various state functions. In this Mohammad Reza Shah was undoubtedly following the example of his father, who made a point of introducing him at an early age to state affairs. The difference between the two reigns was in the range of foreign contacts to which both the ruler and his Crown Prince were exposed. In 1975-76, the Crown Prince was selected to be the principal representative of Iran on such state visits as the celebration in Egypt of the reopening of the Suez Canal, and a journey to Paris at the invitation of President Giscard d'Estaing.

Notwithstanding his often grueling work routine, the Shah has developed a liking for certain hobbies and a moderate amount of recreation. His early interest, sustained throughout his reign, has been in aviation. He became a licensed pilot and never lost interest in flying. During his school days in Switzerland, followed by his education in the Iranian Military Academy, the Shah developed a liking for various outdoor sports, of which skiing has remained his favorite. However, his personal habits have remained modest and unostentatious, and his court has never acquired a reputation for lavish or noisy entertainment. To the extent that time permitted, the Shah would read works of *belles lettres* as well as history and biography.

In concluding this chapter it is permissible to say that since 1925 Iran has benefited from a political leadership that contrasts dramatically with the inept and weak rule of the preceding dynasty. For all practical purposes, Iran during the last decades of Qajar rule was more a territory in a geographical sense than an organized and functioning political entity. Domestic anarchy, foreign encroachments, an empty treasury, a weak army, and general social and economic backwardness were characteristic of that bygone era. The Pahlavis brought a real revolution in all these fields and restored Iran to her rightful place in the family of nations. This progress was achieved under two successive rulers whose careers were remarkable considering the obstacles they had to overcome. The rise of Reza Shah from simple soldier to king was in itself a spectacular achievement, but surely it went beyond the dramatic personal story to affect the well-being of a country thus launched upon the path of modernization. Although as a son of the reigning monarch, Mohammad Reza was born to a unique position of privilege, his progress has been marked by dangers and obstacles that might easily have broken an individual of lesser will power, intelligence, and determination. Ascending the throne at a time of foreign occupation, the new Shah had to face the onslaught of Soviet imperialism in the north of Iran even as the West was surrendering major areas of the globe to Soviet expansionism. During the next decade, the Shah had to face a domestic turmoil of unprecedented proportions. He emerged victorious from both major trials and in his new position of strength was able to launch a bold program of reforms designed to put an end once and for all to the social and economic ills that had plagued the Iranian nation for centuries. In carrying out his struggle and work the Shah took conscious advantage of the historical tradition of his ancient country, a tradition dating back to the Achaemenian antiquity in which the institution of monarchy had originated. In this respect, Iran possessed an advantage over some newer nations, which could not point to the same type of remarkable legacy. In the 1970s, half a century after the installation of the Pahlavi dynasty, this ancient legacy was being revived in its full dimensions.

Appendix

Principles of Iran's White Revolution

ITEM	DATE
The original six points:	Announced by the Shah,
1. Land reform (detailed in the 1962 land reform law)	January 9, 1963, and endorsed by national referendum, January 26, 1963
2. Nationalization of forests	
3. Sale of state-owned enterprises to the public	
4. Workers' profit-sharing in 20 percent of net corporate earnings	
5. Voting and political rights for women	
6. Formation of the Literacy Corps	
Additional three points, 1964-65	
7. Formation of the Health Corps	January 21, 1964
8. Formation of the Reconstruction and Development Corps	September 23, 1964
9. Establishment of Houses of Equity	October 13, 1965
Additional three points, 1967	October 6, 1967
10. Program for nationalization of water resources	
11. Program for urban and rural reconstruction	
12. Administrative revolution (modernization, decentralization)	
Additional five points, 1975	
13. Employee and public ownership extension scheme (up to 99 percent in state-owned enterprises and 49 percent in private firms)	September 9, 1975
14. Price stabilization and campaign against profiteering	September 9, 1975
15. Free education and a daily free meal for all children from kindergarten to eighth grade	mid-December 1975
16. Free nutrition for infants up to the age of two	late December 1975
17. Nation-wide social security (to be extended to rural population)	late December 1975

SOURCES: *Area Handbook for Iran,* American University, Foreign Area Studies, 1971; Mohammad Reza Shah Pahlavi, *The White Revolution,* Tehran: 1967; *Kayhan International; Quarterly Economic Review.*

Notes and Bibliographies

L.P. ELWELL-SUTTON

CHAPTER ONE: NOTES

1. *Ettela'at* (Tehran), September 17, 1941.

2. HIH Shams Pahlavi, *Khaterat-e Reza Shah Pahlavi* [Memories of Reza Shah Pahlavi] (Tehran: 1948).

3. Mohammad Hasan Khan Etemadossaltane, *Attadvin fi ahval-e jebal-e Sharvin* [Treatise on the mountains of Sharvin] (Tehran: 1893), p. 129; reproduced in Hushang Pur-Karim, *Elasht—Zadgah-e a'lahazrat-e Reza Shah-e Kabir* [Elasht, birthplace of HIM Reza Shah the Great] (Tehran: Ministry of Culture and Art, [1971]), p. 37.

4. 'Ali al-Basri, *Yaddashtha-ye a'lahazrat-e Reza Shah-e Kabir* [Memoirs of HIM Reza Shah the Great], trans. Shahram Karimlu (Tehran: Iranian General Staff, 1971), p. 20.

5. Malekosho'ara Bahar, *Tarikh-e mokhtasar-e ahzab-e siyasi* [Short history of the political parties] (Tehran: 1944), vol. 1, p. 77.

6. *Parliamentary Debates*, House of Lords, 5th series, vol. 42, November 16, 1920.

7. Maj.-Gen. Sir Edward Ironside, *High Road to Command*, ed. Lord Ironside (London: Leo Cooper, 1972), p. 163, (hereafter cited as "Ironside").

8. Donald N. Wilber, *Riza Shah Pahlavi*, p. 44, (hereafter cited as "Wilber"); Gen. Hassan Arfa, *Under Five Shahs*, pp. 109-10.

9. Ironside, p. 130; J.M. Balfour, *Recent Happenings in Persia*, p. 188.

10. Ironside, p. 149 (where it is mistakenly described as the "Tabriz *otryad"*).

11. *Documents on British Foreign Policy 1919-1939* (London: 1963), 1st series, vol 13, pp. 731-32.

12. Richard H. Ullman, *Anglo-Soviet Relations 1917-1921*, vol. 3, *The Anglo-Soviet Accord*, p. 389.

13. *Documents on British Foreign Policy*, p. 729.

14. Ironside, p. 117; Wilber, p. 48.

15. Ullman, *Anglo-Soviet Relations*, p. 387.

16. Ironside, pp. 164-65.

17. *Documents on British Foreign Policy*, p. 729.

18. Iranian General Staff, *Tarikh-e artesh-e novin-e Iran* [History of the new army of Iran] (Tehran: n.d.), vol. 1, part 1, pp. 49-50.

19. Hosein Makki, *Tarikh-e bist sale-ye Iran* [Twenty years' history of Iran] (Tehran: 1945), vol. 1, pp. 125-29, (hereafter cited as "Makki, *Iran*"); *Documents on British Foreign Policy,* p. 734.

20. Bahar, *Ahzab-e siyasi,* pp. 185-88.

21. Makki, *Iran,* p. 354.

22. Imperial Court of Iran, Research Center Archives, document no. 711, (hereafter cited as "Imperial Court").

23. A.C. Millspaugh, *The American Task in Persia,* pp. 45-48.

24. Makki, *Iran,* vol. 2, pp. 343-44.

25. Iranian legation in London, telegram no. 794, 11 Saratan 1303 [July 2, 1924], reproduced in Basri, *Reza Shah-e Kabir,* p. 41; Makki, *Iran,* vol. 3, p. 179.

26. Imperial Court, document no. 19.

27. Hosein Makki, *Mokhtasari az zandagani-ye siyasi-ye Soltan Ahmad Shah Qajar* [Sketch of the political life of Ahmad Shah Qajar] (Tehran: 1944), pp. 260-62.

28. Makki, *Iran,* vol. 3, pp. 488-586 (a verbatim record of the debate).

29. Abdorreza Sadeqipur, ed., *Yadgar-e gozashte: Majmu'e-ye sokhanraniha-ye A'lahazrat-e faqid-e Reza Shah-e Kabir* [Memorial of the past: collected speeches of His Late Majesty Reza Shah the Great] (Tehran: Javidan, 1968), pp. 66-67 (hereafter cited as "Sadeqipur").

30. Ibid., pp. 72-74.

31. Ibid., pp. 109, 113-15.

32. Ibid., pp. 91-92.

33. Ibid., p. 158.

34. Ibid., pp. 137-39.

35. Badrolmoluk Bamdad, *Zan-e irani az enqelab-e mashrutiyyat ta enqelab-e safid* [The Iranian woman from the Constitutional Revolution to the White Revolution], (Tehran: Ibn Sina, n.d.), vol. 1, pp. 99.

36. Sadeqipur, pp. 86-87.

37. Ibid., pp. 50-52.

38. Wilber, p. 98; Imperial Court, document no. 3252 (memoir by 'Isa Sadiq).

39. Sadeqipur, p. 164.

40. Wilber, p. 127.

41. Makki, *Iran,* vol. 2, pp. 297-99.

42. Imperial Court, document no. 14.

43. Ibid., document no. 29 (letter from General Staff to Ministry of Foreign Affairs dated 20 Azar 1316 [December 11, 1936]).

44. Ibid., document no. 3249 (memoir by Ali Asghar Hekmat).

45. Ibid., document no. 15.

46. Wipert von Blücher, *Zeitenwende in Iran,* pp. 165-68; Wilber, pp. 175, 186; Imperial Court, document no. 1840.

47. Imperial Court, document no. 1841.

48. Ibid., document no. 3249.

49. Blücher, *Zeitenwende,* p. 331.

50. Sadeqipur, pp. 45-49.

51. Ne'matollah Mehrkhah, *Ketab-e Reza Shah* [The book of Reza Shah] (Tehran: 1946), p. 58.

52. Ibid., pp. 34-36.

53. Ibid., p. 59.

54. Ironside, p. 118.

55. Imperial Court, document no. 3975 (cutting from *Ettela'at,* 24 Mordad 1306 [August 15, 1927]).

56. Ibid., document no. 3249.

57. Iranian General Staff, *artesh-e novin-e Iran,* pp. 144-46.

58. Sadeqipur, pp. 104-6.

59. Arfa, *Under Five Shahs,* p. 236.

CHAPTER ONE: SELECTED BIBLIOGRAPHY*

Aghababian, R. *Législation iranienne actuelle.* Vol. 1: Tehran, 1939; vol. 2: Paris, 1951.

Arasteh, Reza. *Education and Social Awakening in Iran.* Leiden: E.J. Brill, 1962.

Arfa, General Hassan. *Under Five Shahs.* London: John Murray, 1964.

Avery, Peter. *Modern Iran.* London: Ernest Benn, 1965.

Balfour, J.M. *Recent Happenings in Persia.* Edinburgh: Blackwood, 1922.

Banani, Amin. *The Modernization of Iran 1921-1941.* Stanford, Calif.: Stanford University Press, 1961.

Blücher, Wipert von. *Zeitenwende in Iran.* Biberach an der Riss, West Germany: Koehler and Voigtländer, 1949.

Elwell-Sutton, L.P. *Modern Iran.* London: Routledge, 1941.

———. *Persian Oil: A Study in Power Politics.* London: Lawrence and Wishart, 1955.

Essad-Bey. *Reza Schah: Feldherr, Kaiser, Reformator.* Vienna: Rolf Passer, 1936.

———. with Branden, Paul Maerker and Branden, Elsa. *Reza Shah.* London: Hutchinson, 1938.

Fateh, Moustafa Khan. *The Economic Position of Persia.* London: P.S. King and Son, 1926.

Fatemi, Nasrollah Saifpour. *Diplomatic History of Persia 1917-1923.* New York: Russell F. Moore, 1952.

———. *Oil Diplomacy: Powderkeg in Iran.* New York: Whittier Books, 1954.

Filmer, Henry. *The Pageant of Persia.* New York: Bobbs-Merrill, 1936.

Groseclose, Elgin. *Introduction to Iran.* New York: Oxford University Press, 1947.

Haas, William S. *Iran.* New York: Columbia University Press, 1946.

Lenczowski, George. *Russia and the West in Iran 1918-1948.* Ithaca, N.Y.: Cornell University Press, 1949.

*In European languages only.

Mesbah Zadeh, Mostafa. *La politique de l'Iran dans la Société des Nations*. Paris: A. Pedone, 1936.

Migliorini, Elio. *Strade e commercio dell'Iran*. Messina and Milan: Giuseppe Principato, 1939.

Millspaugh, A.C. *The American Task in Persia*. New York: Century Co., 1925.

———. *Americans in Persia*. Washington: Brookings, 1946.

Morton, Rosalie Slaughter. *A Doctor's Holiday in Iran*. New York: Funk and Wagnalls, 1940.

Pahlavi, HIM Mohammed Reza Shah. *Mission for My Country*. London: McGraw-Hill, 1961.

Polacco, Angelo. *L'Iran di Rezà Scià Pahlavi*. Venice: Zanetti Editrice, 1937.

Ramazani, Rouhollah K. *The Foreign Policy of Iran 1500-1941*. Charlottesville, Va.: University of Virginia Press, 1966.

Sadiq, Issa Khan. *Modern Persia and her Educational System*. New York: Columbia University Press, 1931.

Schultze-Holthus, B. *Frührot in Iran*. Esslingen: Bechtle, 1952. English translation, *Daybreak in Iran*. London: Staples, 1954.

Sheean, Vincent. *The New Persia*. New York: Century Co., 1927.

Soheily, Hossein. *Essai sur l'industrialisation de l'Iran*. Montreux: Ganguin and Laubscher, 1950.

Suratgar, Olive. *I Sing in the Wilderness*. London: Edward Stanford, 1951.

Ullman, Richard H. *Anglo-Soviet Relations 1917-1921*. Vol. 3, *The Anglo-Soviet Accord*. Princeton, N.J.: Princeton University Press, 1972.

Upton, Joseph M. *The History of Modern Iran: An Interpretation*. Cambridge, Mass.: Harvard University Press, 1960.

Wilber, Donald N. *Contemporary Iran*. London: Thames and Hudson, 1963.

———. *Riza Shah Pahlavi: The Resurrection and Reconstruction of Iran 1878-1944*. Hicksville, N.Y.: Exposition Press, 1975.

Woodsmall, Ruth Frances. *Moslem Women Enter a New World*. London: George Allen and Unwin, 1936.

PIO FILIPPANI-RONCONI

CHAPTER TWO: NOTES

List of Abbreviations

A.	Arabic
AI.	*Acta Iranica,* 3 vols. (Tehran and Bruxelles: Bibliothèque Pahlavi, distr. by E.J. Brill, 1974).
Ann.	*Annali dell'Istituto Universitario Orientale di Napoli* (Naples: Istituto Univ. Orientale).

Av. *Avesta, The Sacred Books of the Parsis,* ed. by Karl Geldner (Stuttgart: Kohlhammer, 1896).

AZh. *Apyatkar i Zhamaspik,* etc., ed. G. Messina (Rome: Pontifico Istituto Biblico, 1939).

Barth. Bartholomae, Christ., *Altiranisches Wörterbuch* (Berlin: W. de Gruyter, 1961).

Bd. Ankl. *Bundahishn,* ed. Anklesaria (Bombay: 1956).

DD. *Datistan i Denik,* ed. Anklesaria (Bombay: 1911).

Dk. M. *Denkart* ("The Complete Text of. . ."), ed. D.M. Madan (Bombay: 1911).

Inscr. *The Inscriptions in Old Persian Cuneiforms of the Achaemenian Empire* (Tehran: n.d.).

MP. Middle Persian.

NP. Neo-Persian

OI. Old Iranian.

OP. Old Persian.

P. Persian.

Q. *Qur'an* ed. of King Fu'ad (Cairo: 1919).

REA. *Revue des Etudes Arméniennes* (Paris).

Symb. "Le symbolisme cosmique des monuments réligieux," *Orientalia Romana* 14 (Rome: ISMEO, 1957).

V. *Videvdat (Vendidad),* ed. K. Geldner under the title *Vendidad und Prolegomena* (Stuttgart: Kohlhammer, 1895).

Ys. *Yasna.*

Yt. *Yasht. Die Yäst des Awesta,* ed. H. Lommel (Göttingen-Leipzig, 1927).

ZS. *Zatspram. Vičitakiha i Zatspram,* ed. R.C. Zaehner (London: Bulletin of the School of Oriental Studies, IX-X, 1938-39).

1. Yt., 8-34.

2. A. Bausani, *Persia Religiosa* (Milan: 1959), p. 313 et seq.

3. W. Hinz, *Zarathustra* (Stuttgart: 1961), p. 39 et seq.

4. Bd. Ankl., 3: 23-24.

5. Q., 33:72.

6. H. Corbin, "Le temps cyclique dans le Mazdéisme et dans l'Ismaélisme," *Eranos-Jahrbuch* 20: 149 et seq., 204 et seq., 211-16.

7. Yt., 19.9; Corbin, ibid., 152-73; M. Molé, *Culte, mythe et cosmologie dans l'Iran ancien,* p. 529.

8. Corbin, ibid., 199.

9. P. Filippani-Ronconi, "La conception sacrée de la royaute Iranienne," AI. vol. 1, p. 96.

10. Bausani, *Persia Religiosa,* p. 90.

11. Barth., 1151; Yt., 10.2.

12. Barth., 662-68.

13. Ys., 30.9, p. 403, transl. 223.

14. J. Duchesne-Guillemin, *Zoroastre,* pp. 75-76.

15. H. Reichelt, *Awestisches Elementarbuch,* p. 474.

16. Dk. M., 129:7—130:17.

17. Ammianus Marcellinus, ed. V. Gardthausen (Leipzig, 1874-75), 17.5, i et seq.

18. C. Plinius Secondus, *Naturalis Historia,* ed. D. Detlefsen (Berlin: Weidmann, 1866-82), XXX, 2, 16 f.

19. Spiegel, *Die traditionelle Literatur der Parsen,* pp. 327-32; M. Molé; *Culte, mythe et cosmologie dans l'Iran ancien,* p. 40 (hereafter cited as "Molé").

20. Mihir Yasht (Yt. 10) 3: "To those who are not false to the contract grass-land magnate Mithra grants [possession of] fast horses. . . ." *The Avestan Hymn to Mithra,* trans. I. Gershevitch (Cambridge: University Press, 1959).

21. G. Widengren, *The Sacral Kingship of Iran,* pp. 247-48.

22. Molé, p. 469.

23. H. Corbin, *Terre céleste et corps de resurrection,* pp. 168, 192 et seq., 209 et seq.; idem, *Storia della filosofia Islamica,* Italian edition, p. 82.

24. ZS., 27.5.

25. Ibid.

26. AI., vol. 2, pp. 63-68.

27. AZh., 4:13-18.

28. Barth., pp. 976, 1008.

29. Molé, p. 32 et seq.

30. Inscr., D-nb, 86.

31. Dk.M., 7.1:20; Molé, p. 462 et seq.

32. Molé, p. 92, 444 et seq.; DD., 36:1-8; Corbin, *Terre céleste,* pp. 40 et seq., 83.

33. P. Filippani-Ronconi, *Ismaeliti ed "Assassini"* (Milan: 1974), p. 126.

34. Dk.M., 344: 10-13.

35. Dk.M., 349, trans. by R.C. Zaehner, in Zurvan, 373: "this is what is revealed concerning the instrument which the Creator fashioned from the Endless Light and in which He caused creation to be contained: its Avestan name is the Endless Form [*asarok karpak*] and it is twofold." "Endless Form" has been reestablished by Duchesne-Guillemin more properly as "Fire-form," reading the context as *"asro karpak,"* which corresponds to the Av. "Athro kehrp" (*East and West* [Rome 1962], 13: 2).

36. Bd. Ankl., 162: 2-13; Molé, p. 437; J. Duchesne-Guillemin, "Le xvarenah," in Ann., *Sez. linguistica* (Naples: 1963), 5: 19-31. G. Gnoli gives another interpretation of the *agrift khvarrah* in Ann. (Naples: 1963) 13: 295-98. For the seminal aspect of the *khvarenah,* see his "Un particolare aspetto del simbolismo della luce nel Mazdeismoe nel Manicheismo," Ann. (Naples: 1962) 12: 96-128.

37. Dk.M., 349.

38. Yt., 19.34-64.

39. *Historia Romana,* 24.3; Plutarch, *Silla,* 5.9; Dobias, "I primi rapporti dei Romani coi Parti e l'occupazione della Siria," *Archiv Orientalní* (Prague: 1931) 3: 218 et seq.; Plutarch, *Silla,* 5.9.

40. J. Carcopino, *Silla o la Monarchia Mancata,* p. 104 et seq.; A. Piganiol, *Histoire de Rome,* p. 163.

41. Piganiol, ibid.

42. Barth., 42.

43. Piganiol, pp. 442, 452; F. Cumont, *La théologie solaire du paganisme romain* (Acad. des Inscr.) (Brussels: 1913) 12.2: 488; J. Noiville, *Les origines du Natalis Invicti* (REA 1936), p. 146.

44. Piganiol, p. 257.

45. Ibid., pp. 462-63.

46. Widengren, p. 250.

47. Ibid., p. 254.

48. Ibid.

49. F. Pareja, *Islamologia* 1: 111-13.

50. A. Bausani, *I Persiani*, p. 99.

51. I. Shokurzadeh, "Souvenirs de l'Iran ancien dans le folk-lore du Xorasan," AI., vol. 3, 361 et seq

52. AZh., pp. 118-19; P. Filippani-Ronconi, *Ummu'l-kitab* (Naples: 1966), p. 127 et seq.

53. Corbin, *Storia della filosofia Islamica*, Italian edition, pp. 81-82.

54. Ibid., French edition, p. 76.

55. Ibid., pp. 72, 86, 108, 110, 139.

56. The question is extensively treated by our *Ismaeliti ed "Assassini,"* pp. 23-47; see also al-Mutahhar b. Tahir al-Maqdisi, *Kitab al-bad' wa't-tarikh li. . .Ibn Sahl al-Balkhi*, ed. and trans. C. Huart (Paris: Ernest Leroux, 1899-1919), 4: 29 30.

57. Mas'udi, *Muruj adh-dhahab* ("The Golden Prairies"), ed. and trans. Barbier de Meynard (Paris: Imprimerie Nationale, 1861-77), 9: 27 et seq.

58. Bausani, *I Persiani*, pp. 247-54.

59. Corbin, *Storia della filosofia Islamica*, p. 184 et seq., bibl. in 267-68.

60. The question has been extensively dealt with in vol. 2 of E.G. Browne, *A Literary History of Persia*, 4 vols. (Cambridge, England: 1928).

61. T. Gandjei, *Canzoniere di Shah Isma'il Khata'i* (an edition of his Turkish songbook), no. 198 (Naples: Istituto Universitario Orientale, 1959).

62. The principal features of Sohravardi's philosophy, and his revaluation of the Persian metaphysics of light, are described in Corbin, *Storia della filosofia Islamica*, pp. 207-21. As far as his "Mazdaistic" characters are concerned, see H. Corbin, *Les motifs zoroastriens dans la philosophie de Sohrawardi* (Tehran: Publications de la Société d'Iranologie, 1946). The same scholar has edited, commented on, and partly translated the corpus of Sohravardi's metaphysics, besides other works of this author and his disciples.

63. As a matter of fact, Reza Shah was brought to the throne by a wave of popular enthusiasm that actually bordered on rage after some purposeful hints by his collaborators at republican possibilities. This is clearly shown not only by the contemporary press but still more by the formulation of the constitutional law granting him and his descendants the emperorship, as follows. "The Constitutional Monarchy of Iran is conferred on the person of His Majesty the Shahanshah Reza Shah Pahlavi [observe the imperative contradiction of twice calling him a "king," before actually granting him the kingship!] and to his male descendants, generation after generation, *by the Nation* [my emphasis] through the Constitutional Assembly." (21 Azar 1304, Solar Hejira, Assembly Act No. 36.) Furthermore it was established that the person of the Crown Prince was legitimately such only if born of a lady of Iranian stock. Assembly Act No. 37 gave the reasons for this qualification inasmuch as the mother of the Shah, the Empress (Shahbanou), was intended to be the Regent in the case of his minority. This provision is an unmistakable innovation, first, because it enhances the role of womanhood, which until then had been ignored in any Moslem

state; second, because it definitely breaks the link connecting the royalty to some Turkish clan (such as the previous Afshars and Qajars). The posthumous glorification of Reza Shah was brought about by conferring on him the title of "Great" (A. *kabir,* corresponding to the P. *bozorg,* O.P. *wazra-ka:* about this meaning, see note 64 below) on 31 Khordad 1328 S.H., which practically granted to his deceased person the rank of a Roman "Divus Imperator," that is to say, a Sassanid *Bagh-puhr!*

64. M.F. Kanga, "Kingship and religion in Iran," AI., vol. 3, pp. 225-26.

65. The gravity and far-reaching importance of this act, adopted by the joint session of both legislative houses (No. 10, 24 Shahrivar 1344 S.H.), was enhanced by the meaningful speech of the old senator Dr. Shafaq, who declared:

> This title—Aryamehr—is composed of two words, the first being Arya, which is the same that gave birth to the designation of *Iran.* It is worth observing that Iran is the only country in the world that has its own name from the time of yore, a name that is a historical, racial and popular designation. . .since our country was called sixteen centuries ago, during the Sassanian period, either Eran or Eranshahr. . . .This kind of title carries a tremendous meaning, because it was intended by the proponent *to revive* [the word of] *Arya.* As far as the second part is concerned, *Mehr* means "sun," which is the source of light and life. To us Iranians belongs the glory, from time of old, to have always considered light as a manifestation of truth [*haqq,* also "God"], of beauty, friendship [another meaning of *mehr*], inasmuch as we considered evil and impurity to be *Ahriman,* as we named the source of darkness. We called the worshippers of light Ahuramazda-worshippers! In the same sacred religion of ours, Islam, the heavenly Qor'an bears witness that "God is the Light of Heaven and Earth" . . . .From times of yore, this country and its horizons have been named after the light: *we are light-worshippers* [*roshna parast*], which is, by another designation, *God-worshippers.* . . .[author's italics]

66. Ys., 48.5

CHAPTER TWO: SELECTED BIBLIOGRAPHY

Anklesaria, B.T., ed. *Zatspram-i Gosn-jaman.* Bombay: Parsi Punchayet Funds and Properties, 1964.

———, ed. *Bundahishn.* Bombay: Rahnumae Mazdayasnan Sabha, 1956.

Bausani, A. *I Persiani.* Florence: Sansone, 1962.

———. *Persia Religiosa da Zaratustra a Baha'u'llah.* Milan: Adelphi, 1959.

Browne, E.G. *A Literary History of Persia.* Cambridge, England: The University Press, 1928.

Carcopino, J. *Silla o la Monarchia Mancata.* Milan: Longanesi, 1943.

Christensen, Arthur E. *L'Iran sous les Sassanides.* Copenhagen: E. Munkgaard, 1944.

Corbin, Henry. *Les motifs zoroastriens dans la philosophie de Sohrawardi.* Paris: Editions du Courrier, 1946.

———. *Histoire de la philosophie islamique.* Paris: Gallimard, 1964.

———. *Storia della filosofia islamica.* Milan: Adelphi, 1973.

——— *Terre céleste et corps de resurrection de l'Iran Mazdéen à l'Iran Shi'ite, La Barque du Soleil,* Paris: Buchet-Chastel, 1960.

Cumont, Franz. *La théologie solaire du paganisme romain.* Paris: Imprimerie Nationale, 1909. Reissued in Brussels: Academie des Inscriptions, 1913.

———— *The Oriental Religions in Roman Paganism.* Chicago: University of Chicago Press, 1911.

Dhalla, Manckji N. *Zoroastrian Civilization.* New York: Oxford University Press, 1922.

Duchesne-Guillemin, Jacques. "Le xvarenah." *Annali dell' Istituto Universitario Orientale di Napoli.* Sez. linguistica, 5: 19-31. Naples: Istituto Universitario Orientale, 1963.

————, ed. *Zoroastre.* Paris: G.P. Maisoneuve, 1948.

East and West 13, no. 2. Rome: Istituto Italiano per il Medio ed Estremo Oriente (ISMEO), 1962.

Filippani-Ronconi, P. *Ismaeliti ed "Assassini."* Basel: Thoth, 1973; Milan: Poggi, 1974.

———— "La conception sacrée de la royauté Iranienne" in *Acta Iranica.* Tehran and Liège, 1974.

————. *Ummu 'l-kitab.* Naples: Istituto Universitario Orientale, 1966.

Gnoli, G. "Politique religieuse et conception de la royauté sous les Achéménides," in *Acta Iranica,* II, 125 f.

————. "Un particolare aspetto del simbolismo della luce nel Mazdeismo e nel Manicheismo." *Annali dell' Istituto Universitario Orientale di Napoli* 12 (1962): 96-128.

Hinz, W. *Zarathustra.* Stuttgart: W. Kohlhammer, 1961.

Huart, Clément I. *Ancient Persia and Iranian Civilization.* Translated by M.R. Dobie. New York: Alfred A. Knopf, 1927.

Jackson, Abraham. V.W. *Zoroastrian Studies.* New York: Columbia University Press, 1928.

Kanga, M.F. "Kingship and Religion in Iran." *Acta Iranica* 3:228-30. Tehran and Liège, 1974.

Madan, Dhanjishah Meherjibhai. *Dinkard. Pahlavi.* Bombay: Society for the Promotion of Researches into the Zoroastrian Religion, 1911.

Molé, M. *Culte, mythe et cosmologie dans l'Iran ancien.* Paris: Presses Universitaires de France, 1963.

Olmstead, Albert T. *History of the Persian Empire, Achaemenid Period.* Chicago: University of Chicago Press, 1948.

Pareja, F. *Islamologia.* Madrid: Razón y Fe, 1952-54.

Piganiol, André. *Histoire de Rome.* 5th ed. Paris: Presses Universitaires de France, 1949.

Reichelt, H. *Awestisches Elementarbuch.* Heidelberg: C. Winter, 1909.

Shokurzadeh, I. "Souvenirs de l'Iran ancien dans le folk-lore du Xorasan." *Acta Iranica* 3. Tehran and Liège, 1974.

Spiegel, F. *Die traditionelle Literatur der Parsen in Ihrem Zusammenhange mit den angrenzenden Literaturen.* Vienna: for the Deutsche Morgenländische Gesellschaft by K.K. Hof- und Staatsdruckerei, 1860.

Widengren, G. *Sakrales Königtum im Alten Testament und in Judentum.* Stuttgart: W. Kohlhammer, 1955.

———. *The Sacral Kingship in Iran.* Leiden: Brill, 1959.

Zaehner, R.C. *Zurvan, a Zoroastrian Dilemma.* Oxford: Clarendon Press, 1955.

ROGER M. SAVORY

CHAPTER THREE: NOTES

1. Julian Bharier, *Economic Development in Iran 1900-1970*, p. 20 (hereafter cited as "Bharier").

2. Ibid., p. 19.

3. Ali Akbar Siassi, *La Perse au contact de l'Occident*, pp. 179-80 (hereafter cited as "Siassi").

4. Ibid., pp. 135-36, 138-39.

5. Charles S. Prigmore, *Social Work in Iran Since the White Revolution,* p. vii (hereafter cited as "Prigmore").

6. Ibid., p. 19.

7. Bharier, p. 5.

8. C.J. Edmonds, "Luristan: Pish-i-Kuh and Bala Gariveh," *Geographical Journal* 59 (1922): 342.

9. Sir Arnold Wilson, *S.W. Persia,* p. 197.

10. D.N. Wilber, *Contemporary Iran.*

11. Donald N. Wilber, *Riza Shah Pahlavi, The Resurrection and Reconstruction of Iran 1878-1944,* p. 17 (hereafter cited as "Wilber").

12. Amin Banani, *The Modernization of Iran 1921-1941,* p. 38 (hereafter cited as "Banani").

13. Ibid., p. 28.

14. For the text of article 2 of the Fundamental Law, which enunciates this principle, See *Encyclopaedia of Islam,* 2nd ed. s.v. *"Dustur"* [Constitution], p. 653.

15. Banani, p. 17.

16. Wilber, p. 17.

17. Gustav Thaiss, "The Bazaar as a Case Study of Religion and Social Change," in *Iran Faces the Seventies,* ed. Ehsan Yar-Shater, p. 195 (hereafter cited as "Thaiss").

18. Banani, p. 9.

19. Siassi, p. 183.

20. Ibid., p. 186.

21. Banani, p. 102.

22. Ibid., p. 103.

23. Ibid., p. 105.

24. Ibid., p. 71.

25. Ibid., p. 73.

26. Ibid., p. 64.

27. Ibid., p. 63.

28. Ibid., p. 64.

29. Ibid., pp. 64-66.

30. James A. Bill, *The Politics of Iran*, p. 54 (hereafter cited as "Bill").

31. Ibid., p. 54.

32. Ibid., p. 7.

33. Banani, p. 56

34. Ibid.

35. Bharier, p. 5.

36. Ibid., p. 34.

37. Banani, p. 126.

38. Ibid., p. 123.

39. See Peter Avery, *Modern Iran*, p. 285.

40. Wilber, p. 127

41. Ibid., p. 129.

42. *Encyclopaedia of Islam*, 2nd ed., s.v. *"Bast."*

43. Wilber, p. 166.

44. Ibid., p. 173.

45. Ibid., p. 174.

46. Bharier, pp. 195-97.

47. Ibid., p. 85.

48. Gholam Hossein Razi, "Religion and Politics in Iran: A Study in Social Dynamics," p. 346 (hereafter cited as "Razi"). The Thirteenth Majles was convened in November 1941, but most of its members were elected before the Allied invasion of Iran in August 1941. See E. Abrahamian, "The Failure of the Iranian Aristocracy 1941-53," p. 8.

49. Razi, p. 346.

50. See L.P. Elwell-Sutton, *Persian Oil*, pp. 195-96.

51. George Lenczowski, *Russia and the West in Iran 1918-1948: A Study in Big-Power Rivalry*, p. 227.

52. Joseph M. Upton, *The History of Modern Iran: An Interpretation*, p. 90.

53. Bharier, p. 180.

54. Sepehr Zabih, *The Communist Movement in Iran*, p. 163.

55. HIM Mohammed Reza Shah Pahlavi, *Mission for My Country*, p. 57.

56. Ann K.S. Lambton, "Land Reform and the Rural Cooperative Societies," in *Iran Faces the Seventies*, ed. Ehsan Yar-Shater, p. 14 (hereafter cited as "Lambton I").

57. Hafez F. Farmayan, "Politics during the Sixties: A Historical Analysis," in *Iran Faces the Seventies*, ed. Ehsan Yar-Shater, p. 90 (hereafter cited as "Farmayan").

58. Lambton I, p. 15.

59. Ibid., p. 16.

60. Ibid.

61. Mohammad Reza Pahlavi Aryamehr, Shahanshah of Iran, *The White Revolution of Iran,* p. 4.

62. Quoted in Ali Asghar Shamim, *Iran in the Reign of H.M. Mohammad Reza Shah Pahlavi,* trans. Dr. Aladin Pazargadi, n.p., n.d., p. 181.

63. A.K.S. Lambton, *The Persian Land Reform, 1962-1966;* D.R. Denman, *The King's Vista* (Berkhamsted, Hertfordshire, U.K.: Geographical Publications Ltd., 1973) (hereafter cited as "Denman").

64. Prigmore, p. 10.

65. Farmayan, p. 100.

66. Lambton I, p. 17.

67. K.S. McLachlan, "Land Reform in Iran," in *The Cambridge History of Iran,* vol. 1 (1968), pp. 686-87.

68. Lambton I, p. 20.

69. Ibid.

70. Ibid., pp. 21-22.

71. Ibid., p. 34.

72. Ibid.

73. Ibid., p. 23.

74. Ibid., p. 33.

75. Ibid., p. 38.

76. Ibid., p. 39.

77. A.K.S. Lambton, "Land Reform and Rural Co-operative Societies in Persia," *Royal Central Asian Journal* 56 (parts 2 and 3, 1969): 10 (hereafter cited as "Lambton II").

78. Ibid., p. 11.

79. Ibid., p. 26.

80. Ibid., p. 28.

81. Ibid., p. 13.

82. Ibid., p. 4.

83. Denman, p. 142.

84. Ibid., p. 141.

85. Ibid., p. 148.

86. Prigmore, pp. 39-40.

87. For an example of an all-too-typical attitude toward education, on the part of a *kadkhoda* (village headman) and his wife, see Najmeh Najafi, with Helen Hinckley, *Reveille for a Persian Village* (1959), p. 15.

88. Gad Soffer, "The Literacy Corps in Iran—an Evaluation" (Paper prepared for delivery at the Third Annual Meeting of the Middle East Studies Association of North America, Toronto, November 14-15, 1969), p. 7.

89. Ibid., p. 8.

90. Ibid., p. 9.

91. Ibid., pp. 10-11.

92. Ibid., footnote no. 13.

93. Ibid., p. 12.

94. Ibid., p. 1.

95. Bharier, p. 131.

96. Aspen Institute for Humanistic Studies, *Iran: Past, Present and Future,* ed. Jane W. Jacqz, p. 190, table 44 (hereafter cited as "Aspen").

97. Shahpour Rassekh, "Planning for Social Change," in *Iran Faces the Seventies,* ed. Ehsan Yar-Shater, p. 162 (hereafter cited as "Rassekh").
mont").

98. Frédy Bémont, *L'Iran depuis 1962,* p. 72 (hereafter cited as "Bémont").

99. Lambton I, p. 34.

100. *Iran Almanac 1975,* p. 387.

101. Bémont, p. 121.

102. Ibid., p. 131.

103. Farmayan, p. 104.

104. Ibid., pp. 105-6.

105. Ibid., p. 107.

106. Prigmore, p. 21.

107. Bémont, p. 130; also *The Design of Educational Programmes for the Social and Economic Promotion of Rural Women,* p. 12 (hereafter cited as "Design").

108. *The Employment of Women in the Higher Echelons of the Public and Private Sectors,* a report prepared by the Kayhan Research Associates for the Women's Organization of Iran, December 1975, p. 31. Most of the facts in this paragraph have been taken from this report (hereafter cited as "WOI Report").

109. Prigmore, p. 48.

110. Ibid., p. 56.

111. Ibid., p. 51.

112. Ibid., p. 75.

113. Ibid., pp. 75-76.

114. Ibid., pp. 54-55.

115. Article 1 of the Constitution of the Women's Organization of Iran.

116. *Design,* pp. 28-29.

117. Dr. Kokab Moarefi, vice-minister, parliamentary and administrative affairs, Ministry of Social Welfare, *The Iranian Symbol and Structure of Social Development and Welfare Services* (Tehran: July 1975), p. 7 (hereafter cited as "Moarefi I").

118. See Dr. Kokab Moarefi, vice-minister, parliamentary and administrative affairs, Ministry of Social Welfare, "The Concept and Practice of Social Welfare in Iran vis-à-vis Social Planning for Growing Cities" (Paper presented at the International Council on Social Welfare, Hong Kong Regional Conference, September 1-5, 1975), p. 3 (hereafter cited as "Moarefi II").

119. Moarefi I, p. 10.

120. Moarefi II, p. 7.

121. Ibid.

122. Ibid., p. 8.

123. Moarefi I, p. 11.

124. Bharier, p. 180.

125. Ibid., p. 183 (quoting Bank Melli reports).

126. Ibid., p. 186.

127. Ibid., table 8; and p. 188, table 9; *Iran Almanac 1975,* p. 421.

128. Bémont, p. 79.

129. Jahangir Amuzegar and M. Ali Fekrat, *Iran: Economic Development under Dualistic Conditions,* p. 122.

130. The facts contained in the preceding paragraph are based on a statement made on July 17, 1975 by Mr. Hushang Ansary, minister of economic affairs and finance, and on a personal interview with Mr. Behbin of the Plan Organization on January 3, 1976.

131. Personal interview with Prime Minister Hoveyda, January 3, 1976.

132. WOI Report, p. 4; most of the facts in this paragraph have been taken from this report.

133. Ibid.

134. Ibid., p. 18.

135. Audience with HIM Mohammad Reza Pahlavi Aryamehr, Shahanshah of Iran, December 30, 1975.

136. Bill, p. 47.

137. Ibid., p. 48; and p. 41, figure 6.

138. Ibid., pp. 63-67.

139. Ibid., p. 68.

140. Rassekh, p. 159.

141. Thaiss, p. 200.

142. Ibid., p. 199.

143. Rassekh, p. 162.

144. Ibid.

145. Thaiss, p. 201.

146. Rassekh, p. 159.

147. Plan and Budget Organization, *Iran's 5th Development Plan 1973-78, A Revised Summary,* May 1975, pp. 6-7.

148. Based on personal interviews with Dr. Seyyed Hossein Nasr, director, Imperial Academy of Philosophy (January 10, 1976); and Dr. Mehdi Mohaghegh, Faculty of Arts and Science, University of Tehran (January 4, 1976).

149. See Dr. Ehsan Naraghi's thought-provoking paper, "Iran's Culture and the Present-Day World," in Aspen, pp. 421-32.

150. Amir Abbas Hoveyda, prime minister of Iran, in his major address, "The Future of Iran," in Aspen, p. 447.

151. Asghar Fathi, "Marginality, Leadership and Directed Change," *Human Organization* 27 (Summer 1968): 145.

152. Aspen, p. 465.

153. Daniel Yankelovich, "Introduction" to Aspen, p. 6.

CHAPTER THREE: SELECTED BIBLIOGRAPHY

Abrahamian, E. "The Failure of the Iranian Aristrocracy 1941-53." Paper prepared for delivery at the Conference on the Structure of Power in Islamic Iran, University of California, Los Angeles, June 26-28, 1969.

Amuzegar, Jahangir, and Fekrat, Ali M. *Iran: Economic Development under Dualistic Conditions*. Chicago: University of Chicago Press, 1971.

Aspen Institute for Humanistic Studies. *Iran: Past, Present and Future*. Edited by Jane W. Jacqz. New York: 1976.

Avery, Peter. *Modern Iran*. London: Benn, 1965.

Banani, Amin. *The Modernization of Iran 1921-1941*. Stanford Calif.: Stanford University Press, 1961.

Bémont, Fredy. *L'Iran depuis 1962*. Paris: Frédy Bémont, 1971.

Bahrier, Julian. *Economic Development in Iran 1900-1970*. London: Oxford University Press, 1971.

Bill, James A. *The Politics of Iran*. Columbus, Ohio: Charles E. Merrill, 1972.

The Design of Educational Programmes for the Social and Economic Promotion of Rural Women. Tehran: Women's Organization of Iran and International Institute for Adult Literacy Methods, 1975.

Edmonds, C.J. "Luristan: Pish-i-kuh and Bala Gariveh." *Geographical Journal* 59 (1922).

Elwell-Sutton, Laurence P. *Persian Oil: A Study in Power Politics*. London: Lawrence and Wishart, 1955.

The Employment of Women in the Higher Echelons of the Public and Private Sectors. A report prepared by Kayhan Research Associates for the Women's Organization of Iran, December 1975.

Encyclopaedia of Islam. 2nd ed., s.v. "Dustur." Vol. 4, p. 653.

Farmayan, Hafez F. "Politics during the Sixties: A Historial Analysis." In *Iran Faces the Seventies*, edited by Ehsan Yar-Shater. New York: Praeger, 1971.

Lambton, Ann K.S. "Land Reform and Rural Co-operative Societies in Persia." *Royal Central Asian Journal* 56 (1969), parts 2 and 3.

————, "Land Reform and the Rural Cooperative Societies." In *Iran Faces the Seventies*, edited by Ehsan Yar-Shater. New York: Praeger, 1971.

————. *The Persian Land Reform, 1962-1966*. Oxford: Clarendon Press, 1969.

Lenczowski, George. *Russia and the West in Iran 1918-1948: A Study in Big-Power Rivalry*. New York: Greenwood Press, 1968.

McLachlan, K.S. "Land Reform in Iran." In *The Cambridge History of Iran*, edited by A.J. Arberry et al. Vol. 1. Cambridge: Cambridge University Press, 1968.

Moarefi, Kokab. "The Concept and Practice of Social Welfare in Iran vis-a-vis Social Planning for Growing Cities." Paper presented at the International Council on Social Welfare, Hong Kong Regional Conference, September 1-5, 1975.

————. *The Iranian Symbol and Structure of Social Development and Welfare Services*. Tehran: Ministry of Social Welfare, July 1975.

Najafi, Najmeh, and Hinckley, Helen. *Reveille for a Persian Village*. New York: Harper, 1958.

Prigmore, Charles S. *Social Work in Iran since the White Revolution*. University, Ala.: University of Alabama Press, 1976.

Pahlavi, HIM Mohammed Reza Shah. *Mission for My Country.* New York: McGraw-Hill, 1961.

———. *The White Revolution of Iran.* Tehran: Imperial Pahlavi Library, 1967.

Rassekh, Shahpour. "Planning for Social Change." In *Iran Faces the Seventies,* edited by Ehsan Yar-Shater. New York: Praeger, 1971.

Razi, Gholam Hossein. *Religion and Politics in Iran: A Study in Social Dynamics.* Ph.D. dissertation, University of California, 1957.

Shamim, Ali Asghar. *Iran in the Reign of H.M. Mohammed Reza Shah Pahlavi,* translated by Dr. Aladin Pazargadi. Iran: n.d.

Siassi, Ali Akbar. *La Perse au contact de l'Occident.* Paris: 1931.

Soffer, Gad. "The Literacy Corps in Iran—An Evaluation." Paper prepared for delivery at the Third Annual Meeting of the Middle East Studies Association of North America, Toronto, Canada, November 14-15, 1969.

Thaiss, Gustav. "The Bazaar as a Case Study of Religion and Social Change." In *Iran Faces the Seventies,* edited by Ehsan Yar-Shater. New York: Praeger, 1971.

Upton, Joseph M. *The History of Modern Iran: An Interpretation.* Harvard Middle Eastern monographs, no. 2. Cambridge, Mass.: Harvard University Press, 1965.

Wilber, Donald N. *Contemporary Iran.* New York: Praeger, 1963.

———. *Riza Shah Pahlavi, The Resurrection and Reconstruction of Iran 1878-1944.* Hicksville, N.Y.: Exposition Press, 1975.

Wilson, Sir Arnold. *S.W. Persia.* London: Oxford University Press, 1941.

Women's Organization of Iran. *Constitution.*

Yar-Shater, Ehsan, ed. *Iran Faces the Seventies.* New York: Praeger, 1971.

Zabih, Sepehr. *The Communist Movement in Iran.* Berkeley and Los Angeles: University of California Press, 1966.

CHARLES ISSAWI

CHAPTER FOUR: NOTES

1. For fuller details and sources see Charles Issawi, *The Economic History of Iran, 1800-1914;* and Julian Bharier, *Economic Development in Iran.*

2. For fuller details and sources see Issawi, *Economic History of Iran,* "Epilogue," pp. 373-79.

3. *Roads and Road Construction from Achaemenian Era until the Reign of Pahlavi* (n.d.), p. 13.

4. Thus, to take four fields in which Iran lagged behind Egypt and Turkey: by 1974-75, output of electricity had passed the 14,000 million kwh mark; cement production had doubled, standing at 6.7 million tons; sugar output had risen to 860,000 tons; and the number of students in schools had increased to 5.4 million (Bank Markazi Iran, *Gozaresh salaneh* [Annual Report] *1353* (hereafter cited as "Bank Markazi, *Annual Report*").

5. *Petroleum Economist* (London), March 1975.

6. International Labour Office (ILO), *Employment and Income Policy in Iran* (Geneva: 1973) (hereafter cited as "ILO, *Employment and Income*"); Manouchehr Ganji and Abbas Milani, "Iran's Development during the Last 50 Years" (Paper presented at Aspen-Persepolis Symposium, September 15-19, 1975); F. Aminzadeh, "Human Resources Development," Aspen-Persepolis Symposium, q.v.; 1975 estimates obtained from Statistical Center of Iran, Tehran.

7. The objective is "to reduce the fertility rate of women gradually from over seven live births at present to three live births in the course of the next 20 years" (Plan and Budget Organization, *Iran's 5th Development Plan 1973-78, A Revised Summary*), p. 67 (hereafter cited as *Iran's 5th Development Plan*).

8. See ILO, *Employment and Income*, p. 30, for various estimates.

9. *Iran's 5th Development Plan*, pp. 69-71.

10. A sample survey in December 1969-January 1970 showed that nearly 15 percent of the rural employed worked for less than 28 hours a week (ILO, *Employment and Income*, p. 26).

11. Aminzadeh, "Human Resources Development."

12. Bank Markazi, *Annual Report 1353*, p. 218.

13. For a detailed breakdown see *Iran's 5th Development Plan*, pp. 76-77.

14. See the long-term projections in Aminzadeh, "Human Resources Development."

15. This model is expounded in Jahangir Amuzegar and M.A. Fekrat, *Iran: Economic Development under Dualistic Conditions* (Chicago: 1971); see also M.A. Fekrat, "Economic Growth and Development in Iran" (Aspen-Persepolis Symposium, q.v.).

16. Unless otherwise stated, the figures in this section have been taken from Bank Markazi Iran, *National Income of Iran, 1338-50* (Mordad 1353) (hereafter cited as "Bank Markazi, *National Income*"); and Bank Markazi, *Annual Report 1351, 1352, and 1353*.

17. *Iran's 5th Development Plan*, pp. 25-28.

18. M.H. Pesaran, "Income Distribution and Its Major Determinants in Iran" (Aspen-Persepolis Symposium, q.v.).

19. Bank Markazi, *National Income*, pp. 71-73.

20. F. Vakil, "Iran's Basic Macro-Economic Problems," Aspen-Persepolis Symposium, q.v.

21. Pesaran, "Income Distribution."

22. Plan and Budget Organization, *Iran's 5th Development Plan*, p. 165.

23. Ministry of Agriculture, Bookers Agricultural and Technical Services, Ltd., "National Cropping Plan" (August 1975), vol. 1, p. 92.

24. *Iran's 5th Development Plan*, p. 176.

25. Bank Markazi, *Annual Report 1353*.

26. *Salnameh amari 1352 keshvar*, pp. 308-9.

27. Ministry of Agriculture and National Resources, *Agribusiness Opportunities in Iran* (1974), p. 1.

28. *Kayhan* (International Edition), December 30, 1975.

29. Ministry of Agriculture and Natural Resources, "Historical Background and Future Development of the Fertilizer Distribution Company" (July 1975).

30. Ibid.

31. Vezarat-e keshavarzi va manabe'e tabi'i, *Gozaresh fa'aliyate tarhai'i afzayesh tavlidi mahsulate keshavarzi* (Azar. 1353 [1974/75]).

32. Ministry of Agriculture, *Agribusiness Opportunities.*

33. Ministry of Agriculture, "National Cropping Plan," vol. 1, p. 9.

34. "Cotton Exports to East Europe Suffer Decline," *Kayhan* (International Edition), December 30, 1975.

35. Ministry of Agriculture, "National Cropping Plan," vol. 1, p. 60.

36. F. Najmabadi, "Strategies of Industrial Development in Iran" (Aspen-Persepolis Symposium, q.v.).

37. *Iran's 5th Development Plan,* p. 226.

38. Najmabadi, "Strategies of Industrial Development." The production index compiled by the Central Bank rose by 18.4 percent in 1973-74 and 18.8 percent in 1974-75 (Bank Markazi Iran, "Survey of the Selected Manufacturing Industries in 1353," August 1975). reliable series for the period before the Third Plan are scarce, but between 1959-60 and 1962-63 mining and manufacturing production rose by a little over one-third, or at a compound rate of about 18 percent per annum (see table in Charles Issawi, "Iran's Economic Upsurge," *Middle East Journal,* Autumn 1967).

39. Iran's overall supply of energy has grown very rapidly—by 10 percent per annum in the Third Plan, 11.4 percent in the Fourth, and a planned 17.9 percent in the Fifth. Whereas in the two last plans hydroelectric power was the most rapidly growing component, natural gas has now taken the lead. Its share in total primary energy rose from 15.6 percent in 1962-63 to 18 percent in 1972-73, and a planned 23.2 percent in 1977-78. That of oil rose from 60.5 percent in 1962-63 to 71.3 percent in 1972-73, but is due to decline to 70.3 percent in 1977-78; and that of hydroelectricity shows a similar movement, from 0.5 percent to 6.5 percent and 5.1 percent. Coal has played an insignificant, and declining, role (1.1 percent in 1972-73), while noncommercial sources of energy (wood, dung, etc.) have fallen off sharply, from 21.2 percent to 3.4 percent and a planned 0.8 percent (*Iran's 5th Development Plan,* pp. 88-98).

40. ILO, *Employment and Income,* p. 28; Najmabadi, "Strategies of Industrial Development."

41. Bank Markazi, *Annual Report.*

42. *Iran's 5th Development Plan,* pp. 255, 264, 275, 281, and 296.

43. Plan and Budget Organization, *Sectoral Capital Stock for the Iranian Economy* (November 1975).

44. "Foreign Investment in Iran," (Remarks made by A. Qasem Kheradjou, managing director of Industrial and Mining Development Bank of Iran, at UK-Iran Investment Conference, November 27, 1973, in Shiraz).

45. For a descriptive list of the main enterprises see Industrial and Mining Development Bank of Iran (IMDBI), *Fifteenth Annual Report, 1353.*

46. Regionalism has been pursued for social and environmental as well as economic reasons, "growth poles" have been established in Isfahan, Ahwaz, Tabriz, Arak, and other towns, and attempts have been made to set up small and medium-sized plants in the countryside. But industry is still very heavily concentrated in Tehran province which, according to a recent study by the Central Bank, had 54 percent of total employment and contributed 64 percent of value added. The only provinces with a significant industry were Khuzistan (4 percent and 13 percent), Isfahan (11 percent and 4 percent), and East Azarbayjan (7 percent and 2 percent).

47. Najmabadi, "Strategies of Industrial Development."

48. Ibid. Foreign investment has played a significant, but definitely subordinate, part in the private sector: by 1973, the IMDBI had provided financial assistance to seventy-eight joint ventures with a total investment of $979 million, of which $136 million was foreign capital. In the Fourth Plan period, gross foreign investment in Iran was 10 billion rials (about $130 million) and net inflow 6.3 billion rials ($85 million); the main recipients were petrochemicals, tires, pharmaceuticals, chemicals, and the electric and electronic industries. Half the capital was supplied by American investors—14 percent by German and 4 percent by British (Bank Markazi, *Annual Report 1351*, p. 76).

49. IMDBI, *Fifteenth Annual Report, 1353.*

50. See graph in ibid., p. 43.

51. Bharier, *Economic Development in Iran*, pp. 92-98.

52. Imperial Government of Iran, Ministry of Roads and Transportation, *1973-74 Railway Edition, Facts and Figures.*

53. *Eqdamat va barnameha-ye vezarat-e rah va turabari dar dowran barname-ye panjom;* and, more generally, *Fa'allyetha-ye vezarat-e rah dar zamin-e rah, rah ahan, hava pem'i, hava shenasi as bahman mah 1341 ta payn-e sal-e 1350.* (Activities of the Ministry of Roads in the field of roads, railroads, air traffic and meterorology, from the month of Bahman 1341 to the solar year 1350).

54. *The Economist* (London), December 20, 1975.

55. A detailed example may be instructive, viz., that of the public organization, *Shirket Sehami Taraberi Zamini,* charged with transporting goods required by the government (food, cement, steel, etc.) by road from the ports to the center of the country. In 1975 it ordered 4,000 trucks and 12,000 trailers, of which about half had arrived by the end of the year. Training courses, given by American and British instructors, were set up and some 700 drivers had graduated from them after two to four months. The drivers were to be organized in cooperatives, and it was hoped that, eventually, the ownership of the vehicles would be transferred to the drivers.

56. *Iran's 5th Development Plan,* chapter 4.

57. This section is largely based on an unpublished study by Bank Markazi, *Tarikh-e mo'aser-e pul va bankdari dar Iran,* and on the bank's *Annual Reports.*

58. It should, however, be noted that Iran is still very unevenly provided with banking facilities: in Tehran in 1975 there were 512 bank branches per 1 million inhabitants, but in the rest of the country only 181. This reflects the concentration of capital, savings, and business activity in the capital city.

59. Secretariat of the Council of the Stock Exchange, *The Stock Exchange, Esfand 1352* (Tehran).

60. A. Gasem Kheradjou, "Development of the Capital Market and Stock Exchange in Iran" (Iran-UK Financial Conference, 11-12 October 1975).

61. Ibid.

62. Ibid.

63. Between 1970 and 1974, Iran's import price index rose by 42 percent, a figure in line with that of other Middle Eastern and OPEC countries (see Economic Research Institute for the Middle East [Tokyo], "Imported Inflation in the Middle East and OPEC Nations," *Middle East Economic Survey* [Beirut], February 21, 1975).

64. *Salnameh amari 1352 keshvar,* p. 649.

65. One reason for this is that the government has sought to encourage investment by various tax exemptions and rebates.

66. For an appraisal made in 1968 see Charles Issawi, "The Economy: an Assessment of Performance," in *Iran Faces the Seventies,* ed. Ehsan Yar-Shater.

67. International Bank for Reconstruction and Development (IBRD), *World Atlas,* 1974.

68. For a comparison of the availability of foreign exchange in Iran, Egypt, and Turkey in 1960-65, see Issawi, "The Economy· an Assessment."

69. On this subject, see ILO, *Employment and Income,* passim.

70. For comparable figures, see United Nations, *Statistical Yearbook,* and *Monthly Bulletin of Statistics.*

71. Firouz Tofigh, "Development of Iran—a Statistical Note," (Aspen-Persepolis Symposium, q.v.).

72. See Simon Kuznets, *Economic Growth and Structure.*

73. Bank Markazi, *Annual Report 1351,* p. 45.

74. Firouz Vakil, *Determining Iran's Financial Surplus.*

CHAPTER FOUR: SELECTED BIBLIOGRAPHY

Aminzadeh, F. "Human Resources Development." Paper presented at Aspen-Persepolis Symposium, September 15-19, 1975, in Persepolis.

Amuzegar, Jahangir, and Fekrat, M.A. *Iran: Economic Development under Dualistic Conditions.* Chicago: University of Chicago Press, 1971.

Bank Markazi Iran. *Annual Report and Balance Sheet 1351.*

———. *Gozaresh Salaneh 1353.* Tehran: 1974/75.

———. *National Income of Iran, 1338-50* (Mordad 1353).

Bharier, Julian. *Economic Development in Iran, 1900-1970.* London: Oxford University Press, 1971.

Fekrat, M.A. "Economic Growth and Development in Iran." Paper presented at Aspen-Persepolis Symposium, September 15-19, 1975, in Persepolis.

Ganji, Manouchehr, and Milani, Abbas. "Iran's Development during the last 50 Years." Paper presented at Aspen-Persepolis Symposium, September 15-19, 1975, in Persepolis.

"Imported Inflation in the Middle East and OPEC Nations." *Middle East Economic Survey.* Beirut, February 21, 1975.

Industrial and Mining Development Bank of Iran. *Fifteenth Annual Report,* Tehran: 1353 (1974/75).

International Labour Organisation. *Employment and Income Policy in Iran.* Geneva: 1973.

Issawi, Charles. "Iran's Economic Upsurge." *Middle East Journal 21* (Autumn 1967), no. 4.

———. ed. *The Economic History of Iran, 1800-1914.* Chicago: University of Chicago Press, 1971.

Kheradjou, A. Gasem. "Development of the Capital Market and Stock Exchange in Iran." Iran-UK Financial Conference, October 11-12, 1975.

Kuznets, Simon. *Economic Growth and Structure*. New Haven: Yale University Press, 1966.

Ministry of Agriculture and National Resources. *Agribusiness in Iran*. Tehran: 1974.

————. "Historical Background and Future Development of the Fertilizer Distribution Company," Tehran: July 1975.

————. "National Cropping Plan." Vol. 1. Tehran: Bookers Agricultural and Technical Services, Ltd., August 1975.

Ministry of Roads and Transportation. *1973-74 Railway Edition: Facts and Figures.*Tehran: Imperial Government of Iran, n.d.

Najmabadi, F. "Strategies of Industrial Development in Iran." Paper presented at Aspen-Persepolis Symposium, September 15-19, 1975, in Persepolis.

Pesaran, M.H. "Income Distribution and Its Major Determinants in Iran." Paper presented at Aspen-Persepolis Symposium, September 15-19, 1975, in Persepolis.

Plan and Budget Organization. *Iran's 5th Development Plan 1973-78, A Revised Summary*. Tehran: The Organization, May 1975.

————. *Sectoral Capital Stock for the Iranian Economy*. Tehran: The Organization, November 1975.

Roads and Road Construction from Achaemenian Era until the Reign of Pahlavi.

Secretariat of the Council of the Stock Exchange. *The Stock Exchange, Esfand 1352.* Tehran: 1973/74.

Tofigh, Firouz. "Development of Iran—a Statistical Note." Paper presented at Aspen-Persepolis Symposium, September 15-19, 1975, in Persepolis.

Vakil, Firouz. *Determining Iran's Financial Surplus.* Tehran, June 1975.

————. "Iran's Basic Macro-Economic Problems." Paper presented at Aspen-Persepolis Symposium, September 15-19, 1975, in Persepolis.

Yar-Shater, Ehsan, ed. *Iran Faces the Seventies*. New York: Praeger, 1971.

HARALD MEHNER

CHAPTER FIVE: NOTES

1. Bank Melli Iran was established by Reza Shah in 1927 and designated as the central bank with the right of issuing currency, a right previously held by the British-owned Imperial Bank of Persia.

2. Bank Melli, [History of the Iranian Seven Year Plan: Organization—Development and Construction], Bureau of Statistics and Economic and Financial Studies publication no. 98 (Tehran: Bahman-Esfand, 1327), published in Persian, contains documents, letters, and reports about the development and history of planning in Iran, including the mandates for the two previously mentioned consulting companies from the United States.

3. Based on the author's own observations when in summer 1956, he travelled more than 2,000 miles on a motorcycle through Iran without ever leaving dirt roads. The first asphalt road, built during World War II between Qasr Shirin at the Iran-Iraq border and Hamadan, Qazvin, and Bandar Pahlavi, was totally ruined.

4. Together with a German journalist in August 1962, the author had an interview with Mosaddegh for six hours in the village of Ahmedabad, approximately 50 km. west of Tehran, where he was confined. It was the first and only interview by anyone with Mosaddegh after he had been sentenced to life imprisonment in 1957. In his statements about the necessity for and conditions of development in Iran and the country's international requirements and relations, Mosaddegh demonstrated extreme ignorance of economic facts, interdependences, and requirements. This may help to explain the chaotic situation under his premiership of Iran, and the consequences of his development and economic policy.

5. After the end of each of the four plans, the Plan Organization has published final reports about the results, achievements, and problems of the plan in question. The organization has also published special reports, for example in 1968 and 1969, with such titles as *Dam Construction in Iran, Water and Irrigation in Iran, The Sugar Industry in Iran*, and *The Textile Industry in Iran*, as well as a summary study, *Planning in Iran*, in October 1970. Copies of these reports as well as others, including studies and expert reports, are kept in the archives of the Plan and Budget Organization in Tehran.

6. See note 5, above.

7. This situation is characteristic of all large developing countries that have the predominant part of their populations still living in the rural areas.

8. In the third year of the Fifth Plan, approximately $200 million was approved in the annual budget for school food supply, and seven commercial companies were charged with its administration in different provinces of Iran.

9. The original title of the head of the Plan Organization was that of Managing Director. By the time Majidi was appointed to this post, he received the additional title of Minister of State.

10. Information by Governor Mohammad 'Ali Sami'i of Khuzistan on February 21, 1976, in Ahwaz, about regionalization and decentralization projects in that province.

11. Personal interviews with several members of the National Assembly and senators, as well as with local authorities in many parts of Iran since 1960.

12. The way in which the World Bank first became involved is described at the beginning of this section ("Decision Making in the Planning Process").

13. Personal information by Undersecretary Toufigh of the Plan and Budget Organization, general director of the Statistical Center of Iran, on February 19, 1976, in Tehran.

14. See note 10, above.

15. Copies of the two letters dated December 17, 1958, and January 8, 1959, were given to the author by Mr. Ebtehaj on February 26, 1976, in Tehran.

16. Statement of Mr. Mehran, governor of the Central Bank of Iran, in an interview on February 10, 1976, in Tehran.

17. From 1964 to 1976 the auhor has visited the three above-mentioned authorities several times, basing his evaluations on personal observations and interviews.

18. Statement by Mohammad Reza Shah Pahlavi at the session of the Plan Organization on December 29, 1970. This is one of the numerous blunt and increasing-

ly critical statements given by the Shah about the economic and social situation and development of his country.

19. The International Labour Organization has carried out worldwide studies of the labor situation in many developing countries, especially in the rural areas, that offer opportunities for comparative analysis of the countries in question.

CHAPTER FIVE: SELECTED BIBLIOGRAPHY

Amuzegar, Jahangir, and Fekrat, M. Ali. *Iran: Economic Development under Dualistic Conditions*. Chicago: University of Chicago Press, 1971.

Baldwin, George B. *Planning and Development in Iran*. Baltimore, Md.: Johns Hopkins Press, 1967.

Bank Markazi Iran. *Annual Report and Balance Sheet*. Tehran: 1965/66-1973/74.

Bharier, Julian. *Economic Development in Iran 1900-1970*. London: Oxford University Press, 1971.

Farahmand, Sohrab. *Der Wirtschaftsaufbau des Iran*. Publications of the List Gesellschaft, vol. 41. Tübingen: Mohr (Siebeck), 1965.

Gehrke, Ulrich and Mehner, Harald. *Iran: Natur, Bevölkerung, Kultur, Staat und Wirtschaft*. Tübingen and Basel: Horst Erdmann, 1975.

Gittinger, J. Price. *Planning for Agricultural Development: The Iranian Experience*. Washington, D.C.: National Planning Association, 1965.

International Labour Organisation. *Employment and Income Policies for Iran*. Geneva: ILO, 1973.

Jacobs, N. *The Sociology of Development: Iran as an Asian Case Study*. New York: Praeger, 1966.

Kayhan Research Associates. *Iran's 5th Plan: $70 Billion for Development until 1978*. Tehran: Kayhan Press, 1975.

Kiani, Manutschehr. *Ansätze und Möglichkeiten der Geld- und Fiskalpolitik als Finanzierungselemente einer gesamt-wirtschaftlichen Entwicklungspolitik, dargestellt am Beispiel Persiens*. Papers of the Institut für das Spar-, Giro-, und Kreditwesen at Bonn University, vol. 58. Berlin: Duncker und Humblot, 1971.

Ministry of Economy, General Department for Economic Studies. *A Glance at the Fifth Development Plan of Iran*. Tehran: 1974.

Müller, Wilhelm. *Die wirtschaftlichen Entwicklungsprobleme Irans*. Dissertation, Hochschule für Welthandel in Wien, no. 8. Vienna: Verlag Notring, 1971.

Naini, Ahmad. *Entwicklungsplanung in Iran*. Hamburg: Presseverlag Reim, 1975.

Nazari, Hassan. *Der Iran auf dem Wege der Modernisierung: 2500 Jahre Persiens*. Erlangen: VLE-Verlags-GmbH., 1971.

Plan and Budget Organization. *Fourth National Development Plan, 1968-1972*. Tehran: Imperial Government of Iran, 1968.

———. *Review of the Second Seven Year Plan Program of Iran*. Tehran: March 1960.

————. *Iran's 5th Development Plan 1973-1978, Revised: A Summary.* Tehran: May, 1975.

————. *The Budget 1354 and Amendment 1353: A Summary.* Tehran: 1975.

————. *Third Development Plan 1341-1346: Final Report.* Tehran: 1970

Plan Organization, Statistical Center of Iran. *Statistical Yearbook 1972.* Tehran: June 1975.

Samadi, Hadi. *Die Bedeutung der Industrialisierung für die wirtschaftliche Entwicklung des Iran.* Dissertation, Cologne: Universität, Wirtschafts- und Sozialwissenschaftliche Fakultät, 1971.

ROBERT B. STOBAUGH

Chapter Six: Notes

1. This desire for a nation to control its own oil resources has been mentioned by a number of others. For examples, see George Lenczowski, *Middle East Oil in a Revolutionary Age*; idem, "The Oil Producing Countries," in *The Oil Crisis,* ed. Raymond Vernon, p. 59; and William Fulbright's recognition of the OPEC nations' desire for "emancipation," quoted in Zuhayr Mikdashi, "The OPEC Process," in Vernon, *The Oil Crisis,* p. 214. Fariborz Ghadar discusses this trend toward independence by OPEC nations in a somewhat different formulation than mine in his "A Study of the Evolution of Strategy in Petroleum Exporting Nations" (D.B.A. thesis, Harvard Business School, 1976).

2. This early history, from 1907 through 1925, is drawn principally from: George Lenczowski, *The Middle East in World Affairs,* pp. 33-36 (hereafter cited as "Lenczowski 1962"); idem, *Russia and the West in Iran, 1918-1948,* pp. 77-79 (hereafter cited as "Lenczowski 1949"); Benjamin Shwadran, *The Middle East, Oil and the Great Powers,* chapter 2 (hereafter cited as "Shwadran"); Fereidun Fesharaki, *Development of the Iranian Oil Industry,* chapter 1 (hereafter cited as "Fesharaki"); Stephen Hemsley Longrigg, *Oil in the Middle East,* chapters 2, 3, 4 (hereafter cited as "Longrigg"); Nasrollah Saifpour Fatemi, *Oil Diplomacy,* chapters 1-12 (hereafter cited as "Fatemi"); and *New York Times,* 1925.

3. Information regarding this controversy, the subsequent cancelling of the D'Arcy agreement, and the settlement came from: Lenczowski 1962, pp. 186-88; Lenczowski 1949, pp. 79-81; Shwadran, pp. 37-47; Fesharaki, pp. 3-20; G.W. Stocking, *Middle East Oil,* p. 26 (who quotes the Lumely & Lumely decision taken from the *League of Nations Journal*); and *New York Times,* 1932-1933.

4. Fatemi, p. 159.

5. For a text of the agreement, see C. Hurewitz, *Diplomacy in Near and Middle East: A Documentary Record 1914-1956,* pp. 188-96. For summaries, see: Shwadran, pp. 44-46; and Fesharaki, pp. 13-14.

6. The World War II period through 1946 is covered in: Lenczowski 1962, pp. 189-97; Lenczowski 1949, pp. 167-87; Shwadran, pp. 47-62; Fesharaki, pp. 41-42; Longrigg, pp. 122-29, p. 145; Fatemi, chapters 13, 14, 16, 18; and *New York Times,* 1939-1946.

7. Information in this paragraph and subsequent paragraphs related to events leading to this overthrow was drawn from: Lenczowski 1962, pp. 205-18; Longrigg, pp. 124-31; Fatemi, pp. 328-38; Fesharaki, pp. 42-44; Shwadran, pp. 89-117; and *New York Times*, May 1939-February 1950.

8. Anthony Sampson, *The Seven Sisters*, p. 177 (hereafter cited as "Sampson"), audience with the Shah by Sampson.

9. Speech in the Chamber of Deputies, 1848, quoted in Ernest John Knapton, *France: An Interpretive History*, p. 389.

10. Longrigg, p. 157.

11. This account of the nationalization conflict came primarily from periodicals, especially the *New York Times*, February 1950-December 1953, and the *Oil and Gas Journal*, March 1951-August 1953, and periodicals are the source of all quotations here unless otherwise noted. A number of books, however, have accounts; for example, see those listed in notes 2 and 3 above.

12. Sampson, p. 120. This memorandum was to Foreign Secretary Herbert Morrison.

13. Fatemi, p. 379.

14. *New York Times*, May 25, 1951, p. 13.

15. Iran had long had a goal of getting Americans economically interested in Iran in order to provide a counterweight to the Soviet and British influence there. Reza Shah, while prime minister in 1923, was "desirous of introducing healthy competition and shaking off the economic domination of Great Britain and Russia," and granted an oil concession to the U.S.-based Sinclair Exploration Company. For a variety of reasons, for which the Iranians blamed principally the British, the deal was never consummated. See Fatemi, chapter 8. And the present Shah as early as 1945 would have liked to have gotten some oil concessions into American hands (see *New York Times*, November 25, 1945, sec. 4, p. 6). For the sources of the following account of U.S. involvement, see Lenczowski 1962, pp. 200-05, 215-24; Shoshana Klebanoff, *Middle East Oil and U.S. Foreign Policy*, p. 34; Shwadran, pp. 118-20; *New York Times*, February 1950-November 1954; and U.S. Senate, Committee on Foreign Relations, "Multinational Oil Corporations and U.S. Foreign Policy," *Report Together with the Individual Views to the Committee on Foreign Relations* by the Subcommittee on Multinational Corporations, pp. 50-56 (hereafter cited as *"MNC Report"*).

16. *New York Times*, April 16, 1951, p. 1.

17. Venezuela was a special worry, for a poll of Venezuelan oil-field workers showed that 80 percent thought Venezuela should nationalize her oil industry—even though 80 percent thought Venezuela was getting a fair share of the profits and 80 percent thought enough Venezuelans were being employed by the foreign oil companies. See *New York Times*, June 28, 1951, p. 1.

18. This summary of the overthrow in Iran is from *MNC Report*, pp. 57-59; Sampson, pp. 126-28; and Shwadran, p. 115.

19. The subsequent paragraphs referring to the settlement were drawn from: Shwadran, pp. 142-49; Sampson, p. 131; Longrigg, pp. 276-82; *New York Times*, April-November 1954; *Oil and Gas Journal*, March 29, 1954; and *MNC Report*, pp. 56-57.

20. Both President Truman and President Eisenhower took actions to allow the U.S. majors to participate in an Iranian solution without being charged under U.S. antitrust laws. See *MNC Report*, p. 67.

21. Sampson, p. 130.

22. Shwadran, pp. 146-48; and Fesharaki, pp. 51-55.

23. For summary of this act, see Fesharaki, pp. 66-67. For the full text, see *Iran Oil Journal,* issues of September, October, and November 1970.

24. Periodicals used for sources describing NIOC's ventures with foreign oil companies were *Oil and Gas Journal, Iran Oil Journal, Petroleum Economist* (formerly *Petroleum Press Service*), *New York Times,* and *Kayhan* (International Edition). Summaries appear in Lenczowski, *Oil and State in the Middle East,* pp. 10-13; Fesharaki, chapter 4; and Shwadran, chapter 8. A history of NIOC appears in Ghadar, "A Study of the Evolution of Strategy in Petroleum Exporting Nations," appendix 1-A.

25. *New York Times,* April 7, 1957, section 3, p.1.

26. *New York Times,* July 27, 1958, p. 19.

27. Some such comparisons are summarized in Fesharaki, pp. 84-93.

28. The material in this section was drawn from various issues of *Iran Oil Journal, Oil and Gas Journal, Petroleum Economist* (formerly *Petroleum Press Service*), NIOC *Annual Reports,* and summaries in Ghadar, "A Study of the Evolution of Strategy," appendix 1-A; Fesharaki, pp. 174-90, 202-15; and Shwadran, chapter 7.

29. *New York Times,* March 17, 1973, p. 1.

30. *Iran Oil Journal,* August 1971, p. 3.

31. For a full text of the agreement, see *Petroleum Intelligence Weekly,* August 23 and September 3, 1973.

32. Shawdran, p. 151; Fesharaki, pp. 145-47; and *Iran Oil Journal,* various issues.

33. Bijan Mossavar-Rahmani, "Drive for Iran's Own Tanker Fleet Speeds Up," *Kayhan* (International Edition), January 26, 1976; idem, "NIOC, Britain Set Up Joint Fleet of Ten Oil Tankers," *Kayhan* (International Edition), March 9, 1976.

34. Calculated from information in Paul Marshall et al., *Operations Management,* p. 369.

35. *Iran's Fifth Development Plan, 1973-1978,* revised May 1975.

36. Unless otherwise noted, the information in this section was drawn from: *MNC Report,* especially section 5; U.S. Senate, Committee on Foreign Relations, "Multinational Petroleum Companies and Foreign Policy," *Hearings Before the Subcommittee on Multinational Corporations of the Committee on Foreign Relations,* 93rd Congress, part 7, appendix 6 (hereafter cited as *"MNC Hearings"*); and (as a supplementary source), various periodicals, principally the *New York Times* (June 1955-May 1969) and *Iran Oil Journal,* August 1968-March 1969.

37. From a 1956 BBC interview, quoted in *Iran Oil Journal,* August 1968, p. 5.

38. *MNC Report,* p. 102.

39. Ibid., p. 110.

40. *MNC Hearings,* part 8, pp. 571-76. The quotations in this paragraph come from a State Department memorandum rather than being direct quotations of the company executives.

41. *MNC Report,* p. 106.

42. Ibid., p. 112.

43. Ibid., p. 113.

44. Ibid., p. 115.

45. Ibid., p. 117.

46. Ibid., p. 115.

47. *MNC Hearings,* part 5, p. 263.

48. *New York Times,* May 16, 1969, p. 67.

49. Ibid,, p. 73.

50. There were relatively few open-market sales of crude oil during the early part of this period, but prices of refined products corrected for transportation costs and refining margins can be used to impute a price for crude. See M.A. Adelman *The World Petroleum Market,* chapters 5 and 6 (hereafter cited as "Adelman").

51. This and the preceding paragraphs from Adelman, and from Sampson, chapter 8.

52. For reviews of this early history of OPEC, see Zuhayr Mikdashi, *The Community of Oil Exporting Countries—A Study in Governmental Cooperation;* Fuad Rouhani, *A History of OPEC;* and Shwadran, pp. 505-13.

53. *Oil and Gas Journal,* July 30, 1965, p. 132.

54. Interview with U.S. oil executive.

55. First National City Bank, *Energy Memo,* October 1972; also see *MNC Report,* p. 89, which indicated that Saudi Arabia's revenues climbed from about 80 cents a barrel in 1960 to $1.00 in 1970, while Aramco's profits declined from 70 cents down to 30 cents a barrel. Also, see Adelman, p. 183, for data on lower prices. Using the U.S. Consumer Price Index as a correction for inflation, the 1970 per-barrel revenues of the oil-exporting nations were 67 cents in terms of 1961 prices; using the U.S. Export Price Index, the 1970 per-barrel revenues were 72 cents.

56. This section was drawn principally from *MNC Report,* section 6, and related parts; plus *New York Times,* 1970-1972.

57. I estimated the 300 firms from Neil H. Jacoby's statement that 350 entered between 1953 and 1972; see his *Multinational Oil,* p. 126. For market concentration in the world oil industry, see ibid., p. 211, and Adelman, chapter 3. The estimates of production shares come from Adelman, p. 81.

58. *MNC Report,* p. 127.

59. Ibid., pp. 127-28.

60. *MNC Hearings,* part 5, pp. 117, 155.

61. Ibid., p. 170.

62. Ibid., p. 155.

63. *MNC Report,* p. 130.

64. Ibid., p. 131.

65. Ibid.

66. Ibid., p. 132.

67. Ibid.

68. Ibid., p. 134.

69. Ibid., p. 133.

70. Edith Penrose, "The Development of Crisis," in Vernon, *The Oil Crisis,* p. 55.

71. *MNC Report,* p. 134.

72. For a description of this period, see Edith Penrose, "The Development of Crisis," in Vernon, *The Oil Crisis,* pp. 46-50.

73. *MNC Report,* p. 138.

74. For a description of the activities of the OPEC nations during this period, see Lenczowski, "The Oil Producing Countries," in Vernon, *The Oil Crisis,* p. 59; and Lenczowski, *Middle East Oil in a Revolutionary Age.*

75. For a detailed description of such actions, see Stobaugh, "The Oil Companies in Crisis," in Vernon, *The Oil Crisis,* pp. 179-202.

76. *Petroleum Intelligence Weekly,* December 3, 1973.

77. Information in this section about prices bid for oil is from *Petroleum Intelligence Weekly,* various issues between November 1973 and April 1974.

78. Sampson, p. 257 (interview with Dr. Jamshid Amuzegar).

79. *New York Times,* December 22, 1973. Quoted from an interview in *Middle East Economic Survey.*

80. Sampson, p. 258.

81. Interview by author with oil executive.

82. *New York Times,* December 24, 1973, p. 1.

83. Quotations in this paragraph are from articles appearing in the *New York Times,* December 1973.

84. For a discussion of why such adjustments were likely to continue to be needed, see 'Those Awkward Differentials," *The Petroleum Economist,* December 1975, pp. 444-45.

85. For an elaboration of this argument, see Stobaugh, "The Neotechnology Account of International Trade: the Case of Petrochemicals," in Louis T. Wells, Jr., ed., *The Product Life Cycle and International Trade;* and Stobaugh, "The Economics of Energy versus Non-Energy Uses of Petroleum: The Case of Petrochemicals," in Zuhair Mikdashi, ed., *Administration of the Oil Resources of Arab Countries.*

86. The Shah expressed this idea to me at an audience on April 4, 1976.

87. For examples, see my "The Oil Companies in Crisis," in Vernon, *The Oil Crisis,* pp. 179-202.

88. It was reported that NIOC would become a vertically integrated company, controlling its oil "from wellhead to pump," with the implication—at least in the press—that becoming an international oil company was an end in itself; see *Wall Street Journal,* November 27, 1973, p. 1. In fact, a judicious approach to downstream investments by NIOC would be consistent with the foreign investment decisions of U.S.-based multinational enterprises, which usually involved low-risk steps rather than bold leaps forward; see Robert B. Stobaugh et al., *Nine Investments Abroad and Their Impact at Home* (Boston: Harvard Business School Division of Research, 1976), chapter 8.

89. The Shah mentioned this to me at an audience on April 4, 1976.

CHAPTER SIX: SELECTED BIBLIOGRAPHY

Adelman, M.A. *The World Petroleum Market.* Baltimore, Md.: The Johns Hopkins University Press, 1972.

Fatemi, Nasrollah Saifpour. *Oil Diplomacy.* New York: Whittier Books, 1954.

Fesharaki, Fereidun. *Development of the Iranian Oil Industry.* New York: Praeger, 1976.

Ghadar, Fariborz. "A Study of the Evolution of Strategy in Petroleum Exporting Nations." D.B.A. thesis, Harvard Business School, 1976.

Hurewitz, C. *Diplomacy in the Near and Middle East: A Documentary Record.* Vol. 2, 1914-1956. Princeton, N.J.: Van Nostrand, 1956.

Iran's Fifth Development Plan, 1973-78.

Jacoby, Neil H. *Multinational Oil.* New York: Macmillan, 1974.

Klebanoff, Shoshana. *Middle East Oil and U.S. Foreign Policy.* New York: Praeger, 1974.

Knapton, Ernest John. *France—An Interpretive History.* New York: Charles Scribner's Sons, 1971.

Lenczowski, George. *Middle East Oil in a Revolutionary Age.* Washington, D.C.: American Enterprise Institute, 1975.

———. *Oil and State in the Middle East.* Ithaca, N.Y.: Cornell University Press, 1960.

———. *Russia and the West in Iran, 1914-1948.* Ithaca, N.Y.: Cornell University Press, 1949.

———. "The Oil Producing Countries." In *The Oil Crisis,* edited by Raymond Vernon. New York: W.W. Norton, 1976.

———. *The Middle East in World Affairs.* Ithaca, New York: Cornell University Press, 1962.

Longrigg, Stephen Hemsley. *Oil in the Middle East.* London: Oxford University Press, 1968.

Marshall, Paul, et al. *Operations Management.* Homewood, Ill.: Richard D. Irwin, 1975.

Mikdashi, Zuhayr. *The Community of Oil Exporting Countries—A Study in Governmental Cooperation.* London: Allen and Unwin, 1972.

———. "The OPEC Process." In *The Oil Crisis,* edited by Raymond Vernon. New York: W.W. Norton, 1976.

Penrose, Edith. "The Development of Crisis." In *The Oil Crisis,* edited by Raymond Vernon. New York: W.W. Norton, 1976.

Rouhani, Fuad. *A History of OPEC.* New York: Praeger, 1971.

Sampson, Anthony. *The Seven Sisters.* New York: Viking Press, 1957.

Shwadran, Benjamin. *The Middle East, Oil and the Great Powers.* New York: John Wiley and Sons, 1973.

Stobaugh, Robert. "The Economics of Energy versus Non-Energy Uses of Petroleum: The Case of Petrochemicals." In *Administration of the Oil Resources of Arab Countries,* edited by Zuhair Mikdashi. Kuwait: Arab Planning Institute, 1975.

———. "The Neotechnology Account of International Trade: The Case of Petrochemicals." In *The Product Life Cycle and International Trade,* edited by Louis T. Wells, Jr. Boston: Harvard Business School Division of Research, 1972.

———. "The Oil Companies in Crisis." In *The Oil Crisis,* edited by Raymond Vernon. New York: W.W. Norton, 1976.

———, et al. *Nine Investments Abroad and Their Impact at Home.* Boston: Harvard Business School Division of Research, 1976.

Stocking, G.W. *Middle East Oil.* London: Penguin Books, 1971.

U.S. Senate, Subcommittee on Multinational Corporations. "Multinational Oil Corporations and U.S. Foreign Policy." *Report Together with the Individual Views to the Committee on Foreign Relations,* 93rd Congress. Washington, D.C.: U.S. Government Printing Office, 1975.

————. "Multinational Petroleum Companies and Foreign Policy." *Hearings Before the Subcommittee on Multinational Corporations of the Committee on Foreign Relations,* 93rd Congress. Washington, D.C.: U.S. Government Printing Office, 1975.

Vernon, Raymond, ed. *The Oil Crisis.* New York: W.W. Norton, 1976.

D.R. DENMAN

Chapter Seven: Selected Bibliography

Afchar, Hassan. *L'Orientation actuelle du droit rural en Iran.* University of Tehran, 1975.

————[Afshar]. "A Comparative Study of Land Reforms in Iran and Ireland." Ph.D. diss., Department of Land Economy, University of Cambridge, 1972.

Agricultural Cooperative Bank of Iran. *Annual Report for 1349* [1970/71]. Tehran: 1971.

————. *Annual Report for 1351* [1972/73]. Tehran: 1973.

————. *Balance Sheet and Annual Report for 1352* [1973/74]. Tehran: 1974.

————. *Balance Sheet and Annual Report for 1353* [1974/75]. Tehran: 1975.

Agricultural Development Bank of Iran. *Annual Report and Balance Sheet for 1353* [1974/75]. Tehran: 1975.

Arfa, Gen. Hassan. *Under Five Shahs.* London: John Murray, 1964.

Avery, Peter. *Modern Iran.* London: Ernest Benn, 1965.

Banani, Amin. *The Modernization of Iran 1921-41.* Stanford, Calif.: Stanford University Press, 1961.

Bank Omran, Iran. *The Pahlavi Domain Lands Distribution Programme: Objectives, Accomplishments and Needs.* Tehran, 1958.

Dadgar, M., and Saroukhanian, G. *The Health Corps in Iran: An Approach to the Better Distribution of Health Resources in Remote Areas.* London: J. and A. Churchill, 1971.

Denman, D.R. *Origins of Ownership.* London: George Allen and Unwin, 1958.

————. *Rural Land Systems.* London: FIG/RICS, 1968.

————. *The King's Vista.* Berkhamsted, Hertfordshire, U.K.: Geographical Publications Ltd., 1973.

El-Ghonemy, Mohamad Riad. "Land Policy in the Near East." Rome: FAO, 1967.

————. "Land Reform and Economic Development in the Near East." *Land Economics*, February 1968.

Goodarzy, Karim. *Highlights of Iran Land Reform Programme.* Taiwan: Land Reform Training Institute, March 1970.

————. *Iran Land Reform: A Decade of Progress.* Taiwan: Land Reform Training Institute, March 1970.

Institute for Economic Research, University of Tehran. "The Age of the Rural Labor Force and Land Reform." *Tahqiqat-e Eqtesadi*, vol. 7 (1970).

Iran, Ministry of Agriculture. *Report of the Extension Service.* Tehran: 1969.

Iran, Ministry of Cooperation and Rural Affairs. *Land Reform Programme.* Tehran: 1972.

————. *Land Reform in Iran: A Decade of Progress.* Tehran: 1972.

Iran, Ministry of Education. *Education Corps Organization.* Tehran: 1968.

————. *The Education Corps Magazine.* Tehran: Summer 1971.

Iran, Ministry of Health. *The Health Corps in Action.* Tehran: 1971.

Iran, Ministry of Information. *Nationalization of Forests and Pastures.* Tehran: 1970.

————. *Revolution in Iran's Agricultural System.* Tehran: 1970.

Iran, Ministry of Land Reform and Rural Cooperation. "Report on Iran to FAO Inter-Regional Seminar." Warsaw, Poland: October 1969.

————. "Cooperative Movement in Iran." Unpublished memorandum, Tehran, 1970.

Iran, Pahlavi Estate Information Department. *Distribution of Pahlavi Estates among the Peasants.* Tehran: 1956.

Khatibi, N. "Land Reform in Economic Development, with Special Reference to the Experience of Iran." Faculty of Agricultural Science, *Centennial Symposium Proceedings, 1967.* American University of Beirut, 1967.

Lambton, A.K.S. *Landlord and Peasant in Persia.* 2nd ed. London: Oxford University Press, 1969.

————. *The Persian Land Reform, 1962-66.* London: Oxford University Press, 1969.

Najafi, B. "Foreign Investment in Iran with Particular Reference to Agriculture." Ph.D. diss., Department of Land Economy, University of Cambridge, 1975.

Pahlavi, HIM Mohammad Reza Shah. *Mission for My Country.* London: Hutchinson, 1961.

————. *The White Revolution.* Tehran: Imperial Pahlavi Library, 1967.

————. "Universal Welfare Legion." Address to Harvard University reported in *Taavon* (Iran), July 1968.

Price, O.T.W. *Towards a Comprehensive Iranian Agricultural Policy.* Tehran: International Bank for Reconstruction and Development, Agricultural and Rural Development Advisory Mission, 1975.

Ram, Hushang. *The Development Bank's Programme for Rural Cooperatives.* Tehran: Bank Omran, 1960.

Ramesh Sanghvi, *Aryamehr: The Shah of Iran.* London: Macmillan, 1969.

Shams, H.Z. "Allocation of Resources under Agrarian Reform in Iran." Ph.D. diss., Department of Land Economy, University of Cambridge, 1973.

Valian, A.A. "Implementation of Land Reform in Iran." Paper read at World Land Reform Conference, Rome, June 1966.

————. "Land Reform Programme in Iran." Paper read at Congress of the International Academy of Comparative Law, Pescara, Italy, September 1970.

WILHELM EILERS

Chapter Eight: Notes

1. So already the lament by R. Ker Porter, *Travels in Georgia, Persia, Armenia. ...*, Vol. 1 (1821), pp. 400 et seq.

2. His activities have often been described. Cf. F. Adamiyyat, *Amir-e Kabir va-Iran,* 2nd ed. (Tehran: 1955); H. Makki, *Zendegani-ye Amir-e Kabir* (Tehran: 1944).

3. The teachers were supposed to publish books for teaching purposes. A remaining fruit of these endeavors is J.L. Schlimmer, *Terminologie medico-pharmaceutique. . .*(Tehran: 1874), reprinted under no. 330 of the *Entesharat-e Daneshgah-e Tehran* (Tehran: 1330 [1951]).

4. E.G. Browne, *The Press and Poetry of Modern Persia* (Cambridge: University Press, 1914); A. Kasravi, *Tarikh-e mashrutiyat-e Iran,* 3 vols. (Tehran: 1319-23[1940-44]).

5. Text and British interpretation by Percy Sykes, *A History of Persia,* 2nd ed., vol. 2 (121), pp. 410 et seq.; cf. W. Litten, *Persien: Von der "pénétration pacifique" zum Protektorat* (Berlin and Leipzig: 1920).

6. Author of *Nazar-e mutafakkeran-e islami dar bara-ye tabi'at, Entesharat-e Daneshgah-e Tehran,* no. 890 (Tehran: 1342 [1963]); and *Three Muslim Sages* (1964), *An Introduction to Islamic Cosmological Doctrines* (1964), *Ideals and Realities of Islam* (1966), *Sufi Essays,* and other writings. We still remember his excellent "Elements of Continuity in the Life of Mysticism and Philosophy in Iran" (paper delivered at the International Congress of Iranology, Shiraz, October 1971).

7. He has contributed to our subject through several writings, including: Isa Sadiq, *Ravish-e novin dar amuzesh va parvaresh* (Tehran: 1951); *Sair-e farhang dar Iran va maghreb zamin* (Tehran: 1953); and *Tarikh-e farhang-e Iran* (Tehran: 1959).

8. M. Mahludji, *"Die Frauenbildung in Iran und ihr kulturgeschichtlicher Hintergrund,"* (diss., Cologne, 1965).

9. Farman of Isfand 1st, 1352.

10. See note 9, above.

11. Introduced by the *Qanun-e khedamat-e ejtema'i-ye zanan.*

12. Cf. *Hadafha-ye sepah-e danesh,* ed. by the Ministry of Education, 1967. There is also a journal of the Literacy Corps, *Nashriye-ye sepah-e danesh.*

13. Cf. the official published report, "Universal Welfare Legion of Iran, Shul Project 1971."

14. Cf. B. Pazargad, *Pishahangi-ye Iran* (Tehran: 1315 [1936]).

15. On this Seventh Ramsar Conference (September 3-4, 1974), see *Iran Almanac,* 14th ed., 1975, p. 411.

16. Famous for his publication *Ganj-e sokhan,* an anthology of Persian poetry from Rudaki to Bahar, with an introduction, in three volumes (Tehran: 1339-40 [1960-61]), reprinted under nos. 598, 653, and 672 of the *Entesharat-e Daneshgah-e Tehran.*

17. There is a magnificent edition of the *Kolliyat-e Shams* by the first dean of the Theological Faculty in Tehran, Professor Badi'ozzaman Furuzanfar, in seven volumes (1336-45 [1957-66]). In his honor was published no. 89 of the *Majalle-ye daneshkade-ye adabiyat va 'ulum-e insani* (1354 [1975]).

18. See for example note 3, above.

19. *"Ta'ziya, das persische Passionsspiel,"* compiled by Davoud Monchi-Zadeh, *Acta Societatis Literarum Humaniorum Regiae Upsalensis* 44:4 (Uppsala: 1967); L.P. Elwell-Sutton, *Tarikhche-ye te'atr dar Iran,* in *Sukhan,* 1335 (1956), pp. 288 et seq., 383 et seq.

20. 'Ali-Naqi Vaziri, *Musiqi-ye nazari,* 3 parts (Tehran: 1313 [1934]).

CHAPTER EIGHT: SELECTED BIBLIOGRAPHY*

Allgemeine Statistik des Auslandes. *Länderkurzberichte: Iran 1975.* Wiesbaden: Statistisches Bundesamt, July 1975.

Andalib, Mandana. *Das heutige iranische Erziehungswesen und seine Probleme.* Ph.D. diss., Tübingen: 1971.

Darbar-e shahanshahi. *Umur-e ejtema'i, sazman-e shahanshahi, bazrasi-ye amuzesh-e ali va pizhuheshe 'elmi,* no. 45, *"Arzyabi-ye gostaresh-e amuzesh-e ali-ye Iran"* (Seyyed Mohammad Taqi-ye Tyyib), 1353 [1974]; and no. 49, *"Dauraha-ye far 'i-ye amuzeshi dar daneshgaha va mo'assesat-e amuzesh-e ali"* ('Abbas-e Shifati), 1353 [1974].

Davidian, Zaven N., director, International Relations Department, University of Isfahan. "Iran in the Service of World Peace: On the Occasion of the 2500th Anniversary Celebration of the Founding of the Iranian Empire." Tehran: 1971.

Educational Statistics 1975. Tehran: Ministry of Education.

Gehrke, Ulrich, and Mehner, Harald. *Iran: Natur, Bevölkerung, Geschichte, Kultur, Staat, Wirtschaft.* Tübingen and Basel: 1975.

Iran Almanac 1975 and Book of Facts. 14th ed. Tehran: Echo of Iran, 1976.

Mahbubi-Ardakani, Hosein. *Tarikh-e tahavvol-e daneshgah-e Tehran va mo'assesat-e ali-ye amuzesh-e Iran dar 'asr-e khojaste-ye Pahlavi.* Tehran: 1350 [1971].

Pahlavi, Mohammad Reza Shah Aryamehr. *Enqelab-e sefid.*Tehran: 1966.

———. "Universal Welfare Legion." Text of the address at Harvard University on June 13, 1968, when His Imperial Majesty received an Honorary Doctor of Laws degree.

*Not mentioned here are general works on Persian history and literature or articles and information published by newspapers and journals. Thanks are due to government ministries and other official sources for their kind help.

Rahnama-ye daneshgah-e Tehran sale-e tahsili 1353-54. Tehran: Daftar-e motala 'ati-ye amuzeshi-ye daneshgah-e Tehran, 1353 [1974].

Salnameh-ye amari 1352 keshvar. Tehran: Sazman-e barname va buje-ye markazi-ye amar-e Iran, no. 394, 1353 [1974].

PETER CHELKOWSKI

CHAPTER NINE: NOTES

1. E.G. Browne, *A Literary History of Persia,* vol. 2, p. 86.

2. F. Machalski, "Muhammad Taqi Bahar as a Painter of Nature," in *Iran Society Silver Jubilee Souvenir,* p. 237.

3. Ibid.

4. Ibid., p. 234.

5. M. Roushangiar, *Az Nima Ta Baad*(Tehran: 1347[1968]), p. 11 (hereafter cited as "Roushangiar").

6. Ibid.

7. J. Kritzeck, *Modern Islamic Literature from 1800 to the Present* (hereafter cited as "Kritzeck"). Poem translated by A.J. Arberry.

8. Roushangiar, pp. 42-50.

9. On the title page Farrokhzad's name does not appear. M. Roushangiar is the editor but he gives full credit for the collection to Farrokhzad. The publishers are Morvarid and Khaneye Ketab (Tehran: 1347 [1968]).

10. Roushangiar, p. 171.

11. Ibid., pp. 93-94.

12. Ibid., p. 33.

13. This strong statement by Farrokhzad appears on the outside hardback cover of the book *Az Nima Ta Baad.*

14. Kritzeck, pp. 188-89. Poem translated by Bahram Jamalpur.

15. G. Squires and R. Nematollahi, "Contemporary Iranian Poetry," *Poésie Vivante 28* (1968): 10.

16. G. Tikku, "Furugh-i- Farrukhzad: A New Direction in Persian Poetry," *Studia Islamica 26* (1967): 149-73.

17. Ibid., p. 172.

18. Squires and Nematollahi, "Contemporary Iranian Poetry," p. 11.

19. M.A. Jamalzadeh, *Yeki Bud, Va Yeki Nabud* (Tehran: 1333 [1954]), p.9.

20. Kritzeck, pp. 211-16.

21. Ibid.

22. Ibid.

23. Translation by Z. Rastegar and P. Chelkowski.

24. W. Lentz, *Goethes Noten und Abhandlungen zum Westöstlichen Divan,* p. 118.

CHAPTER NINE: SELECTED BIBLIOGRAPHY

Armajani, Yahya. "Islamic Literature in Post-war Iran." In *The World of Islam: Studies in Honor of Philip K. Hitti,* edited by James Kritzeck and R. Bayly Winder. Princeton, N.J.: Princeton University Press, 1959.

Browne, E. G. *A Literary History of Persia.* Cambridge: Cambridge University Press, 1964.

Chelkowski, Peter J., ed. *Iran: Continuity and Variety.* New York: New York University Press and the Center for Near Eastern Studies, 1971.

Jamalzadeh, Mohammad 'Ali. *Yeki Bud, Va Yeki Nabud.* Tehran: 1333 (1913).

Kritzeck, J. *Modern Islamic Literature from 1800 to the Present.* New York: Holt, Rinehart and Winston, 1970.

Lentz, W. *Goethes Noten und Abhandlungen zum Westöstlichen Divan.* Hamburg: J.J. Augustin, 1955.

Machalski, Franciszek. "Muhammad Taqi Bahar as a Painter of Nature." In *Iran Society Silver Jubilee Souvenir.*

Roushangiar, M. *Az Nima Ta Baad.* Tehran: 1347 (1927).

Rypka, Jan, et al. *History of Iranian Literature.* New York: Humanities Press, 1968.

Squires, G., and Nematollahi, R. "Contemporary Iranian Poetry." *Poésie Vivante 28* (1968).

Tikku, Girdhari L. "Furugh-i Farrukhzad: A New Direction in Persian Poetry." *Studia Islamica 26* (1967).

————, ed. "Some socio-religious themes in modern Persian fiction." In *Islam and Its Cultural Divergence: Studies in Honor of Gustave E. Von Grunebaum.* Urbana, Ill.: University of Illinois Press, 1971.

WILLIAM E. GRIFFITH

CHAPTER TEN: NOTES

1. A.T. Olmstead, *History of the Persian Empire.*

2. P.M. Sykes, *A History of Persia,* 2 vols.

3. Sepehr Zabih, *The Communist Movement in Iran.*

4. The two standard works on Iranian foreign policy, both excellent, are: Rouhollah K. Ramazani, *The Foreign Policy of Iran, 1500-1941* and *Iran's Foreign Policy, 1941-1973,* a more historical survey; and Shahram Chubin and Sepehr Zabih, *The Foreign Relations of Iran,* a more contemporary analysis. This essay relies primarily on both. See also Peter Avery, *Modern Iran;* E.A. Bayne, *Persian Kingship in Transition;* George Lenczowski, *Russia and the West in Iran 1918-1948;* and Richard W. Cottam, *Nationalism in Iran.* I have also benefited greatly from conversations in Tehran, in July 1974 and March 1975, and especially in January 1976

from an audience with HIM Shah Mohammad Reza Pahlavi and from conversations with HE Prime Minister Amir Abbas Hoveyda, HE Minister of the Court Assadollah Alam, HE Ambassador Amir Khosrow Afshar, and Dr. Abbas Amirie and Dr. Shahram Chubin of the Institute for International Political and Economic Studies.

5. In addition to the works by Ramazani and Chubin (note 4, above), see Donald N. Wilber, *Riza Shah Pahlavi: The Resurrection and Reconstruction of Iran.*

6. See Mohammed H. Haikal's interview with the Shah in *Kayhan* (Weekly International Edition), September 20, 1975, pp. 4-5.

7. William E. Griffith, "The Fourth Middle Eastern War, the Energy Crisis, and U.S. Policy," mimeo., MIT Center for International Studies Paper C/73-15.

8. See the most recent long analyses from Oman by Thankmar, Freiherr von Münchhausen, in the *Frankfurter Allgemeine Zeitung,* June 21, 1975; and by Eric Pace from Muscat in the *New York Times,* January 11, 1976. See also the extracts from a captured PFLO document, indicating their defeats, in *Al-Nahar,* June 10, 1975 (summarized in *Afro-Asian Affairs* [London], no. 13, July 16, 1975, p. 3).

9. William E. Griffith, "Soviet Influence in the Middle East," *Survival,* vol. 18, no. 1 (January/February 1976): 2-9.

10. See field correspondence by A.H. [Arnold Hottinger] from Baghdad in the *Neue Zürcher Zeitung,* June 14-15, 17, 18, 1975; and, regarding the Kurdish problem, from Erbil in ibid., June 10, 1975, and from Suleimaniye, ibid., June 26, 1975; idem, "Kurdistan After the Revolt," *Swiss Review of World Affairs,* July 1975, pp. 13-14; Ian Seymour," "Iraqi Oil Policy in Focus," *Middle Eastern Economic Survey,* vol. 18, no. 35 (June 20, 1975), supplement, pp. 1-5; Oles M. Smolansky, "The Soviet Union and the Middle East: The Post-October Period," *Current History,* vol. 69 (October 1975): 117-20; and Shahram Chubin and Mohammad Fard-Saidi, *Recent Trends in Middle East Politics and Iran's Foreign Options.*

11. William E. Griffith, "Le Moyen-Orient: avant la prochaine guerre," *Politique Etrangère,* no. 2 (1975): 117-40; idem, "The Great Powers, the Indian Ocean, and the Persian Gulf," MIT Center for International Studies Paper C/75-8, also in *Jerusalem Journal of International Affairs,* no. 2 (1976), and in Abbas Amirie, ed., *The Persian Gulf and Indian Ocean in International Politics.* See also in general Alvin J. Cottrell and R. M. Burrell, eds., *The Indian Ocean: Its Political, Economic, and Military Importance;* Geoffrey Jukes, *The Indian Ocean in Soviet Naval Policy,* Adelphi Paper no. 87; Rouhollah K. Ramazani, *The Persian Gulf: Iran's Role;* idem, "Emerging Patterns of Regional Relations in Iranian Foreign Policy," *Orbis,* vol. 18, no. 4 (Winter 1975); R.M. Burrell, *The Persian Gulf,* The Washington Papers, no. 1; Udo Steinbach, "Iran's Foreign Policy Renaissance," *Aussenpolitik* (English ed.), vol 25, no. 3 (1974), pp. 316-30; W.A.C. Adie, *Oil, Politics, and Seapower: The Indian Ocean Vortex,* National Strategy Information Center, strategy paper no. 24. For the Soviet Navy in general and the Indian Ocean in particular, see Michael MccGwire, ed., *Soviet Naval Developments:* Michael MccGwire et al., ed., *Soviet Naval Policy.* See also Norman Polmar, *Soviet Naval Power: Challenge for the 1970s,* National Strategy Information Center, strategy paper no. 13, rev. ed. I benefited greatly from the September 1974 Dalhousie University seminar on Soviet naval developments at Halifax, Nova Scotia, the papers of which will be published by Praeger. I have also benefited from conversations in Karachi and Quetta in August 1974, including in Quetta with Prime Minister Zulfikar Ali Bhutto and with Nawab Akhtar Bukhti.

12. For the former view see James Bill, *The Politics of Iran: Groups, Classes and Modernization;* Marvin Zonis, *The Political Elite of Iran.* For the latter, see Samuel

Huntington, "Political Development and Political Decay," *World Politics* 17 (April 1965): 386-430.

13. Griffith, "Soviet Influence in the Middle East," (note 8, above).

CHAPTER TEN: SELECTED BIBLIOGRAPHY

Adie, W.A.C. *Oil, Politics and Seapower: The Indian Ocean Vortex*, National Strategy Information Center, strategy paper no. 24. New York: Crane Russak, 1975.

Amirie, Abbas. *The Persian Gulf and Indian Ocean in International Politics*. Tehran: Institute for Political and Economic Studies, 1976.

Avery, Peter. *Modern Iran*. London: Benn, 1965.

Bayne, E.A. *Persian Kingship in Transition*. New York: American Universities Field Staff, 1968.

Bill, James. *The Politics of Iran: Groups, Classes and Modernization*. Columbus, Ohio: Merrill, 1972.

Burrell, R.M. *The Persian Gulf*. The Washington Papers, no. 1. New York: Library Press, 1972.

Chubin, Shahram, and Saidi, Mohammad Fard. *Recent Trends in Middle East Politics and Iran's Foreign Policy Options*. Tehran: Institute for International Political and Economic Studies, 1975.

Chubin, Shahram, and Zabih, Sepehr. *The Foreign Relations of Iran*. Berkeley and Los Angeles: University of California Press, 1974.

Cottam, Richard W. *Nationalism in Iran*. Pittsburgh, Pa.: University of Pittsburgh Press, 1964.

Cottrell, Alvin J. and Burrell, R.M. (eds.) *The Indian Ocean: Its Political, Economic, and Military Importance*. New York: Praeger, 1972.

Griffith, William E. "Le Moyen-Orient: Avant la Prochaine Guerre." *Politique Etrangère*, no. 2, 1975.

————. "The Fourth Middle Eastern War, the Energy Crisis, and U.S. Policy." Paper C/73-15, Massachusetts Institute of Technology, Center for International Studies. Mimeographed. Cambridge, Mass.: The Center, November, 1973.

————. "The Great Powers, the Indian Ocean, and the Persian Gulf." Paper C/75-8, Massachusetts Institute of Technology, Center for International Studies. Mimeographed. Cambridge, Mass.: The Center, 1975.

————. "Soviet Influence in the Middle East." *Survival* 18, no. 1 (January-February 1976).

Huntington, Samuel. "Political Development and Political Decay." *World Politics* 17 (April 1965).

Jukes, Geoffrey. *The Indian Ocean in Soviet Naval Policy*. Adelphi Paper no. 87. London: International Institute for Strategic Studies, May 1972.

Lenczowski, George. *Russia and the West in Iran 1918-1948.* Ithaca, N.Y.: Cornell University Press, 1949.

MccGwire, Michael, ed. *Soviet Naval Developments.* New York: Praeger, 1973.

———, et al., eds. *Soviet Naval Policy.* New York: Praeger, 1974.

Olmstead, A.T. *History of the Persian Empire.* Chicago: University of Chicago Press, 1948.

Polmar, Norman. *Soviet Naval Power, Challenge for the 1970s.* National Strategy Information Center, strategy paper no. 13, rev. ed. New York: Crane Russak, 1975.

Ramazani, Rouhollah K. "Emerging Patterns of Regional Relations in Iranian Foreign Policy." *Orbis* 18, no. 4 (Winter 1975).

———. *Iran's Foreign Policy, 1941-1973.* Charlottesville, Va.: University Press of Virginia, 1975.

———. *The Foreign Policy of Iran, 1500-1941.* Charlottesville, Va.: University Press of Virginia, 1966.

———. *The Persian Gulf: Iran's Role.* Charlottesville, Va.: University Press of Virginia, 1972.

Seymour, Ian. "Iraqi Oil Policy in Focus." *Middle East Economic Survey* 18, no. 35 (June 20, 1975), and supplement.

Smolansky, Oles M. "The Soviet Union and the Middle East: The Post-October Period." *Current History* 69 (October 1975).

Steinbach, Udo. "Iran's Foreign Policy Renaissance." *Aussenpolitik* 25 (1974), no. 3. English edition.

Sykes, P.M. *A History of Persia.* 2 vols. London: Macmillan, 1915.

Wilber, Donald N. *Riza Shah Pahlavi: The Resurrection and Reconstruction of Iran, 1878-1944.* New York: Exposition Press, 1975.

Zabih, Sepehr. *The Communist Movement in Iran.* Berkeley and Los Angeles: University of California Press, 1966.

Zonis, Marvin. *The Political Elite of Iran.* Princeton, N.J.: Princeton University Press, 1971.

ALVIN J. COTTRELL

Chapter Eleven: Notes

1. His Imperial Majesty Mohammed Reza Shah Pahlavi, Shahanshah of Iran, *Mission for My Country,* chapter 2 (hereafter cited as *"Mission for My Country"*).

2. Ibid.

3. A very good discussion of military training during Reza Shah's reign is contained in J.C. Hurewitz, *Middle East Politics: The Military Dimension,* published for the Council on Foreign Relations, pp. 266-73.

4. Ibid.

5. For further details of these campaigns see *Survey of International Affairs 1925*, vol. 1, "The Islamic World Since the Peace Settlement," pp. 534-43.

6. *Mission for My Country*, chapter 2.

7. Donald N. Wilber, *Riza Shah Pahlavi: The Resurrection and Reconstruction of Iran 1878-1944*, p. 144.

8. Hassan Arfa, *Under Five Shahs*, p. 436.

9. Ibid., p. 437.

10. Richard N. Frye, *Persia*, p. 102.

11. A concise historical account of this important historical juncture in Iran's political and military evolution can be found in Harvey H. Smith et al., *Area Handbook for Iran*, DA PAM no. 550-68.

12. *Mission for My Country*, p. 74.

13. Ibid.

14. There is an excellent account of the events during this most crucial historical juncture in Iranian history in a little-known volume by Michael Sheehan, *Iran: The Impact of United States Interests and Policies 1941-1954*, chapter 4.

15. See United States Department of State Bulletin, vol. 14, March 17, 1946, p. 435.

16. Harry S. Truman, *Year of Decisions*, p. 523.

17. Joseph M. Jones, *The Fifteen Weeks (February 21-June 5, 1947)*, pp. 133-34.

18. For a detailed description of the evolution of CENTO, see George Lenczowski, *The Middle East in World Affairs*, p. 159 and passim.

19. Cited in Rouhollah K. Ramazani, *Iran's Foreign Policy 1941-1973: A Study of Foreign Policy in Modernizing Nations*, p. 254.

20. Ibid., p. 259.

21. Ibid., p. 260.

22. *New York Times*, February 12, 1959.

23. Yahya Armajani, *Iran*, p. 169.

24. *Mission for My Country*, pp. 105-15.

25. Ramazani, *Iran's Foreign Policy*, p. 318.

26. R.M. Burrell and Alvin J. Cottrell, *Iran, the Arabian Peninsula and the Indian Ocean*, p. 13.

27. Quoted from the Shah's address to the graduates of the Armed Forces Staff College and the National Defense College, September 11, 1971. Text by courtesy of the Imperial Court.

28. *Kayhan* (Weekly International Edition), November 9, 1974.

29. *Kayhan* (Weekly International Edition), November 18, 1972, cited in Ramazani, *Iran's Foreign Policy*, p. 428.

30. See Amir Taheri, "Policies of Iran in the Persian Gulf Region," in Abbas Amirie, ed., *The Persian Gulf and Indian Ocean in International Politics*, p. 265.

31. Ray Vickers, "The Mideast's Forgotten War," *Wall Street Journal*, April 18, 1974.

32. See John Duke Anthony, "Insurrection and Intervention: The War In Dhofar," in Amirie, ed., *The Persian Gulf*.

33. Eric Pace, "Shah of Iran Uses Oman to Train Armed Forces," *New York Times*, January 25, 1976.

34. Joseph Fitchett of the *London Observer*, reporting in the *Washington Post*, January 12, 1976.

35. Pace, "Shah of Iran Uses Oman."

36. D.L. Price, "Oman: Insurgency and Development," *Conflict Studies*. No. 53, January 1976, p. 9.

37. Fred Halliday, *Arabia Without Sultans*, p. 483.

38. Eric Pace, "Omanis Expect Iranian Force to Remain to Oppose Yemenis," *New York Times*, January 14, 1976.

39. Ranulph Fiennes, *Where Soldiers Fear to Tread*, pp. 242-43.

40. As an example of criticism of Iran's policy see William Safire, "Mr. Ford's Secret Sellout," *New York Times*, February 4, 1976; idem, "Son of 'Secret Sellout'," *New York Times*, February 12, 1976.

41. "Iran and Iraq Agree on Plan Ending Dispute," *Kayhan* (Weekly International Edition), March 15, 1975.

42. Audience at Niavaran Palace, May 28, 1972.

43. *New Times*, Moscow, April 1972.

44. *Mission for My Country*, p. 314.

45. Many of the American-supplied personnel carriers were armed with advanced wire-guided antitank missiles. Iran also had French antitank missiles. See R.D.M. Furlong, "Iran—A Power To Be Reckoned With," *International Defense Review*, June 1973, p. 724.

46. Ibid., p. 726. The Soviet systems included the ZU-23 dual-purpose twin 23 mm towed cannon; the ZSU-23-4 self-propelled radar-controlled antiair guns are still on order. The ZSU-57-2 antiair tanks mounting twin 57 mm cannon and the 85 mm M-44 towed gun are part of the artillery equipment. The American artillery systems ranged from the small 75mm M1A1 mountain pack howitzers, the 105 mm M101s and the 203 M115s—both towed—to the more modern self-propelled 175 mm M103 and 203 mm M110s. There were two relatively new Soviet surface-to-surface systems: the M-46 130 mm towed gun and the 40-tube 122 mm BM-21 version of the truck-carried Katyusha rocket family.

47. International Institute for Strategic Studies, *The Military Balance, 1975-76*, p. 90.

48. Henry Stanhope writes that Iran's number of Chieftain tanks is "more than twice as many as Britain itself can afford to buy or to man." See his "Iran's Defense Budget," *Defence Journal* (Karachi), vol. 2 (April-May 1976), p. 42.

49. Richard Burt, "Power and the Peacock Throne," *Round Table*, December 25, 1975, p. 354. Helicopter systems included the 202 Bell Sea Cobra, armed with the TOW missile; the Bel Isfahan twin-turbine troop assault chopper; and the Agusta Bell Jet Rangers.

50. D.L. Price, "Iran's Military Role," Paper for the Institute for the Study of Conflict, p. 13.

51. Iranian Ministry of Information, *Iran* (Iran: the Ministry, 1969), p. 103. As early as 1925, the Iranian government sent officers abroad for pilot training, and by 1950 some forty fighters formed the core of the army's air arm.

52. International Institute for Strategic Studies, *The Military Balance*, p. 33. Several of the F-4E versions were fitted with the AIM-7 Sparrow long-range intercept missile. For ground strikes the F-4Es were armed with Maverick air-to-surface missiles, of which Iran in 1973 bought some 2,500 from the United States. An order for

close to 260 F-4s and another 180 F-5s had been placed.

53. Furlong, "Iran—A Power To Be Reckoned With," p. 728.

54. Ibid., p. 729. Air transport units included six transport squadrons of C-130s and two light squadrons of the Fokker-72, the Beech C-45, the Douglas C-47, and the Beaver. Helicopter carriers counted the Super Frelons, Chinooks, Jet Rangers, and Huskies.

55. The air-defense mission had traditionally been covered by interceptor aircraft. In the early seventies, however, the IIAF acquired Rapier surface-to-air missile batteries and a Hawk surface-to-air missile battalion to help cover the medium-altitude air defense. The Tigercat surface-to-air missile provides low-level close-in air defense. The Swiss Oerlikon cannon and the Soviet-supplied antiair defense guns supplemented the SAM systems. Iran's air defense capability was further underwritten by an early warning system around Tehran, Mashhad and Tabriz. The surveillance radars were originally built under a CENTO program. Four early warning radars were continuously operative. As part of a U.S. aid project a new radar network was being installed that included Westinghouse AN/TPS-43-S band stacked beam radars and mobile Marconi S300 radars. Ibid., pp. 728, 729.

56. Ibid., p. 729.

57. Iranian Ministry of Information, *Iran*, p. 103.

58. *Jane's All the World's Fighting Ships, 1975-76*, p. 179 et seq. The destroyer *Artemiz* was armed with a quadruple Seacat antiair missile launcher, with 4.5-inch and 40 mm antiair guns.

59. Ibid.

60. International Institute for Strategic Studies, *The Military Balance, 1975-76*, p. 33. These latter were armed with the Harpoon surface-to-surface cruise missile. Six of the British patrol craft were Wellington BN-7s, and the rest were Winchester SR-N6s.

61. The naval air force consisted of six fixed-wing Shrike Commanders, 5 AB-205 Hueys, 14 AB-206 A Jet Rangers, 6 AB-212s, and 10 Agusta-Sikorsky SH-3D Sea Kings.

62. Richard Burt, "Power and the Peacock Throne," p. 349.

63. International Institute for Strategic Studies, *Strategic Survey 1971*, p. 45.

64. Ibid., p. 40.

65. Lewis M. Simons, "Iran Seen Overspending for Gulf Military Role," *Washington Post*, February 28, 1976.

66. Audience at Niavaran Palace, January 13, 1976.

67. Audience on the Iranian island of Kish, March 27, 1975.

68. *On the Occasion of The Official Visit of Their Imperial Majesties Mohammad Reza Pahlavi Aryamehr Shahanshah of Iran and Farah Pahlavi Shahbanou of Iran to Singapore, Australia, New Zealand, Indonesia and India, September 1974* (n.p., n.d.), pp. 14-15.

69. Ibid., pp. 17-18.

CHAPTER ELEVEN: SELECTED BIBLIOGRAPHY

Anthony, John Duke. "Insurrection and Intervention: The War In Dhofar." In *The Persian Gulf and Indian Ocean in International Politics,* edited by Abbas Amirie. Tehran: Institute for International Political and Economic Studies, 1975.

Arfa, General Hassan. *Under Five Shahs.* London: John Murray, 1964.

Armajani, Yahya. *Iran.* Englewood Cliffs, N.J.: Prentice-Hall, 1972.

Burrell, R.M., and Cottrell, Alvin J. *Iran, the Arabian Peninsula and the Indian Ocean.* New York: National Strategy Information Center, 1972.

Burt, Richard. "Power and the Peacock Throne." *Round Table,* December 25, 1975.

Fiennes, Ranulph. *Where Soldiers Fear to Tread.* London: Hodder and Stoughton, 1975.

Frye, Richard N. *Persia.* London: George Allen and Unwin, 1960.

Furlong, R.D.M. "Iran—A Power To Be Reckoned With," *International Defense Review,* June 1973.

Halliday, Fred. *Arabia Without Sultans.* England: Penguin Books, 1974.

Hurewitz, J.C. *Middle East Politics: The Military Dimension.* Published for the Council on Foreign Relations. New York: Praeger, 1969.

International Institute for Strategic Studies. *The Military Balance, 1975-76.* London: IISS, 1975.

———. *Strategic Survey 1971.* London: IISS, 1972.

Jane's All the World's Fighting Ships, 1975-76. New York: Franklin Watts, 1975.

Jones, Joseph M. *The Fifteen Weeks.* New York: Viking Press, 1955.

Lenczowski, George. *The Middle East in World Affairs.* Ithaca, N.Y.: Cornell University Press, 1962.

D.L. Price. "Oman: Insurgency and Development." No. 53, January 1975. London: Institute for the Study of Conflict, 1975.

On the Occasion of the Official Visit of Their Imperial Majesties Mohammad Reza Pahlavi Aryamehr Shahanshah of Iran and Farah Pahlavi Shahbanou of Iran to Singapore, Australia, New Zealand, Indonesia and India, September 1974. Washington, D.C.: Imperial Embassy of Iran, 1974.

Pace, Eric. "Omanis Expect Iranian Force to Remain to Oppose Yemenis." *New York Times,* January 14, 1976.

———. "Shah of Iran Uses Oman to Train Armed Forces." *New York Times,* January 25, 1976.

Pahlavi, HIM Mohammed Reza Shah. *Mission for My Country.* London: Hutchinson, 1961.

Price, D.L. "Iran's Military Role." Paper for the Institute for the Study of Conflict, 1975.

Ramazani, Rouhollah K. *Iran's Foreign Policy 1941-1973: A Study of Foreign Policy in Modernizing Nations.* Charlottesville, Va.: University Press of Virginia, 1975.

Safire, William. "Mr. Ford's Secret Sellout," *New York Times,* February 4, 1976.

———. "Son of 'Secret Sellout'." *New York Times,* February 12, 1976.

Sheehan, Michael. *Iran: The Impact of United States Interests and Policies 1941-1954.* Brooklyn, N.Y.: Theo. Gaus's Sons, 1968.

Simmons, Lewis M. "Iran Seen Overspending for Gulf Military Role." *Washington Post,* February 28, 1976.

Smith, Harvey, et al. *Area Handbook for Iran.* DA PAM no. 550-68. Washington, D.C.: U.S. Government Printing Office, 1971.

Stanhope, Henry. "Iran's Defense Budget." *Defence Journal* (Karachi) 2, April-May, 1976.

Survey of International Affairs, 1925. Vol. 1, "The Islamic World Since the Peace Settlement." London: Royal Institute of International Affairs, 1927.

Taheri, Amir. "Policies of Iran in the Persian Gulf Region." In *The Persian Gulf and Indian Ocean in International Politics,* edited by Abbas Amirie. Tehran: Institute for International Political and Economic Studies, 1975.

Truman, Harry S. *Year of Decisions.* New York: Doubleday, 1955.

Vickers, Ray. "The Mideast's Forgotten War." *Wall Street Journal,* April 18, 1975.

Wilber, Donald N. *Riza Shah Pahlavi: The Resurrection and Reconstruction of Iran 1878-1944.* Hicksville, N.Y.: Exposition Press, 1975.

GEORGE LENCZOWSKI

CHAPTER TWELVE: NOTES

1. English text of both documents in Helen Miller Davis, *Constitutions, Electoral Laws, Treaties of States in the Near and Middle East,* rev. ed., p. 104 et seq. (hereafter cited as "Davis"). Another version, with minor differences, may be found in Amos Peaslee, *Constitutions of Nations* (The Hague: M. Nijhoff, 1965), p. 396 et seq.

2. Davis, p. 122.

3. The newly elected and appointed Senate was convoked for the first time on February 9, 1950.

4. Davis, pp. 115-16.

5. Ibid., p. 123.

6. Ibid., p. 114.

7. Texts in Peaslee, *Constitutions of Nations,* pp. 396 and 407.

8. Text in *Kayhan* (International Edition) (Tehran), Sept. 9, 1967, p. 5.

9. For a fuller discussion, see Lawrence Lockhart, "The Constitutional Laws of Persia: An Outline of Their Origin and Development," *Middle East Journal* 13, no. 4 (Autumn 1959); 372 et seq. See also Mehdi Tohidipur, "Das Werden und der Inhalt der Iranischen Verfassung," *Verfassung und Recht in Übersee* 7: 189-206.

10. Edward G. Browne, *The Persian Revolution of 1905-1909;* idem, *The Persian Crisis of December, 1911; How It Arose and Whither It May Lead Us.*

11. For a more comprehensive treatment of this period, see George Lenczowski, *Russia and the West in Iran, 1918-1948;* idem, *Supplement* to the above (1954).

12. Jahangir Amuzegar, "Nationalism Versus Economic Growth," *Foreign Affairs* 44, no. 4 (July 1966): 651-61.

13. For the enumeration of the points of the program, see chapter 3 of this book.

14. For a comprehensive treatment of this subject, see Sepehr Zabih, *The Communist Movement in Iran.*

15. For details, see George Lenczowski, "The Communist Movement in Iran," *Middle East Journal* 1, no. 1 (January 1947): 29-45.

16. For a more detailed treatment, see William Eagleton, Jr., *The Kurdish Republic of 1946.*

17. For a brief discussion of this subject, see A. Farmanfarma, "Constitutional Law of Iran," *American Journal of Comparative Law* 3, no. 2 (April 1954): 241-47.

18. For a text of the Shah's speech, see *Kayhan* (International Edition), March 8, 1975, p. 4 et seq.

19. L.P. Elwell-Sutton, "Political Parties in Iran: 1941-1948," *Middle East Journal* 3, no. 1 (January 1949): 45-62.

20. General Hassan Arfa, *Under Five Shahs,* chapters 6, 9, 11.

21. For a discussion of this subject, see T. Cuyler Young, "The Race between Russia and Reform in Iran," *Foreign Affairs* 28 (January 1950): 3-14.

22. From the Shah's speech at Harvard University, in *Twelve Speeches by His Imperial Majesty Mohammad Reza Pahlavi Aryamehr Shahanshah of Iran on Ideological Basis of Iran's National and International Policy,* p. 63 (hereafter cited as "Twelve Speeches").

23. Ibid., p. 34.

24. Ibid., p. 42.

25. His Imperial Majesty Mohammad Reza Pahlavi Aryamehr Shahanshah of Iran, *The White Revolution,* p. 12 (hereafter cited as *"The White Revolution"*).

26. Ibid., pp. 14-15.

27. "In Iran there is magic in the notion of a King. . . .Our kingship is really an imperial principle, not imperialistic in the foreign expansionist sense, but in the sense of rule and communion between the Shah and the people—the notion of rule which is *Shahanshahi.*" From an audience with HIM Shah Mohammad Reza Pahlavi, Niavaran Palace, April 4, 1976.

28. Ibid. Similarly, the Shah stated in 1967: "None of the ideologies based on enmity and antagonism or crushing a class or classes for the benefit of other classes. . .is acceptable to us. . . ." (*The White Revolution,* p. 20).

29. These three principles were specifically mentioned by the Shah when announcing the creation of the Rastakhiz party (*Kayhan* [International Edition]), March 8, 1975).

30. *The White Revolution,* pp. 6-7.

31. Ibid., p. 8.

32. HIM Mohammed Reza Shah Pahlavi Shahanshah of Iran, *Mission for My Country,* p. 75 (hereafter cited as *Mission for My Country*).

33. Ibid., p. 77.

34. Ibid., p. 91.

35. Ibid., p. 116.

36. Ibid., p. 49.

37. Ibid., p. 66.

38. In this sense, see Richard W. Cottam, *Nationalism in Iran,* chapter 16, pp. 286-311.

39. Carl J. Friedrich and Zbigniew K. Brzezinski, *Totalitarian Dictatorship and Autocracy* (Cambridge, Mass.: Harvard University Press, 1956), Chapter 6.

40. *Mission for My Country,* p. 162.

41. Ibid., p. 178.

42. In this sense, see Sidney and Beatrice Webb, *Soviet Communism: A New Civilization* (New York: C. Scribner's Sons, 1936).

43. It may be appropriate to quote here the Shah's own testimony on this subject:

The Free World felt deeply concerned over the crisis that developed in my country prior to the fall of Mossadegh and his Tudeh allies. I have, therefore, sometimes been asked if America or Britain helped finance the movement that overthrew Mossadegh. Of course it was well known that a foreign power helped establish the Tudeh party, and that from the beginning it was aided with foreign funds; so it was easy to believe that those who were opposed to the Tudeh and to Mossadegh were also subsidized. Rumors flow unusually free in my country, and one had it that ordinary people who rose against Mossadegh in some instances received American dollars or (according to another version) British pounds for help.

Although I was abroad at the climax of the uprising, I was in constant touch with the situation during those days, and of course lived with it before and after my short absence. I do not deny that payments could in some case conceivably have been made. I frankly have no firm evidence either way. But I think this is certainly true: it takes much more than money to impel people to do what Iran's loyal citizens did during those days. In overturning Mossadegh and the Tudeh, they staged a revolution that was inspired by indigenous nationalism. I have told how many of them advanced unarmed against the fire of tanks and machine guns. Women and children as well as men gave up their lives in that way. I doubt if those brave people expected or received payment for their patriotism. I credit them with ideals of a nobler sort (*Mission for My Country*, p. 107).

44. For a more detailed discussion of this subject, see Shahram Chubin and Sepehr Zabih, *The Foreign Relations of Iran*, Chapter 2; and Rouhollah K. Ramazani, *Iran's Foreign Policy, 1941-1973*. Also George Lenczowski, "United States' Support for Iran's Independence and Integrity, 1945-1959," *Annals of the American Academy of Political and Social Science* 401 (May 1972): 45-55.

45. *Mission for My Country*, p. 105.

46. Ibid., p. 129.

47. Arthur M. Schlesinger, Jr., *The Imperial Presidency* (Boston: Houghton Mifflin, 1973).

48. For a fuller discussion of this period, see Peter Avery, *Modern Iran;* Cottam, *Nationalism in Iran;* Leonard Binder, *Iran: Political Development in a Changing Society;* and Donald N. Wilber, *Iran: Past and Present.*

49. *Mission for My Country*, p. 125.

50. Ibid., p. 124.

51. In his addresses and messages to the UNESCO World Congress of Ministers of Education, Tehran, September 8, 1965; the United Nations, October 24, 1965; the University of Sofia, September 1, 1966; the Malaysian National Assembly, January 19, 1968; Harvard University, June 13, 1968; also *Twelve Speeches*, pp. 22, 30, 40, 48, 54, 59.

52. Ibid., p. 38.

53. Ibid., p. 66.

54. *Mission for My Country*, p. 164.

55. In a remark to the author during the audience in Saadabad Palace, September 8, 1971.

56. *Mission for My Country*, p. 54.

57. *The White Revolution* p. 16.

58. Author's audience in Niavaran Palace, April 6, 1976.

59. *Mission for My Country*, p. 328.

60. Ibid., p. 321.

61. For a fuller discussion, see James A. Bill, *The Politics of Iran: Groups, Classes and Modernization*; idem, "The Plasticity of Informal Politics: The Case of Iran," *Middle East Journal* 27 (Spring 1973): 131-51. The same theme is further developed by Bill in "The Patterns of Elite Politics in Iran," in George Lenczowski, ed., *Political Elites in the Middle East* (Washington, D.C.: American Enterprise Institute, 1975).

62. *Mission for My Country*, p. 326.

63. Ibid, p. 323.

CHAPTER TWELVE: SELECTED BIBLIOGRAPHY

Abrahamian, Ervand. "Communism and Communalism in Iran: The Tudeh and the Firqah-i Dimukrat." *International Journal of Middle East Studies* 1, no. 4 (October 1970).

Alavi, Bozorg. *Kämpfendes Iran.* Berlin: Dietz, 1955.

Algar, Hamid. *Religion and State in Iran 1785-1906.* Berkeley and Los Angeles: University of California Press, 1969.

Amuzegar, Jahangir. "Nationalism Versus Economic Growth." *Foreign Affairs* 44, no. 4 (July 1966).

Arfa, General Hassan. *Under Five Shahs.* London: John Murray, 1964.

Avery, Peter. *Modern Iran.* New York: Praeger, 1965.

Baldwin, George B. "The Foreign-Educated Iranian." *Middle East Journal* 17, no. 3 (Summer 1963).

Banani, Amin. *The Modernization of Iran, 1921-1941.* Stanford, Calif.: Stanford University Press, 1961.

Bayne, E.A. *Persian Kingship in Transition: Conversations with a Monarch Whose Office Is Traditional and Whose Goal is Modernization.* New York: American Universities Field Staff, 1968.

Bill, James. *The Politics of Iran: Groups, Classes and Modernization.* Columbus, Ohio: Charles E. Merrill, 1972.

————. "The Social and Economic Foundations of Power in Contemporary Iran." *Middle East Journal* 17, no. 4 (Autumn 1963).

Bill, James A., and Leiden, Carl. *The Middle East: Politics and Power.* Boston: Allyn and Bacon, 1974.

Binder, Leonard. *Iran: Political Development in a Changing Society.* Berkeley and Los Angeles: University of California Press, 1962.

————. "The Cabinet in Iran." *Middle East Journal* 16, no. 1 (Winter 1962).

Blücher, Wipert von. *Zeitenwende in Iran: Erlebnisse und Beobachtungen.* Biberach an der Riss: Koehler Voigtländer, 1949.

Brammer, Lawrence M. "Problems of Iranian University Students," *Middle East Journal* 18, no. 4 (Autumn 1964).

Browne, Edward G. *The Persian Crisis of December, 1911; How It Arose and Whither It May Lead Us.* Compiled for the use of the Persia Committee. Cambridge: Cambridge University Press, 1912.

———. *The Persian Revolution of 1905-1909.* Cambridge: Cambridge University Press, 1910.

Chubin, Shahram, and Zabih, Sepehr. *The Foreign Relations of Iran.* Berkeley and Los Angeles: University of California Press, 1974.

Cottam, Richard W. *Nationalism in Iran.* Pittsburgh, Pa.: University of Pittsburgh Press, 1964.

———. "Political Party Development in Iran." *Iranian Studies* 1, no. 3 (1968).

Davis, Helen Miller. *Constitutions, Electoral Laws, Treaties of States in the Near and Middle East.* Rev. ed. Durham, N.C.: Duke University Press, 1953.

Dupree, Louis. "Democracy and the Military Base of Power." *Middle East Journal* 22, no. 1 (1968).

Eagleton, William, Jr. *The Kurdish Republic of 1946.* London: Oxford University Press, 1963.

Elwell-Sutton, L.P. "Political Parties in Iran: 1941-1948." *Middle East Journal* 3, no. 1 (January 1949).

———. *Modern Iran.* London: G. Routledge, 1941.

Farmanfarma, A. "Constitutional Law of Iran." *American Journal of Comparative Law* 3, no. 2 (April 1954).

Gable, Richard W. "Culture and Administration in Iran." *Middle East Journal* 13, no. 4 (Autumn 1959).

Keddie, Nikki R. "The Iranian Power Structure and Social Change 1800-1969." *International Journal of Middle East Studies* 2, no. 1 (January 1971).

Lenczowski, George. "The Communist Movement in Iran." *Middle East Journal* 1, no. 1 (January 1947).

———. *Russia and the West in Iran, 1918-1948.* Ithaca, N.Y.: Cornell University Press, 1949; with a *Supplement,* 1954.

———. "United States' Support for Iran's Independence and Integrity, 1945-1959." *Annals of the American Academy of Political and Social Science,* May 1972.

Lockhart, Lawrence. "The Constitutional Laws of Persia: An Outline of Their Origin and Development." *Middle East Journal* 13, no. 4 (Autumn 1959).

Miller, William Green. "Political Organization in Iran: From Dowreh to Political Party." *Middle East Journal* 23, nos. 2 and 3 (Spring and Summer 1969).

On the Occasion of the Official Visit of Their Imperial Majesties Mohammad Reza Pahlavi Aryamehr Shahanshah of Iran and Farah Pahlavi Shahbanou of Iran to Singapore, Australia, New Zealand, Indonesia and India, September 1974. Washington, D.C.: Imperial Embassy of Iran, 1974.

Pahlavi Aryamehr, HIM Mohammad Reza Shahanshah of Iran. *The White Revolution.* Tehran: Imperial Pahlavi Library, 1967.

———. *Mission for My Country.* New York, Toronto, London: McGraw-Hill, 1960.

Ramazani, Rouhollah K. *Iran's Foreign Policy, 1941-1973.* Charlottesville, Va.: University of Virginia Press, 1975.

Razi, G. Hossein. "Genesis of Party in Iran: A Case Study of the Interaction between the Political System and Political Parties." *Iranian Studies* 3, no. 2 (Spring 1970).

———. "The Press and Political Institutions of Iran." *Middle East Journal* 22, no. 4 (Autumn 1968).

Roosevelt, Archie, Jr. "The Kurdish Republic of Mahabad." *Middle East Journal* 1, no. 3 (July 1947).

Rossow, Robert, Jr. "The Battle of Azerbaijan, 1946." *Middle East Journal* 10, no. 1 (Winter 1956).

Sahebajam, Freidoune. *Mohamad Reza Pahlavi, Shah d'Iran.* Paris: Berger-Levrault, 1971.

Sanghvi, Ramesh. *Arya Mehr, the Shah of Iran: A Political Biography.* London: Macmillan, 1968.

Tavallali, Djamchid. *Le Parlement Iranien.* Lausanne: Imprimerie des Arts et Métiers, 1954.

Tohidipur, Mehdi. "Das Werden und der Inhalt der Iranischen Verfassung." In *Verfassung und Recht in Übersee.* Hamburg: Institut für Internationale Angelegenheiten der Universität Hamburg, 1974.

Twelve Speeches by His Imperial Majesty Mohammad Reza Pahlavi Aryamehr Shahanshah of Iran on Ideological Basis of Iran's National and International Policy. Tehran: Pahlavi Library, 1971.

Upton, Joseph M. *The History of Modern Iran: An Interpretation.* Cambridge, Mass.: Harvard University Press, 1960.

Warne, William E. *Mission for Peace: Point Four in Iran.* Indianapolis, Ind.: Bobbs-Merrill, 1956.

Weinbaum, Marvin G. "Iran Finds a Party System: The Institutionalization of Iran Novin." *Middle East Journal* 27, no. 4 (1973).

Westwood, Andrew F. "Elections and Politics in Iran." *Middle East Journal* 15, no. 2 (Spring 1961).

Wilber, Donald N. *Iran: Past and Present.* 7th ed. Princeton, N.J.: Princeton University Press, 1975.

———. *Riza Shah Pahlavi: The Resurrection and Reconstruction of Iran, 1878-1944.* Hicksville, N.Y.: Exposition Press, 1975.

Young, T. Cuyler, "Iran in Continuing Crisis." *Foreign Affairs* 40, no. 2 (January 1962).

——. "The Race between Russia and Reform in Iran." *Foreign Affairs,* January 1950.

———. "The Social Support of Current Iranian Policy." *Middle East Journal* 6, no. 2 (Spring 1952).

Zabih, Sepehr. *The Communist Movement in Iran.* Berkeley and Los Angeles: University of California Press, 1966.

Zonis, Marvin. *The Political Elite of Iran.* Princeton, N.J.: Princeton University Press, 1971.

———. "The Political Elite of Iran: A Second Stratum?" In *Political Elites and Political Development in the Middle East,* edited by Frank Tachau. New York: John Wiley, 1975.

Selected Glossary of Persian Terms

amlak—[crown] lands

artesh—army

'aruz—classical rules of poetic style

Aryamehr—The Light (Sun) of the Aryans

ba'er—neglected yet cultivable lands

barzegar—cultivator without implements or animals; a farmer

bast—political sanctuary in a protected area such as mosque or foreign embassy

bonyad—foundation

chador—woman's veil

dabestan—elementary school

dabirestan—secondary school

edareh—administration

espahbad—military governor

farangi ma'ab—a person affecting Western manners

farman—decree, rescript

feda'iyyan-e eslam—fighters (devotees) for Islam (often called "fedayan Islam" in the Western press)

gavband—villager owning oxen and implements but not working fields himself (i.e., a middleman)

hajji—a title applied to those who have successfully performed a pilgrimage to Mecca

kargar-e keshavarzi—landless farmworkers

khaleseh—land of public domain

Khan—courtesy title of Turkish-Mongol origin; a tribal chief

khordehmalekin—minor landowners; squatters

khoshneshin—village squatters

khvarenah—divine grace

madraseh—Moslem school usually attached to a mosque

Majles—National Assembly

maktab—a lower-grade traditional school

markaz—center

mashrutiyyat—constitutional government

mavat—dead lands

melk—private property of land

melli—national

mojtahed—a Shi'a Islamic doctor

molla—Moslem cleric ("mulla")

mosha' communal property

mosha'ereh—traditional poetry recitation contest

nasaq—village arable land

'olama—Islamic religious scholars (a collective noun)

qanat—underground water canal

rastakhiz—resurrection, resurgence

ruhowzi—type of folk entertainment of secular character

sardar-e sepah—commander of the army

sazeman—organization

sepah-e behdasht—Health Corps

sepah-e danesh—Literacy Corps

sepah-e tarvij va abadani—Reconstruction and Development Corps

seyyed—descendant of the Prophet through his daughter, Fatima

Shahanshah—King of Kings; a great king

Shahbanou—Empress (Queen)

Shah-nameh—The Book of Kings (by Ferdowsi)

Shari'a—Quranic law

shaykh—chief ("sheikh")

ta'ziyeh—ritual drama based on traditions of Persian Islam

toman—currency unit equal to 10 rials

tudeh—masses

vaqf (pl. *owqaf*)—endowment for charitable, public, or private purposes

vazir—minister

vezarat—ministry

zare' (pl. *zare'in*)—cultivator with customary rights of land use; a farmer

zurkhaneh—"house of strength" (traditional athletic club)

Index